T0349018

Java Microservices and Containers in the Cloud

With Spring Boot, Kafka, PostgreSQL, Kubernetes, Helm, Terraform and AWS EKS

Binildas A. Christudas

Apress®

Java Microservices and Containers in the Cloud: With Spring Boot, Kafka, PostgreSQL, Kubernetes, Helm, Terraform and AWS EKS

Binildas A. Christudas
NBCRA 45, Christbin
Thiruvananthapuram, Kerala, India

ISBN-13 (pbk): 979-8-8688-0554-7 ISBN-13 (electronic): 979-8-8688-0555-4
https://doi.org/10.1007/979-8-8688-0555-4

Copyright © 2024 by Binildas A. Christudas

Managing Director, Apress Media LLC: Welmoed Spahr
Acquisitions Editor: James Robinson-Prior & Divya Modi
Development Editor: James Markham
Coordinating Editor: Gryffin Winkler
Copy Editor: Kezia Endsley

Cover designed by eStudioCalamar

Cover image by Unsplash.com

Distributed to the book trade worldwide by Apress Media, LLC, 1 New York Plaza, New York, NY 10004, U.S.A. Phone 1-800-SPRINGER, fax (201) 348-4505, e-mail orders-ny@springer-sbm.com, or visit www.springeronline.com. Apress Media, LLC is a California LLC and the sole member (owner) is Springer Science + Business Media Finance Inc (SSBM Finance Inc). SSBM Finance Inc is a **Delaware** corporation.

For information on translations, please e-mail booktranslations@springernature.com; for reprint, paperback, or audio rights, please e-mail bookpermissions@springernature.com.

Apress titles may be purchased in bulk for academic, corporate, or promotional use. eBook versions and licenses are also available for most titles. For more information, reference our Print and eBook Bulk Sales web page at http://www.apress.com/bulk-sales.

Any source code or other supplementary material referenced by the author in this book is available to readers on GitHub (https://github.com/Apress). For more detailed information, please visit https://www.apress.com/gp/services/source-code.

If disposing of this product, please recycle the paper

To Sowmya Hubert, Ann S. Binil, and Ria S. Binil

Table of Contents

About the Author

 **Binildas A. Christudas** is an experienced architect and developer, specializing in building distributed software solutions for the airlines, hospitality, and telecommunications domains since the inception of Java. He currently heads technology services as a vice president at IBS Software, a leader in the airline cargo software domain. Binildas is engaged in architecting highly resilient and highly available software solutions for some of the world's largest cruise and airline companies. He specializes in ensuring data consistency across distributed and decentralized systems, encompassing various scenarios such as cross-region deployments across major public clouds.

Binildas is a mechanical engineer from the College of Engineering, Trivandrum (CET) with a post-graduate degree in systems from the Institute of Management Kerala (IMK). Leveraging over 25 years of experience in distributed systems, he currently dedicates his focus to architecting conflict-free, replicated, and eventually consistent systems that handle streaming data and big data. He is the author of Practical Microservices Architectural Patterns by Apress and Service Oriented Java Business Integration by Packt. Binildas was the captain of the Kerala University power lifting team and was the national champion during his studies. He has also been awarded a patent for "A Method and a System for Facilitating Multitenancy of Services" by the USPTO. Binil can be contacted through www.linkedin.com/in/binildasca/.

About the Technical Reviewer

Yogesh Sharma is a dynamic software developer based in Pune, India, currently honing his skills at Nice Actimize. With a keen interest in complex event processing (CEP), low-code/no-code (LCNC) programming, and progressive application development, Yogesh is always eager to experiment with cutting-edge technologies and innovative solutions. Outside of work, he is a devoted father, spending quality time with his son. Together, they explore the exciting worlds of DIY rocketry and rollerblading, fostering creativity and a love for learning.

Acknowledgments

A big thanks to Apress Media for having trust in me and giving me the opportunity to write this book. Nirmal Selvaraj, Dulcy Nirmala and Divya Modi have been very helpful in making the process seamless.

The tech-friendly workplace at IBS Software has been a boon to me. Many thanks to Mr. V. K. Mathews, founder and executive chairman, IBS Group, for providing consistent motivation throughout my career. I also want to thank Mr. Arun Hrishikesan, Senior VP at Innovation Ecosystem, IBS, for his constant motivation and support, especially in providing his broader views on technology areas, which influenced the content and style of this book to a great extent. Thanks also to Christopher Branagan, CTO, IBS, for his many years of mentoring.

I also want to thank Arun Prasanth from IBS for discussing aspects of this book with me.

Thanks to my wife, Sowmya Hubert, and my daughters, Ann S. Binil and Ria S. Binil, who sacrificed so much. A huge thanks is due to my father, Christudas Y., and my mother, Azhakamma J., for their selfless support, which helped me get where I am today. Also, a note of thanks to my in-laws, Hubert Daniel and Pamala Percis. Finally, thanks to my sister, Dr. Binitha, her husband, Dr. Segin Chandran, and their daughter, Aardra B. S.

Introduction

Microservices promise the holy grail: concurrent releases and selective scalability. How can you do that in a cloud-native manner? Can microservices do away with synchronous RPC and adopt asynchronous, message-based interactions? When you do that, how do you guarantee user experience with the same synchronous mode of interaction? In this book, you will learn about these non-trivial patterns and practices, all with production grade example code that you can use as templates to start your own work.

With 25 years of experience, I teach you the otherwise hard-to-understand hexagonal and onion architectures and demonstrate them with concrete samples in Spring Boot. If you know enough Java and Spring, you can learn basic to advanced concepts, including replicating instances of the same microservice and correlating request and responses from concurrent users to the same instance, in RPC and in messaging styles. You will learn to do this in standalone Java processes, in Docker containers, in Kubernetes, and in AWS Cloud using the Elastic Kubernetes Service (EKS).

What's inside:

- Build a simple microservice in Spring Boot

- Learn about HATEOAS, hexagonal, and onion architectures, with code example

- Build multiple microservices interacting over RPC and messaging

- Use asynchronous patterns at every tier, yet corelate concurrent user requests to the same instance or to different instances

- Learn about CI and CD and Helm packaging, with code examples

- Build Docker packages and deploy them to Kubernetes

- Deploy microservices to AWS EC2 and EKS

Spring Boot helps developers create applications that just run. When minimal configuration is required to create an application, even novice Java developers can do it. There is no reason why this simplicity should constrain developers in addressing complex enterprise requirements, and that is where microservice architecture using Spring Boot helps. In addition to rapidly deploying, patching, or scaling applications, containers provide solutions that can also support agile and DevOps efforts to accelerate development, test, and production cycles. The cloud helps companies scale and adapt at speed, accelerate innovation, and drive business agility, without heavy upfront IT investment. What if you could equip even a novice developer with all that is required to help enterprises do all these? This book just does that, and more.

## CHAPTER 1

Microservices for the Enterprise

It has been more than a decade since the original ideas and variants of microservices were discussed and considered. Today, this architectural style is the norm, not the exception. Its tools and frameworks have matured enough and the architecture principles have been tested and proven, both on-premises and on the cloud. There is sufficient clarity on how this software architecture distinguishes itself from its predecessors, so this chapter discusses only a few key points that have not been discussed elsewhere.

This chapter starts by looking at an overview of the computing paradigm and explaining where the current trends of microservices fit in. You will learn that microservices is yet another form of distributed computing, but the true benefits of microservices are reaped when you provide a decentralized capability in business transaction processing for the microservices components. Decentralization brings autonomy to peer microservices, which brings a distinguishable feature to the business transactions, called *eventual consistency*. Eventually consistent systems are more fault tolerant and provide reliability to end-to-end business transactions, which happen over the otherwise relatively less stable HTTP-based transport protocol. The chapter next looks at the boundaries between microservices and "not so micro" services, covered in the service

© Binildas A. Christudas 2024
B. A. Christudas, *Java Microservices and Containers in the Cloud*,
https://doi.org/10.1007/979-8-8688-0555-4_1

granularity discussion. Before I close this chapter, I also introduce the notion of the *hexagonal architecture* with an example. There are more examples of the hexagonal architecture in Chapter 2 as well.

This chapter covers the following topics:

- Different computing architecture paradigms

- Eventually consistent software systems

- Service granularity

- The hexagonal architecture metaphor

- Your first Java microservice in code

Computing Architecture Paradigms

It's important to understand the distributed nature of services in a microservices style of architecture, so this section explains what this architecture is and how it differentiates itself from other more familiar counterparts.

Centralized Computing

Compared to minicomputers or personal computers, which are common and commoditized today, mainframes have more processing power. Early versions of mainframe computers had a large cabinet, called a *main frame,* which housed the central processing unit and main memory. Mainframe computers are characterized by interactive user terminals operating as timesharing computers, supporting hundreds of users simultaneously along with batch processing. Mainframes are used for business transaction processing, like airline reservation, banking, and so on. A transaction encompasses a set of operations including disk I/O, operating system calls, and other forms of data transfer from one subsystem to another, as shown in Figure 1-1.

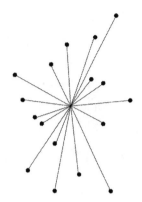

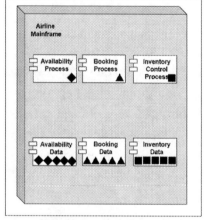

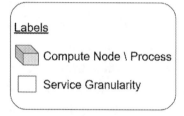

Mainframe Architecture

Figure 1-1. *Centralized computing*

As depicted, mainframes are centralized computers operating in timesharing mode, supporting hundreds of users simultaneously along with batch processing. Users access mainframes through keyboard/typewriter terminals and specialized text terminal CRT displays with integral keyboards. *Green screen* is the common name for those monochrome monitors used for user access, since they traditionally used a green "P1" phosphor screen.[1]

---

[1] Monochrome monitors are commonly available in three colors: If the P1 phosphor is used, the screen is green monochrome. If the P3 phosphor is used, the screen is amber monochrome. If the P4 phosphor is used, the screen is white monochrome (known as "page white").

3

Transaction processing or *batch processing* was offered as a service by the central mainframe system, so this architecture is best categorized under the *centralized computing paradigm*, where a central computer makes all the decisions regarding the successful completion of the business transaction, end to end.

Distributed Computing

Next came the *distributed computing* paradigm, where the different components of the compute system were located on different networked computers, and they communicated and coordinated their actions by passing messages to one another. While doing so, typically, one of the nodes or computers acted as a coordinator for the business transaction— it coordinated (or orchestrates) elementary computing components of the overall business transaction on different networked computers and decided on the success or failure of the transaction.

Distributed computing comes in different variants. The major ones are listed here:

- *Client–server*: In a client-server architecture, clients request and receives data from the servers and display it to the users. The client machine hosts most of the rules and validations required for the business logic to complete. Thick clients are characteristic of this architecture, and client-binary distribution is a hassle here

- *Three-tier*: A three-tier architectures move the client intelligence to a middle tier so that stateless and thin clients can be used. This simplifies application deployment to a single middleware server, and client binary distribution is zero or minimal. Most web applications are three-tier.

- *n-tier*: An N-tier architecture, also known as a multi-tier architecture, is a software engineering design pattern that separates an application into logical layers and physical tiers. Each layer has a specific responsibility and functionality, and the tiers are usually separated by physical or logical boundaries, such as different servers, processes, or networks.

- *Peer-to-peer*: In this architecture, there are no particular machines that provide a service or manage the network resources. Instead all responsibilities are uniformly divided among all the machines, known as peers. Each peer can serve as a client and as a server. Examples of this architecture include BitTorrent. The bitcoin network is also a kind of peer to peer, but bitcoin network fits more into another computing paradigm called *decentralized architecture,* which is explained shortly.

- *Microservices*: Microservices are a kind of distributed architecture where functional units are identified as the basis for distribution. Because of that, more than one microservice is needed in many cases to complete a single business transaction. Microservices with additional design capabilities can be classified into another class of computing paradigm, called *decentralized*, which is discussed later in this chapter.

Figure 1-2 represents a distributed architecture. Here, the client, business, and database processes are separated by the network.

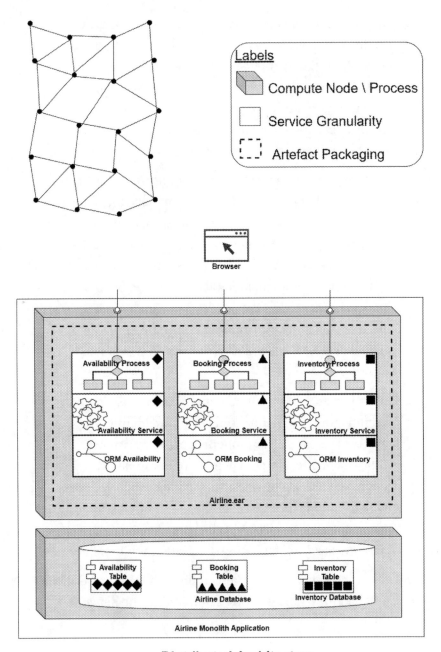

Distributed Architecture

Figure 1-2. *Distributed computing*

In Figure 1-2, a single middle tier server is shown. This server is composed of a set of business modules:

- *Availability*: A module that helps to plan a flight, during which a traveler can enter the travel dates and destinations and get a list of all available flights from different airlines, through what is called an Internet Booking Engine (IBE). The traveler can browse through this list, compare the prices, and then decide which one to book.

- *Booking*: The booking module helps the traveler book a flight and create a Passenger Name Record (PNR) for travel in the shortlisted flight.

- *Inventory*: When a booking is completed for seats in a flight, the seat inventory should be reduced in the Inventory module.

In some cases, the middle tier server will also connect to other third-party systems like a Global Distribution System (GDS) such as Amadeus or Sabre, thus exhibiting the distributed computing paradigm in the truest sense. This is depicted in the distributed mesh notation in Figure 1-2.

Decentralized Computing

In decentralized computing, application services are carried out by individual computing devices or nodes on a distributed network, with no central location. This approach to software development (and distribution) affords developers great flexibility and savings, since they don't have to create a central control point. Bitcoin, Ethereum, and Uniswap are a few protocols that use decentralized computing.

Figure 1-3 depicts a microservices architecture, which is obviously distributed. Different components of the end-to-end business transactions could also be spread across different components, so in a way this is decentralized.

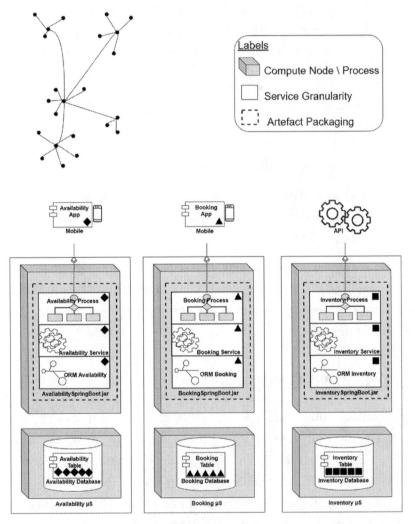

Distributed (and Decentralized) Architecture

Figure 1-3. *Decentralized computing*

I do not discuss the intricacies of why Figure 1-3 depicts a microservices architecture, since I assume readers are familiar with those basics. Here are a few of the characteristics of this architecture:

- *Distributed*: The business application is divided and distributed based on functionality (airline shopping, booking, and inventory management are the functionalities).

- *Independent*: Each of the microservices can be developed and deployed independent of the others (provided you maintain API compatibility for inter-microservices communication).

- *Availability*: If one of the microservices is not running, users can still get functionality from the application through other microservices that are running (if Booking is down, a user can still do some shopping).

Thus, in a way, a microservices architecture with the appropriate design primitives can also function as a decentralized application (even though the nomenclature of decentralized is more applicable to applications involving blockchains).

Eventually Consistent Software Systems

It's important to understand the distributed nature of services in a microservices style of architecture. This section explains what this is and how it's different from other more familiar counterpart architectures.

Atomic Consistency

Figure 1-4 is the distributed architecture shown in Figure 1-2, but here a user is booking a flight.

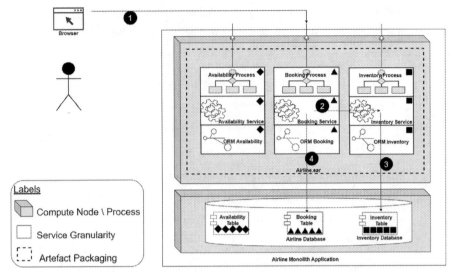

ACID Transactions

Figure 1-4. *ACID transactions*

Referring to Figure 1-4, a typical flight booking business transaction happens like this:

1. The browser sends the user transaction to the business tier server.

2. Since the transaction is a flight booking, it is intercepted by the Booking module. Before you perform the booking, the booking module sends an update inventory request to the Inventory module to reduce the seat inventory, after starting an ACID[2] transaction.

---

[2] ACID stands for Atomicity, Consistency, Isolation, and Durability. If a database operation has these ACID properties, it can be called an ACID transaction, and data storage systems that apply these operations are called transactional systems.

3. Within the previously started ACID transaction, the Inventory module updates the inventory database table.

4. If the inventory update is successful, the booking module will create a booking in its database table, within the same transaction context.

If the booking and the inventory tables are in the same database, and if the booking and the inventory components are two modules in the same middle tier server, the transaction is a local transaction. That means the two table updates will either be successful or rolled back in an atomic (ACID) manner.

Eventual Consistency

This section considers the same flight booking scenario in a microservices architecture, where the processing is distributed. See Figure 1-5.

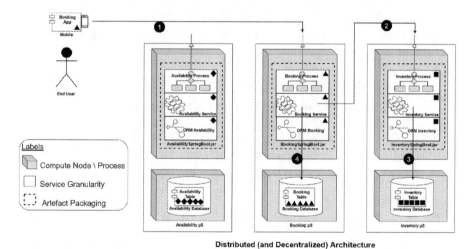

Figure 1-5. *Inter-microservice transactions*

The same flight booking business transaction scenario now happens like this:

1. The Booking app will send the user transaction to the business tier server.

2. Since the transaction is booking a flight, it is intercepted by the booking microservice. Before you perform the booking, the booking microservice sends an update inventory request to the inventory microservice to reduce the seat inventory. However, you can't start a global transaction and send the update inventory request in the same global transaction. This is because the update inventory request is typically a synchronous REST invocation, and distributed transactions across microservices are not encouraged. Without a distributed transaction context, a success or a failure for the update inventory request is received by the booking microservice.

3. The Inventory module updates the inventory database table and sends a success or a failure.

4. If the inventory update is successful, the booking microservices will create a booking in its database table and send back a success message to the end user.

Here, there is a catch. If by chance the attempt to update the inventory database table is successful, but the booking microservices fails to create a booking in the booking database table, there is an issue in the consistency in data across these two tables. You need manual intervention to correct this and bring these two microservices back to eventually consistent.

Eventually Consistent, Decentralized Systems

I have initiated a discussion on how to make microservices eventually consistent. I have also discussed how to deal with the scenario when the update inventory database table is successful, but the booking microservices fails to create a booking in the booking database table. Now consider the converse scenario—what if the inventory microservice is not running and the booking microservices cannot complete the booking? This scenario occurs when the synchronous style REST invocation from the booking microservices to the inventory microservice cannot complete, so the booking creation will also fail.

Figure 1-6 shows an improvisation over the architecture shown in Figure 1-5, by plugging in an event based channel.

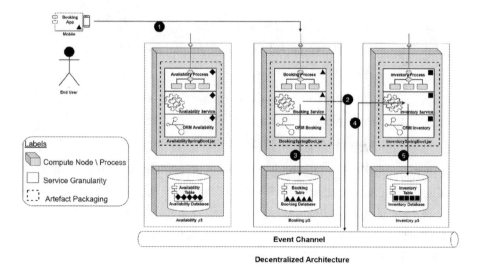

Decentralized Architecture

Figure 1-6. *Decentralized microservices*

Here, the microservices are not tightly coupled. Instead, you can use a loosely coupled JMS or AMQP style messaging protocol. The sequence of the flight booking business transaction could then be as follows:

1. The browser sends the user transaction to the business tier server.

2. Since the transaction is a flight booking, it is intercepted by the booking microservice. Before you perform the booking, the Booking module sends a "flight booked" message to the messaging channel.

3. The booking microservice will create a booking in its database table and provide the response to the end user.

4. The "flight booked" message will be picked up by any other interested microservices—the inventory microservice in this case.

5. The inventory microservices update the inventory database table and optionally sends a success or failure message to the messaging channel.

It is possible to improve the reliability of this business transaction by keeping Steps 2 and 3 in the scope of a transaction. Regardless of that, one notable change in the design is that the business transaction is spanned across multiple microservices, and the successful completion of the transaction is determined by the overall completion of transactions by these different microservices, eventually. No single microservice is solely responsible for controlling the complete end-to-end flow. Instead, each microservice performs its own part, thus making the architecture truly decentralized.

Note that this discussion assumed that enough inventory exists. There can be more complex scenarios in which inventory is limited, but this is beyond the scope here.

Service Granularity

A proper appreciation of the different levels of granularity for a services architecture will help you understand their possibilities and limitations, so this section looks at these service granularities.

Monolith

Figure 1-7 illustrates a typical monolith architecture. In this architecture, the functional modules are only logically separated, but they are all physically packaged into a single .ear (enterprise archive) archive.

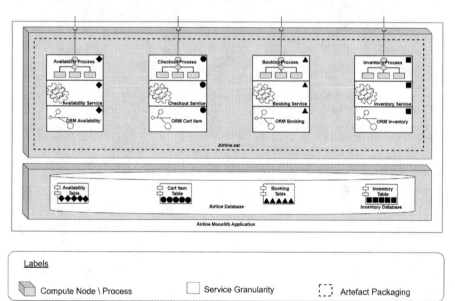

Figure 1-7. *A monolith architecture*

Many times, a monolith architecture communicates with a database in a different node, and all the functional modules are coupled tightly to this single database.

Macroservice

The macroservice architecture shown in Figure 1-8 is a packaging improvement over the monolith architecture.

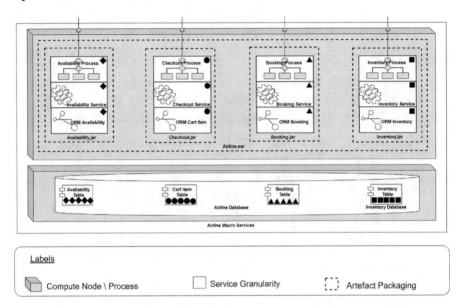

Figure 1-8. A macroservice architecture

In the macroservice architecture, different functional modules are packaged separately, into separate .jars (Java archives). The deployment schema of a macroservice architecture is similar to that of a monolith. All of the Java archives are placed in a single .ear or .war (web archive) and then deployed in a single node.

Mini Service

A mini service architecture is a genuine attempt to improvise over a monolith or macroservice. Figure 1-9 depicts a mini service architecture.

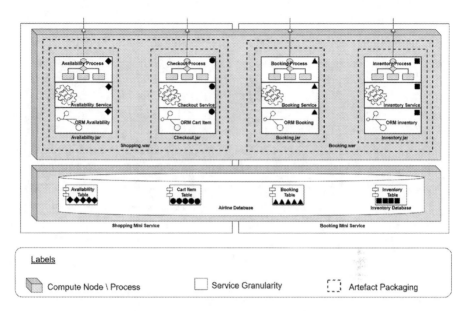

Figure 1-9. *A mini service architecture*

As shown in Figure 1-9, a mini service architecture will also package modules into separate archives, similar to a macroservice architecture. Further, some of these archives can also be packaged into separate deployable archives. However, in many cases, these deployment archives are deployed in the same node due to architectural constraints like dependent libraries, communication modes, and so on.

Microservices

The microservice architecture attempts to provide complete flexibility in terms of development, deployment, and release, as shown in Figure 1-10.

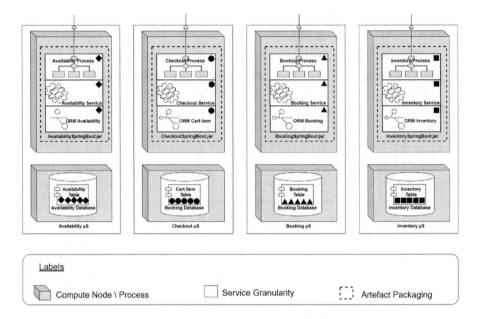

Figure 1-10. *A microservice architecture*

One notable advantage of the microservices architecture is that it promotes polyglot technologies. This gives each microservice the flexibility to adopt its own implementation technology and architecture, yet still exposing and interacting with peer microservices using standard protocols.

The Hexagonal Architecture Metaphor

When learning about loosely coupled systems, especially in the context of microservices, it's helpful to discuss the *hexagonal architecture*. I do that in this section.

To understand this metaphor, I start the discussion with the typical layered architecture.

Layered Architecture

A layered architecture refers to the typical software architecture organization that's followed to separate concerns, mainly those of communication, as shown in Figure 1-11.

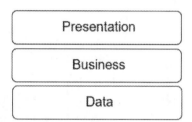

Figure 1-11. Layered architecture

In the layered architecture in Figure 1-11, the top and bottom layers are simply entry/exit points to/from the application.

The Ports and Adapter Architecture

The ports and adapter architecture was mentioned by Alistair Cockburn on his blog in 2005. It reads as follows:

"Allow an application to equally be driven by users, programs, automated test or batch scripts, and to be developed and tested in isolation from its eventual runtime devices and databases."

To explain further, think about an application as the central artefact of a system, where all input reaches and all output leaves the application through a port(s) that isolates the application from all kinds of external tools, technologies, and delivery mechanisms. The application should have no knowledge of who/what is sending input or receiving output. This is intended to protect the applications against the evolution of technology and business requirements, since such an evolution can make applications obsolete shortly after they are developed.

To understand the ports and adapters architecture, first turn the layered architecture from the typical North-South orientation to an East-West orientation, as shown in Figure 1-12.

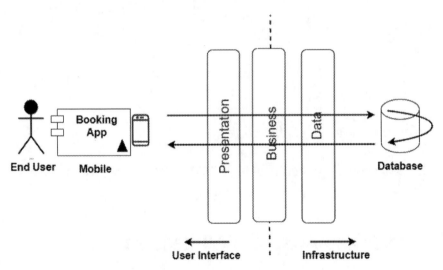

Figure 1-12. *The layered architecture, orientation changed*

Figure 1-12 shows the typical application flow, which starts from the code in the user interface, through the application core to the infrastructure code, back to the application core, finally delivering a response to the user interface.

The ports and adapters architecture solves the problem of safeguarding and reusing the inner layers (business layer) by using an abstraction layer, implemented as a port and an adapter.

- *Ports*: A port is a consumer-agnostic entry and exit point to/from the application. In Java, it is a Java interface. Or in more abstract terms, it could be an HTTP REST interface or a JMS or AMQP messaging interface.

- *Adapter*: An adapter class implements an interface known to its clients and provides access to an instance of a class not known to its clients. An adapter object provides the functionality promised by an interface without having to assume what class is used to implement that interface.

The ports and adapters architecture explicitly identifies three fundamental blocks of code in a system:

1. *Interface*: Code that makes it possible to run a user interface, regardless of the type of user interface it might be.

2. *Business*: The business logic code, or application core, which is used by the user interface to make things happen.

3. *Infrastructure*: The infrastructure code that connects the application core to tools like a database, a message queue, or a third-party API.

In the current orientation in Figure 1-12, the adapters on the left side, representing the UI, are called the *primary* or *driving* adapters because they initiate an action on the application. The adapters on the right side, representing the connections to the backend resources, are called the *secondary* or *driven* adapters because they always react to an action of a primary adapter.

The primary or driving adapters provide services (to the user interface), whereas the secondary or driven adapters consume services (from the infrastructure). Hence on the left side, both the port and its concrete implementation (the use case) belong inside the application. On the right side, the port belongs inside the application, but its concrete implementation belongs outside. It wraps around some external infrastructure from some provider.

Hexagonal Architecture

Figure 1-12 shows two sides—one side an entry to the application using the user interface and the other side an exit from the application into an infrastructure. Thus, although there are two symmetrical sides (left and right) of the application, each side can have several entry/exit points. For example, an API (say REST API) and a Graphical User Interface (GUI) can be two different entry/exit points on the left side of the application, while a database and a message queue can be two different entry/exit points on the right side of the application. To represent that this application can have multiple entry/exit points, you draw the application diagram with several sides. The diagram could have been any polygon with several sides, but the choice turned out to be a hexagon, hence the name hexagonal architecture.

Microservice Metamodel

I can now extend the notion of the hexagonal architecture to a microservice, since many of the aspects discussed in the ports and adapters section make sense in the context of a microservice. This is shown in Figure 1-13.

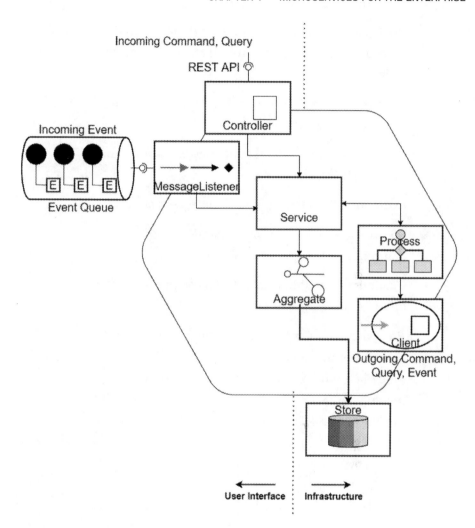

Figure 1-13. *The microservices metamodel*

You can now compare the microservice metamodel shown in Figure 1-13 to that of a Java Spring-based microservice with the following components:

- *REST controller*: An HTTP-based REST based controller class, annotated with @RestController.

- *POJO service*: The core business logic. This class should be shielded from any entry/exit changes to facilitate reuse.

- *ORM repository*: An ORM repository class handling persistence logic to a database.

- *Aggregate entity*: Domain entity based on the domain model, which is reusable.

- *Data store*: The infrastructure's persistent storage.

- *Message listener*: A JMS or an AMQP-based controller class.

- *Client program*: Program that will use ports to exit to other kinds of infrastructure.

- *Process*: A complex business modeling would call for a process modeling, which is optional. If a process modelling is involved, the abstract metamodel relationship between a process and service is as shown in Figure 1-14.

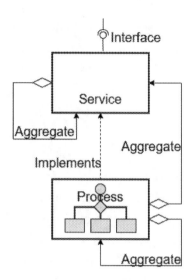

Figure 1-14. *Process vs. service relationship*

- A service exposes a service interface.

- A service can be an aggregate of other services.

- A process aggregates and orchestrates many services, or even other processes.

- A process also exposes a service interface.

Subsequent discussions follow the microservices metamodel shown in Figure 1-13 to represent many of the upcoming scenarios.

Your First Java Microservice

I am sure you have had enough theory, so it's time to build your first microservice in Java.

This example uses Spring Boot to build the Java microservices. The project codebase can be imported into any of your favorite IDEs, but they could also be built and run without an IDE and with the help of commands in a Windows or Mac terminal. Subsequent chapters use a similar approach, since discussion on which IDE to use and how to use a specific IDE is beyond the scope of this book. I assume you are either already familiar with those steps or can refer to an introductory Java or JEE book.

Spring Boot

Spring Boot uses an opinionated view of the Spring platform and many third-party Java libraries so that it is straightforward to create standalone, production-grade, Spring-based applications that you can "just run." Spring Boot follows many conventions and usage patterns followed by developers, which they have been leveraging while using Spring and other third-party libraries. Therefore, most Spring Boot applications need very little Spring configuration. Again, the intention is not to cover Spring Boot in detail; that is outside the scope of this chapter. Readers already familiar with Java or Spring should have no problem getting started by visiting the Spring Boot home page.

Design Your First Hexagonal Microservice

This section starts with a trimmed-down version of the hexagonal microservice view shown in Figure 1-13. The same is shown in Figure 1-15.

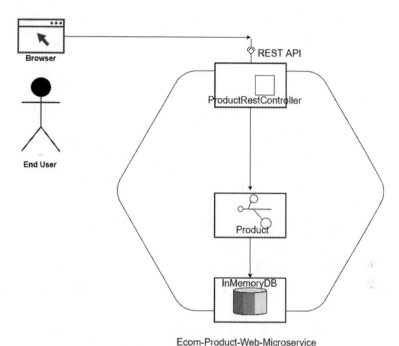

Ecom-Product-Web-Microservice

Figure 1-15. *Product web microservice*

Consider Figure 1-15 using the language of ports and adapters. An HTTP port is used, which is nothing more than a specification of how the user's browser can use the application core. This port (interface) belongs inside the business logic as a REST controller. The Product entity fulfills the application core. See Figure 1-16.

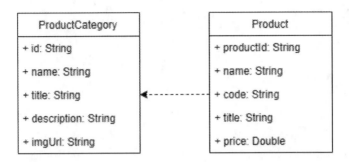

Figure 1-16. *Product web microservice core entities*

In Figure 1-15, I have intentionally stripped off the service and the process components from Figure 1-13 to make the first sample rather simple. Next, you'll use a database adapter to connect to an in-memory DB. Again, to keep the first example simple, I haven't designed an adapter. Instead, I used a direct dependency to an in-memory database class. In the next chapter, you will look at how to use an adapter in the right manner.

`ProductRestController` is the primary or driver adapter, which wraps around an HTTP port. You use it to tell the application core what to do. It translates whatever comes from delivery mechanism (a browser request in this case) into a method call in the application core.

Code Organization

The source code for this book is available on GitHub via the book's product page, located at `www.apress.com/9798868805547`. The code for the sample is organized as shown in Listing 1-1, inside the `ch01\ch01-01` folder. This follows the standard Maven structure, so `pom.xml` is in the root of the directory.

Listing 1-1. Spring Boot Source Code Organization

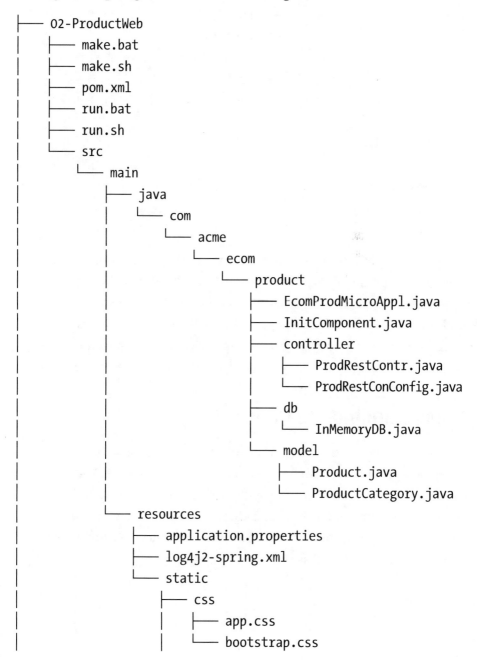

```
├── 02-ProductWeb
│   ├── make.bat
│   ├── make.sh
│   ├── pom.xml
│   ├── run.bat
│   ├── run.sh
│   └── src
│       └── main
│           ├── java
│           │   └── com
│           │       └── acme
│           │           └── ecom
│           │               └── product
│           │                   ├── EcomProdMicroAppl.java
│           │                   ├── InitComponent.java
│           │                   ├── controller
│           │                   │   ├── ProdRestContr.java
│           │                   │   └── ProdRestConConfig.java
│           │                   ├── db
│           │                   │   └── InMemoryDB.java
│           │                   └── model
│           │                       ├── Product.java
│           │                       └── ProductCategory.java
│           └── resources
│               ├── application.properties
│               ├── log4j2-spring.xml
│               └── static
│                   ├── css
│                   │   ├── app.css
│                   │   └── bootstrap.css
```

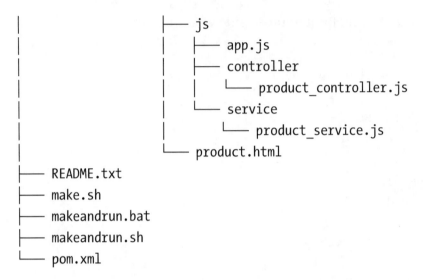

```
|                           ├── js
|                           |   ├── app.js
|                           |   ├── controller
|                           |   |   └── product_controller.js
|                           |   └── service
|                           |       └── product_service.js
|                           └── product.html
├── README.txt
├── make.sh
├── makeandrun.bat
├── makeandrun.sh
└── pom.xml
```

The ch01\ch01-01\02-ProductWeb\src\main\java folder contains the source code for the microservice. The ch01-01\02-ProductWeb\src\main\resources folder contains the configurations for the microservice as well as the source code for the web app, which will help the end users interact with the microservice using a browser interface. The topmost folder also contains scripts that will help you build and run the microservice.

Understanding the Code

I keep the domain entity very simple for this first example. The entity is a typical product that can be listed on an e-commerce site. Multiple products fall into a product category, so on the site you can first show product categories and users can explore or browse through the product categories to see all products available under the selected category. Let's look at these entities first, as shown in Listing 1-2.

Listing 1-2. Product/Product Category Domain Model (ch01\
ch01-01\02-ProductWeb\src\main\java\com\acme\ecom\product\
model\Product.java)

```java
public class Product {

    @Id
    private String productId;
    private String name;
    private String code;;
    private String title;
    private Double price;
}

public class ProductCategory {

    @Id
    private String id;
    private String name;
    private String title;
    private String description;
    private String imgUrl;
}
```

These entities are straightforward, hence they are not explained
further. Next, consider the REST-capable HTTP port, using a Spring
RestController, as shown in Listing 1-3.

Listing 1-3. REST Based HTTP Port for getAllProducts (ch01\
ch01-01\02-ProductWeb\src\main\java\com\acme\ecom\product\
controller\ProductRestController.java)

```
@RestController
public class ProductRestController{

    @Autowired
    private InMemoryDB inMemoryDB;

    @RequestMapping(value = "/productsweb",
        method = RequestMethod.GET,
        produces = {MediaType.APPLICATION_JSON_VALUE})
    public ResponseEntity<List<Product>> getAllProducts() {

        List<Product> products = inMemoryDB.getAllProducts();
        if(products.isEmpty()){
            return new ResponseEntity<List<Product>>(
            HttpStatus.NOT_FOUND);
        }
        List<Product> list = new ArrayList<Product> ();
        for(Product product:products){
            list.add(product);
        }
        return new ResponseEntity<List<Product>>(list,
            HttpStatus.OK);
    }
}
```

getAllProducts is a Java method that will return a list of all products in
the database, defined through an abstract protocol and format of delivery
declared in the HTTP-based REST port. A concrete implementation of
this port is then injected (or used to intercept) by Spring and used in the
Controller in the runtime. They translate the JSON-formatted data payload

from the HTTP delivery channel into a getAllProducts method call in the application core. To retrieve the products, the getAllProducts delegates a call to an InMemoryDB class.

The remainder of the REST controller's implementation is shown in Listing 1-4.

Listing 1-4. REST Based HTTP Port for getAllProducts (ch01\ch01-01\02-ProductWeb\src\main\java\com\acme\ecom\product\controller\ProductRestController.java)

```java
public class ProductRestController{

    @RequestMapping(value = "/productsweb/{productId}",
        method = RequestMethod.GET,
        produces = MediaType.APPLICATION_JSON_VALUE)
    public ResponseEntity<Product> getProduct(@PathVariable(
        "productId") String productId) {

        Product product = inMemoryDB.getProduct(productId);
        if (product == null) {
            return new ResponseEntity<Product>(
                HttpStatus.NOT_FOUND);
        }
        return new ResponseEntity<Product>(product,
            HttpStatus.OK);
    }

    @RequestMapping(value = "/productsweb",
        method = RequestMethod.POST,
        produces = MediaType.APPLICATION_JSON_VALUE)
    public ResponseEntity<Product> addProduct(
        @RequestBody Product product) {
```

```
    Product productFound = inMemoryDB.getProduct(
        product.getProductId());
    if (null != productFound) {
        return new ResponseEntity<Product>(
            HttpStatus.CONFLICT);
    }
    inMemoryDB.addProduct(product);
    return new ResponseEntity<Product>(product,
        HttpStatus.OK);
}

@RequestMapping(value = "/productsweb/{productId}",
    method = RequestMethod.DELETE,
    produces = MediaType.APPLICATION_JSON_VALUE)
public ResponseEntity<Product> deleteProduct(
    @PathVariable("productId")String productId) {

    Product productFound = inMemoryDB.getProduct(
        productId);
    if (productFound == null) {
        return new ResponseEntity<Product>(
            HttpStatus.NOT_FOUND);
    }
    inMemoryDB.deleteProduct(productId);
    return new ResponseEntity<Product>(
        HttpStatus.NO_CONTENT);
}

@RequestMapping(value = "/productsweb/{productId}",
    method = RequestMethod.PUT,
    produces = MediaType.APPLICATION_JSON_VALUE)
public ResponseEntity<Product> updateProduct(
    @PathVariable("productId")String productId,
    @RequestBody Product product) {
```

```java
    Product currentProduct = inMemoryDB.getProduct(
        productId);
    if (currentProduct == null) {
        return new ResponseEntity<Product>(
            HttpStatus.NOT_FOUND);
    }
    currentProduct.setName(product.getName());
    currentProduct.setCode(product.getCode());
    currentProduct.setTitle(product.getTitle());
    currentProduct.setPrice(product.getPrice());
    Product newProduct = inMemoryDB.updateProduct(
        currentProduct);
    return new ResponseEntity<Product>(newProduct,
        HttpStatus.OK);
    }
}
```

Here, given a `productId`, the `getProduct` method will retrieve the details of a specific product. `addProduct` will create a new product and `deleteProduct` will remove a product from the in-memory DB. `updateProduct` will update a product with a new set of values.

Build and Run the Code

The `ch01\ch01-01` folder contains the Maven scripts required to build and run the examples. This example is the simplest microservice anyone could think of, since there are no dependencies to external resources like databases or message queues. It's still a fully functional microservice demonstrating the complete CRUD (Create, Read, Update, and Delete) functionality, so building the sample and bringing up the microservices is a breeze. Assuming you have Java and Maven installed in your machine, you can open a command terminal, go to the `ch01\ch01-01` folder, and execute the commands in Listing 1-5.

Listing 1-5. Commands to Build and Run the Microservice

```
mvn -Dmaven.test.skip=true clean package
java -jar -Dserver.port=8080 ./02-ProductWeb/target/Ecom-
Product-Web-Microservice-0.0.1-SNAPSHOT.jar
```

Alternatively, there is a shell script for a Mac terminal and a Windows batch script that will help you build and run the application in a single go, as shown in Listing 1-6.

Listing 1-6. Build and Run the Microservice Using Scripts

```
(base) binildass-MacBook-Pro:ch01-01 binil$ pwd
/Users/binil/binil/code/mac/mybooks/docker-04/Code/ch01/ch01-01
binildass-MacBook-Pro:ch01-01 binil$ sh makeandrun.sh
[INFO] Scanning for projects...
[INFO] ------------------------------------------------------------
[INFO] Reactor Build Order:
[INFO]
[INFO] Ecom-Product-Web-Microservice                      [jar]
[INFO] Ecom                                               [pom]
[INFO]
[INFO] --------<com.acme.ecom.product:Ecom-Product-Web-Micro
[INFO] Building Ecom-Product-Web-Mi 0.0.1-SNAPSHOT     [1/2]
[INFO] ------------------------------[ jar ]--------------
[INFO]
...
[INFO]
[INFO] Ecom-Product-Web-Microservice .... SUCCESS [  1.705 s]
[INFO] Ecom ............................. SUCCESS [  0.019 s]
[INFO] ------------------------------------------------------------
[INFO] BUILD SUCCESS
[INFO] ------------------------------------------------------------
```

```
[INFO] Total time:  1.902 s
[INFO] Finished at: 2023-12-13T11:32:38+05:30
[INFO] ------------------------------------------------------------

  .   ____
 /\\ / ___'_ _ _ _ _(_)_ _ _ _ \ \ \ \
( ( )\___ | '_ | '_| | '_ \/ _` | \ \ \ \
 \\/  ___)| |_)| | | | | | || (_| |  ) ) ) )
  '  |____| ._|_| |_|_| |_\__, | / / / /
 =========|_|==============|___/=/_/_/_/
 :: Spring Boot ::                (v3.2.0)

2023-12-13 11:32:39 INFO  Startup…:50 - Starting EcomProd...
2023-12-13 11:32:39 DEBUG StartupInfoLogger.logStarting:51 -
Running with Spring Boot v3.2.0, Spring v6.1.1
2023-12-13 11:32:39 INFO  SpringApp…:653 - No active ...
2023-12-13 11:32:40 INFO  InMemoryDB.initDB:71 - Start
2023-12-13 11:32:40 INFO  InMemoryDB.initDB:92 - Ending.
2023-12-13 11:32:40 INFO  Initial...init:35 - Start
2023-12-13 11:32:40 DEBUG Initial...init:37 - Doing Nothing...
2023-12-13 11:32:40 INFO  Initial….init:39 - End
2023-12-13 11:32:40 INFO  Start…:56 - Started EcomProd...
2023-12-13 11:32:46 INFO  ProdRest...getAllProducts:64 - Start
2023-12-13 11:32:46 DEBUG ProductRest...lambda$getAll$0:74 -
Product [productId=1, ...
2023-12-13 11:32:46 DEBUG ProductRestController.
lambda$getAllProducts$0:74 - Product [productId=2, ...
2023-12-13 11:32:46 INFO  ProdRest.getAllProducts:75 – Ending
...
```

You can see from the log that the application is built and deployed, and it is in the running state. Now it's time to test the application.

Test the Microservice Using UI

Once the microservice is up, you can access the web application using your browser and pointing to http://localhost:8080/product.html (see Figure 1-17).

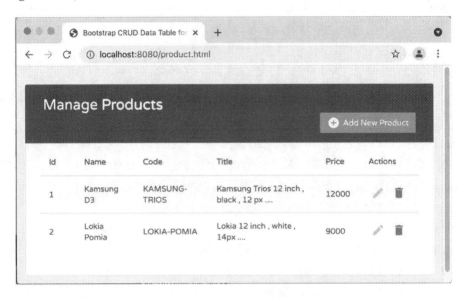

Figure 1-17. *Accessing the microservice using a browser*

Typing this URL using the browser will render the UI app that's packaged inside the resources folder inside the project. From the browser UI, you can add a new product by clicking the Add New Product button and entering the details (see Figure 1-18).

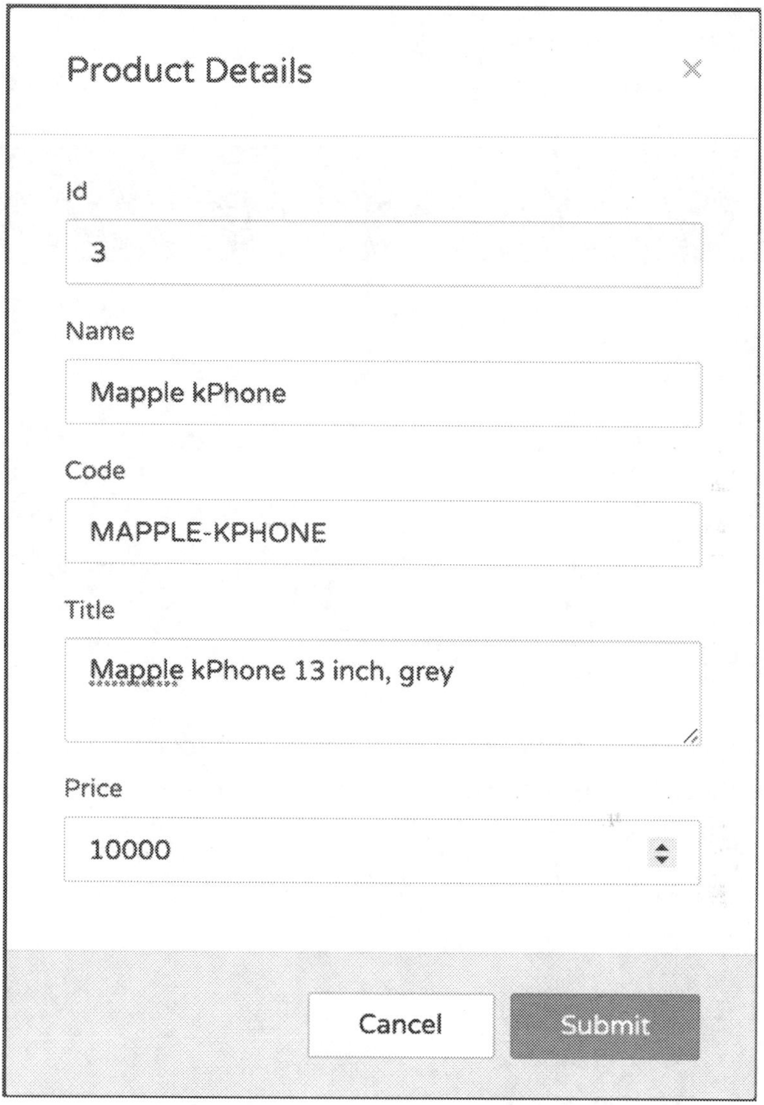

Figure 1-18. *Adding a new product*

Input some meaningful values for all the fields in the UI and click the Submit button, which will ask the microservice to create a new product in the in-memory DB. The newly added product will also be listed in the refreshed screen, as shown in Figure 1-19.

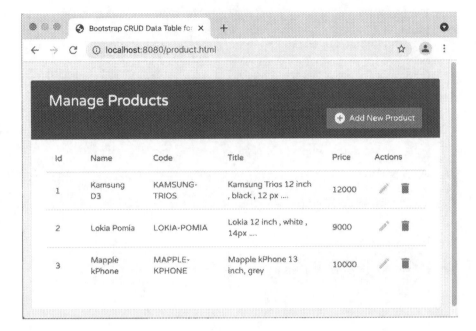

Figure 1-19. *Listing the newly added product*

You can now attempt to edit (update) the newly added product by clicking the Edit icon on the right side of each listed product entry. See Figure 1-20.

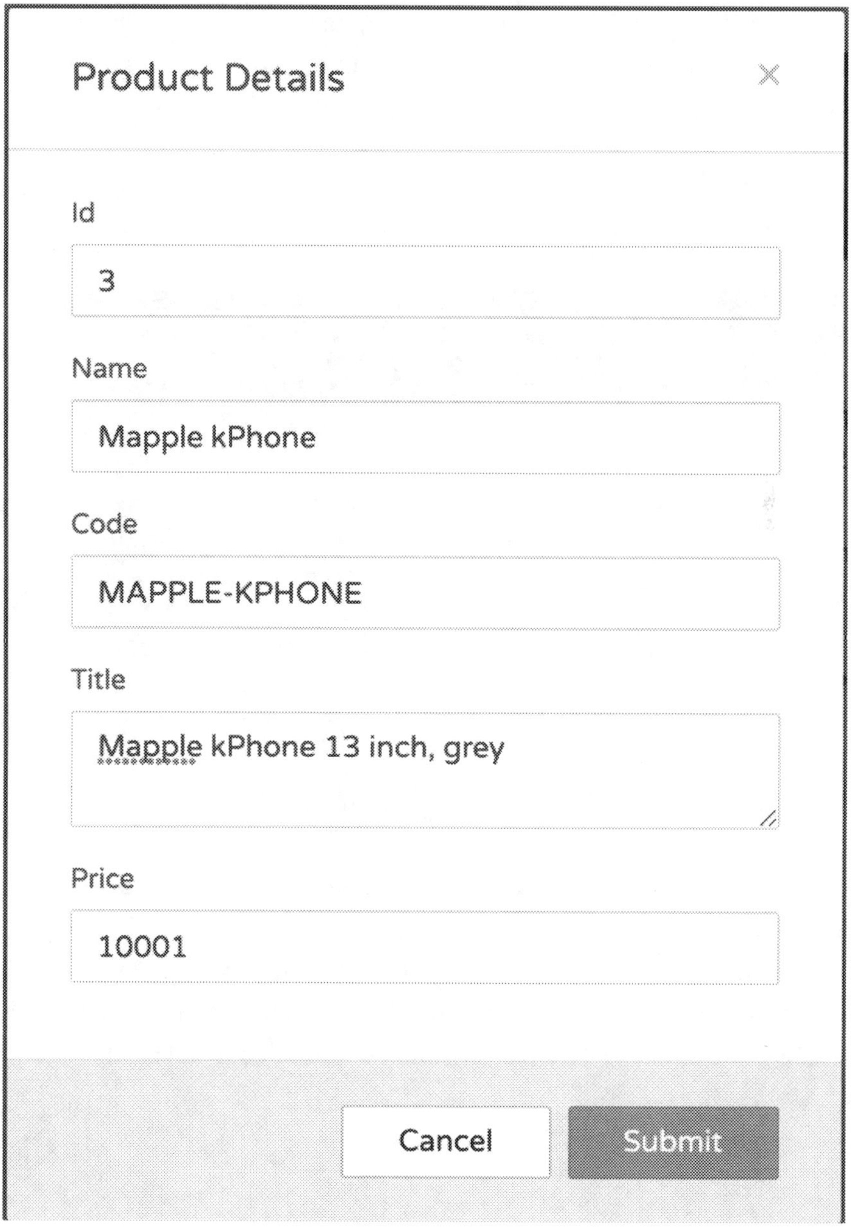

Product Details ✕

Id

3

Name

Mapple kPhone

Code

MAPPLE-KPHONE

Title

Mapple kPhone 13 inch, grey

Price

10001

Cancel   Submit

Figure 1-20. *Update the product*

As shown in Figure 1-20, without changing the product ID, make some valid changes to some of the fields—price in this example. Clicking the Submit button to have the changes take effect. See Figure 1-21.

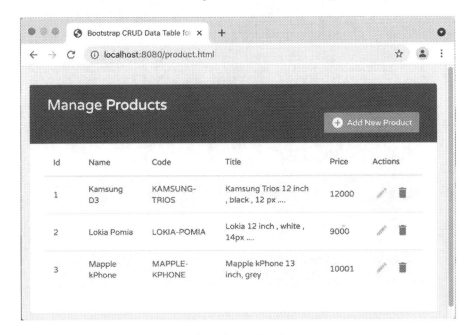

Figure 1-21. *Listing the updated product*

The changes made to the product are listed in the refreshed screen, as shown in Figure 1-21.

Last but not the least, you might also want to test the Delete functionality, which you can do by clicking the Delete icon on the far right side of each product and then confirming your action. See Figure 1-22.

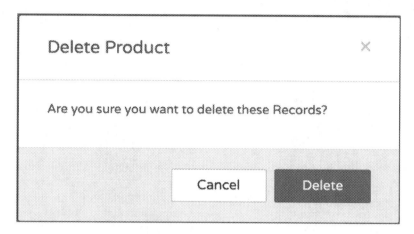

Figure 1-22. *Confirming Delete*

Test the Microservice Using cURL

You may also want to use cURL or Postman to test all the methods implemented in the microservice. Refer to Appendix A for detailed instructions.

Summary

In this chapter, I purposefully tried to avoid defining microservices, since many definitions and viewpoints exist in the industry. Instead, I attempted to look at microservices from some less common perspectives with a view to understand how they fit into the bigger computing paradigm. This chapter also considered how the distinguishing features help provide superior capabilities in executing business transactions. I also attempted to show, with examples, what a hexagonal architecture is. I continue this discussion in the next two chapters, with more examples, so that you can clearly appreciate the design structure and qualities your microservices will have if you adopt the principles of a hexagonal architecture.

CHAPTER 2

More Hands-on Microservices

You coded your first and simplest microservice in the last chapter. That example used a simple data structure as an in-memory database. This chapter extends that example by creating a few more microservices, each one in increasing order of complexity. This will enable you to build on your prior learnings. You will interact with a few real databases and firm up your knowledge of the ports and adapters architecture introduced in Chapter 1.

This chapter is fully hands-on, but the examples are still simple, so you don't have to understand complex business or entity relationships. Instead, the examples emphasize on learning technologies and architecture variations.

This chapter covers the following concepts, each with running examples:

- First, you will enhance the microservice example from the previous chapter to interact with a MongoDB.

- I introduce the Spring Cloud next.

- I move on to a discussion of HAL and HATEOAS.

- As a final example, you will implement a HATEOAS-based microservice using Spring Boot.

© Binildas A. Christudas 2024
B. A. Christudas, *Java Microservices and Containers in the Cloud*,
https://doi.org/10.1007/979-8-8688-0555-4_2

Microservices Using MongoDB and RestTemplate

As mentioned, you will enhance the microservice you created in the last chapter. You will have two microservices—a consumer and a provider microservice—communicating each other using the REST protocol. The provider microservice also interacts with a NoSQL database, MongoDB.

Design the Microservices

This example uses the hexagonal microservice design depicted in Figure 1-13 in Chapter 1. This is shown again in Figure 2-1.

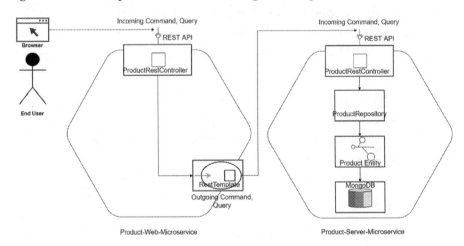

Figure 2-1. *Consumer and provider microservice design*

Both of the microservices shown in Figure 2-1 use HTTP ports at the REST interfaces, which are specification of how a user's browser or some other HTTP client can use the application core. These ports (interfaces) belong inside the business logic of the respective microservices as REST controllers. An adapter is provided by Spring runtime, which provides the functionality promised by the REST interface. A request from the browser will hit the Product Web microservice, which is the consumer microservice. The Product Web microservice doesn't perform any business logic; instead, it delegates the calls to the Product Server microservice, which is the provider microservice. The objective of keeping the Product Web microservice simple is to demonstrate how to initiate inter-microservice communication so that you can use and extend this template for real-world cases.

The RestTemplate in the Product Web microservice is another port, which again is nothing more than a specification on how it is used by the application core. A concrete-driven adapter that implements the RestTemplate port is injected into the application core by Spring wherever and wherever the port is required (type-hinted).

The Product entity fulfills the application core in the Product Server microservice. Here again, I avoided the typical layering of service and component stereotype classes to keep the overall complexity of the example simple.

ProductRepository is the third port used by the Product Server microservice. The purpose of the Product Server microservice is to persist data. So you create a persistence interface that meets its needs, with methods to do CRUD operations in a NoSQL collection using the ID of the entity. At that point, whenever and wherever the application needs to execute CRUD operations, the application core will need an object that implements the persistence interface that you defined, which is supplied by Spring runtime.

Code Organization

The source code for this book is available on GitHub via the book's product page, located at www.apress.com/9798868805547. The code for the example is organized as shown in Listing 2-1, inside the ch02\ch02-01 folder. This follows the standard Maven structure, so pom.xml is in the root of the directory.

Listing 2-1. Spring Boot Source Code Organization

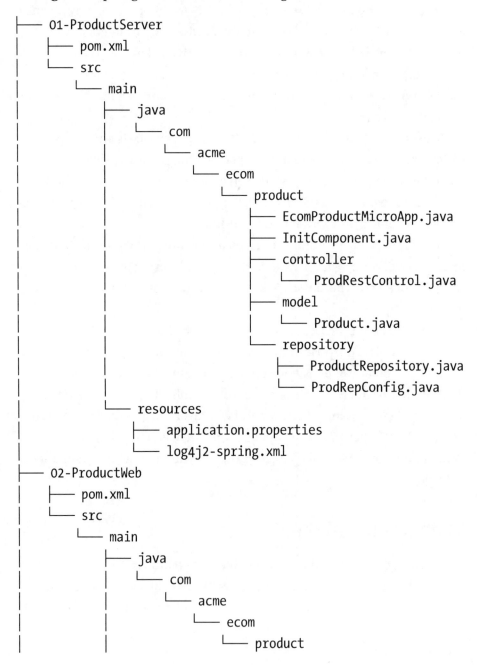

```
├── 01-ProductServer
│   ├── pom.xml
│   └── src
│       └── main
│           ├── java
│           │   └── com
│           │       └── acme
│           │           └── ecom
│           │               └── product
│           │                   ├── EcomProductMicroApp.java
│           │                   ├── InitComponent.java
│           │                   ├── controller
│           │                   │   └── ProdRestControl.java
│           │                   ├── model
│           │                   │   └── Product.java
│           │                   └── repository
│           │                       ├── ProductRepository.java
│           │                       └── ProdRepConfig.java
│           └── resources
│               ├── application.properties
│               └── log4j2-spring.xml
├── 02-ProductWeb
│   ├── pom.xml
│   └── src
│       └── main
│           ├── java
│           │   └── com
│           │       └── acme
│           │           └── ecom
│           │               └── product
```

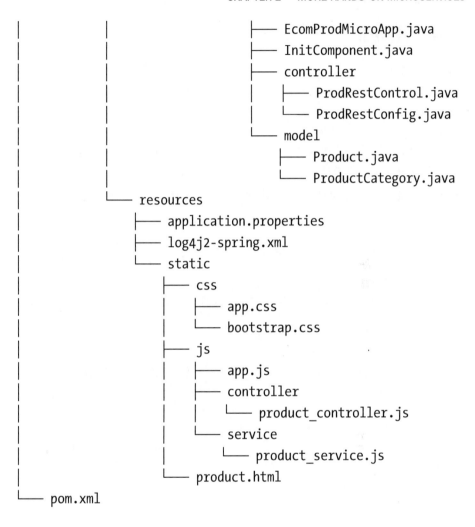

```
|                    |                         ├── EcomProdMicroApp.java
|                    |                         ├── InitComponent.java
|                    |                         ├── controller
|                    |                         |    ├── ProdRestControl.java
|                    |                         |    └── ProdRestConfig.java
|                    |                         └── model
|                    |                              ├── Product.java
|                    |                              └── ProductCategory.java
|                    └── resources
|                         ├── application.properties
|                         ├── log4j2-spring.xml
|                         └── static
|                              ├── css
|                              |    ├── app.css
|                              |    └── bootstrap.css
|                              ├── js
|                              |    ├── app.js
|                              |    ├── controller
|                              |    |    └── product_controller.js
|                              |    └── service
|                              |         └── product_service.js
|                              └── product.html
└── pom.xml
```

Note   The names of a few of the Java classes in Listing 2-1 has been shortened for formatting purposes.

The ch02\ch02-01 folder contains the source code for the consumer and provider microservices. The topmost folder also contains scripts that will help you build the microservices together. There are also scripts in this folder to clean up the projects at the end.

Understanding the Code

Let's look at the provider microservice—the Product Server microservice—first. Listing 2-2 starts with the REST-capable HTTP port, using a Spring RestController.

Listing 2-2. REST Based HTTP Port for getAllProducts Product Server (ch02\ch02-01\01-ProductServer\src\main\java\com\acme\ ecom\product\controller\ProductRestController.java)

```
@RestController
public class ProductRestController {

    @Autowired
    private ProductRepository productRepository;

    @RequestMapping(value = "/products",
        method = RequestMethod.GET,
        produces = {MediaType.APPLICATION_JSON_VALUE})
    public ResponseEntity<List<Product>> getAllProducts() {

        List<Product> products = productRepository.findAll();
        if(products.isEmpty()){
            return new ResponseEntity<List<Product>>(
                HttpStatus.NOT_FOUND);
        }
        List<Product> list = new ArrayList<Product> ();
        for(Product product:products){
            list.add(product);
        }
        list.forEach(item->LOGGER.debug(item.toString()));
        return new ResponseEntity<List<Product>>(list,
            HttpStatus.OK);
    }
}
```

getAllProducts is a Java method that will return a list of all products in the MongoDB database, defined through an abstract protocol and the format of delivery declared in the HTTP-based REST port. A concrete implementation of this port is then injected (or used to intercept) by Spring and used in the Controller edge in the runtime. They translate the JSON formatted Request data payload from the HTTP delivery channel into a getAllProducts method call in the application core. To retrieve the products, getAllProducts delegates calls to the driven port, ProductRepository.

The remainder of the implementation of the REST controller in the Product Server microservice is very similar to the code in Listing 1-4 in Chapter 1 (with the single exception that instead of the in-memory database, the ProductRepository port is used to interact with a MongoDB repository), so I do not repeat the full code here.

This example introduces the abstract port to interact with the MongoDB, as shown in Listing 2-3.

Listing 2-3. Abstract Port to MongoDB Repository (ch02\ ch02-01\01-ProductServer\src\main\java\com\acme\ecom\ product\repository\ProductRepository.java)

```
@RepositoryRestResource(collectionResourceRel = "productdata",
path = "productdata")
public interface ProductRepository extends
        MongoRepository<Product, String> {

    public List<Product> findByCode(
        @Param("code") String  code);
}
```

Since this port extends MongoRepository, all of the default CRUD method declarations are inherited by default. Therefore, you need to only declare the custom methods—findByCode in this example.

The code for the main class of the Product Server microservice is shown in Listing 2-4.

Listing 2-4. Product Server Microservice Main class (ch02\ ch02-01\01-ProductServer\src\main\java\com\acme\ecom\ product \EcomProductMicroserviceApplication.java)

```
@SpringBootApplication
public class EcomProductMicroserviceApplication {

    public static void main(String[] args) {

        SpringApplication.run(
            EcomProductMicroserviceApplication.class, args);
    }
}
```

Listing 2-5 shows the Product Server microservice configuration file.

Listing 2-5. The Product Server Microservice Config File (ch02\ ch02-01\01-ProductServer\src\main\resources\application. properties)

```
spring.data.mongodb.uri=mongodb://localhost:27017/test
server.port=8081
spring.application.name = product-server
```

This URL points to the MongoDB database.

Next, you will look at the consumer microservice, that is, the Product Web microservice. Listing 2-6 shows the REST-capable HTTP port, using a Spring RestController.

Listing 2-6. REST Based HTTP Port for getAllProducts Product Web
(ch02\ch02-01\02-ProductWeb\src\main\java\com\acme\ecom\
product\controller\ProductRestController.java)

```java
@RestController
public class ProductRestController{

    @Value("${acme.PRODUCT_SERVICE_URL}")
    private String PRODUCT_SERVICE_URL;

    @Autowired
    private RestTemplate restTemplate;

    @RequestMapping(value = "/productsweb",
        method = RequestMethod.GET,
        produces = {MediaType.APPLICATION_JSON_VALUE})
    public ResponseEntity<List<Product>> getAllProducts() {

        ParameterizedTypeReference<List<Product>>
            responseTypeRef = new ParameterizedTypeReference<
                List<Product>>() {};
        ResponseEntity<List<Product>> entity =
            restTemplate.exchange(PRODUCT_SERVICE_URL,
                HttpMethod.GET, (HttpEntity<Product>) null,
                responseTypeRef);
        List<Product> productList = entity.getBody();
        return new ResponseEntity<List<Product>>(productList,
            HttpStatus.OK);
    }
}
```

The value for PRODUCT_SERVICE_URL is configured in application.
properties to point to the URL for the provider microservice, as follows:

```
acme.PRODUCT_SERVICE_URL = http://localhost:8081/products
```

53

The adapter to realize the inter-microservice communication is defined in the Product Web microservice by defining the `RestTemplate` configured in Spring in the configuration class, as shown in Listing 2-7.

Listing 2-7. REST Template Configuration in Product Web ch02\ch02-01\02-ProductWeb\src\main\java\com\acme\ecom\product\controller\ProductRestControllerConfiguration.java)

```
@Bean
    RestTemplate restTemplate() {
        ObjectMapper mapper = new ObjectMapper();
        mapper.configure(
            DeserializationFeature.FAIL_ON_UNKNOWN_PROPERTIES,
                false);
        MappingJackson2HttpMessageConverter converter =
            new MappingJackson2HttpMessageConverter();
        converter.setSupportedMediaTypes(
            MediaType.parseMediaTypes("application/json"));
        converter.setObjectMapper(mapper);
        return new RestTemplate(Arrays.asList(converter));
    }
}
```

From now on, whenever the Product Web microservice needs to communicate to the external API of the Product Server microservice, you need an object that implements the `RestTemplate` interface that you defined, and Spring provides you with that.

The rest of the implementation of the Product Web microservice REST controller is shown in Listing 2-8.

Listing 2-8. REST based HTTP Port for CRUD methods of Product Web (ch02\ch02-01\02-ProductWeb\src\main\java\com\acme\ ecom\product\controller\ProductRestController.java)

```
public class ProductRestController{

    @RequestMapping(value = "/productsweb/{productId}",
        method = RequestMethod.GET,
        produces = MediaType.APPLICATION_JSON_VALUE)
    public ResponseEntity<Product> getProduct(@PathVariable(
            "productId") String productId) {

        String uri = PRODUCT_SERVICE_URL + "/" + productId;
        Product product = restTemplate.getForObject(uri,
            Product.class);
        return new ResponseEntity<Product>(product,
            HttpStatus.OK);
    }

    @RequestMapping(value = "/productsweb",
        method = RequestMethod.POST,
        produces = MediaType.APPLICATION_JSON_VALUE)
    public ResponseEntity<Product> addProduct(
            @RequestBody Product product) {

        Product productNew = restTemplate.postForObject(
            PRODUCT_SERVICE_URL,
            product, Product.class);
        return new ResponseEntity<Product>(product,
            HttpStatus.OK);
    }

    @RequestMapping(value = "/productsweb/{productId}",
        method = RequestMethod.DELETE,
        produces = MediaType.APPLICATION_JSON_VALUE)
```

```
public ResponseEntity<Product> deleteProduct(
        @PathVariable("productId")String productId) {

    restTemplate.delete(PRODUCT_SERVICE_URL + "/" +
        productId);
    return new ResponseEntity<Product>(
        HttpStatus.NO_CONTENT);
}

@RequestMapping(value = "/productsweb/{productId}",
    method = RequestMethod.PUT,
    produces = MediaType.APPLICATION_JSON_VALUE)
public ResponseEntity<Product> updateProduct(
        @PathVariable("productId")String productId,
        @RequestBody Product product) {

    String uri = PRODUCT_SERVICE_URL + "/" + productId;
    restTemplate.put(uri, product, Product.class);
    Product updatedProduct = restTemplate.getForObject(
        uri, Product.class);
    return new ResponseEntity<Product>(updatedProduct,
        HttpStatus.OK);
}
}
```

Given a productId, the getProduct method will retrieve the details of a specific product. addProduct will create a new product and deleteProduct will remove a product from the MongoDB database. updateProduct will update a product with a new set of values.

Build and Run the Microservice

The ch02\ch02-01 folder contains the Maven scripts required to build these examples. As a first step, you need to bring up the MongoDB server. Refer to Appendix B to learn how to set up a MongoDB server and bring it up. You need to execute the commands shown in Listing 2-9 to bring up MongoDB.

Listing 2-9. Bringing Up the MongoDB Server

```
(base) binildass-MBP:bin binil$ pwd
/Users/binil/Applns/mongodb/mongodb-macos-x86_64-4.2.8/bin
(base) binildass-MBP:bin binil$ mongod --dbpath /usr/local/var/
mongodb --logpath /usr/local/var/log/mongodb/mongo.log
```

Next, open a command terminal and go to the ch02\ch02-01 folder. Execute the commands shown in Listing 2-10 to build the microservices together.

Listing 2-10. Building and Running the Microservices

```
(base) binildass-MBP:ch02-01 binil$ pwd
/Users/binil/binil/code/mac/mybooks/docker-03/ch02/ch02-01
binildass-MacBook-Pro:ch02-01 binil$ sh make.sh
[INFO] Scanning for projects...
[INFO] ------------------------------------------------------
[INFO] Reactor Build Order:
[INFO]
[INFO] Ecom-Product-Server-Microservice          [jar]
[INFO] Ecom-Product-Web-Microservice             [jar]
[INFO] Ecom                                      [pom]
[INFO]
...
[INFO]
```

```
[INFO] Ecom-Product-Server-Microservice  SUCCESS [  1.834 s]
[INFO] Ecom-Product-Web-Microservice ... SUCCESS [  0.425 s]
[INFO] Ecom .......................... SUCCESS [  0.040 s]
[INFO] -----------------------------------------------------
[INFO] BUILD SUCCESS
[INFO] -----------------------------------------------------
[INFO] Total time:  2.491 s
[INFO] Finished at: 2023-12-20T08:26:08+05:30
[INFO] -----------------------------------------------------
binildass-MacBook-Pro:ch02-01 binil$
```

Alternatively, you can take two command terminals and change the directory to the top-level folder of the microservices. First, build and run the Product Server microservice using the make.sh and the run.sh scripts, as shown in Listing 2-11.

Listing 2-11. Building and Running the Product Server Microservice Using Scripts

```
(base) binildass-MacBook-Pro:01-ProductServer binil$ pwd
/Users/binil/binil/code/mac/mybooks/docker-03/ch02/ch02-01/01-
ProductServer
binildass-MacBook-Pro:01-ProductServer binil$ sh make.sh
[INFO] Scanning for projects...
[INFO]
...
[INFO] -----------------------------------------------------
[INFO] BUILD SUCCESS
[INFO] -----------------------------------------------------
[INFO] Total time:  2.136 s
[INFO] Finished at: 2023-12-20T08:18:18+05:30
[INFO] -----------------------------------------------------
binildass-MacBook-Pro:01-ProductServer binil$
```

```
binildass-MacBook-Pro:01-ProductServer binil$ sh run.sh


  .    ___                             _            __ _ _
 /\\ / ___'_ __ _ _(_)_ __  __ _  \ \ \ \
( ( )\___ | '_ | '_| | '_ \/ _` | \ \ \ \
 \\/  ___)| |_)| | | | | || (_| |  ) ) ) )
  '  |____| ._|_| |_|_| |_\__, | / / / /
 =========|_|==============|___/=/_/_/_/
 :: Spring Boot ::                (v3.2.0)

2023-12-20 08:21:18 INFO  Start.log:50 - Starting EcomProd...
2023-12-20 08:21:18 DEBUG Start.log:51 - Run with Boot v3.2.0
2023-12-20 08:21:18 INFO  SpringApp.log:653 - No active ...
2023-12-20 08:21:19 INFO  InitComponent.init:45 - Start
2023-12-20 08:21:19 INFO  InitComponent.init:67 - End
2023-12-20 08:21:20 INFO  Start.log:56 - Started EcomProd...
```

Next, build and run the Product Web microservice, as shown in Listing 2-12.

Listing 2-12. Building and Running the Product Web Microservice Using Scripts

```
(base) binildass-MacBook-Pro:02-ProductWeb binil$ pwd
/Users/binil/binil/code/mac/mybooks/docker-03/ch02/ch02-01/02-
ProductWeb
binildass-MacBook-Pro:02-ProductWeb binil$ sh make.sh
...
binildass-MacBook-Pro:02-ProductWeb binil$ sh run.sh
[INFO] Scanning for projects...
[INFO]
...
2023-12-20 08:23:46 INFO  SpringApp.log:653 - No active ...
2023-12-20 08:23:47 INFO  InitComponent.init:37 - Start
```

```
2023-12-20 08:23:47 DEBUG InitComponent.init:39 - Do Nothing
2023-12-20 08:23:47 INFO  InitComponent.init:41 - End
2023-12-20 08:23:47 INFO  StartupInfoLogger.logStarted:56 -
Started EcomProduct...
```

Now that both microservices are up and running, you can test the microservices.

Testing the Microservices

Once both microservices are up and running, you can inspect your MongoDB server using the mongo terminal to make sure the Product Server microservice has inserted a few products into the MongoDB server during the microservice startup (see Listing 2-13). Refer to Appendix B to learn how to use the mongo terminal.

Listing 2-13. Inspecting the MongoDB Server Using a Mongo Shell

```
> show collections
product
> db.product.find()
{ "_id" : ObjectId("619e1a5b21b6e123a375641c"), "name" :
"Kamsung D3", "code" : "KAMSUNG-TRIOS", "title" : "Kamsung
Trios 12 inch , black , 12 px ....", "price" : 12000, "_class"
: "com.acme.ecom.product.model.Product" }
{ "_id" : ObjectId("619e1a5b21b6e123a375641d"), "name" : "Lokia
Pomia", "code" : "LOKIA-POMIA", "title" : "Lokia 12 inch ,
white , 14px ....", "price" : 9000, "_class" : "com.acme.ecom.
product.model.Product" }
>
```

When all is set, you can access the web application using your browser and pointing to http://localhost:8080/product.html.

To test the CRUD operations, follow the instructions described in the subsection, "Test the Microservices Using UI" in the last section of Chapter 1, titled "Your First Java Microservice."

Microservices Using Spring Cloud

Spring Cloud is built over Spring Boot. Spring Cloud provides many common patterns in distributed, microservices ecosystems that can help you integrate the core services as a set of loosely coupled services. Spring Cloud also provides many powerful tools that enhance the behavior of Spring Boot applications to implement those patterns. This section looks at one such pattern with code so that you can appreciate the benefits it provides.

Design the Microservices

This section slightly modifies the previous microservice example to introduce Spring Cloud.

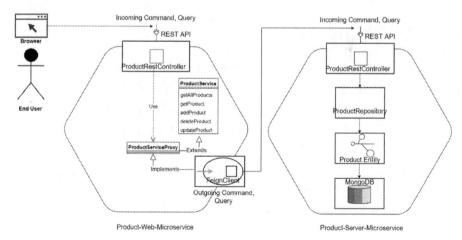

Figure 2-2. *Microservices design with Spring Cloud Feign client*

As explained in the previous example, in both microservices shown in Figure 2-2, you use HTTP ports at the REST interfaces, which specify how a user's browser or another HTTP client can use the application core. These ports (interfaces) belong inside the business logic of the respective microservices as REST controllers. Requests from the browser will hit the Product Web microservice, which is the consumer microservice. The Product Web microservice doesn't perform any business logic; instead, it delegates calls to the Product Server microservice, the provider microservice.

The FeignClient port in the Product Web microservice is another port, which again is nothing more than a specification of how it is used by the application core. A concrete driven adapter that implements the FeignClient port is injected into the application core by Spring Cloud wherever and wherever the port is required (type-hinted).

The Product entity fulfills the application core in the Product Server microservice.

The rest of the ports and adapters in the Product Server microservice function exactly similar as the previous example.

Understanding the Code

The source code for this book is available on GitHub via the book's product page, located at www.apress.com/9798868805547. The source code for this example is organized inside the ch02\ch02-02 folder. The source code is similar to the previous example. The Product Server microservice is similar; however, there are a few changes in the Product Web microservices, which you look at here. Instead of the RestTemplate, this example uses FeignClient. Listing 2-14 shows how to specify FeignClient.

Listing 2-14. The Service Interface for the Product Server
Microservice (ch02\ch02-02\02-ProductWeb\src\main\java\com\
acme\ecom\product\api\ProductService.java)

```java
public interface ProductService {

    @RequestMapping(value = "/products",
        method = RequestMethod.GET,
        produces = MediaType.APPLICATION_JSON_VALUE)
    public ResponseEntity<Resources<Resource<Product>>>
        getAllProducts();

    @RequestMapping(value = "/products/{productId}",
        method = RequestMethod.GET,
        produces = MediaType.APPLICATION_JSON_VALUE)
    public ResponseEntity<Resource<Product>> getProduct(
        @PathVariable("productId") String productId);

    @RequestMapping(value = "/products",
        method = RequestMethod.POST,
        produces = MediaType.APPLICATION_JSON_VALUE)
    public ResponseEntity<Resource<Product>> addProduct(
        @RequestBody Product product);

    @RequestMapping(value = "/products/{productId}",
        method = RequestMethod.DELETE,
        produces = MediaType.APPLICATION_JSON_VALUE)
    public ResponseEntity<Resource<Void>> deleteProduct(
        @PathVariable("productId") String productId);
    @RequestMapping(value = "/products/{productId}",
        method = RequestMethod.PUT,
        produces = MediaType.APPLICATION_JSON_VALUE)
```

```
public ResponseEntity<Resource<Product>> updateProduct(
    @PathVariable("productId") String productId ,
    @RequestBody Product product);
}
```

The first thing you'll do here is define a service interface, as shown in Listing 2-14. Based on this service interface, you can declare an abstract FeignClient, which is a declarative web service client. The nice thing about using Feign is that you don't have to write any code for calling the service, other than an interface definition, as shown in Listing 2-15.

Listing 2-15. The Feign Client Interface for the Product Server Microservice (ch02\ch02-02\02-ProductWeb\src\main\java\com\acme\ecom\product\client\ProductServiceProxy.java)

```
@FeignClient(name="the-name", url = "http://localhost:8081")
public interface ProductServiceProxy extends ProductService{

}
```

A name must be specified for all clients, which is the name of the service with the optional protocol prefix.

You then declare this FeignClient in pom.xml, as shown in Listing 2-16.

Listing 2-16. The Feign Client Dependency in Maven (ch02\ch02-02\02-ProductWeb\pom.xml)

```
<dependencies>
    <dependency>
        <groupId>org.springframework.cloud</groupId>
        <artifactId>
            spring-cloud-starter-openfeign
        </artifactId>
```

```
    <version>4.1.0</version>
  </dependency>
</dependencies>
```

You can use application properties to configure Feign clients; however, I am keeping this example simple, without configuring the Feign client with such details. See Listing 2-17.

Listing 2-17. The Ribbon Configuration (ch02\ch02-02\02-ProductWeb\src\main\resources\application.properties)

```
feign:
    client:
        config:
            default:
                connectTimeout: 5000
                readTimeout: 5000
                loggerLevel: basic
```

Build and Run the Microservice

The ch02\ch02-02 folder contains the Maven scripts required to build the examples. As a first step, you need to bring up the MongoDB server. Refer to Appendix B to learn how to set up a MongoDB server and bring it up. You need to execute the commands shown in Listing 2-18 to bring MongoDB up.

Listing 2-18. Bringing Up the MongoDB Server

```
(base) binildass-MBP:bin binil$ pwd
/Users/binil/Applns/mongodb/mongodb-macos-x86_64-4.2.8/bin
(base) binildass-MBP:bin binil$ mongod --dbpath /usr/local/var/
mongodb --logpath /usr/local/var/log/mongodb/mongo.log
```

Next, take two command terminals and change the directory to the top-level folder of both microservices. Then, build and run the Product Server microservice using the make.sh and the run.sh scripts, as shown in Listing 2-19.

Listing 2-19. Build and Run Product Server Microservice Using Scripts

```
(base) binildass-MacBook-Pro:01-ProductServer binil$ pwd
/Users/binil/binil/code/mac/mybooks/docker-04/Code/ch02/
ch02-02/01-ProductServer
(base) binildass-MacBook-Pro:01-ProductServer binil$ sh make.sh
[INFO] Scanning for projects...
[INFO]
...
2023-12-20 09:28:00 INFO  InitializationComp.init:45 - Start
2023-12-20 09:28:01 INFO  InitializationComp.init:67 - End
2023-12-20 09:28:01 INFO  Start.log:56 - Started EcomProd...
```

As a next step, build and run the Product Web microservice, as shown in Listing 2-20.

Listing 2-20. Build and Run Product Web Microservice Using Scripts

```
(base) binildass-MacBook-Pro:02-ProductWeb binil$ pwd
/Users/binil/binil/code/mac/mybooks/docker-04/Code/ch02/
ch02-02/02-ProductWeb
(base) binildass-MacBook-Pro:02-ProductWeb binil$ sh make.sh
[INFO] Scanning for projects...
...
```

```
2023-12-20 09:32:00 INFO  InitComponent.init:37 - Start
2023-12-20 09:32:00 DEBUG InitComponent.init:39 - Do Nothing.
2023-12-20 09:32:00 INFO  InitComponent.init:41 - End
2023-12-2009:32:00 INFO Start.log:56 - Started EcomProduct...
```

Now that both microservices are up and running, you can now test the microservices.

Testing the Microservices

Once both microservices are up and running, you can access the web application using your browser. Point to this URL:

```
http://localhost:8080/product.html
```

To test the CRUD operations, follow the instructions described in the subsection, "Test the Microservices Using UI" in the last section of Chapter 1, titled "Your First Java Microservice."

Now that you have experienced the flavor of Spring Boot and Spring Cloud, the next section looks at one more important concept in REST-based microservices—HATEOAS and HAL.

HATEOAS and HAL

Hypermedia as the Engine of Application State (HATEOAS) is a constraint of the REST application architecture, which decouples the client from the server. Such a decoupling enables server functionality to evolve independently. The following section investigates this more, again with working examples.

HATEOAS Explained

HATEOAS advocates a user agent that implements HTTP to make an HTTP request of a REST API through a simple URL. Once bootstrapped, all subsequent requests the user agent may make are discovered inside the responses to each request. The media types used for these representations, and the link relations each response may contain, are standardized. The client transitions through the application states by selecting from the links within a representation or by manipulating the representation in other ways afforded by its media type. In other words, the resources available and the actions applicable to these resources are discovered, and subsequent transitions are orchestrated accordingly. In this way, RESTful interaction is driven by hypermedia, rather than out-of-band information.

As an example, the GET request in Listing 2-21 fetches a product resource, requesting details in a JSON representation.

Listing 2-21. HATEOAS Response Format

```
GET /productdata/61a7a51467964f330f6560fa HTTP/1.1
Host: ecom.acme.com

{
    "productId" : "61a7a51467964f330f6560fa",
    "name" : "Lokia Pomia",
    "code" : "LOKIA-POMIA",
    "title" : "Lokia 12 inch , white , 14px ....",
    "price" : 9000.0,
    "_links" : {
        "self" : {
            "href" : "http://localhost:8081/productdata/61"
        },
```

```
    "product" : {
        "href" : "http://localhost:8081/productdata/61"
    }
    "buy" : " http://localhost:8081/productdata/61/buy"
  }
}
```

The response contains the follow-up link to buy the product. Later, when the stock of this product SKU is zero, the "Buy" link may not be available, or to rephrase, in its current state, the Buy link is not available. Hence, the term Engine of Application State. The possible actions vary as the state of the resource varies.

HATEOS thus provides context-driven responses using hypermedia controls, which indicate which operations are possible, or for that matter not possible, based on the presence or absence of these links. This helps avoid transporting state-related fields between servers and clients.

HAL Explained

Hypertext Application Language (HAL) is an Internet standard (a "work in progress") convention for defining hypermedia such as links to external resources within JSON or XML data. HAL is structured to represent elements based on the concepts of Resources and Links. Resources consist of URI links, embedded resources, your standard JSON or XML data, and non-URI links. Links have a target URI, the name of the link (referred to as rel), and optional properties designed to be mindful of deprecation and content negotiation.

To summarize, the HAL model revolves around two simple concepts.

- Resources, which contain:

    - Links to relevant URIs

- Embedded resources

- State

- Links:

  - A target URI

  - A relation, or rel, to the link

  - A few other optional properties to help with depreciation, content negotiation, and so on

With that little introduction, you can now get into the action with some code.

Microservices Using HATEAOS and HAL

This section uses a working example to show how things fit together. You will modify the microservices example to demonstrate both HATEOAS and HAL.

Design the Microservices

This example reuses the hexagonal microservice view shown in Figure 2-1 and described earlier. A few of the differences are as follows:

- The Product Web microservice will be enhanced to exhibit HATEOAS capability.

- The Product Server microservice will be enhanced to demonstrate HAL.

You will be leveraging the Spring HATEOAS project for creating hypermedia-driven REST web services. The intention is to easily create REST representations that follow the principle of HATEOAS so the API can guide the client through the application by returning relevant information about the next potential steps, along with each response.

Code Organization

The source code for this book is available on GitHub via the book's product page, located at www.apress.com/9798868805547.. The code for this example is organized as shown in Listing 2-22, inside the ch02\ch02-03 folder. This follows the standard Maven structure, so pom.xml is in the root of the directory. Code organization for the relevant portion of the Product Web microservice alone is shown, since you already saw the Product Server microservice code.

Listing 2-22. Spring Boot Source Code Organization

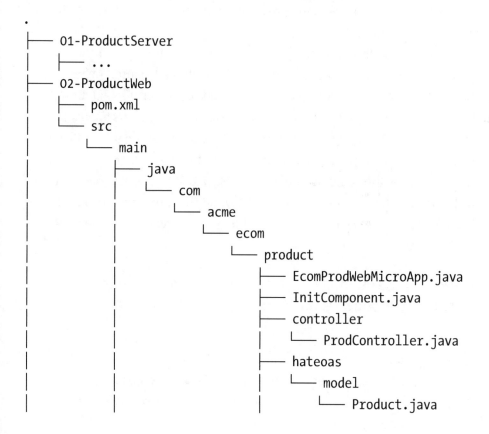

```
.
├── 01-ProductServer
│   ├── ...
├── 02-ProductWeb
│   ├── pom.xml
│   └── src
│       └── main
│           ├── java
│           │   └── com
│           │       └── acme
│           │           └── ecom
│           │               └── product
│           │                   ├── EcomProdWebMicroApp.java
│           │                   ├── InitComponent.java
│           │                   ├── controller
│           │                   │   └── ProdController.java
│           │                   ├── hateoas
│           │                   │   └── model
│           │                   │       └── Product.java
```

```
|              |                    └── model
|              |                        └── Product.java
|              └── resources
└── pom.xml
```

One difference you want to note is the hateoas subfolder in the Product entity model. I will explain the reason for this folder in the next section.

Understanding the Code

Let's look at the changes in the provider microservice—the Product Server microservice—first.

Much of the implementation of the REST controller in the Product Server microservice is similar to the code in Listings 1-3 and 1-4 in Chapter 1, with the exception that instead of the in-memory database, the ProductRepository and ProductCategoryRepository ports are used to interact with a MongoDB repository, so I do not repeat the full code here. However, this example does introduce a HAL browser. The HAL browser was created by the same person who developed HAL and it provides an in-browser GUI to traverse your REST API. It is easy to integrate a HAL browser into your Maven project by adding the relevant dependency—see Listing 2-23.

Listing 2-23. HAL Browser Dependency in Maven (ch02\ch02-03\01-ProductServer\pom.xml)

```
<dependencies>
    <dependency>
        <groupId>org.springframework.data</groupId>
        <artifactId>spring-data-rest-hal-explorer</artifactId>
    </dependency>
</dependencies>
```

There are a few changes in the Product Web microservice, and I will discuss them. Listing 2-24 shows the HATEOAS variant of the Product entity.

Listing 2-24. HATEOAS Variant of Product Entity (ch02\ch02-03\02-ProductWeb\src\main\java\com\acme\ecom\product\hateoas\model\Product.java)

```
public class Product extends RepresentationModel<Product> {

    private String productId;
    private String name;
    private String code;;
    private String title;
    private Double price;
}
```

The Product extends from the RepresentationModel class to inherit the add() method. Once you create a link, you can easily set that value to the resource representation without adding any new fields to it.

Next, let's look at the Controller class methods. The code in Listing 2-25 shows how to build HATEOAS hyperlinks based on the getProduct() method of the ProductRestController.

Listing 2-25. HATEOAS REST Controller (ch02\ch02-03\02-ProductWeb\src\main\java\com\acme\ecom\product\controller\ProductRestController.java)

```
public class ProductRestController{

    private static final Logger LOGGER = LoggerFactory.
    getLogger(ProductRestController.class);

    @Value("${acme.PRODUCT_SERVICE_URL}")
    private String PRODUCT_SERVICE_URL;
```

```
@Autowired
public RestTemplate restTemplate;

@Autowired
private ModelMapper modelMapper;

@RequestMapping(value = "/productsweb/{productId}",
    method = RequestMethod.GET,
    produces = MediaType.APPLICATION_JSON_VALUE)
public ResponseEntity<com.acme.ecom.product.hateoas.model.
Product>
        getProduct(@PathVariable("productId")
            String productId) {

    String uri = PRODUCT_SERVICE_URL + "/" + productId;
    com.acme.ecom.product.model.Product productRetreived =
        restTemplate.getForObject(uri,
            com.acme.ecom.product.model.Product.class);
    com.acme.ecom.product.hateoas.model.Product
        productHateoas = convertEntityToHateoasEntity(
            productRetreived);
    productHateoas.add(linkTo(methodOn(
        ProductRestController.class).getProduct(
        productHateoas.getProductId())).withSelfRel());
    return new ResponseEntity<
        com.acme.ecom.product.hateoas.model.Product>(
        productHateoas, HttpStatus.OK);
}

private com.acme.ecom.product.hateoas.model.Product
    convertEntityToHateoasEntity(
        com.acme.ecom.product.model.Product product){
            return  modelMapper.map(
```

```
        product,
        com.acme.ecom.product.hateoas.
            model.Product.class);
    }
}
```

WebMvcLinkBuilder offers great support for Spring MVC controllers. The methodOn() obtains the method mapping by making dummy invocations of the target method on the proxy controller and sets the productId as the path variable of the URI.

WebMvcLinkBuilder also simplifies building URIs by avoiding hard-coding the links. The code in Listing 2-25 shows how to build the product self-link using the WebMvcLinkBuilder class.

You use the ModelMapper to implicitly map a HATEOAS Product instance to a non-HATEOAS Product API instance. When the map method is called, the source and target types are analyzed to determine which properties implicitly match. Data is then mapped according to these matches. Even when the source and target objects and their properties are different, ModelMapper can do its best to determine reasonable matches between properties if a configured matching strategy exists.

Again, for brevity, I do not list the rest of the methods for the ProductRestController. You can refer to them in the code repository.

Build and Run the Microservice

The ch02\ch02-03 folder contains the Maven scripts required to build the examples. As a first step, you need to bring up the MongoDB server. Refer to Appendix B to learn how to set up MongoDB server and bring it up. You need to execute the commands shown in Listing 2-26 to bring up MongoDB.

Listing 2-26. Bringing up the MongoDB Server

```
(base) binildass-MBP:bin binil$ pwd
/Users/binil/Applns/mongodb/mongodb-macos-x86_64-4.2.8/bin
(base) binildass-MBP:bin binil$ mongod --dbpath /usr/local/var/
mongodb --logpath /usr/local/var/log/mongodb/mongo.log
```

Next, take two command terminals and change the directory to the top-level folder of both microservices. Build and run the Product Server microservice using the make.sh and the run.sh scripts, as shown in Listing 2-27.

Listing 2-27. Build and Run Product Server Microservice Using Scripts

```
(base) binildass-MBP:01-ProductServer binil$ pwd
/Users/binil/binil/code/mac/mybooks/docker-03/ch02/ch02-03/01-
ProductServer
(base) binildass-MBP:01-ProductServer binil$ sh make.sh
[INFO] Scanning for projects...
[INFO]
...
2023-12-20 10:33:45 INFO  InitComponent.init:42 - Start
2023-12-20 10:33:45 INFO  InitComponent.init:62 - End
2023-12-20 10:33:45 INFO  Start.log:56 - Started EcomProd...
```

Next, build and run the Product Web microservice, as shown in Listing 2-28.

Listing 2-28. Build and Run Product Web Microservice
Using Scripts

```
(base) binildass-MBP:02-ProductWeb binil$ pwd
/Users/binil/binil/code/mac/mybooks/docker-03/ch02/ch02-03/02-
ProductWeb
(base) binildass-MBP:02-ProductWeb binil$ sh make.sh
[INFO] Scanning for projects...
[INFO]
...
2023-12-20 10:36:29 INFO  InitComponent.init:37 - Start
2023-12-20 10:36:29 DEBUG InitComponent.init:39 - Do Nothing
2023-12-20 10:36:29 INFO  InitComponent.init:41 - End
2023-12-20 10:36:29 INFO  Start.log:56 - Started EcomProd...
```

Now that the microservices are up and running, you can test the
microservices.

Testing the Microservice

Once both microservices are up and running, you can access the web
application using your browser and pointing to this URL:

```
http://localhost:8080/product.html
```

To test the CRUD operations, follow the instructions described in
the subsection, "Test the Microservices Using UI" in the last section of
Chapter 1, titled "Your First Java Microservice."

Recall that you enabled the HAL browser, so Spring will auto-configure
the browser and make it available via the default endpoint (see Figure 2-3).
You can access the HAL browser at:

```
http://localhost:8081/
```

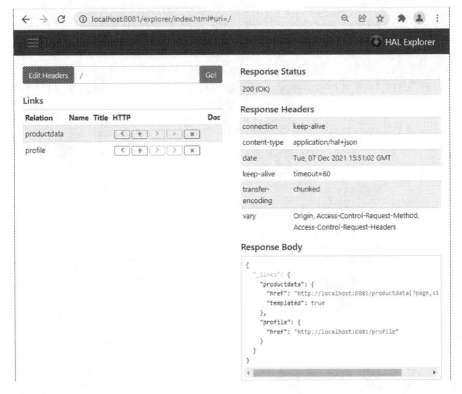

Figure 2-3. *The HAL browser*

You can now try the various options with the HAL browser.

Summary

In Chapter 1, you saw examples of the hexagonal architecture. This chapter continued that discussion, with more complex microservice examples. You also saw more examples of ports and adapters. By now, you should be able to relate these concepts to the many interfaces you use to expose services at the edge as well as many other interfaces you use to invoke other services from the edge (of microservices). This notion of ports and adapters provided by the hexagonal architecture is a great way to think the loosely coupled way of inter-microservice interactions too. You saw how a Feign client provides for that in a smart manner with very little application-specific code. To complete this discussion on flexibility and loose coupling, the chapter also covered HATEOAS. The next chapter moves on to more interesting aspects in component-based architectures

CHAPTER 3

Onion and Hexagonal Architecture in Practice

Chapter 1 introduced the hexagonal architecture. You also saw a few examples in Chapter 1 and 3 that explained how the concepts of abstract ports are realized by lightweight containers like Spring and Spring Boot to provide on-demand adapters at runtime. This chapter expands on those concepts by introducing the Onion architecture, with more precise and concrete examples.

This chapter covers the following concepts:

- Extends the notion of hexagonal architecture in microservices using Spring Boot and PostgreSQL.

- Demonstrates hexagonal architecture in action, by plugging in MongoDB in place of PostgreSQL.

- Introduces the concept of the Onion architecture.

- Introduces GraphQL as a technology means to demonstrate the Onion architecture.

- Demonstrates with example the complementary nature of the Hexagonal and Onion architectures.

© Binildas A. Christudas 2024
B. A. Christudas, *Java Microservices and Containers in the Cloud,*
https://doi.org/10.1007/979-8-8688-0555-4_3

Microservices Using PostgreSQL and RestTemplate

In this section, you will tweak the first example of microservices you saw in Chapter 2, but to connect to a PostgreSQL database instead of MongoDB. You will have the same two microservices—a consumer and a provider microservice—communicating with each other using the REST protocol. The provider microservice also interacts with a PostgreSQL, instead of the MongoDB. Refer to Figure 2-1 in Chapter 2 for the overall design.

Design the Microservice

You will reuse the hexagonal microservice view shown in Figure 2-1 in Chapter 2. There are a few differences with this design, as follows:

- The Product Server microservice connects to a PostgreSQL database.

- You'll use Liquibase to initialize the PostgreSQL database.

- The Product entity is less verbose due to the use of the Lombok library.

- You'll use separate entity models—the ProductOR for the Repository interactions and the Product for the REST interface.

- You'll use the mapstruct library to transform entities between the ProductOR and Product structures.

Understanding the Code

The source code for this book is available on GitHub via the book's product page, located at www.apress.com/9798868805547. The source code for this example is organized inside the ch03\ch03-01 folder. You will look at the provider microservice—that is, the Product Server microservice—first. Listing 3-1 shows the changed repository used to interact with the PostgreSQL.

Listing 3-1. The Abstract Port for Product Server Microservice to Interact with PostgreSQL (ch03\ch03-02\01-ProductServer\ src\main\java\com\acme\ecom\product\repository\ ProductRepository.java)

```
@RepositoryRestResource(collectionResourceRel = "productdata",
    path = "productdata")
public interface ProductRepository extends
        CrudRepository<ProductOR, Long> {

    public List<ProductOR> findByCode(@Param("code")
        String code);
}
```

This port (interface) provides for generic CRUD operations on a repository, a PostgreSQL in this case. Note that MongoRepository interacts with MongoDB for all the examples in Chapter 2. However, this example opts for a more generic type of MongoRepository in the way of CrudRepository . There is a reason for doing this. I want to demonstrate how a generic port (the driven port with CrudRepository) can be adapted to connect to different kinds of databases—more specifically to a PostgreSQL database in this example and to a MongoDB database in the next example.

CrudRepository is a Spring Data interface for generic CRUD operations on a repository of a specific type. It provides several methods out-of-the-box to interact with a database. The specific adapter for this port, an adapter to a PostgreSQL database, is provided by Spring based on the configuration in pom.xml (see Listing 3-2).

Listing 3-2. The Adapter Hint to Product Server Microservice (ch03\ ch03-02\01-ProductServer\ pom.xml)

```
<dependencies>
    <dependency>
        <groupId>org.postgresql</groupId>
        <artifactId>postgresql</artifactId>
        <version>42.2.19</version>
        <scope>runtime</scope>
    </dependency>
</dependencies>
```

Listing 3-3 shows the REST-capable HTTP port, using a Spring RestController.

Listing 3-3. REST Based HTTP Port for getAllProducts Product Server (ch03\ch03-02\01-ProductServer\src\main\java\com\acme\ ecom\product\controller\ProductRestController.java)

```
@RestController
public class ProductRestController {

    @Autowired
    private ProductRepository productRepository;

    @Autowired
    private ProductMapper mapper;
```

```
@ApiOperation(value="View a list of all products",
    response = Product.class,
    responseContainer = "List")
@RequestMapping(value = "/products",
    method = RequestMethod.GET,
    produces = {MediaType.APPLICATION_JSON_VALUE})
public ResponseEntity<List<Product>> getAllProducts() {

    Iterable<ProductOR> iterable =
        productRepository.findAll();
    List<Product> list = new ArrayList<Product> ();
    for(ProductOR productOR:iterable){
        list.add(mapper.entityToApi(productOR));
    }
    if(list.size() == 0){
        return new ResponseEntity<List<Product>>(
            HttpStatus.NOT_FOUND);
    }
    return new ResponseEntity<List<Product>>(list,
        HttpStatus.OK);
    }
}
```

The REST controller has CRUD methods that synchronize the
state of the Product entity with those in the PostgreSQL database. The
getAllProducts is a Java method that returns a list of all products in
the PostgreSQL database, defined through an abstract protocol and
format of delivery declared in the HTTP-based REST port. A concrete
implementation of this port is then injected (or used to intercept) by
Spring and used in the controller in the runtime. They translate the JSON
formatted Request data payload from the HTTP delivery channel into a

getAllProducts method call in the application core. To retrieve the actual product entities, the getAllProducts delegates call to the driven port, ProductRepository.

There are two new utility libraries I need to discuss here. The first one is ProductMapper, shown in Listing 3-4.

Listing 3-4. Product Entity Mapper (ch03\ch03-02\01-ProductServer\src\main\java\com\acme\ecom\product\controller\ProductMapper.java)

```
@Mapper(componentModel = "spring")
public interface ProductMapper {

    Product entityToApi(ProductOR entity);
    ProductOR apiToEntity(Product api);
}
```

This API contains functions that automatically map between two Java Beans, the ProductOR and the Product in this case. With MapStruct, you only need to create the interface, and the library will automatically create a concrete implementation during compile time based on the declaration in pom.xml. See Listing 3-5.

Listing 3-5. Configuring the Mapper in ProductRestController (ch03\ch03-02\01-ProductServer\pom.xml)

```
<dependencies>
    <dependency>
        <groupId>org.mapstruct</groupId>
        <artifactId>mapstruct</artifactId>
        <version>1.5.5.Final</version>
    </dependency>
</dependencies>
```

When you trigger the MapStruct processing by executing a mvn clean install, it will generate the implementation class under /target/ generated-sources/annotations/.

The rest of the implementation of the REST controller in the Product Server microservice is very similar to Listing 1-4 in Chapter 1 (with the single exception that instead of the in-memory database, the ProductRepository port is used to interact with a PostgreSQL repository), so I do not repeat the full code here.

Let's now look at the Entity classes. The Product entity class, which is exposed in the API of the Product Server microservice, is shown in Listing 3-6.

Listing 3-6. The Product Entity (ch03\ch03-02\01-ProductServer\ src\main\java\com\acme\ecom\product\model\Product.java)

```
@Builder
@Data
@NoArgsConstructor
@AllArgsConstructor
public class Product{

    @ApiModelProperty(position = 1)
    private String productId;

    @ApiModelProperty(position = 2)
    private String name;

    @ApiModelProperty(position = 3)
    private String code;;

    @ApiModelProperty(position = 4)
    private String title;

    @ApiModelProperty(position = 5)
    private Double price;
}
```

Project Lombok's @Builder is a useful mechanism for using the Builder pattern without writing boilerplate code. You can apply this annotation to a class or a method.

@Data is a convenient shortcut annotation that bundles the features of @ToString, @EqualsAndHashCode, @Getter/@Setter, and @RequiredArgsConstructor together. That is, @Data generates all the boilerplate that is normally associated with Plain Old Java Objects (POJO) and beans, mainly the getters for all fields, setters for all non-final fields, and the appropriate toString, equals, and hashCode implementations that involve the fields of the class, a constructor that initializes all final fields, and all non-final fields with no initializer that have been marked with @NonNull, in order to ensure the field is never null.

Listing 3-7 shows the ProductOR entity class used by the ProductRepository of the Product Server microservice to persist the data in the PostgreSQL database.

Listing 3-7. The ProductOR Entity (ch03\ch03-02\01-ProductServer\src\main\java\com\acme\ecom\product\model\ProductOR.java)

```
import javax.persistence.Id;

@Data
@NoArgsConstructor
@Entity
@Table(name ="product")
public class ProductOR{

    @GeneratedValue(strategy = GenerationType.IDENTITY)
    @Id
    @Column(name = "productid")
    private Long productId;
```

```
@Column(name = "prodname")
private String name;

@Column(name = "code")
private String code;;

@Column(name = "title")
private String title;

@Column(name = "price")
private Double price;
}
```

You use JPA for persistence. Entities in JPA are nothing but POJOs annotated with @Entity representing data that can be persisted to the database. An entity represents a table stored in a database. Every instance of an entity represents a row in the table. You must specify @Entity annotation at the class level. You must also ensure that the entity has a no-arg constructor and a primary key. The entity name defaults to the name of the class. You can change its name using the name element @Entity(name="product"). In some cases, the name of the table in the database and the name of the entity will not be the same. In these cases, you can specify the table name using the @Table annotation.

Each JPA entity must have a primary key that uniquely identifies it. The @Id annotation defines the primary key. You can generate the identifiers in multiple ways, specified by the @GeneratedValue annotation. You can choose from four ID-generation strategies with the strategy element. The value can be AUTO, TABLE, SEQUENCE, or IDENTITY.

You can also use the @Column annotation to mention the details of a column in the table. The @Column annotation has many elements, including name, length, nullable, and unique.

There is another reason to introduce the ProductOR entity. I want to demonstrate that while using the ports and adapters architecture, you can reuse the core entities and core business services to the maximum.

In other words, I want to demonstrate that `Product` entity used in this example is reused in the next example too, which will assert the capability to plugging in different driven adapters at runtime, still reusing the core. To do that, the `ProductOR` entity will take care of all adapter (database) specific details.

The JPA dependency is mentioned in the Maven configuration. See Listing 3-8.

Listing 3-8. The JPA Dependency in Maven (ch03\ch03-02\01-ProductServer\ pom.xml)

```
<dependencies>
    <dependency>
    <groupId>org.springframework.boot</groupId>
    <artifactId>spring-boot-starter-data-jpa</artifactId>
    </dependency>
</dependencies>
```

The `pom.xml` file also reveals the Liquibase dependency. The core component in using Liquibase is the `changeLog` file, which is an XML file that keeps track of all changes that need to run to update the DB. See Listing 3-9.

Listing 3-9. The Liquibase Change Log (ch03\ch03-02\01-ProductServer\src\main\resources\db\changelog\db.changelog-master.xml)

```
<databaseChangeLog>
    <changeSet id="1" author="Binildas">
        <sqlFile path="01_init_product.sql"
            relativeToChangelogFile="true"
            splitStatements="true"
```

```
        stripComments="true"/>
      <comment>Create table with Product info</comment>
    </changeSet>
</databaseChangeLog>
```

Here, it calls the `01_init_product.sql` file, which includes the script to create a product table if it doesn't exist.

Listing 3-10 shows the Product Server Microservice main application class.

Listing 3-10. Product Server Microservice Main Application (ch03\ch03-01\01-ProductServer\src\main\java\com\acme\ecom\ product\ EcomProductMicroserviceApplication.java)

```
@SpringBootApplication
@EnableJpaRepositories("com.acme.ecom.product.repository")
public class EcomProductMicroserviceApplication {

    public static void main(String[] args) {

        SpringApplication.run(
            EcomProductMicroserviceApplication.class, args);
    }
}
```

To activate the Spring JPA repository support, this example uses the `@EnableJpaRepositories` annotation and specifies the package that contains the DAO interfaces.

Listing 3-11 shows the Product Server Microservice configuration file.

Listing 3-11. The Liquibase Change Log (ch03\ch03-02\01-
ProductServer\src\main\resources\application.properties)

```
spring.application.name = product-server
server.port=8081
spring.datasource.url=jdbc:postgresql://${DB_SERVER}/
${POSTGRES_DB}
spring.datasource.username=${POSTGRES_USER}
spring.datasource.password=${POSTGRES_PASSWORD}
spring.liquibase.change-log=classpath:/db/changelog/
db.changelog-master.xml
spring.jpa.properties.hibernate.jdbc.lob.non_contextual_
creation=true
spring.jpa.show-sql=true
```

This file expects the PostgreSQL database configuration parameters
through the environment context of the Product Server microservice.

The Product Web microservice code is very similar to the Product Web
microservice code you saw in Chapter 2. I do not repeat the code here;
instead, you are advised to refer to Listings 2-6 through 2-8 in Chapter 2.

Build and Run the Microservice

The ch03\ch03-01 folder contains the Maven scripts required to build the
examples. As a first step, you need to bring up the PostgreSQL server. Refer
to Appendix C to learn how to set up PostgreSQL server and bring it up.
You need to execute the commands in Listing 3-12 to bring up PostgreSQL.

Listing 3-12. Bringing Up PostgreSQL Server

```
binildass-MacBook-Pro:~ binil$ pg_ctl -D /Library/
PostgreSQL/12/data start
```

Next, take two command terminals and change the directory to the top-level folder of both microservices. Then build and run the Product Server microservice using the make.sh and run.sh scripts, as shown in Listing 3-13.

Listing 3-13. Build and Run Product Server Microservice Using Scripts

```
binildass-MacBook-Pro:01-ProductServer binil$ pwd
/Users/binil/binil/code/mac/mybooks/docker-04/Code/ch03/
ch03-01/01-ProductServer
binildass-MacBook-Pro:01-ProductServer binil$
binildass-MacBook-Pro:01-ProductServer binil$ sh make.sh
[INFO] Scanning for projects...
[INFO]
[INFO] -< com.acme.ecom.product:Ecom-Product-Server-Micro >-
...
[INFO] ------------------------------------------------------------
[INFO] BUILD SUCCESS
[INFO] ------------------------------------------------------------
[INFO] Total time:  3.026 s
[INFO] Finished at: 2024-01-03T12:36:02+05:30
[INFO] ------------------------------------------------------------
binildass-MacBook-Pro:01-ProductServer binil$

binildass-MacBook-Pro:01-ProductServer binil$ sh run.sh


  .   ____          _            __ _ _
 /\\ / ___'_ __ _ _(_)_ __  __ _ \ \ \ \
( ( )\___ | '_ | '_| | '_ \/ _` | \ \ \ \
 \\/  ___)| |_)| | | | | || (_| |  ) ) ) )
  '  |____| .__|_| |_|_| |_\__, | / / / /
 =========|_|==============|___/=/_/_/_/
 :: Spring Boot ::                (v3.2.0)
```

```
2024-01-03 12:37:17 INFO  Start.log:50 - Starting EcomProdM…
2024-01-03 12:37:20 INFO  InitComponent.init:47 - Start...
2024-01-03 12:37:20 DEBUG InitComponent.init:51 - Delete...
Hibernate: select pco1_0.categoryid,pco1_0.description,pco1_0.
imgurl,pco1_0.name,pco1_0.title from productcategory pco1_0
Hibernate: select po1_0.productid,po1_0.category,po1_0.
code,po1_0.prodname,po1_0.price,po1_0.title from product po1_0
2024-01-03 12:37:20 DEBUG InitializationComponent.init:56 -
Creating initial data on start...
Hibernate: insert into productcategory
(description,imgurl,name,title) values (?,?,?,?)
Hibernate: insert into productcategory
(description,imgurl,name,title) values (?,?,?,?)
Hibernate: insert into product (category,code,prodname,price,ti
tle) values (?,?,?,?,?)
Hibernate: insert into product (category,code,prodname,price,ti
tle) values (?,?,?,?,?)
Hibernate: insert into product (category,code,prodname,price,ti
tle) values (?,?,?,?,?)
Hibernate: insert into product (category,code,prodname,price,ti
tle) values (?,?,?,?,?)
2024-01-03 12:37:20 INFO  InitComponent.init:105 - End
2024-01-03 12:37:21 INFO  Start.log:56 - Started EcomProd...
...
```

Note the initialization is being done by inserting a few rows into the PostgreSQL DB while the Product Server microservice starts up. Next, build and run the Product Web microservice, as shown in Listing 3-14.

Listing 3-14. Build and Run Product Web Microservice
Using Scripts

```
binildass-MacBook-Pro:02-ProductWeb binil$ pwd
/Users/binil/binil/code/mac/mybooks/docker-04/Code/ch03/
ch03-01/02-ProductWeb
binildass-MacBook-Pro:02-ProductWeb binil$ sh make.sh
[INFO] Scanning for projects...
[INFO]
...
binildass-MacBook-Pro:02-ProductWeb binil$

binildass-MacBook-Pro:02-ProductWeb binil$ sh run.sh
...
2024-01-03 12:43:58 INFO  Startup.log:50 - Starting EcomProd
...
2024-01-03 12:43:59 INFO  InitComponent.init:36 - Start
2024-01-03 12:43:59 DEBUG InitComponent.init:38 - Do Nothing
2024-01-03 12:43:59 INFO  InitComponent.init:40 - End
2024-01-03 12:43:59 INFO  Startup.log:56 - Started EcomProd
...
```

Now that both microservices are up and running, you can test the
microservices.

Testing the Microservice

Once both microservices are up and running, you can inspect your
PostgreSQL server using the psql terminal to make sure the Product Server
microservice inserted a few products into the PostgreSQL server during the
microservice startup process. Refer to Appendix C to learn how to use the
psql terminal.

Listing 3-15. Inspecting the PostgreSQL Server Using a psql Shell

```
postgres=# connect productdb
You are now connected to database "productdb" as user "postgres".
productdb=# select * from product;
 productid |   prodname   |  code   |    title      | price
-----------+--------------+---------+---------------+-----
         1 | Kamsung D3   | KAMSUNG | Kamsung Tr..  | 12000
         2 | Lokia Pomia  | LOKIA   | Lokia 1.      |  9009
(2 rows)

productdb=#
```

When all is set, you can access the web application using your browser. Point to this URL:

```
http://localhost:8080/product.html
```

To test the CRUD operations, follow the instructions described in the subsection, "Test the Microservices Using UI" in the last section of Chapter 1, titled "Your First Java Microservice."

Once you have executed the test cases in this example, you can move on to the next example, which is intended to demonstrate one of the many great flexibilities of the hexagonal architecture—plug and play.

Microservices Using MongoDB and CrudRepository

This example tweaks the first example of microservices you saw in Chapter 2 to connect to a MongoDB, using the CrudRepository instead of the MongoRepository. You have the same two microservices—a consumer and a provider microservice—communicating with each other using the REST protocol. The provider microservice also interacts with a MongoDB. Refer to Figure 2-1 in Chapter 2 for the overall design.

Hexagonal Architecture Revisited

I reused the hexagonal microservice view shown in Figure 2-1 in Chapter 2. However, you will be using CrudRepository instead of MongoRepository. I want to demonstrate how a generic port (the driven port with CrudRepository in this case) can be "adapted using suitable adaptors" to connect to different kinds of databases—more specifically to a MongoDB database in this example.

Further, I introduced the ProductOR entity in the last example. The reason for this is that I want to demonstrate that while using the ports and adapters architecture, you can reuse the core entities and business services to the maximum. In other words, I want to demonstrate that you will retain and reuse a Product entity from the last example in this example too, which will assert the capability to plug in different driven adapters at runtime.

Understanding the Code

The source code for this book is available on GitHub via the book's product page, located at www.apress.com/9798868805547. The code for this example is organized inside the ch03\ch03-02 folder. You will look at the provider microservice—that is, the Product Server microservice—first. Listing 3-16 starts with the changed Repository used to interact with the PostgreSQL.

Listing 3-16. The Abstract Port for Product Server Microservice to Interact with MongoDB (ch03\ch03-02\01-ProductServer\src\main\java\com\acme\ecom\product\repository\ProductRepository.java

```
@RepositoryRestResource(collectionResourceRel = "productdata",
path = "productdata")
public interface ProductRepository extends
        CrudRepository<ProductOR, String> {
```

```
    public List<ProductOR> findByCode(@Param("code")
        String  code);
    public List<ProductOR> findByCategory(@Param("category")
        String  category);
}
```

This example retains the CrudRepository for generic CRUD operations on a repository of a specific type. The specific adapter for this port, an adapter to a MongoDB database, is provided by Spring based on the configuration in pom.xml; see Listing 3-17.

Listing 3-17. The Product Server Microservice Maven File (ch03\ ch03-02\01-ProductServer\pom.xml)

```
<dependencies>
    <dependency>
        <groupId>org.springframework.boot</groupId>
        <artifactId>spring-boot-starter-data-mongodb
        </artifactId>
    </dependency>
    <dependency>
        <groupId>javax.persistence</groupId>
        <artifactId>javax.persistence-api</artifactId>
        <version>2.2</version>
    </dependency>
</dependencies>
```

I also changed the persistence dependency to its API alone.

The rest of the implementation of the REST controller in the Product Server microservice is very similar to the code in Listing 1-4 in Chapter 1 (with the single exception that instead of the in-memory database, the ProductRepository port is used to interact with a MongoDB repository), hence I do not repeat the full code here.

The Product entity class is similar to the previous example, as shown in Listing 3-6. I have retained this class as the API entity, hence I have its counterpart ProductOR to manage the DB interactions. The code for ProductOR is very similar to that shown in the previous example in Listing 3-7 with subtle differences, which are commented out and replaced with new code in Listing 3-18.

Listing 3-18. The ProductOR Entity (ch03\ch03-02\01-ProductServer\src\main\java\com\acme\ecom\product\model\ProductOR.java)

```
import org.springframework.data.annotation.Id;
//import javax.persistence.Id;

    @Data
    @NoArgsConstructor
    @Entity
    @Table(name ="product")
    public class ProductOR{

    @GeneratedValue(strategy = GenerationType.IDENTITY)
    @Id
    @Column(name = "productid")
    //private Long productId;
    private String productId;

    @Column(name = "prodname")
    private String name;

    @Column(name = "code")
    private String code;;

    @Column(name = "title")
    private String title;
```

```
@Column(name = "price")
private Double price;

@Column(name = "category")
private String category;
```

}

If you ask MongoDB to auto-generate an ID for the Long type, it will complain, so I changed the ID to String. Next, I changed the @Id annotation from javax.persistence to that of springframework so that the ID value is exposed through the API methods. ProductOR thus shields the impedance mismatch across databases from the Product entity class. This makes the Product entity reusable.

The rest of the classes in the Product Server microservice are similar to what you saw in the previous example. The code for the Product Web microservice is also unchanged from the previous example, so it's not repeated here.

Build and Run the Microservice

The ch03\ch03-02 folder contains the Maven scripts required to build the examples. As a first step, you need to bring up the MongoDB server. Refer to Appendix B to learn how you can set up a MongoDB server and bring it up. You need to execute the commands in Listing 3-19 to bring up MongoDB.

Listing 3-19. Bringing Up the MongoDB Server

```
(base) binildass-MBP:bin binil$ pwd
/Users/binil/Applns/mongodb/mongodb-macos-x86_64-4.2.8/bin
(base) binildass-MBP:bin binil$ mongod --dbpath /usr/local/var/
mongodb --logpath /usr/local/var/log/mongodb/mongo.log
```

Next, take two command terminals and change the directory to the top-level folder of both microservices. Then, build and run the Product Server microservice using the make.sh and run.sh scripts, as shown in Listing 3-20.

Listing 3-20. Build and Run Product Server Microservice Using Scripts

```
binildass-MacBook-Pro:01-ProductServer binil$ pwd
/Users/binil/binil/code/mac/mybooks/docker-04/Code/ch03/
ch03-02/01-ProductServer
binildass-MacBook-Pro:01-ProductServer binil$ sh make.sh
[INFO] Scanning for projects...
[INFO]
...
binildass-MacBook-Pro:01-ProductServer binil$
binildass-MacBook-Pro:01-ProductServer binil$ sh run.sh
...
2024-01-03 13:13:59 INFO  Startup.log:50 - Starting EcomProd
...
2024-01-03 13:14:01 INFO  InitComponent.init:47 - Start...
2024-01-03 13:14:01 DEBUG InitComponent.init:51 - Delete ...
2024-01-03 13:14:01 DEBUG InitComponent.init:56 - Create init
2024-01-03 13:14:01 INFO  InitComponent.init:105 - End
2024-01-03 13:14:01 INFO  Startup.log:56 - Started EcomProd
...
```

Next, build and run the Product Web microservice, as shown in Listing 3-21.

Listing 3-21. Build and Run Product Web Microservice
Using Scripts

```
binildass-MacBook-Pro:02-ProductWeb binil$ pwd
/Users/binil/binil/code/mac/mybooks/docker-04/Code/ch03/
ch03-02/02-ProductWeb
binildass-MacBook-Pro:02-ProductWeb binil$ sh make.sh
[INFO] Scanning for projects...
[INFO]
...
binildass-MacBook-Pro:02-ProductWeb binil$
binildass-MacBook-Pro:01-ProductServer binil$ sh run.sh
...
2024-01-03 13:17:09 INFO  Startup.log:50 - Starting EcomProd
...
2024-01-03 13:17:10 INFO  InitComponent.init:37 - Start
2024-01-03 13:17:10 DEBUG InitComponent.init:39 - Do Nothing
2024-01-03 13:17:10 INFO  InitComponent.init:41 - End
2024-01-03 13:17:10 INFO  Startup.log:56 - Started EcomProd...
...
```

Now that both microservices are up and running, you can test the
microservices.

Testing the Microservices

Once both microservices are up and running, you can inspect your
MongoDB server using the Mongo terminal to make sure the Product
Server Microservice inserted a few products into the MongoDB server
during the microservice startup. See Listing 3-22.

Listing 3-22. Inspect MongoDB Server Using a Mongo Shell

```
> db.productOR.find()
{ "_id" : ObjectId("61a5e3bc80e0e72c72097305"), "name"
: "Kamsung Mobile", "code" : "KAMSUNG-TRIOS", "title" :
"Tablet Trios 12 inch , black , 12 px ....", "price" : 12000,
"category" : "Mobile", "_class" : "com.acme.ecom.product.model.
ProductOR" }
{ "_id" : ObjectId("61a5e3bc80e0e72c72097306"), "name" : "Lokia
Mobile", "code" : "LOKIA-POMIA", "title" : "Lokia 12 inch ,
white , 14px ....", "price" : 9000, "category" : "Mobile", "_
class" : "com.acme.ecom.product.model.ProductOR" }
{ "_id" : ObjectId("61a5e3bc80e0e72c72097307"), "name" :
"Mapple Mobile", "code" : "MAPPLE-EPHONE", "title" : "Mapple
7 inch, purple, 14px ....", "price" : 8000, "category" :
"Mobile", "_class" : "com.acme.ecom.product.model.ProductOR" }
{ "_id" : ObjectId("61a5e3bc80e0e72c72097308"), "name" :
"Mapple Tablet", "code" : "MAPPLE-PAD", "title" : "Mapple
11 inch , grey, 140px ....", "price" : 19000, "category" :
"Tablet", "_class" : "com.acme.ecom.product.model.ProductOR" }
>
```

When all is set, you can access the web application using your browser. Point to this URL:

```
http://localhost:8080/product.html
```

To test the CRUD operations, follow the instructions described in the subsection, "Test the Microservices Using UI" in the last section of Chapter 1, titled "Your First Java Microservice."

It's now time to consolidate your learning so far and introduce the next concept, the Onion architecture.

The Onion Architecture

The layering principle enables software architects to separate concerns. Software architects have been successfully building layered software architectures for decades, and today these layered principles have gained traction with the widespread adoption of the microservices architecture. Let's look at what layering has to do with onions.

Onion Architecture Design

In the ports and adapters architecture explained in the previous chapters, you learned about defining abstract ports and adapters that shield the core business services and entities from the context and intent of the software. In other words, these ports and adapters isolate the software application core from the infrastructure and peripheral concerns by writing adapter code so that the infrastructure and peripheral code does not leak into the application core. The Onion architecture depicts enterprise applications with multiple layers, and some of these layers in the business logic might be recognizable from the principles of domain driven design. A typical Onion architecture is depicted in Figure 3-1.

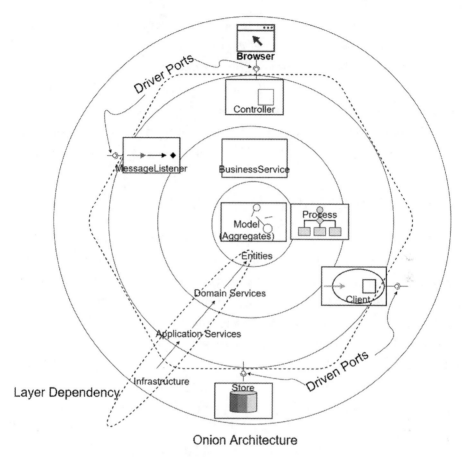

Figure 3-1. *Onion architecture*

Referring to Figure 3-1, the two core principles in software architecture are:

- Outer layers depend on inner layers

- Outer layers are transparent to inner layers

Referring to Figure 3-1, the direction of coupling of layers is toward the center, providing you with an independent object model (domain model), which in its core depends on nothing. This inner layer contains the data and the logic to manipulate data that is specific to the domain of the application itself.

Many times, you'll also encounter logic that involves multiple entities, and such domain logic may not belong to a specific entity. Such logic could also be reused, so that calls for another layer, called the Business Services layer. These Business services—aka domain services—have the role of receiving a set of entities and performing some business logic on them. Such domain services could aggregate more domain services and business entities too (refer to Figure 1-14 in Chapter 1).

Onion vs. Hexagonal Architecture

The ports and adapters defined in the hexagonal architecture are a means to isolate the software application core from the infrastructure and peripheral concerns. These peripherals could be a user interface, whatever type of user interface it might be, like a browser, a mobile device, a scanner, and so on. Similarly, infrastructure code could connect the application core to tools like a database, a third-party system, a printer, and so on. The infrastructure layer, which becomes the outermost onion ring, depicts this in the Onion architecture in Figure 3-1. You can also visualize them as being placed in the boundary of the hexagon, as abstract ports and adapters.

These ports and adapters are connected to the inner layers through what we call *application services*. These are technical services handling protocol and format transformations and optimizations. For example, a REST controller is an application service exposing entities as JSON through an HTTP transport. Similarly, persistence abstractions to a specific type of database could be done using a repository interface, as you saw in the first two examples in this chapter, which again are kinds of application services. Thus, this second layer of the onion are the inner, reusable layers.

Having discussed enough theory, let's look at some practical examples. If you turn back to the two previous examples in this chapter, you can visualize how the domain entities (Product) are reused across different persistence abstractions across a PostgreSQL and a MongoDB database, which are driven interfaces. I will now extend the same example further to demonstrate how ports can be defined to allow multiple driver abstractions. To be more specific, you have seen how a REST interface to the microservices provides fine abstractions as driver ports. I will plug in another port, one using a GraphQL technology, to the same microservices in the outermost ring of the onion so that inner rings of the same onion can be reused.

GraphQL

GraphQL is an open-source data query and manipulation language for APIs, and a runtime for fulfilling queries with existing data. GraphQL was developed internally by Facebook in 2012. The GraphQL project was later moved from Facebook to the newly established GraphQL Foundation, hosted by the non-profit Linux Foundation. I will quickly go through GraphQL so you can appreciate the next example in this chapter.

GraphQL Explained

GraphQL enables clients to ask for exactly what they need and nothing more, thus making it easier to evolve APIs over time. It allows clients to define the structure of the required data, and the same structure of the data is returned from the server, therefore preventing excessively large amounts of data from being returned. It is highly desirable in low profile devices like mobiles, IOT, and so on. It allows the client to navigate to child resources in a single request, and thus enables multiple queries in a single request.

GraphQL uses the notion of named queries and mutations instead of a standard mandatory set of actions. This helps to put the control where it belongs, with the API developer on specifying what is possible, and with the API consumer on what is desired. Listing 3-23 shows an example query.

Listing 3-23. A GraphQL Query

```
query {
    products(count: 10, offset: 0) {
        productId
        code
        productCategory {
            id
            name
            title
        }
    }
}
```

This GraphQL query is intended to do the following:

- Request the ten most recently added products

- For each product, request the productId and code

- For each product request, its productCategory, returning the id, name, and title of the corresponding product category

In a traditional REST API, this either requires 11 requests—one for the initial products query and ten for their corresponding productCategory—or it needs to include the productCategory details along with the post details, making the payload large.

Onion Architecture Microservice Example

This example tweaks the previous example of microservices. It uses the same two microservices—a consumer and a provider microservice—communicating with each other using the REST protocol. The provider microservice also interacts with a MongoDB. The consumer microservice exposes an additional port based on GraphQL.

Onion Design for the Microservice

If you superimpose the hexagonal microservice view shown in Figure 2-1 in Chapter 2 on to the Onion architecture view in Figure 3-1 in this chapter, you get Figure 3-2.

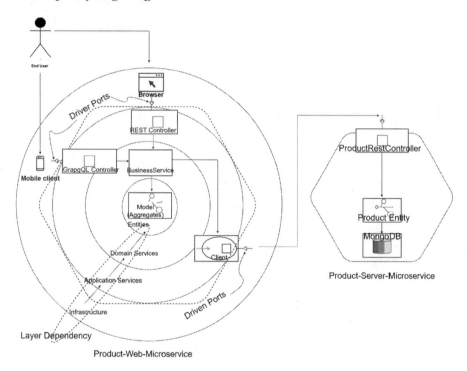

Figure 3-2. *Onion architecture for the Consumer and Provider microservices*

In both microservices shown in Figure 3-2, you use HTTP ports at the REST interfaces, which specify how a user's browser or some other HTTP client can use the application core. For the Product Web microservice, you specify an additional port based on GraphQL. You can also define a business service intended to demonstrate that the business service instances from the inner layers are reused by the outer layers of the Onion architecture, just like how they reuse the business entity classes.

Code Organization

The source code for this book is available on GitHub via the book's product page, located at www.apress.com/9798868805547. The code for this example is organized as shown in Listing 3-24, inside the ch03\ch03-03 folder. This follows the standard Maven structure, so pom.xml is in the root of the directory. Code organization for the relevant portion of the Product Web microservice alone is shown, since the Product Server microservice is similar to what you have seen already.

Listing 3-24. Spring Boot Source Code Organization

```
./ch03-03/
├── 01-ProductServer
│   ├── ...
│   .
├── 02-ProductWeb
│   ├── pom.xml
│   └── src
│       └── main
│           ├── java
│           │   └── com
│           │       └── acme
│           │           └── ecom
│           │               └── product
│           │                   ├── EcomProductApp.java
│           │                   ├── InitComponent.java
│           │                   ├── config
│           │                   │   └── SwaggerConfig.java
│           │                   ├── controller
│           │                   │   ├── GraphQLController.java
│           │                   │   ├── RestController.java
│           │                   │   └── RestControlConf.java
```

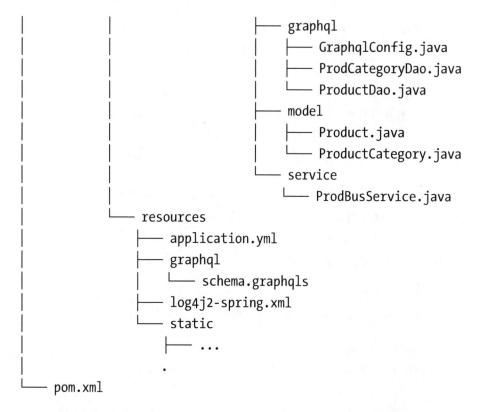

```
|            |                    ├── graphql
|            |                    |   ├── GraphqlConfig.java
|            |                    |   ├── ProdCategoryDao.java
|            |                    |   └── ProductDao.java
|            |                    ├── model
|            |                    |   ├── Product.java
|            |                    |   └── ProductCategory.java
|            |                    └── service
|            |                        └── ProdBusService.java
|            └── resources
|                ├── application.yml
|                ├── graphql
|                |   └── schema.graphqls
|                ├── log4j2-spring.xml
|                └── static
|                    ├── ...
|                    .
└── pom.xml
```

I added the following new folders and files, which are explained next:

ch03\ch03-03\02-ProductWeb\src\main\java\com\acme\ecom\
product\graphql
ch03\ch03-03\02-ProductWeb\src\main\java\com\acme\ecom\
product\service
ch03\ch03-03\02-ProductWeb\src\main\resources\graphql\schema.
graphqls

Understanding the Code

This section looks at the changes in the provider microservice—that is, the
Product Server microservice—first.

Much of the REST controller's implementation in the Product Server microservice is similar to the code in Listing 1-4 in Chapter 1 (with the exception that instead of the in-memory database, the `ProductRepository` and `ProductCategoryRepository` ports are used to interact with a MongoDB repository), hence I do not repeat the full code here. However, I introduced two new methods for `ProductRestController,` as shown in Listing 3-25.

Listing 3-25. REST Based HTTP Port for Product Category Based Queries in Product Server (ch03\ch03-03\01-ProductServer\ src\main\java\com\acme\ecom\product\controller\ ProductRestController.java)

```
@RestController
public class ProductRestController {

    @Autowired
    private ProductRepository productRepository;

    @Autowired
    private ProductCategoryRepository
        productCategoryRepository;

    @RequestMapping(value =
        "/productsbycat/{productcategoryname}",
        method = RequestMethod.GET,
        produces = {MediaType.APPLICATION_JSON_VALUE})
    public ResponseEntity<List<Product>>
            getProductsByCategory(
        @PathVariable("productcategoryname") String
            productCategoryName) {

        List<ProductOR> productORs =
            productRepository.findByCategory(
                productCategoryName);
```

```java
    if(productORs.isEmpty()){
        return new ResponseEntity<
            List<Product>>(HttpStatus.NOT_FOUND);
    }
    List<Product> list = new ArrayList<Product> ();
    for(ProductOR productOR:productORs){
        list.add(productMapper.entityToApi(productOR));
    }
    return new ResponseEntity<
        List<Product>>(list, HttpStatus.OK);
}

@RequestMapping(value =
    "/category/{category}", method = RequestMethod.GET,
    produces = MediaType.APPLICATION_JSON_VALUE)
public ResponseEntity<ProductCategory> getCategory(
    @PathVariable("category") String category) {

    List<ProductCategoryOR> productCategoryORs =
        productCategoryRepository.findByName(category);
    if(productCategoryORs.isEmpty()){
        return new ResponseEntity<ProductCategory>(
            HttpStatus.NOT_FOUND);
    }
    ProductCategoryOR firstProductCategoryOR =
        productCategoryORs.iterator().next();
    return new ResponseEntity<ProductCategory>(
        productCategoryMapper.entityToApi(
            firstProductCategoryOR), HttpStatus.OK);
    }
}
```

These two new methods use their respective repositories to retrieve corresponding entities, which will be utilized by the GraphQL implementation, which I explain soon.

Listing 3-26 looks at the consumer microservice—the Product Web microservice. This starts with the REST capable HTTP port, using a Spring RestController.

Listing 3-26. REST Based HTTP Port for getAllProducts Product Web (ch03\ch03-03\02-ProductWeb\src\main\java\com\acme\ ecom\product\controller\ProductRestController.java)

```
@CrossOrigin
@RestController
public class ProductRestController{

    @Autowired
    private ProductBusinessService productBusinessService;

    @RequestMapping(value = "/productsweb",
        method = RequestMethod.GET,
        produces = {MediaType.APPLICATION_JSON_VALUE})
    public ResponseEntity<List<Product>> getAllProducts() {

        List<Product> productList =
            productBusinessService.getAllProducts();
        return new ResponseEntity<
            List<Product>>(productList, HttpStatus.OK);
    }
}
```

The notable aspect in the Product Web microservice is that it delegates all calls to a ProductBusinessService. Here, the ProductRestController is an application service class, whereas the ProductBusinessService

is a business service class. The rest of the methods in the
ProductRestController are not repeated here for brevity. Listing 3-27
inspects the business service class.

Listing 3-27. The Product Business Service (ch03\ch03-03\02-
ProductWeb\src\main\java\com\acme\ecom\product\service\
ProductBusinessService.java)

```java
@Service
public class ProductBusinessService{

    @Value("${acme.PRODUCT_SERVICE_BY_CAT_URL}")
    private String PRODUCT_SERVICE_BY_CAT_URL;

    @Value("${acme.PRODUCT_CATEGORY_URL}")
    private String PRODUCT_CATEGORY_URL;

    @Autowired
    private RestTemplate restTemplate;

    public List<Product> getProductsForCategory(String name) {

        ParameterizedTypeReference<List<Product>>
            responseTypeRef = new ParameterizedTypeReference<
                List<Product>>() {};
        ResponseEntity<List<Product>> entity =
            restTemplate.exchange(
                PRODUCT_SERVICE_BY_CAT_URL + "/" + name,
                HttpMethod.GET, (HttpEntity<Product>) null,
                responseTypeRef);
        List<Product> productList = entity.getBody();
        return productList;
    }
```

```
    public ProductCategory getProductCategory(
            String productCategoryName) {

        String uri = PRODUCT_CATEGORY_URL + "/" +
            productCategoryName;
        ProductCategory productCategory =
            restTemplate.getForObject(uri,
                ProductCategory.class);
        return productCategory;
    }
}
```

@Service annotates classes at the service layer, which are special cases of @Component. You may mark the beans with @Service to indicate that they're holding the business logic. The typical implementation pattern within the product business service is shown in Listing 3-27. You can see that the calls are directed to the respective methods in the Product Server microservice.

You have now come to the GraphQL implementation. GraphQL should have a schema describing the API. You need to have these .graphqls or .gqls schema files under the src/main/resources/graphql/** location so that Spring Boot can pick them up automatically. See Listing 3-28.

Listing 3-28. The Product GraphQL Schema (ch03\ch03-03\02-ProductWeb\src\main\resources\graphql\schema.graphqls)

```
type Product {
    productId: ID!
    name: String!
    code: String!
    title: String!
    price: Float!
    productCategory: ProductCategory!
}
```

```
type ProductCategory {
    id: ID!
    name: String!
    title: String!
    description: String!
    imgUrl: String!
    products: [Product]!
}

# The Root Query for the application
type Query {
    products(count: Int, offset: Int): [Product]!
}

# The Root Mutation for the application
type Mutation {
    writeProduct(name: String!, code: String!, title: String!,
price: Float!, category: String!) : Product!
}
```

This scheme is made up of type definitions. Each type has one or more fields, which each take zero or more arguments and return a specific type. The ! at the end of some names indicates that they are non-nullable types. The graph shows the way these fields are nested with each other.

The GraphQL schema in Listing 3-28 is for the Product definitions, describing a product, a category of the product, and a root query to get the most recently added products. There must be exactly one root query, and up to one root mutation. The root query needs to have special beans defined in the Spring context to handle the various fields in this root query.

Next, you need to resolve the root query. As stated, it needs to have specially annotated methods to handle the various fields. You do this by annotating the handler methods with @QueryMapping annotations and then placing them inside standard `@Controller` components in the application. This registers the annotated classes as data-fetching components in the GraphQL application, as shown in Listing 3-29.

Listing 3-29. The Root Query Resolver (/ch03/ch03-03/02-ProductWeb/src/main/java/com/acme/ecom/product/controller/ProductGraphQLController.java)

```
@Controller
public class ProductGraphQLController {

    private ProductDao productDao;
    private ProductCategoryDao productCategoryDao;

    public ProductGraphQLController(ProductDao productDao,
            ProductCategoryDao productCategoryDao) {

        this.productDao = productDao;
        this.productCategoryDao = productCategoryDao;
    }

    @QueryMapping
    public List<Product> products(@Argument int count,
            @Argument int offset) {

        return productDao.getProducts(count, offset);
    }
}
```

As you can see, I define the method products, which I'll use to handle any GraphQL queries for the Products field in the schema defined earlier. The method should also have parameters annotated with @Argument that correspond to the related parameters in the schema. The method must return the right return type for the type in the GraphQL scheme. You can use any simple types like Int, String, List, and so on, with the equivalent Java types, and the GraphQL runtime just maps them automatically.

Any complex type in the GraphQL server is represented by a corresponding Java bean. The same Java class will always represent the same GraphQL type. Any fields or methods on the Java bean that don't map onto the GraphQL schema will be silently ignored without causing any problems. In this case, Product and ProductCategory are both non-trivial to load. Hence the @SchemaMapping annotation maps the handler method to a field with the same name in the schema and uses it as the DataFetcher for that field, as shown in Listing 3-30.

Listing 3-30. The Root Query Resolver (/ch03/ch03-03/02-ProductWeb/src/main/java/com/acme/ecom/product/controller/ProductGraphQLController.java)

```java
@Controller
public class ProductGraphQLController {

    @SchemaMapping
    public ProductCategory productCategory(Product product) {

        return productCategoryDao.getProductCategory(
            product.getCategory());
    }

    @SchemaMapping
    public List<Product> products(
            ProductCategory productCategory) {

        return productDao.getProductsForCategory(
            productCategory.getName());
    }
}
```

If the client doesn't request a field explicitly, the GraphQL Server won't do the work to retrieve it. In this case, if the client retrieves a product and doesn't ask for the ProductCategory field, the productCategory() method won't be executed, and the productCategoryDao call won't be made.

Listing 3-31 shows the Data Fetcher class.

Listing 3-31. Product Data Fetcher (/ch03/ch03-03/02-ProductWeb/src/main/java/com/acme/ecom/product/graphql/ProductDAO.java)

```java
public class ProductDao {

    @Autowired
    private ProductBusinessService productBusinessService;

    public List<Product> getProducts(int count, int offset) {

        List<Product> productList =
            productBusinessService.getAllProducts();
        return productList.stream().skip(offset).
            limit(count).collect(Collectors.toList());
    }
}
```

This Data Fetcher delegates calls to the product business service you have already seen. You will later see that the instances of this product business service are pooled or reused regardless of through which port the client request is reaching the server.

Once you have defined the abstract GraphQL based port, Spring Boot GraphQL Starter offers an elegant way to get a GraphQL server running, by defining the respective dependencies in pom.xml, as shown in Listing 3-32.

Listing 3-32. The Product Web Microservice Maven Dependency (ch03\ch03-03\02-ProductWeb\pom.xml)

```
<dependencies>
    <dependency>
        <groupId>org.springframework.boot</groupId>
        <artifactId>spring-boot-starter-graphql</artifactId>
    </dependency>

    <dependency>
        <groupId>org.springframework.boot</groupId>
        <artifactId>spring-boot-starter-web</artifactId>
    </dependency>
</dependencies>
```

GraphQL is transport-agnostic. Hence I've included the web starter in this config. This will expose the GraphQL API over HTTP using Spring MVC on the default `/graphql` endpoint.

GraphQL also has a nice companion UI tool called GraphiQL. This UI can communicate with any GraphQL-compliant server and execute queries and mutations against it. See Figure 3-3.

Figure 3-3. *GraphiQL query browser*

Lastly, you need to configure the Product Web microservice, as shown in Listing 3-33.

Listing 3-33. The Product Web Microservice Configuration (ch03\ ch03-03\02-ProductWeb\src\main\resources\application.yml)

```
spring:
    application:
        name: product-web
    graphql:
        graphiql:
            enabled: true
```

```
server:
    port: 8080
acme:
    PRODUCT_SERVICE_URL: http://localhost:8081/products
    PRODUCT_CATEGORY_URL: http://localhost:8081/category
    PRODUCT_SERVICE_BY_CAT_URL: http://localhost:8081/
productsbycat
```

Most of these configurations here are trivial. What you need to look explicitly at is the GraphQL's companion tool, GraphiQL. This UI tool can communicate with any GraphQL Server and helps to develop and consume against a GraphQL API. Spring GraphQL comes with a default GraphQL page that is exposed at the /graphiql endpoint. This endpoint is disabled by default, but it can be turned on by enabling the spring. graphql.graphiql.enabled property, which is done in Listing 3-33. This works as a quick but neat in-browser way to write and test queries, particularly during development and testing.

Build and Run the Microservice

The ch03\ch03-03 folder contains the Maven scripts required to build these examples. As a first step, you need to bring up the MongoDB server. Refer to Appendix B to learn how to set up MongoDB server and bring it up. You need to execute the commands in Listing 3-34 to bring up MongoDB.

Listing 3-34. Bringing Up the MongoDB Server

```
(base) binildass-MBP:bin binil$ pwd
/Users/binil/Applns/mongodb/mongodb-macos-x86_64-4.2.8/bin
(base) binildass-MBP:bin binil$ mongod --dbpath /usr/local/var/
mongodb --logpath /usr/local/var/log/mongodb/mongo.log
```

Next, take two command terminals and change the directory to the top-level folder of both microservices. Then, build and run the Product Server microservice using the make.sh and run.sh scripts, as shown in Listing 3-35.

Listing 3-35. Build and Run Product Server Microservice Using Scripts

```
(base) binildass-MacBook-Pro:01-ProductServer binil$ pwd
/Users/binil/binil/code/mac/mybooks/docker-04/Code/ch03/
ch03-03/01-ProductServer
(base) binildass-MacBook-Pro:01-ProductServer binil$ sh make.sh
[INFO] Scanning for projects...
[INFO]
...
binildass-MacBook-Pro:01-ProductServer binil$

binildass-MacBook-Pro:01-ProductServer binil$ sh run.sh
...
2024-01-21 20:44:22 INFO  Startup.log:50 - Starting EcomProd
...
2024-01-21 20:44:23 INFO  InitComponent.init:47 - Start...
2024-01-21 20:44:23 DEBUG InitComponent.init:51 – Delete…
2024-01-21 20:44:23 DEBUG InitComponent.init:56 – Create…
2024-01-21 20:44:23 INFO  InitComponent.init:105 - End
2024-01-21 20:44:24 INFO  Startup.log:56 - Started EcomProd
```

Next, build and run the Product Web microservice, as shown in Listing 3-36.

Listing 3-36. Build and Run Product Web Microservice
Using Scripts

```
(base) binildass-MacBook-Pro:02-ProductWeb binil$ pwd
/Users/binil/binil/code/mac/mybooks/docker-04/Code/ch03/
ch03-03/02-ProductWeb
(base) binildass-MacBook-Pro:02-ProductWeb binil$ sh make.sh
[INFO] Scanning for projects...
[INFO]
...
binildass-MacBook-Pro:02-ProductWeb binil$

binildass-MacBook-Pro:02-ProductWeb binil$ sh run.sh
...
2024-01-21 20:46:04 INFO  Startup.log:50 - Starting EcomProd
...
2024-01-21 20:46:05 INFO  InitComponent.init:37 - Start
2024-01-21 20:46:05 DEBUG InitComponent.init:39 - Do Nothing
2024-01-21 20:46:05 INFO  InitComponent.init:41 - End
2024-01-21 20:46:06 INFO  Startup.log:56 - Started EcomProd….
...
```

Now that both microservices are up and running, you can test the
microservices.

Testing the Microservice

Once both microservices are up and running, you can inspect your
MongoDB server using the Mongo terminal to make sure the Product
Server microservice inserted a few products into the MongoDB server
during the microservice startup. See Listing 3-37.

Listing 3-37. Inspecting MongoDB Server Using a Mongo Shell

```
> db.productOR.find()
{ "_id" : ObjectId("61a71908b1690955cc51afff"), "name"
: "Kamsung Mobile", "code" : "KAMSUNG-TRIOS", "title" :
"Tablet Trios 12 inch , black , 12 px ....", "price" : 12000,
"category" : "Mobile", "_class" : "com.acme.ecom.product.model.
ProductOR" }
{ "_id" : ObjectId("61a71908b1690955cc51b000"), "name" : "Lokia
Mobile", "code" : "LOKIA-POMIA", "title" : "Lokia 12 inch ,
white , 14px ....", "price" : 9000, "category" : "Mobile", "_
class" : "com.acme.ecom.product.model.ProductOR" }
{ "_id" : ObjectId("61a71908b1690955cc51b001"), "name" :
"Mapple Mobile", "code" : "MAPPLE-EPHONE", "title" : "Mapple
7 inch, purple, 14px ....", "price" : 8000, "category" :
"Mobile", "_class" : "com.acme.ecom.product.model.ProductOR" }
{ "_id" : ObjectId("61a71908b1690955cc51b002"), "name" :
"Mapple Tablet", "code" : "MAPPLE-PAD", "title" : "Mapple
11 inch , grey, 140px ....", "price" : 19000, "category" :
"Tablet", "_class" : "com.acme.ecom.product.model.ProductOR" }
> db.productCategoryOR.find()
{ "_id" : ObjectId("61a71908b1690955cc51affd"), "name" :
"Mobile", "title" : "Mobiles and Tablet", "description" :
"Mobile phones", "imgUrl" : "mobile.jpg", "_class" : "com.acme.
ecom.product.model.ProductCategoryOR" }
{ "_id" : ObjectId("61a71908b1690955cc51affe"), "name" :
"Tablet", "title" : "Tablet like pads", "description" : "Tablet
pads", "imgUrl" : "tablet.jpg", "_class" : "com.acme.ecom.
product.model.ProductCategoryOR" }
>
```

When all is set, you can access the web application using your browser. Point to this URL:

```
http://localhost:8080/product.html
```

To test the CRUD operations, follow the instructions described in the subsection, "Test the Microservices Using UI" in the last section of Chapter 1, titled "Your First Java Microservice." Before you try to test more methods, let's pause to inspect a few other aspects.

When you fire this URL in the browser, you need to pay attention to the Product Web microservice terminal, as shown in Listing 3-38.

Listing 3-38. Inspecting the Product Web Microservice Terminal

```
...
2024-01-21 20:47:47 INFO  ProductRestController.
getAllProducts:70 - Start
2024-01-21 20:47:47 INFO  ProductBusinessService.
getAllProducts:64 - Start. I am instance: com.acme.ecom.
product.service.ProductBusinessService@528729a9
2024-01-21 20:47:47 INFO  ProductBusinessService.
getAllProducts:69 - Ending...
2024-01-21 20:47:47 INFO  ProductRestController.
getAllProducts:74 - Ending...
```

As a next step, test the GraphQL based port.

In a command terminal, execute a cURL command targeted to the GraphQL port, as shown in Listing 3-39.

Listing 3-39. cURL Request to GraphQL Endpoint

```
curl --request POST 'localhost:8080/graphql' --header
'Content-Type: application/json' --data-raw '{"query":"query
{products(count: 2, offset: 0) {productId name code}}"}'
```

Again, you need to pay attention to the Product Web microservice terminal, as shown in Listing 3-40.

Listing 3-40. Inspecting the Product Web Microservice Terminal

```
...
2024-01-21 20:51:05 INFO  ProductGraphQLController.
products:54 - Start
2024-01-21 20:51:05 INFO  ProductDao.getProducts:54 - Start
2024-01-21 20:51:05 INFO  ProductBusinessService.
getAllProducts:64 - Start. I am instance: com.acme.ecom.
product.service.ProductBusinessService@528729a9
2024-01-21 20:51:05 INFO  ProductBusinessService.
getAllProducts:69 - Ending...
2024-01-21 20:51:05 INFO  ProductDao.getProducts:56 - Ending...
```

As mentioned, you can see from the Product Web microservice terminal that the instances of the product business service are pooled or reused regardless of which port the client request is reaching the server.

You can execute more variants of this request using the cURL commands in Listing 3-41.

Listing 3-41. More cURL Requests to GraphQL Endpoint

```
curl --request POST 'localhost:8080/graphql' --header
'Content-Type: application/json' --data-raw '{"query":"query
{products(count: 2, offset: 0) {productId code productCategory
{id name title}}}"}'

curl --request POST 'localhost:8080/graphql' --header
'Content-Type: application/json' --data-raw '{"query":"query
{products(count: 2, offset: 0) {productId code productCategory
{id name products {productId}}}}"}'
```

Alternatively, access the GraphiQL UI from this URL:

```
http://localhost:8080/graphiql
```

Fire this Request to get the response in the GraphiQL UI (see Figure 3-4):

```
{products(count: 2, offset: 0) {productId name code}}
```

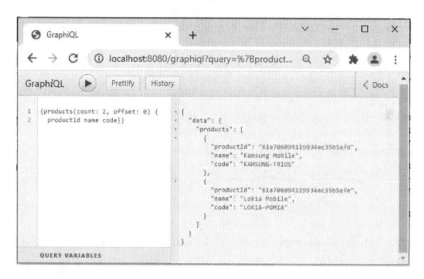

Figure 3-4. *GraphiQL top-level query*

You can next fire the following Request to get a more detailed response in the GraphiQL UI (see Figure 3-5):

```
{products(count: 2, offset: 0) {productId code productCategory
{id name title}}}
```

Figure 3-5. *GraphiQL first-level dependency query*

A further detailed response can be received in the GraphiQL UI by firing this request (see Figure 3-6):

```
{products(count: 2, offset: 0) {productId code productCategory
{id name products {productId}}}}
```

Figure 3-6. *GraphiQL second-level dependency query*

Observe the server-side logs when you execute these queries. It will be evident that the single query from the client device is mapped to multiple internal server side calls. If you alternate sending requests to the REST Controller and the GraphQL Controller that forms the outer onion rings, you can also identify from the server-side logs that the Service class (and for that matter, the entity classes) that forms the inner onion rings and their instances are being reused. Here, you have the Onion architecture in action!

Summary

I started this chapter by looking into how the pluggable nature of ports and adaptors comes into play in enterprise applications by showcasing the plugging in of a MongoDB in place of PostgreSQL. This plugin is a key characteristic of the hexagonal architecture. Next, you looked at the complementary nature of the hexagonal architecture and the Onion architecture. I demonstrated once again a flexible way of adding more ports in a hexagonal architecture so that the core of the application remains undisturbed. Equally important is the layered notion in the Onion architecture, where the outer layers depend on the inner layers, and as you move more and more toward the inner layers, you explore the core of the business domain where reusability of the core is a desirable objective. You should now have a solid understanding of the options available in the Microservices Architecture paradigm. You are now equipped to learn about the next-level concepts of events and messaging in microservices, which are covered in Chapter 4.

CHAPTER 4

Message Oriented Microservices

In the previous chapters of this book, you saw microservices interacting with each other and human actors (end users) interacting with the edge microservice using a client device (a browser). Because microservices are "micro" in nature, multiple microservices must often communicate with each other to meet useful business functionalities. These inter-microservices communications can be within a business domain or across business domains.

Microservices are distributed parts of an application that run on multiple processes or services, sometimes even across multiple servers or hosts or even across multiple geographies. Each service instance is typically a computer process. Therefore, inter-microservice communications happen using an inter-process communication (IPC) protocol such as HTTP or AMQP, or using a binary protocol like TCP, depending on the nature of these microservices.

Inter-microservice communication using REST is simple and straightforward. REST in its simplest form is synchronous, in that the client sends a request and waits for a response from the service. Hence the client code or the client-side thread can only continue its task when it receives the HTTP response from the server. While this is okay, there are alternate paradigms that you can use to achieve inter-microservice

© Binildas A. Christudas 2024
B. A. Christudas, *Java Microservices and Containers in the Cloud*,
https://doi.org/10.1007/979-8-8688-0555-4_4

communication, but in a more flexible and scalable manner. This chapter introduces message-oriented microservices, whereby microservices can communicate over messaging backbones.

This chapter covers the following concepts:

- Characteristics of microservices

- REST-based request-response style inter-microservices communication

- The need for a flexible schema for inter-microservices communication

- Introduction to messaging channels

- Inter-microservices communication using messaging channels

- Bringing flexibility to the request-response style interaction of a web browser

Characteristics of Microservices

This section starts by looking at typical characteristics of a microservice application, which will help you understand the need for a new paradigm for inter-microservice communication.

Microservices Are Autonomous

You know that microservices communicate each other, since a single microservice alone may not be sufficient to fulfill an end-to-end business use case. At the same time, one of the goals of the microservices architecture is that each microservice is autonomous and is available to the client consumer, even when the other microservices that are part of the end-to-end application flow are down or unhealthy. This is in addition to the basic principle that a microservice owns and encapsulates its own data.

When microservices communicate using REST in the typical synchronous style, they are said to be communicating in a point-to-point fashion. Thus, an HTTP transport is a point-to-point channel, which ensures that only one receiver will receive a particular message (see Figure 4-1).

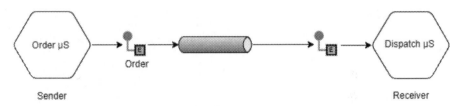

Sender   Receiver

Figure 4-1. *Point-to-point communication*

Figure 4-1 represents an Order microservice. The order is created and then sent to the Dispatch microservice. When you make a call from the Order microservice to the Dispatch microservices (such as performing an HTTP request for a dispatch order event), this call chain can provide a response to a client application. This architecture won't be resilient enough when some of these microservices fail. To rephrase, if the provider microservice cannot respond within SLA, the consumer microservice will receive an error.

Microservices Are Evolutionary

A better alternative is to employ loose coupling between microservices. You can substitute the HTTP channel with a messaging channel. Here again, the message queue is point-to-point, so you need to use message topics, which are one-to-many. Topics provide Publish-Subscribe semantics, which deliver a copy of a particular event to each subscribed receiver.

In a Publish-Subscribe channel, one input channel splits into multiple output channels, one for each subscriber microservice. When an event is published into the channel, the Publish-Subscribe channel delivers a copy of the message to be delivered to each of the output channels. Each output channel has only one subscriber microservice, which is only allowed to consume a message once. In this way, each subscriber only gets the message once; consumed copies disappear from their channels. See Figure 4-2.

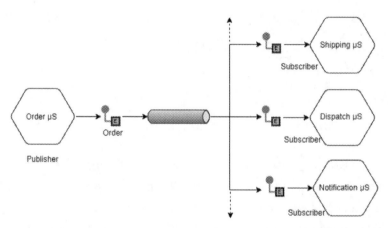

Figure 4-2. *Publish-subscribe channel*

This Publish-Subscribe channel not only brings more autonomy to individual microservices, but it also allows the microservices application to evolve at its own pace over time. In other words, as you can see in Figure 4-2, when the microservices application grows over time and you need to add more microservices, you don't need to disturb the existing architecture; you don't even need to restart the existing application deployment!

The Honeycomb Analogy

The discussions so far bring us to the analogy of a honeycomb for the microservices architecture. The microservices application architecture starts to grow from the first, single microservice to many more microservices, just like a honeycomb is built (see Figure 4-3).

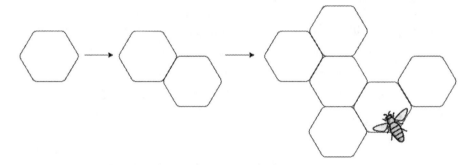

Figure 4-3. *Microservices honeycomb analogy*

The next section looks at the messaging infrastructure as a medium for inter-microservice communication.

Async, Still Request-Reply

I purposefully omitted another important aspect in the previous section, which is the need to have Request Reply semantics for typical inter-microservices communication. Messaging channels are asynchronous, rather typically one way, or request alone. How do you then get the corresponding reply? This section discusses this issue.

Async Request

HTTP channels are not only synchronous, but they also provide a mechanism for the sender to receive a reply or response. However, as discussed, to realize the full benefits of a message-based architecture, the event delegation mechanism must be inherently asynchronous. There may however be many use cases where a synchronous styled request-reply semantic is still needed. The challenge is then to mimic request-reply semantics over message channels, which are otherwise one-way channels.

Async Request-Reply

When an application sends a message, how can it get a corresponding response from the receiver through messaging channels? The Request-Reply Enterprise Integration pattern provides a proven mechanism for synchronous styled message exchange over asynchronous channels (see Figure 4-4).

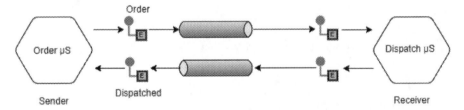

Figure 4-4. *Request reply over async*

The solution is to send a pair of request-reply messages, each on its own channel. However, there is a problem. A service provider or a receiver (or a server role microservice) can accept requests in a well-known channel that it can advertise. But what about a client's channel address? Multiple clients can connect to the same microservice process in the server role, and it's not possible for the server to know or remember the reply channel, since clients come and go, and many more new clients might appear in the future. Instead, one proven way is for the request message to contain a return address that indicates where to send the reply message (see Figure 4-5).

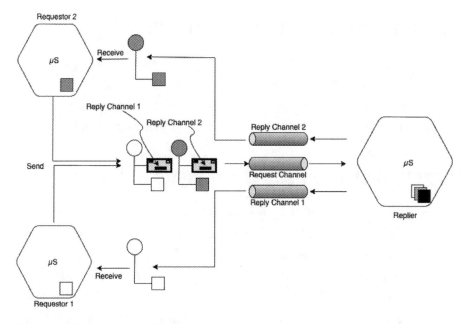

Figure 4-5. *Return address pattern*

By attaching the return address along with the request, the replier does not need to know or remember where to send the reply. It can just inspect and infer that from the request. If different messages to the same replier require replies to different places, the replier can infer where to send the corresponding reply for each request. This encapsulates the knowledge of what channels to use for requests and replies within the requestor, so those decisions do not have to be hard-coded within the replier. A return address is placed in the header of a message because it's not part of the data being transmitted, and the message transport infrastructure doesn't need to inspect the payload.

The next section demonstrates this process in code.

Sync Over Async Microservices

In this example, you will tweak the same set of microservices you saw earlier. A consumer and a provider microservice will communicate with each other using a messaging channel. The provider microservice stores the entity in an in-memory database, to keep the example simple.

Design Microservices Over Async Channel

This example slightly modifies the hexagonal microservice view shown in Figure 2-1 in Chapter 2 so that both microservices communicate through an async messaging channel instead of the HTTP channel. Apache Kafka is used as the messaging channel, which is inherently asynchronous. Remember, the objective is to simulate synchronous styled communication over the Kafka-based async channel. See Figure 4-6.

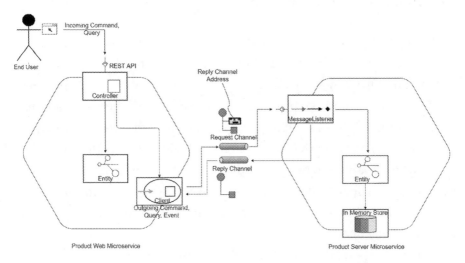

Figure 4-6. *Microservices communicate over async channel*

The end user request from the browser will reach the Product Web microservice first. The Product Web microservice will delegate the request to the Product Server microservice, but through a message channel.

The Product Server microservice could automatically know which channel to send replies to the Product Web microservice, but as discussed earlier, hard-coded assumptions make the software less flexible and more difficult to maintain. In this case, a single Product Server microservice instance could be processing calls from several different requestor types and/ or even from multiple instances of the same requestor type, so the reply channel is not the same for every message. It depends on which requestor sent that request message. You can use the return address pattern in this case.

Note that the Product Server microservice in this example is using a messaging port, in contrast to the HTTP port used in previous examples. This further validates the aspect of how different ports and adapters in the hexagonal architecture can be plugged in easily, as and when required.

Understanding the Code

The source code for this book is available on GitHub via the book's product page, located at www.apress.com/9798868805547. The code for this example is organized inside the ch04\ch04-01 folder. This section looks at the changes in the consumer microservice—that is, the Product Web microservice—first.

The core component used is the ReplyingKafkaTemplate<K,V,R> from Spring, which extends the behavior of a KafkaTemplate to provide request-reply semantics. To set this up, you need a producer (ProducerFactory) and a KafkaMessageListenerContainer. Listing 4-1 shows how to do this using a Kafka Configuration class.

Listing 4-1. Kafka Configuration for Message Producer (ch04\
ch04-01\02-ProductWeb\src\main\java\com\acme\ecom\product\
KafkaConfig.java)

```
@Configuration
public class KafkaConfig {

    @Bean
    public Map<String, Object> producerConfigs() {
        // config values goes here
    }

    @Bean
    public Map<String, Object> consumerConfigs() {
        // config values goes here
    }

    @Bean
    public ProducerFactory<String, String> producerFactory() {
        return new DefaultKafkaProducerFactory<>(
            producerConfigs());
    }

    @Bean
    public KafkaTemplate<String, String> kafkaTemplate() {
        return new KafkaTemplate<>(producerFactory());
    }

    @Bean
    public ReplyingKafkaTemplate<String, String, Products>
            replyKafkaTemplate(ProducerFactory<
            String, String> pf, KafkaMessageListenerContainer<
            String, Products> container){
```

```
        return new ReplyingKafkaTemplate<>(pf, container);
}

@Bean
public KafkaMessageListenerContainer<String, Products>
        replyContainer(
        ConsumerFactory<String, Products> cf) {

    ContainerProperties containerProperties =
        new ContainerProperties(requestReplyTopic);
    return new KafkaMessageListenerContainer<>(cf,
        containerProperties);
}

@Bean
public ConsumerFactory<String, Products>
        consumerFactory() {

    return new DefaultKafkaConsumerFactory<>(
        consumerConfigs(),
        new StringDeserializer(),new JsonDeserializer<>(
            Products.class));
}

@Bean
public KafkaListenerContainerFactory<
        ConcurrentMessageListenerContainer<
        String, Products>>
            kafkaListenerContainerFactory() {

    ConcurrentKafkaListenerContainerFactory<String,
        Products> factory =
        new ConcurrentKafkaListenerContainerFactory<>();
```

```
    factory.setConsumerFactory(consumerFactory());
    factory.setReplyTemplate(kafkaTemplate());
    return factory;
}

@Bean
public KafkaAdmin admin() {
    Map<String, Object> configs = new HashMap<>();
    configs.put(ConsumerConfig.BOOTSTRAP_SERVERS_CONFIG,
        bootstrapServers);
    return new KafkaAdmin(configs);
}

@Bean
public NewTopic requestTopic() {
    Map<String, String> configs = new HashMap<>();
    configs.put("retention.ms", replyTimeout.toString());
    return new NewTopic(requestReplyTopic, 2, (short) 1).
        configs(configs);
}
}
```

To understand the event transport mechanics, consider how a typical event (aka, a message) will look:

> Event key: "Ria"
>
> Event value: "Made a payment of $300 to Ann"
>
> Event timestamp: "Sep. 25, 2021 at 3:06 p.m."

There is an originator for an event, and events are typically time series data. If you look at the template for sending an event, the ReplyingKafkaTemplate <K, V, R> offers a return object or a reply object once the message is consumed by the Kafka listener from the provider or producer side. The type parameters represent:

- K – The key type

- V – The outbound data type

- R – The reply data type

Here, the event timestamp shown in the example event could be an optional metadata header. Keys are used to determine the partition in a log in the messaging infrastructure to which a message is appended. Value is the actual payload of the message. When a new event is published to a topic, it is appended to one of the topic's partitions. Events with the same event key (e.g., a Customer ID or Account ID) are written to the same partition, and Kafka guarantees that any consumer of a given topic-partition will always read that partition's events in the same order as they were written.

The key and/or value can be null, too. If the key is null, then a random partition will be selected. If the value is null, it can have special "delete" semantics if you enabled the log-compaction policy instead of the log-retention policy for a topic.

Using the key to direct to a partition is the default strategy of the producer. Specifying the key so that all events on the same key go to the same partition is important for proper ordering of message processing, if you have multiple consumers in a consumer group[1] on a topic. Without a key, two messages on the same key could go to different partitions and be processed by different consumers in the group, out of order.

Ultimately, the producer chooses which partition to use. If you specify the partition parameter, it will be used, and the key will be "ignored" even though it's still written into the topic. This allows you to have a customized

---

[1] A Kafka consumer group is a set of consumers that cooperate to consume data from some topics. The partitions of all the topics are divided among the consumers in the group.

partitioning even if you have keys. In other words, the order guarantees come not from the key but from messages being in the same partition. To restate, the routing of messages to partitions doesn't have to be key-based. You can explicitly specify a partition when creating a `ProducerRecord`.

This example defines the bean as `ReplyingKafkaTemplate<String, String, Products>`, where you will send a `String` type request to Kafka and then get the `Products` type object as the reply data type. You will create the Products and the included DTO classes in the next section. To summarize, you set up a `ReplyingKafkaTemplate` that sends request messages with `String` keys and receives reply messages with `String` keys. The `ReplyingKafkaTemplate` needs to be backed by a `Request ProducerFactory`, a `ReplyConsumerFactory`, and a `MessageListenerContainer`, with corresponding consumer and producer configs, which was done in the `KafkaAdmin` in Listing 4-1.

When you define a `KafkaAdmin` bean in the application context, it can automatically add topics to the broker. To do that, you need to add a `NewTopic @Bean` for each topic to the application context.

The `ContainerProperties` contains runtime properties for a listener container. Even though you specify the reply address using `requestReplyTopic`, you will later see that this example explicitly sets the return address while sending the message. It creates a single-threaded message listener container using the Java consumer.

The REST controller class, which is used in `ReplyingKafkaTemplate`, is configured in `KafkaAdmin` in Listing 4-2.

Listing 4-2. Kafka Configuration for Message Producer (ch04\
ch04-01\02-ProductWeb\src\main\java\com\acme\ecom\product\
controller\ProductRestController.java)

```
@RestController
public class ProductRestController{

    @Autowired
    ReplyingKafkaTemplate<String, String,Products>
    kafkaTemplate;

    @Value("${kafka.topic.request-topic}")
    private String requestTopic;

    @Value("${kafka.topic.requestreply-topic}")
    private String requestReplyTopic;

    @RequestMapping(value = "/productsweb",
        method = RequestMethod.GET,
        produces = {MediaType.APPLICATION_JSON_VALUE})
    public ResponseEntity<Resources<Resource<Product>>>
            getAllProducts() throws InterruptedException,
            ExecutionException {

        ProducerRecord<String, String> record =
            new ProducerRecord<String,
            String>(requestTopic, "All");
        record.headers().add(new RecordHeader(
            KafkaHeaders.REPLY_TOPIC,
            requestReplyTopic.getBytes()));
        RequestReplyFuture<String, String, Products>
            sendAndReceive =
                kafkaTemplate.sendAndReceive(record);
```

```
    ConsumerRecord<String, Products> consumerRecord =
        sendAndReceive.get();
    return new ResponseEntity(consumerRecord.value().
        getProducts(), HttpStatus.OK);
  }
}
```

The REST controller receives the requests from the client device, the browser in this case. Inside the controller, the requestReplyKafkaTemplate generates and sets a KafkaHeaders. CORRELATION_ID header. The CorrelationId should be consumed by the provider microservice and return the same in the header. You need to set the KafkaHeaders.REPLY_TOPIC header on the request explicitly, even though the same reply topic was redundantly wired into the replyListenerContainer in the KafkaConfig earlier.

The sendAndReceive method of ReplyingKafkaTemplate sends a request and receives a reply with the default timeout. It gives you a RequestReplyFuture, on which you can call the get, which will wait if necessary for the computation to complete and then retrieve its result. Products in this case.

Next, look at the Products class. See Listing 4-3.

Listing 4-3. The Container Class to Return Collection of Product Entities (ch04\ch04-01\02-ProductWeb\src\main\java\com\acme\ ecom\product\model\Products.java)

```
public class Products {

    private List<Product> products;

    public List<Product> getProducts() {
        return products;
    }
```

```
public void setProducts(List<Product> products) {
    this.products = products;
}
}
```

Products is just a container wrapper that holds a collection of Product instances.

The Product Web microservices configuration is shown in Listing 4-4, where the requestreply-topic refers to the topic to which the provider is supposed to send the response.

Listing 4-4. The Product Web Microservices Configuration (ch04\ch04-01\02-ProductWeb\src\main\resources\application. properties)

```
server.port=8080
spring.kafka.bootstrap-servers: localhost:9092
spring.kafka.consumer.auto-offset-reset: earliest
spring.kafka.consumer.group-id: product-web
kafka.topic.requestreply-topic: product-req-reply-topic
kafka.topic.request-topic=product-req-topic
kafka.request-reply.timeout-ms: 20000
```

On the Product Server microservice side, a regular KafkaListener is listening on the request topic. See Listing 4-5.

Listing 4-5. The Product Web Microservices Configuration (ch04\ch04-01\01-ProductServer\src\main\java\com\acme\ecom\product\kafka\client\ProductListener.java)

```
@Component
public class ProductListener {

    @KafkaListener(topics = "${kafka.topic.request-topic}")
    @SendTo
```

149

```java
    public Products listen(String request) {

        List<Product> productList = getAllTheProducts();
        Products products = new Products();
        products.setProducts(productList);
        return products;

    }
}
```

This listener is decorated with an additional @SendTo annotation, to provide the reply message. The Product instances retrieved by the getAllTheProducts() method and returned by the listener method is automatically wrapped into a reply message. The CORRELATION_ID is added, and the reply is posted on the topic specified by the REPLY_ TOPIC. The @KafkaListener is used to subscribe to the request Kafka topic. Using the annotation, the @SendTo annotation enables the listener method to send a response to another reply topic. Figure 4-7 illustrates the dynamics of these interactions and is marked with labels in the order of event flow.

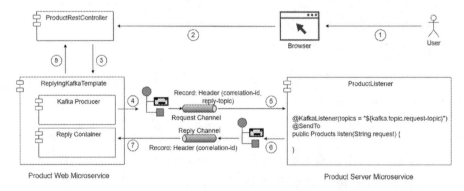

Figure 4-7. *Replying Kafka template*

You have a KafkaConfig for the provider microservice too, but it's simple and straightforward compared to the consumer microservice, so it's not listed here.

Build and Run the Microservice

The ch04\ch04-01 folder contains the Maven scripts required to build these examples. As a first step, you need to bring up the Kafka broker. Refer to Appendix D to learn to set up the Kafka server and bring it up. You need to execute the commands in Listing 4-6 to bring up Kafka from the Kafka installation location.

Listing 4-6. Commands to Bring Up Kafka Broker

```
bin/zookeeper-server-start.sh config/zookeeper.properties
bin/kafka-server-start.sh config/server.properties
```

Next, take two command terminals and change the directory to the top-level folder of both microservices. Then, build and run the Product Server microservice using the make.sh and run.sh scripts, as shown in Listing 4-7.

Listing 4-7. Commands to Build and Run the Product Server Microservice

```
(base) binildass-MacBook-Pro:01-ProductServer binil$ pwd
/Users/binil/binil/code/mac/mybooks/docker-04/Code/ch04/
ch04-01/01-ProductServer
(base) binildass-MacBook-Pro:01-ProductServer binil$ sh make.sh
[INFO] Scanning for projects...
[INFO]
...
binildass-MacBook-Pro:01-ProductServer binil$

binildass-MacBook-Pro:01-ProductServer binil$ sh run.sh
```

```
  .    ___               _                  __ _ _
 /\\ / / __ '_ __ _ _(_)_ _  __ _ \ \ \ \
( ( )\__ | '_ | '_| | | '_ \/ _` | \ \ \ \
 \\/  ___)| |_)| | | | | | || (_| |  ) ) ) )
  '   |___| ._|_| |_|_| |_\_, | / / / /
 =========|_|==============|___/=/_/_/_/
 :: Spring Boot ::                (v3.2.0)
```

2024-01-23 11:43:59 INFO Startup.log:50 - Starting EcomProd
...
2024-01-23 11:44:00 INFO InitComponent.init:43 - Start
2024-01-23 11:44:00 INFO InitComponent.init:44 - Doing
Nothing...
2024-01-23 11:44:00 INFO InitComponent.init:66 - End
2024-01-23 11:44:01 INFO Startup.log:56 - Started EcomProd
2024-01-23 11:56:03 DEBUG ProductListener.
listenWithHeaders:58 - Received request : All
...

Next, build and run the Product Web microservice, as shown in
Listing 4-8.

Listing 4-8. Commands to Build and Run the Product Web
Microservice

```
(base) binildass-MacBook-Pro:02-ProductWeb binil$ pwd
/Users/binil/binil/code/mac/mybooks/docker-04/Code/ch04/
ch04-01/02-ProductWeb
(base) binildass-MacBook-Pro:02-ProductWeb binil$ sh make.sh
[INFO] Scanning for projects...
[INFO]
...
```

```
binildass-MacBook-Pro:02-ProductWeb binil$

binildass-MacBook-Pro:02-ProductWeb binil$ sh run.sh
...
2024-01-23 11:54:08 INFO  StartupInfoLogger.logStarting:50 -
Starting EcomProductWebMicro...
...
2024-01-23 11:54:10 INFO  StartupInfoLogger.logStarted:56 -
Started EcomProductWebMicro...
```

Now that both microservices are up and running, you can test the microservices.

Testing the Microservice

When all is set, you can access the web application using your browser (see Figure 4-8). Point to this URL:

```
http://localhost:8080/product.html
```

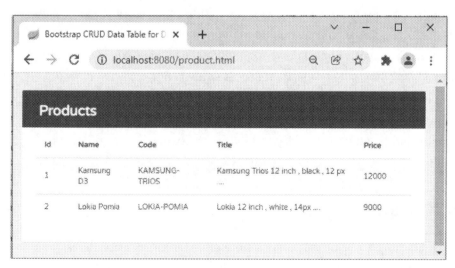

Figure 4-8. *Testing the microservices*

When you fire the URL in the browser, the request hits the REST controller of the Product Web microservice. From then onwards, the flow is as shown in Figure 4-7.

For the completeness of this example, you may also want to list and see the request and the response queues created in the broker, as shown in Listing 4-9.

Listing 4-9. List the Queues Created in Kafka Broker

```
binildass-MacBook-Pro:kafka_2.13-2.5.0 binil$ sh ./bin/kafka-
topics.sh --zookeeper localhost:2181 --list
__consumer_offsets
product-req-reply-topic
product-req-topic
binildass-MacBook-Pro:kafka_2.13-2.5.0 binil$
```

SEDA and Microservices

Having discussed and executed the examples on how you can perform inter-microservice communications over an async messaging backbone, it's now time to understand the bigger picture of what you are targeting. The SEDA (Staged Event Driven Architecture) concept is used for allowing services to be well-conditioned to be loaded, preventing resources from being overcommitted when demand exceeds service capacity. You will investigate that next and corelate the concept to your enterprise microservices using messaging infrastructure.

SEDA Architecture

In SEDA, applications consist of a network of event-driven stages connected by explicit queues. This architecture allows services to be well-conditioned to load, preventing resources from being overcommitted when demand exceeds service capacity. SEDA uses a set of dynamic resource controllers to keep stages within their operating regime, despite large fluctuations in load. This is explained in the paper titled "SEDA: An Architecture for Well-Conditioned, Scalable Internet Services" by Matt Welsh, David Culler, and Eric Brewer. The architecture is shown in Figure 4-9, adapted from this paper.

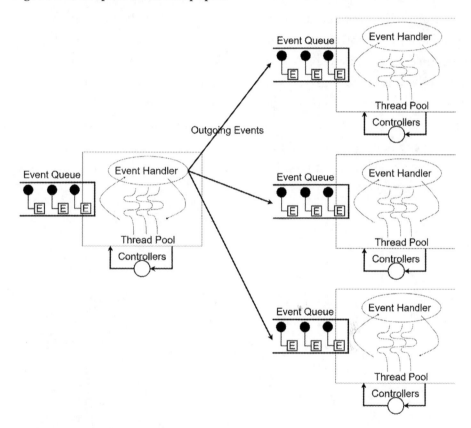

Figure 4-9. *A SEDA stage*

A stage consists of an incoming event queue, a thread pool, and an application-supplied event handler. The stage's operation is managed by the controller, which adjusts resource allocations and scheduling dynamically. Many such stages can be chained together to create a loosely coupled, end-to-end application continuum.

Microservices Architecture as a Network of Stages

A microservices-based architecture can be designed as a network of stages, interconnected by event queues. Each microservice can be envisioned as a stage. These event queues are finite; that is, an enqueue operation may fail if the queue wants to reject new entries, say, because it reached a threshold. Caller microservices can use backpressure (by blocking on a full queue) or load shedding (by dropping events) when enqueue operations fail. Alternately, the microservices can take some service-specific action, such as sending an error to the user, or performing an alternate function, such as invoking a Hystrix callback, and so on.

What if you attempt to represent inter-microservice interaction using a SEDA style? See Figure 4-10.

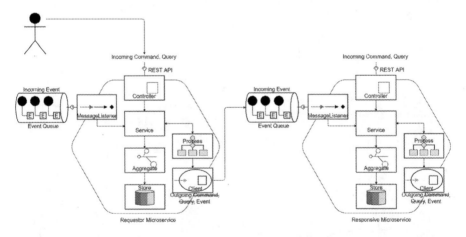

Figure 4-10. *Async based microservices architecture as a network of stages*

Introducing queues between two microservices in this manner will provide isolation, modularity, and independent load management, but may increase latency. Further, if the provider microservice is not up and running, the promise the consumer microservice can provide to the end user may have to be fulfilled later (or eventually), which will lead to a different user experience from that of the traditional means of executing use cases.

Note the blocking manner by which the Product Web microservice has been executing its request it received from the browser. Typical containers in application servers like in Apache Tomcat normally use a server thread per client request. Under increased load conditions, this necessitates that containers have many threads to serve all the client requests. This limits scalability, which can arise due to running out of memory or exhausting the pool of container threads. Java EE has added asynchronous processing support for servlets and filters from the Servlet 3.0 spec onwards.

The next section shows you how you can leverage this to isolate resources from undue blocking with the help of an example.

Async HTTP on Sync over Async Microservices

In this example, you will tweak the same previous set of microservices used in this chapter. A consumer and a provider microservice will communicate with each other using a messaging channel. The provider microservice stores the entity in an in-memory database, to keep the example simple. Moreover, when the browser sends a request to the first (consumer) microservice, the example will use async HTTP instead of sync HTTP.

Understanding the Code

The source code for this book is available on GitHub via the book's product page, located at www.apress.com/9798868805547. The source code for this example is organized inside the ch04\ch04-02 folder. Listing 4-10 looks at the changes in the consumer microservice—that is, the Product Web microservice—first.

Listing 4-10. Product Web Microservice REST Controller (ch04\
ch04-02\02-ProductWeb\src\main\java\com\acme\ecom\product\
controller\ProductRestController.java)

```java
public class ProductRestController{

    @RequestMapping(value = "/productsweb", method =
    RequestMethod.GET,
        produces = {MediaType.APPLICATION_JSON_VALUE})
    public DeferredResult<Products>  getAllProducts()
            throws InterruptedException, ExecutionException {

        LOGGER.info("Start");
        LOGGER.debug("Thread : " + Thread.currentThread());
        DeferredResult<Products> deferredResult =
            new DeferredResult<>();
        ProducerRecord<String, String> record =
            new ProducerRecord<String, String>(
                requestTopic, "All");
        record.headers().add(new RecordHeader(
            KafkaHeaders.REPLY_TOPIC,
            requestReplyTopic.getBytes()));
        record.headers().forEach(header ->
            LOGGER.debug(header.key() + ":" +
            header.value().toString()));
        RequestReplyFuture<String, String, Products>
            sendAndReceive =
            replyingKafkaTemplate.sendAndReceive(record);
        SendResult<String, String> sendResult =
            sendAndReceive.getSendFuture().get();
```

```
LOGGER.debug("Request success -> " + sendResult);
sendResult.getProducerRecord().headers().forEach(
    header -> LOGGER.debug(header.key() + " : " +
        new String(header.value())));

sendAndReceive.addCallback(
    new ListenableFutureCallback<
        ConsumerRecord<String, Products>>() {

        @Override
        public void onFailure(Throwable ex) {
            LOGGER.debug(Thread.currentThread().
                toString());
            LOGGER.error(ex.getMessage());
        }
        @Override
        public void onSuccess(ConsumerRecord<
            String, Products> consumerRecord) {

            long secondsToSleep = 2;
            LOGGER.debug("Starting to Sleep Seconds :
                " + secondsToSleep);
            try{
                Thread.sleep(1000 * secondsToSleep);
            }
            catch(Exception e) {
                //Logger.error("Error : " + e);
            }
            LOGGER.debug("Awakening from Sleep...");
            LOGGER.debug(Thread.currentThread().
                toString());
```

```
                    deferredResult.setResult(
                        consumerRecord.value());
            }
        }
    );
    LOGGER.debug("Thread : " + Thread.currentThread());
    LOGGER.info("Ending...");
    return deferredResult;
    }
}
```

As you can see, the getAllProducts method in the REST controller is asynchronous. This means that the HTTP main thread that initiated to serve the getAllProducts needn't be blocked until the method is completed. There is also a sleep of two seconds so that you can visualize these methods in the command terminal.

A six-second sleep is also included in the Product Server microservice, as shown in Listing 4-11.

Listing 4-11. Product Server Microservice Message Listener ch04\
ch04-02\01-ProductServer\src\main\java\com\acme\ecom\
product\kafka\client\ProductListener.java)

```
public class ProductListener {

    @KafkaListener(topics = "${kafka.topic.request-topic}")
    @SendTo
    public Products listenConsumerRecord(ConsumerRecord<
            String, String> record){

        long secondsToSleep = 6;

        LOGGER.info("Start");
```

```
//print all headers
record.headers().forEach(header ->
    LOGGER.debug(header.key() + ":" +
        new String(header.value())));

String brand = record.key();
String request = record.value();
LOGGER.debug("Listen; brand : " + brand);
LOGGER.debug("Listen; request : " + request);
List<Product> productList = getAllTheProducts();
Products products = new Products();
products.setProducts(productList);

LOGGER.debug("Starting to Sleep Seconds : " +
    secondsToSleep);
try{
    Thread.sleep(1000 * secondsToSleep);
}
catch(Exception e) {
    LOGGER.error("Error : " + e);
}
LOGGER.debug("Awakening from Sleep...");
LOGGER.info("Ending...");

    return products;
    }
}
```

This sleep delay of six seconds enables the caller (Product Web) microservice to feel the delay. Hence the HTTP main thread "Thread[http-nio-8080-exec-5,5,main]" in the Product Web microservice that initiated to serve the getAllProducts from the caller microservice is taken away from the service for this request. Another thread "Thread[ForkJoinPool.commonPool-worker-1,5,main]" completes the request later, as explained in the next section and shown in Listing 4-14.

Build and Run the Microservice

The ch04\ch04-02 folder contains the Maven scripts required to build the examples. As a first step, you need to bring up the Kafka broker. Refer to Appendix D to learn how to set up the Kafka server and bring it up. You need to execute the commands in Listing 4-12 to bring up Kafka from the Kafka installation location.

Listing 4-12. Commands to Bring Up Kafka Broker

```
bin/zookeeper-server-start.sh config/zookeeper.properties
bin/kafka-server-start.sh config/server.properties
```

Next, take two command terminals and change the directory to the top-level folder of both microservices. Then, build and run the Product Server microservice using the make.sh and run.sh scripts, as shown in Listing 4-13.

Listing 4-13. Commands to Build and Run the Product Server Microservice

```
binildass-MacBook-Pro:01-ProductServer binil$ pwd
/Users/binil/binil/code/mac/mybooks/docker-04/Code/ch04/
ch04-02/01-ProductServer
binildass-MacBook-Pro:01-ProductServer binil$ sh make.sh
[INFO] Scanning for projects...
[INFO]
...
binildass-MacBook-Pro:01-ProductServer binil$
binildass-MacBook-Pro:01-ProductServer binil$ sh run.sh
```

```
...
2024-02-20 19:14:19 INFO  ProductListener.
listenConsumerRecord:50 - Start
2024-02-20 19:14:19 DEBUG ProductListener.lambda$listenConsumer
Record$0:53 - kafka_replyTopic:product-req-reply-topic
2024-02-20 19:14:19 DEBUG ProductListener.lambda$listenConsumer
Record$0:53 - kafka_correlationId:◆upI<JN◆rI54◆($
2024-02-20 19:14:19 DEBUG ProductListener.
listenConsumerRecord:57 - Listen; brand : null
2024-02-20 19:14:19 DEBUG ProductListener.
listenConsumerRecord:58 - Listen; request : All
2024-02-20 19:14:19 DEBUG ProductListener.
listenConsumerRecord:63 - Starting to Sleep Seconds : 6
2024-02-20 19:14:25 DEBUG ProductListener.
listenConsumerRecord:70 - Awakening from Sleep...
2024-02-20 19:14:25 INFO  ProductListener.
listenConsumerRecord:71 - Ending...
```

Next, build and run the Product Web microservice, as shown in
Listing 4-14.

Listing 4-14. Commands to Build and Run the Product Web
Microservice

```
binildass-MacBook-Pro:02-ProductWeb binil$ pwd
/Users/binil/binil/code/mac/mybooks/docker-04/Code/ch04/
ch04-02/02-ProductWeb
binildass-MacBook-Pro:02-ProductWeb binil$ sh make.sh
[INFO] Scanning for projects...
[INFO]
...
binildass-MacBook-Pro:02-ProductWeb binil$
```

```
binildass-MacBook-Pro:02-ProductWeb binil$ sh run.sh
...
2024-02-20 19:14:19 INFO  ProductRestController.
getAllProducts:70 - Start
2024-02-20 19:14:19 DEBUG ProductRestController.
lambda$getAllProducts$0:74 - kafka_replyTopic:[B@47139a13
2024-02-20 19:14:19 DEBUG ProductRestController.
getAllProducts:76 - Thread : Thread[http-nio-8080-exec-5,5,main]
2024-02-20 19:14:19 DEBUG ProductRestController.
getAllProducts:78 - Request success -> SendResult [producerRe
cord=ProducerRecord(topic=product-req-topic, partition=null,
headers=RecordHeaders(headers = [RecordHeader(key = kafka_
replyTopic, value = [112, 114, ...
2024-02-20 19:14:19 DEBUG ProductRestController.
lambda$getAllProducts$1:79 - kafka_replyTopic : product-req-
reply-topic
2024-02-20 19:14:19 DEBUG ProductRestController.
lambda$getAllProducts$1:79 - kafka_correlationId : �upI<JN�
rI54�($
2024-02-20 19:14:19 DEBUG ProductRestController.
lambda$getAllProducts$1:79 - __TypeId__ : java.lang.String
2024-02-20 19:14:19 DEBUG ProductRestController.
getAllProducts:80 - Thread : Thread[http-nio-8080-exec-5,5,main]
2024-02-20 19:14:19 DEBUG ProductRestController.
lambda$getAllProducts$2:86 - Thread[ForkJoinPool.commonPool-
worker-1,5,main]
2024-02-20 19:14:19 DEBUG ProductRestController.
getAllProducts:142 - Thread : Thread[http-nio-8080-exec-5,5,main]
2024-02-20 19:14:19 INFO  ProductRestController.
getAllProducts:143 - Ending...
```

2024-02-20 **19:14:25** DEBUG ProductRestController.
lambda$getAllProducts$2:88 - Thread[**ForkJoinPool.commonPool-
worker-1**,5,main]
2024-02-20 19:14:25 DEBUG ProductRestController.
lambda$getAllProducts$3:98 - Starting to Sleep Seconds: 2
2024-02-20 19:14:27 DEBUG ProductRestController.
lambda$getAllProducts$3:105 - Awakening from Sleep...
2024-02-20 **19:14:27** DEBUG ProductRestController.
lambda$getAllProducts$3:106 - Thread[**ForkJoinPool.commonPool-
worker-2**,5,main]

Now that both microservices are up and running, you can test the
microservices.

Testing the Microservice

When all is set, you can access the web application using your browser and
pointing to this URL:

http://localhost:8080/product.html

You may have to wait a bit, because the browser will be rendered
with the data *eventually*, due to the sleep delays you provisioned in both
microservices.

After executing the test, carefully observe the multiple threads
being logged in the Product Web microservice command terminal
in Listing 4-14. You need to correlate those logs with the logs in the
Product Web microservice command terminal in Listing 4-13. This
correlation is depicted in Table 4-1.

Table 4-1. *Event Log for the Async HTTP on Sync Over Async Example*

Sl. No.	Timestamp	Microservice	LOC[2]	Thread	Event
1	19:14:19	Product Web	76	http-nio-8080-exec-5	Before Invoke Product Web
2	19:14:19	Product Server	50	-	Product Server Invoked
3	19:14:19	Product Server	63	-	Product Server Start 6s sleep
4	19:14:19	Product Web	80	http-nio-8080-exec-5	Proceeds after Invocation
5	19:14:19	Product Web	86	ForkJoinPool. commonPool-worker-1	New Pooled Thread Spun
6	19:14:19	Product Web	143	http-nio-8080-exec-5	Exiting
7	19:14:25	Product Server	70	-	Product Server finishes sleep, returns
8	19:14:25	Product Web	88	ForkJoinPool. commonPool-worker-1	Received response from Product Server

(continued)

---

[2] LOC means Line (Number) of Code.

Table 4-1. (*continued*)

Sl. No.	Timestamp	Microservice	LOC²	Thread	Event

9	19:14:25	Product Web	98	`ForkJoinPool.`
				`commonPool-`
				`worker-1`
					Product Web
					Start 2s sleep

10	19:14:27	Product Web	106	`ForkJoinPool.`
				`commonPool-`
				`worker-1`
					Product
					Server
					finishes sleep,
					Exits

A few aspects of interest are listed here:

- As the first step (Sl. No. 1), the worker thread in the Product Web microservice (`http-nio-8080-exec-5`) invokes the Product Server microservice.

  - Since this invocation is asynchronous (`sendAndReceive.getSendFuture()` is async), the worker thread will not wait for a response from the Product Server microservice.

  - In Steps 4 and 6, the worker thread in the Product Web microservice exits.

- As a result of invocation in Step 1, the Product Server microservice gets the hit more or less at the same time as shown in Step 2.

  - The Product Server microservice then goes to sleep for six seconds.

  - While the Product Server microservice sleeps, the invoker worker thread in the Product Web microservice doesn't wait. Instead, it exits in Steps 4 and 6.

- In parallel, as shown in Step 5, the sendAndReceive. get() method for the response is blocked, but this is in a newly pooled thread.

- After the six seconds of sleep, the Product Server microservice completes its sleep in Step 7. The newly pooled thread of the Product Web microservice receives the response in Step 8.

- In Step 9, this pooled thread of Product Web microservice starts two seconds of sleep. The rest of the steps are not that important, so you can ignore them.

You have not only seen sync style over async channel, but also learned how to release the main worker thread and leverage a pooled thread to continue the processing when the response is available in the message channel.

You also learned about another aspect. You might have observed with patience that the browser rendered the data only eventually, after a few seconds of delay, due to the sleep delays you provisioned in both microservices. The interesting fact is the HTTP worker thread that was serving the socket connection from the browser also doesn't wait. Instead, when the response from the Product Web microservice is available in the HTTP channel, a pooled thread from the HTTP server is attached in order to stream this response back to the browser. This is done under the hood by DeferredResult.

Summary

The objective of this chapter was to introduce events and inter-microservice communication through message channels. You learned how to do this effectively. By using the return address pattern, you can weave the correlated request and response interactions together to provide synchronous user experiences over the asynchronous channels. You also learned about effective programming practices, which enable you to avoid tying up resources unless otherwise absolutely required.

By leveraging the Servlet 3 spec of utilizing Async processing at the HTTP level, you also attempted to better manage the HTTP worker threads from a dedicated pool, which can become exhausted otherwise. Incrementing the HTTP thread pool size to a number larger than the optimum will also lead to system resources exhaustion, acting against scalability. An asynchronous servlet enables your application to process incoming requests in an asynchronous manner. A given HTTP worker thread handles an incoming request, and instead of processing the actual workload, it passes the request to another background—a pooled thread—which in turn is responsible for processing the workload and sending the response back to the client. The initial HTTP worker thread can return to the HTTP thread pool as soon as it passes the workload to the background thread, so it becomes available to process more requests from the socket. All of these concepts were demonstrated in the code, but you are not equipped enough yet. What will happen when concurrent requests arrive at the same topic to be consumed by multiple instances of the same type of microservice? The next chapter opens Pandora's box.

CHAPTER 5

Microservices Integration in Practice

You have seen how messaging middleware can play a key role in providing a bridge for microservices to communicate to each other in a loosely coupled manner. You have seen a few hands-on examples. Some engineers are still skeptical about whether they can use events and event paradigms for inter-microservices communication in comparison to the manner they use synchronous REST style. This chapter throws some light onto some of these issues. This chapter is hands on. It's best if you read Chapter 4 before this chapter, so that you understand the basics of running examples over the event infrastructure. Although, the chapter does provide step-by-step instructions if you want to start with this chapter.

The following topics are covered in this chapter:

- Scalability schema in the context of microservices

- The sync over async challenge

- Types of microservices vs. instances of the same types of microservice

- Sequential microservice consumers

- Parallel microservice consumers

© Binildas A. Christudas 2024
B. A. Christudas, *Java Microservices and Containers in the Cloud,*
https://doi.org/10.1007/979-8-8688-0555-4_5

Microservices Scalability in the Cloud

Thinking in terms of production quality and scalability is indispensable in microservices architecture for today's operations, especially when public cloud is the norm. There needs to be a paradigm shift in your mindset on how to scale services when you move from the monolith to the microservices architecture. This section quickly reviews some of these aspects, which sets the stage for further discussions and examples in this chapter.

Vertical Scalability

Vertical scalability has been practiced traditionally, especially during the monolith architecture days when developers used to increase the core or CPU of the machines hosting the applications. See Figure 5-1.

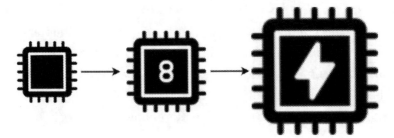

Figure 5-1. *Vertical scalability*

Vertically scaling the application is comparatively straightforward, since it doesn't disrupt existing deployment topology. A "lift and shift" of the existing process to a different host machine with more compute power is a straightforward step. However, to scale applications beyond that limit, vertical scalability doesn't help, since you will be limited by the comparatively slow rate of advancements happening in the chip and memory technologies.

Horizontal Scalability

Horizontally scaling (see Figure 5-2) is orthogonal to vertical scaling in that, instead of increasing the capacity of the existing compute or memory modules, you improve the overall compute and\or memory by incorporating more modules.

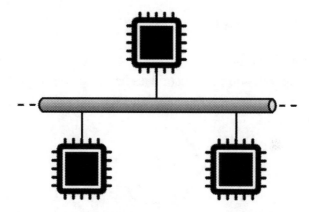

Figure 5-2. *Horizontal scalability*

Microservices Scalability

Typically, microservices represents a functional domain or a portion of a functional domain. Just like any application, microservices applications also grow over time. A balance between the size of a single microservice and the number of these microservices is required to affect an efficient operational schema.

Just like with vertical scalability, it's possible to add more functionality to the existing microservice, as shown in Figure 5-3.

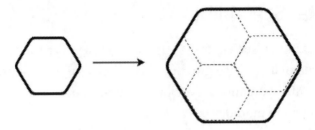

Figure 5-3. *Microservices vertical growth*

Endlessly adding more and more functionality to an existing microservice will transition microservices back to a monolith system. Instead, more microservice types can be added, as shown in Figure 5-4.

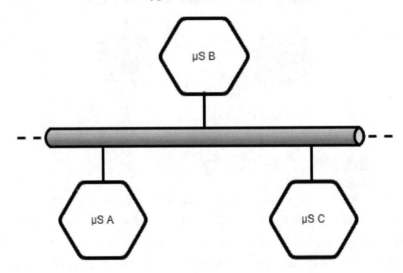

Figure 5-4. *Microservices horizontal growth*

When you want to address scalability in operations, you also need to address the growing volumes of traffic. This necessitates cloning multiple instances of the microservice and routing traffic in a load-balanced manner, as shown in Figure 5-5.

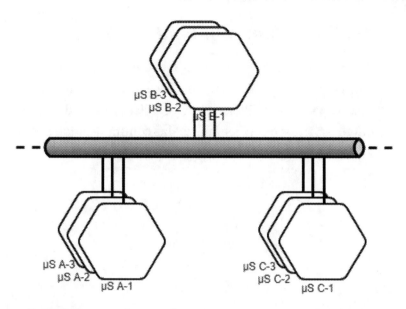

Figure 5-5. *Microservices scale out*

Routing requests to different types of microservices and distributing the load to multiple instances of the same type of microservice is straightforward in a typical HTTP-based transport, but it's non-trivial over message-based infrastructure. Let's investigate that next.

Sync over Async Dynamics

The messaging style of communication is inherently asynchronous, and messaging channels are one way. Both properties, when combined, bring a set of complexities for the developers to handle, especially if they have to mimic synchronous style, inter-microservice communication over asynchronous natured event channels.

Publisher Subscriber Combinations

Chapter 4 briefly described the return address pattern in Figure 4-5. When microservices communicate, the same microservice can send messages to different microservices, and different microservices can send messages to the same microservice. We can generalize this communication pattern, as shown in Figure 5-6.

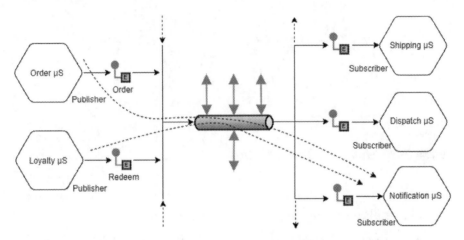

Figure 5-6. *Different kinds of microservices communicating*

Referring again to Figure 4-5 in Chapter 4, each publisher microservice can have its own return address and, in that manner, response messages can be directed to the corresponding sender.

Publisher Subscriber Instance Combinations

When you want to scale out microservices, this introduces more complexity if you need to send synchronous styled communications over an async channel.

If you have multiple instances of the same microservice, you must make sure that the reply is sent to the correct microservice instance. The Spring Kafka documentation suggests that each consumer use a unique reply topic so that reply messages are not interchanged.

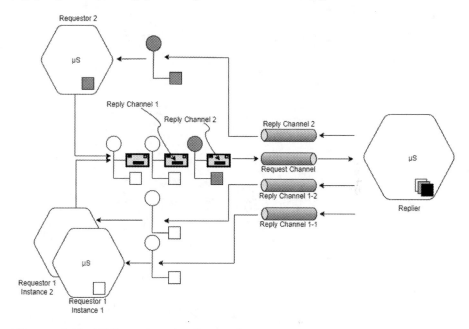

Figure 5-7. *Different reply channels*

Figure 5-7 depicts each consumer using a unique reply topic so that reply messages are not interchanged across consumers. A particular request thread from a specific requestor instance receives the response corresponding to the right request. The solution works, but it's not elegant. Topics are managed objects, and they need housekeeping. Even if the housekeeping could be automated (like with dynamic queues), it's not nice to have tens of hundreds of topics just like that.

A better solution is to leverage partitions of *topics*, a feature provided by Kafka. As suggested by the Spring Kafka documentation, each consumer can use an additional KafkaHeaders.REPLY_PARTITION header value, which is sent with the request. It's a four-byte field containing a BIG-ENDIAN representation of the partition integer.

The schema can be represented as shown in Figure 5-8.

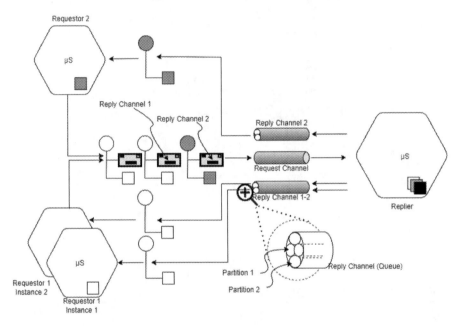

Figure 5-8. *Different reply partitions*

Kafka partitions are the main concurrency mechanism in Kafka. A topic is divided into one or more partitions, enabling producer and consumer loads to be scaled. The consumers are shared evenly across the partitions, allowing for the consumer load to be linearly scaled by increasing both consumers and partitions. You can use this feature for the reply address.

The next section illustrates these topics with code.

Microservices Sequential Processing

In this example, you see how to tweak the same set of microservices shown in Chapter 4. A consumer and a provider microservice communicate with each other using a messaging channel. The provider microservice stores the entity in an in-memory database, to keep the example simple. Moreover, when the browser sends the request to the first (consumer) microservice, it uses async HTTP.

The complexity of this example compared to the example in Chapter 4 is that this example uses multiple instances of consumer and provider microservices and multiple clients while testing the service. When the same kinds of requests from different users reach the single instance of the (message consumer) microservice, the requests are serviced one by one, in sequence.

Design Sequential Processing Microservices

I slightly modify the hexagonal microservice view shown in Figure 2-1 in Chapter 2 so that both microservices communicate through an async channel. This example uses Apache Kafka as the messaging channel, which is inherently asynchronous. Remember, the objective is to mimic synchronous styled communication over the Kafka-based async channel, as well as demonstrate that multiple consumer types or multiple instances of the same consumer type can connect to one or more instances of the provider microservice and still get the responses corresponding to the respective request alone. See Figure 5-9.

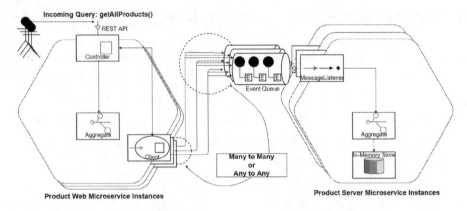

Figure 5-9. *Microservice design over async channel using partitions*

A few observations to note are as follows:

- There are multiple instances of the Product Web
  (Request Consumer) microservice provisioned. If this
  schema works, it should work for different types of
  microservices too.

- There are multiple instances of the Product Server
  (Request Provider) microservice provisioned. Hence,
  events can be picked up for processing by any instance
  in a round robin manner.

- Even though the Product Web is the Request Consumer
  and the Product Server is the Request Provider from the
  Service Consumer and Service Provider perspective,
  they are both playing the role of Message Sender
  and Message Consumer at the same time over the
  Kafka topics.

- Figure 5-9 shows instances of the Product Server
  microservice listening to different topics, even though
  in this example, it listens to the same topic but
  leverages different partitions.

Understanding the Code

The source code for this book is available on GitHub via the book's product page, located at www.apress.com/9798868805547. The source code for the example is organized inside the ch05\ch05-01 folder. This section looks at the changes in the consumer microservice—that is, the Product Web microservice, first.

As explained earlier, using separate topics for different clients is not an elegant solution, since you should leverage the REPLY_PARTITION explicitly. The consumer microservice in that case will need to know which partition it is assigned to. Explicit configuration to select a specific partition can be provided as follows:

```
@Value("${kafka.topic.product.reply.partition}")
private int replyPartition;
```

As shown in Listing 4-2 in Chapter 4, you now need to set the parameters explicitly, like those in Listing 5-1.

Listing 5-1. Static Configuration of Reply Topic and Partition

```
productRecord.headers().add(new RecordHeader(
    KafkaHeaders.REPLY_TOPIC, requestReplyTopic.getBytes()));
productRecord.headers().add(new RecordHeader(
    KafkaHeaders.REPLY_PARTITION,
    intToBytesBigEndian(replyPartition)));
RequestReplyFuture<String, RequestReply,
    RequestReply> sendAndReceive =
        requestReplyKafkaTemplate.sendAndReceive(
            productRecord);
...
```

However, this kind of static configuration will not help you in cases of dynamic horizontal scaling (adding more instances of the same microservice), so you would need a schema to address this.

Bjorn Beskow from Callista Enterprise wrote a nice blog and provided a utility library on the Internet to do this, hence you will utilize that for this example. The requirement is to dynamically manage the Reply topic and the Reply partition required to implement the Return Address pattern, and this library does exactly that. The Reply topic needs to be wired into RequestReplyTemplate, so you don't need to handle it through the API while sending the record. For the Reply partition, you retrieve the partition(s) on which the reply topic listener has been assigned and pass that partition info. The utility library is available in this source code subfolder:

ch05\ch05-01\kafka-request-reply-util

A detailed explanation of the implementation of this utility is beyond the scope of this book. You are directed to refer to the blog for more information. Instead, this section looks at how to use this utility and implement the functionality. Listing 5-2 shows the configurations to use the utility library.

Listing 5-2. Kafka Configuration for the Product Web Microservice (ch05\ch05-01\02-ProductWeb\src\main\java\com\acme\ecom\ product\KafkaConfig.java)

```
import se.callista.blog.synch_kafka.request_reply_util.
    CompletableFutureReplyingKafkaOperations;
import se.callista.blog.synch_kafka.request_reply_util.
    CompletableFutureReplyingKafkaTemplate;

@Configuration
public class KafkaConfig {
```

```
@Value("${spring.kafka.bootstrap-servers}")
private String bootstrapServers;

@Value("${spring.kafka.consumer.group-id}")
private String groupId;

@Value("${kafka.topic.product.request}")
private String requestTopic;

@Value("${product.topic.request.numPartitions}")
private int numPartitions;

@Value("${kafka.topic.product.reply}")
private String replyTopic;

@Value("${kafka.request-reply.timeout-ms}")
private Long replyTimeout;

@Bean
public CompletableFutureReplyingKafkaOperations<
        String, String, Products> replyKafkaTemplate() {

    CompletableFutureReplyingKafkaTemplate<String,
        String, Products> requestReplyKafkaTemplate =
            new CompletableFutureReplyingKafkaTemplate<>(
                requestProducerFactory(),
                    replyListenerContainer());

    requestReplyKafkaTemplate.setDefaultTopic(
        requestTopic);
    requestReplyKafkaTemplate.setDefaultReplyTimeout(
        Duration.of(replyTimeout, ChronoUnit.MILLIS));
    return requestReplyKafkaTemplate;
}
```

```
@Bean
public NewTopic replyTopic() {

    Map<String, String> configs = new HashMap<>();
    configs.put("retention.ms", replyTimeout.toString());
    return new NewTopic(replyTopic, numPartitions,
        (short) 1).configs(configs);
}
}
```

As you saw in Chapter 4, ReplyingKafkaTemplate <K, V, R> offers a Return object or a Reply object once the message is consumed by the Kafka listener from the provider or producer side. The type parameters represent:

- K – Key type

- V – Outbound data type

- R – Reply data type

When you have multiple sender microservices instances, you must make sure that the response is sent to the correct sender microservices instance. The Spring Kafka documentation suggests that each sender microservices use a unique topic, or that an additional KafkaHeaders. REPLY_PARTITION header value be sent with the request. Topics are administered objects. You can also set the REPLY_PARTITION explicitly. The REPLY_PARTITION header denotes a partition number on which to send the reply. The sender microservices will then need to know which partition it is assigned to. The documentation suggests using explicit configuration to select a specific partition. Listing 5-3 shows one possible configuration.

Listing 5-3. Kafka Configuration for the Product Web Microservice, Specifying Partition

```
@Configuration
public class KafkaConfig {

    @Value("${kafka.topic.product.reply}")
    private String replyTopic;

    @Value("${kafka.topic.product.reply.partition}")
    private int replyPartition;

    @Bean
    public KafkaMessageListenerContainer<String,
            RequestReply> replyListenerContainer() {

        ContainerProperties containerProperties =
            new ContainerProperties(replyTopic);
        TopicPartitionInitialOffset initialOffset =
            new TopicPartitionInitialOffset(replyTopic,
                replyPartition);
        return new KafkaMessageListenerContainer<>(
            replyConsumerFactory(),
            containerProperties, initialOffset);
}
```

An additional `KafkaHeaders.REPLY_PARTITION` header value can be sent with the request, which is a four-byte field containing a BIG-ENDIAN representation of the partition integer, as shown in Listing 5-4.

Listing 5-4. Kafka Message Exchange for the Product Web
Microservice, Specifying Partition

```
record.headers().add(new RecordHeader(KafkaHeaders.REPLY_TOPIC,
    requestReplyTopic.getBytes()));
record.headers().add(new RecordHeader(KafkaHeaders.REPLY_
PARTITION, intToBytesBigEndian(replyPartition)));
RequestReplyFuture<String, RequestReply, RequestReply>
sendAndReceive =
    requestReplyKafkaTemplate.sendAndReceive(record);
```

Using separate topics for different sender microservices is clearly
not very flexible, as mentioned. The configuration and the programming
needed is extensive, and the APIs are low level. Moreover, when you
need to dynamically scale the number of sender microservices, this way
of static configuration is not what you need. Hence, you can use the `Par`
`titionAwareReplyingKafkaTemplate<K, V, R>` utility, which extends
`ReplyingKafkaTemplate<K, V, R>`. It also implements `PartitionAware`
`ReplyingKafkaOperations<K, V, R>`. Subsequently, `CompletableFuture`
`ReplyingKafkaTemplate<K, V, R>` extends `PartitionAwareReplyingKafka`
`Template<K, V, R>`.

You can enhance the Return Address pattern by passing the
partition along with the Reply topic. The Reply topic is wired into the
`RequestReplyTemplate`, and hence needn't be present in the API. For the
partition info, you retrieve which partition(s) the reply topic listener has
been assigned and pass that partition along automatically. This eliminates
the need for the client to care about these headers. As mentioned earlier,
Bjorn Beskow from Callista Enterprise placed this utility library on the
Internet to do this, and it's used in Listing 5-5.

Listing 5-5. Encapsulating Partition Info in Kafka Message Exchange (ch05\ch05-01\kafka-request-reply-util\src\ main\java\se\callista\blog\synch_kafka\request_reply_util\ PartitionAwareReplyingKafkaTemplate.java)

```java
public class PartitionAwareReplyingKafkaTemplate<K, V, R>
      extends ReplyingKafkaTemplate<K, V, R> {

   public PartitionAwareReplyingKafkaTemplate(
         ProducerFactory<K, V> producerFactory,
         GenericMessageListenerContainer<K, R>
         replyContainer) {
      super(producerFactory, replyContainer);
   }

   private TopicPartition
         getFirstAssignedReplyTopicPartition() {

      if (getAssignedReplyTopicPartitions() != null &&
            getAssignedReplyTopicPartitions().iterator().
               hasNext()) {
         TopicPartition replyPartition =
            getAssignedReplyTopicPartitions().iterator().
               next();
         if (this.logger.isDebugEnabled()) {
            this.logger.debug("Using partition " +
               replyPartition.partition());
         }
         return replyPartition;
      } else {
         throw new KafkaException("Illegal state: No reply
            partition is assigned to this instance");
      }
   }
```

```
protected RequestReplyFuture<K, V, R> doSendAndReceive(
        ProducerRecord<K, V> record) {

    TopicPartition replyPartition =
        getFirstAssignedReplyTopicPartition();
    record.headers()
        .add(new RecordHeader(KafkaHeaders.REPLY_TOPIC,
            replyPartition.topic().getBytes()))
            .add(new RecordHeader(
                KafkaHeaders.REPLY_PARTITION,
                intToBytesBigEndian(
                    replyPartition.partition()))));
    return super.sendAndReceive(record);
  }
}
```

Listing 5-5 is slightly non-trivial, so I attempt to explain it with the help of Figure 5-10, which depicts the complete abstraction provided by `CompletableFutureReplyingKafkaTemplate`.

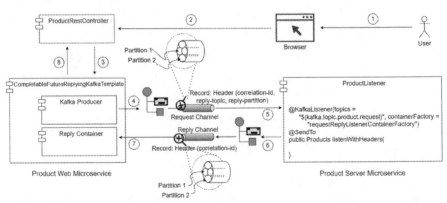

Figure 5-10. *CompletableFutureReplyingKafkaTemplate abstraction*

The labelled steps are in sequence in Figure 5-10, so you can simply follow those steps to understand the explanation provided earlier.

Next, we will look at the REST controller for the Product Web microservice. This is shown in Listing 5-6.

Listing 5-6. REST Controller for the Product Web Microservice (ch05\ch05-01\02-ProductWeb\src\main\java\com\acme\ecom\ product\controller\ProductRestController.java)

```java
@CrossOrigin
@RestController
public class ProductRestController{

    private static final String REQUEST_PAYLOAD = "All";
        //Get All Data

    @Value("${spring.application.name:product-web}")
    private String appName;

    @Value("${kafka.topic.product.pinnedToPartition:false}")
    private boolean pinnedToPartition;

    @Value("${kafka.topic.product.request}")
    private String requestTopic;

    @Autowired
    private CompletableFutureReplyingKafkaOperations<String,
        String, Products> replyingKafkaTemplate;

    @RequestMapping(value = "/productsweb", method =
        RequestMethod.GET,
        produces = {MediaType.APPLICATION_JSON_VALUE})
    public DeferredResult<Products> getAllProducts()
            throws InterruptedException, ExecutionException {

        DeferredResult<Products> deferredResult =
            new DeferredResult<>();
        CompletableFuture<Products> completableFuture = null;
```

189

```
    if(pinnedToPartition){
        completableFuture = replyingKafkaTemplate.
            requestReply(requestTopic,
                appName, REQUEST_PAYLOAD);
    }
    else{
        completableFuture = replyingKafkaTemplate.
            requestReply(requestTopic, REQUEST_PAYLOAD);
    }
    completableFuture.thenAccept(products ->
        deferredResult.setResult(products))
        .exceptionally(ex -> {
            LOGGER.error(ex.getMessage());
            return null;
        });

    return deferredResult;
    }
}
```

Similar to ReplyingKafkaTemplate, CompletableFutureReplyingKaf
kaOperations<K, V, R> offers a Return or Reply object once the message
is consumed by the Kafka listener from the provider or producer side. The
type parameters represent:

- K – Key type

- V – Outbound data type

- R – Reply data type

Next, we introduce a Boolean flag pinnedToPartition, intended to
demonstrate the various test cases. This flag can be configured in the
application.yml configuration file for the Product Web microservice. See
Listing 5-7.

Listing 5-7. Configuration for the Product Web Microservice (ch05\
ch05-01\02-ProductWeb\src\main\resources\application.yml)

```
server:
    port: 8080
spring:
    application:
        name: product-web
    autoconfigure:
        exclude: org.springframework.boot.autoconfigure.kafka.
            KafkaAutoConfiguration
    kafka:
        bootstrap-servers: localhost:9092
        consumer:
            auto-offset-reset: earliest
            group-id: product-web
kafka:
    topic:
        product:
            request: product-req-topic
            pinnedToPartition: true
            reply: product-req-reply-topic
    request-reply:
        timeout-ms: 60000
product:
    topic:
        request:
            numPartitions: 2
```

If pinnedToPartition is configured with false, the sender microservices are intended to send request messages to receiver microservices in a random, load balanced manner, as shown here:

```
completableFuture = replyingKafkaTemplate.
requestReply(requestTopic, REQUEST_PAYLOAD);
```

Instead, if pinnedToPartition is configured with true, the sender microservices are intended to send request messages to receiver microservices in a fixed or pinned manner, as shown here:

```
completableFuture = replyingKafkaTemplate.
requestReply(requestTopic, appName,
    REQUEST_PAYLOAD);
```

As you saw in Chapter 4, the producer chooses which partition to use. If you specify the partition parameter, it will be used, and the key will be "ignored" even though the key will still be written into the topic. Routing of messages to partitions doesn't have to be key-based. You can explicitly specify a partition when creating a ProducerRecord too. When pinnedToPartition is configured with true, the underlying utility library uses the overloaded version of requestReply(String topic, K key, V value) so that a value for the key can be specified, as shown in Listing 5-8.

Listing 5-8. CompletableFutureReplyingKafkaTemplate Utility (ch05\ch05-01\kafka-request-reply-util\src\main\ java\se\callista\blog\synch_kafka\request_reply_util\ CompletableFutureReplyingKafkaTemplate.java)

```
package se.callista.blog.synch_kafka.request_reply_util;

public class CompletableFutureReplyingKafkaTemplate<K, V, R>
    extends PartitionAwareReplyingKafkaTemplate<K, V, R>
    implements CompletableFutureReplyingKafkaOperations<
    K, V, R> {
```

```
@Override
public CompletableFuture<R> requestReply(String topic,
        V value) {
    return adapt(sendAndReceive(topic, value));
}

@Override
public CompletableFuture<R> requestReply(String topic,
        K key, V value) {
    return adapt(sendAndReceive(topic, key, value));
}

@Override
public CompletableFuture<R> requestReply(String topic,
        Integer partition, K key, V value) {
    return adapt(sendAndReceive(topic, partition,
        key, value));
}
}
```

You can configure the same values for the key by providing the same values for the appName through the run scripts in the root folder of the Product Web microservice:

```
-Dspring.application.name=product-web-1
-Dspring.application.name=product-web-1
```

In Listing 5-7, note the configuration numPartitions: 2. The number 2 is arbitrary, but it should be more than the number of (instances of) requester microservices, because otherwise the system will throw errors. Moreover, shared partitions cannot guarantee that the requestor (instance of) microservice will receive the corresponding response.

In the Product Server microservice, the main component is ProductListener, as shown in Listing 5-9.

Listing 5-9. Product Server Message Listener (ch05\ch05-01\01-
ProductServer\src\main\java\com\acme\ecom\product\kafka\
client\ProductListener.java)

```
@Component
public class ProductListener {

    @KafkaListener(topics = "${kafka.topic.product.request}",
        containerFactory =
            "requestReplyListenerContainerFactory")
    @SendTo
    public Products listenWithHeaders(
            @Payload String requestor,
            @Header(KafkaHeaders.REPLY_TOPIC)
                String replyTopic,
            @Header(KafkaHeaders.REPLY_PARTITION)
                int replyPartitionId,
            @Header(KafkaHeaders.RECEIVED_TOPIC)
                String receivedTopic,
            @Header(KafkaHeaders.RECEIVED_PARTITION_ID)
                int receivedPartitionId,
            @Header(KafkaHeaders.CORRELATION_ID)
                String correlationId,
            @Header(KafkaHeaders.OFFSET) String offset){

        LOGGER.info("Start");
        LOGGER.debug("Listen; Request from : " + requestor);
        LOGGER.debug("Listen; replyTopic : " + replyTopic);
        LOGGER.debug("Listen; replyPartitionId : " +
            replyPartitionId);
        LOGGER.debug("Listen; receivedTopic : " +
            receivedTopic);
```

```
LOGGER.debug("Listen; receivedPartitionId : " +
    receivedPartitionId);
LOGGER.debug("Listen; correlationId : " +
    correlationId);
LOGGER.debug("Listen; offset : " + offset);

List<Product> productList = getAllTheProducts();
Products products=new Products();
products.setProducts(productList);

LOGGER.info("Ending...");
return products;
    }
}
```

ProductListener contains logging information, which will help you debug the headers and other parameters. It also fetches a collection of Product entities from an in-memory DB and returns it to the Reply channel.

The rest of the code is very similar to Listing 4-11 from Chapter 4, so it's not repeated here. Instead, Listing 5-10 shows a snippet of the configuration for the Product Server microservice.

Listing 5-10. Configuration for Product Server Microservice (ch05\ch05-01\01-ProductServer\src\main\resources\application.yml)

```
product:
  topic:
    request:
      numPartitions: 3
```

This example is demonstrated with three instances of the Product Server microservice.

Build and Run the Microservice Sequential Processing

The ch05\ch05-01 folder contains the Maven scripts required to build the examples. As a first step, you need to bring up the Kafka broker. Refer to Appendix D to learn how to set up Kafka server and bring the server up. You need to execute the commands in Listing 5-11 to bring up Kafka from the Kafka installation location.

Listing 5-11. Commands to Bring Up Kafka Broker

```
bin/zookeeper-server-start.sh config/zookeeper.properties
bin/kafka-server-start.sh config/server.properties
```

Next, build and install the utility library from the Callista Enterprise, as shown in Listing 5-12.

Listing 5-12. Commands to Build and Install the Utility Library from the Callista Enterprise

```
(base) binildass-MacBook-Pro:kafka-request-reply-util
binil$ pwd
/Users/binil/binil/code/mac/mybooks/docker-04/Code/ch05/
ch05-01/kafka-request-reply-util
(base) binildass-MacBook-Pro:kafka-request-reply-util binil$
mvn clean install
[INFO] Scanning for projects...
[INFO]
[INFO] -< se.callista.blog.synch_kafka:kafka-req...-util >-
[INFO] Building Kafka Request Reply utility 0.0.1-SNAPSHOT
[INFO] --------------------------------[ jar ]-------------
[INFO]
...
```

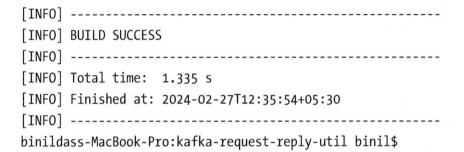

```
[INFO] ------------------------------------------------------
[INFO] BUILD SUCCESS
[INFO] ------------------------------------------------------
[INFO] Total time:  1.335 s
[INFO] Finished at: 2024-02-27T12:35:54+05:30
[INFO] ------------------------------------------------------
binildass-MacBook-Pro:kafka-request-reply-util binil$
```

Next, take five command terminals—three for the Product Server and two for the Product Web microservice—and change the directory to the top-level folder of both microservices.

Build the Product Server microservice using the make.sh scripts, as shown in Listing 5-13.

Listing 5-13. Commands to Build the Product Server Microservice

```
binildass-MacBook-Pro:01-ProductServer binil$ pwd
/Users/binil/binil/code/mac/mybooks/docker-04/Code/ch05/
ch05-01/01-ProductServer
binildass-MacBook-Pro:01-ProductServer binil$ sh make.sh
[INFO] Scanning for projects...
[INFO]
...
```

Next, build the Product Web microservice, as shown in Listing 5-14.

Listing 5-14. Commands to Build the Product Web Microservice

```
binildass-MacBook-Pro:02-ProductWeb binil$ pwd
/Users/binil/binil/code/mac/mybooks/docker-04/Code/ch05/
ch05-01/02-ProductWeb
binildass-MacBook-Pro:02-ProductWeb binil$ sh make.sh
[INFO] Scanning for projects...
[INFO]
...
```

Now that the Product Server microservice is built, you can run it using the run1.sh, run2.sh and run3.sh scripts in the root folder of the microservice, in three different terminals. See Listings 5-15 through 5-17.

Listing 5-15. Commands to Run the Product Server Microservice: Instance 1

```
binildass-MacBook-Pro:01-ProductServer binil$ pwd
/Users/binil/binil/code/mac/mybooks/docker-04/Code/ch05/
ch05-01/01-ProductServer
binildass-MacBook-Pro:01-ProductServer binil$ sh run1.sh


  .   ____          _            __ _ _
 /\\ / ___'_ __ _ _(_)_ __  __ _ \ \ \ \
( ( )\___ | '_ | '_| | '_ \/ _` | \ \ \ \
 \\/  ___)| |_)| | | | | || (_| |  ) ) ) )
  '  |____| .__|_| |_|_| |_\__, | / / / /
 =========|_|==============|___/=/_/_/_/
 :: Spring Boot ::                (v3.2.0)
...
2024-02-28 17:41:09 INFO   InitComponent.init:43 - Start
2024-02-28 17:41:09 INFO   InitComponent.init:44 - Do Nothing
2024-02-28 17:41:09 INFO   InitComponent.init:66 - End
2024-02-28 17:41:11 INFO   Logger.log:56 - Started EcomProd...
...
```

Listing 5-16. Commands to Run the Product Server Microservice: Instance 2

```
binildass-MacBook-Pro:01-ProductServer binil$ pwd
/Users/binil/binil/code/mac/mybooks/docker-04/Code/ch05/
ch05-01/01-ProductServer
```

```
binildass-MacBook-Pro:01-ProductServer binil$ sh run2.sh
...
2024-02-28 17:41:11 INFO  Logger.log:56 - Started EcomProd...
...
```

Listing 5-17. Commands to Run the Product Server Microservice:
Instance 3

```
binildass-MacBook-Pro:01-ProductServer binil$ pwd
/Users/binil/binil/code/mac/mybooks/docker-04/Code/ch05/
ch05-01/01-ProductServer
binildass-MacBook-Pro:01-ProductServer binil$ sh run3.sh
...
2024-02-28 17:41:19 INFO  InitComponent.init:43 - Start
2024-02-28 17:41:19 INFO  InitComponent.init:44 - Do Nothing
2024-02-28 17:41:19 INFO  InitComponent.init:66 - End
2024-02-28 17:41:20 INFO  Logger.log:56 - Started EcomProd...
2024-02-28 17:52:23 INFO  ProductListener.
listenWithHeaders:57 - Start
2024-02-28 17:52:23 DEBUG ProductListener.
listenWithHeaders:58 - Listen; Request from : All
2024-02-28 17:52:23 DEBUG ProductListener.
listenWithHeaders:59 - Listen; replyTopic : product-req-
reply-topic
2024-02-28 17:52:23 DEBUG ProductListener.
listenWithHeaders:60 - Listen; replyPartitionId : 0
2024-02-28 17:52:23 DEBUG ProductListener.
listenWithHeaders:61 - Listen; receivedTopic : product-
req-topic
2024-02-28 17:52:23 DEBUG ProductListener.
listenWithHeaders:62 - Listen; receivedPartitionId : 0
...
```

2024-02-28 **17:52:29** INFO ProductListener.
listenWithHeaders:80 - **Ending...**
2024-02-28 **17:52:29** INFO ProductListener.
listenWithHeaders:57 - **Start**
2024-02-28 17:52:29 DEBUG ProductListener.
listenWithHeaders:58 - Listen; Request from : All
2024-02-28 17:52:29 DEBUG ProductListener.
listenWithHeaders:59 - Listen; replyTopic : product-req-
reply-topic
2024-02-28 17:52:29 DEBUG ProductListener.
listenWithHeaders:60 - Listen; replyPartitionId : 1
2024-02-28 17:52:29 DEBUG ProductListener.
listenWithHeaders:61 - Listen; receivedTopic : product-
req-topic
2024-02-28 17:52:29 DEBUG ProductListener.
listenWithHeaders:62 - Listen; receivedPartitionId : 0
...
2024-02-28 **17:52:35** INFO ProductListener.
listenWithHeaders:80 - **Ending...**

Once all three instances of the Product Server microservice are running, you can bring up the two Product Web microservice instances, as shown in Listings 5-18 and 5-19.

Listing 5-18. Commands to Run the Product Web Microservice: Instance 1

```
binildass-MacBook-Pro:02-ProductWeb binil$ pwd
/Users/binil/binil/code/mac/mybooks/docker-04/Code/ch05/
ch05-01/02-ProductWeb
binildass-MacBook-Pro:02-ProductWeb binil$ sh run1.sh
...
2024-02-28 17:48:02 INFO  Logger.log:56 - Started EcomProd...
```

```
2024-02-28 17:52:23 INFO  ProductRestController.
getAllProducts:69 - Start
2024-02-28 17:52:23 DEBUG ProductRestController.
getAllProducts:70 - Application Name : product-web-1
2024-02-28 17:52:23 DEBUG ProductRestController.
getAllProducts:71 - PinnedToPartition? : true
2024-02-28 17:52:23 DEBUG ProductRestController.
getAllProducts:72 - Thread : Thread[http-nio-8080-
exec-1,5,main]
2024-02-28 17:52:23 DEBUG LogAccessor.debug:191 - Using Request
partition : null
2024-02-28 17:52:23 DEBUG LogAccessor.debug:191 - Using Request
key : product-web-1
2024-02-28 17:52:23 DEBUG LogAccessor.debug:191 - Using Reply
partition : 0
2024-02-28 17:52:23 DEBUG LogAccessor.debug:313 - Sending:
ProducerRecord(topic=product-req-topic...
...
2024-02-28 17:52:27 INFO  ProductRestController.
getAllProducts:98 - Ending
2024-02-28 17:52:29 DEBUG LogAccessor.debug:313 - Received:
product-req-reply-topic-0@0 with correlationId: ec3cceaa-
d7e4-4544-add2-4b98ce5e3709
```

Listing 5-19. Commands to Run the Product Web Microservice:
Instance 2

```
binildass-MacBook-Pro:02-ProductWeb binil$ pwd
/Users/binil/binil/code/mac/mybooks/docker-04/Code/ch05/
ch05-01/02-ProductWeb
binildass-MacBook-Pro:02-ProductWeb binil$ sh run2.sh
...
```

```
2024-02-28 17:50:27 INFO  Logger.log:56 - Started EcomProd...
2024-02-28 17:52:23 INFO  ProductRestController.
getAllProducts:69 - Start
2024-02-28 17:52:23 DEBUG ProductRestController.
getAllProducts:70 - Application Name : product-web-1
2024-02-28 17:52:23 DEBUG ProductRestController.
getAllProducts:71 - PinnedToPartition? : true
2024-02-28 17:52:23 DEBUG ProductRestController.
getAllProducts:72 - Thread : Thread[http-nio-8081-
exec-1,5,main]
2024-02-28 17:52:23 DEBUG LogAccessor.debug:191 - Using Request
partition : null
2024-02-28 17:52:23 DEBUG LogAccessor.debug:191 - Using Request
key : product-web-1
2024-02-28 17:52:23 DEBUG LogAccessor.debug:191 - Using Reply
partition : 1
2024-02-28 17:52:23 DEBUG LogAccessor.debug:313 - Sending:
ProducerRecord(topic=product-req-topic...
...
2024-02-28 17:52:27 INFO  ProductRestController.
getAllProducts:98 - Ending
2024-02-28 17:52:35 DEBUG LogAccessor.debug:313 - Received:
product-req-reply-topic-1@0 with correlationId: 8403edb7-
e702-4e05-8341-ed7a2b2bd3ba
```

Now that both microservices are up and running, you are ready to test the microservices.

Testing Sequential Request Processing

When all is set, you can access the web application using cURL clients.

To test the processing of requests in sequential order within a single partition, you need to configure the `pinnedToPartition` with a `true` value, which is shown in Listing 5-7.

For testing, the intention is to fire more than one request to the Product Web microservices instance concurrently. Since you have pinned requests from the Product Web microservices to the same partition, you know the request messages will be picked up by a single instance of the Product Server microservice.

You can now use two separate terminals to run cURL client commands concurrently (more or less), as shown in Listings 5-20 and 5-21.

Listing 5-20. Commands to Test Using cURL: Client 1

```
binildass-MacBook-Pro:02-ProductWeb binil$ pwd
/Users/binil/binil/code/mac/mybooks/docker-04/Code/ch05/
ch05-01/02-ProductWeb
binildass-MacBook-Pro:02-ProductWeb binil$ sh curlrun1.sh
Firing http://127.0.0.1:8080/productsweb and waiting...
-------------------------------------------
Current date: Wed Feb 28 17:52:23 IST 2024
===========================================
{"products":[{"productId":"1","name":"Kamsung ...
-------------------------------------------
Current date: Wed Feb 28 17:52:29 IST 2024
===========================================
Response from http://127.0.0.1:8080/productsweb received.
binildass-MacBook-Pro:02-ProductWeb binil$
```

Listing 5-21. Commands to Test Using cURL: Client 2

```
binildass-MacBook-Pro:02-ProductWeb binil$ pwd
/Users/binil/binil/code/mac/mybooks/docker-04/Code/ch05/
ch05-01/02-ProductWeb
binildass-MacBook-Pro:02-ProductWeb binil$ sh curlrun2.sh
Firing http://127.0.0.1:8081/productsweb and waiting...
-------------------------------------------
Current date: Wed Feb 28 17:52:23 IST 2024
===========================================
{"products":[{"productId":"1","name":"Kamsung ...
-------------------------------------------
Current date: Wed Feb 28 17:52:35 IST 2024
===========================================
Response from http://127.0.0.1:8081/productsweb received.
binildass-MacBook-Pro:02-ProductWeb binil$
```

Listings 5-20 and 5-21 show that you can send requests from clients more or less concurrently (at time 17:52:23). Listings 5-18 and 5-19 further show that the same instance of the Product Web microservice has also attempted to relay these requests to the Product Server microservice more or less concurrently:

```
2024-02-28 17:52:23 DEBUG LogAccessor.debug:313 - Sending:
ProducerRecord(topic=product-req-topic...
2024-02-28 17:52:23 DEBUG LogAccessor.debug:313 - Sending:
ProducerRecord(topic=product-req-topic...
```

However, careful observation of Listing 5-17 will reveal that the Product Server microservice performs computation against the messages received sequentially, which is the order in which messages arrive at the Product Server microservice:

```
...
2024-02-28 17:52:23 INFO  ProductListener.
listenWithHeaders:57 - Start
...
2024-02-28 17:52:29 INFO  ProductListener.
listenWithHeaders:80 - Ending...
2024-02-28 17:52:29 INFO  ProductListener.
listenWithHeaders:57 - Start
...
2024-02-28 17:52:35 INFO  ProductListener.
listenWithHeaders:80 - Ending...
```

When you bring up more instances of the Product Web microservice, if you want to make sure they are all pinned to the same Topic partition, you need to tweak the default values for the appName configured through the run scripts in the root folder of the Product Web microservice. The default values are as follows:

```
-Dspring.application.name=product-web-1
-Dspring.application.name=product-web-1
```

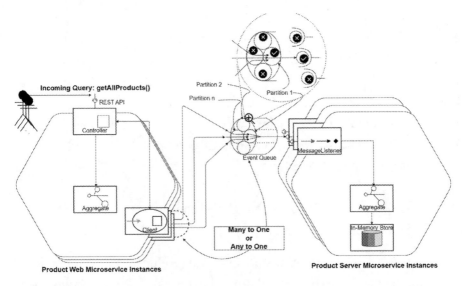

Figure 5-11. *Microservice instances pinned to the same message topic partition*

In doing so, as shown in Figure 5-11, messages from all the instances of the Product Web microservice can be pinned to be delivered to the same partition, say Partition 1 (shown with a tick mark). Consequently, messages from all the instances of the Product Web microservice can be served by a single instance of the Product Server microservice.

The message processing schema of the (Product Server) microservice instance processing messages in sequence, and hence in order, is shown in Figure 5-12.

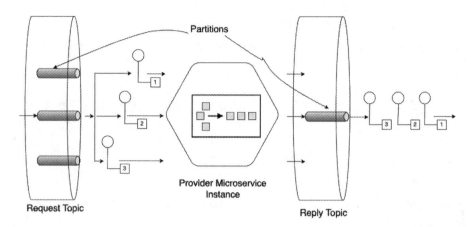

Figure 5-12. *Microservice processing requests in sequence*

Before I conclude, the next section inspects the assignment of partitions that were configured in Listings 5-7 and 5-10.

Inspecting the Microservice Partition assignment

This section starts by looking at the different topics created automatically when you bring the microservice instances up. See Listing 5-22.

Listing 5-22. Commands to List the Kafka Topics

```
binildass-MacBook-Pro:kafka_2.13-2.5.0 binil$ sh bin/kafka-
topics.sh --zookeeper localhost:2181 --list
__consumer_offsets
product-req-reply-topic
product-req-topic
binildass-MacBook-Pro:kafka_2.13-2.5.0 binil$
```

With reference to the number of partitions configured for the Product Web microservice in Listing 5-7, the partition assignments are shown in Listing 5-23.

Listing 5-23. Assignment of Kafka Topic Partitions for the Product Web Microservice

```
binildass-MacBook-Pro:kafka_2.13-2.5.0 binil$ bin/kafka-
consumer-
groups.sh --bootstrap-server localhost:9092 --describe --group
product-web

GROUP           TOPIC                      PARTITION  CURRENT-
OFFSET  LOG-END-OFFSET  LAG                CONSUMER-ID
                HOST            CLIENT-ID
product-web    product-req-reply-topic 1          0
0               0                consumer-product-web-1-
c457cc3e-cf76-4788-9230-19c89f016333 /127.0.0.1      consumer-
product-web-1
product-web    product-req-reply-topic
0          0                0                0          consumer-
product-web-1-347b84e6-d51a-4561-b5d1-3ec54378a47c /127.0.0.1
consumer-product-web-1
binildass-MacBook-Pro:kafka_2.13-2.5.0 binil$
```

With reference to the number of partitions configured for the Product Server microservice in Listing 5-10, the partition assignments are shown in Listing 5-24.

Listing 5-24. Assignment of Kafka Topic Partitions for the Product Server Microservice

```
binildass-MacBook-Pro:kafka_2.13-2.5.0 binil$ bin/
kafka-consumer-groups.sh --bootstrap-server localhost:
9092 --describe --group product-server

GROUP              TOPIC              PARTITION  CURRENT-
OFFSET  LOG-END-OFFSET  LAG                CONSUMER-
ID               HOST       CLIENT-ID
product-server  product-req-topic 2        0            0
0               consumer-product-server-1-f2ae14f5-3964-4a6f-89
7e-954d3c447669 /127.0.0.1    consumer-product-server-1
product-server  product-req-topic 1        0            0
0               consumer-product-server-1-865f46aa-
a4fe-4031-830d-8c182f74cb42 /127.0.0.1    consumer-
product-server-1
product-server  product-req-topic 0        0            0
0               consumer-product-server-1-436a6f12-2073-4c43-
a201-0981ed94f286 /127.0.0.1    consumer-product-server-1
binildass-MacBook-Pro:kafka_2.13-2.5.0 binil$
```

This extra partition assignment information can help you if you need to explore with the demonstration code further.

Microservices Parallel Processing

This slightly altered example leverages the same set of microservices in Chapter 4, which are tweaked to demonstrate the sequential processing in the just previous sample. A consumer and a provider microservice communicate with each other using a messaging channel. The provider microservice stores the entity in an in-memory database, to keep the example simple. Moreover, when the browser sends requests to the first (consumer) microservice, the example uses async HTTP.

The objective here is to demonstrate that when the same kind of requests from different users or microservice consumers reaches a cluster of instances of a single type of provider microservice, the requests can also be serviced in parallel to improve system scalability.

Design Parallel Processing Microservices

Figure 5-13 shows a modified version of the Hexagonal microservice view shown in Figure 2-1 in Chapter 2. This allows both microservices to communicate through an async channel. Apache Kafka is again used as the messaging channel, which is inherently asynchronous.

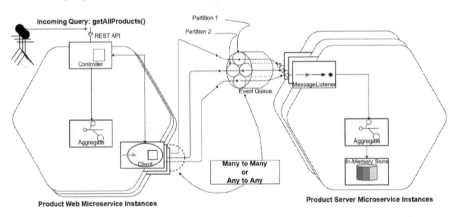

Figure 5-13. *Microservice instances load balanced to many topic partitions*

The more partitions a topic has, the higher the concurrency you can achieve and therefore the higher the potential throughput. In Kafka, each partition must be allocated to only one consumer. So, you can have a maximum of one consumer per partition. This means that you can only have as many consumers (in a single consumer group) as there are partitions for a topic, but you may have fewer. If there are fewer consumers than partitions, consumers may process records from one or more partitions. To summarize, the maximum throughput will be achieved when you have one consumer per partition, or when you have as many consumers as there are partitions.

Parallelism and Thread Safety

Figure 5-14 portrays the discussions in the previous section. You have seen that you can only have as many consumers (in a single consumer group) as there are partitions for a topic. If you have more consumers than the number of partitions, extra consumers may not be assigned with a partition.

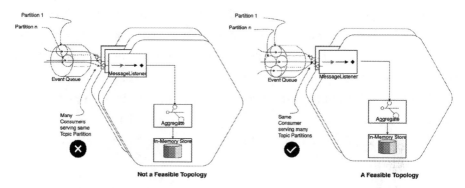

Figure 5-14. *Microservice consumers vs. partition assignment*

Kafka producers are thread-safe and can be shared among multiple threads. However, Kafka consumers are not thread-safe by design. Hence, you can't share the same consumer instance among multiple threads. The default Kafka consumer is single-threaded, so it can only process records sequentially, as you saw in the example in the previous section. So, how can you increase parallelism?

Because single-threaded consumers can't concurrently process regardless of being assigned to multiple partitions, the straightforward solution is to increase the number of partitions and consumers simultaneously, which is what you will attempt in this section. However, this design has its own caveats, since for high-transactional systems it is not feasible to have too many consumers, requiring as many partitions to support as there are consumers, potentially millions. In such scenarios, you need to adopt a heterogenous strategy of decoupling the consumption and acknowledgment of messages from time-consuming message processing, which is not in the scope of this demonstration.

Understanding the Code

The source code for this book is available on GitHub via the book's product page, located at www.apress.com/9798868805547. The source code for this example is organized inside the ch05\ch05-02 folder. This code is the same as the first example in this chapter, but it's configured differently. This section looks at the changes in the consumer microservice—the Product Web microservice.

The main parts of the Product Web microservice configuration are shown in Listing 5-25.

Listing 5-25. Configuration for the Product Web Microservice (ch05\ch05-02\02-ProductWeb\src\main\resources\ application.yml)

```
server:
    port: 8080
spring:
    ...
    kafka:
        bootstrap-servers: localhost:9092
```

```
consumer:
        auto-offset-reset: earliest
        group-id: product-web
kafka:
    topic:
        product:
            request: product-req-topic
            pinnedToPartition: false
            reply: product-req-reply-topic
    request-reply:
        timeout-ms: 60000
product:
    topic:
        request:
            numPartitions: 3
```

The pinnedToPartition is configured with false, since you leave the assignment of Product Web microservice instances to the available partitions in the underlying library.

You can configure values for the appName through the run scripts in the root folder of the Product Web microservice:

```
-Dspring.application.name=product-web-1
-Dspring.application.name=product-web-2
-Dspring.application.name=product-web-3
```

Since the pinnedToPartition is configured with false, you are not leveraging the appName for any partition stickiness, so it doesn't matter whether you configure the same values or different values for the spring. application.name.

In Listing 5-25, you may notice the configuration numPartitions: 3. The number is arbitrary, but it should be more than the number of (instances of) requester microservices, since otherwise the system will throw errors. The number of instances for the Product Server microservices is also three.

Build and Run the Microservice Parallel Processing

The ch05\ch05-02 folder contains the Maven scripts required to build the examples. As a first step, you need to bring up the Kafka broker. Refer to Appendix D to learn how to set up Kafka server and bring it up. Subsequently, you also need to build and install the utility library from Callista Enterprise, as mentioned in the previous example in this chapter.

Next, take six command terminals—three for the Product Server and three for the Product Web microservice—and change the directory to the top-level folder of both microservices.

Build the Product Server microservice using the make.sh scripts, as shown in Listing 5-26.

Listing 5-26. Commands to Build the Product Server Microservice

```
binildass-MacBook-Pro:01-ProductServer binil$ pwd
/Users/binil/binil/code/mac/mybooks/docker-04/Code/ch05/
ch05-02/01-ProductServer
binildass-MacBook-Pro:01-ProductServer binil$ sh make.sh
[INFO] Scanning for projects...
[INFO]
...
```

Next, build the Product Web microservice, as shown in Listing 5-27.

Listing 5-27. Commands to build the Product Web Microservice

```
binildass-MacBook-Pro:01-ProductServer binil$ pwd
/Users/binil/binil/code/mac/mybooks/docker-04/Code/ch05/
ch05-02/02-ProductWeb
binildass-MacBook-Pro:02-ProductWeb binil$ sh make.sh
[INFO] Scanning for projects...
[INFO]
...
```

In the first step, you bring up the three instances of the Product Server microservices one by one. You begin by running the Product Server microservices instance 1, as shown in Listing 5-28.

Listing 5-28. Commands to Run the Product Server Microservice Instance 1

```
binildass-MacBook-Pro:01-ProductServer binil$ pwd
/Users/binil/binil/code/mac/mybooks/docker-04/Code/ch05/
ch05-02/01-ProductServer
binildass-MacBook-Pro:01-ProductServer binil$ sh run1.sh
...
2024-02-29 19:52:16 INFO  ProductListener.
listenWithHeaders:57 - Start
...
2024-02-29 19:52:23 INFO  ProductListener.
listenWithHeaders:80 - Ending...
```

Next, you run the Product Server microservices instance 2, as shown in Listing 5-29.

Listing 5-29. Commands to Run the Product Server Microservice Instance 2

```
binildass-MacBook-Pro:01-ProductServer binil$ pwd
/Users/binil/binil/code/mac/mybooks/docker-04/Code/ch05/
ch05-02/01-ProductServer
binildass-MacBook-Pro:01-ProductServer binil$ sh run2.sh
...
2024-02-29 19:52:17 INFO  ProductListener.
listenWithHeaders:57 - Start
...
2024-02-29 19:52:23 INFO  ProductListener.
listenWithHeaders:80 - Ending...
```

Lastly, you run the Product Server microservices instance 3, as shown in Listing 5-30.

Listing 5-30. Commands to Run the Product Server Microservice Instance 3

```
binildass-MacBook-Pro:01-ProductServer binil$ pwd
/Users/binil/binil/code/mac/mybooks/docker-04/Code/ch05/
ch05-02/01-ProductServer
binildass-MacBook-Pro:01-ProductServer binil$ sh run3.sh
...
2024-02-29 19:52:16 INFO  ProductListener.
listenWithHeaders:57 - Start
...
2024-02-29 19:52:22 INFO  ProductListener.
listenWithHeaders:80 - Ending...
```

In the second step, you bring up the three instances of the Product Web microservice one by one. First, run the Product Web microservice instance 1, as shown in Listing 5-31.

Listing 5-31. Commands to Run the Product Web Microservice
Instance 1

```
binildass-MacBook-Pro:02-ProductWeb binil$ pwd
/Users/binil/binil/code/mac/mybooks/docker-04/Code/ch05/
ch05-02/02-ProductWeb
binildass-MacBook-Pro:02-ProductWeb binil$ sh run1.sh
...
2024-02-29 19:52:16 INFO  ProductRestController.
getAllProducts:69 - Start
...
2024-02-29 19:52:16 DEBUG LogAccessor.debug:313 - Sending:
ProducerRecord(topic=product-req-topic,...
...
2024-02-29 19:52:22 DEBUG LogAccessor.debug:313 - Received:
product-req-reply-topic-2@0 with correlationId:
c67dd6d1-83ed-479c-99b4-708f603b48dc
```

Listing 5-32 shows the Product Web microservice instance 2.

Listing 5-32. Commands to Run the Product Web Microservice
Instance 2

```
binildass-MacBook-Pro:02-ProductWeb binil$ pwd
/Users/binil/binil/code/mac/mybooks/docker-04/Code/ch05/
ch05-02/02-ProductWeb
binildass-MacBook-Pro:02-ProductWeb binil$ sh run2.sh
...
2024-02-29 19:52:16 INFO  ProductRestController.
getAllProducts:69 - Start
...
2024-02-29 19:52:16 DEBUG LogAccessor.debug:313 - Sending:
ProducerRecord(topic=product-req-topic,...
```

```
...
2024-02-29 19:52:23 DEBUG LogAccessor.debug:313 - Received:
product-req-reply-topic-0@0 with correlationId: 2045c904-
b6c8-4608-a21b-684943f4ab30
```

As a last step, run the Product Web microservices instance 3, as shown in Listing 5-33.

Listing 5-33. Commands to Run the Product Web Microservice Instance 3

```
binildass-MacBook-Pro:02-ProductWeb binil$ pwd
/Users/binil/binil/code/mac/mybooks/docker-04/Code/ch05/
ch05-02/02-ProductWeb
binildass-MacBook-Pro:02-ProductWeb binil$ sh run3.sh
...
2024-02-29 19:52:17 INFO  ProductRestController.
getAllProducts:69 - Start
...
2024-02-29 19:52:17 DEBUG LogAccessor.debug:313 - Sending:
ProducerRecord(topic=product-req-topic,...
...
2024-02-29 19:52:23 DEBUG LogAccessor.debug:313 -
Received: product-req-reply-topic-1@0 with correlationId:
3bdb5077-8f14-46a0-ae7c-3585dc8a9fce
```

Now that both microservices are up and running, you can test the microservices.

Testing Parallel Request Processing

When all is set, you can access the web application using cURL clients.

To test the processing of requests in parallel, you need to configure the pinnedToPartition with a false value, which is done in Listing 5-25.

For testing, the intention is to fire more than one request to the Product Web microservices concurrently. You can now use three separate terminals to run cURL client commands concurrently (more or less), as shown in Listings 5-34 through 5-36.

Listing 5-34. Commands to Test Using cURL: Client 1

```
binildass-MacBook-Pro:02-ProductWeb binil$ pwd
/Users/binil/binil/code/mac/mybooks/docker-04/Code/ch05/
ch05-02/02-ProductWeb
binildass-MacBook-Pro:02-ProductWeb binil$ sh curlrun1.sh
Firing http://127.0.0.1:8080/productsweb and waiting...
------------------------------------------------
Current date: Thu Feb 29 19:52:16 IST 2024
================================================
{"products":[{"productId":"1","name":"Kamsung ...
------------------------------------------------
Current date: Thu Feb 29 19:52:22 IST 2024
================================================
Response from http://127.0.0.1:8080/productsweb received.
binildass-MacBook-Pro:02-ProductWeb binil$
```

Listing 5-35. Commands to Test Using cURL: Client 2

```
binildass-MacBook-Pro:02-ProductWeb binil$ sh curlrun2.sh
Firing http://127.0.0.1:8081/productsweb and waiting...
------------------------------------------------
Current date: Thu Feb 29 19:52:16 IST 2024
================================================
{"products":[{"productId":"1","name":"Kamsung...
------------------------------------------------
```

```
Current date: Thu Feb 29 19:52:23 IST 2024
=============================================
Response from http://127.0.0.1:8081/productsweb received.
binildass-MacBook-Pro:02-ProductWeb binil$
```

Listing 5-36. Commands to Test Using cURL: Client 3

```
binildass-MacBook-Pro:02-ProductWeb binil$ sh curlrun3.sh
Firing http://127.0.0.1:8082/productsweb and waiting...
---------------------------------------------
Current date: Thu Feb 29 19:52:17 IST 2024
=============================================
{"products":[{"productId":"1","name":"Kamsung...
---------------------------------------------
Current date: Thu Feb 29 19:52:23 IST 2024
=============================================
Response from http://127.0.0.1:8082/productsweb received.
binildass-MacBook-Pro:02-ProductWeb binil$
```

Careful observation of Listings 5-34 through 5-36 will show that the program can fire cURL clients more or less concurrently with the Product Web microservice instances. Subsequently, from Listings 5-31 through 5-33, it's clear that the different Product Web microservice instances can also relay these requests more or less at the same time to different Product Server microservice instances in a load balanced manner.

```
2024-02-29 19:52:16 INFO  ProductRestController.
getAllProducts:69 - Start
2024-02-29 19:52:16 INFO  ProductRestController.
getAllProducts:69 - Start
2024-02-29 19:52:17 INFO  ProductRestController.
getAllProducts:69 - Start
```

Next, observe the processing of requests in different instances of the Product Server microservice in Listings 5-28 through 5-30. They show that message processing happens more or less concurrently in a load balanced manner:

```
2024-02-29 19:52:16 INFO  ProductListener.
listenWithHeaders:57 - Start
2024-02-29 19:52:17 INFO  ProductListener.
listenWithHeaders:57 - Start
2024-02-29 19:52:16 INFO  ProductListener.
listenWithHeaders:57 - Start
```

The message processing schema of the microservice instance is processing messages concurrently, and could be processing out of order, as shown in Figure 5-15.

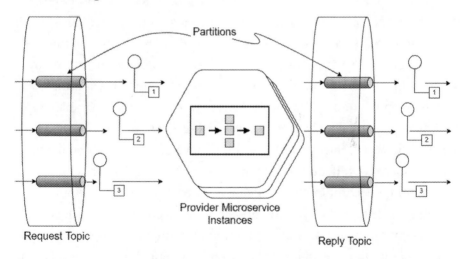

Figure 5-15. *Microservice consumer vs. partition assignments*

When the microservices are up and running, you can also access the web application using your browser and pointing to the URL:

```
http://localhost:8080/product.html
http://localhost:8081/product.html
http://localhost:8082/product.html
```

You might have to wait at the browser console a bit, since the browser is rendered with the data only eventually, due to the sleep delays provisioned in the microservices.

Summary

One major benefit of an event-driven architecture using a message-oriented microservice is decoupling the event producer microservice from the event consumer microservice, allowing for more flexible and evolvable systems. Relying on a synchronous Request-Reply semantics is the exact opposite, where the producer and consumer microservices are tightly coupled. This should only be used when needed. If synchronous Request-Reply is required, an HTTP-based protocol is much simpler, more straightforward, and more efficient than using an asynchronous channel like Apache Kafka. Having said this, there may be scenarios when using synchronous styled Request-Reply makes sense. You might need to wisely choose from the combination of available choices for the job at hand. The examples in this chapter have demonstrated the retrieval of a collection of Product entities over a messaging channel. You might now naturally think about whether the style of inter-microservice interactions explained in this chapter could be used in real life to cover full-fledged business use cases, and this is what Chapter 6 covers.

CHAPTER 6

Production Grade Message Oriented Microservices

Chapter 4 explained how messaging middleware can play a key role in providing a bridge for microservices to communicate with each other in a loosely coupled manner. Messaging channels are typically characterized by the asynchronous style of interaction, but Chapters 4 and 5 attempted to show how a synchronous user experience can be attained, even over asynchronous messaging channels. This is the first step in providing confidence that loosely coupled, messaging-based microservice interactions can be leveraged to implement many, if not all, your functional use cases. As mentioned in Chapter 5, many engineers are still skeptical on whether they can use events and the event paradigm for inter-microservices communication in a synchronous manner to implement a full data management paradigm. This chapter attempts to address that skepticism.

This chapter is fully hands on, with examples. An overview and working experience with the examples in Chapter 5 is required for you to quickly understand the enhanced examples in this chapter.

© Binildas A. Christudas 2024
B. A. Christudas, *Java Microservices and Containers in the Cloud*,
https://doi.org/10.1007/979-8-8688-0555-4_6

This chapter covers the following concepts:

- Protocols and message formats for message exchange

- Full CRUD (create, read, update, delete) functionality across microservices using Kafka in between

- CRUD using MongoDB and PostgreSQL DB

- A quick look at a few integration-patterns

Inter-Microservices Wire Level Options

There are pros and cons when we talk about message-oriented microservices. One of the main aspects relates to the inter-microservice communication format options. Let's investigate those in the next section.

XML-RPC and SOAP

XML-RPC and SOAP have been the cornerstone of remote service invocation using web services for more than a decade. A web service is described by a WSDL (Web Services Description Language) document, which acts as the contract between the service provider and service consumer. A WSDL document describes how the web service is bound to a messaging protocol—in the case of the web services, the SOAP protocol.

A WSDL SOAP binding can be either an RPC-oriented binding or a document-oriented binding.

- **RPC-oriented style:** Web services that use the RPC (Remote Procedure Call)-oriented style are interface-driven. Here the client applications invoke a web service method (call a remote procedure) by sending parameter values of the request and receiving parameter values of the response. The body of the

SOAP request includes a wrapper XML element for this method. The parameters of this method are embedded as child elements inside this wrapper element.

- **Document-oriented style:** Web services that use the document-oriented style are document (more precisely, XML document) driven. Here, the client applications send parameters to the web service as XML documents, instead of as discrete sets of parameter values. The body of the SOAP request and response messages contain one or more XML documents. The document-oriented style is flatter than the RPC-oriented style and does not require the use of wrapper elements.

REST and JSON-RPC

In the recent past, whenever somebody wanted to start building an HTTP API, they pretty much exclusively used REST as the de facto architectural style, over alternative approaches such as XML-RPC and SOAP. REST specifies a client-server relationship, where server-side data is made available through representations of data in simple formats, often JSON and XML. These representations for resources or collections of resources are then potentially modifiable, with actions or more precisely with HTTP actions. Relationships between data are made discoverable via a method known as *hypermedia*. Hypermedia is fundamental to REST and is essentially just the concept of providing links to other resources. In the section titled "HATEOAS and HAL" in Chapter 2, you have learned about this.

JSON-RPC is a remote procedure call protocol encoded in JSON. It is like the XML-RPC protocol, defining only a few data types and commands. JSON-RPC allows for notifications (data sent to the server that does not require a response) and for multiple calls to be sent to the server, which may be answered asynchronously.

RPC vs. Messaging

The fundamental difference between these two protocols is that an RPC framework is synchronous. You make a call, and you aren't done until you receive the response. Messaging on the other hand is asynchronous. You send the message, and either you don't expect a response, or you don't know when it will come back, if at all!

If your caller needs information from a response from the service(s) you are requesting or calling, you should use an RPC, because you can't return to your caller until you have the information you need from the provider. If your caller doesn't need information from a downstream service, you can use messaging. Fire your message and forget it, since you are not expecting (rather, cannot expect) to receive a response.

RPC Style Messaging

As described, a messaging paradigm tries to enforce a fire-and-forget messaging style, but it is possible to use properly designed message queues to perform and mimic RPC, as explained in Chapter 5. Figure 5-7 in Chapter 5 depicts different reply channels for microservice communications, whereas Figure 5-8 depicts different reply partitions for microservices communicating with each other. In both scenarios, you can simulate synchronous style request-responses between participating microservices across messaging channels.

Unlike with the XML-RPC or SOAP scenario, when microservices communicate over plain messaging channels, they are not hard bound to a strict message invocation schema—a WSDL kind of mechanism which acts as the contract between the service provider and service consumer is missing. Hence, you need to weave a mechanism to specify "what action to perform." HTTP provides standard verbs to provide semantic meaning for the intention of the action being taken.

HTTP Methods for CRUD on Resources

RPC-based APIs are great for actions (that is, procedures or commands), whereas REST-based APIs are great for modeling your domain (that is, resources or entities), making CRUD (create, read, update, delete) available for all your data. REST uses HTTP methods such as GET, POST, PUT, DELETE, OPTIONS and, hopefully, PATCH, to provide semantic meaning for the intention of the action being taken.

The main methods in HTTP you can leverage for implementing REST are listed here:

- GET: GET is the simplest HTTP operation and its intention is to retrieve a resource from the server. 200 OK is the status code for a successful operation. All GET operations should be *idempotent*, which means regardless of how many times you repeat the operation with the same parameters, there should not be any change in state for the resource.

- POST: HTTP POST provides an option for clients to send information to the server. POST is recommended for creating a new resource (even though it can also update an existing resource).

- PUT:[1] HTTP PUT also provides an option for clients to send information to the server; however, the usage semantics of PUT are slightly different from that of POST, as per HTTP. Using PUT, you can send a "new object" to the server to be placed at a location in the server represented by the URI, so the intent should be to replace the resource with a new one. A PUT request is idempotent as far as a single client is concerned. If only a subset of data elements is provided in a PUT request, the rest will be replaced with empty or null.

- DELETE: DELETE allows clients to remove a resource from the server. The URI identifies the resource to be deleted. The resource may not have to be removed immediately; instead, it can be done by an asynchronous or long-running operation behind the scenes.

REST is not only CRUD, but things are done through mainly CRUD-based operations.

RPC, however, does not strictly follow standard HTTP verbs. Most use only GET and POST, with GET being used to retrieve information and POST being used for everything else. It is common to see RPC APIs using something like POST /deleteBar, with a body of { "id": 10 }, instead of the REST approach, which would be DELETE /bars/10.

---

[1] As per strict HTTP specifications, the difference between a POST and PUT is in how the server interprets the URI. In a POST, the URI normally identifies an object on the server that can process the included data. In a PUT, the URI identifies a resource in which the server should place the data. So a POST URI generally indicates a program or script that can do processing; a PUT URI is usually the path and name for a resource.

JSON (JavaScript Object Notation) is an open standard file format and data interchange format that uses human-readable text to store and transmit data objects consisting of attribute–value pairs and arrays (or other serializable values). If you want to continue using this format, instead of sync style HTTP transport, you can use async style messaging transport. But when you don't use standard HTTP, you miss the opportunity to use standard HTTP verbs and any of their associated advantages.

The next section looks at two examples demonstrating a few of these discission items. Specifically, we will adhere to REST for the end point APIs and we will attempt to stick to JSON for inter-microservice communication over Kafka.

CRUD Microservices Over Kafka on MongoDB

This example tweaks the same set of microservices in Chapter 5. A consumer and a provider microservice communicate with each other using Kafka as the messaging channel. The provider microservice stores the entity in a MongoDB database. Moreover, when the browser sends the request to the first (consumer) microservice, it uses async HTTP. Even though it uses async HTTP, the example emulates a sync-style user experience at the browser level.

As with the example in Chapter 5, this example is demonstrated with multiple instances of the consumer and provider microservices, and it uses multiple clients while testing the service.

This example introduces a new functional feature. It emulates a full CRUD (Create, Read, Update and Delete) feature through the microservice interactions, using Kafka as the messaging channel.

Design CRUD Over Async Channel on MongoDB

This example uses the modified version of the hexagonal microservice view shown in Figure 2-1 in Chapter 2, which you also visited in Chapter 5, so that both microservices communicate through an async channel. Apache Kafka is used as the messaging channel, which is inherently asynchronous. The objectives of this example are multifold:

- To invoke synchronous-style communication over the Kafka-based async channel.

- To demonstrate that multiple consumer types or multiple instances of the same consumer type can connect to one or more instances of the provider microservice and still receive the right responses corresponding to the respective request alone.

- To demonstrate that the full set of CRUD actions can be orchestrated over the async channel.

- To provide a sync-style experience to the users at the browser end, even though the example uses async HTTP.

- To demonstrate that the browser can consume from fully compliant HATEOAS interfaces.

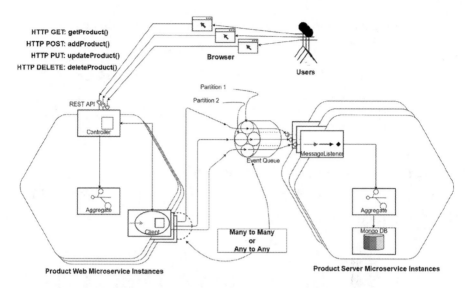

Figure 6-1. *Microservice design over async channel using partitions*

As shown in Figure 6-1, this example will leverage Kafka partitions as the main concurrency mechanism in the async channel between the microservices. This async topic is divided into one or more partitions, five in this case, enabling the producer and consumer loads to be scaled. The consumers are shared evenly across the partitions, allowing for the consumer load to be linearly scaled by increasing the provider instances and their provisioned partitions.

Understanding the Source Code

The source code for this book is available on GitHub via the book's product page, located at www.apress.com/9798868805547. The code for this example is organized inside the ch06\ch06-01 folder. Much of the source code for this example is similar to that in ch05\ch05-01. I explained in detail how to set up consumer and provider microservices that communicate with each other using a messaging channel. This section covers only the changes.

The main class to inspect is a new container class for the Product entity (see Listing 6-1), which has the following functions:

- Acts as a container to transport collections of resources between microservices

- Acts as a schema specification

Listing 6-1. The Container Class for Product Entity (ch06\ch06-01\02-ProductWeb\src\main\java\com\acme\ecom\product\model\Products.java)

```java
public class Products {

    public static final String CREATE = "Create";
    public static final String DELETE = "Delete";
    public static final String DELETE_ALL = "Delete_All";
    public static final String UPDATE = "Update";
    public static final String RETREIVE_ALL = "Retreive_All";
    public static final String RETREIVE_DETAILS =
        "Retreive_Details";

    public static final String SUCCESS = "Success";
    public static final String FAILURE = "Failure";

    private String operation;
    private List<Product> products;

    public String getOperation() {
        return operation;
    }
    public void setOperation(String operation) {
        this.operation = operation;
    }
```

```
public List<Product> getProducts() {
    return products;
}
public void setProducts(List<Product> products) {
    this.products = products;
}
}
```

The Products class lists counterparts for CRUD HTTP verbs as constant literals. The attribute operation is used to specify the action intended to be performed during the request phase. In the response phase, the same operation specifies the outcome of the request processing as "Success" or "Failure". Next, the products collection may contain one or more Product entity. In the request phase, the products attribute contains one Product entity, whose attribute values correspond to the parameters of the operation to be performed. In the response phase of the operation, the same products collection may contain one or more Product entities corresponding to the response of the performed operation.

This method of piggybacking the request and response parameters and operations as payload is not the best, most elegant way, but it does the job.

Listing 6-2 shows the configuration class used by the Product Web microservice.

Listing 6-2. Kafka Configuration for Product Web Microservice (ch06\ch06-01\02-ProductWeb\src\main\java\com\acme\ecom\ product\KafkaConfig.java)

```
@Configuration
public class KafkaConfig {

    @Bean
    public CompletableFutureReplyingKafkaOperations<String,
            Products, Products> replyKafkaTemplate() {
```

```java
        CompletableFutureReplyingKafkaTemplate<String,
            Products, Products>
            requestReplyKafkaTemplate = new
                CompletableFutureReplyingKafkaTemplate<>(
                    requestProducerFactory(),
                    replyListenerContainer());
    requestReplyKafkaTemplate.setDefaultTopic(
        requestTopic);
    requestReplyKafkaTemplate.setDefaultReplyTimeout(
        Duration.of(replyTimeout, ChronoUnit.MILLIS));
    return requestReplyKafkaTemplate;
}

@Bean
public ConsumerFactory<String, Products>
        replyConsumerFactory() {

    JsonDeserializer<Products> jsonDeserializer =
        new JsonDeserializer<>();
    jsonDeserializer.addTrustedPackages(
        Products.class.getPackage().getName());
    return new DefaultKafkaConsumerFactory<>(
        consumerConfigs(), new StringDeserializer(),
        jsonDeserializer);
}

@Bean
public KafkaMessageListenerContainer<String, Products>
        replyListenerContainer() {
```

```
    ContainerProperties containerProperties =
        new ContainerProperties(replyTopic);
    return new KafkaMessageListenerContainer<>(
        replyConsumerFactory(), containerProperties);
    }
}
```

This code configures CompletableFutureReplyingKafkaTemplate, specifying that Products is sent as the request and Products is expected as the response.

Listing 6-3 inspects a single method in the Product Web controller. Other methods are implemented in a similar fashion, so that code is not replicated here for brevity.

Listing 6-3. REST Controller for Product Web Microservice (ch06\ ch06-01\02-ProductWeb\src\main\java\com\acme\ecom\product\ controller\ProductRestController.java)

```
@RestController
public class ProductRestController{

    @Autowired
    private CompletableFutureReplyingKafkaOperations<String,
            Products, Products> replyingKafkaTemplate;

    @RequestMapping(value = "/productsweb",
        method = RequestMethod.GET,
        produces = {MediaType.APPLICATION_JSON_VALUE})
    public DeferredResult<ResponseEntity<CollectionModel<
            com.acme.ecom.product.hateoas.model.Product>>>
            getAllProducts(){

        DeferredResult<ResponseEntity<CollectionModel<
            com.acme.ecom.product.hateoas.model.Product>>>
            deferredResult = new DeferredResult<>();
```

```
    Products productsRequest = new Products();
    productsRequest.setOperation(Products.RETREIVE_ALL);

    CompletableFuture<Products> completableFuture =
        replyingKafkaTemplate.requestReply(
            requestTopic, productsRequest);

    completableFuture.thenAccept(products -> {
        List<com.acme.ecom.product.model.Product>
            productList = products.getProducts();
    CollectionModel<com.acme.ecom.product.hateoas.
        model.Product> result = CollectionModel.of(
            list, links);
    deferredResult.setResult(new ResponseEntity<
        CollectionModel<com.acme.ecom.product.
            hateoas.model.Product>>(result,
                HttpStatus.OK));
        return deferredResult;
    }
}
```

While sending the request message to retrieve all the products from the Product Server microservice, you specify the operation as Products.RETREIVE_ALL. Even though you send an empty Products collection productsRequest along with the request, it's not relevant or used here. However, for a few other methods, you could use this same productsRequest collection to send request parameters. You then use CompletableFutureReplyingKafkaOperations, which was configured in the previous step to send the request message and to receive its corresponding response message in a synchronous style, even though the underlying request and response message semantics are two separate asynchronous messages.

Note   A detailed explanation of `CompletableFutureReplying` `KafkaOperations` and its usage pattern appears in Chapter 5.

On the Product Server microservice side, you must also configure and specify the `Products` container class as passing to and from the wire, as shown in Listing 6-4.

Listing 6-4. Kafka Configuration for Product Server Microservice (ch06\ch06-01\01-ProductServer\src\main\java\com\acme\ecom\ product\KafkaConfig.java)

```
@Configuration
@EnableKafka
public class KafkaConfig {

    @Bean
    public ConsumerFactory<String, Products>
            requestConsumerFactory() {

        JsonDeserializer<Products> jsonDeserializer =
            new JsonDeserializer<>();
        jsonDeserializer.addTrustedPackages(Products.class.
            getPackage().getName());
        return new DefaultKafkaConsumerFactory<>(
            consumerConfigs(), new StringDeserializer(),
            jsonDeserializer);
    }

    @Bean
    public KafkaListenerContainerFactory<
            ConcurrentMessageListenerContainer<String,
            Products>> requestReplyListenerContainerFactory(){
```

```
    ConcurrentKafkaListenerContainerFactory<String,
        Products> factory =
        new ConcurrentKafkaListenerContainerFactory<>();
    factory.setConsumerFactory(requestConsumerFactory());
    factory.setReplyTemplate(replyTemplate());
    return factory;
    }
}
```

The ProductListener is the message listener at the Product Server microservice. ProductListener first resolves which operation to perform by inspecting the operation attribute and invoking the respective method. See Listing 6-5.

Listing 6-5. Kafka Listener for Product Server Microservice (ch06\ch06-01\01-ProductServer\src\main\java\com\acme\ecom\product\kafka\client\ProductListener.java)

```
@Component
public class ProductListener {

    @Autowired
    private ProductRepository productRepository;

    @KafkaListener(topics = "${kafka.topic.product.request}",
            containerFactory =
                "requestReplyListenerContainerFactory")
    @SendTo
    public Products listenWithHeaders(

        ConsumerRecord<String, Products> record){
        Products productsRequest = record.value();
        Products productsResponse = resolveAndExecute(
            productsRequest);
```

```java
    return productsResponse;
}

private Products resolveAndExecute(Products products) {

    Products productsToReturn = null;
    if(products.getOperation().equals(
            Products.RETREIVE_DETAILS)){
        productsToReturn = getProduct(products);
    }
    else if(products.getOperation().equals(
            Products.RETREIVE_ALL)){
        productsToReturn = getAllProducts(products);
    }
    else if(products.getOperation().equals(
            Products.CREATE)){
        productsToReturn = createProduct(products);
    }
    else if(products.getOperation().equals(
            Products.UPDATE)){
        productsToReturn = updateProduct(products);
    }
    else if(products.getOperation().equals(
            Products.DELETE)){
        productsToReturn = deleteProduct(products);
    }
    else {
        LOGGER.debug("Inside else. Undefined Operation!");
    }
    return productsToReturn;
}
```

```
private Products getAllProducts(Products products) {

    Products productsToReturn = new Products();
    List<Product> productListToReturn =
        productRepository.findAll();
    productsToReturn.setOperation(Products.SUCCESS);
    productsToReturn.setProducts(productListToReturn);
    return productsToReturn;
}

//other code goes here
}
```

Here again a single method is shown in the `ProductListener`, called `getAllProducts`. Other methods are implemented in similar ways, so their code is not replicated here.

You are also advised to refer to the second example in the section titled "Microservices Using MongoDB and CrudRepository" in Chapter 3, which explains how the Product Server microservice connects to a MongoDB to perform the complete set of CRUD operations.

Build and Run the Microservice

The `ch06\ch06-01` folder contains the Maven scripts required to build the examples. As a first step, you need to bring up the Kafka broker. Refer to Appendix D to learn how to set up a Kafka server and bring it up. You need to execute the commands in Listing 6-6 to bring up Kafka from the Kafka installation location.

Listing 6-6. Commands to Bring Up Kafka Broker

```
bin/zookeeper-server-start.sh config/zookeeper.properties
bin/kafka-server-start.sh config/server.properties
```

As a next step, you need to bring up the MongoDB server. Refer to Appendix B to learn how to set up a MongoDB server and bring it up. You need to execute the commands in Listing 6-7 to bring up MongoDB.

Listing 6-7. Commands to Bring Up MongoDB

```
(base) binildass-MBP:bin binil$ pwd
/Users/binil/Applns/mongodb/mongodb-macos-x86_64-4.2.8/bin
(base) binildass-MBP:bin binil$ mongod --dbpath /usr/local/var/
mongodb --logpath /usr/local/var/log/mongodb/mongo.log
```

Next, you need to build and install the utility library from Callista Enterprise (see Listing 6-8). Refer to Chapter 5 for a brief introduction to this library.

Listing 6-8. Commands to Build and Install the Utility Library from Callista Enterprise

```
binildass-MacBook-Pro:kafka-request-reply-util binil$ pwd
/Users/binil/binil/code/mac/mybooks/docker-04/Code/ch06/
ch06-01/kafka-request-reply-util
(base) binildass-MacBook-Pro:kafka-request-reply-util binil$
mvn clean install
[INFO] Scanning for projects...
[INFO]
...
```

Next, use two command terminals and change the directory to the top-level folder of both microservices. First, build the Product Server microservice using the make.sh scripts, as shown in Listing 6-9.

Listing 6-9. Commands to Build the Product Server Microservice

```
binildass-MacBook-Pro:01-ProductServer binil$ pwd
/Users/binil/binil/code/mac/mybooks/docker-04/Code/ch06/
ch06-01/01-ProductServer
binildass-MacBook-Pro:01-ProductServer binil$ sh make.sh
...
```

Next, build the Product Web Microservice, as shown in Listing 6-10.

Listing 6-10. Commands to Build the Product Web Microservice

```
binildass-MacBook-Pro:02-ProductWeb binil$ pwd
/Users/binil/binil/code/mac/mybooks/docker-04/Code/ch06/
ch06-01/02-ProductWeb
binildass-MacBook-Pro:02-ProductWeb binil$ sh make.sh
...
```

This example tests three instances of the Product Server microservice and another three instances of the Product Web microservice.

To start, bring up the first instance of the Product Server microservice, as shown in Listing 6-11.

Listing 6-11. Commands to Run the Product Server Microservice Instance 1

```
(base) binildass-MacBook-Pro:01-ProductServer binil$ pwd
/Users/binil/binil/code/mac/mybooks/docker-04/Code/ch06/
ch06-01/01-ProductServer
(base) binildass-MacBook-Pro:01-ProductServer binil$ sh run1.sh
...
```

Next, you'll bring up the second instance of the Product Server microservice, as shown in Listing 6-11.

Listing 6-12. Commands to Run the Product Server Microservice
Instance 2

```
(base) binildass-MacBook-Pro:01-ProductServer binil$ pwd
/Users/binil/binil/code/mac/mybooks/docker-04/Code/ch06/
ch06-01/01-ProductServer
(base) binildass-MacBook-Pro:01-ProductServer binil$ sh run2.sh
...
```

Finally, bring up the third instance of the Product Server microservice,
as shown in Listing 6-13.

Listing 6-13. Commands to Run the Product Server Microservice
Instance 3

```
(base) binildass-MacBook-Pro:01-ProductServer binil$ pwd
/Users/binil/binil/code/mac/mybooks/docker-04/Code/ch06/
ch06-01/01-ProductServer
(base) binildass-MacBook-Pro:01-ProductServer binil$ sh run3.sh
...
```

Next, run the instances of the Product Web microservice. As a first step,
Listing 6-14 shows how to run the first instance.

Listing 6-14. Commands to Run the Product Web Microservice
Instance 1

```
(base) binildass-MacBook-Pro:02-ProductWeb binil$ pwd
/Users/binil/binil/code/mac/mybooks/docker-04/Code/ch06/
ch06-01/02-ProductWeb
(base) binildass-MacBook-Pro:02-ProductWeb binil$ sh run1.sh
...
```

Next, bring up the second instance of the Product Web microservice, as
shown in Listing 6-15.

Listing 6-15. Commands to Run the Product Web Microservice Instance 2

```
(base) binildass-MacBook-Pro:02-ProductWeb binil$ pwd
/Users/binil/binil/code/mac/mybooks/docker-04/Code/ch06/
ch06-01/02-ProductWeb
(base) binildass-MacBook-Pro:02-ProductWeb binil$ sh run2.sh
...
```

As a last step, bring up the third instance of the Product Web microservice, as shown in Listing 6-16.

Listing 6-16. Commands to Run the Product Web Microservice Instance 3

```
(base) binildass-MacBook-Pro:02-ProductWeb binil$ pwd
/Users/binil/binil/code/mac/mybooks/docker-04/Code/ch06/
ch06-01/02-ProductWeb
(base) binildass-MacBook-Pro:02-ProductWeb binil$ sh run3.sh
...
```

Figure 6-2 shows the process of accessing multiple instances of these microservices.

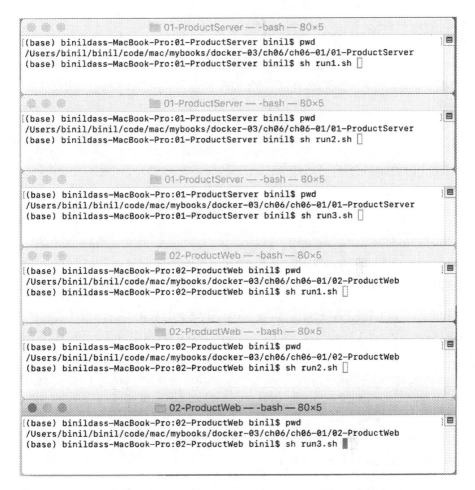

Figure 6-2. *Testing the microservices using multiple instances*

Now that both microservices are up and running, you can test the microservices.

Testing the Microservices

In order to test these microservices, refer to the "Testing Parallel Request Processing" section in Chapter 5. Alternatively, you can use the following section.

There is more than one way to test these microservices. One way is to use three browser instances and point to the URLs in Listing 6-17 to test the microservices.

Listing 6-17. Testing the Microservice Using Browsers

```
http://localhost:8080/product.html
http://localhost:8081/product.html
http://localhost:8082/product.html
```

Follow the detailed instructions described in the section titled "Test the Microservice Using UI" in Chapter 1 to test the CRUD operations.

Alternatively, you can now take three (or even more) separate terminals to run cURL client commands concurrently. Listing 6-17 shows cURL clients sending requests to the Product Web microservice.

Listing 6-18. cURL Clients that Fire Requests to the Product Web Microservice at Different Ports

```
binildass-MacBook-Pro:~ binil$ curl http://localhost:8080/
productsweb
binildass-MacBook-Pro:~ binil$ curl http://localhost:8081/
productsweb
binildass-MacBook-Pro:~ binil$ curl http://localhost:8082/
productsweb
```

You can also endurance-test the microservices by keeping the cURL clients firing continuously, as shown in Listings 6-19 through 6-21.

Listing 6-19. Endurance Test Using cURL Client 1

```
(base) binildass-MacBook-Pro:02-ProductWeb binil$ pwd
/Users/binil/binil/code/mac/mybooks/docker-04/Code/ch06/
ch06-01/02-ProductWeb
(base) binildass-MacBook-Pro:02-ProductWeb binil$ sh
loopcurl1.sh
{"_embedded":{"products":[{"productId":"1","name":"
Kamsung D3","code":"KAMSUNG-TRIOS","title":"Kamsung
Trios 12 inch , black , 12 px ....","price":12000.0,"_
links":{"self":{"href":"/products/1"}}},{"productId":"2","name
":"Lokia Pomia","code":"LOKIA-POMIA","title":"Lokia 12 inch ,
white , 14px ....","price":9000.0,"_links":{"self":{"href":"/
products/2"}}}]},"_links":{"self":{"href":"/productsweb"},"get
AllProducts":{"href":"/productsweb"}}}
-----------------------------------------
Current date: Mon Dec 13 13:37:04 IST 2021
=========================================
...
```

Listing 6-20. Endurance Test Using cURL Client 2

```
(base) binildass-MacBook-Pro:02-ProductWeb binil$ pwd
/Users/binil/binil/code/mac/mybooks/docker-04/Code/ch06/
ch06-01/02-ProductWeb
(base) binildass-MacBook-Pro:02-ProductWeb binil$ sh
loopcurl2.sh
...
```

Listing 6-21. Endurance Test Using cURL Client 3

```
(base) binildass-MacBook-Pro:02-ProductWeb binil$ pwd
/Users/binil/binil/code/mac/mybooks/docker-04/Code/ch06/
ch06-01/02-ProductWeb
(base) binildass-MacBook-Pro:02-ProductWeb binil$ sh
loopcurl3.sh
...
```

This completes the first example. This example has attempted to demonstrate many of the concepts covered in the book so far. For the completeness of this discussion, the next section covers a PostgreSQL version of this example.

CRUD Microservices Over Kafka on PostgreSQL

This example tweaks the same set of microservices you saw in the previous section. A consumer and provider microservice communicate with each other using Kafka as the messaging channel. The provider microservice stores the entity in a PostgreSQL database instead of in MongoDB. When the browser sends a request to the first (consumer) microservice, it uses async HTTP. Even though the code uses async HTTP, it emulates a sync-style user experience at the browser level.

As with the previous example, this example aims to demonstrate multiple instances of the consumer and provider microservices and uses multiple clients while testing this service.

Design CRUD Over Async Channel on PostgreSQL

This example uses the modified version of the hexagonal microservice view shown in Figure 2-1 in Chapter 2, which was revisited in Chapter 5 and tweaked slightly in the previous example. Here, both microservices communicate through an async channel. The example uses Apache Kafka as the messaging channel, which is inherently asynchronous.

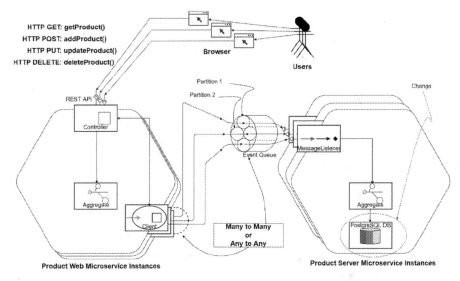

Figure 6-3. *Microservice design over async channel using partitions*

The noticeable change from the previous example is that the provider microservice stores the entity in a PostgreSQL database instead of using a MongoDB database. This change is marked in Figure 6-3.

Understanding the Source Code

The source code for this book is available on GitHub via the book's product page, located at www.apress.com/9798868805547. The code for this example is organized inside the ch06\ch06-02 folder.

The only change in the code from the previous example is that the provider microservice stores the entity in a PostgreSQL database instead of using a MongoDB database. The code needed for the provider microservice to store the entity in a PostgreSQL database and perform complete CRUD operations is described in detail in the section titled "Understanding the Code" in the first example in Chapter 3. You are directed to refer to that section for explanations.

Build and Run the Microservice

The ch06\ch06-02 folder contains the Maven scripts required to build these examples. As a first step, you need to bring up the Kafka broker. Refer to Appendix D to learn how to set up a Kafka server and bring it up. You need to execute the commands in Listing 6-22 to bring up Kafka from the Kafka installation location.

Listing 6-22. Commands to Bring Up Kafka Broker

```
bin/zookeeper-server-start.sh config/zookeeper.properties
bin/kafka-server-start.sh config/server.properties
```

Next, you need to bring up the PostgreSQL DB server. Refer to Appendix C to learn how to set up PostgreSQL server and bring it up. You need to execute the commands in Listing 6-23 to bring up PostgreSQL.

Listing 6-23. Bringing Up PostgreSQL Server

```
binildass-MacBook-Pro:~ binil$ pg_ctl -D /Library/
PostgreSQL/12/data start
```

Next, you need to build and install the utility library from Callista Enterprise (see Listing 6-24). Refer to Chapter 5 for a brief introduction to this library.

Listing 6-24. Commands to Build and Install the Utility Library from Callista Enterprise

```
binildass-MacBook-Pro:kafka-request-reply-util binil$ pwd
/Users/binil/binil/code/mac/mybooks/docker-04/Code/ch06/
ch06-02/kafka-request-reply-util
(base) binildass-MacBook-Pro:kafka-request-reply-util binil$
mvn clean install
[INFO] Scanning for projects...
[INFO]
...
```

Next, use two command terminals and change the directory to the top-level folder of both microservices. Then build the Product Server microservice using the make.sh scripts, as shown in Listing 6-25.

Listing 6-25. Commands to Build the Product Server Microservice

```
binildass-MacBook-Pro:01-ProductServer binil$ pwd
/Users/binil/binil/code/mac/mybooks/docker-04/Code/ch06/
ch06-02/01-ProductServer
binildass-MacBook-Pro:01-ProductServer binil$ sh make.sh
...
```

Next, build the Product Web microservice, as shown in Listing 6-26.

Listing 6-26. Commands to Build the Product Web Microservice

```
binildass-MacBook-Pro:02-ProductWeb binil$ pwd
/Users/binil/binil/code/mac/mybooks/docker-04/Code/ch06/
ch06-02/02-ProductWeb
binildass-MacBook-Pro:02-ProductWeb binil$ sh make.sh
...
```

You will test using three instances of the Product Server microservice and another three instances of the Product Web microservice.

First, bring up the first instance of the Product Server microservice, as shown in Listing 6-27.

Listing 6-27. Commands to Run the Product Server Microservice Instance 1

```
binildass-MacBook-Pro:01-ProductServer binil$ pwd
/Users/binil/binil/code/mac/mybooks/docker-04/Code/ch06/
ch06-02/01-ProductServer
binildass-MacBook-Pro:01-ProductServer binil$ sh run1.sh


  .   ____          _            __ _ _
 /\\ / ___'_ __ _ _(_)_ __  __ _ \ \ \ \
( ( )\___ | '_ | '_| | '_ \/ _` | \ \ \ \
 \\/  ___)| |_)| | | | | || (_| |  ) ) ) )
  '  |____| .__|_| |_|_| |_\__, | / / / /
 =========|_|==============|___/=/_/_/_/
 :: Spring Boot ::                (v3.2.0)

2023-05-16 22:02:45 INFO  StartupInfoLogger.logStarting:51
- Starting EcomProductServerMicroservice...
...
Running Changeset: db/changelog/initial-schema_inventory.
xml::product::Binildas
Running Changeset: db/changelog/initial-schema_inventory.
xml::addAutoIncrement...
Running Changeset: db/changelog/initial-schema_inventory.
xml::insert-product-01::Binildas
Running Changeset: db/changelog/initial-schema_inventory.
xml::insert-product-02::Binildas
```

```
UPDATE SUMMARY
Run:                      4
Previously run:           0
Filtered out:             0
-------------------------------
Total change sets:        4
```

Liquibase: Update has been successful.
2024-03-04 17:52:57 INFO InitializationComponent.
init:42 - Start
2024-03-04 17:52:57 INFO InitializationComponent.init:70 - End
2024-03-04 17:52:58 INFO StartupInfoLogger.logStarted:56 -
Started EcomProductServerMicroserviceApplication in 4.665
seconds (process running for 5.577)

Next, bring up the second instance of the Product Server microservice, as shown in Listing 6-28.

Listing 6-28. Commands to Run the Product Server Microservice Instance 2

```
binildass-MacBook-Pro:01-ProductServer binil$ pwd
/Users/binil/binil/code/mac/mybooks/docker-04/Code/ch06/
ch06-02/01-ProductServer
binildass-MacBook-Pro:01-ProductServer binil$
java -jar -Dserver.port=8084 -DDB_SERVER=127.0.0.1:
5432 -DPOSTGRES_DB=productdb -DPOSTGRES_USER=postgres -DPOSTGRES_
PASSWORD=postgre -Dspring.kafka.consumer.group-id=product-
server ./target/Ecom-Product-Server-
Microservice-0.0.1-SNAPSHOT.jar
...
```

Finally, bring up the third instance of the Product Server microservice, as shown in Listing 6-29.

Listing 6-29. Commands to Run the Product Server Microservice
Instance 3

```
binildass-MacBook-Pro:01-ProductServer binil$
java -jar -Dserver.port=8085 -DDB_SERVER=127.0.0.1:
5432 -DPOSTGRES_DB=productdb -DPOSTGRES_USER=postgres -DPOSTGRES_
PASSWORD=postgre -Dspring.kafka.consumer.group-id=product-server
./target/Ecom-Product-Server-Microservice-0.0.1-SNAPSHOT.jar
...
```

Next, run the instances of the Product Web microservice. As a first step,
run the first instance. See Listing 6-30.

Listing 6-30. Commands to Run the Product Web Microservice
Instance 1

```
binildass-MacBook-Pro:02-ProductWeb binil$ pwd
/Users/binil/binil/code/mac/mybooks/docker-04/Code/ch06/
ch06-02/02-ProductWeb
binildass-MacBook-Pro:02-ProductWeb binil$ sh run1.sh
```

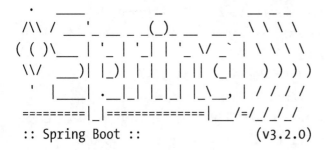

```
  ::  Spring Boot ::                (v3.2.0)
```

```
2024-03-04 17:54:06 INFO  StartupInfoLogger.logStarted:56 -
Started EcomProductWebMicroserviceApplication in 2.322 seconds
(process running for 2.981)
...
```

Next, bring up the second instance of the Product Web microservice, as shown in Listing 6-31.

Listing 6-31. Commands to Run the Product Web Microservice Instance 2

```
binildass-MacBook-Pro:02-ProductWeb binil$ pwd
/Users/binil/binil/code/mac/mybooks/docker-04/Code/ch06/
ch06-02/02-ProductWeb
binildass-MacBook-Pro:02-ProductWeb binil$ java -jar target/
Ecom-Product-Microservice-0.0.1-SNAPSHOT.jar  -Dserver.
port=8081
...
```

As a last step, bring up the third instance of the Product Web microservice, as shown in Listing 6-32.

Listing 6-32. Commands to Run the Product Web Microservice Instance 3

```
binildass-MacBook-Pro:02-ProductWeb binil$ java -jar target/
Ecom-Product-Microservice-0.0.1-SNAPSHOT.jar  -Dserver.
port=8082
...
```

Now that both microservices are up and running, you can test the microservices.

Testing the Microservice

To test the microservices, you are directed to refer to the "Testing Parallel Request Processing" section in Chapter 5. Alternatively, we will follow as below.

There is more than one way to test these microservices. One way to test them is to use three browser instances to point to the URLs shown in Listing 6-33.

Listing 6-33. Testing the Microservice Using Browsers

```
http://localhost:8080/product.html
http://localhost:8081/product.html
http://localhost:8082/product.html
```

Follow the detailed instructions described in the section "Test the Microservice Using UI" in Chapter 1 to test these CRUD operations.

Alternatively, you can now use three (or more) separate terminals to run cURL client commands concurrently. Listing 6-34 shows the cURL clients sending requests to the Product Web microservice.

Listing 6-34. cURL Clients to Fire Requests to Product Web Microservice at Different Ports

```
binildass-MacBook-Pro:~ binil$ curl http://localhost:8080/
productsweb
...

binildass-MacBook-Pro:~ binil$ curl http://localhost:8081/
productsweb
...

binildass-MacBook-Pro:~ binil$ curl http://localhost:8082/
productsweb
...
```

You can also endurance-test the microservices by keeping the cURL clients firing continuously, as shown in Listings 6-35 through 6-37.

Listing 6-35. Endurance Test Using cURL Client 1

```
(base) binildass-MacBook-Pro:02-ProductWeb binil$ pwd
/Users/binil/binil/code/mac/mybooks/docker-04/Code/ch06/
ch06-02/02-ProductWeb
(base) binildass-MacBook-Pro:02-ProductWeb binil$ sh
loopcurl1.sh
...
```

Listing 6-36. Endurance Test using cURL Client 2

```
(base) binildass-MacBook-Pro:02-ProductWeb binil$ pwd
/Users/binil/binil/code/mac/mybooks/docker-04/Code/ch06/
ch06-02/02-ProductWeb
(base) binildass-MacBook-Pro:02-ProductWeb binil$ sh
loopcurl2.sh
...
```

Listing 6-37. Endurance Test using cURL Client 3

```
(base) binildass-MacBook-Pro:02-ProductWeb binil$ pwd
/Users/binil/binil/code/mac/mybooks/docker-04/Code/ch06/
ch06-03/02-ProductWeb
(base) binildass-MacBook-Pro:02-ProductWeb binil$ sh
loopcurl3.sh
...
```

This completes the second example, using PostgreSQL.

Before I close this chapter, the next section quickly explains an important concept called *integration patterns*. They show how such standard and defined patterns provide value to architectures involving Message Oriented Middleware (MOM).

Aggregating Responses from Multiple Microservices

All through the previous chapters and the previous sections in this chapter, you have seen different combinations in which you can mix and match the transport connectivity options between microservices to simulate different message exchange patterns. To complete this discussion, this section looks at an integration pattern called an *aggregator*. You can use this pattern to aggregate responses from multiple microservices.

Aggregator Integration Pattern

Let's first look at what an aggregator pattern is. An *aggregator* is a stateful filter used to collect and store individual messages until a complete set of related messages has been received. The aggregator can then filter, compose, and publish a single message distilled from the individual messages. See Figure 6-4.

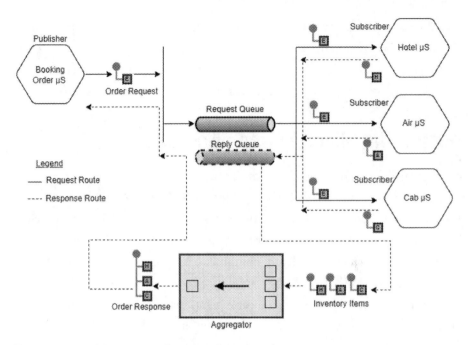

Figure 6-4. *Aggregator integration pattern*

Figure 6-4 depicts a typical travel booking scenario done by travel agents. The Booking Order microservice is used by the travel agent to fulfill the booking request on behalf of a traveler. The Booking Order microservice can also be used by a traveler directly through the web or mobile apps. Assuming the booking has to be done for a combined itinerary involving hotel accommodations, air travel, and airport drop-off and pickup, these individual fulfillment inventory items will be owned by different third-party providers—a Hotel microservice, an Air microservice, and a Cab microservice, in this case. These different inventory owner microservices will pick up the booking request and try to fulfill the respective booking component and send a response message back to the reply queue. Now comes the part of the aggregator.

The aggregator, being a stateful filter, can wait for multiple replies until a timeout. The aggregator can then compose from the individual response messages and publish a single message to the Booking Order microservice. The next section looks at some working code to show this pattern.

Design the Microservice Aggregator

This example uses the now-familiar Product Web and Product Server microservices domain. As shown in Figure 6-5, users interact with the Product Web microservice from a browser. The Product Web microservice in turn invokes the Product Server microservice. The Product Server microservice retrieves data from a database, from an in-memory database in this example, and sends the response.

Inter-microservice communication happens over a messaging channel.

Moreover, the request message is relayed to more than one service provider. The objective is to enable the Product Web microservice to relay requests to more than one service provider and receive responses from all or many of these service providers. The Product Web microservice acts as an aggregator and stores individual messages until a complete set of related messages has been received. The aggregator can then filter, compose, and publish a single message distilled from the individual messages to the browser. See Figure 6-5.

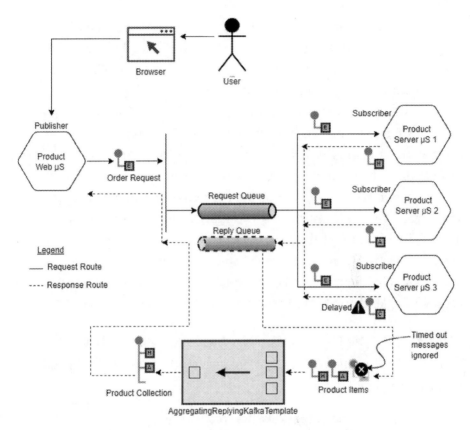

Figure 6-5. *Microservices aggregator*

To keep the complexity of the example under control, it does not use different kinds of provider microservices. Instead, the example uses different instances of the same kind of microservice. However, note that nothing prevents you from having different kinds of provider microservices responding to the same request message.

Understanding the Source Code

The source code for this book is available on GitHub via the book's product page, located at www.apress.com/9798868805547. The code for this example is organized inside the ch06\ch06-03 folder, which was explained in detail. The additional wiring plugs in an aggregator between the two microservices and the mechanism used to relay the single request from the Product Web microservice to more than one (instance of the) provider microservice, which you will see in the code in this section.

Spring Kafka provides AggregatingReplyingKafkaTemplate, a replying template that aggregates multiple replies with the same correlation ID. AggregatingReplyingKafkaTemplate is a listener that handles a batch of incoming Kafka messages. The list of batch messages is created from the consumer records object returned by a poll. AggregatingReplyingKafkaTemplate extends the behavior of ReplyingKafkaTemplate<K,V,R> from Spring, which extends the behavior of KafkaTemplate to provide request-reply semantics. You saw this in detail in Chapter 4, so I only explain the additional features of AggregatingReplyingKafkaTemplate, as configured in Listing 6-38.

Listing 6-38. The Product Web Kafka Configuration (ch06\ ch06-03\02-ProductWeb\src\main\java\com\acme\ecom\product\ KafkaConfig.java)

```
import org.springframework.kafka.requestreply.
AggregatingReplyingKafkaTemplate;

@Configuration
public class KafkaConfig {

    @Value("${product.topic.reply.numProviders}")
    private int numProviders;

    @Value("${product.topic.reply.aggregatingTimeout}")
    private long aggregatingTimeout;
```

```
@Bean
public AggregatingReplyingKafkaTemplate<String, String,
        Products> replyKafkaTemplate(ProducerFactory<
        String, String> pf,
        KafkaMessageListenerContainer<String,
        Collection<ConsumerRecord<String, Products>>>
        replyContainer){

    AggregatingReplyingKafkaTemplate<String, String,
        Products> replyTemplate =
        new AggregatingReplyingKafkaTemplate<>(pf,
                replyContainer,(list, timeout) -> {

            LOGGER.debug("list.size() : {}; timeout : {}",
                list.size(), timeout);
            return (list.size() == numProviders) ||
                (timeout);
        });

    replyTemplate.setReturnPartialOnTimeout(true);
    replyTemplate.setSharedReplyTopic(true);
    replyTemplate.setDefaultReplyTimeout(
        java.time.Duration.ofSeconds(aggregatingTimeout));
    return replyTemplate;
}

@Bean
public KafkaMessageListenerContainer<String, Collection<
        ConsumerRecord<String, Products>>>
        replyContainer(ConsumerFactory<String,
        Collection<ConsumerRecord<String, Products>>> cf){

    ContainerProperties containerProperties =
        new ContainerProperties(requestReplyTopic);
```

```
    containerProperties.setAckMode(AckMode.MANUAL);
    return new KafkaMessageListenerContainer<String,
        Collection<ConsumerRecord<
        String, Products>>>(cf, containerProperties);
  }
}
```

The `replyContainer` bean creates properties for a container that will subscribe to the specified topic—`requestReplyTopic` in this case. You can configure this listener container to consume more than one topic. The replies must then contain the correlation ID header (used to aggregate). The framework will create a container that subscribes to all topics matching the specified pattern to get dynamically assigned partitions.

Using the `replyContainer`, you configure an `AggregatingReplyingKafkaTemplate`, specifying that you expect a collection of `ConsumerRecord`-containing `Products`. Then you set `replyTemplate.setReturnPartialOnTimeout(true)`, which simply means that the template will consult the release strategy upon timeout. The template does this with the timeout argument set to `true`, to tell the strategy it's a timeout rather than a delivery call. When it's set to `true`, it releases a partial result. You can also take many actions and look at (and possibly modify) the list to decide whether you want to release or discard.

In this case, you run the following test:

```
return (list.size() == numProviders) || (timeout);
```

One more parameter (`numProviders`) is configured in this example. You set `numProviders` (in this case, in `application.properties`) to 3, as shown in Listing 6-39. This is because you have three instances of the Product Server microservice. Once you receive response messages from the three Product Server microservice instances, you no longer want to wait for more responses.

By specifying `replyTemplate.setSharedReplyTopic(true)`, you indicate that multiple templates are using the same topic for replies. This simply changes logs for unexpected replies to debug instead of error.

The `replyTemplate.setDefaultReplyTimeout()` will set a timeout to check this release strategy in this example.

Listing 6-39. The Product Web Kafka Configuration (ch06\ch06-03\02-ProductWeb\src\main\resources\application.properties)

```
product.topic.reply.numProviders: 3
product.topic.reply.aggregatingTimeout: 6
```

You can tweak this value by changing the value for `aggregatingTimeout` in `application.properties` of the Product Web microservice to test different scenarios. Listing 6-40 shows the dynamics of the aggregator code.

Listing 6-40. The Product Web REST Controller (ch06\ch06-03\02-ProductWeb\src\main\java\com\acme\ecom\product\controller\ProductRestController.java)

```
@RestController
public class ProductRestController{

    @Autowired
    AggregatingReplyingKafkaTemplate<String, String, Products>
        kafkaTemplate;

    @Value("${kafka.topic.request-topic}")
    private String requestTopic;

    @Value("${kafka.topic.requestreply-topic}")
    private String requestReplyTopic;
```

```java
@RequestMapping(value = "/productsweb", method =
        RequestMethod.GET,
        produces = {MediaType.APPLICATION_JSON_VALUE})
public ResponseEntity<List<Product>> getAllProducts()
        throws InterruptedException,
        ExecutionException, TimeoutException {

    ProducerRecord<String, String> record =
        new ProducerRecord<String, String>(
            requestTopic, "All");
    record.headers().add(new RecordHeader(
        KafkaHeaders.REPLY_TOPIC,
        requestReplyTopic.getBytes()));
    RequestReplyFuture<String, String, Collection<
            ConsumerRecord<String, Products>>>
        sendAndReceive =
            kafkaTemplate.sendAndReceive(record);

    SendResult<String, String> sendResult =
        sendAndReceive.getSendFuture().get();
    sendResult.getProducerRecord().headers().forEach(
        header -> LOGGER.trace(header.key() + ":" +
            header.value().toString()));

    sendAndReceive.getSendFuture().get(30,
        TimeUnit.SECONDS);
    ConsumerRecord<String, Collection<ConsumerRecord<
            String, Products>>>
        consumerRecords = sendAndReceive.get();

    Collection<ConsumerRecord<String,
            Products>> consumerRecord =
        consumerRecords.value();
    List<Product> products =new ArrayList<Product>();
```

```
for(ConsumerRecord<String, Products>
        temp:consumerRecord) {
    products.addAll(temp.value().getProducts());
}
return new ResponseEntity(products, HttpStatus.OK);
}
}
```

For an explanation of the code in Listing 6-40, see the section titled "Sync over Async Microservices" in Chapter 4. Here, I explain only the new code for fulfilling the aggregation. sendAndReceive sends the request and AggregatingReplyingKafkaTemplate receives a ConsumerRecord, which by itself is a Collection of ConsumerRecords containing a Collection of Products retrieved from each instance of the Product Server microservice (a Collection of Collection)!

You can disassemble the ConsumerRecord of Collection of ConsumerRecord of Collection of Products, flatten it, and aggregate it into a single ArrayList and return. Note that you are not doing any filtering, de-duplication, or any such transformations here. However, you are free to do any further processing based on your requirements.

Build and Run the Microservice

The ch06\ch06-03 folder contains the Maven scripts required to build the examples. First, you need to bring up the Kafka broker. Refer to Appendix D to learn how to set up Kafka server and bring it up. You need to execute the commands in Listing 6-41 to bring up Kafka from the Kafka installation location.

Listing 6-41. Commands to Bring Up Kafka Broker

```
bin/zookeeper-server-start.sh config/zookeeper.properties
bin/kafka-server-start.sh config/server.properties
```

Next, use two command terminals and change the directory to the top-level folder of both microservices. Then build the Product Server microservice using the make.sh scripts, as shown in Listing 6-42.

Listing 6-42. Commands to Build the Product Server Microservice

```
(base) binildass-MacBook-Pro:01-ProductServer binil$ pwd
/Users/binil/binil/code/mac/mybooks/docker-04/Code/ch06/
ch06-03/01-ProductServer
(base) binildass-MacBook-Pro:01-ProductServer binil$ sh make.sh
[INFO] Scanning for projects...
[INFO]
...
```

Next, build the Product Web microservice, as shown in Listing 6-43.

Listing 6-43. Commands to Build the Product Web Microservice

```
(base) binildass-MacBook-Pro:02-ProductWeb binil$ pwd
/Users/binil/binil/code/mac/mybooks/docker-04/Code/ch06/
ch06-03/02-ProductWeb
(base) binildass-MacBook-Pro:02-ProductWeb binil$ sh make.sh
[INFO] Scanning for projects...
[INFO]
...
```

You will test this example with three instances of the Product Server microservice and a single instance of the Product Web microservice.

Listing 6-44 shows how to bring up the first instance of the Product Server microservice.

Listing 6-44. Commands to Run the Product Server Microservice Instance 1

```
(base) binildass-MacBook-Pro:01-ProductServer binil$ pwd
/Users/binil/binil/code/mac/mybooks/docker-03/ch06/ch06-03/01-
ProductServer
(base) binildass-MacBook-Pro:01-ProductServer binil$
java -jar -Dserver.port=8081 -Dspring.kafka.consumer.group-
id=product-server1 -Dcom.acme.ecom.product.kafka.client
.productlistener.sleeptimeout=2 ./target/Ecom-Product-Server-
Microservice-0.0.1-SNAPSHOT.jar
...
```

Next, bring up the second instance of the Product Server microservice, as shown in Listing 6-45.

Listing 6-45. Commands to Run the Product Server Microservice Instance 2

```
(base) binildass-MacBook-Pro:01-ProductServer binil$ pwd
/Users/binil/binil/code/mac/mybooks/docker-03/ch06/ch06-03/01-
ProductServer
(base) binildass-MacBook-Pro:01-ProductServer binil$
java -jar -Dserver.port=8082 -Dspring.kafka.consumer.group-
id=product-server2 -Dcom.acme.ecom.product.kafka.client
.productlistener.sleeptimeout=10 ./target/Ecom-Product-Server-
Microservice-0.0.1-SNAPSHOT.jar
```

Finally, bring up the third instance of the Product Server microservice, as shown in Listing 6-46.

Listing 6-46. Commands to Run the Product Server Microservice
Instance 3

```
(base) binildass-MacBook-Pro:01-ProductServer binil$ pwd
/Users/binil/binil/code/mac/mybooks/docker-03/ch06/ch06-03/01-
ProductServer
(base) binildass-MacBook-Pro:01-ProductServer binil$
java -jar -Dserver.port=8083 -Dspring.kafka.consumer.group-
id=product-server3 -Dcom.acme.ecom.product.kafka.client.pr
oductlistener.sleeptimeout=3 ./target/Ecom-Product-Server-
Microservice-0.0.1-SNAPSHOT.jar
...
```

Note one aspect in Listings 6-44 through 6-46:—the value passed
for the environment variable `spring.kafka.consumer.group-id`. The
example configures different values for this so that the message consumers
(or the provider microservices) are in different groups (`group.id`). If they
are all in the same group, only one of them will consume the request. By
specifying all three instances of the Product Server microservices to be
in different consumer groups, all of them will consume the same request
message.

Next, run the Product Web microservice instance, as shown in
Listing 6-47.

Listing 6-47. Commands to Run the Aggregator—the Product Web
Microservice Instance

```
(base) binildass-MacBook-Pro:02-ProductWeb binil$ pwd
/Users/binil/binil/code/mac/mybooks/docker-03/ch06/ch06-03/02-
ProductWeb
(base) binildass-MacBook-Pro:02-ProductWeb binil$ sh run.sh
```

```
      .   ___           _            __ _ _
     /\\ / ___'_ __ _ _(_)_ __  __ _ \ \ \ \
    ( ( )\___ | '_ | '_| | '_ \/ _` | \ \ \ \
     \\/  ___)| |_)| | | | | || (_| |  ) ) ) )
      '  |____| .__|_| |_|_| |_\__, | / / / /
     =========|_|==============|___/=/_/_/_/
     :: Spring Boot ::                (v3.2.0)
```

2022-05-22 10:41:45 INFO org.springframework.boot.
StartupInfoLogger.logStarting:55 - Starting EcomProductWeb...
2022-05-22 10:41:45 DEBUG org.springframework.boot.
StartupInfoLogger.logStarting:56 - Running with Spring Boot ...
2022-05-22 10:41:45 INFO org.springframework.boot.
SpringApplication.logStartupProfileInfo:651 - No active ...
2022-05-22 10:41:47 INFO org.springframework.boot.
StartupInfoLogger.logStarted:61 - Started EcomProductWeb...
2022-05-22 10:41:57 INFO com.acme.ecom.product.controller.
ProductRestController.getAllProducts:71 - Start
2022-05-22 10:41:57 INFO com.acme.ecom.product.controller.
ProductRestController.getAllProducts:72 - Thread :
Thread[http-nio-8080-exec-5,5,main]
2022-05-22 10:41:59 DEBUG com.acme.ecom.product.KafkaConfig.
lambda$replyKafkaTemplate$0:129 - **list.size() : 1;**
timeout : false
2022-05-22 10:42:00 DEBUG com.acme.ecom.product.KafkaConfig.
lambda$replyKafkaTemplate$0:129 - **list.size() : 2;**
timeout : false
2022-05-22 10:42:03 DEBUG com.acme.ecom.product.KafkaConfig.
lambda$replyKafkaTemplate$0:129 - **list.size() : 2;**
timeout : true
2022-05-22 10:42:03 DEBUG com.acme.ecom.product.controller.
ProductRestController.getAllProducts:83 - Reply success ...

271

```
2022-05-22 10:42:03 INFO   com.acme.ecom.product.controller.
ProductRestController.getAllProducts:84 - Thread :
Thread[http-nio-8080-exec-5,5,main]
```

Refer to Listings 6-44 through 6-46, where the sleeptimeout is configured for the three Product microservice instances respectively as:

-Dcom.acme.ecom.product.kafka.client.productlistener.
sleeptimeout=2
-Dcom.acme.ecom.product.kafka.client.productlistener.
sleeptimeout=10
-Dcom.acme.ecom.product.kafka.client.productlistener.
sleeptimeout=3

Now, referring to Listing 6-30, you have configured the following in the Product Web microservice so that it will time out in six seconds:

product.topic.reply.aggregatingTimeout: 6

It will receive responses from the Product Server microservice instances 1 and 3 alone.

Testing the Microservice

When all is set, you can access the web application using your browser and pointing to this URL (see Figure 6-6):

http://localhost:8080/product.html

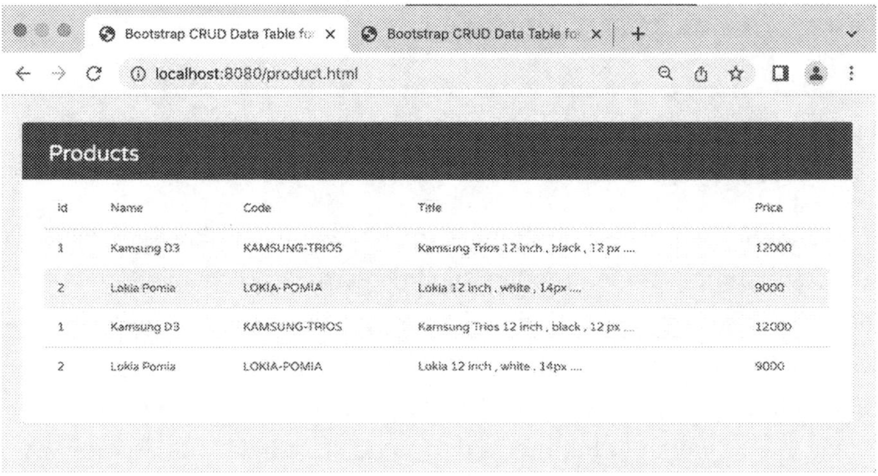

Figure 6-6. *Testing the microservices, showing results from two of the three service providers*

As described, the example uses three instances of the Product Server microservice instead of three different microservice types, so all of them will reply with the same response. But in Listing 6-45, there is a delay called `sleeptimeout=10` for one of the Product Server microservices. Listing 6-39 shows `aggregatingTimeout: 6` for the Product Web microservice, so the `AggregatingReplyingKafkaTemplate` of the Product Web microservice will not wait for the response from this instance of the Product Server microservice.

Since you are not doing any filtering, de-duplication, or any such transformation, you'll see duplicated line items from the responses of two instances of the Product Server microservices.

Listing 6-48 shows the logging by the `AggregatingReplyingKafkaTemplate` on the Product Web microservice.

273

Listing 6-48. Aggregator Times Out

```
list.size() : 1; timeout : false
list.size() : 2; timeout : false
list.size() : 2; timeout : true
```

Listing 6-48 shows what is happening when the template is consulting the release strategy upon timeout. The first two lines correspond to when responses are received from the two instances of the Product Web microservice within the timeout limit. The third line corresponds to when the template does this with the timeout argument set to true, to tell the strategy it's a timeout rather than a delivery call, so it will not wait for any more responses.

This aggregated response is shown in Figure 6-6.

In real life, you may not statically configure product.topic. reply.numProviders, as is done in in Listing 6-39. Instead, you have to dynamically form the value of numProviders based on the minimum number of service providers you expect until there's a timeout. The typical production design is shown in Figure 6-7, where the travel agent or travel aggregator has contracts with multiple air, hotel, cab and other ancillary service providers. Travel search parameters are relayed to all or preferred inventory providers and the responses from all or many of these preferred providers are aggregated. Filtering, de-duplication, or any transformations can be applied and the result set sorted again, based on a similar set of rules and responses sent to the Booking Service provider Web microservice.

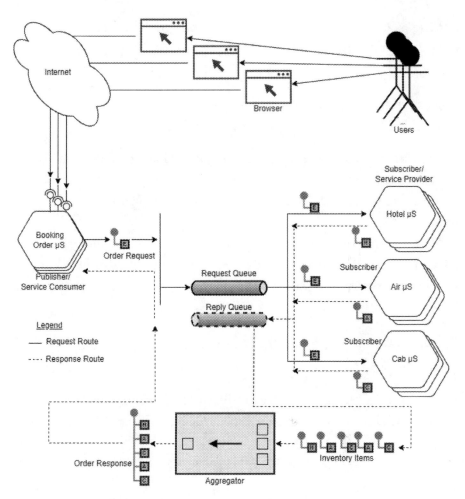

Figure 6-7. *Booking aggregator connected to third-party inventory providers*

I will now change the test condition. Let's increase the aggregating timeout, as shown in Listing 6-49.

Listing 6-49. The Product Web Kafka Configuration (ch06\
ch06-03\02-ProductWeb\src\main\resources\application.
properties.

```
product.topic.reply.numProviders: 3
product.topic.reply.aggregatingTimeout: 15
```

You increase the aggregating timeout by adjusting the value in Listing 6-49 so that you are sure you will receive responses from all three instances of the Product Server microservice before the timeout, as configured in Listings 6-44 through 6-46.

You have not made any changes to the Product Server microservice, so you could repeat the test with the same running instances of it. But you need to rebuild and rerun the Product Web microservice, as shown in Listing 6-50.

Listing 6-50. Rebuild and Run Product Web Microservice
Using Scripts

```
(base) binildass-MacBook-Pro:02-ProductWeb binil$ pwd
/Users/binil/binil/code/mac/mybooks/docker-03/ch06/ch06-03/02-
ProductWeb
(base) binildass-MacBook-Pro:02-ProductWeb binil$ sh make.sh
...

(base) binildass-MacBook-Pro:02-ProductWeb binil$ sh run.sh


  .   ____          _            __ _ _
 /\\ / ___'_ __ _ _(_)_ __  __ _ \ \ \ \
( ( )\___ | '_ | '_| | '_ \/ _` | \ \ \ \
 \\/  ___)| |_)| | | | | || (_| |  ) ) ) )
  '  |____| .__|_| |_|_| |_\__, | / / / /
 =========|_|==============|___/=/_/_/_/
 :: Spring Boot ::                (v3.2.0)
```

```
2022-05-22 10:53:48 INFO  org.springframework.boot.
StartupInfoLogger.logStarting:55 - Starting EcomProductWeb...
2022-05-22 10:53:48 DEBUG org.springframework.boot.
StartupInfoLogger.logStarting:56 - Running with Spring Boot ...
2022-05-22 10:53:48 INFO  org.springframework.boot.
SpringApplication.logStartupProfileInfo:651 - No active ...
2022-05-22 10:53:50 INFO  org.springframework.boot.
StartupInfoLogger.logStarted:61 - Started EcomProductWeb...
2022-05-22 10:54:02 INFO  com.acme.ecom.product.controller.
ProductRestController.getAllProducts:71 - Start
2022-05-22 10:54:02 INFO  com.acme.ecom.product.controller.
ProductRestController.getAllProducts:72 - Thread :
Thread[http-nio-8080-exec-5,5,main]
2022-05-22 10:54:04 DEBUG com.acme.ecom.product.KafkaConfig.
lambda$replyKafkaTemplate$0:129 - list.size() : 1;
timeout : false
2022-05-22 10:54:05 DEBUG com.acme.ecom.product.KafkaConfig.
lambda$replyKafkaTemplate$0:129 - list.size() : 2;
timeout : false
2022-05-22 10:54:12 DEBUG com.acme.ecom.product.KafkaConfig.
lambda$replyKafkaTemplate$0:129 - list.size() : 3;
timeout : false
2022-05-22 10:54:12 DEBUG com.acme.ecom.product.controller.
ProductRestController.getAllProducts:83 - Reply success ...
2022-05-22 10:54:12 INFO  com.acme.ecom.product.controller.
ProductRestController.getAllProducts:84 - Thread :
Thread[http-nio-8080-exec-5,5,main]
```

You can now test the application by accessing the web application using your browser and pointing to this URL (see Figure 6-8):

```
http://localhost:8080/product.html
```

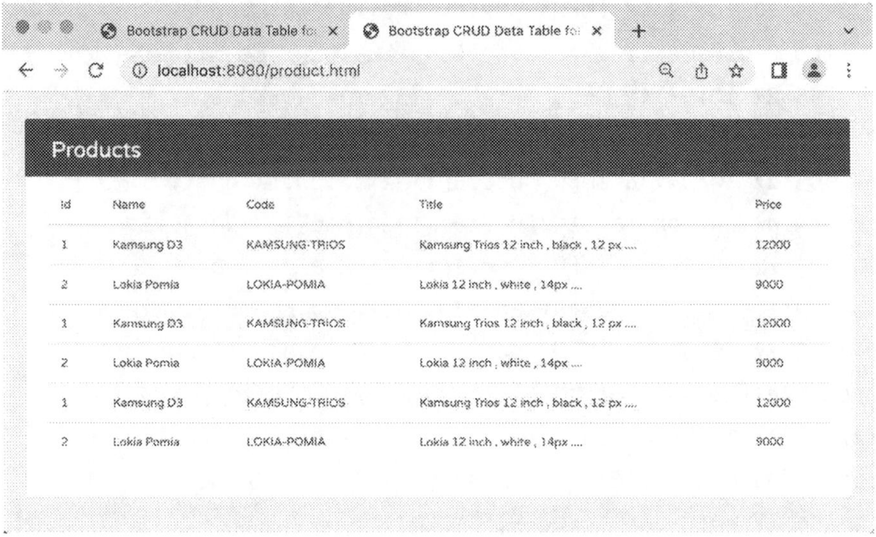

Figure 6-8. *Testing the microservices, showing results from all the service providers*

If you observe Listing 6-50, you can see that even though the timeout has not occurred, since you received responses from all expected instances of the Product Server microservices, you can terminate waiting at the third delivery call, as shown in Listing 6-51.

Listing 6-51. Aggregator Times Out

```
list.size() : 1; timeout : false
list.size() : 2; timeout : false
list.size() : 3; timeout : false
```

You can see duplicated line items from the three instances of the Product Server microservices in Figure 6-8.

Summary

Starting with the simplest of the microservices in Chapter 1, you have come a long way in understanding multiple variants of microservices architectures. You have tried and tested many concurrency and integration patterns, with familiar SQL and NoSQL databases. The examples in these chapters can be extracted to use as templates and modified for your daily production use cases. The stage is now set to begin the next journey to Containers, which are covered in the next chapter.

CHAPTER 7

Introducing Docker

Resource and time sharing are not new and were generally believed to originate in the IBM mainframe days of the late 1960s and early 1970s. Virtualization was made possible for organizations and individuals to use a computer resource without owning one. The capacity of a single server is so large that it is almost impossible for the majority of general-purpose workloads to effectively use it, so shared use among a large group of applications and users makes sense. The goal was to increase the efficiency of the users and the expensive computer resources they shared and this paved the road to virtualization.

Containers are a form of operating system virtualization. Containers have no or lean operating system images, but greatly utilize the host operating system. A set of characteristics make containers attractive, especially in deploying microservice-based applications, and they are explored in this chapter.

The following topics are covered in this chapter:

- Virtualization in general

- Introduction to containers

- Docker in detail

- Compiling, packaging, and running a Java app without a local Java Installation

- Running your first Java container

© Binildas A. Christudas 2024
B. A. Christudas, *Java Microservices and Containers in the Cloud*,
https://doi.org/10.1007/979-8-8688-0555-4_7

Different Types of Virtualization

This discussion begins with the traditional mode of application deployment and then moves to various ways of virtualization so that you can appreciate some of the advantages containers offer as compared to peer methods of virtualizations.

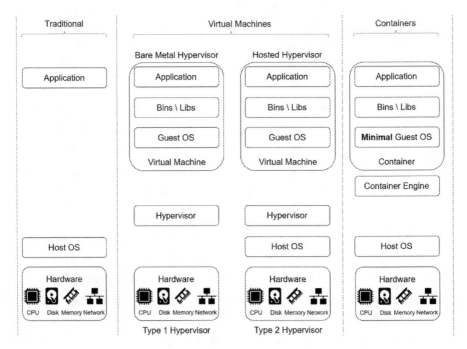

Figure 7-1. *Traditional vs. VMs vs. containers*

Referring to Figure 7-1, first consider the different modes of virtualizations and application deployment.

Traditional Deployment

In the traditional or classical mode of application deployment, organizations used physical servers. Every time the business needed a new application, the IT department would buy a new server. Since many times nobody knew the performance requirements of the new application, and to provide enough headroom for future business volume growth, the IT department would over-purchase. They used guesswork to determine the model and size of the server to buy.

The typical lifecycle of provisioning application software flows like this:

1. Get the physical servers ready in the data center.

2. Install or use an existing operating system.

3. Install any additional tools needed by your application software.

4. Install any dependencies for your software.

5. Run your software.

6. Retire your application.

7. Repurpose or recycle server hardware.

A much better way to utilize capital expenses is to use virtualization, which is discussed next.

Virtualization

When VMware, Inc. brought the Virtual Machine (VM) concept, IT departments no longer needed to procure a new, oversized server every time they needed a new application. Instead, IT could run new apps on existing servers that were sitting around with spare capacity. Virtualization allows IT to run multiple VMs on a single physical server. Each VM includes a full copy of an operating system, the application, necessary binaries, and libraries.

The essential component in the virtualization stack is the *hypervisor*, also called the Virtual Machine Monitor (VMM). It creates a virtual platform on the host computer, on top of which multiple guest operating systems are executed and monitored. These multiple operating systems are either different instances of the same operating system, or different operating systems. They share the hardware resources offered by the same, single host. Hypervisors have classifications:

- **Type 1, native or bare metal:** Native hypervisors run directly on the host's hardware to control the hardware, and to monitor the guest OS. Consequently, the guest OS runs on a separate level above the hypervisor. Examples: Oracle VM, Microsoft Hyper-V, VMWare ESX, and Xen.

- **Type 2, hosted:** Hosted hypervisors run within a traditional OS. Hosted hypervisors add a distinct software layer to top of the host OS, and the guest OS becomes a third software level above the hardware. Examples: Oracle VM VirtualBox, VMWare Server and Workstation, Microsoft Virtual PC, KVM, QEMU, and Parallels.

The fact that every VM requires its own dedicated operating system (OS) is a major flaw. Every OS consumes CPU, RAM, and other resources. Every OS needs licensing, patching, and monitoring. There are other challenges too, a few of which are listed here:

- Operating system images are heavyweight—in the GBs.

- It is a slow-to-boot-up process.

- The applications are not portable.

- Spinning up a virtual machine may take 1–2 minutes.

Docker Container was introduced in 2013 to address these drawbacks.

Containers

Containers use OS level virtualization. They do not require their own full-blown OS. Instead, all containers on a single host share the host's OS. This frees up huge amounts of system resources, including CPU, RAM, and storage. It also reduces potential licensing costs and reduces the overhead of OS patching and other maintenance. Container abstraction at the OS layer packages code and dependencies together.

Containers are also fast to start and ultra-portable. Containers are very lightweight and can spin up in a few seconds or milliseconds. Container workloads can be moved from laptops to the cloud, and then to VMs or bare metal in your data center quickly and easily.

Containers in Detail

Understanding containers is essential for understanding the rest of this chapter, hence this section is devoted to containers.

History of Containers

Let's consider a brief history of containers. Around 2000, Jails, an early implementation of container technology, was added to FreeBSD. The next year, the Linux VServer project made running several general-purpose Linux servers on a single box a reality. This separated the userspace environment into distinct units—called Virtual Private Servers—so that each VPS looked and felt like a real server to the processes contained within. In 2006, the "Generic Process Containers" was put forward. This was renamed Cgroups (Control Groups) and it allowed processes to be grouped together and ensured that each group got a share of memory, CPU, and disk I/O while at the same time preventing any one container from monopolizing any of these resources. Adding to this is the notion of Kernel namespaces, which separated it from user namespaces. User namespaces allow a process to have its own set of users and allow a process to have root privileges inside a container, but not outside. In 2008, IBM created the Linux Containers Project (LXC). LXC 1.0 was released in 2014. SELinux and Seccomp are two new features:

- **Seccomp:** Seccomp is a Linux kernel feature for limiting the system calls that a task can use. This allows an underutilized CPU to be rented out to untrusted guests without fearing they will abuse other resources, which is a good fit for container use case.

- **SELinux:** SELinux has an access control schema for "labeling processes, files, and devices and at defining rules on how labeled processes interact with labeled processes, files, and devices." Linux containers, as a group of processes, are a good match for hardening with SELinux, another idea that maps to the container use case.

Docker built on all of these features incrementally and wrapped the LXC userspace tools to make them even easier for developers to use. In June 2015, Docker the company open sourced Docker to OCI (Open Container Initiative) under the auspices of the Linux Foundation. Docker initially used the LXC driver, then moved to libcontainer, which is now renamed runc.

Container Internals

The namespace is a Kernel level feature. This function of the OS allows global resources, like network and disks among processes, to be shared. When global resources were wrapped in namespaces, they become visible only to those processes that run in the same namespace. For example, when you get a portion of disk and put it in one namespace, processes running in another namespace can't see or access it. Similarly, processes in one namespace can't access anything in memory that is allocated to another namespace, and so on. Of course, processes in namespace A can't see or talk to processes in namespace B. This way, global resources can be virtualized and isolated. Docker works in this manner—each Docker container runs in its own namespace but uses the same kernel as all the other containers. The isolation happens because the kernel knows the namespace that was assigned to the process. During an API call, it makes sure that the process can only access resources in its own namespace.

Virtualization vs. Containerization

Having looked at the different levels of virtualization options, this section investigates the underlying details. See Figure 7-2.

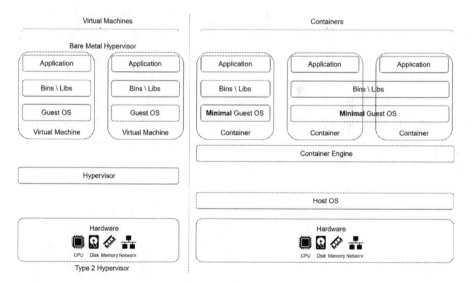

Figure 7-2. *VMs vs. containers*

Figure 7-2 compares and contrasts the similarities and differences between virtualization and containerization. This discussion is limited to Type 2 virtualization, which gives more contrast compared to containerization, even though almost all the aspects are applicable to Type 1 virtualization also.

In this case of virtualization, the VM manager takes over the CPU ring 0 (which is also called the "root mode" in newer CPUs) and intercepts all privileged calls made by the guest OS to create the illusion that the guest OS has its own hardware. Virtualization thus allows you to run two completely different OSes on the same (single) underlying hardware. Each guest OS goes through the processes of bootstrapping, kernel loading, and so on. The guest OS can't get full access to either the host OS or to other guest OSs and hence can't mess things up. This provides tighter security.

You may now be able to appreciate that while you could run multiple OS in virtualized hardware, you can't run completely different OSes in containers like in virtualization. However, you can run different distros of Linux because they all share the same kernel. This means, since containers share the same kernel as the host, you can run an Arch image on an Ubuntu host.

A system call (commonly abbreviated as *syscall*) is the programmatic way in which a program requests services from the kernel of the operating system on which it is executed. This may include hardware-related services (for example, accessing a hard disk drive or accessing the device's I\O ports), creation and execution of new processes, and communication with integral kernel services such as process scheduling. syscalls provide an essential interface between a process and the operating system. Containers have access to the kernel of the host. Since the kernel is the only part that communicates with the hardware, as long as your OS uses the good syscall, you can run any Linux distribution inside your container. For the same the reason, you can't use Windows inside a container since it's not using the same syscall.

Docker Concepts

This section talks about Docker concepts and Docker containers.

Layered Filesystems

Docker is based on *aufs* (short for *advanced multi-layered unification filesystem*), which implements Unionfs, a union mount for Linux filesystems. Unionfs is a filesystem service for Linux, FreeBSD, and NetBSD which implements a union mount for other filesystems. It allows files and directories of separate filesystems, known as *branches*, to be transparently overlaid, forming a single coherent filesystem. Several Linux distributions have chosen aufs as a replacement for UnionFS.

A *union mount* is a mount that allows several filesystems to be mounted at one time and appear as one filesystem. The union mount overlays the filesystems on top of one another so that the resulting filesystem may contain files and subdirectories from any or all of the underlying filesystems. In Docker vocabulary, each of these filesystems is called an *image*.

Docker Images

A Docker image is made up of filesystems layered over each other, as shown in Figure 7-3.

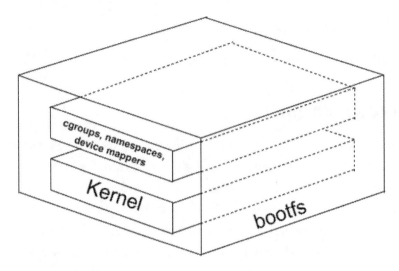

Figure 7-3. *Docker bootfs*

At the base of the image is a boot filesystem, bootfs, which resembles the typical Linux/UNIX boot filesystem. When a container is booted, it is moved into memory, and the boot filesystem is unmounted to free up the RAM used by the initrd disk image. This is like a typical Linux virtualization stack so far. A Docker user may never interact with the boot filesystem.

On top of the boot filesystem, Docker layers a root filesystem, rootfs. This rootfs can be one or more operating systems (e.g., a Debian or Ubuntu). See Figure 7-4.

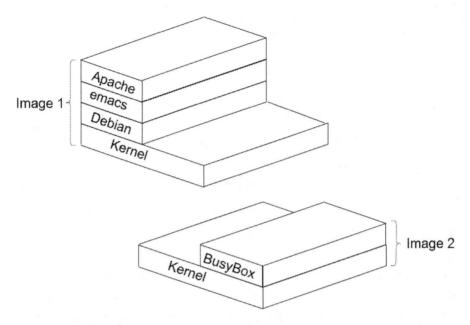

Figure 7-4. *Docker images*

In traditional Linux boot, the root filesystem is mounted read-only and then switched to read-write after the boot is finished and an integrity check is conducted. In the Docker world, the root filesystem stays in read-only mode, and Docker leverages union mount to add more read-only filesystems over the root filesystem.

Docker organizes the common parts of the operating system as read-only. Any common parts are shared among all of your containers. See Figure 7-5.

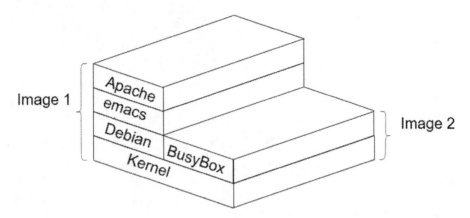

Figure 7-5. *Docker images sharing layers*

Sharing these common parts provides storage and runtime efficiency. To make it clear, if you have a 1GB container image and use a traditional VM method, you will need 1GB times the number of VMs you want. Since Docker shares the bulk of the 1GB between all the containers, if you have 1,000 containers, you still might only need a little over 1GB of space for all these containers (assuming they are all running the same OS image).

Docker images are layered on top of one another. The image on the top is the parent image; you can traverse from one layer to its parent and so on until you reach the bottom of the image stack, where the final image is called the base image. See Figure 7-6.

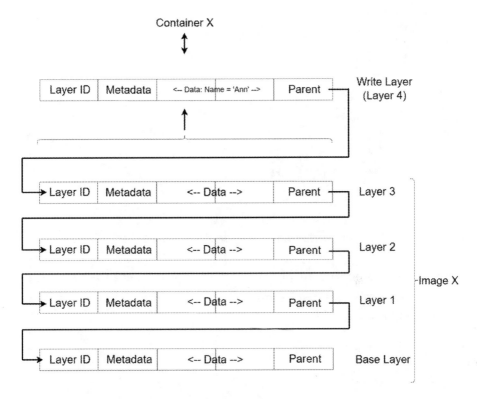

Figure 7-6. *Anatomy of a Docker image*

Docker Images vs. Containers

Docker images are read-only templates used to build containers. Containers are deployed instances created from those templates. Images and containers are closely related and are essential in powering the Docker software platform.

When a container is launched from an image, Docker mounts a read-write filesystem on the top. In this read-write layer, whatever processes you want the Docker container to run will execute. Figures 7-6 through 7-8 represents this process.

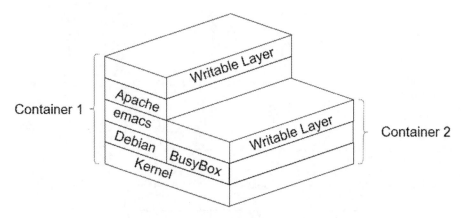

Figure 7-7. *Docker containers sharing image layers*

Even if containers share the same images (layers), once they are instantiated from their image templates, they are separate and isolated, as shown in Figure 7-8.

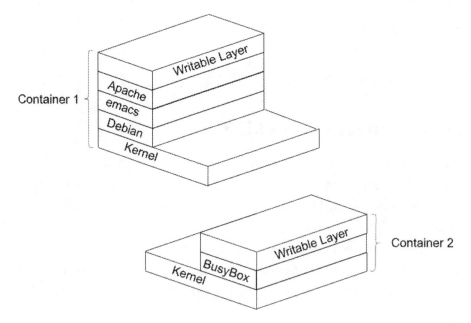

Figure 7-8. *Docker container isolation*

When a container starts, the initial read-write layer is empty. As changes occur, they are applied to this read-write layer, as shown in Figure 7-9.

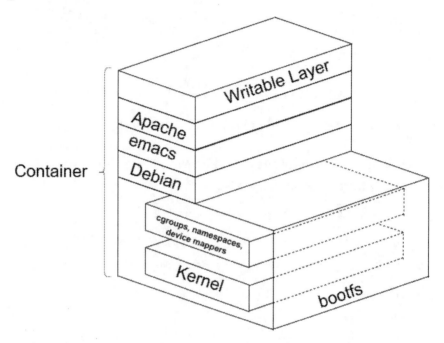

Figure 7-9. *Docker container write layer*

To make it clear, if you want to change a file, that file will be copied from the read-only layer below into the read-write layer. The read-only version of the file will still exist, but it will be hidden underneath the copy by the overlays above it. See Figure 7-10.

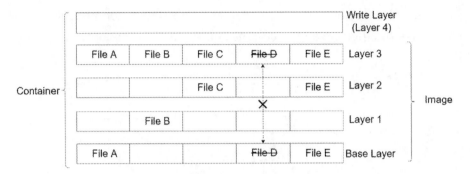

Figure 7-10. *The process of a Docker container write*

Each container can apply its own changes to its container read-write layer because they are isolated. See Figure 7-11.

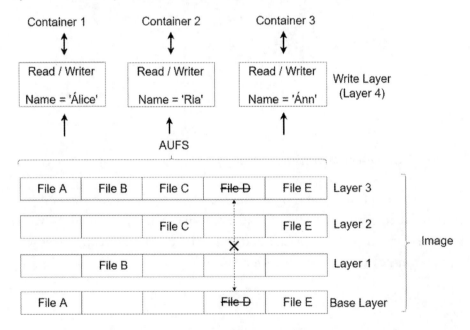

Figure 7-11. *The process of a Docker container copy on write*

This pattern is traditionally called "copy on write" and is one of the features that makes Docker so powerful. Each read-only image layer is read-only—these images never change. When a container is created,

296

Docker builds from the stack of images and adds the read-write layer on top. Figure 7-11 shows the process of adding data to a container. Once you make your changes and commit them using Docker, Docker creates a new image. This image contains only the differences from the base. When you want to run this new image, you can make changes to that container, as represented in Figure 7-12.

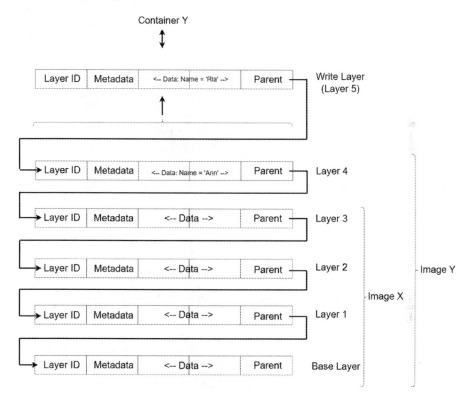

Figure 7-12. *The process of a Docker container commit*

Docker Registry

The Docker Registry is a repository that stores your Docker images (see Figure 7-13). It can be private or public, and it can be local or remote. A Docker Registry facilitates easy sharing of Docker images between different development environments and runtimes. Once you have built your image, you can either run it on the computer you've built it on, or you can push (upload) the image to a registry and subsequently pull (download) it to the same computer or to another computer and run it there.

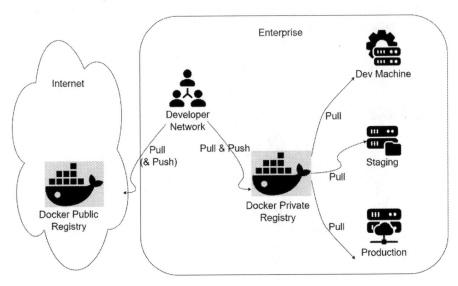

Figure 7-13. *The Docker Registry*

Docker Hub is an example of a public registry. Private registries can be set up using many methods, like a private Docker Registry on JFrog Bintray. There are also remote repositories, which serve as caching proxies for a Docker Registry managed at a remote site such as Docker Hub or JFrog Bintray. Images are stored and updated in remote Docker Registries according to various configuration parameters that control the caching and proxying behavior.

Development environment tools like JFrog Artifactory can act as intermediaries between developer machines and remote Docker Registries. Since they fully implement the Docker Registry API specification, they can act as proxies to any public or private Docker

Registry such as Docker Hub, JFrog Bintray, or other private Docker Registries. When an image is first requested by a developer machine, it is downloaded, and while doing this, Artifactory can store it in a local cache. Upon receiving subsequent requests for the image, Artifactory conducts a smart checksum search for it, and if the image has already been downloaded and is available in the local cache, the locally cached copy is provided. In this manner, each image is only downloaded once and is locally available to all other developers in the organization. This not only reduces network traffic but also effectively screens you from any issues with the network and other remote Docker Registries, thus providing you with a consistent, reliable, and continuous access to (remote) Docker images.

Hello World Tomcat in Docker

I'm sure you've read enough theory, so this section helps you learn by doing things. You will learn to run a "Docker Hello World" program in this section.

I assume that you have Docker Daemon running on your host. If not, refer to Appendix E to set up a Docker Daemon on your Mac machine (without Docker Desktop). If you have Docker Desktop on any of the OSes on your machine, that will also do.

Run Tomcat Container

The first step is to start the Minikube single-node Kubernetes cluster so that you have a Docker Daemon up (see Listing 7-1). Refer to Appendix E for a quick reference to the container commands.

Listing 7-1. Starting Minikube

```
(base) binildass-MacBook-Pro:~ binil$ pwd
/Users/binil
(base) binildass-MacBook-Pro:~ binil$ minikube start
  minikube v1.25.2 on Darwin 12.4
...
  Done! kubectl is now configured to use "minikube" cluster and
  "default" namespace by default
(base) binildass-MacBook-Pro:~ binil$
```

Next, set the Minikube environment variables in your work terminal as shown in Listing 7-2.

Listing 7-2. Setting Minikube Environment in Terminal

```
(base) binildass-MacBook-Pro:~ binil$ eval $(minikube
docker-env)
(base) binildass-MacBook-Pro:~ binil$
```

This points the Docker client toward Minikube's Docker environment since you are using the Docker Daemon in the Minikube VM. This setup is used for most of the Docker examples in this book. The minikube docker-env command returns a set of Bash environment variable exports to configure your local host environment to reuse the Docker Daemon inside the Minikube instance. Passing this output through eval causes bash to evaluate these exported variables and put them into effect. This will build the Docker image using Minikube's Docker instance and then push the image to Minikube's Docker Registry. It will also set up your deployment in Minikube to use this image. These variables will thus help your Docker CLI (where you write Docker commands) connect with the Docker Daemon in the VM created by the Minikube.

Instead, if you are using Docker Daemon from the Docker Desktop or a similar installation, you don't need to set up this environment configuration.

To list all the containers you have on your system, either running or stopped, execute the docker ps command shown in Listing 7-3.

Listing 7-3. Listing Docker Containers

```
(base) binildass-MacBook-Pro:~ binil$ docker ps
CONTAINER ID   IMAGE          COMMAND
CREATED         STATUS         PORTS    NAMES
24eea7cbd5b2   e1482a24335a   "/dashboard --insecu..."
5 minutes ago  Up 5 minutes              k8s_kubernetes-
c091fe0efebc   6e38f40d628d   "/storage-provisioner"
 5 minutes ago  Up 5 minutes              k8s_storage-
...
(base) binildass-MacBook-Pro:~ binil$ docker ps
```

The Docker client will list a table containing container IDs (a unique ID that you can use to refer to the container in other commands), creation date, the command used to start a container, status, exposed ports, and a name. The name can be assigned by you or Docker can pick an arbitrary name.

Next, you can run a container. To run a container, use this docker run command:

```
docker run [OPTIONS] IMAGE [COMMAND] [ARG...]
```

Listing 7-4 shows the code to bring up a Tomcat container.

Listing 7-4. Tomcat Container Starting Up

```
(base) binildass-MacBook-Pro:~ binil$ docker run -it -p
8080:8080 tomcat
Unable to find image 'tomcat:latest' locally
latest: Pulling from library/tomcat
67e8aa6c8bbc: Downloading
[========>                              ]    9.653MB/54.95MB
627e6c1e1055: Download complete
0670968926f6: Downloading
[====================================>] 8.059MB/10.88MB
5a8b0e20be4b: Downloading
[==>                                    ]   3.226MB/54.58MB
7a93fb438607: Waiting
400f1e54bef0: Waiting
f0b65b53f1a4: Waiting
dc9d1a029c69: Waiting
42a9874765c5: Waiting
52140cf8a5cf: Waiting
```

The stdin, stdout, and ttys are related concepts and an
understanding will help you. stdin and stdout are the input and output
streams of a process. A pseudo-terminal (also known as a tty or a pts)
connects a user's "terminal" with the stdin and stdout stream, commonly
(but not necessarily) through a shell such as bash. The word "terminal"
is used in quotes since we really don't use a terminal in the same
sense today.

As seen in Listing 7-4, you'll often use -t and -i together when you run
processes in interactive mode, such as when starting a bash shell. In the
case of the shell, your intention is to issue commands and read the output.

In Docker, the -i or --interactive (for keeping STDIN stream open, even if not attached) and -t or -tty (for attaching a pseudo-tty) switches are commonly used together as -it, which will help you allocate a pseudo -tty console for the process running in the container.

The -it combination will attach the command line to the container after it starts. This way you can see what's going on in the running container in your shell console and interact with the container, if needed.

When the command in Listing 7-4 is executed, Docker will determine if the image is available on your local machine. If it's not, the image will be pulled from the remote repository. The Docker engine uses the image and adds a writable layer on top of the image's layers stack. Subsequently, it initializes the image's name, ID, and resource limits, such as CPU and memory. In this phase, Docker will also set up the container's IP address by finding and attaching an available IP address from an IP pool. The last step of the execution is the actual command, passed as the last parameter of the docker run command. See Listing 7-5.

Listing 7-5. Tomcat Container Running

```
(base) binildass-MacBook-Pro:~ binil$ docker run -it -p
8080:8080 tomcat
Unable to find image 'tomcat:latest' locally
latest: Pulling from library/tomcat
67e8aa6c8bbc: Pull complete
627e6c1e1055: Pull complete
0670968926f6: Pull complete
5a8b0e20be4b: Pull complete
7a93fb438607: Pull complete
400f1e54bef0: Pull complete
f0b65b53f1a4: Pull complete
dc9d1a029c69: Pull complete
42a9874765c5: Pull complete
```

```
52140cf8a5cf: Pull complete
Digest: sha256:fe703c02e16ea7d3e8d7bdf5a0c03957f2d4a313cfa9
ae44878a3ad12e633ccf
Status: Downloaded newer image for tomcat:latest
Using CATALINA_BASE:   /usr/local/tomcat
Using CATALINA_HOME:   /usr/local/tomcat
Using CATALINA_TMPDIR: /usr/local/tomcat/temp
Using JRE_HOME:        /usr/local/openjdk-11
Using CLASSPATH:       /usr/local/tomcat/bin/bootstrap.jar:/
usr/local/tomcat/bin/tomcat-juli.jar
Using CATALINA_OPTS:
...
26-May-2022 14:33:47.952 INFO [main] org.apache.catalina.
startup.Catalina.start Server startup in [100] milliseconds
```

Listing 7-5 shows a Tomcat container running. Since the -it option has been used, Docker will capture and provide the container output, which is displayed in the console. When you run this command, Docker will install tomcat:latest from the Tomcat public repository hosted on Docker Hub and run the software. After Docker has installed and started running Tomcat, one line of seemingly random characters will be written to the terminal. This blob of characters is a unique identifier of the container that was just created to run Tomcat. Every time you invoke the docker run command and create a new container, that newly created container will get a unique identifier like this.

You can now list the Docker containers again, as shown in Listing 7-6.

Listing 7-6. Listing Docker Containers

```
(base) binildass-MacBook-Pro:~ binil$ docker ps
CONTAINER ID  IMAGE   COMMAND  CREATED  STATUS  PORTS    NAMES
5b621bcd9dd1  tomcat  "catalina.sh run"  About a minute
ago   Up About a minute   0.0.0.0:8080->8080/tcp
priceless_chebyshev
...
(base) binildass-MacBook-Pro:~ binil$
```

You can see the Tomcat container which you just started, along with other containers. To access Tomcat, as mentioned in Appendix E, you must get the minikube IP first. See Listing 7-7.

Listing 7-7. Finding Minikube IP

```
(base) binildass-MacBook-Pro:ch07-01 binil$ minikube ip
192.168.64.5
(base) binildass-MacBook-Pro:ch07-01 binil$
```

You can now access the Tomcat using the curl command, as shown in Listing 7-8.

Listing 7-8. Accessing Tomcat Container

```
(base) binildass-MacBook-Pro:ch07-01 binil$ curl
http://192.168.64.5:8080
HTTP Status 404 - Not Found...
(base) binildass-MacBook-Pro:ch07-01 binil$
```

You may also use a browser, as shown in Figure 7-14.

Figure 7-14. *Accessing "No Web App" in a Tomcat container*

You might think that you made a mistake while installing the Docker image when you see the 404 error. But this is not an error and it was designed to behave like this due to security concerns raised by the Docker community. You can find this security information on the Tomcat image official documentation in Docker Hub. See Figure 7-15.

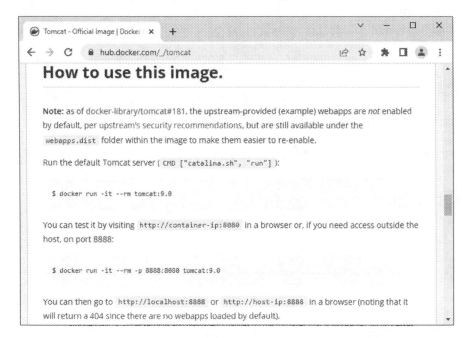

Figure 7-15. *Docker Tomcat notice*

You can stop the Tomcat container by using the code in Listing 7-9.

Listing 7-9. Stopping Tomcat Container

```
(base) binildass-MacBook-Pro:~ binil$ docker stop 5b62
5b62
(base) binildass-MacBook-Pro:~ binil$
```

Note that 5b62 are the first four characters of the container ID in Listing 7-6. This container, when stopped, will retain all settings and filesystem changes (in the top layer that is writeable). All processes running in the container will be stopped and you will lose everything in memory. If you now attempted to access the Tomcat using the curl command, you would get the response shown in Listing 7-10.

Listing 7-10. Attempt to Access Tomcat Container

```
(base) binildass-MacBook-Pro:~ binil$ curl
http://192.168.64.5:8080
curl: (7) Failed to connect to 192.168.64.5 port 8080:
Connection refused
(base) binildass-MacBook-Pro:~ binil$
```

Build and Run Java App without Java

The aim of this section is to compile, package, deploy, and run a Java app without a Java SDK or Java runtime in your development machine. How do you do that? You might have already guessed, since you are learning to use Docker, right? Use Docker!

Using a Maven Container

You can run the official Maven Docker image as a container and further compile, package, and deploy a Java application. Let's see how to use that here. First, set the Minikube environment variables in your terminal as mentioned in Listing 7-2. Next, run Docker, as shown in Listing 7-11.

Listing 7-11. Running Maven Container

```
(base) binildass-MacBook-Pro:~ binil$ docker run --rm -it maven
mvn --version
Unable to find image 'maven:latest' locally
latest: Pulling from library/maven
d5fd17ec1767: Pull complete
...
Status: Downloaded newer image for maven:latest
Apache Maven 3.8.5 (3599d3414f046de2324203b78ddcf9b5e4388aa0)
Maven home: /usr/share/maven
Java version: 17.0.3, vendor: Eclipse Adoptium, runtime: /opt/
java/openjdk
Default locale: en_US, platform encoding: UTF-8
OS name: "linux", version: "4.19.202", arch: "amd64",
family: "unix"
(base) binildass-MacBook-Pro:~ binil$
```

Listing 7-11 creates a Maven container and runs the maven command in it. The --rm parameter will remove the container once the command has been completed.

Creating a Maven Archetype

In this section, you create a new web application project Product Web of type maven-archetype-webapp. See Listing 7-12.

Listing 7-12. Creating maven-archetype-webapp with the Maven Container

```
(base) binildass-MacBook-Pro:~ binil$ docker run --rm -it -v
$(pwd):/workfolder -w /workfolder maven mvn archetype:
generate -DgroupId=com.acme.ecom.product -DartifactId=
ProductWeb -DarchetypeArtifactId=maven-archetype-webapp -Dintera
ctiveMode=false
[INFO] Scanning for projects...
Downloaded from central: ...
...
[INFO] ----------------------------------------------------------
[INFO] Using following parameters for creating project from Old
(1.x) Archetype: maven-archetype-webapp:1.0
[INFO] ----------------------------------------------------------
[INFO] Parameter: basedir, Value: /workfolder
[INFO] Parameter: package, Value: com.acme.ecom.product
[INFO] Parameter: groupId, Value: com.acme.ecom.product
[INFO] Parameter: artifactId, Value: ProductWeb
[INFO] Parameter: packageName, Value: com.acme.ecom.product
[INFO] Parameter: version, Value: 1.0-SNAPSHOT
[INFO] project created from Old (1.x) Archetype in dir:
/workfolder/ProductWeb
[INFO] ----------------------------------------------------------
[INFO] BUILD SUCCESS
[INFO] ----------------------------------------------------------
[INFO] Total time:  02:02 min
[INFO] Finished at: 2022-05-26T14:53:54Z
[INFO] ----------------------------------------------------------
(base) binildass-MacBook-Pro:~ binil$
```

-v $(pwd):/workfolder mounts the current directory as /workfolder
in the container. -w /workfolder changes the current working directory
for the container to /workfolder. When you run the -DartifactId=
ProductWeb command, you will have a new project with a new directory
called ProductWeb, which is created in the mounted volume. It's preserved
after you destroy the container, since the mounted directory is not within
the container but actually refers to a folder in the host machine.

There is a catch here. If you are using Docker Desktop or a similar
Docker Daemon, you will find the newly project created in the ProductWeb
folder in the host machine. However, this example uses a Docker Daemon
inside Minikube, so to see the newly created project, you need to look
inside the virtual machine hosting minikube. See Listing 7-13.

Listing 7-13. Log in to Minikube VM

```
(base) binildass-MacBook-Pro:~ binil$ pwd
/Users/binil
(base) binildass-MacBook-Pro:~ binil$ minikube ssh
```

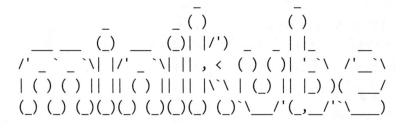

```
$ cd /Users/binil/binil/code/mac/mybooks/docker-03/ch07/ch07-01
$ ls
ProductWeb
$ cd ProductWeb/
$ ls
pom.xml   src
$
```

```
(base) binildass-MacBook-Pro:~ binil$ tree ProductWeb/
ProductWeb/
├── pom.xml
└── src
    └── main
        ├── resources
        └── webapp
            ├── WEB-INF
            │   └── web.xml
            └── index.jsp

5 directories, 3 files
(base) binildass-MacBook-Pro:~ binil$
```

Inside the Minikube host, this is inside the /Users/binil/binil/code/ mac/mybooks/docker-03/ch07/ch07-01 folder, since that's where the current working folder is (assuming that is your working folder). You might have to tweak it according to the path in your machine, since this example can be built and run from any folder.

Build and Package Using Maven Container

Here, you don't make any changes to the Maven web app project. You see how to build and package it. In a terminal where you set the Minikube environment variables, as mentioned in Listing 7-2, you can run Docker again, as shown in Listing 7-14.

Listing 7-14. Build and Package Web App Using Maven Container

```
(base) binildass-MacBook-Pro:~ binil$ docker run
--rm -it -v $(pwd)/ProductWeb:/DockerHostProductWeb -w /
DockerHostProductWeb maven:3.8.5-jdk-11 mvn clean package
[INFO] Scanning for projects...
```

```
[INFO]
[INFO] ---------< com.acme.ecom.product:ProductWeb01 >----
[INFO] Building ProductWeb Maven Webapp 1.0-SNAPSHOT
[INFO] ------------------------------[ war ]-----------
Downloading from central: https://repo.maven.apache.org/
maven2/...
...
[INFO] Packaging webapp
[INFO] Assembling webapp [ProductWeb01] in [/DockerHost
ProductWeb/target/ProductWeb]
[INFO] Processing war project
[INFO] Copying webapp resources [/DockerHostProductWeb/src/
main/webapp]
[INFO] Webapp assembled in [13 msecs]
[INFO] Building war: /DockerHostProductWeb/target/
ProductWeb.war
[INFO] WEB-INF/web.xml already added, skipping
[INFO] ---------------------------------------------------
[INFO] BUILD SUCCESS
[INFO] ---------------------------------------------------
[INFO] Total time:  02:07 min
[INFO] Finished at: 2022-05-26T17:17:19Z
[INFO] ---------------------------------------------------
(base) binildass-MacBook-Pro:~ binil$
```

Here, -v $(pwd)/ProductWeb:/DockerHostProductWeb will mount
the /Users/binil/binil/code/mac/mybooks/docker-03/ch07/ch07-01/
ProductWeb path as DockerHostProductWeb for the container. -w /
DockerHostProductWeb will set DockerHostProductWeb as the current
working directory, and the Maven container executes the command. The
command will create a directory called target in the location of your

project (inside /Users/binil/binil/code/mac/mybooks/docker-03/
ch07/ch07-01/ProductWeb in Minikube VM) and it should contain
your build. Since you set the artifact ID to be ProductWeb, it should look
something like Listing 7-15.

Listing 7-15. Web App Project Folder Exploded After Build

```
(base) binildass-MacBook-Pro:~ binil$ tree ProductWeb/
ProductWeb/
├── pom.xml
├── src
│   └── main
│       ├── resources
│       └── webapp
│           ├── WEB-INF
│           │   └── web.xml
│           └── index.jsp
└── target
    ├── ProductWeb
    │   ├── META-INF
    │   ├── WEB-INF
    │   │   ├── classes
    │   │   └── web.xml
    │   └── index.jsp
    ├── ProductWeb.war
    ├── classes
    └── maven-archiver
        └── pom.properties

12 directories, 7 files
(base) binildass-MacBook-Pro:~ binil$
```

Deploy Webapp Using Maven Container

You can simply add your application build to Tomcat's webapps directory (in the case of the official Docker image, that is /usr/local/tomcat/webapps) to deploy your app. Based on the build name added to the webapps directory, Tomcat maps this application to a specific route. If you were to add ProductWeb.war to webapps as product-web.war, you could access it on /product-web path for the Tomcat URL. If you want to deploy your application without any extra paths, you have to use an artefact named ROOT. See Listing 7-16.

Listing 7-16. Deploy Web App Project Using Maven Container

```
(base) binildass-MacBook-Pro:~ binil$ docker run -it -p
8080:8080 -v $(pwd)/ProductWeb/target/ProductWeb.war:/usr/
local/tomcat/webapps/productapp.war tomcat
Using CATALINA_BASE:   /usr/local/tomcat
Using CATALINA_HOME:   /usr/local/tomcat
Using CATALINA_TMPDIR: /usr/local/tomcat/temp
Using JRE_HOME:        /usr/local/openjdk-11
Using CLASSPATH:       /usr/local/tomcat/bin/bootstrap.jar:/
usr/local/tomcat/bin/tomcat-juli.jar
Using CATALINA_OPTS:
...
26-May-2022 17:41:34.052 INFO [main] org.apache.catalina.
startup.HostConfig.deployWAR Deploying web application archive
[/usr/local/tomcat/webapps/productapp.war]
26-May-2022 17:41:34.307 INFO [main] org.apache.catalina.
startup.HostConfig.deployWAR Deployment of web application
archive [/usr/local/tomcat/webapps/productapp.war] has finished
in [255] ms
```

26-May-2022 17:41:34.310 INFO [main] org.apache.coyote.
AbstractProtocol.start Starting ProtocolHandler ["http-nio-8080"]
26-May-2022 17:41:34.329 INFO [main] org.apache.catalina.
startup.Catalina.start Server startup in [339] milliseconds

In the previous section, you saw how to run a Tomcat container. Let's repeat that here again as in Listing 7-16. Note that the Tomcat image is not downloaded this time, since it's already downloaded, as in Listing 7-5. You can go to /productapp on port 8080 for your Docker environment and see the output of your web application using a browser, as shown in Figure 7-16.

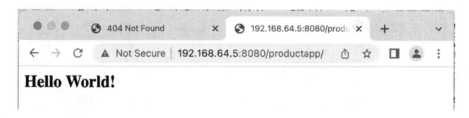

Figure 7-16. *Access a web app in the Tomcat container*

Note that 192.168.64.5 is the IP for the Minikube. You can also access the application using cURL, as in Listing 7-17.

Listing 7-17. Access Web App in Tomcat Using cURL

```
(base) binildass-MacBook-Pro:~ binil$ curl
http://192.168.64.5:8080/productapp/
<html>
<body>
<h2>Hello World!</h2>
</body>
</html>
(base) binildass-MacBook-Pro:~ binil$
```

Once that's done, you can stop the Tomcat container using the code in Listing 7-18.

Listing 7-18. Stopping Tomcat Container

```
(base) binildass-MacBook-Pro:~ binil$ docker ps
CONTAINER
ID   IMAGE     COMMAND              CREATED           STATUS
PORTS                         NAMES
a198aabd9464   tomcat  "catalina.sh run"   8 minutes ago
Up 8 minutes   0.0.0.0:8080->8080/tcp   happy_gould
..
(base) binildass-MacBook-Pro:~ binil$ docker stop a198
a198
(base) binildass-MacBook-Pro:~ binil$
```

That was a simple example to demonstrate how you can build, package, deploy, and run a Java application without even having Java installed on your host machine! The next section moves to the next concept—Docker Compose.

Build and Run Java App with Docker Compose

The objective here is to compile, package, deploy, and run a Java app using Docker Compose. I include more details and examples of Docker Compose in a later chapter. Let's just run this example for the completion of our discussion.

Using Docker Compose

The source code for this book is available on GitHub via the book's product page, located at www.apress.com/9798868805547. The code for this example is organized inside the ch07\ch07-01 folder. Refer to Appendix E on Docker to make sure you have installed Docker Compose. Docker Compose uses the file shown in Listing 7-19.

Listing 7-19. Docker Compose YML File

```
version: '2'
services:
    web:
        image: tomcat
        ports:
            - "8080:8080"
        volumes:
            - ./ProductWeb/target/ProductWeb.war:
                /usr/local/tomcat/webapps/ROOT.war
            - ./ProductWeb/target/ProductWeb:
                /usr/local/tomcat/webapps/ROOT
```

If you want to deploy your application without any extra paths, you have to place an artifact named ROOT. That is done by the directory mounting in Listing 7-19. Then you run Docker to package, as in an earlier example, and subsequently run docker-compose, both commands in one go. docker-compose will fetch the docker-compose.yml, as shown in Listing 7-20.

Listing 7-20. Run Tomcat Container using Docker Compose

```
(base) binildass-MacBook-Pro:ch07-01 binil$ docker
run --rm -it -v $(pwd)/ProductWeb:/ProductWebDockerHost -w /
ProductWebDockerHost maven:3.8.5-jdk-11 mvn package && docker-
compose up
[INFO] Scanning for projects...
[INFO]
[INFO] ------< com.acme.ecom.product:ProductWeb >--------

WARNING: All illegal access operations will be denied in a
future release
[INFO] Packaging webapp
[INFO] Assembling webapp [ProductWeb] in [/ProductWebDocker
Host/target/ProductWeb]
[INFO] Processing war project
[INFO] Copying webapp resources [/ProductWebDockerHost/src/
main/webapp]
[INFO] Webapp assembled in [16 msecs]
[INFO] Building war: /ProductWebDockerHost/target/
ProductWeb.war
[INFO] WEB-INF/web.xml already added, skipping
[INFO] ------------------------------------------------
[INFO] BUILD SUCCESS
[INFO] ------------------------------------------------
[INFO] Total time:  01:56 min
[INFO] Finished at: 2022-05-26T18:04:38Z
[INFO] ------------------------------------------------
[+] Running 2/0
 ⠿ Network ch07-01_default  Created                0.1s
 ⠿ Container ch07-01-web-1   Created                0.0s
Attaching to ch07-01-web-1
```

...
ch07-01-web-1 | 26-May-2022 18:04:40.683 INFO [main] org.
apache.catalina.startup.HostConfig.deployWAR Deploying web
application archive [/usr/local/tomcat/webapps/ROOT.war]
ch07-01-web-1 | 26-May-2022 18:04:41.016 INFO [main] org.
apache.catalina.startup.HostConfig.deployWAR Deployment of web
application archive [/usr/local/tomcat/webapps/ROOT.war] has
finished in [333] ms
ch07-01-web-1 | 26-May-2022 18:04:41.020 INFO [main] org.
apache.coyote.AbstractProtocol.start Starting ProtocolHandler
["http-nio-8080"]
ch07-01-web-1 | 26-May-2022 18:04:41.054 INFO [main] org.
apache.catalina.startup.Catalina.start Server startup in [465]
milliseconds

Next, access the application http://192.168.64.5:8080. See
Figure 7-17.

Figure 7-17. *Access the web app in a Tomcat container*

You can also access the application using cURL, as shown in
Listing 7-21.

Listing 7-21. Access Web App in Tomcat Container Using cURL

```
(base) binildass-MacBook-Pro:ch07-01 binil$ curl
http://192.168.64.5:8080/
<html>
<body>
<h2>Hello World!</h2>
</body>
</html>
(base) binildass-MacBook-Pro:ch07-01 binil$
```

Build the First Java Microservice with Docker

In this section, you investigate using Docker to deploy a more serious microservice. For that, you use the same microservice deployed in the section titled "Your First Java Microservice" in Chapter 1.

Dockerizing the Microservice Using Jib

Jib is an open-source Java tool maintained by Google for building Docker images of Java-based applications. Jib simplifies containerization, since with it, you don't need to write a Dockerfile (you will learn what a Dockerfile is in the next section), which you saw in the previous example. Moreover, you don't even have to have Docker installed to create and publish Docker Images. Google publishes Jib as both a Maven and a Gradle plugin—you use Maven here.

Understanding the Source Code

The source code for this book is available on GitHub via the book's product page, located at www.apress.com/9798868805547. The code for this example is organized inside the ch07\ch07-02 folder. Much of the source code in this example is similar to that in ch01\ch01-01. This section does not discuss the code of the microservice since it's described in Chapter 1, but it does look into the deployment aspects. Jib will catch any changes you make to the source code of your application each time you build. This saves you separate Docker build/push commands and simplifies adding this to a CI pipeline, but I do not expand on those aspects. You also need to set yourself up locally to authenticate with the Docker repository you want to deploy to. This is done in the Maven settings.xml file, as shown in Listing 7-22.

Listing 7-22. Maven Settings File

```
(base) binildass-MacBook-Pro:~ binil$ vi /Users/binil/.m2/
settings.xml
...
<settings>
    </servers>
        <server>
            <id>registry.hub.docker.com</id>
            <username>binildas</username>
            <password>********</password>
        </server>
    </servers>
</settings>
...
(base) binildass-MacBook-Pro:~ binil$
```

As you might have guessed, I created an account in the Docker Hub public repository, whose credentials I configured in Listing 7-22. Further, the Maven plugin configuration is shown in Listing 7-23.

Listing 7-23. The Maven Module Configurations (ch07\ch07-02\ pom.xml)

```
<?xml version="1.0" encoding="UTF-8"?>
<project>
    <build>
        <pluginManagement>
            <plugins>
                <plugin>
                    <groupId>com.google.cloud.tools</groupId>
                    <artifactId>jib-maven-plugin</artifactId>
                    <version>3.4.1</version>
                </plugin>
            </plugins>
        </pluginManagement>
    </build>
</project>
```

Jib makes a number of reasonable guesses about what you want, like the FROM and the ENTRYPOINT (which you look at next section). Spring Boot exposes port 8080 by default, but if you want to make your application run on port 8081 and make it exposable through a container, you can do this by configuring jib and making appropriate changes in Boot. Further, you can use Jib to make it exposable in the image. Also, by default, Jib uses the distro-less Java image. If you want to run the application on a different base image, such as alpine-java, you can configure it in a similar way. This section does not go into any of these options, but shows the Docker Hub configuration alone, as in Listing 7-24.

Listing 7-24. The Maven Build Configurations (ch07\ch07-02\02-
ProductWeb\pom.xml)

```xml
<?xml version="1.0" encoding="UTF-8"?>
<project>
    <build>
        <plugins>
            <plugin>
                <groupId>org.springframework.boot</groupId>
                <artifactId>
                    spring-boot-maven-plugin
                </artifactId>
            </plugin>
            <plugin>
                <groupId>com.google.cloud.tools</groupId>
                <artifactId>jib-maven-plugin</artifactId>
                <version>3.2.0</version>
                <configuration>
                    <to>
                        <image>
                registry.hub.docker.com/binildas/product-web
                        </image>
                    </to>
                </configuration>
            </plugin>
        </plugins>
    </build>
</project>
```

Build and Push Images to Docker Hub

The ch07\ch07-02 folder contains the Maven scripts required to build, containerize, and push an image to Docker Hub.

With the Jib plugin, you can use your local Docker instance to build the image from the configuration using this command:

```
mvn compile jib:dockerBuild
```

However, you can even build your image without the locally running Docker:

```
mvn compile jib:build
```

This is shown in Listing 7-25.

Listing 7-25. Build and Create an Image of Product Server Microservice and Push the Image

```
(base) binildass-MacBook-Pro:ch07-02 binil$ pwd
/Users/binil/binil/code/mac/mybooks/docker-04/ch07/ch07-02
(base) binildass-MacBook-Pro:ch07-02 binil$ mvn compile
jib:build
[INFO] Scanning for projects...
...
[INFO] Containerizing application to registry.hub.docker.com/
binildas/product-web...
[WARNING] Base image 'eclipse-temurin:8-jre' does not use a
specific image digest - build may not be reproducible
[INFO] Using credentials from Maven settings file for registry.
hub.docker.com/binildas/product-web
[INFO] The base image requires auth. Trying again for eclipse-
temurin:8-jre...
[WARNING] The system does not have docker-credential-
desktop CLI
```

[WARNING]   Caused by: Cannot run program "docker-credential-
desktop": error=20, Not a directory
...
[INFO] Using base image with digest: sha256:ca34c4ad9cb6b4fcbfb
1ee24c94539901a6266fa585bef4ecfb57bc53468f6f9
[INFO]
[INFO] Container entrypoint set to [java, -cp, /app/
resources:/app/classes:/app/libs/*, com.acme.ecom.product.
EcomProductMicroserviceApplication]
[INFO]
[INFO] Built and pushed image as registry.hub.docker.com/
binildas/product-webNFO]
...
[INFO] -< com.acme.ecom.product:Ecom-Product-Microservice >-
[INFO] Building Ecom
0.0.1-SNAPSHOT   [2/2]
[INFO] -----------------------------[pom]------------
[INFO]
[INFO] --- jib-maven-plugin:3.2.0:build (default-cli) @ Ecom-
Product-Microservice ---
[INFO] Skipping containerization because packaging is 'pom'...
[INFO] ---
[INFO] Reactor Summary for Ecom 0.0.1-SNAPSHOT:
[INFO]
[INFO] Ecom-Product-Web-Microservice ....
SUCCESS [01:52 min]
[INFO] Ecom ....
SUCCESS [0.064 s]
[INFO] ---
[INFO] BUILD SUCCESS
[INFO] ---

```
[INFO] Total time:  01:52 min
[INFO] Finished at: 2022-05-27T10:30:39+05:30
[INFO] -----------------------------------------------------
(base) binildass-MacBook-Pro:ch07-02 binil$
```

Executing this Maven build will build the Docker image without using your Docker Daemon and will push the image to Docker Hub.

Docker Hub Registry and Repository

As described previously, the component in Docker's distribution system is the registry. Images that you build can be pushed and stored in a remote registry for others to use. The Docker Hub is an example of the publicly available registry. It is free and serves a huge, constantly growing collection of existing images. See Figure 7-18.

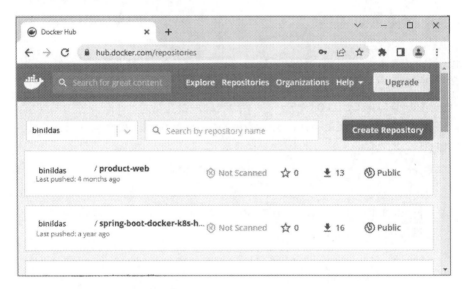

Figure 7-18. *Docker Hub Registry*

Figure 7-18 shows the Docker Hub registry login interface and many image repositories in it. The repository is a collection (namespace) of related images, which provides different versions of the same application or service. It's a collection of different Docker images with the same name and different tags. product-web is one such repository that I pushed as a result of the jib build command in Listing 7-25. Since the app is named product-web and my username (or namespace) for the registry is binildas, this image is placed in the binildas/product-web repository. See Figure 7-19.

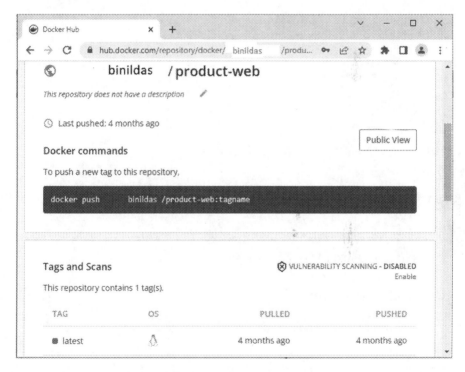

Figure 7-19. *Docker repository*

You can select a specific tag of a repository and delete it. See Figure 7-20.

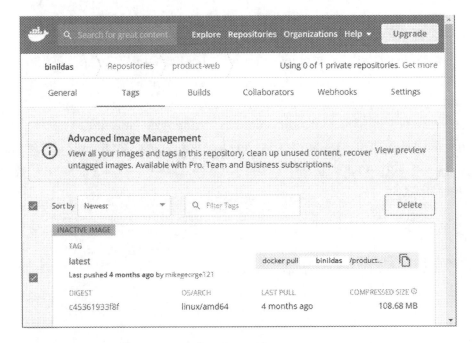

Figure 7-20. *Deleting a Docker Repository*

Pull Image and Run Container

The next step is to start the Minikube single-node Kubernetes cluster so that you have a Docker Daemon up. See Listing 7-26.

Listing 7-26. Start Minikube

```
(base) binildass-MacBook-Pro:ch07-02 binil$ minikube start
...
(base) binildass-MacBook-Pro:ch07-02 binil$
```

Next, set the Minikube environment variables in your terminal, as shown in Listing 7-27.

Listing 7-27. Setting Minikube Environment

```
(base) binildass-MacBook-Pro:ch07-02 binil$ pwd
/Users/binil/binil/code/mac/mybooks/docker-04/ch07/ch07-02
(base) binildass-MacBook-Pro:ch07-02 binil$ eval
$(minikube docker-env)
(base) binildass-MacBook-Pro:ch07-02 binil$
```

Next, we will run the Product Web microservice in Docker.

Listing 7-28. Running Product Web Microservice using Docker

```
(base) binildass-MacBook-Pro:ch07-02 binil$ docker run -it -p
8080:8080 binildas/product-web
Unable to find image ' binildas /product-web:latest' locally
latest: Pulling from binildas/product-web
125a6e411906: Pull complete
42222acc001c: Pull complete
4da85a7c2f39: Pull complete
ebcc7b1a7ad2: Pull complete
4edc7728a946: Pull complete
9a2bc4698b49: Pull complete
68af01cc5861: Pull complete
f3636ebea575: Pull complete
Digest: sha256:56254d5a6e84cbe625013d245d8fa7dfe157722d0a6dd5
0d434f8e63dfc339ad
Status: Downloaded newer image for binildas/product-web:latest
```

```
  .   ____          _            __ _ _
 /\\ / ___'_ __ _ _(_)_ __  __ _ \ \ \ \
( ( )\___ | '_ | '_| | '_ \/ _` | \ \ \ \
 \\/  ___)| |_)| | | | | || (_| |  ) ) ) )
  '  |____| .__|_| |_|_| |_\__, | / / / /
 =========|_|==============|___/=/_/_/_/
 :: Spring Boot ::                (v3.0.6)
```

329

```
2022-05-27 05:12:40 INFO  StartupInfoLogger.logStarting:55 -
Starting EcomProductMicroserviceA...
2022-05-27 05:12:40 DEBUG StartupInfoLogger.logStarting:56 -
Running with Spring Boot ...
2022-05-27 05:12:40 INFO  SpringApplication.
logStartupProfileInfo:662 - No active ...
2022-05-27 05:12:41 INFO  InitializationComponent.
init:37 - Start
2022-05-27 05:12:41 DEBUG InitializationComponent.init:39 -
Doing Nothing...
2022-05-27 05:12:41 INFO  InitializationComponent.init:41 - End
2022-05-27 05:12:42 INFO  StartupInfoLogger.logStarted:61 -
Started EcomProductMicroservice...
2022-05-27 05:16:03 INFO  ProductRestController.
getAllProducts:63 - Start
2022-05-27 05:16:03 DEBUG ProductRestController.
lambda$getAllProducts$0:73 - Product [productId=1, ...
2022-05-27 05:16:03 DEBUG ProductRestController.
lambda$getAllProducts$0:73 - Product [productId=2, ...
```

In the step in Listing 7-28, I built using Jib so I directly pushed the Product Web microservice image to Docker Hub. No traces of that is in the local registry. Why, when I attempted to run the Product Web microservice in Docker in Listing 7-28, did it first pull the image to the local registry and then start the container? You can now inspect the Docker Registry, where you will find that the image has been pulled from Docker Hub and is made available in the local registry. See Listing 7-29.

Listing 7-29. Inspecting Local Docker Registry

```
(base) binildass-MacBook-Pro:ch07-02 binil$ docker images
REPOSITORY              TAG     IMAGE ID        CREATED         SIZE
...
binildas/product-web   latest  b547edfdc0be    52 years ago    247MB
(base) binildass-MacBook-Pro:ch07-02 binil$
```

Ignore the label that the image has been created "52 years ago," I am not sure why it's displayed so. Once the container is running, you can list the running containers, as shown in Listing 7-30.

Listing 7-30. List the Running Containers

```
(base) binildass-MacBook-Pro:ch07-02 binil$ docker ps
CONTAINER ID    IMAGE                   COMMAND
CREATED         STATUS       PORTS                  NAMES
e95b2b5eb64e    binildas/product-web    "java -cp /app/resou..."
6 minutes ago   Up 6 minutes  0.0.0.0:8080->8080/tcp   loving_williams
...
(base) binildass-MacBook-Pro:ch07-02 binil$
```

To access the Product Web microservice, as mentioned in Appendix E, you have to get the minikube IP first, which is done in Listing 7-31.

Listing 7-31. Finding Minikube IP

```
(base) binildass-MacBook-Pro:ch07-02 binil$ minikube ip
192.168.64.5
(base) binildass-MacBook-Pro:ch07-02 binil$
```

You can now access the Product Web microservice using your browser with the URL formed with the Minikube IP. See Figure 7-21.

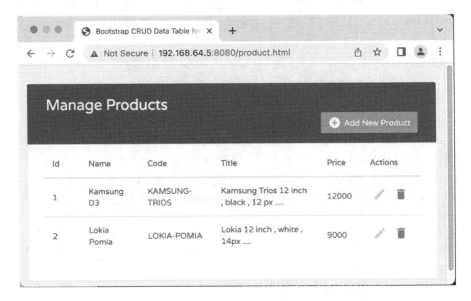

Figure 7-21. *Testing Product Web microservice container*

Refer to the section titled "Test the Microservice using UI" in Chapter 1 to test the Product Web microservice container.

You can now stop the Product Web microservice container, as shown in Listing 7-32.

Listing 7-32. Stopping Product Web Microservice Container

```
(base) binildass-MacBook-Pro:ch07-02 binil$ docker stop e95b
e95b
(base) binildass-MacBook-Pro:ch07-02 binil$
```

Note that e95b are the first four characters of the ID of the Product Web Microservice container shown in Listing 7-30.

You can now remove the Product Web microservice container, as shown in Listing 7-33.

Listing 7-33. Removing Product Web Microservice Container

```
(base) binildass-MacBook-Pro:ch07-02 binil$ docker rm e95b
e95b
(base) binildass-MacBook-Pro:ch07-02 binil$
```

You can also remove the Product Web Microservice image from the local Docker Registry, as shown in Listing 7-34.

Listing 7-34. Removing Product Web Microservice Image

```
(base) binildass-MacBook-Pro:ch07-02 binil$ docker rmi b547
Untagged: binildas/product-web:latest
Untagged: binildas/product-web@sha256:56254d5a6e84cbe625013d24
5d8fa7dfe157722d0a6dd50d434f8e63dfc339ad
Deleted: sha256:b547edfdc0be94d5a44b168ff13f515aa916d63534a
2d6075e000ab829a363e8
...
(base) binildass-MacBook-Pro:ch07-02 binil$
```

Again note that b547 are the first four characters of the ID of the Product Web Microservice image in Listing 7-29.

Build a Microservice Using a Dockerfile

This section explains how to deploy a microservice using a Dockerfile. It uses the same microservice deployed in the section titled "Your First Java Microservice" in Chapter 1.

Dockerfiles

A *Dockerfile* is a recipe using a plain text file to build a Docker Image. Each Dockerfile specifies a base image that the Docker engine will use to build upon. The Dockerfile then contains a series of instructions on how to build the image. You instruct Docker to create a Docker image based on the Dockerfile. The docker build command runs within a build context. The build's context has the files at a specified location, which can be a PATH or an URL. The PATH is a directory in your local filesystem and the URL is a Git repository location. The context is processed recursively. PATH also includes any subdirectories. The URL will include the repository and its submodules.

Understanding the Source Code

The source code for this book is available on GitHub via the book's product page, located at www.apress.com/9798868805547. The code for this example is organized inside the ch07\ch07-03 folder. Much of the source code in this example is similar to the code in ch01\ch01-01. Hence, this section does not review the microservice code. It looks at several deployment aspects, especially those using the Dockerfile. See Listing 7-35.

Listing 7-35. The Dockerfile (ch07\ch07-03\Dockerfile)

```
FROM openjdk:8-jdk-alpine
VOLUME /tmp
ARG JAR_FILE
COPY ${JAR_FILE} ecom.jar
ENTRYPOINT ["java","-jar","/ecom.jar"]
```

This Dockerfile contains the following information:

- FROM: As the base for this image, you'll take the Java-enabled Alpine Linux by openjdk, an official repository containing an open-source implementation of the Java platform, Standard Edition.

- VOLUME: This points to /tmp, because that is where the Spring Boot application creates working directories by default. The effect is to create a temporary file on your host under /var/lib/docker and link it to the container under /tmp. This is essential when running the container as a non-root user.

- ARG: This is also known as a build-time variable. They are only available from the moment they are "announced" in the Dockerfile with an ARG instruction until the moment the image is built. Running containers can't access values of ARG variables.

- COPY: Docker copies the Jar file into the image.

- ENTRYPOINT: This will be the executable to start when the container is booting. Defined as JSON-Array since you'll use an ENTRYPOINT in combination with a CMD for some application arguments.

The single script in Listing 7-36 is used to automate this build process.

Listing 7-36. The Docker Build Script (ch07\ch07-03\ makeandrun.sh)

```
mvn -Dmaven.test.skip=true clean package
docker build  --build-arg JAR_FILE=02-ProductWeb/target/
*.jar -t binildas/product-web .
docker push binildas/product-web
```

```
sleep 10
docker rmi binildas/product-web
sleep 10
docker run -p 8080:8080  --name product-web binildas/
product-web
```

Build and Run the Microservice Using a Dockerfile

The next step is to start the Minikube single-node Kubernetes cluster so that you have a Docker Daemon up. See Listing 7-37.

Listing 7-37. Starting Minikube

```
(base) binildass-MacBook-Pro:ch07-03 binil$ minikube start
...
(base) binildass-MacBook-Pro:ch07-03 binil$
```

Next, set the Minikube environment variables in your terminal, as shown in Listing 7-38.

Listing 7-38. Setting Minikube Environment in Terminal

```
(base) binildass-MacBook-Pro:ch07-03 binil$ pwd
/Users/binil/binil/code/mac/mybooks/docker-04/ch07/ch07-03
(base) binildass-MacBook-Pro:ch07-03 binil$ eval $(minikube
docker-env)
(base) binildass-MacBook-Pro:ch07-03 binil$
```

Next, you can try to run the Product Web microservice in Docker. As you see in Listing 7-36, you use the docker push command. To facilitate this, you need to log in to Docker Hub in your current terminal. See Listing 7-39.

Listing 7-39. Log in to Docker Terminal

```
(base) binildass-MacBook-Pro:ch07-03 binil$ docker login
Login with your Docker ID to push and pull images from Docker
Hub. If you don't have a Docker ID, head over to https://hub.
docker.com to create one.
Username: binildas
Password:
Error saving credentials: error storing credentials - err:
exec: "docker-credential-desktop": executable file not found in
$PATH, out: ``
(base) binildass-MacBook-Pro:ch07-03 binil$
```

The error in Listing 7-39 happens because you are not dealing with the host filesystem, but with the filesystem in your Minikube VM. Hence, if you try to push the Docker Image to Docker Hub, you might not be successful. See Listing 7-40.

Listing 7-40. Log in to Docker Terminal

```
(base) binildass-MacBook-Pro:ch07-03 binil$ sh makeandrun.sh

(base) binildass-MacBook-Pro:ch07-03 binil$ pwd
/Users/binil/binil/code/mac/mybooks/docker-04/ch07/ch07-03
(base) binildass-MacBook-Pro:ch07-03 binil$ docker push
binildas/product-web
Using default tag: latest
The push refers to repository [docker.io/binildas/product-web]
2c54cf7f9c27: Preparing
ceaf9e1ebef5: Preparing
9b9b7f3d56a0: Preparing
f1b5933fe4b5: Preparing
denied: requested access to the resource is denied
(base) binildass-MacBook-Pro:ch07-03 binil$
```

As mentioned, there is an error in Listing 7-40, so set aside the makeandrun.sh automation script and try this manually, step by step. See Listings 7-41 and 7-42.

Listing 7-41. Build and Package Product Web Microservice

```
(base) binildass-MacBook-Pro:ch07-03 binil$ pwd
/Users/binil/binil/code/mac/mybooks/docker-04/ch07/ch07-03
(base) binildass-MacBook-Pro:ch07-03 binil$ mvn -Dmaven.test.
skip=true clean package
[INFO] Scanning for projects...
...
[INFO] Ecom-Product-Web-Microservice ... SUCCESS [  1.622 s]
[INFO] Ecom ......................... SUCCESS [  0.017 s]
[INFO] ------------------------------------------------
[INFO] BUILD SUCCESS
[INFO] ------------------------------------------------
[INFO] Total time:  1.796 s
[INFO] Finished at: 2022-05-27T11:50:50+05:30
[INFO] ------------------------------------------------
(base) binildass-MacBook-Pro:ch07-03 binil$
```

Listing 7-42. Build an Image of Product Web Microservice

```
(base) binildass-MacBook-Pro:ch07-03 binil$ docker
build  --build-arg JAR_FILE=02-ProductWeb/target/*.jar -t
binildas/product-web .
Sending build context to Docker daemon  21.68MB
Step 1/5 : FROM openjdk:8-jdk-alpine
---> a3562aa0b991
Step 2/5 : VOLUME /tmp
---> Running in b33ed0a15fb0
```

```
Removing intermediate container b33ed0a15fb0
---> 388ef9de0cd0
Step 3/5 : ARG JAR_FILE
---> Running in cdab850cc040
Removing intermediate container cdab850cc040
---> 9c06159a60bf
Step 4/5 : COPY ${JAR_FILE} ecom.jar
---> 9ed33fae3b42
Step 5/5 : ENTRYPOINT ["java","-jar","/ecom.jar"]
---> Running in 0949e3c49a48
Removing intermediate container 0949e3c49a48
---> 079251d7b3b0
Successfully built 079251d7b3b0
Successfully tagged binildas/product-web:latest
(base) binildass-MacBook-Pro:ch07-03 binil$
```

Since you utilized the Docker Daemon in Minikube (refer to Appendix E), the image is crated in the local registry of the Docker Daemon. You should also push this to Docker Hub. Since you are not dealing with the host filesystem but with the one in your Minikube VM, you need to log in to the VM and execute the push. See Listing 7-43.

Listing 7-43. Push Image of Product Web Microservice

```
(base) binildass-MacBook-Pro:ch07-03 binil$ pwd
/Users/binil/binil/code/mac/mybooks/docker-04/ch07/ch07-03
(base) binildass-MacBook-Pro:ch07-03 binil$ minikube ssh
```

```
$ docker login
Login with your Docker ID to push and pull images from Docker
Hub. If you don't have a Docker ID, head over to https://hub.
docker.com to create one.
Username: binildas
Password:
WARNING! Your password will be stored unencrypted in /home/
docker/.docker/config.json.
Configure a credential helper to remove this warning. See
https://docs.docker.com/engine/reference/commandline/
login/#credentials-store

Login Succeeded
$ docker push binildas/product-web
Using default tag: latest
The push refers to repository [docker.io/binildas/product-web]
2c54cf7f9c27: Pushed
ceaf9e1ebef5: Layer already exists
9b9b7f3d56a0: Layer already exists
f1b5933fe4b5: Layer already exists
latest: digest: sha256:420cc888c575f695b5f2b84092b6bfa73d153
bc0937cb846a28366ff14fa1f04 size: 1159
$ exit
logout
(base) binildass-MacBook-Pro:ch07-03 binil$
```

To make sure you actually pushed the image, you can remove the local
image and attempt to run the Product Web microservice container, as
shown in Listing 7-44.

Listing 7-44. Remove Image of Product Web Microservice
from Local

```
(base) binildass-MacBook-Pro:ch07-03 binil$ pwd
/Users/binil/binil/code/mac/mybooks/docker-04/ch07/ch07-03
(base) binildass-MacBook-Pro:ch07-03 binil$ docker rmi
binildas/product-web
Untagged: binildas/product-web:latest
Untagged: binildas/product-web@sha256:420cc888c575f695b5f2b8409
2b6bfa73d153bc0937cb846a28366ff14fa1f04
Deleted: sha256:079251d7b3b01df698620fc9648125c62b220de7f03
1e3610d06970d994ca2ed
...
(base) binildass-MacBook-Pro:ch07-03 binil$
```

Next, run the Microservice container, as shown in Listing 7-45.

Listing 7-45. Run Product Web Microservice Container

```
(base) binildass-MacBook-Pro:ch07-03 binil$ docker run -p
8080:8080  --name product-web binildas/product-web
Unable to find image 'binildas/product-web:latest' locally
latest: Pulling from binildas/product-web
e7c96db7181b: Already exists
f910a506b6cb: Already exists
c2274a1a0e27: Already exists
fa880b6dd374: Pull complete
Digest: sha256:420cc888c575f695b5f2b84092b6bfa73d153bc0937cb84
6a28366ff14fa1f04
Status: Downloaded newer image for binildas/product-web:latest
```

```
  .   ____          _            __ _ _
 /\\ / ___'_ __ _ _(_)_ __  __ _ \ \ \ \
( ( )\___ | '_ | '_| | '_ \/ _` | \ \ \ \
 \\/  ___)| |_)| | | | | || (_| |  ) ) ) )
  '  |____| .__|_| |_|_| |_\__, | / / / /
 =========|_|==============|___/=/_/_/_/
 :: Spring Boot ::                (v3.0.6)
```

2022-05-27 06:40:30 INFO StartupInfoLogger.logStarting:55 -
Starting EcomProductMicroservice...
2022-05-27 06:40:30 DEBUG StartupInfoLogger.logStarting:56 -
Running with Spring Boot ...
2022-05-27 06:40:30 INFO SpringApplication.
logStartupProfileInfo:662 - No active ...
2022-05-27 06:40:31 INFO InitializationComponent.
init:37 - Start
2022-05-27 06:40:31 DEBUG InitializationComponent.init:39 -
Doing Nothing...
2022-05-27 06:40:31 INFO InitializationComponent.init:41 - End
2022-05-27 06:40:32 INFO StartupInfoLogger.logStarted:61 -
Started EcomProductMicroser...
2022-05-27 06:42:49 DEBUG ProductRestController.
lambda$getAllProducts$0:73 - Product [productId=1...
2022-05-27 06:42:49 DEBUG ProductRestController.
lambda$getAllProducts$0:73 - Product [productId=2...

In Listing 7-45, you are pulling the image from the Docker Hub Registry. You can now access the Product Web microservice using a browser with the URL formed with the Minikube IP:

http://192.168.64.5:8080/product.html

Summary

Containers are great at packaging, shipping, and getting the code executed from a target environment without having to set many application-specific settings on the target machine. You can treat a container as a black box. To demonstrate that, this chapter included examples of building, packaging, and executing Java code without a local Java SDK, but with just a Maven in a container! You also learned about various ways to handle containers in order to interact with simple microservices. You are now in a better position to appreciate what a container is. The next chapter covers more serious microservices, also using containers.

CHAPTER 8

Microservice Containers

The initial chapters introduced microservices, which are self-contained, independent application units, each fulfilling related business functionalities from a specific domain. Each of them, or a collection of them together, can be considered an application in its own. In a multi-microservice application, you create many microservices for your app. What if you decide to build several microservices with different technology stacks? Your team will soon be in trouble, as developers have to manage even more environments than they would have been dealing with in a classical monolithic application development scenario. With Docker, it's possible to manage, deploy, and even reduce performance overhead of hundreds if not thousands of microservices on the same server. Docker containers require fewer computing resources than virtual machines, and containers also provide required isolation so that disparate technologies can coexist, side by side. Thus, containers are a natural fit with microservices.

© Binildas A. Christudas 2024
B. A. Christudas, *Java Microservices and Containers in the Cloud,*
https://doi.org/10.1007/979-8-8688-0555-4_8

Chapter 7 introduced how to run application containers using Docker images. This chapter continues that discussion, but with microservices examples that reflect real-life scenarios. Multiple microservices will interact, which means they need to communicate with each other. This chapter covers the following concepts:

- Microservice containers connecting with each other

- Microservice containers connecting to a PostgreSQL database on a host machine

- Microservice containers connecting to PostgreSQL in a container

- Microservice containers connecting to MongoDB in a container

To understand inter-container communications, you need to understand the networking options between containers, which is covered next.

Container Networking

Docker provides different ways to configure networking so that your containers can communicate with the outside world, whether with another server or with another Docker container. The next section briefly looks at these options.

Links

When you install Docker, Docker defaults to a bridge network that is created automatically. Docker's networking subsystem is pluggable, using drivers. Before Docker introduced the networking feature, the Docker link feature enabled containers to discover each other and securely transfer information about one container to another. With the introduction of the Docker networking feature, you can still create links, but they behave differently compared to the default bridge network and the other user-defined networks. Even though the link option works, it is a legacy feature. The first example uses links; however, this feature may eventually be removed so you are advised to use other options (network) for this functionality. One feature that user-defined networks do not support, which you can do with a link today, is share environment variables between containers. But volumes provide better options to share environment variables between containers in a more controlled way.

Networks

There are multiple types of networks. I only mention them here because detailed explanations are beyond the scope of this book.

- Bridge networks are best when you need multiple containers to communicate on the same Docker host.

- Host networks are best when the network stack should not be isolated from the Docker host, but you want other aspects of the container to be isolated.

- Overlay networks are best when you need containers running on different Docker hosts to communicate, or when multiple applications work together using swarm services.

- Macvlan networks are best when you are migrating from a VM setup or need your containers to look like physical hosts on your network, each with a unique MAC address.

- Third-party network plugins allow you to integrate Docker with specialized network stacks.

You will look at working code soon so that you can learn by doing.

Since you will be looking at multiple scenarios of container communications in this chapter, it makes sense to also understand how to inspect container logs, which is covered next.

Container Logs

You learned that Docker is an operating system-level virtualization platform and hence it allows you to run multiple applications containers in the same host at the same time. It facilitates the separation of applications and infrastructure, but when you have many applications in the same infrastructure, you need a way to troubleshoot when things don't go as intended. Docker Logs helps you here.

Console Output Logging

When you run a container, you can immediately see the STDOUT logs in the console. You saw this in Listing 7-28 in Chapter 7, which is reproduced in Listing 8-1 here.

Listing 8-1. Running Product Web Microservice Using Docker

```
(base) binildass-MacBook-Pro:ch07-02 binil$ docker run -it -p
8080:8080 binildas/product-web
...
f3636ebea575: Pull complete
Digest: sha256:56254d5a6e84cbe625013d245d8fa7dfe157722d0a6dd5
0d434f8e63dfc339ad
Status: Downloaded newer image for binildas/product-web:latest
```

```
  .   ____          _            __ _ _
 /\\ / ___'_ __ _ _(_)_ __  __ _ \ \ \ \
( ( )\___ | '_ | '_| | '_ \/ _` | \ \ \ \
 \\/  ___)| |_)| | | | | || (_| |  ) ) ) )
  '  |____| .__|_| |_|_| |_\__, | / / / /
 =========|_|==============|___/=/_/_/_/
 :: Spring Boot ::                (v3.2.0)
```

2022-05-27 05:12:40 INFO StartupInfoLogger.logStarting:55 -
Starting EcomProductMicroserviceA...
2022-05-27 05:12:40 DEBUG StartupInfoLogger.logStarting:56 -
Running with Spring Boot ...

This command follows the logs like the Linux shell `tail -f` command. In Linux, with `--follow` (`-f`), `tail` defaults to following the file descriptor.

From Listing 7-30 in Chapter 7, you learned that the container ID is e95b2b5eb64e. You can use these IDs to view the container logs, as shown in Listing 8-2.

Listing 8-2. Viewing Product Web Microservice Container Logs

```
(base) binildass-MacBook-Pro:~ binil$ eval $(minikube
docker-env)
(base) binildass-MacBook-Pro:~ binil$ docker logs e95b2b5eb64e
...
```

In Listing 8-2, the logs will contain the data of the output stream with the timestamp. However, this command doesn't contain the continuous log output. To view the continuous log output of your container, you need to use the `-follow` option in the `docker logs` command, as shown in Listing 8-3.

Listing 8-3. Viewing Product Web Microservice Container Logs
Continuously

```
(base) binildass-MacBook-Pro:~ binil$ eval $(minikube
docker-env)
(base) binildass-MacBook-Pro:~ binil$ docker logs --follow
e95b2b5eb64e
```
...

This –follow option is a very useful Docker option, since it allows you
to monitor the live logs of a container.

With this little introduction, it's time to move on to the code.

Microservice and MongoDB Containers Using Links

This example reuses the microservices from the section titled
"Microservices Using MongoDB and CrudRepository" in Chapter 3.
It uses the same two microservices—a consumer and a provider
microservice communicating each other using the REST protocol.
The provider microservice also interacts with a MongoDB. Refer to
Figure 2-1 in Chapter 2 for the overall design.

Designing the Container Topology

From this design in Figure 2-1 in Chapter 2, you also need to define a
container-based deployment topology. This is shown in Figure 8-1.

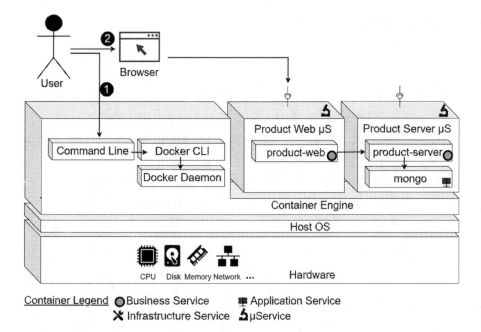

Figure 8-1. *Microservices container topology design*

A consumer and a provider microservice communicate with each other using the REST protocol. Product Web microservice is the consumer microservice, which will be deployed as a single container. The provider microservice also interacts with a NoSQL database, MongoDB. Therefore, the deployment involves two containers—one for the Product Server component and the other for the MongoDB component. Here, the Product Web and Product Server containers provide business services, whereas the Mongo container provides application services for persisting data.

Also note another aspect in Figure 8-1. The Product Server and MongoDB containers are grouped together and are so called as a single microservice, the Product Server microservice. This follows the standard conventions of microservices, where you define that a microservice is a self-contained unit owning its own data.

351

Also note two kinds of interactions with the user doing with the deployment:

- The command-line interface, or CLI, runs in what is called userspace memory, as a deployment management interface. This program runs just like other programs that run on top of the operating system. Programs running in the userspace can't modify kernel space memory. The operating system is the interface between the user programs and the hardware that the computer is running on.

- The user uses a browser to access the business functionality from the business services

Docker Engine and Docker CLI are two programs running in the userspace when you run Docker. Figure 8-1 shows three containers running. Each container is running as a child process of the Docker engine, wrapped with a container, and the delegate process is running in its own memory subspace of the userspace. Programs running inside a container cannot access memory and resources scoped by the neighbor container.

Further, in a way Figure 8-1 represents a logical view of microservices deployment too. While at an infrastructure architecture level the container deployment makes more sense, it's the microservice architecture view that is more relevant to the application architect, hence I have shown that in the figure. That is why even though Product Server and MongoDB are deployed as two separate containers, I have logically grouped them together to represent the single Product Server microservice. This specific instance of MongoDB is wholly owned by the Product Server microservice, and entities outside the Product Server microservice may not be concerned about this MongoDB instance for any reason.

Understanding the Source Code

The source code for this book is available on GitHub via the book's product page, located at www.apress.com/9798868805547. The code for this example is organized inside the ch08\ch08-01 folder. The source code in this example is similar to ch03\ch03-02, which was explained in detail in Chapter 3. What you need to understand more is the deployment schema, which is covered in the next section.

Run Containers Using Dockerfiles

Chapter 7 introduced how to build Docker images of microservices. This section extends that knowledge by building multiple microservice images.

The first step is to start Minikube single-node Kubernetes cluster so that you have a Docker Daemon up. Refer to Appendix E for a quick reference to the container commands.

```
(base) binildass-MacBook-Pro:~ binil$ minikube start

(base) binildass-MacBook-Pro:~ binil$ eval $(minikube docker-env)
```

Note   For all the examples in this chapter, I assume the previous two steps that connect to the Docker Daemon to be executed if you are using the Minikube single-node Kubernetes cluster.

Listing 8-4 shows the commands organized into a single utility script.

Listing 8-4. Script to Build and Run Microservices Docker Containers (ch08\ch08-01\makeandrun.sh)

```
mvn -Dmaven.test.skip=true clean package
docker build  --build-arg JAR_FILE=02-ProductWeb/
target/*.jar -t ecom/product-web .
docker build  --build-arg JAR_FILE=01-ProductServer/target/*.
jar -t ecom/product-server .
docker run -d -it -p 27017:27017 --name mongo mongo:3.6
docker run -d -p 8081:8081  --link mongo:mongo --name product-
server ecom/product-server
docker run -d -p 8080:8080  --link product-server:product-
server --name product-web ecom/product-web
```

The first line builds both microservices and packages them into .jar files, one by one. The second and third lines build Docker images using the .jar files. This build utilizes the Dockerfile you saw in Listing 7-35 in Chapter 7, which is reproduced here in Listing 8-5.

Listing 8-5. The Dockerfile (ch08\ch08-01\Dockerfile)

```
FROM openjdk:8-jdk-alpine
VOLUME /tmp
ARG JAR_FILE
COPY ${JAR_FILE} ecom.jar
ENTRYPOINT ["java","-jar","/ecom.jar"]
```

The Dockerfile is template-enabled, so that the actual value of the .jar file can be parameterized along with the build command. See Listing 8-6.

Listing 8-6. The Dockerfile Build and Run Commands

```
(base) binildass-MacBook-Pro:ch08-01 binil$ pwd
/Users/binil/binil/code/mac/mybooks/docker-03/ch08/ch08-01
(base) binildass-MacBook-Pro:ch08-01 binil$ eval $(minikube
docker-env)
(base) binildass-MacBook-Pro:ch08-01 binil$ sh makeandrun.sh
[INFO] Scanning for projects...
[INFO] ------------------------------------------------------
[INFO] Reactor Build Order:
[INFO]
...
Sending build context to Docker daemon   67.45MB
Step 1/5 : FROM openjdk:8-jdk-alpine
...
Successfully tagged ecom/product-web:latest
...
Successfully tagged ecom/product-server:latest
e0e9a00ce90dac5076991a67611c938458049f915ff472fed96afe9b9ce
03c80c666627fafda58611a9648b5c443010663311a6453187ccffd35a6
f19bb132fa30fedbf2f2cf8c9a6f6b082280993829a536deac8b1d3f3ff
(base) binildass-MacBook-Pro:ch08-01 binil$
```

In Listing 8-4, the second and third command use the same
Dockerfile as in Listing 8-5, but they utilize different .jar file paths
during the build, and thus they build ecom/product-web:latest and
ecom/product-server:latest and run the corresponding containers.
Listing 8-6 reveals three containers instantiated from the last three log
lines. Two are for the two business microservices (Product Server and
Product Web) and the third line is for the MongoDB container you
instantiated.

The MongoDB is an independent container. As shown in Figure 8-1, the Product Server depends on MongoDB and Product Web depends on Product Server. These dependencies are specified explicit using links in the deployment scripts in Listing 8-4.

Once the containers are up and running, you can list the running containers. See Listing 8-7.

Listing 8-7. List the Running Containers

```
(base) binildass-MacBook-Pro:ch08-01 binil$ eval $(minikube
docker-env)
(base) binildass-MacBook-Pro:ch08-01 binil$ docker ps
CONTAINER
ID    IMAGE                  COMMAND                      CREATED
STATUS              PORTS                     NAMES
f19bb132fa30   ecom/product-web       "java -jar /ecom.
jar"      About a minute ago
Up 59 seconds       0.0.0.0:8080->8080/tcp    product-web
03c80c666627   ecom/product-server   "java -jar /ecom.
jar"      About a minute ago
Up About a minute   0.0.0.0:8081->8081/tcp    product-server
e0e9a00ce90d   mongo:3.6                "docker-
entrypoint.s..."  About a minute ago
Up About a minute  0.0.0.0:27017->27017/tcp  mongo
...
(base) binildass-MacBook-Pro:ch08-01 binil$
```

Since the-d option is for running the containers, they are running as background daemon child processes. It would be convenient to keep watching the terminal logs while you access the application.

Note the container IDs from Listing 8-7. You can use these IDs to view the logs, as shown in Listings 8-8 and 8-9.

Listing 8-8. Product Server Container Logs

```
(base) binildass-MacBook-Pro:~ binil$ eval $(minikube
docker-env)
(base) binildass-MacBook-Pro:~ binil$ docker logs --follow
03c80c666627

  .   ____          _            __ _ _
 /\\ / ___'_ __ _ _(_)_ __  __ _ \ \ \ \
( ( )\___ | '_ | '_| | '_ \/ _` | \ \ \ \
 \\/  ___)| |_)| | | | | || (_| |  ) ) ) )
  '  |____| .__|_| |_|_| |_\__, | / / / /
 =========|_|==============|___/=/_/_/_/
 :: Spring Boot ::                (v3.2.0)

...
2022-05-30 04:44:31 INFO  InitComponent.init:68 - Start...
2022-05-30 04:44:31 DEBUG InitComponent.init:72 - Deleting all
existing data on start...
2022-05-30 04:44:31 DEBUG InitComponent.init:77 - Creating
initial data on start...
2022-05-30 04:44:31 INFO  InitComponent.init:126 - End
2022-05-30 04:44:36 INFO  Startup.log:61 - Started EcomProd...
...
```

Listing 8-8 shows the Product Server container logs. Similarly,
Listing 8-9 shows the product Web container logs.

Listing 8-9. Product Web Container Logs

```
(base) binildass-MacBook-Pro:~ binil$ eval $(minikube
docker-env)
(base) binildass-MacBook-Pro:~ binil$ docker logs --follow
f19bb132fa30
```

```
  .   ___          _            __ _ _
 /\\ / ___'_ __ _ _(_)_ __  __ _ \ \ \ \
( ( )\___ | '_ | '_| | '_ \/ _` | \ \ \ \
 \\/  ___)| |_)| | | | | || (_| |  ) ) ) )
  '  |____| .__|_| |_|_| |_\__, | / / / /
 =========|_|==============|___/=/_/_/_/
 :: Spring Boot ::              (v3.2.0)

...
2022-05-30 04:44:30 INFO  InitComponent.init:58 - Start
2022-05-30 04:44:30 DEBUG InitComponent.init:60 - Doing
Nothing...
2022-05-30 04:44:30 INFO  InitComponent.init:62 - End
2022-05-30 04:44:35 INFO  Startup.log:61 - Started EcomProd...
```

Testing the Microservice Containers

Once the microservices are up and running, you can access the Product Web microservice. However, as mentioned in Appendix E, you have to get the Minikube IP first. See Listing 8-10.

Listing 8-10. Finding Minikube IP

```
(base) binildass-MacBook-Pro:ch07-02 binil$ minikube ip
192.168.64.5
(base) binildass-MacBook-Pro:ch07-02 binil$
```

You can now access the Product Web microservice using a browser with the URL formed with the Minikube IP.

```
http://192.168.64.5:8080/product.html
```

Refer to the section titled "Test the Microservice Using UI" in Chapter 1 to test the Product Web microservice container. While you test the microservices, keep watching the log windows.

Once you complete the testing process, you can stop and remove the microservice containers and clean the environment. The environment cleanup steps are automated in the script in Listing 8-11.

Listing 8-11. Script Automating the Environment Cleanup (ch08\ch08-01\clean.sh)

```
mvn -Dmaven.test.skip=true clean
docker stop product-web
docker stop product-server
docker stop mongo
docker rm product-web
docker rm product-server
docker rm mongo
docker rmi -f ecom/product-web
docker rmi -f ecom/product-server
```

You can execute the script in Listing 8-12 to stop and remove the microservice containers and clean the environment.

Listing 8-12. Stopping Microservice Containers and Cleaning the Environment

```
(base) binildass-MacBook-Pro:ch08-01 binil$ pwd
/Users/binil/binil/code/mac/mybooks/docker-03/ch08/ch08-01
(base) binildass-MacBook-Pro:ch08-01 binil$ sh clean.sh
[INFO] Scanning for projects...
[INFO] ------------------------------------------------
[INFO] Reactor Build Order:
[INFO]
[INFO] Ecom-Product-Server-Microservice     [jar]
[INFO] Ecom-Product-Web-Microservice        [jar]
[INFO] Ecom                                 [pom]
```

```
[INFO]
...
product-web
product-server
mongo
product-web
product-server
mongo
Untagged: ecom/product-web:latest
Deleted: sha256:42ce83c1cbcb195e66db8b9541f7bd391764d075
9d99753725a0b97d34d2b2fd
...
Untagged: ecom/product-server:latest
...
(base) binildass-MacBook-Pro:ch08-01 binil$
```

The next example slightly modifies the current example to use a network in place of a link.

Microservice and MongoDB Containers Using a Network

In this section, you are going to reuse the same microservices visited in the section titled "Microservices Using MongoDB and CrudRepository" in Chapter 3, which you ran in the previous section of this chapter. You will have the same two microservices—a consumer and a provider microservice communicating each other using the REST protocol. The provider microservice also interacts with a MongoDB. Refer to Figure 2-1 in Chapter 2 for the overall design.

Designing the Container Topology

You reuse the deployment schema defined in the previous example in this chapter, as shown in Figure 8-1. The only change is that you will replace link with net for the network connectivity option between the containers.

Understanding the Source Code

The source code for this book is available on GitHub via the book's product page, located at www.apress.com/9798868805547. The code for this example is organized inside the ch08\ch08-02 folder. The source code in this example is very similar to ch03\ch03-02, which I explained in detail in Chapter 3, and which you deployed in the previous example of this chapter.

Run Containers Using Dockerfiles

You will modify the scripts alone in the previous example in this chapter. Listing 8-13 shows the commands organized into a single script.

Listing 8-13. Script to Build and Run Microservices Docker Containers (ch08\ch08-02\makeandrun.sh)

```
mvn -Dmaven.test.skip=true clean package
docker build  --build-arg JAR_FILE=02-ProductWeb/target/
*.jar -t ecom/product-web .
docker build  --build-arg JAR_FILE=01-ProductServer/target/*.
jar -t ecom/product-server .
docker network create ecom-network
docker pull mongo:3.6
docker run -d -it -p 27017:27017 --name mongo  --net=ecom-
network  mongo:3.6
```

```
docker run -d -p 8081:8081   --net=ecom-network --name product-
server ecom/product-server
docker run -d -p 8080:8080   --net=ecom-network --name product-
web ecom/product-web
```

Note the network creation command. This is the simplest form of the create network command, and yet it will probably be the one you will use most often. It takes a default driver (you haven't specified a driver, hence the default one will be used, which is bridge). When you create the network, an ID is created. You can later use this identifier to refer to this network when connecting containers to it or when inspecting the network's properties.

The Dockerfile for this example is the same Dockerfile you used in the previous example, which is shown in Listing 8-5.

Listing 8-14 builds the microservices and docker images and then runs the containers.

Listing 8-14. Executing the Script to Build and Run the Microservices

```
(base) binildass-MacBook-Pro:ch08-02 binil$ pwd
/Users/binil/binil/code/mac/mybooks/docker-03/ch08/ch08-02
(base) binildass-MacBook-Pro:ch08-02 binil$ eval $(minikube
docker-env)
(base) binildass-MacBook-Pro:ch08-02 binil$ sh makeandrun.sh
[INFO] Scanning for projects...
...
a9f5da94581b4f3a492938734edca433c1fc6afbe954ad4e28ead4621dd
d762e59b315dfece79e7b98deb6b01796a9210b9536ede1f36a98af67af
b51443e6a5d0cfcc16efc54e52858353ce5aa0ada1a23012dc88dfa49f0
(base) binildass-MacBook-Pro:ch08-02 binil$
```

You need to newly create the `ecom-network` in Listing 8-13, so you need to view the creation status. See Listing 8-15.

Listing 8-15. Listing the Docker Networks

```
(base) binildass-MacBook-Pro:ch08-02 binil$ docker network ls
NETWORK ID        NAME               DRIVER     SCOPE
435b063e810b      bridge             bridge     local
129e1b5f4de5      ecom-network       bridge     local
28731f4db9e0      host               host       local
2480825a3deb      none               null       local
(base) binildass-MacBook-Pro:ch08-02 binil$
```

The `network ls` command simply lists networks available for your containers. It will output the network identifier, its name, the driver being used, and a scope of the network.

To list all the containers you have on your system, execute the `docker ps` command. See Listing 8-16.

Listing 8-16. Listing the Docker Containers

```
(base) binildass-MacBook-Pro:ch08-02 binil$ docker ps
CONTAINER
ID    IMAGE    COMMAND    CREATED      STATUS     PORTS        NAMES
b51443e6a5d0    ecom/product-web        "java -jar /ecom.jar"
3 minutes ago    Up 3 minutes    0.0.0.0:8080->8080/tcp
roduct-web
d762e59b315d    ecom/product-server     "java -jar /ecom.jar"
3 minutes ago    Up 3 minutes    0.0.0.0:8081->8081/
tcp    t-server
a9f5da94581b    mongo:3.6    "docker-entrypoint.s..."
3 minutes ago    Up 3 minutes    0.0.0.0:27017->27017/tcp    mongo
...
(base) binildass-MacBook-Pro:ch08-01 binil$
```

You can now list the details of the ecom-network you previously created, as shown in Listing 8-17.

Listing 8-17. Inspecting a Particular Docker Network

```
(base) binildass-MacBook-Pro:ch08-02 binil$ docker network
inspect ecom-network
[
    {
        "Name": "ecom-network",
        "Id": "129e1b5f4de5a5c2bff188496f0148eed01204924d0c09
c0be9be9d1f4e9557e",
        "Created": "2022-06-02T10:06:06.119442393Z",
        "Scope": "local",
        "Driver": "bridge",
        "EnableIPv6": false,
        "IPAM": {
            "Driver": "default",
            "Options": {},
            "Config": [
                {
                    "Subnet": "172.20.0.0/16",
                    "Gateway": "172.20.0.1"
                }
            ]
        },
        "Internal": false,
        "Attachable": false,
        "Ingress": false,
        "ConfigFrom": {
            "Network": ""
        },
```

```
"ConfigOnly": false,
"Containers": {
    "a9f5da94581b4f3a492938734edca433c1fc6afbe954a
    d4e28ead4621ddf5d92": {
        "Name": "mongo",
        "EndpointID": "f2093e54a61c65800ca1a3da8f0092
        7704fbeab12cf39df142ca3
        6746321aba6",
        "MacAddress": "02:42:ac:14:00:02",
        "IPv4Address": "172.20.0.2/16",
        "IPv6Address": ""
    },
    "b51443e6a5d0cfcc16efc54e52858353ce5aa0ada1a230
    12dc88dfa49f01c79d": {
        "Name": "product-web",
        "EndpointID": "9ca35c49812d5adc0c0d13585f0d7e7
        b007948e531951549625a78ae2f1fc225",
        "MacAddress": "02:42:ac:14:00:04",
        "IPv4Address": "172.20.0.4/16",
        "IPv6Address": ""
    },
    "d762e59b315dfece79e7b98deb6b01796a9210b9536ede1f3
    6a98af67afb2aa2": {
        "Name": "product-server",
        "EndpointID": "3990604146f3bc7c327606ab77b2de9f
        818c687a2f5a0bc5eaa86b64cfe5e3e0",
        "MacAddress": "02:42:ac:14:00:03",
        "IPv4Address": "172.20.0.3/16",
        "IPv6Address": ""
    }
},
"Options": {},
```

```
        "Labels": {}
    }
]
(base) binildass-MacBook-Pro:ch08-02 binil$
```

As you can see in Listing 8-17, the newly created network uses the bridge driver, as is evident in "Driver": "bridge". Even if you haven't explicitly asked for it, it's the default. The Containers section lists the three containers to which you earlier connected this network.

Note the container IDs from Listing 8-16. You can use these IDs to view the logs.

Listing 8-18. Viewing Product Server Container Logs

```
(base) binildass-MacBook-Pro:ch08-02 binil$ docker
logs --follow d762e59b315d
...
2022-06-02 10:06:24 INFO  StartupInfoLogger.logStarted:61 -
Started EcomProductMicroserviceApplication in 10.378 seconds
(JVM running for 11.925)
...
```

Listing 8-18 shows the Product Server container logs. Similarly, Listing 8-19 shows the Product Web container logs.

Listing 8-19. Viewing Product Web Container Logs

```
(base) binildass-MacBook-Pro:ch08-02 binil$ docker
logs --follow b51443e6a5d0
...
2022-06-02 10:06:23 INFO  StartupInfoLogger.logStarted:61 -
Started EcomProductMicroserviceApplication in 9.058 seconds
(JVM running for 10.648)
...
```

Once the containers are up and running, you can test the application.

Testing the Microservice Containers

Since both microservices are up and running, you can access the Product Web microservice. However, as mentioned in Appendix E, you have to get the minikube IP first. See Listing 8-20.

Listing 8-20. Finding Minikube IP

```
(base) binildass-MacBook-Pro:ch07-02 binil$ minikube ip
192.168.64.5
(base) binildass-MacBook-Pro:ch07-02 binil$
```

You can now access the Product Web microservice using a browser with the URL formed with the Minikube IP.

```
http://192.168.64.5:8080/product.html
```

Refer to the section titled "Test the Microservice Using UI" in Chapter 1 to test the Product Web microservice container. While you test the microservices, keep watching the log windows.

Once you complete the testing process, stop and remove the microservice containers and clean the environment. The environment cleanup steps are automated in a script, as shown in Listing 8-21.

Listing 8-21. Script Automating the Environment Cleanup (ch08\ch08-02\clean.sh)

```
mvn -Dmaven.test.skip=true clean
docker stop product-web
docker stop product-server
docker stop mongo
docker rm product-web
docker rm product-server
```

```
docker rm mongo
docker rmi -f ecom/product-web
docker rmi -f ecom/product-server
docker network rm ecom-network
```

You can now execute this script to stop and remove the microservice containers and clean the environment. See Listing 8-22.

Listing 8-22. Stopping Microservice Containers and Cleaning the Environment

```
(base) binildass-MacBook-Pro:ch08-02 binil$ sh clean.sh
[INFO] Scanning for projects...
[INFO] ------------------------------------------------
[INFO] Reactor Build Order:
[INFO]
[INFO] Ecom-Product-Server-Microservice      [jar]
[INFO] Ecom-Product-Web-Microservice         [jar]
[INFO] Ecom                                  [pom]
[INFO]
...
product-web
product-server
mongo
product-web
product-server
mongo
Untagged: ecom/product-web:latest
...
Untagged: ecom/product-server:latest
...
ecom-network
(base) binildass-MacBook-Pro:ch08-02 binil$
```

Microservice Container with PostgreSQL in Host

This example reuses the microservices from the section titled "Microservices Using PostgreSQL and RestTemplate" in Chapter 3. It includes the same two microservices—a consumer and a provider microservice communicating each other using the REST protocol. The provider microservice in this case interacts with a PostgreSQL database. Refer to Figure 2-1 in Chapter 2 for the overall design with the exception that this example uses a PostgreSQL database.

Designing the Container Topology

For this new design, you need to slightly tweak the container-based deployment topology in Figure 8-1. This is shown in Figure 8-2. The Product Web and Product Server microservices are containerized, but the plan here is to use a PostgreSQL database running outside a Docker container, directly on the host operating system.

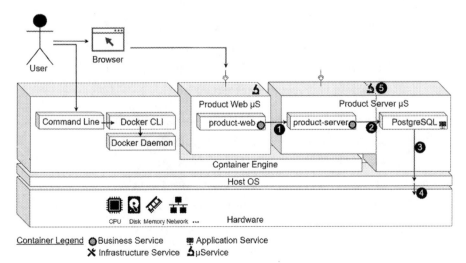

Figure 8-2. *Microservices container topology design*

There are a few aspects to be noted with respect to the numbered labels in Figure 8-2:

1. The Product Web microservice connects to the Product Server microservice using networks between containers.

2. To connect to the PostgreSQL database, it is not enough that the Product Server microservice uses container networking alone, instead you need to explicitly tell the Product Server microservice container about the IP details of the host machine where you are running PostgreSQL database.

3. The PostgreSQL database is not containerized, so it doesn't use any kind of virtualization. Instead, PostgreSQL is running directly on the host OS.

4. PostgreSQL directly uses the host machine resources, especially for the data storage requirements.

5. The Product Server microservice is not a physical organization; it's a virtual grouping of the Product Server microservice container and the PostgreSQL database in the host machine together.

Let's now look at why you need this kind of deployment architecture. Orchestration tools like Docker are created with the assumption that they are stateless, which means that they should not save any data during the run. If containers are stateful they might end up having several containers of a certain type act differently even if they are instantiated from the same image. However, databases store state, so they are stateful. Because of this, a deployment architecture like the one shown in Figure 8-2 could work. Of course, for production purposes, this single database instance (or cluster) will be instead in a public cloud, perhaps as a DBaaS (Database as a Service) instead of the local host machine (assuming that you are using a cloud-based deployment).

Understanding the Source Code

The source code for this book is available on GitHub via the book's product page, located at www.apress.com/9798868805547. The code for this example is organized inside the ch08\ch08-03 folder. Much of the source code in this example is similar to that in ch03\ch03-01, which was explained in detail in Chapter 3, in the section titled "Microservices Using PostgreSQL and RestTemplate." You saw the deployment schema of multiple interacting microservices in the previous two example, so, in this example, emphasis is on connecting to a non-containerized database.

Container to PostgreSQL in Host Configuration

Since the Postgres database is running on the host system, you need to allow the Docker container running the Product Server microservice to connect to a local PostgreSQL database. Assuming you don't want the container to share the network with the host (using --network host parameter while running it), the database and the container need to be configured to communicate.

Refer to these sections in Appendix C on PostgreSQL:

- Opening a PostgreSQL server for remote clients

- Opening PostgreSQL on a host machine for Docker clients

Those configurations should be enough to create a Postgre database running on a host system work with a containerized app.

Run Containers Using Dockerfiles

The ch08\ch08-03 folder contains the Maven scripts required to build
the examples. As a first step, you need to bring up the PostgreSQL server.
This example assumes you already have a PostgreSQL server running, and
you have configured it as mentioned previously. You need to execute the
following commands in Listing 8-23 to bring up PostgreSQL.

Listing 8-23. Bringing Up the PostgreSQL Server

```
binildass-MacBook-Pro:~ binil$ pg_ctl -D /Library/
PostgreSQL/12/data start
```

If you have already made the configurations required for the Postgres
database running on a host system work with a containerized app in the
previous section, you now need to tell the container about the host's IP
address. You can pass the host's IP using the --add-host option, which is
done in Listing 8-25. In this case, the host is a name of the host machine,
and it will be added to the container's /etc/hosts file. Inside the Docker
container, you can use the name host to connect to the host system. You
need to have the IP of the host where PostgreSQL is running, which you
find in Listing 8-24.

Listing 8-24. Finding the IP of PostgreSQL Host Machine

```
binildass-MacBook-Pro:~ binil$ ipconfig getifaddr en0
192.168.29.96
binildass-MacBook-Pro:~ binil$
```

The Dockerfile in this example is the same Dockerfile used in the
previous example, which is shown in Listing 8-5.

Next, build the microservices and Docker images and then run the
containers. You will modify the scripts in the previous example in this
chapter. Listing 8-25 organizes the commands into a single script.

Listing 8-25. Script to Build and Run Microservices Docker Containers (ch08\ch08-03\makeandrun.sh)

```
mvn -Dmaven.test.skip=true clean package
docker build  --build-arg JAR_FILE=01-ProductServer/target/
*.jar -t ecom/product-server .
docker build  --build-arg JAR_FILE=02-ProductWeb/target/
*.jar -t ecom/product-web .
docker network create ecom-network
docker run -d -p 8081:8081 --net=ecom-network --add-
host=host:192.168.29.96 --name product-server -e DB_
SERVER=host:5432 -e POSTGRES_DB=productdb -e POSTGRES_
USER=postgres -e POSTGRES_PASSWORD=postgre ecom/product-server
docker run -d -p 8080:8080 --net=ecom-network --name product-
web -e acme.PRODUCT_SERVICE_URL=http://product-server:8081/
products ecom/product-web
```

To build the microservices and the Docker images and then run the containers, you need to execute the script in Listing 8-25, as shown in Listing 8-26.

Listing 8-26. Executing the Docker Container Build and Run Commands

```
(base) binildass-MacBook-Pro:ch08-03 binil$ pwd
/Users/binil/binil/code/mac/mybooks/docker-03/ch08/ch08-03
(base) binildass-MacBook-Pro:ch08-03 binil$ eval $(minikube
docker-env)
(base) binildass-MacBook-Pro:ch08-03 binil$ sh makeandrun.sh
[INFO] Scanning for projects...
[INFO] ------------------------------------------------
[INFO] Reactor Build Order:
[INFO]
```

```
[INFO] Ecom-Product-Server-Microservice    [jar]
[INFO] Ecom-Product-Web-Microservice       [jar]
[INFO] Ecom                                 [pom]
[INFO]
...
Sending build context to Docker daemon   83.36MB
Step 1/5 : FROM openjdk:8-jdk-alpine
---> a3562aa0b991
...
Successfully tagged ecom/product-server:latest
...
Successfully tagged ecom/product-web:latest
3b852d90e2b71ac7f5c5a2a49d445c7daa3a37d9a695efd316f3c89107c
c89e8b5749fe45c235280d03a666de4fce9c7a7ddb46a147bc507b92c06
71e9c4b442275a4645009d046a506289271dd48a86b83d83683b13d5721
(base) binildass-MacBook-Pro:ch08-03 binil$
```

To list all the containers you have on your system now, execute the docker ps command, as shown in Listing 8-27.

Listing 8-27. Listing Docker Containers

```
(base) binildass-MacBook-Pro:~ binil$ docker ps
CONTAINER ID   IMAGE                 COMMAND
CREATED        STATUS         PORTS                 NAMES
71e9c4b44227   ecom/product-web      "java -jar /ecom.jar"
3 minutes ago  Up 3 minutes   0.0.0.0:8080->8080/tcp   product-web
c89e8b5749fe   ecom/product-server   "java -jar /ecom.jar"
3 minutes ago  Up 3 minutes   0.0.0.0:8081->8081/tcp   product-server
...
(base) binildass-MacBook-Pro:ch08-01 binil$
```

Note the container IDs from Listing 8-27. You can use these IDs to view the logs, as shown in Listing 8-28.

Listing 8-28. Viewing Product Server Container Logs

```
(base) binildass-MacBook-Pro:~ binil$ docker logs --follow
c89e8b5749fe


  .   ____              _            __ _ _
 /\\ / ___'_ __ _ _(_)_ __  __ _ \ \ \ \
( ( )\___ | '_ | '_| | '_ \/ _` | \ \ \ \
 \\/  ___)| |_)| | | | | || (_| |  ) ) ) )
  '  |____| .__|_| |_|_| |_\__, | / / / /
 =========|_|==============|___/=/_/_/_/
 :: Spring Boot ::                (v3.2.0)

...
Creating 2 new products in DB during initialization
Hibernate: insert into product (code, prodname, price, title)
values (?, ?, ?, ?)
Hibernate: insert into product (code, prodname, price, title)
values (?, ?, ?, ?)
2022-05-30 07:18:02 INFO  InitializationComponent.init:74 - End
2022-05-30 07:18:04 INFO  StartupInfoLogger.logStarted:61 -
Started EcomProductMicroserviceApplication in 13.101 seconds
(JVM running for 15.006)
```

Listing 8-28 shows the Product Server container logs. Similarly, Listing 8-29 shows the Product Web container logs.

Listing 8-29. Viewing Product Web Container Logs

```
(base) binildass-MacBook-Pro:~ binil$ docker logs --follow
71e9c4b44227
...
2022-05-30 07:18:00 INFO  StartupInfoLogger.logStarted:61 -
Started EcomProductMicroserviceApplication in 8.835 seconds
(JVM running for 10.646)
```

Once the containers are up and running, you are ready to test the application.

Testing the Microservice Containers

Since both microservices are up and running, you can access the Product Web microservice. However, as mentioned in Appendix E, you must get the Minikube IP first. See Listing 8-30.

Listing 8-30. Finding Minikube IP

```
(base) binildass-MacBook-Pro:ch07-02 binil$ minikube ip
192.168.64.5
(base) binildass-MacBook-Pro:ch07-02 binil$
```

You can now access the Product Web microservice using a browser with the URL formed with the Minikube IP (see Figure 8-3).

```
http://192.168.64.5:8080/product.html
```

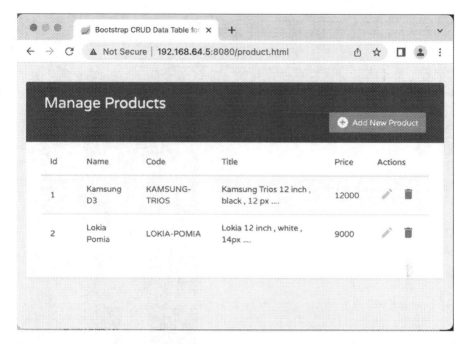

Figure 8-3. *Accessing the microservices container using a browser*

Refer to the section titled "Test the Microservice Using UI" in Chapter 1 to test the Product Web microservice container. While you test the microservices, keep watching the log windows.

You can add a new product to the application for testing, as shown in Figure 8-4.

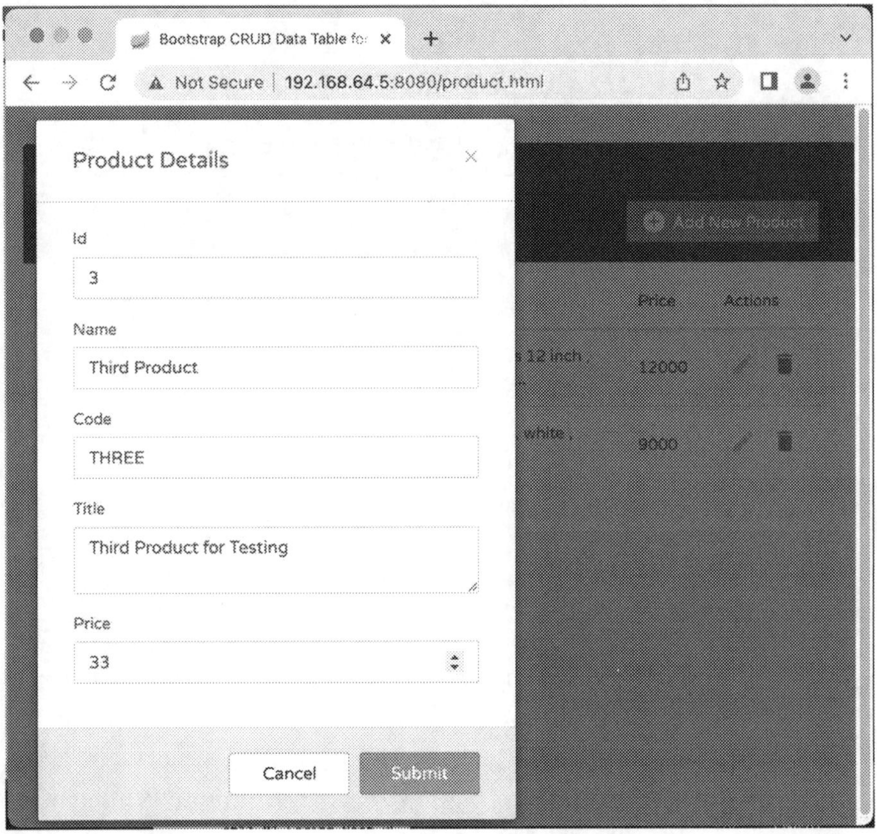

Figure 8-4. *Adding a new product to test the microservice*

Refresh your browser to view the newly added product, as shown in Figure 8-5.

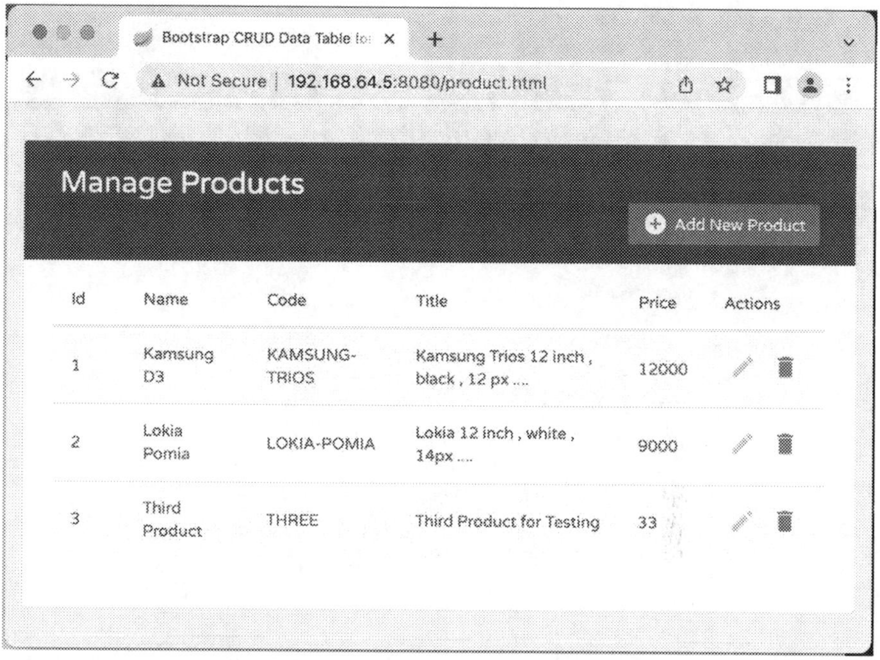

Figure 8-5. *Refreshing the browser to view the newly added product*

To make sure everything went as expected and your Product Server microservice has in fact persisted the data to the PostgreSQL database in the host machine, you can now inspect the PostgreSQL database. Refer to the section titled "Create Database in PostgreSQL Using pgAdmin" in Appendix C on how to use pgAdmin to interact with a PostgreSQL database. You can see this in Figure 8-6.

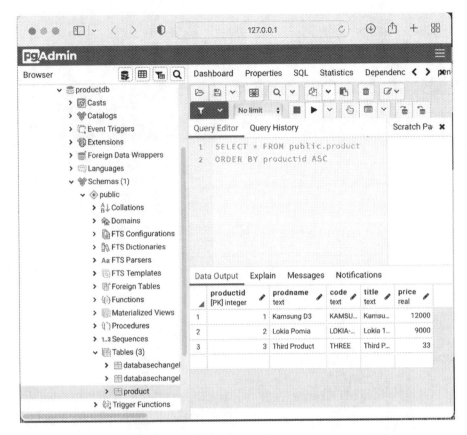

Figure 8-6. *Viewing the newly added product using pgAdmin*

Once you complete the testing process, you can stop and remove the microservice containers and clean the environment. The environment cleanup is automated in a script, as shown in Listing 8-31.

Listing 8-31. Script Automating the Environment Cleanup (ch08\ch08-03\clean.sh)

```
mvn -Dmaven.test.skip=true clean
docker stop product-web
docker stop product-server
docker rm product-web
```

```
docker rm product-server
docker rmi -f ecom/product-web
docker rmi -f ecom/product-server
docker network rm ecom-network
```

You can execute this script to stop and remove the microservice containers and clean the environment. See Listing 8-32.

Listing 8-32. Stopping Microservice Containers and Cleaning the Environment

```
(base) binildass-MacBook-Pro:ch08-03 binil$ sh clean.sh
[INFO] Scanning for projects...
...
product-web
product-server
product-web
product-server
Untagged: ecom/product-web:latest
...
Untagged: ecom/product-server:latest
...
ecom-network
(base) binildass-MacBook-Pro:ch08-03 binil$
```

Microservice and PostgreSQL in Container

You learned why it's better to state-handle applications, including databases, to be deployed outside a Docker container, since containers are designed to be more efficient in stateless kind of operations. However, there are use cases where you might like to have your database in a container, such as in cases of rapid testing. In this section, you learn how to modify the example from the previous section to be fully deployed within a container infrastructure.

Designing the Container Topology

For the current design, you need to slightly tweak the container-based deployment topology shown in Figure 8-1 and replace MongoDB with PostgreSQL. This is shown in Figure 8-7. The Product Web and Product Server microservices are containerized, and the Product Server microservice will connect to a PostgreSQL database, again deployed as a container.

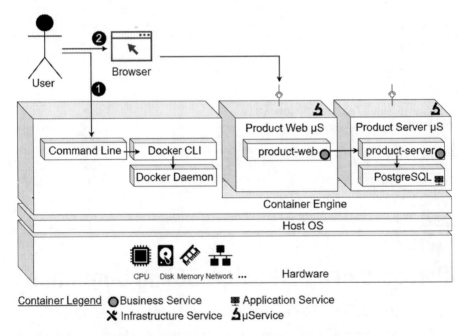

Figure 8-7. *Container deployment topology for microservices*

Here again, the Product Web and Product Server containers provide business services, whereas the PostgreSQL container provides application services for persisting state.

Understanding the Source Code

The source code for this book is available on GitHub via the book's product page, located at www.apress.com/9798868805547. The code for this example is organized inside the ch08\ch08-04 folder. The source code in this example is very similar to ch03\ch03-01, which was explained in detail in Chapter 3, in the section titled "Microservices Using PostgreSQL and RestTemplate." You also saw the deployment schema of multiple interacting microservices using a PostgreSQL database in the previous example. This section looks specifically into connecting to a containerized PostgreSQL database alone.

Connecting from a containerized microservice to a containerized PostgreSQL server is rather straightforward, so there is very little change to be made while running the containers alone. You will learn about that in the next section.

Run Containers Using Dockerfiles

The ch08\ch08-04 folder contains the Maven scripts required to build the examples. As a first step, you need to bring up the PostgreSQL server. The Dockerfile for this example is the same Dockerfile used in the previous three examples, and it is shown in Listing 8-5.

Next, build the microservices and the Docker images and then run the containers. You will modify the scripts in the previous example in this chapter. Listing 8-33 organizes the commands into a single script.

Listing 8-33. Script to Build and Run Microservices Docker Containers (ch08\ch08-04\makeandrun.sh)

```
mvn -Dmaven.test.skip=true clean package
docker build  --build-arg JAR_FILE=01-ProductServer/target/
*.jar -t ecom/product-server .
docker build  --build-arg JAR_FILE=02-ProductWeb/target/
*.jar -t ecom/product-web .
docker network create ecom-network
docker run -d --net=ecom-network --name postgres-docker -e
POSTGRES_DB=productdb -e POSTGRES_USER=postgres -e POSTGRES_
PASSWORD=postgre -p 5432:5432 -d postgres:15.3-alpine3.18
docker run -d -p 8081:8081 --net=ecom-network --name
product-server -e DB_SERVER=postgres-docker:5432 -e
POSTGRES_DB=productdb -e POSTGRES_USER=postgres -e POSTGRES_
PASSWORD=postgre ecom/product-server
docker run -d -p 8080:8080 --net=ecom-network --name product-
web -e acme.PRODUCT_SERVICE_URL=http://product-server:8081/
products ecom/product-web
```

This section explains the Docker Run command for PostgreSQL server alone, since the rest of the commands have been explained.

```
docker run -d --net=ecom-network --name postgres-docker -e
POSTGRES_DB=productdb -e POSTGRES_USER=postgres -e POSTGRES_
PASSWORD=postgre -p 5432:5432 -d postgres:9.6-alpine
```

Here is what this does:

- This first line pulls the Postgres Docker image from Docker Hub.

- It then sets POSTGRES_DB, which is an optional environment variable used to define a different name for the default database that is created when the image starts. If it is not specified, the value of POSTGRES_USER will be used.

- It then sets the POSTGRES_USER, which is an optional environment variable used in conjunction with POSTGRES_PASSWORD to set a user and its password. This variable will create the specified user with superuser power and a database with the same name (which I have overridden). If it is not specified, the default user of postgres will be used.

- It then sets the POSTGRES_PASSWORD, which is an environment variable required for you to use the PostgreSQL image. It must not be empty or undefined. This environment variable sets the superuser password for PostgreSQL. The default superuser is defined by the POSTGRES_USER environment variable.

- It then names (--name) the Docker container to be postgres-docker.

- It maps the container's internal 5432 port to external 5432 port, so you'll be able to enter it from outside.

- It then enables to run the Docker container in the background (-d).

If you want to enter into the database using a GUI application (like pgAdmin, psql, or so), you should now be able to do so.

You can build the microservices and the docker images and then run the containers, as shown in Listing 8-34.

Listing 8-34. The Dockerfile Build and Run Commands

```
(base) binildass-MacBook-Pro:ch08-01 binil$ pwd
/Users/binil/binil/code/mac/mybooks/docker-03/ch08/ch08-04
(base) binildass-MacBook-Pro:ch08-04 binil$ sh makeandrun.sh
[INFO] Scanning for projects...
[INFO] ------------------------------------------------------
[INFO] Reactor Build Order:
[INFO]
[INFO] Ecom-Product-Server-Microservice                  [jar]
[INFO] Ecom-Product-Web-Microservice                     [jar]
[INFO] Ecom                                              [pom]
[INFO]
...
Sending build context to Docker daemon  82.32MB
Step 1/5 : FROM openjdk:8-jdk-alpine
...
Successfully tagged ecom/product-server:latest
...
Successfully tagged ecom/product-web:latest
e5f38c5b37460b3889e284a7d1ccb4f7c32f6147516f81b90d26a8fbeb8
Unable to find image 'postgres:9.6-alpine' locally
9.6-alpine: Pulling from library/postgres
59bf1c3509f3: Pull complete
...
Status: Downloaded newer image for postgres:9.6-alpine
72d0bc450b9057b7c21bcd30ad3dffc4a1e04fd79415b9cd254057785cf
e309c7db0b1f72f96bf8ba19999f0e471aaff47cce056e8d757a3d3713a
f624b4b3fd732135948d61b23c07d31c54c07e7bc5e370a57485e7cfd7b
(base) binildass-MacBook-Pro:ch08-04 binil$
```

To list all the containers you have on your system now, execute the docker ps command, as shown in Listing 8-35.

Listing 8-35. Listing Docker Containers

```
(base) binildass-MacBook-Pro:~ binil$ docker ps
CONTAINER ID    IMAGE                 COMMAND
CREATED          STATUS        PORTS                  NAMES
f624b4b3fd73    ecom/product-web      "java -jar /ecom.jar"
2 minutes ago   Up 2 minutes  0.0.0.0:8080->8080/tcp    product-web
e309c7db0b1f    ecom/product-server   "java -jar /ecom.jar"
2 minutes ago   Up 2 minutes  0.0.0.0:8081->8081/tcp    product-server
72d0bc450b90    postgres:9.6-alpine   "docker-entrypoint.s..."
2 minutes ago   Up 2 minutes  0.0.0.0:5432->5432/tcp    postgres-docker
...
(base) binildass-MacBook-Pro:~ binil$
```

Note the container IDs from Listing 8-35. You can use these IDs to view the logs, as shown in Listings 8-36 and 8-37.

Listing 8-36. Product Server Container Logs

```
(base) binildass-MacBook-Pro:~ binil$ docker logs --follow
e309c7db0b1f
```

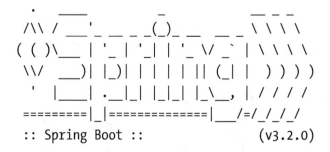

```
  .   ____          _            __ _ _
 /\\ / ___'_ __ _ _(_)_ __  __ _ \ \ \ \
( ( )\___ | '_ | '_| | '_ \/ _` | \ \ \ \
 \\/  ___)| |_)| | | | | || (_| |  ) ) ) )
  '  |____| .__|_| |_|_| |_\__, | / / / /
 =========|_|==============|___/=/_/_/_/
 :: Spring Boot ::                (v3.2.0)
```

...

Creating 2 new products in DB during initialization
Hibernate: insert into product (code, prodname, price, title)
values (?, ?, ?, ?)
Hibernate: insert into product (code, prodname, price, title)
values (?, ?, ?, ?)
2022-05-30 10:29:35 INFO InitializationComponent.init:74 - End
2022-05-30 10:29:37 INFO StartupInfoLogger.logStarted:61 -
Started EcomProductMicroserviceApplication in 12.887 seconds
(JVM running for 15.075)
...

Listing 8-36 shows the Product Server container logs. Note two rows
are inserted as initial data in the database. Similarly, Listing 8-37 shows the
product Web container logs.

Listing 8-37. Product Web Container Logs

(base) binildass-MacBook-Pro:~ binil$ docker logs --follow
f624b4b3fd73
...
2022-05-30 10:29:34 INFO StartupInfoLogger.logStarted:61 -
Started EcomProductMicroserviceApplication in 8.81 seconds (JVM
running for 10.568)
...

Once the containers are up and running, you can test the application.

Testing the Microservice Containers

Since the microservices and database containers are up and running now,
you can access the Product Web microservice. However, as mentioned in
Appendix E, you have to get the minikube IP first. See Listing 8-38.

Listing 8-38. Finding Minikube IP

```
(base) binildass-MacBook-Pro:ch07-02 binil$ minikube ip
192.168.64.5
(base) binildass-MacBook-Pro:ch07-02 binil$
```

You can now access the Product Web microservice using a browser with the URL formed with the Minikube IP.

```
http://192.168.64.5:8080/product.html
```

Refer to the section titled "Test the Microservice Using UI" in Chapter 1 to test the Product Web microservice container. While you test the microservices, keep watching the log windows.

You can also access the PostgreSQL server in the Docker container using the psql terminal. Refer to the Appendix C section titled "Run Commands Against PostgreSQL Server Using psql" to get an overview of various terminal commands. See Listing 8-39.

Listing 8-39. psql Terminal Access

```
(base) binildass-MacBook-Pro:~ binil$ docker exec -it postgres-
docker bash
bash-5.1# psql -U postgres
psql (9.6.24)
Type "help" for help.

postgres=# \list
                                List of databases
    Name     |   Owner    | Encoding |   Collate   |   Ctype     |
-------------+------------+----------+-------------+-------------+-
 postgres    | postgres   | UTF8     | en_US.utf8  | en_US.utf8  |
 productdb   | postgres   | UTF8     | en_US.utf8  | en_US.utf8  |
 template0   | postgres   | UTF8     | en_US.utf8  | en_US.utf8  |
```

```
postgres=CTc/postgres
(4 rows)

postgres=# \conninfo
You are connected to database "postgres" as user "postgres" via
socket in "/var/run/postgresql" at port "5432".
postgres=# \c productdb
You are now connected to database "productdb" as user
"postgres".
productdb=# \conninfo
You are connected to database "productdb" as user "postgres"
via socket in "/var/run/postgresql" at port "5432".
productdb=# select * from product;
 productid |  prodname   |
code    |    title               | price
-----------+-------------+---------------+------------------
        1 | Kamsung D3  | KAMSUNG | Kamsung Trios 12 in..
        2 | Lokia Pomia | LOKIA   | Lokia 12 inch..
(2 rows)
```

After verifying the initial data created by Product Server microservice in the PostgreSQL container, you can add a new product to the application for testing purposes, as shown in Figure 8-8.

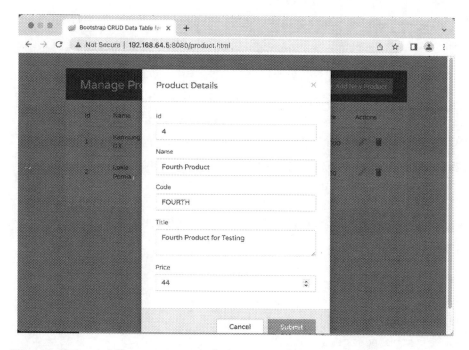

Figure 8-8. *Adding a new product to test the microservice*

Refresh your browser to view the newly added product. You can also refresh your terminal query to access the PostgreSQL server in the Docker container using the psql terminal, as shown in Listing 8-40.

Listing 8-40. psql Terminal Access

```
productdb=# select * from product;
 productid | prodname    |
code    |    title             | price
-----------+-------------+---------------+------------------
        1 | Kamsung D3  | KAMSUNG | Kamsung Trios 12 in..
        2 | Lokia Pomia | LOKIA   | Lokia 12 inch..
        3 | Fourth Prod | FOURTH  | Fourth Product for
(3 rows)
productdb=# \q
```

```
bash-5.1# exit
exit
(base) binildass-MacBook-Pro:~ binil$
```

As in Listing 8-40, you can verify that the newly inserted product through the Product Web microservice web app is safely persisted in the PostgreSQL database inside the container. Once you complete testing the microservices, you can then stop and remove the microservice containers and clean the environment using the script shown in Listing 8-41.

Listing 8-41. Script Automating the Environment Cleanup (ch08\ch08-04\clean.sh)

```
mvn -Dmaven.test.skip=true clean
docker stop product-web
docker stop product-server
docker stop postgres-docker
docker rm product-web
docker rm product-server
docker rm postgres-docker
docker rmi -f ecom/product-web
docker rmi -f ecom/product-server
docker network rm ecom-network
```

You can execute the script shown in Listing 8-42 to stop and remove the microservice containers and clean the environment.

Listing 8-42. Stopping Microservice Containers and Cleaning the Environment

```
(base) binildass-MacBook-Pro:ch08-04 binil$ sh clean.sh
...
product-web
product-server
```

```
postgres-docker
product-web
product-server
postgres-docker
Untagged: ecom/product-web:latest
...
Untagged: ecom/product-server:latest
...
ecom-network
(base) binildass-MacBook-Pro:ch08-04 binil$
```

You have now seen many examples exploring different scenarios of using containers with SQL and No SQL databases. Next, the chapter extends this learning to one more aspect—container storage.

Container Storage

Chapter 7 explained that the Docker container filesystem is predominantly read-only and is a kind of temporary by default. When you start up a Docker image by running the container, you're placing a read-write layer on top of the lower layer file stack. You can create, modify, and delete files as you wish. Only when you commit the changes back into the image do they become persisted. This is not very convenient when it comes to storing and retrieving data, which is supposed to be non-volatile. A better option is to separate the container lifecycle from the data it manages. You can keep these separate, so that the data managed (or being used) by your application is not destroyed or tied to the container lifecycle and can thus be reused.

Separating long-lived data from containers is done via volumes, which this section investigates. Volumes are not part of the union filesystem, and so the write operations are instant and as fast as possible and there is no need to commit any changes. Since volumes live outside of the union filesystem, they exist as normal directories and files on the host filesystem.

Volumes

Volumes are the preferred mechanism for persisting data generated by and used by Docker containers. Volumes are better than a container's writable layer in persisting long-term data. Volumes do not increase the size of the containers using them, and the volume's contents exist outside the lifecycle of a given container.

There are two ways to create volumes:

- Specify the -v option when running an image.

- Use the command to create a volume prior to starting a container.

Let's look at the first option here, which you will also use in the next example.

```
docker run  -d -it -p 27017:27017 --name mongo  --net=ecom-
network -v /Users/binil/dockerbook/ch08-05/mongodata:/data/
db  mongo:3.6
```

You can create a volume using the -v switch and instruct Docker that the host directory /Users/binil/dockerbook/ch08-05/mongodata should be mapped into the /data/db directory in the running Mongo container.

Let's straight look into an example.

Microservice and MongoDB Containers Using File Mount

This example reuses the same microservices from the section titled "Microservices using MongoDB and CrudRepository" in Chapter 3. The same two microservices are used—a consumer and a provider microservice communicating each other using the REST protocol. The provider microservice also interacts with a MongoDB. Different from the first two MongoDB examples in this chapter, this example uses volumes to persist the Mongo database data. Refer to Figure 2-1 in Chapter 2 for the overall design.

Designing the Container Topology

This example reuses the deployment schema defined in the first example in this chapter. However, there is a change—you will use volume mount here. See Figure 8-9.

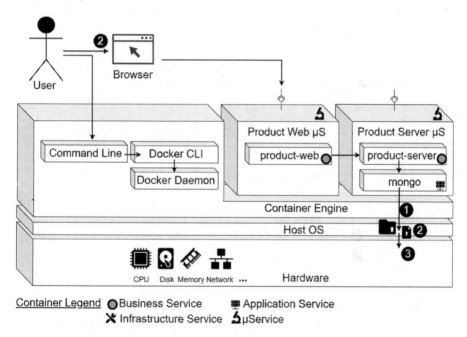

Figure 8-9. *Container deployment topology for microservice*

This example uses the -v options so that the directory on the host operating system will be available for the container in this modified example. The volume created in this manner is a kind of mapped directory. This mapped directory will be available for the container and it is also available from the host operating system. Any files already in the mapped directory will also be available inside the container; they will not be deleted during the mapping step. Referring to the numbered labels in Figure 8-9, you may note these aspects:

- Since you have mapped the volume using the –v option, the persistence-related commands from the Mongo container are delegated to the filesystem abstraction.

- The filesystem abstraction of the operating system can organize the Mongo database's data into files, directories, and other related constructs.

- At the hardware layer, a storage device is used to retain digital data, which could be a magnetic disk, a semiconductor device, and so on.

Since this example uses a persistence mechanism outside the container, so you must also verify that the data persisted to the storage has the capability to overcome container lifecycle.

Understanding the Source Code

The source code for this book is available on GitHub via the book's product page, located at www.apress.com/9798868805547. The code for this example is organized inside the ch08\ch08-05 folder. Much of the source code in this example is similar to ch03\ch03-02, which was explained in detail in Chapter 3. Also, the source code for this example is like the first two examples in this chapter. Compared to the second example in this chapter, the change is that you will use the -v options so that the directory on the host operating system will be available for the container.

Run Containers Using Dockerfiles

The ch08\ch08-05 folder contains the Maven scripts required to build the examples. As a first step, you need to bring up the PostgreSQL server. The Dockerfile for this example is the same Dockerfile used in the previous four examples, and it is shown in Listing 8-5.

Next, build the microservices and the docker images and then run the containers. You need to modify the scripts from the previous example. Listing 8-43 shows the commands organized into a single script.

Listing 8-43. Script to Build and Run Microservices Docker Containers (ch08\ch08-05\makeandrun.sh)

```
mvn -Dmaven.test.skip=true clean package
docker build  --build-arg JAR_FILE=02-ProductWeb/target/
*.jar -t ecom/product-web .
docker build  --build-arg JAR_FILE=01-ProductServer/target/
*.jar -t ecom/product-server .
docker network create ecom-network
docker pull mongo:3.6
docker run  -d -it -p 27017:27017 --name mongo  --net=ecom-
network -v /Users/binil/dockerbook/ch08-05/mongodata:/data/
db  mongo:3.6
docker run -d -p 8081:8081  --net=ecom-network --name product-
server ecom/product-server
docker run -d -p 8080:8080  --net=ecom-network --name product-
web ecom/product-web
```

One extra aspect you need to note here is the additional step of creating a folder for hosting the data files and pointing that file as the volume for the Mongo container. The folder is auto-created in the Minikube VM, since this example uses Docker within Minikube. Remember, all of this will be lost when you stop the Minikube. If you are using Docker in a host machine, you can manually create this folder too.

Listing 8-44 shows you how to build the microservices and Docker images and then run the containers.

Listing 8-44. The Dockerfile Build and Run Commands

```
(base) binildass-MacBook-Pro:ch08-05 binil$ eval $(minikube
docker-env)
(base) binildass-MacBook-Pro:ch08-05 binil$ sh makeandrun.sh
...
Successfully tagged ecom/product-web:latest
Successfully tagged ecom/product-server:latest
(base) binildass-MacBook-Pro:ch08-05 binil$
```

To list all the containers you have on your system now, execute the `docker ps` command, as shown in Listing 8-45.

Listing 8-45. List the Docker Containers

```
(base) binildass-MacBook-Pro:~ binil$ docker ps
CONTAINER ID    IMAGE                   COMMAND
CREATED         STATUS        PORTS                         NAMES
5e4c172b0e83    ecom/product-web     "java -jar /ecom.jar"
50 seconds ago   Up 50 seconds   0.0.0.0:8080->8080/tcp      product-web
24f369a0359d    ecom/product-server "java -jar /ecom.jar"
51 seconds ago   Up 50 seconds   0.0.0.0:8081->8081/tcp      product-server
bf4ccedcd7b4    mongo:3.6            "docker-entrypoint.s..."
51 seconds ago   Up 51 seconds   0.0.0.0:27017->27017/tcp   mongo
...
(base) binildass-MacBook-Pro:~ binil$
```

Now you can inspect if and how the data folder is created. Since the Docker environment is within Minikube, you need to investigate the Minikube VM for this data folder, as shown in Listing 8-46.

Listing 8-46. Inspecting the Volume Folder Created

```
(base) binildass-MacBook-Pro:~ binil$ minikube ssh
```

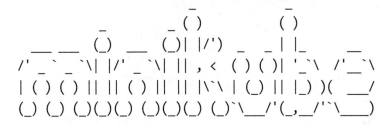

```
$ ls /Users/binil/dockerbook/ch08-05/mongodata
WiredTiger                          diagnostic.data
WiredTiger.lock                     index-1--7375842170208132306.wt
WiredTiger.turtle                   index-10--7375842170208132306.wt
WiredTiger.wt                       index-3--7375842170208132306.wt
WiredTigerLAS.wt                    index-5--7375842170208132306.wt
_mdb_catalog.wt                     index-6--7375842170208132306.wt
collection-0--7375842170208132306.wt  index-8--7375842170208132306.wt
collection-2--7375842170208132306.wt  journal
collection-4--7375842170208132306.wt  mongod.lock
collection-7--7375842170208132306.wt  sizeStorer.wt
collection-9--7375842170208132306.wt  storage.bson
$
```

You can see that the Mongo container has initialized with everything required during the container startup.

Note the container IDs from Listing 8-45. You can use these IDs to view the logs, as shown in Listing 8-47.

Listing 8-47. Product Server Container Logs

```
(base) binildass-MacBook-Pro:~ binil$ docker logs --follow
24f369a0359d

...
2022-05-30 13:55:07 INFO  InitializationComponent.init:47 -
Start...
2022-05-30 13:55:07 DEBUG InitializationComponent.init:51 -
Deleting all existing data on start...
2022-05-30 13:55:07 DEBUG InitializationComponent.init:56 -
Creating initial data on start...
2022-05-30 13:55:08 INFO  InitializationComponent.
init:105 - End
2022-05-30 13:55:12 INFO  StartupInfoLogger.logStarted:61 -
Started EcomProductMicroserviceApplication in 9.964 seconds
(JVM running for 11.603)
...
```

Listing 8-47 shows the Product Server container logs. Note that two rows are inserted as initial data in the database. Similarly, Listing 8-48 shows the Product Web container logs.

Listing 8-48. Product Web Container Logs

```
(base) binildass-MacBook-Pro:~ binil$ docker logs --follow
5e4c172b0e83
...
2022-05-30 13:55:11 INFO  StartupInfoLogger.logStarted:61 -
Started EcomProductMicroserviceApplication in 8.539 seconds
(JVM running for 10.306)
...
```

Once the containers are up and running, you can test the application.

Testing the Microservice Containers

Since the microservices and database containers are up and running, you can access the Product Web microservice. However, as mentioned in Appendix E, you must get the minikube IP first. See Listing 8-49.

Listing 8-49. Finding Minikube IP

```
(base) binildass-MacBook-Pro:ch07-02 binil$ minikube ip
192.168.64.5
(base) binildass-MacBook-Pro:ch07-02 binil$
```

You can now access the Product Web microservice using a browser with the URL formed with the Minikube IP.

```
http://192.168.64.5:8080/product.html
```

Refer to the section titled "Test the Microservice Using UI" in Chapter 1 to test the Product Web microservice container. While you test the microservices, keep watching the log windows.

Now bring down the running Mongo container, shown in Listing 8-50.

Listing 8-50. Removing the Mongo Container

```
(base) binildass-MacBook-Pro:~ binil$ docker rm -f bf4ccedcd7b4
```

Next, you can bring up a new Mongo container with the same volume attached, as shown in Listing 8-51.

Listing 8-51. Running a New Mongo Container

```
(base) binildass-MacBook-Pro:~ binil$ docker run -d -it -p
27017:27017 --name mongo  --net=ecom-network -v /Users/binil/
dockerbook/ch08-05/mongodata:/data/db  mongo:3.6
```

List the newly created Mongo container and assert that it's a new container (ID). See Listing 8-52.

Listing 8-52. Listing DockerContainers

```
(base) binildass-MacBook-Pro:~ binil$ docker ps
CONTAINER ID    IMAGE      COMMAND                  CREATED
STATUS          PORTS                     NAMES
a3b84961b0a7    mongo:3.6  "docker-entrypoint.s..."  11 seconds ago
Up 10 seconds   0.0.0.0:27017->27017/tcp    mongo
...
(base) binildass-MacBook-Pro:~ binil$
```

Now access the Product Web microservice using a browser with the URL formed with the Minikube IP.

```
http://192.168.64.5:8080/product.html
```

You can now verify that the date that has been originally created and managed by the earlier Mongo container is still safe. Once you complete testing the microservices, you can then stop and remove the microservice containers and clean the environment. See Listing 8-53.

Listing 8-53. Stopping Microservice Container and Cleaning
Environment

```
(base) binildass-MacBook-Pro:ch08-05 binil$ sh clean.sh
[INFO] Scanning for projects...
[INFO] -------------------------------------------------
[INFO] Reactor Build Order:
[INFO]
[INFO] Ecom-Product-Server-Microservice     [jar]
[INFO] Ecom-Product-Web-Microservice        [jar]
[INFO] Ecom                                 [pom]
[INFO]
...
product-web
product-server
mongo
product-web
product-server
mongo
Untagged: ecom/product-web:latest
...
Untagged: ecom/product-server:latest
...
ecom-network
(base) binildass-MacBook-Pro:ch08-05 binil$
```

Summary

You started your container and Docker journey in Chapter 7, and in this chapter, you extended that learning by exploring multiple combinations of microservice containers and database containers that interact with each other. There is one thing left, which is the containerization of the message broker. This is covered in the next chapter, where I demonstrate Kafka containers with the help of Docker Compose. Don't miss the next chapter, since you will then be equipped with the basic tools you need to create serious microservice applications on containers.

CHAPTER 9

Composing Multi-Service Containers

As microservices applications grow beyond a handful of services, we often need some way to define inter-dependency and inter-connectivity options between these services. We also need an elegant way to manage these services. Tools like Docker Compose and Kubernetes have quickly become commonplace for these types of requirements. This chapter looks at Docker Compose, followed by Kubernetes in the next chapter.

Docker Compose is used for easily defining and running multi-container Docker applications or microservices. In the previous two chapters, you learned how to effectively utilize Docker to containerize applications. When it comes to microservices, any trivial application will have more than a dozen microservices, which is many more compared to the classical single .ear or single .jar kind of monolith deployments. With Docker Compose, you can use a single YAML file to configure your microservice application's services. Then, with a single command, you create and start all the services from your YAML configuration. The following concepts are covered in this chapter.

- A quick introduction to Docker Compose

© Binildas A. Christudas 2024
B. A. Christudas, *Java Microservices and Containers in the Cloud*,
https://doi.org/10.1007/979-8-8688-0555-4_9

- Composing microservices and database containers together

- Adding message broker containers to the composition

- Demonstrating Full CRUD functionality across composed containers

As has been mentioned, the objective is to explain and demonstrate aspects in gradually increasing levels of complexity. So, the code examples start from where the last chapter stopped. It's best to read Chapter 8 before you read this chapter, so that you are acquitted with the basics of running container infrastructure. This chapter provides step-by-step instructions if you want to start straight into this chapter.

Introducing Docker Compose

As explained, when using Docker for containerization, managing many different containers can quickly become cumbersome. Docker Compose is a tool that helps you overcome this problem and handle multiple containers at once.

Using Docker Compose for packaging and deployment management is basically a three-step process:

1. You define your application's environment with a Dockerfile so that it can be reproduced anywhere.

2. You define the services that make up your application in docker-compose.yml so that they can be run together in an isolated environment.

3. As the final step, you run docker compose up, and this command starts and runs your entire app.

The next section delves into how this compose file looks.

Docker Compose YAML

In Docker Compose, you declare rules declared within a single docker-compose.yml configuration file. These YAML rules are both human-readable and machine-optimized, and hence verbal enough for you to declare the interdependencies of multiple containers. This helps you manage multiple microservices in a single application's deployment landscape.

In a Docker Compose YAML file, you need to specify the version of the Compose file format, at least one service, and optionally volumes and networks. The general format is shown in Listing 9-1.

Listing 9-1. Docker Compose YAML Format

```
version: "3"
services:
  ...
  ...
volumes:
  ...
networks:
  ...
```

Volumes, as explained in the previous chapters, are physical areas of disk space in the host computer shared between the host and a container, or even between containers. In other words, a volume is a shared directory in the host, visible from containers that have access.

Networks define the communication path and rules between containers, and between a container and the host. Shared or common network zones will make containers' services discoverable by each other, while private zones will segregate them into virtual sandboxes.

Services are typically logical groupings of related container services. As an example, a web application with different tiers could be declared, as shown in Listing 9-2.

Listing 9-2. Docker Composing Typical 3 Tier Service

```
services:
    app:
        image: my-js-app
        ...
    backend:
        image: my-boot-app
        ...
    db:
        image: mongo
        ...
```

There are many more constructs available in Docker Compose, and in line with the theme of this book, you will learn by doing things.

Docker Compose Use Cases

Even though there are more tools available for managing containerized applications, Docker Compose has its use in a few scenarios, such as:

- Developer environment: One of the best use cases for Docker Compose is in enabling developers to "getting started," which is highly useful for new entrants to a project. Docker Compose can reduce a multi-page "developer getting started guide" into a single machine-readable Compose file and a few commands that anyone can bring up using a single button. The

Docker Compose file provides a way to document and configure all the application's service dependencies (databases, message queues, caches, web service APIs, presentation apps, etc.). Using the Compose command-line tool, you can create and start one or more containers for each dependency with a single `docker-compose up` command.

- Automating test environments: Test automation is an essential part of any Continuous Deployment or Continuous Integration process and Docker Compose provides a convenient way to create and destroy testing environments custom defined for your test suite.

You can create and destroy these environments in a few commands within a Compose file:

```
docker-compose up
./run_your tests
docker-compose down
```

As mentioned, you will learn best by doing things, so let's jump straight to concrete coding examples.

Composing Microservice with PostgreSQL Containers

Chapter 8 explained why it's better to deploy state-handling applications including databases outside Docker container, since containers are designed to be more efficient in stateless kinds of operations. There can still be use cases where you'd want your database within a container, such as in cases of rapid testing. In Chapter 8, you saw a full-fledged

microservice interaction with a PostgreSQL database, all in Docker
containers. Refer to Figure 2-1 in Chapter 2 for the overall design of it. In
this section, you will modify that example to be fully deployed within a
container infrastructure using Docker Compose.

Composing the Container Topology

For this composition, you need a complete container-based deployment
topology, as shown in Figure 9-1. The Product Web and Product Server
microservices are both containerized, and the Product Server microservice
will connect to a PostgreSQL database, again deployed within a container.

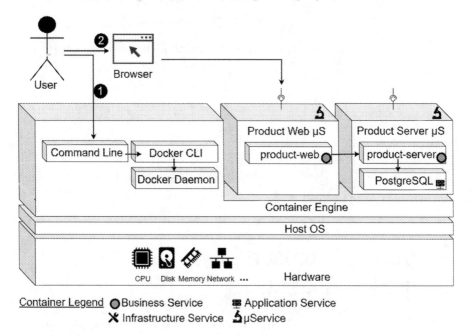

Figure 9-1. *Composing microservice containers*

Here, the Product Web and Product Server containers provide business
services, whereas the PostgreSQL container provides application services
for persisting state.

Understanding the Source Code

The source code for this book is available on GitHub via the book's product page, located at www.apress.com/9798868805547. The code for this example is organized inside the ch09\ch09-01 folder. Much of the source code in this example is similar to ch03\ch03-01, which was explained in detail in Chapter 3 in the section titled "Microservices Using PostgreSQL and RestTemplate" and in Chapter 8 in the section titled "Microservice and PostgreSQL in Container." You saw the deployment schema of these multiple interacting microservices using a PostgreSQL database in the previous chapter, so this section looks specifically into composing them using Docker Compose.

Connecting from a containerized microservice to a containerized PostgreSQL server is rather straightforward, so there are very few changes to be made when running the containers alone. The next section investigates those changes.

Listing 9-3 shows the source code organization for this example.

Listing 9-3. Example 09-01 Source Code Organization

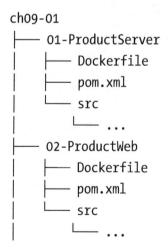

```
ch09-01
├── 01-ProductServer
│   ├── Dockerfile
│   ├── pom.xml
│   └── src
│       └── ...
├── 02-ProductWeb
│   ├── Dockerfile
│   ├── pom.xml
│   └── src
│       └── ...
```

```
├── README.txt
├── clean.sh
├── docker-compose.yml
├── makeandrun.sh
└── pom.xml
```

A concise representation of the source code organization for the example inside the ch09-01 folder is shown in Listing 9-3. Of interest here are docker-compose.yml and the Dockerfile placed inside the two project folders.

Listing 9-4. The Docker Compose YAML File (ch09\ch09-01\ docker-compose.yml)

```yaml
version: "3"

services:

    db:
        image: "postgres:9.6-alpine"
        container_name: postgres-docker
        volumes:
            - product-data:/var/lib/postgresql/data
        ports:
            - 5432:5432
        environment:
            - POSTGRES_DB=productdb
            - POSTGRES_USER=postgres
            - POSTGRES_PASSWORD=postgre
        networks:
            - ecom-network

    server:
        build: ./01-ProductServer
        image: ecom/product-server
```

```yaml
    container_name: product-server
    ports:
        - "8081:8081"
    depends_on:
        - "db"
    environment:
        - DB_SERVER=postgres-docker:5432
        - POSTGRES_DB=productdb
        - POSTGRES_USER=postgres
        - POSTGRES_PASSWORD=postgre
    networks:
        - ecom-network

web:
    build: ./02-ProductWeb
    image: ecom/product-web
    container_name: product-web
    depends_on:
        - "server"
    ports:
        - "8080:8080"
    environment:
        - acme.PRODUCT_SERVICE_URL=http://product-
          server:8081/products
    networks:
        - ecom-network

volumes:
    product-data:

networks:
    ecom-network:
```

There are three services defined here, each one an abstract definition of a computing resource within an application that can be scaled/replaced independent of other components. Each service is backed by a container and run by the platform according to the replication requirements and placement constraints. Each of these services backed by containers are defined by a Docker image and a set of runtime arguments. All containers within a service are identically created with these arguments.

You need to build an image of the server and the web from the source code by reading its Dockerfile. You can use the `build` keyword, passing the path to the Dockerfile as the value. When you specify `./01-ProductServer` and `./02-ProductWeb`, you mention that relative to the current directory (where you have the `docker-compose.yml`), go in one more folder into each of these mentioned folders to find the corresponding Dockerfile.

When the image you need for the service (as in the case of `db`) has already been published (by you or by others) in Docker Hub or another Docker Registry, it's called using the `image` attribute, by specifying the image name and tag. But when you can specify the image name in conjunction with the `build` attribute, as in the case of server and web, you name the image, making it available to other services.

To reach a container from the host, the ports of the services must be exposed declaratively through the `ports` keyword, as if you were using 8080 for `web`, 8081 for `server` and 5432 for `db`. This also allows you to choose to expose the port differently in the host, if required.

The three containers—`web`, `server`, and `db`—communicate between themselves in networks created implicitly or through configurations by Docker Compose, as you do in the example. A service can communicate with another service on the same network by simply referencing it by container name and port (for example, `product-server:8081`), if you've made the port accessible through the `expose` keyword.

Docker manages both anonymous and named volumes, automatically mounting them in self-generated directories in the host. product-data is a named volume accessible to the db service. /var/lib/postgresql/ data is the path it's mapped to, which will be used by the postgres-docker container.

You might also need to create a dependency chain between these services, so that some services are loaded before (and unloaded after) the other ones. You can achieve this result through the depends_on keyword. You want the db to be loaded before you load the server because you have the initialization script in server, inserting the initial load data to the db.

Providing the required environment variables is easy in Compose. You can define static and dynamic environment variables, the latter with the ${} notation. For example: DB_SERVER=postgres-docker:5432.

As explained, relative to the current directory (where the docker-compose.yml is located), the Dockerfile is found here:

```
build: ./01-ProductServer
```

Listing 9-5 shows this file.

Listing 9-5. The Dockerfile (ch09\ch09-01\01-ProductServer\ Dockerfile)

```
FROM maven:3.6.1-jdk-8-slim AS build
RUN mkdir -p /workspace
WORKDIR /workspace
COPY pom.xml /workspace
COPY src /workspace/src
RUN mvn -f pom.xml clean package

FROM openjdk:8-alpine
COPY --from=build /workspace/target/*.jar app.jar
EXPOSE 8081
ENTRYPOINT ["java","-jar","app.jar"]
```

A multi-stage build file is used here. With multi-stage builds, you can use multiple FROM statements in your Dockerfile. Each FROM instruction can use a different base, and each begins a new stage of the build. You can selectively copy artifacts from one stage to another.

You can name your stages by adding an AS <NAME> to the FROM instruction. The name build is used in this example. This name can be used in the second stage in the COPY instruction. This means that even if the instructions in your Dockerfile are reordered later, the COPY doesn't break.

Run Containers Using Docker Compose

The ch09\ch09-04 folder contains the scripts required to build and run these examples. The first step is to start a Minikube single-node Kubernetes cluster so that you have a Docker Daemon up. Refer to Appendix E for a quick reference to the container commands. See Listing 9-6.

Listing 9-6. Starting Minikube

```
(base) binildass-MacBook-Pro:~ binil$ pwd
/Users/binil
(base) binildass-MacBook-Pro:~ binil$ minikube start
  minikube v1.25.2 on Darwin 12.4
...
  Done! kubectl is now configured to use "minikube" cluster and
"default" namespace by default
(base) binildass-MacBook-Pro:~ binil$
```

You also need to set the Minikube environment variables in your work terminal.

Note   For all the examples in this chapter, I assume the previous
two steps connected to the Docker Daemon have been executed if
you are using the Minikube single-node Kubernetes cluster.

Listing 9-7 shows a simple script containing a single command that
builds and runs the complete application with all the defined containers.

Listing 9-7. The Script to Build and Run Microservices Docker
Containers (ch09\ch09-01\makeandrun.sh)

```
docker-compose up
```

You can build the microservices and the Docker images and then run
the containers, as shown in Listing 9-8.

Listing 9-8. Executing the Docker Compose Up Command

```
(base) binildass-MacBook-Pro:ch09-01 binil$ pwd
/Users/binil/binil/code/mac/mybooks/docker-03/ch09/ch09-01
(base) binildass-MacBook-Pro:~ binil$ eval $(minikube
docker-env)
(base) binildass-MacBook-Pro:ch09-01 binil$ sh makeandrun.sh
[+] Running 0/2
 ⁝⁝ web Error
 ⁝⁝ server Error
[+] Building 58.4s (16/20)
 => [ecom/product-server internal] load build context
 => => transferring context: 5.06kB
 => [ecom/product-web internal] load build context
 => => transferring context: 4.92kB
 => CACHED [ecom/product-web build 2/6] RUN mkdir -p /workspace
 => CACHED [ecom/product-web build 3/6] WORKDIR /workspace
```

```
=> CACHED [ecom/product-server build 4/6] COPY pom.xml
   /workspace
=> [ecom/product-server build 5/6] COPY src /workspace/src
=> CACHED [ecom/product-web build 4/6] COPY pom.xml /workspace
=> [ecom/product-web build 5/6] COPY src /workspace/src
=> [ecom/product-server build 6/6] RUN mvn -f pom.xml
   clean package
=> => # erxml/jackson/core/jackson-core/2.11.4/jackson-
       core-2.11.4.pom (4.9 kB
=> => #   at 6.2 kB/s)
=> => # Downloading from central: https://repo.maven.apache.
       org/maven2/com/fas
=> => # terxml/jackson/datatype/jackson-datatype-jdk8/2.11.4/
       jackson-datatype-
=> => # jdk8-2.11.4.pom
=> => # Progress (1): 2.2 kB
=> [ecom/product-web build 6/6] RUN mvn -f pom.xml clean
   package          56.6s
=> => # Downloaded from central: https://repo.maven.apache.
       org/maven2/com/fast
=> => # erxml/jackson/datatype/jackson-datatype-jsr310/2.11.4/
       jackson-datatype
=> => # -jsr310-2.11.4.pom (4.5 kB at 6.0 kB/s)
=> => # Downloading from central: https://repo.maven.apache.
       org/maven2/com/fas
=> => # terxml/jackson/module/jackson-module-parameter-
       names/2.11.4/jackson-mo
=> => # dule-parameter-names-2.11.4.pom
```

If this is the first time you are running this command, the microservices will be built first using Maven. This is shown in Listing 9-8. The completion of the docker-compose up command is shown in Listing 9-9.

Listing 9-9. Execution of the Docker Compose Up Command: Completed

```
(base) binildass-MacBook-Pro:ch09-01 binil$ docker-compose up
[+] Running 0/2
 ⠿ web Error
 ⠿ server Error
[+] Building 381.2s (21/21) FINISHED
...
 => [ecom/product-web stage-1 2/2] COPY --from=build
    /workspace/target/*.
 => [ecom/product-server] exporting to image
 => => exporting layers
 => => writing image sha256:76407061fc0df84b795e7aa818e4eca
       8189ba2d4e76f6
 => => naming to docker.io/ecom/product-web
 => => writing image sha256:05dc3a6cbb0248e6353beac61240a7f8115
       5c47264644
 => => naming to docker.io/ecom/product-server
 => [ecom/product-server stage-1 2/2] COPY --from=build
    /workspace/target
[+] Running 4/2
 ⠿ Network ch09-01_ecom-network   Created
 ⠿ Container postgres-docker      Created
 ⠿ Container product-server       Created
 ⠿ Container product-web          Created
Attaching to postgres-docker, product-server, product-web
postgres-docker  |
postgres-docker  | PostgreSQL Database directory appears to
contain a database; Skipping initialization
...
```

```
product-server  |  .      ___                          _ _ _
product-server  | /\\ / ___'_ __ _ _(_)_ __  __ _ \ \ \ \
product-server  | ( ( )\___ | '_ | '_| | '_ \/ _` | \ \ \ \
product-server  |  \\/  ___)| |_)| | | | | | || (_| |  ) ) ) )
product-server  |  '  |____| .__|_| |_|_| |_\__, | / / / /
product-server  | =========|_|==============|___/=/_/_/_/
product-server  |  :: Spring Boot ::                (v3.2.0)
product-server  |
product-server  | 2022-06-04 13:15:31 INFO  StartupInfoLogger.
logStarting:55 - Starting EcomProductMicroserviceApplication
v0.0.1-SNAPSHOT using Java 1.8.0_212 on 67bec9c678c1 with PID 1
(/app.jar started by root in /)
...
product-web    |
product-web    |  .      ___                          _ _ _
product-web    | /\\ / ___'_ __ _ _(_)_ __  __ _ \ \ \ \
product-web    | ( ( )\___ | '_ | '_| | '_ \/ _` | \ \ \ \
product-web    |  \\/  ___)| |_)| | | | | | || (_| |  ) ) ) )
product-web    |  '  |____| .__|_| |_|_| |_\__, | / / / /
product-web    | =========|_|==============|___/=/_/_/_/
product-web    |  :: Spring Boot ::                (v3.2.0)
product-web    |
...
product-web    | 2022-06-04 13:15:50 INFO  StartupInfoLogger.
logStarted:61 - Started EcomProductMicroserviceApplication in
20.779 seconds (JVM running for 24.665)
product-server  | 2022-06-04 13:15:52
INFO  InitializationComponent.init:45 - Start
...
product-server  | Hibernate: insert into product (code,
prodname, price, title) values (?, ?, ?, ?)
```

```
product-server    | Hibernate: insert into product (code,
prodname, price, title) values (?, ?, ?, ?)
product-server    | 2022-06-04 13:15:53
INFO  InitializationComponent.init:74 - End
product-server    | 2022-06-04 13:15:59 INFO  StartupInfoLogger.
logStarted:61 - Started EcomProductMicroserviceApplication in
30.06 seconds (JVM running for 33.926)
```

Listing 9-9 shows that the .jar files generated as a result of maven build are used to generate Docker images, and subsequently all three containers (postgres-docker, product-server, and product-web) are started.

In my Minikube-based Docker environment on the Mac, I received the following error when I tried to build the example the first time:

```
"exec: "docker-credential-desktop.exe": executable file not
found in $PATH, out:"
```

I changed credsStore to credStore in ~/.docker/config.json:

```
(base) binildass-MacBook-Pro:~ binil$ sudo nano ~/.docker/
config.json
```

Make this change, then press Control+X to quit. Enter Y to save the modified buffer. You also need to open a new terminal after making these changes (and of course set the minikube env).

Once the containers are up and running, you can test the application.

Testing the Microservice Containers

Since the microservices and database containers are up and running now, you can access the Product Web microservice. However, as mentioned in Appendix E, you have to get the Minikube IP first. See Listing 9-10.

Listing 9-10. Finding Minikube IP

```
(base) binildass-MacBook-Pro:ch07-02 binil$ minikube ip
192.168.64.5
(base) binildass-MacBook-Pro:ch07-02 binil$
```

You can now access the Product Web microservice using a browser with the URL formed with the Minikube IP.

```
http://192.168.64.5:8080/product.html
```

Refer to the section titled "Test the Microservice Using UI" in Chapter 1 to test the Product Web microservice container.

While you test the microservices, keep watching the log windows. To determine the container IDs and keep watching the log windows, refer to Chapter 8.

Once you complete testing the microservices, you can then stop and remove the microservice containers and clean the environment. To stop the containers, use this command:

```
docker-compose down
```

This command is included in Listing 9-11.

Listing 9-11. The Script to Bring Down Microservices Docker Containers (ch09\ch09-01\clean.sh)

```
docker-compose down
docker rmi -f ecom/product-web
docker rmi -f ecom/product-server
```

You can execute this script to stop and remove the microservice containers and clean the environment, as shown in Listing 9-12.

Listing 9-12. Stopping Microservice Containers and Cleaning the Environment

```
(base) binildass-MacBook-Pro:ch09-01 binil$ pwd
/Users/binil/binil/code/mac/mybooks/docker-03/ch09/ch09-01
(base) binildass-MacBook-Pro:ch09-01 binil$ sh clean.sh
[+] Running 4/4
 :: Container product-web          Removed 0.3s
 :: Container product-server       Removed 0.3s
 :: Container postgres-docker      Removed 0.2s
 :: Network ch09-01_ecom-network   Removed 0.0s
Untagged: ecom/product-web:latest
Deleted: sha256:76407061fc0df84b795e7aa818e4eca8189ba2d4e76f6cc
9adbb1d34aa14a1c3
Untagged: ecom/product-server:latest
Deleted: sha256:05dc3a6cbb0248e6353beac61240a7f81155c4726464457
eec808fa06f08bebd
(base) binildass-MacBook-Pro:ch09-01 binil$
```

You can also watch the logs in the server side console while executing the clean.sh script, as shown in Listing 9-13.

Listing 9-13. Server-side Logs While Cleaning the Environment

```
...
product-web exited with code 143
product-web exited with code 0
product-server exited with code 143
product-server exited with code 0
...
postgres-docker | LOG:  database system is shut down
postgres-docker exited with code 0
(base) binildass-MacBook-Pro:ch09-01 binil$
```

Composing Microservice with MongoDB Containers

This example again reuses the microservices from the section titled "Microservices Using MongoDB with CrudRepository" in Chapter 3. It uses the same two microservices—a consumer and a provider microservice communicating with each other using the REST protocol. The provider microservice also interacts with a MongoDB. Chapter 8 showed a full-fledged microservice example interacting with a MongoDB database, all in Docker containers. Refer to Figure 2-1 in Chapter 2 for the overall design. In this section, you modify that example to be fully deployed within a container infrastructure using Docker Compose.

Composing the Container Topology

For this composition, you need a complete container-based deployment topology, as shown in Figure 9-2. The Product Web and Product Server microservices are containerized, and the Product Server microservice will connect to a MongoDB database, again deployed within a container.

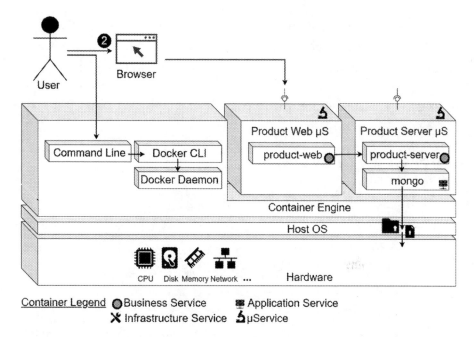

Figure 9-2. *Composing microservice containers*

Here also, the Product Web and Product Server containers provide business services, whereas the PostgreSQL container provides application services for persisting state.

Understanding the Source Code

The source code for this book is available on GitHub via the book's product page, located at www.apress.com/9798868805547. The code for this example is organized inside the ch09\ch09-02 folder. Much of the source code in this example is similar to ch03\ch03-02, which was explained in detail in Chapter 3, in the section titled "Microservices Using MongoDB and CrudRepository," and in Chapter 8, in the section titled "Microservice and MongoDB Containers Using File Mount." You saw the container-based deployment schema of these multiple interacting microservices in the previous chapter, so this section looks specifically into composing them using Docker Compose.

Let's start by looking at the docker-compose.yml file. The section describing the web service is the same as the one in Listing 9-4, so it's not repeated here. The rest of the configuration is shown in Listing 9-14.

Listing 9-14. The Docker Compose YAML File (ch09\ch09-02\ docker-compose.yml)

```
version: "3"

services:

    db:
        image: mongo:3.6
        container_name: mongo
        ports:
            - "27017:27017"
        volumes:
            - "db-data:/data/db"
        networks:
            - ecom-network

    server:
        build: ./01-ProductServer
        image: ecom/product-server
        container_name: product-server
        ports:
            - "8081:8081"
        depends_on:
            - "db"
        networks:
            - ecom-network
        environment:
            - spring.data.mongodb.uri=mongodb://192.168.64.5:
              27017/test
```

```
web:
    ...

volumes:
    db-data:
        driver: local
        driver_opts:
            o: bind
            type: none
            device: /home/docker/binil/mongodata

networks:
    ecom-network:
```

All the sections here are shown in the previous example and have been explained. Note that this example uses a named volume db-data, which uses a mounted folder from the host. You can reuse the folder created for the example in Chapter 8. The folder is auto-created in the Minikube VM, since I use Docker in Minikube in the example in Chapter 8. If you have difficulty in creating this folder, one easy hack is to execute the example in Chapter 8 and, without restarting the Minikube, try building this example. Remember, all of this will be lost when you stop the Minikube. Optionally, you can create a new folder, which is explained as the first step in next section. If you are using Docker in a host machine, you can manually create this folder too, but in the host machine.

Run Containers Using Docker Compose

The ch09\ch09-02 folder contains the scripts required to build and run the examples. The first step is to start a Minikube single-node Kubernetes cluster so that you have a Docker Daemon up. Refer to Appendix E for a quick reference to the container commands.

Assuming the Minikube single-node Kubernetes cluster is up and running, as a next step, you need to create this new folder for the Mongo data you configured in docker-compose.yml in Listing 9-14. This is done in Listing 9-15.

Listing 9-15. Creating a Local Folder Acting as Volume Mount for Mongo Data

```
(base) binildass-MacBook-Pro:mongodata binil$ minikube ssh
```

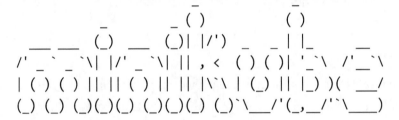

```
$ pwd
/home/docker
$ cd /home/docker
$ mkdir -p binil/mongodata
$ ls
binil
$ cd binil/mongodata/
$ ls
$ pwd
/home/docker/binil/mongodata
```

Listing 9-16 shows you how to build the microservices and the Docker images and then run the containers.

Listing 9-16. Executing the Docker Compose Up Command

```
(base) binildass-MacBook-Pro:ch09-02 binil$ pwd
/Users/binil/binil/code/mac/mybooks/docker-03/ch09/ch09-02
(base) binildass-MacBook-Pro:ch09-02 binil$ sh makeandrun.sh
[+] Running 0/2
 :: server Error
 :: web Error
[+] Building 324.8s (21/21) FINISHED
...
 => [ecom/product-server build 6/6] RUN mvn -f pom.xml
    clean package
 => [ecom/product-web build 6/6] RUN mvn -f pom.xml
    clean package
 => [ecom/product-web stage-1 2/2] COPY --from=build
    /workspace/target/*.
 => [ecom/product-server] exporting to image
 => => exporting layers
 => => writing image sha256:dc88e223b86907868d6e9ed2bd9837295b2
    6afed551f3
 => => naming to docker.io/ecom/product-web
 => => writing image sha256:d1ec2ce63b03cb6df7eaeee522fe271c0
    ac24d76b8f47
 => => naming to docker.io/ecom/product-server
 => [ecom/product-server stage-1 2/2] COPY --from=build
    /workspace/target
[+] Running 4/2
 :: Network ch09-02_ecom-network   Created
 :: Container mongo                 Created
 :: Container product-server        Created
 :: Container product-web           Created
Attaching to mongo, product-server, product-web
```

```
mongo              | 2022-06-04T14:57:12.181+0000 I CONTROL
                     [initandlisten] MongoDB starting :
                     pid=1 port=27017 dbpath=/data/db 64-bit
                     host=872d52dbcb22
...
product-web        | 2022-06-04 14:57:24 INFO  StartupInfoLogger.
                     logStarted:61 - Started EcomProduct
                     MicroserviceApplication in 9.386 seconds
                     (JVM running for 11.156)
product-server     | 2022-06-04 14:57:25 INFO  StartupInfoLogger.
                     logStarted:61 - Started EcomProduct
                     MicroserviceApplication in 10.909 seconds
                     (JVM running for 12.848)
```

Once the containers are up and running, you can test the application.

Testing the Microservice Containers

Since the microservices and database containers are up and running now, you can access the Product Web microservice. However, as mentioned in Appendix E, you must get the Minikube IP first. See Listing 9-17.

Listing 9-17. Finding Minikube IP

```
(base) binildass-MacBook-Pro:ch07-02 binil$ minikube ip
192.168.64.5
(base) binildass-MacBook-Pro:ch07-02 binil$
```

You can now access the Product Web microservice using a browser with the URL formed with the Minikube IP.

```
http://192.168.64.5:8080/product.html
```

Refer to the section titled "Test the Microservice Using UI" in Chapter 1 to test the Product Web microservice container.

While you test the microservices, keep watching the log windows. To determine the container IDs and keep watching the log windows, refer to Chapter 8.

Once you complete testing the microservices, you can then stop and remove the microservice containers and clean the environment. To stop the containers you need to use this command:

```
docker-compose down
```

It's included in the script in Listing 9-18.

Listing 9-18. The Script to Bring Down Microservices Docker Containers (ch09\ch09-02\clean.sh)

```
docker-compose down
docker rmi -f ecom/product-web
docker rmi -f ecom/product-server
```

You can execute this script to stop and remove the microservice containers and clean the environment, as shown in Listing 9-19.

Listing 9-19. Stopping Microservice Containers and Cleaning the Environment

```
(base) binildass-MacBook-Pro:ch09-02 binil$ sh clean.sh
[+] Running 3/3
[+] Running 4/4oduct-web        Removed
 :: Container product-web        Removed
 :: Container product-server     Removed
 :: Container mongo              Removed
 :: Network ch09-02_ecom-network Removed
Untagged: ecom/product-web:latest
```

```
Deleted: sha256:dc88e223b86907868d6e9ed2bd9837295b26afed551f37f...
Untagged: ecom/product-server:latest
Deleted: sha256:d1ec2ce63b03cb6df7eaeee522fe271c0ac24d76b8f47be...
(base) binildass-MacBook-Pro:ch09-02 binil$
```

This completes the example.

At this point, you have seen two examples using Docker Compose. These are real improvements over similar examples in Chapter 8 in terms of management of containers.

Having added this improvisation into your toolkit, it's time now to investigate more complex scenarios including more containers. In the next section, you add the Kafka broker to the container composition.

Composing Microservice with PostgreSQL and Kafka

In Chapter 8, in the section titled "Microservice and PostgreSQL in Container," you saw a full-fledged microservice example interaction with a PostgreSQL database, all in Docker containers. This section shows you how to modify that example so those containers can talk to each other using a messaging middleware, Kafka. You will also make the changes required to fully deploy all services within a container infrastructure using Docker Compose.

Composing the Container Topology

For the current design, you need a complete container-based deployment topology, as shown in Figure 9-3. The Product Web and Product Server microservices are containerized, and the Product Server microservice will connect to a PostgreSQL database, again deployed within a container. All communications between the Product Web microservice and the Product Server microservice are through Kafka.

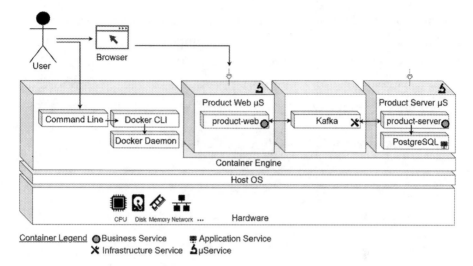

Figure 9-3. *Composing microservice containers*

Here, the Product Web and Product Server containers provide business services, whereas the Mongo container provides application services for persisting state. Kafka containers provide infrastructure services, so they are not shown as part of any specific (business) microservice.

Understanding the Source Code

The source code for this book is available on GitHub via the book's product page, located at www.apress.com/9798868805547. The code for this example is organized inside the ch09\ch09-03 folder, as shown in Listing 9-20. Much of the source code in this example is similar to ch03\ch03-01, which was explained in detail in Chapter 3, in the section titled "Microservices Using PostgreSQL and RestTemplate." In the section titled "CRUD Microservices over Kafka on PostgreSQL" in Chapter 6, you saw the code required for the Product Web microservice and the Product Server microservice to communicate with each other over the Kafka messaging channel, so those details are not covered again here. Further, you also saw the Docker Compose-based deployment of the topology of a major portion of Figure 9-3 in the section titled "Composing Microservice with PostgreSQL Containers." This section explores the Kafka container and its deployment with the other microservices using the Docker Compose tool.

Listing 9-20 shows the source code organization for this example.

Listing 9-20. Example 09-03 Source Code Organization

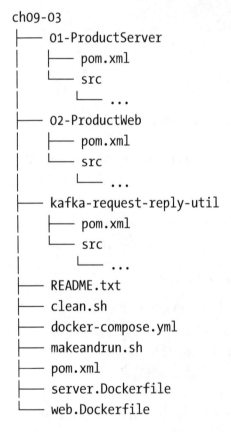

```
ch09-03
├── 01-ProductServer
│   ├── pom.xml
│   └── src
│       └── ...
├── 02-ProductWeb
│   ├── pom.xml
│   └── src
│       └── ...
├── kafka-request-reply-util
│   ├── pom.xml
│   └── src
│       └── ...
├── README.txt
├── clean.sh
├── docker-compose.yml
├── makeandrun.sh
├── pom.xml
├── server.Dockerfile
└── web.Dockerfile
```

A concise representation of the source code organization for the example inside the ch09-03 folder is shown in Listing 9-20. docker-compose.yml, server.Dockerfile, and web.Dockerfile are all placed in the parent folder, and they are referred appropriately from the docker-compose.yml file in Listing 9-21.

Listing 9-21. The Docker Compose YAML File (ch09\ch09-03\
docker-compose.yml)

```
version: "3"

services:

    zookeeper:
        image: bitnami/zookeeper:latest
        container_name: zookeeper
        ports:
            - '2181:2181'
        networks:
            - ecom-network
        environment:
            - ALLOW_ANONYMOUS_LOGIN=yes

    kafka:
        image: bitnami/kafka:latest
        container_name: kafka
        ports:
            - '9092:9092'
        networks:
            - ecom-network
        environment:
            - KAFKA_CFG_ZOOKEEPER_CONNECT=zookeeper:2181
            - ALLOW_PLAINTEXT_LISTENER=yes
        depends_on:
            - zookeeper

    db:
        image: "postgres:9.6-alpine"
        container_name: postgres-docker
```

```yaml
      volumes:
        - product-data:/var/lib/postgresql/data
      ports:
        - 5432:5432
      environment:
        - POSTGRES_DB=productdb
        - POSTGRES_USER=postgres
        - POSTGRES_PASSWORD=postgre
      networks:
        - ecom-network

  server:
    build:
      context: .
      dockerfile: server.Dockerfile
    image: ecom/product-server
    container_name: product-server
    ports:
      - "8081:8081"
    depends_on:
      - "db"
    environment:
      - DB_SERVER=postgres-docker:5432
      - POSTGRES_DB=productdb
      - POSTGRES_USER=postgres
      - POSTGRES_PASSWORD=postgre
      - spring.kafka.bootstrap-servers=kafka:9092
    networks:
      - ecom-network

  web:
    build:
      context: .
```

```
        dockerfile: web.Dockerfile
    image: ecom/product-web
    container_name: product-web
    depends_on:
        - "server"
    ports:
        - "8080:8080"
    environment:
        - spring.kafka.bootstrap-servers=kafka:9092
    networks:
        - ecom-network

volumes:
    product-data:

networks:
    ecom-network:
```

For the server and the web service, the build scripts `server.Dockerfile` and `web.Dockerfile` are referred from the current context of the `docker-compose.yml`, including the relative file paths, so Docker Compose will find these files appropriately during the build. The rest of the aspects of `db`, `web`, and `server` were explained in the first example in this chapter. `zookeeper` and `kafka` are the two new containers being configured here, and those configurations are self-explanatory.

As explained earlier, relative to the current directory (where the `docker-compose.yml` is located), the Dockerfile called `server.Dockerfile` is found here:

```
build:
    context: .
    dockerfile: server.Dockerfile
```

You can now investigate this file, as shown in Listing 9-22.

Listing 9-22. The Dockerfile (ch09\ch09-03 \server.Dockerfile)

```
FROM maven:3.6.1-jdk-8-slim AS prebuild
RUN mkdir -p /workspace
WORKDIR /workspace
COPY ./kafka-request-reply-util .
RUN mvn clean install

FROM maven:3.6.1-jdk-8-slim AS build
COPY --from=prebuild /root/.m2 /root/.m2
COPY ./01-ProductServer .
RUN mvn clean package

FROM openjdk:8-alpine
COPY --from=build ./target/*.jar app.jar
EXPOSE 8081
ENTRYPOINT ["java","-jar","app.jar"]
```

This is a three-stage build. In the first stage, you build the kafka-request-reply-util, and in the second stage, you use that .jar dependency for the Maven build for the Product Server microservice. In the third stage, you use the .jar of the Product Server microservice to build the Docker image. This image is named based on the docker-compose.yml file in Listing 9-21, under the server service, and the respective container is run.

A similar explanation holds true for the web.Dockerfile file of the Product Web microservice, so it's not repeated here.

Run Containers Using Docker Compose

The ch09\ch09-03 folder contains the scripts required to build and run the examples. The first step is to start a Minikube single-node Kubernetes cluster so that you have a Docker Daemon up. Refer to Appendix E for a quick reference to the container commands.

Assuming the Minikube single-node Kubernetes cluster is up and running, the simple script in Listing 9-23 contains a single command to build and run the complete application with all the defined containers.

Listing 9-23. The Script to Build and Run Microservices Docker Containers (ch09\ch09-03\makeandrun.sh)

```
docker-compose up
```

Listings 9-24 through 9-27 build the microservices and the Docker images and then run the containers.

Listing 9-24. The Docker Compose Up Command – Prebuild Stage

```
(base) binildass-MacBook-Pro:ch09-03 binil$ pwd
/Users/binil/binil/code/mac/mybooks/docker-03/ch09/ch09-03
(base) binildass-MacBook-Pro:~ binil$ eval $(minikube
docker-env)
(base) binildass-MacBook-Pro:ch09-03 binil$ sh makeandrun.sh
[+] Running 0/2
 ⠿ web Error
 ⠿ server Error
[+] Building 145.4s (12/24)
...
 => CACHED [ecom/product-web prebuild 2/5] RUN mkdir -p
    /workspace
 => CACHED [ecom/product-web prebuild 3/5] WORKDIR /workspace
```

```
=> [ecom/product-web prebuild 4/5] COPY ./kafka-request-
   reply-util .
=> [ecom/product-web prebuild 5/5] RUN mvn clean install
=> => # Downloaded from central: https://repo.maven.apache.
      org/maven2/org/apac
=> => # he/maven/maven-toolchain/2.0.9/maven-toolchain-
      2.0.9.pom (3.5 kB at 5.
=> => # 7 kB/s)
...
```

Listing 9-24 shows the start of the build, where the kafka-request-reply-util library is getting Maven built. The build continues in Listing 9-25.

Listing 9-25. The Docker Compose Up Command – Build Start Stage

```
(base) binildass-MacBook-Pro:ch09-03 binil$ pwd
/Users/binil/binil/code/mac/mybooks/docker-03/ch09/ch09-03
(base) binildass-MacBook-Pro:ch09-03 binil$ sh makeandrun.sh
...
=> CACHED [ecom/product-server build 2/4] COPY --from=prebuild
/root/.m2
=> [ecom/product-server build 3/4] COPY ./01-ProductServer
=> [ecom/product-server build 4/4] RUN mvn clean package
=> => # -build-configuration-parent-11.0.10.Final.pom
=> => # Downloaded from central: https://repo.maven.apache.
      org/maven2/org/infi
=> => # nispan/infinispan-build-configuration-parent/11.0.10.
      Final/infinispan-
=> => # build-configuration-parent-11.0.10.Final.pom
      (13 kB at 23 kB/s)
```

```
=> => # Downloading from central: https://repo.maven.apache.
    org/maven2/org/jbo
=> => # ss/jboss-parent/36/jboss-parent-36.pom
...
```

In Listing 9-25, you can see that the .jar generated from building the kafka-request-reply-util library is copied into the build context of the product-server and product-web microservices, and the product-server and product-web microservices are both getting built. The build continues in Listing 9-26.

Listing 9-26. The Docker Compose Up Command – Build Precompletion Stage

```
(base) binildass-MacBook-Pro:ch09-03 binil$ pwd
/Users/binil/binil/code/mac/mybooks/docker-03/ch09/ch09-03
(base) binildass-MacBook-Pro:ch09-03 binil$ sh makeandrun.sh
...
=> [ecom/product-web build 4/4] RUN mvn clean package
=> [ecom/product-web stage-2 2/2] COPY --from=build
    ./target/*.jar app.j
=> [ecom/product-web] exporting to image
=> => exporting layers
=> => writing image sha256:7c979090f142559b149b6b7f1518189
    fb33a85af0eadd
=> => naming to docker.io/ecom/product-web
```

Listing 9-26 has almost completed the packaging of the kafka-request-reply-util library and the product-server and product-web microservices and is heading toward the next stage of creating Docker images, which is shown in Listing 9-27.

Listing 9-27. The Completed Docker Compose Up Command

```
(base) binildass-MacBook-Pro:ch09-03 binil$ pwd
/Users/binil/binil/code/mac/mybooks/docker-03/ch09/ch09-03
(base) binildass-MacBook-Pro:ch09-03 binil$ sh makeandrun.sh
[+] Running 0/2
 ⠿ web Error                             6.4s
 ⠿ server Error                          6.4s
[+] Building 480.1s (24/25)
...
 ⠿ Network ch09-03_ecom-network   Created   0.1s
 ⠿ Container zookeeper            Created   0.1s
 ⠿ Container postgres-docker      Created   0.0s
 ⠿ Container product-server       Created   0.0s
 ⠿ Container kafka                Created   0.0s
 ⠿ Container product-web          Created   0.0s
Attaching to kafka, postgres-docker, product-server,
product-web, zookeeper
postgres-docker  |
postgres-docker  | PostgreSQL Database directory appears to
contain a database; Skipping initialization
...
zookeeper        | zookeeper 12:40:10.68
zookeeper        | zookeeper 12:40:10.68 Welcome to the Bitnami
                   zookeeper container

...
kafka            | [2022-06-05 12:40:16,663] INFO Session
                   establishment complete on server
                   zookeeper/172.19.0.3:2181, session id =
                   0x1000008b2470000, negotiated timeout =
                   18000 (org.apache.zookeeper.ClientCnxn)
```

```
kafka             | [2022-06-05 12:40:16,667] INFO [ZooKeeper
                    Client Kafka server] Connected. (kafka.
                    zookeeper.ZooKeeperClient)
product-server    |
product-server    |   .    ____          _            __ _ _
product-server    |  /\\ / ___'_ __ _ _(_)_ __  __ _ \ \ \ \
product-server    | ( ( )\___ | '_ | '_| | '_ \/ _` | \ \ \ \
product-server    |  \\/  ___)| |_)| | | | | || (_| |  ) ) ) )
product-server    |   '  |____| .__|_| |_|_| |_\__, | / / / /
product-server    |  =========|_|==============|___/=/_/_/_/
product-server    |  :: Spring Boot ::              (v3.2.0)
product-server    |
...
product-web       |
product-web       |   .    ____          _            __ _ _
product-web       |  /\\ / ___'_ __ _ _(_)_ __  __ _ \ \ \ \
product-web       | ( ( )\___ | '_ | '_| | '_ \/ _` | \ \ \ \
product-web       |  \\/  ___)| |_)| | | | | || (_| |  ) ) ) )
product-web       |   '  |____| .__|_| |_|_| |_\__, | / / / /
product-web       |  =========|_|==============|___/=/_/_/_/
product-web       |  :: Spring Boot ::              (v3.2.0)
product-web       |
...
product-web       | 2022-06-05 12:40:26 INFO  StartupInfoLogger.
                    logStarted:61 - Started EcomProductWeb
                    MicroserviceApplication in 10.874 seconds
                    (JVM running for 14.179)
...
product-server    | 2022-06-05 12:40:33 INFO  StartupInfoLogger.
                    logStarted:61 - Started EcomProductServer
                    MicroserviceApplication in 17.581 seconds
                    (JVM running for 21.825)
```

```
product-web      | 2022-06-05 12:40:42
                   INFO  ProductRestController.
                   getAllProducts:77 - Start
product-web      | 2022-06-05 12:40:42 INFO  ProductRest
                   Controller.getAllProducts:111 - Ending
...
```

Listing 9-27 shows the five containers up and running, as well as the microservices log indicating that they are executing user-initiated transactions from the web browser.

Once the containers are up and running, you can test the application.

Testing the Microservice Containers

Once the five containers are up and running, you can access the Product Web microservice. However, as mentioned in Appendix E, you have to get the Minikube IP first. See Listing 9-28.

Listing 9-28. Finding Minikube IP

```
(base) binildass-MacBook-Pro:ch07-02 binil$ minikube ip
192.168.64.5
(base) binildass-MacBook-Pro:ch07-02 binil$
```

You can now access the Product Web microservice using a browser with the URL formed with the Minikube IP.

```
http://192.168.64.5:8080/product.html
```

Refer to the section titled "Test the Microservice Using UI" in Chapter 1 to test the Product Web microservice container.

While you test the microservices, keep watching the log windows. To determine the container IDs and keep watching the log windows, refer to Chapter 8.

Once you have tested the microservices, you can stop and remove the microservice containers and clean the environment using the script in Listing 9-29.

Listing 9-29. The Script to Bring Down Microservices Docker Containers (ch09\ch09-03\clean.sh)

```
docker-compose down
docker rmi -f ecom/product-web
docker rmi -f ecom/product-server
```

You can execute this script to stop and remove the microservice containers and clean the environment, as shown in Listing 9-30.

Listing 9-30. Stopping Microservice Containers and Cleaning the Environment

```
(base) binildass-MacBook-Pro:ch09-01 binil$ pwd
/Users/binil/binil/code/mac/mybooks/docker-03/ch09/ch09-03
(base) binildass-MacBook-Pro:ch09-03 binil$ sh clean.sh
[+] Running 6/5
 ⠿ Container kafka               Removed    1.1s
 ⠿ Container product-web         Removed    0.3s
 ⠿ Container product-server      Removed    0.3s
 ⠿ Container postgres-docker     Removed    0.1s
 ⠿ Container zookeeper           Removed    0.5s
 ⠿ Network ch09-03_ecom-network  Removed    0.0s
Untagged: ecom/product-server:latest
Deleted: sha256:41ff845a1401143729e9979ad6239d5298
bb8556536d0fd...
Untagged: ecom/product-web:latest
Deleted: sha256:7c979090f142559b149b6b7f1518189fb33a85af
0eaddae...
```

```
(base) binildass-MacBook-Pro:ch09-03 binil$
```

You can also watch the logs in the server-side console while executing the clean.sh script, as shown in Listing 9-31.

Listing 9-31. Server-side Logs While Cleaning the Environment

```
...
product-web exited with code 143
product-web exited with code 0
...
product-server exited with code 143
kafka           | [2022-06-05 12:44:34,332] INFO [KafkaServer
id=1001] shut down completed (kafka.server.KafkaServer)
product-server exited with code 0
...
postgres-docker | LOG:  database system is shut down
postgres-docker exited with code 0
postgres-docker exited with code 0
kafka exited with code 143
kafka exited with code 0
zookeeper exited with code 143
(base) binildass-MacBook-Pro:ch09-03 binil$
```

This completes the example of composing microservices with PostgreSQL and Kafka containers.

For the completeness, the next section covers composing microservices with MongoDB and Kafka containers.

Composing Microservices with MongoDB and Kafka

Here again this example reuses the microservices from the section titled "Microservices Using MongoDB with CrudRepository" in Chapter 3.

This example uses the same two microservices—a consumer and a provider microservice. However, they communicate with each other using a Kafka messaging channel.

Composing the Container Topology

For this current design, you need a complete container-based deployment topology, as shown in Figure 9-4. The Product Web and Product Server microservices are containerized, and the Product Server microservice will connect to a MongoDB database, again deployed within a container. All communications between the Product Web microservice and the Product Server microservice are through Kafka.

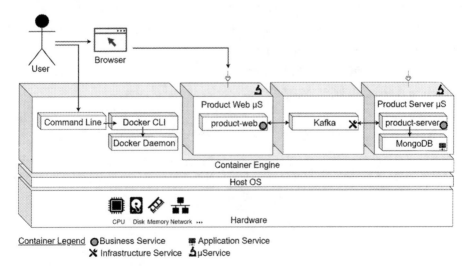

Figure 9-4. *Composing microservice containers*

447

Here, the Product Web and Product Server containers provide business services, whereas the Mongo container provides application services for persisting state. Kafka containers provide infrastructure services, so they are not shown as part of any specific (business) microservice.

Understanding the Source Code

The source code for this book is available on GitHub via the book's product page, located at www.apress.com/9798868805547. The code for this example is organized inside the ch09\ch09-04 folder and the code organization is shown in Listing 9-20. Much of the source code in this example is similar to ch03\ch03-02, which was explained in detail in Chapter 3, in the section titled "Microservices Using MongoDB and CrudRepository." In the section titled "CRUD Microservices over Kafka on MongoDB" in Chapter 6, you saw the code required for the Product Web and Product Server microservices to communicate with each other over the Kafka messaging channel, so those details are not covered again here. Further, you also saw Docker Compose-based deployment of the topology of a major portion of Figure 9-4 in the section titled "Composing Microservice with MongoDB Containers."

A major part of the docker-compose.yml file is similar to the one shown in Listing 9-21. Listing 9-32 shows only the changes.

Listing 9-32. The Docker Compose YAML File (ch09\ch09-04\ docker-compose.yml)

```
version: "3"

services:

...
    db:
        image: mongo:3.6
```

```
container_name: mongo
ports:
    - "27017:27017"
networks:
    - ecom-network
```

. . .

In fact, the MongoDB configuration in Listing 9-32 has become simpler in this case.

The Dockerfile for the microservices is similar to the previous example in Listing 9-22. This too is configured as a three-stage build.

Run Containers Using Docker Compose

The ch09\ch09-04 folder contains the scripts required to build and run these examples. The first step is to start a Minikube single-node Kubernetes cluster so that you have a Docker Daemon up. Refer to Appendix E for a quick reference to the container commands.

Assuming the Minikube single-node Kubernetes cluster is up and running, Listing 9-33 shows the simple script that contains a single command to build and run the complete application with all the defined containers.

Listing 9-33. The Script to Build and Run Microservices Docker Containers (ch09\ch09-04\makeandrun.sh)

```
docker-compose up
```

Listing 9-34 builds the microservices and the Docker images and then runs the containers.

Listing 9-34. The Completed Docker Compose Up Command

```
(base) binildass-MacBook-Pro:ch09-04 binil$ pwd
(base) binildass-MacBook-Pro:ch09-04 binil$ sh makeandrun.sh
[+] Running 0/2
 :: server Error
 :: web Error
[+] Building 402.1s (24/25)
...
 => [ecom/product-server prebuild 4/5] COPY ./kafka-request-
    reply-util
 => [ecom/product-server prebuild 5/5] RUN mvn clean install
 => [ecom/product-server build 2/4] COPY --from=prebuild
    /root/.m2 /root/
 => [ecom/product-server build 3/4] COPY ./01-ProductServer.
...
 => [ecom/product-web build 4/4] RUN mvn clean package
 => [ecom/product-web stage-2 2/2] COPY --from=build
    ./target/*.jar app.j
 => [ecom/product-server] exporting to image
 => => exporting layers
...
[+] Running 6/4
 :: Network ch09-04_ecom-network   Created
 :: Container mongo                 Created
 :: Container zookeeper             Created
 :: Container kafka                 Created
 :: Container product-server        Created
 :: Container product-web           Created
Attaching to kafka, mongo, product-server, product-web,
zookeeper
zookeeper          | zookeeper 13:38:33.77
```

```
zookeeper       | zookeeper 13:38:33.77 Welcome to the Bitnami
                  zookeeper container
...
mongo           | 2022-06-05T13:38:34.066+0000 I CONTROL
                  [initandlisten] MongoDB starting : pid=1
                  port=27017 dbpath=/data/db 64-bit
                  host=87f677f2efd6
...
kafka           | kafka 13:38:35.16
kafka           | kafka 13:38:35.16 Welcome to the Bitnami kafka
                  container
...
kafka           |
kafka           | kafka 13:38:35.60 INFO  ==> ** Starting Kafka **
...
product-server  |
product-server  | .   ____          _            __ _ _
kafka           | [2022-06-05 13:38:39,863] INFO [ZooKeeperClient
                  Kafka server] Waiting until connected. (kafka.
                  zookeeper.ZooKeeperClient)
product-server  | /\\ / ___'_ __ _ _(_)_ __  __ _ \ \ \ \
product-server  | ( ( )\___ | '_ | '_| | '_ \/ _` | \ \ \ \
product-server  | \\/  ___)| |_)| | | | | || (_| |  ) ) ) )
product-server  |  '  |___| .__|_| |_|_| |_\__, | / / / /
product-server  | =========|_|==============|___/=/_/_/_/
product-server  | :: Spring Boot ::                (v3.2.0)
product-server  |
...
product-server  | 2022-06-05 13:38:40 INFO  StartupInfo
                  Logger.logStarting:55 - Starting EcomProduct
                  ServerMicroserviceApplication v0.0.1-SNAPSHOT
                  using Java 1.8.0_212 on 0ee4c7da5620 with PID 1
                  (/app.jar started by root in /)
```

```
product-web    |
product-web    |  .   ___              _            ___ _ _
product-web    | /\\ / ___'_ __ _ _(_)_ __  __ _ \ \ \ \
product-web    | ( ( )\__ | '_ | '_| | '_ \/ _` | \ \ \ \
product-web    | \\/  ___)| |_)| | | | | | || (_| |  ) ) ) )
product-web    |  '  |____| .__|_| |_|_| |_\__, | / / / /
product-web    | =========|_|==============|___/=/_/_/_/
product-web    |  :: Spring Boot ::              (v3.2.0)
product-web    |
...
product-web    | 2022-06-05 13:38:40 INFO  StartupInfoLogger.
                 logStarting:55 - Starting EcomProductWeb
                 MicroserviceApplication v0.0.1-SNAPSHOT using
                 Java 1.8.0_212 on 4acbe5c92061 with PID 1
                 (/app.jar started by root in /)
kafka          | [2022-06-05 13:38:40,890] INFO
KafkaConfig values:
...
```

Listing 9-34 shows all five containers up and running, as well as the microservices log indicating they are waiting to respond to the transactions initiated from the web browser.

Once the containers are up and running, you can test the application.

Testing the Microservice Containers

Once all five containers are up and running, you can access the Product Web microservice. However, as mentioned in Appendix E, you have to get the Minikube IP first. See Listing 9-35.

Listing 9-35. Finding Minikube IP

```
(base) binildass-MacBook-Pro:ch07-02 binil$ minikube ip
192.168.64.5
(base) binildass-MacBook-Pro:ch07-02 binil$
```

You can now access the Product Web microservice using a browser with the URL formed with the Minikube IP.

```
http://192.168.64.5:8080/product.html
```

Refer to the section titled "Test the Microservice Using UI" in Chapter 1 to test the Product Web microservice container.

While you test the microservices, keep watching the log windows. To determine the container IDs and keep watching the log windows, refer to Chapter 8.

Once the testing is complete, you can stop and remove the microservice containers and clean the environment using the script in Listing 9-36.

Listing 9-36. The Script to Bring Down Microservices Docker Containers (ch09\ch09-04\clean.sh)

```
docker-compose down
docker rmi -f ecom/product-server
docker rmi -f ecom/product-web
```

You can execute the script in Listing 9-37 to stop and remove the microservice containers and clean the environment.

Listing 9-37. Stopping Microservice Containers and Cleaning the Environment

```
(base) binildass-MacBook-Pro:ch09-04 binil$ sh clean.sh
[+] Running 6/5
 ⠿ Container kafka            Removed      1.5s
 ⠿ Container product-web      Removed      0.4s
```

```
:: Container product-server      Removed      0.4s
:: Container mongo               Removed      0.3s
:: Container zookeeper           Removed      0.5s
:: Network ch09-04_ecom-network  Removed      0.0s
Untagged: ecom/product-server:latest
Deleted: sha256:d0cb4d2302a2891120ae3f5b28616ebaaa85a
5f25177f2c...
Untagged: ecom/product-web:latest
Deleted:
sha256:b54513d0dc3a3d5b791c988114aebb7c46dbfee106d6f0d...
(base) binildass-MacBook-Pro:ch09-04 binil$
```

You can also watch the logs in the server side console while executing the clean.sh script.

Summary

Chapter 7 introduced Docker containers and Chapter 8 explained how Docker containers can be used to better manage microservice applications. Tools like Docker Compose and Kubernetes help you further when you have more than a handful of microservices as a part of your aggregate application. This chapter showed how Docker Compose helps you when you have many business microservices, application services, and infrastructure services. Many of these services can be deployed as separate containers and this is where Docker Compose helps you manage their dependencies and lifecycles during deployment and operations. You don't need to stop with Docker; you can also consider full-fledged container orchestration tools including but not limited to Kubernetes. You'll do that in the next chapter.

CHAPTER 10

Microservices with Kubernetes

Chapter 1 discussed various levels of service granularity. As you keep splitting services into finer services, you are in fact increasing the number of moving parts in your architecture. This kind of divide-and-conquer approach in splitting to finer services is attempting to decrease the risk of an individual service failure bringing down your entire application. But on the other hand, as you increase the number of moving parts, you also increase the number of links between these moving parts, thus increasing the blast area prone to failures.

Monolithic applications consist of components and modules that are all tightly coupled and must be developed, deployed, operated, and managed as one entity, because they all run as a single process. Running a monolithic application usually requires one or a few powerful servers that can provide enough resources to run the application. When the load on the application increases, you can *vertically* scale (by increasing hardware specs) or *horizontally* scale (by introducing more replicas of the process) the application.

When you move from monolithic to microservices, most of these scaling principles are applicable, but since you have increased the number of moving parts, the overall complexity also increases many fold. In fact, the degree of complexity keeps increasing more than proportional to the new elements. You might have seen this in the chapters on Docker, where I talked

© Binildas A. Christudas 2024
B. A. Christudas, *Java Microservices and Containers in the Cloud*,
https://doi.org/10.1007/979-8-8688-0555-4_10

about images and containers, which are over and above the classical existing .jar formatted artifacts. You need a toolset and an ecosystem to better manage your application binaries in their static form (.jar and images) and in their dynamic form (containers). This topic is covered in this chapter.

The following concepts are covered in this chapter.

- Introduction to the Kubernetes architecture

- Selected Kubernetes deployment aspects

- Traffic and state management in Kubernetes

- Composing microservices and database containers together in Kubernetes

- Demonstrating Full CRUD functionality across the containers composed in Kubernetes

The World of Kubernetes

The act of splitting monolithic applications into finer, independently deployable components called microservices, packaging them as container images, and instantiating them into containers is the way forward. Each microservice is packaged into an image and runs as an independent process in the container. Each microservice communicates with other microservices through well-defined interfaces (APIs).

Figure 10-1 shows the different modes of virtualizations and application deployments from Chapter 7. In the containerized mode, the business applications are instantiated as containers over a container runtime. Docker is the container runtime used in this book. In a microservices-based architecture, you have many containers. To be specific, you may have one or more containers from the same Docker image or from different Docker images. When you have many such containers, this is where you need a container management tool or a container orchestration tool like Kubernetes.

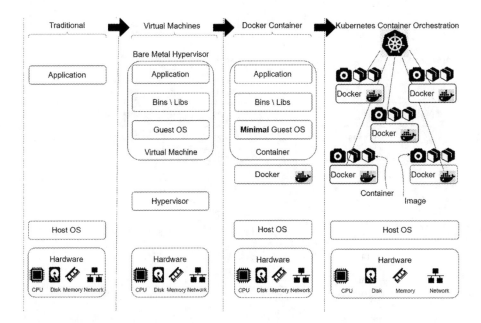

Figure 10-1. *The Kubernetes ecosystem*

Running containers is like running processes, which require their own housekeeping to be performed. Starting and stopping your containerized applications, rolling out updates, maintaining service levels, scaling containers to meet varying loads, securing access, and so on, are just a few of the many such housekeeping jobs to be performed. This section looks at how Kubernetes helps in this regard.

Kubernetes Architecture

Kubernetes is a container orchestrator. It manages running containers. A Kubernetes architecture is composed of multiple nodes, which are classified into master nodes and worker nodes. The master nodes host the Kubernetes Control Plane, whereas the worker nodes host your actual container applications.

457

You can investigate these nodes with the help of Figure 10-2.

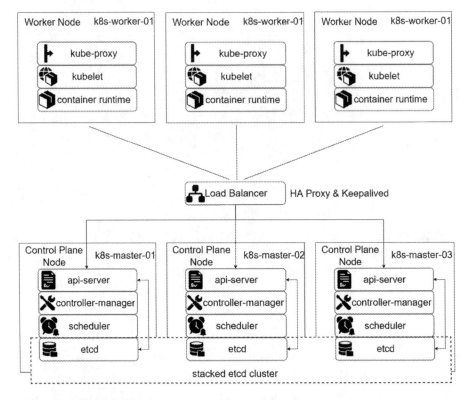

Figure 10-2. *The Kubernetes architecture*

The next section looks at the Kubernetes architecture at a high level.

The Control Plane

The master node hosts the Kubernetes Control Plane; it also controls and manages the Kubernetes system. The components of the Kubernetes Control Plane are listed here:

- The Kubernetes API server: The developer and the other components of the Kubernetes Control Plane communicate with the Control Plane using the Kubernetes API Server.

- The Scheduler: Schedules the jobs or workloads into the worker nodes of your Kubernetes cluster.

- The Control Manager: Performs Kubernetes cluster-level functions, such as replicating instances, keeping track of worker nodes, and so on.

- etcd: A reliable, distributed, and persistent data store that stores the cluster configurations.

The Node

The nodes, or the worker nodes, run your containerized applications. The major components are listed here:

- Container runtime: Runs your containers. Docker, rkt, and so on, are different container runtimes.

- The Kubelet: Talks to the API server of the Control Plane and manages containers on the respective nodes.

- The kube-proxy: Otherwise known as the Kubernetes Service Proxy, this load balances network traffic between application components.

Figure 10-2 depicts the Control Plane and the worker nodes. When you set up a Kubernetes cluster on-premises for a production environment, it is recommended that you deploy it in high availability (HA) mode. High availability means installing Kubernetes master or Control Plane in HA mode, as shown in Figure 10-2.

Kubernetes Deployment

You use different kinds of API objects to deploy workloads in Kubernetes. This section briefly looks into a few of them.

Containers

In the previous two chapters on Docker, you learned how a container works. When it comes to Kubernetes, you use those same containers as the basic unit of work. Any workload or application that runs in Kubernetes, must run inside a container. This container could be a Docker container, a rkt container, or a virtual machine (VM) managed by Virtlet.

When containers are orchestrated using Kubernetes, Kubernetes needs additional information for container management, such as a restart policy, a liveness probe, and so on. Kubernetes architecture abstracts for such additional requirements into what is called a *pod*.

Pods

Pods are the smallest deployable unit in Kubernetes. A pod will contain a container but can run multiple containers (meaning multiple applications) within it too. A pod is a wrapper on top of one or more running containers. Using pods, Kubernetes controls, monitors, and operates the containers.

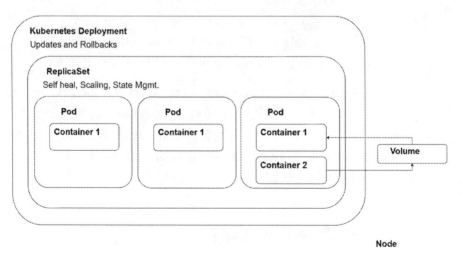

Figure 10-3. *Kubernetes deployment*

Containers in a pod run on a "logical host," since they lie in the same node (i.e., they use the same network namespace and the same IPC namespace). They can also use shared volumes, as depicted in Figure 10-3.

When an application requires more than one container running on the same host, and when those containers need to efficiently communicate ensuring data locality, they can be in the same pod. This provides process isolation; it's easier to troubleshoot the container because logs from different processes are not mixed.

ReplicaSets

Kubernetes allows you to imperatively or declaratively define and create a *ReplicaSet*. A ReplicaSet is a set of replicas (pods) maintained with their revision history. A ReplicaSet's job is to constantly monitor the list of running pods and make sure the running number of pods of a certain specification always match the desired number. Thus, a ReplicaSet is used to define and manage a collection of identical pods that are running on different cluster nodes. A ReplicaSet defines which container images are used by the containers running inside a pod and how many instances of the pod will run in the cluster, among other things.

Deployment

Deployment is a higher-level resource meant for deploying applications and updating them declaratively. When you create a Deployment, one or more ReplicaSet resources are created underneath. When using a Deployment, the actual pods are created and managed by the Deployment's ReplicaSets, not by the Deployment directly. See Figure 10-4.

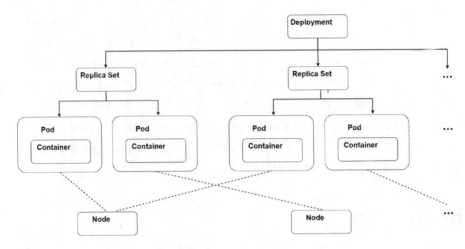

Figure 10-4. *Kubernetes deployment across nodes*

Accessing Kubernetes Services

Having looked at the deployment schema adopted with Kubernetes, this section looks at the access mechanism for accessing the workloads deployed in Kubernetes.

Accessing Kubernetes Deployments

In Kubernetes, pods are created and destroyed to match the desired state of your cluster, as specified in your deployment descriptor. Pods are temporary resources. When you use a Deployment to run your Kubernetes application, it can create and destroy pods on the fly. When pods are created, each pod gets its own IP address. When you use a Deployment, the set of pods running in one moment in time can be different than the set of pods running the same application a moment later.

Upon creation, pods are assigned an IP address. These IP addresses are visible in the cluster, which allows access from within the cluster. Other pods in the cluster can access that IP address and inter-pod communication can happen. When a pod dies, a new pod will be created that comes into service with a new IP address and anything trying to communicate with the dead pod somehow needs to know about this new address. Kubernetes provides a "service," which is an abstract way to expose an application running on a set of pods as a network service.

Kubernetes Service

The pods you saw earlier from the Deployment object can be killed or scaled up and down, so you can't rely on their IP addresses because they are not persistent. Once a pod is defined, it will exhibit the following essential but not so straight characteristics:

- Pods are ephemeral: Pods are like "tellers in a bank" in the sense that you are not served by the same teller (person) every time. Similarly pods can come and go. During scale up or scale down, pods may come and go, and if a crash occurs, pods might go and may be re-created.

- Post create IP: Kubernetes assigns an IP address to a pod after the pod has been scheduled and started. So clients can't know the IP address of the pod upfront.

- Dynamic IP list: Scaling out means more than one pod of the same type may provide the same service. Each of these (dynamic) pods has its own IP address and it may not be practical for clients to bind to a dynamic list of IPs easily. Rather, all these pods should be accessible through a single address.

To solve these problems, a service gives those pods a stable IP. In a more general sense, a *service* is an abstraction that defines a logical set of pods and a policy by which you have access to them. When a service is created, it publishes its own virtual address as an environment variable to every pod. Services not only abstract access to pods, but they can also abstract access to DBs, external hosts, or even other services. A Kubernetes service is a resource you create to make a single, stable entry point to a group of pods providing the same service. Each service is an IP address and port combination that don't change during the lifetime of the service. As shown in Figure 10-5, a Kubernetes service can be backed by a single pod or many replicas of the same pod. External clients can reach any of the pods of the same service by a single service name. Similarly, a frontend pod or, for that matter a frontend service, can also reach any of the pods of the same backend service by a single service name. Figure 10-5 shows two services—product-web and product-server.

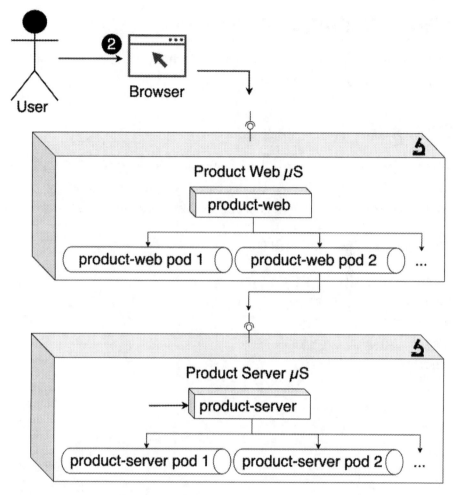

Figure 10-5. *Kubernetes services*

Here, the browser or the client device should know the service (name) of the frontend microservice—the Product Web microservice. In a similar manner, the frontend microservice should know the service (name) of the backend microservice—the Product Server microservice.

Traffic Routing to Kubernetes

There are different ways to get external traffic into your Kubernetes cluster. This section looks at how each of them works.

Cluster IP

As the name implies, this provides access only inside the Kubernetes cluster. Other apps inside your cluster can access this, but there is no external access to the service. Cluster IP is described in Listing 10-1.

Listing 10-1. The ClusterIP Definition

```
apiVersion: v1
kind: Service
metadata:
  name: product-web
spec:
  selector:
    app: product-web
  type: ClusterIP
  ports:
  - name: http
    port: 80
    targetPort: 80
    protocol: TCP
```

You might now wonder how you access the service externally? The answer is to use a Kubernetes proxy, as shown in Figure 10-6.

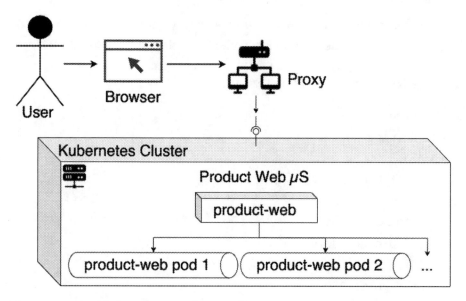

Figure 10-6. *Kubernetes proxy to ClusterIP*

You can start a Kubernetes proxy with this command:

```
(base) binildass-MacBook-Pro:ch10-01 binil$ kubectl
proxy --port=8080
```

This will create a proxy server or application-level gateway between the localhost and the Kubernetes API server. All incoming data enters through one port and is forwarded to the remote Kubernetes API server port.

NodePorts

When you expose the service as a NodePort service, each cluster node opens a port on the node itself (hence the name) and redirects traffic received on that port to the respective service. The service is not only accessible at the internal cluster IP and port, but also through a dedicated port on all nodes or virtual machines.

A NodePort is thus the most primitive way to get external traffic directly to your service. The definition of a NodePort is shown in Listing 10-2.

Listing 10-2. The NodePort Definition

```
apiVersion: v1
kind: Service
metadata:
  name: product-server-nodeport
spec:
  selector:
    app: product-server
  ports:
    - nodePort: 30002
      port: 8081
      targetPort: 8081
  type: NodePort
```

In Listing 10-2, 30002 is specified as the nodePort. You can only use ports 30000 to 32767, and if it's not specified, a random port is used.

As shown in Figure 10-7, since a service spans across nodes, a connection received on a port of the first node might be forwarded either to the pod running on the same first node or to one of the pods running on the other nodes.

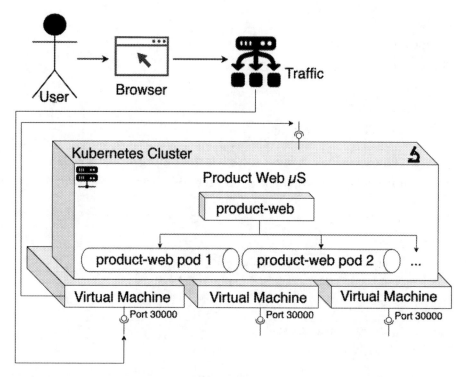

Figure 10-7. *Node port in Kubernetes*

Load Balancer

Using a load balancer, you can expose services to the Internet. This makes the service accessible through a dedicated load balancer, provisioned from the cloud infrastructure that Kubernetes is running on. See Listing 10-3.

Listing 10-3. The LoadBalancer Definition

```
apiVersion: v1
kind: Service
metadata:
  name: product-web
spec:
```

```
selector:
  app: product-web
type: LoadBalancer
ports:
  - port: 8765
    targetPort: 80
```

When you use a load balancer, there is no routing or filtering, and all the traffic you specify will be forwarded to the service, as shown in Figure 10-8.

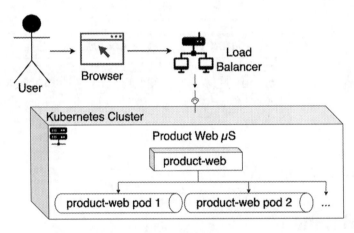

Figure 10-8. *Load balancer in Kubernetes*

The downside of the load balancer is that each service you expose will get its own IP address, and you must pay for one load balancer each for all services exposed.

Ingress

An *ingress* can expose multiple services through a single IP address. Ingress operates at the HTTP level (network layer 7), so it's cost efficient. There are many kinds of ingress with different capabilities. See Figure 10-9.

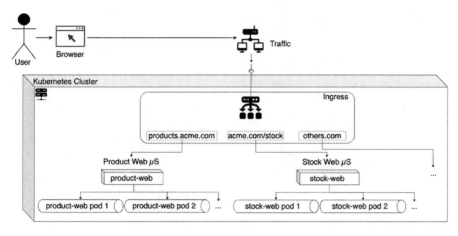

Figure 10-9. *Ingress in Kubernetes*

Listing 10-4 defines an ingress with two rules.

Listing 10-4. The Ingress Definition

```
apiVersion: networking.k8s.io/v1
kind: Ingress
metadata:
  name: ingress-service
  annotations:
    kubernetes.io/ingress.class: nginx
spec:
  rules:
    - host: "adminer.acme.test"
      http:
        paths:
          - path: /
            pathType: Prefix
            backend:
              service:
```

```
                name: adminer
                port:
                    number: 8080
     - host: "products.acme.test"
       http:
         paths:
            - path: /
              pathType: Prefix
              backend:
                service:
                    name: product-web
                    port:
                        number: 8080
```

The rules in Listing 10-4 ensure that all HTTP requests received by the Ingress controller, in which the products.acme.test host is requested, will be sent to the product-web service on port 8080 and that all HTTP requests in which the adminer.acme.test host is requested will be sent to the adminer service on port 8080.

State Management

When you look at pods and deployments in detail, you know that Kubernetes pods are to be designed for scaling out, even elastically. There is a downside to scaling architectures.

Scale Out vs. State Management

Although it is desirable to have elastic scale out architectures, state management poses issues. If the components are to be truly stateless, they are to be like "tellers in a bank" in the sense that you are not served by the same teller (person) every time. Similarly, every subsequent transaction could be served by any other instance of the similar component. This means, except your client device and your persistent store, every other intermediate component must be stateless. You cannot avoid state in the client tier, since then you cannot do any personalization, which will inhibit user experience. Similarly, for non-trivial applications, some kind of state has to be managed and you would typically do that in some kind of database.

StatefulSets

To solve the issue of state management, a *StatefulSet* represents a set of pods that are unique, persistent, and have a stable pod name (see Figure 10-10). In the case of the non-stateful DeploymentSet, whenever you deploy a pod, upon every deployment or restart you will get a different pod name—something like `product-server-6fb88b6849-6mrf5` or `product-web-5dfc886d6d-zvm8p`. In such cases, the pod name will change when it restarts. And on the next restart, it could be anything, like `product-web-5dfc886d6d-4qw45` or `product-server-6fb88b6849-dwkcf`. If you want a stable pod name, a StatefulSet can be used. Then, even when the deployment restarts, you will get the same pod name (such as `mongo-cluster-0`).

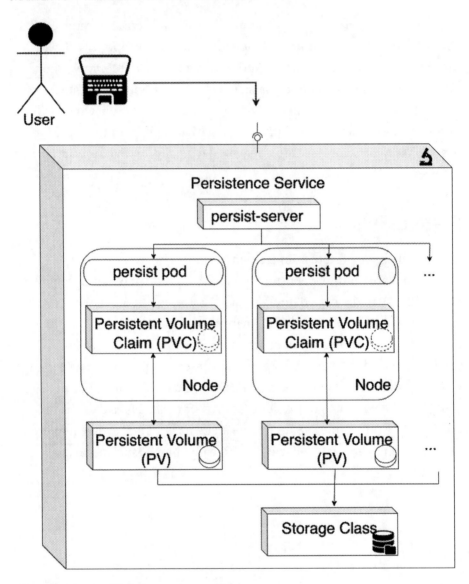

Figure 10-10. *Kubernetes stateful sets*

Persistent Volume Claim

A *persistent volume claim* (PVC) is a declaration by the pod for a need for storage that can at some point in the lifecycle of the pod become available or satisfied. A persistent volume claim promises that it will at some point "translate" into some platform specific storage volume that your application will be able to use, with one of defined characteristics, such as class, size, and access mode (ROX: ReadOnlyMany, RWO: ReadWriteOnce, and RWX: ReadWriteMany).

In this manner you can abstract linking of a particular storage implementation away from your pods/deployments. Your application in typical cases specify something like "I need persistent storage of default class and size Y." Later, during the time when the "promise" is fulfilled at runtime, you can link an EBS device, an EFS store, and so on, and your core manifests are the same in both cases.

Persistent Volume

A *persistent volume* (PV) is a piece of storage in the Kubernetes cluster that has been provisioned by the server/storage/cluster administrator or dynamically provisioned using some storage classes. It is a resource in the cluster just like a node. So, the persistent volume is the actual product or options that you get back from Kubernetes that you asked for. If Kubernetes does not have what you asked for, it will try to create it on the fly for you.

In the section illustrating the first example in this chapter, especially in Listings 10-11 through 10-14, you will come across how all these concepts of state management are affected with running examples.

Kubernetes Clusters

As you have seen, a Kubernetes cluster is a set of nodes that run containerized applications. Kubernetes clusters allow containers to run across multiple machines and environments—virtual, physical, cloud-based, or on-premises. Creating a Kubernetes cluster from scratch is a non-trivial task. Adding to the complexity, there are multiple options and tools to select from.

As an easier path, there is Minikube, which is a local Kubernetes tool, focusing on making it easy to learn and develop for Kubernetes. You do need other and better options to run production workloads.

Minikube

As stated, Minikube is local Kubernetes. It is rather easy to set up a single-node, local Kubernetes using Minikube. Moreover, a local Kubernetes will also speed up the cycle time of code, test, deploy, and debug cycle on the developer machine before you commit changes to your teams environment. Minikube will also enable developers to develop and test containerized applications in Windows and Mac environments, which are the preferred development machine OSes among application developers.

Appendix E on container tools provides detailed instructions to install and bring up Minikube in a Mac environment.

The next section gets into some code. You will deploy the first application into a Minikube-based local Kubernetes cluster.

Microservices and MongoDB in Kubernetes

This example reuses the microservices from the section titled "Microservices Using MongoDB and CrudRepository" in Chapter 3. It uses the same two microservices—a consumer and a provider microservice communicating with each other using the REST protocol. The provider microservice also interacts with a MongoDB. You will use volumes to persist the Mongo database data. Refer to Figure 2-1 in Chapter 2 for the overall design.

Design Microservices Deployment Topology

This example reuses the deployment schema defined in the second example in Chapter 9, shown in Figure 9-2. The one change is that this example uses Kubernetes.

The deployment topology of the microservices is shown in Figure 10-11.

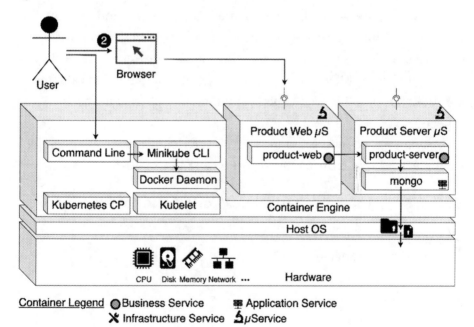

Figure 10-11. *Kubernetes-based deployment topology for microservices*

Here, the Product Web and Product Server containers provide business services, whereas the Mongo container provides application services for persisting state.

Understanding the Source Code

The source code for this book is available on GitHub via the book's product page, located at www.apress.com/9798868805547. The source code for the example is organized inside the ch10\ch10-01 folder. Much of the source code in this example is similar to ch03\ch03-02, which was explained in detail in Chapter 3, in the section titled "Microservices Using MongoDB and CrudRepository." You also saw the Docker-based deployment of the topology in Figure 8-9, in the section titled "Microservice and MongoDB Containers Using File Mount" in Chapter 8. The Docker Compose-based deployment of the topology was also shown in Figure 9-2, in the section titled "Composing Microservice with MongoDB Containers" in Chapter 9. For those reasons, this section gets right into the Kubernetes-specific aspects.

A summarized representation of the source code organization for the example inside the ch10-01 folder is shown in Listing 10-5.

Listing 10-5. Example 10-01 Source Code Organization

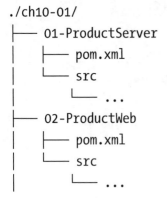

```
./ch10-01/
├── 01-ProductServer
│   ├── pom.xml
│   └── src
│       └── ...
├── 02-ProductWeb
│   ├── pom.xml
│   └── src
│       └── ...
```

```
├── Dockerfile
├── README.txt
├── clean.sh
├── makeandrun.sh
├── mongo-deployment.yml
├── mongo-service.yml
├── mongo-volume-claim.yml
├── mongo-volume.yml
├── pom.xml
├── product-server-deployment.yml
├── product-server-service.yml
├── product-web-deployment.yml
└── product-web-service.yml
```

This Dockerfile is like the one from the section titled "Build Microservice Using Dockerfile" of Chapter 7, so I do not repeat the explanation here. There are a set of .yml files as well.

Creating the Kubernetes resources is done by posting a JSON or YAML manifest to the Kubernetes's REST endpoint. This helps to version-control these resource definitions.

The first resource I investigate is a pod, which is a collocated group of containers. It represents the basic building block in Kubernetes. You always deploy and operate on a pod of containers. It's very common for pods to contain only a single container, but if you think you have closely related containers, you may have more than one container in a pod. Sidecar containers are one such example, where a log and a data change watcher can be in the same pod of the main container.

Subsequently, even though you can host a multi-tier application (such as ProductWeb and ProductServer) in a single pod, the recommended way is to use separate pods for each tier. The reason for that is simple—you can scale out tiers independently and distribute them across clusters. See Listing 10-6.

Listing 10-6. The Pod Definition YAML File for Product Web (ch10\ch10-01\product-web-deployment.yml)

```
---
apiVersion: apps/v1
kind: Deployment
metadata:
  name: product-web
  labels:
    app: product-web
    group: frontend
spec:
  replicas: 1
  selector:
    matchLabels:
      app: product-web
  template:
    metadata:
      labels:
        app: product-web
    spec:
      containers:
      - name: product-web
        image: ecom/product-web
        ports:
        - containerPort: 8080
        imagePullPolicy: Never
        env:
          - name: acme.PRODUCT_SERVICE_URL
            value: http://product-server:8081/products
```

In the pod definition in Listing 10-6, the first line is a separator, and it is optional. If you're trying to define multiple structures in a single file, the separator is required. The metadata contains the name, namespace, labels, and other information about the Kubernetes pod.

Listing 10-6 shows the pod descriptor for the Product Web microservice. Here, Spec includes the actual description of the Kubernetes pod's contents, such as the pod's containers, number of replicas, the image, volumes, and other data.

Note the containerPort: 8080. Even if you don't assign a port, clients can still connect to the pod. If the app binds to 127.0.0.1, it will effectively prevent traffic to the pod, whereas 0.0.0.0 allows traffic to the pod on all interfaces, even if the port isn't listed in the pod spec explicitly. But if you define the ports explicitly, everyone using your cluster can quickly see which ports each pod exposes. Explicitly defining ports also allows you to assign a name to each port, which can be handy.

The Product Web microservice is dependent on the appropriate value for an environment variable acme.PRODUCT_SERVICE_URL, whose value you set as the service URL for the dependent Product Server microservice, which you will see in Listing 10-9.

In the same manner you created a pod, the easiest way to create a Kubernetes service is to post a JSON or YAML manifest to the Kubernetes's REST endpoint, as shown by the Kubernetes service of the Product Web microservice in Listing 10-7.

Listing 10-7. The Service Definition YAML File for Product Web (ch10\ch10-01\product-web-service.yml)

```
apiVersion: v1
kind: Service
metadata:
  name: product-web
spec:
```

```
selector:
  app: product-web
ports:
  - protocol: TCP
    port: 8080
    targetPort: 8080
type: LoadBalancer
```

In Listing 10-7, the service has a name, product-web. The port refers to which port this service will be available on and the targetPort is the container port to which the request will be forwarded, to avail the service. So, to summarize, you're defining a service called product-web, which will accept requests on port 80 and route each request to port 8080 of one of the pods matching the app=product-web label selector. You can also see that a LoadBalancer is defined for easy access to the services.

Listing 10-8 shows the pod description for the Product Server microservice.

Listing 10-8. The Pod Definition YAML File for Product Server (ch10\ch10-01\product-server-deployment.yml)

```
apiVersion: apps/v1
kind: Deployment
metadata:
  name: product-server
  labels:
    app: product-server
    group: backend
spec:
  replicas: 1
  selector:
    matchLabels:
```

```
      app: product-server
  template:
    metadata:
      labels:
        app: product-server
    spec:
      containers:
      - name: product-server
        image: ecom/product-server
        ports:
        - containerPort: 8081
        imagePullPolicy: Never
        env:
          - name: spring.data.mongodb.uri
            value: mongodb://mongo:27017/test
```

One notable aspect here is that the Product Server microservice is dependent on the appropriate value for an environment variable spring.data.mongodb.uri, whose value is set as the service URL for the dependent Mongo DB, which you will see in Listing 10-15.

Listing 10-9 shows the service description for the Product Server microservice.

Listing 10-9. The Service Definition YAML File for Product Server (ch10\ch10-01\product-server-service.yml)

```
apiVersion: v1
kind: Service
metadata:
  name: product-server
spec:
  selector:
```

```
    app: product-server
  ports:
    - protocol: TCP
      port: 8081
      targetPort: 8081

---

apiVersion: v1
kind: Service
metadata:
  name: product-server-nodeport
spec:
  selector:
    app: product-server
  ports:
    - nodePort: 30002
      port: 8081
      targetPort: 8081
  type: NodePort
```

There is no need for the Product Server microservice to be accessed by any external clients, so I omitted the LoadBalancer type of service definition, which you saw in Listing 10-7 for Product Web microservice. A ClusterIP would have been enough, but an additional NodePort was defined, the advantage of which I explain in the "Test the Microservices" section.

The third component in Figure 10-11 is the MongoDB. Listing 10-10 shows the pod definition for the MongoDB.

Listing 10-10. The Pod Definition YAML File for MongoDB Server
(ch10\ch10-01\mongo-deployment.yml)

```yaml
apiVersion: apps/v1
kind: StatefulSet
metadata:
  name: mongo-cluster
  labels:
    app: mongo
spec:
  replicas: 1
  serviceName: "mongo"
  selector:
    matchLabels:
      app: mongo
  template:
    metadata:
      labels:
        app: mongo
      annotations:
        sidecar.istio.io/inject: "false"
    spec:
      volumes:
        - name: data-db
          persistentVolumeClaim:
            claimName: mongo-data-db
      terminationGracePeriodSeconds: 10
      containers:
        - name: mongo
          image: mongo:4.2.24
          volumeMounts:
            - mountPath: /data/db
```

```
            name: data-db
            readOnly: false
        ports:
          - containerPort: 27017
```

This example specifies using mongo:4.2.24 as the image based on which the pod is created. Note that the pod is defined as a StatefulSet. The Mongo pod has to manage data or state in the MongoDB, so you need a stateful set. It also defines a persistentVolumeClaim—mongo-data-db. The next section looks at the description of this PVC.

Listing 10-11. The Persistent Volume Claim Definition for MongoDB (ch10\ch10-01\mongo-volume-claim.yml)

```
apiVersion: v1
kind: PersistentVolumeClaim
metadata:
  name: mongo-data-db
spec:
  storageClassName: manual
  accessModes:
    - ReadWriteOnce
  resources:
    requests:
      storage: 3Gi
```

Now you create the PersistentVolumeClaim. The MongoDB pod uses PersistentVolumeClaim to request physical storage. You request a volume of at least 3GB, so it can provide read-write access for at least one node. Once you execute the scripts in the next section, you can inspect the PersistentVolumeClaim, as shown in Listing 10-12.

Listing 10-12. Listing the Details of the Persistent Volume Claim

```
(base) binildass-MacBook-Pro:~ binil$ kubectl get pvc
mongo-data-db
NAME            STATUS   VOLUME          CAPACITY
ACCESS MODES    STORAGECLASS   AGE
mongo-data-db   Bound    mongo-data-db   10Gi
RWO             manual         2m32s
(base) binildass-MacBook-Pro:~ binil$
```

Once you create the `PersistentVolumeClaim`, the Kubernetes Control Plane looks for a `PersistentVolume` that satisfies the claim's requirements. See Listing 10-13.

Listing 10-13. The Persistent Volume Definition for MongoDB (ch10\ch10-01\mongo-volume.yml)

```
apiVersion: v1
kind: PersistentVolume
metadata:
  name: mongo-data-db
  labels:
    type: local
spec:
  storageClassName: manual
  capacity:
    storage: 10Gi
  accessModes:
    - ReadWriteOnce
  hostPath:
    path: "/home/docker/binil/mongodata"
```

With this, the Control Plane can find this PersistentVolume with the same storage class using the storageClassName, so it binds the claim to the volume. After you execute the scripts in the next section, you can inspect the PersistentVolume, as shown in Listing 10-14.

Listing 10-14. Listing the Details of the Persistent Volume

```
(base) binildass-MacBook-Pro:~ binil$ kubectl get pv
mongo-data-db
NAME          CAPACITY ACCESS MODES RECLAIM STATUS CLAIM
STORAGECLASS              AGE
mongo-data-db 10Gi     RWO            Retain  Bound
mongo-data-db manual     44s
(base) binildass-MacBook-Pro:~ binil$
```

As far as Kubernetes knows, mongo-data-db PV is just some piece of storage somewhere and its lifecycle is independent on the pod that's using it. So, even if the pod goes away—say it crashes or hits a memory limit and is killed due to an Out of Memory error—the storage is still there, ready to be used by your MongoDB pod when it regenerates. So this persistent volume will persist no matter what happens with the pod (sort of), since the RECLAIM policy is Retain, as you can see in Listing 10-14. When the PVC is deleted, Kubernetes will handle the PV according to the RECLAIM policy of the PV.

The last aspect left is defining the MongoDB service, which is done in Listing 10-15.

Listing 10-15. The Description for MongoDB Service (ch10\ ch10-01\mongo-service.yml)

```
apiVersion: v1
kind: Service
metadata:
  name: mongo
```

```
spec:
  selector:
    app: mongo
  ports:
    - protocol: TCP
      port: 27017
      targetPort: 27017

---

apiVersion: v1
kind: Service
metadata:
  name: mongo-nodeport
spec:
  selector:
    app: mongo
  ports:
    - nodePort: 30001
      port: 27017
      targetPort: 27017
  type: NodePort
```

As with the Product Server Service description in Listing 10-9, a ClusterIP would have been enough, but this example defined an additional NodePort, the advantage of which I explain in the "Test the Microservices" section.

Run Microservices in Kubernetes

The ch10\ch10-01 folder contains the scripts required to build and run the examples. The first step is to start a Minikube single-node Kubernetes cluster. Refer to Appendix E for a quick reference to the Kubernetes setup and commands. See Listing 10-16.

Listing 10-16. Starting Minikube

```
(base) binildass-MacBook-Pro:~ binil$ pwd
/Users/binil
(base) binildass-MacBook-Pro:~ binil$ minikube start
  minikube v1.25.2 on Darwin 12.4
...
  Done! kubectl is now configured to use "minikube" cluster and
  "default" namespace by default
(base) binildass-MacBook-Pro:~ binil$
```

You must also set the Minikube environment variables in your work terminal.

Note   For all the examples in this chapter, I assume that the previous two steps connected to the Docker Daemon have been executed if you are using the Minikube single-node Kubernetes cluster.

As the next step, you need to create this new folder for Mongo data you configured in mongo-volume.yml. See Listing 10-17.

Listing 10-17. Creating a Local Folder Acting as Volume Mount for Mongo Data

```
(base) binildass-MacBook-Pro:mongodata binil$ minikube ssh
```

490

```
$ pwd
/home/docker
$ cd /home/docker
$ mkdir -p binil/mongodata
$ ls
binil
$ cd binil/mongodata/
$ ls
$ pwd
/home/docker/binil/mongodata
$ ls
$
```

The simple script called makeandrun.sh contains a single command to build and run the complete application with all the defined deployments, and it is shown in Listing 10-18.

Listing 10-18. The Script to Build and Run Microservices in Kubernetes (ch10\ch10-01\makeandrun.sh)

```
mvn -Dmaven.test.skip=true clean package
docker build  --build-arg JAR_FILE=02-ProductWeb/target/
*.jar -t ecom/product-web .
docker build  --build-arg JAR_FILE=01-ProductServer/target/*.
jar -t ecom/product-server .
# docker network create ecom-network
# docker pull mongo:4.2.24
kubectl create -f mongo-volume.yml
kubectl create -f mongo-volume-claim.yml
kubectl create -f mongo-deployment.yml
kubectl create -f mongo-service.yml
kubectl create -f product-server-deployment.yml
kubectl create -f product-server-service.yml
```

```
kubectl create -f product-web-deployment.yml
kubectl create -f product-web-service.yml
minikube service product-web --url
sleep 3
kubectl get pods
kubectl get services
```

In Appendix E, you might have noticed that I used this command from Listing E-22:

```
kubectl apply -f https://raw.githubusercontent.com/scriptcamp/
minikube/main/nginx.yaml
```

This is declarative management, whereby you specify the required outcome, not the individual steps needed to achieve that outcome. This command applies a configuration to a resource by filename or stdin. The resource name must be specified. JSON and YAML formats are accepted.

However, Listing 10-18 uses kubectl create. This is an imperative way of specification, meaning that you give a series of instructions or steps to reach the goal. You specify what and how you should reach the goal. The kubectl create command also creates a resource from a file or from stdin. JSON and YAML formats are accepted.

You can now execute the script shown in Listing 10-19.

Listing 10-19. Executing the Script to Build and Run Microservice Pods in Kubernetes

```
(base) binildass-MacBook-Pro:ch10-01 binil$ pwd
/Users/binil/binil/code/mac/mybooks/docker-04/Code/ch10/ch10-01
(base) binildass-MacBook-Pro:ch10-01 binil$ eval $(minikube
docker-env)
(base) binildass-MacBook-Pro:ch10-01 binil$ sh makeandrun.sh
[INFO] Scanning for projects...
```

```
[INFO] ------------------------------------------------------------
[INFO] Reactor Build Order:
[INFO]
[INFO] Ecom-Product-Server-Microservice    [jar]
[INFO] Ecom-Product-Web-Microservice       [jar]
[INFO] Ecom                                [pom]
[INFO]
...
[INFO]
[INFO] Ecom-Product-Server-Microservice .. SUCCESS [   3.687 s]
[INFO] Ecom-Product-Web-Microservice ..... SUCCESS [   0.842 s]
[INFO] Ecom ............................. SUCCESS [   0.043 s]
[INFO] ------------------------------------------------------------
[INFO] BUILD SUCCESS
[INFO] ------------------------------------------------------------
[INFO] Total time:  4.836 s
[INFO] Finished at: 2023-05-25T19:18:03+05:30
[INFO] ------------------------------------------------------------
...
persistentvolume/mongo-data-db created
persistentvolumeclaim/mongo-data-db created
statefulset.apps/mongo-cluster created
service/mongo created
service/mongo-nodeport created
deployment.apps/product-server created
service/product-server-nodeport created
deployment.apps/product-web created
service/product-web created
http://192.168.64.6:30503
...
(base) binildass-MacBook-Pro:ch10-01 binil$
```

Once the pods are running, you can inspect the data folder created in Listing 10-20 and see that it has been initialized. This is because you are initializing a few rows of data in MongoDB using the InitializationComponent class in the Product Server microservice.

Listing 10-20. Inspecing the Local Folder Acting as Volume Mount for Mongo Data

```
(base) binildass-MacBook-Pro:~ binil$ minikube ssh
```

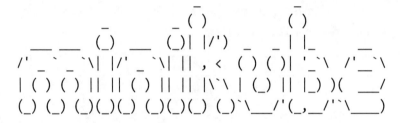

```
$ pwd
/home/docker
$ cd /home/docker/binil/mongodata
$ ls
WiredTiger                               diagnostic.data
WiredTiger.lock                          index-1-840414156336134639.wt
WiredTiger.turtle                        index-11-840414156336134639.wt
WiredTiger.wt                            index-3-840414156336134639.wt
WiredTigerLAS.wt                         index-5-840414156336134639.wt
_mdb_catalog.wt                          index-6-840414156336134639.wt
collection-0-840414156336134639.wt       index-9-840414156336134639.wt
collection-10-840414156336134639.wt      journal
collection-2-840414156336134639.wt       mongod.lock
collection-4-840414156336134639.wt       sizeStorer.wt
collection-8-840414156336134639.wt       storage.bson
$
```

Once all the pods have been created, how do you know if it's running? You can list the pods to see their status, as shown in Listing 10-21.

Listing 10-21. Listing the Status of the Kubernetes Pods

```
(base) binildass-MacBook-Pro:~ binil$ kubectl get pods
NAME                            READY STATUS    RESTARTS AGE
mongo-cluster-0                 1/1   Running   0        3m53s
product-server-6fb88b6849-q2pfx 1/1   Running   0        3m52s
product-web-5dfc886d6d-8cl7t    1/1   Running   0        3m52s
(base) binildass-MacBook-Pro:~ binil$
```

The kubectl exec command allows you to remotely run arbitrary commands inside an existing container of a pod. This will help when you want to examine the contents, state, and/or environment of a container. You can inspect the environment variables of the Product Web pod in Listing 10-22 by referencing the pod name from Listing 10-21.

Listing 10-22. Listing the Environment Variables for Product Web Microservice

```
(base) binildass-MacBook-Pro:~ binil$ kubectl exec product-
web-5dfc886d6d-8cl7t env
...
acme.PRODUCT_SERVICE_URL=http://product-server:8081/products
```

The command in Listing 10-22 will spit out all the environment variables that you configured in Listing 10-6.

Next, list the Kubernetes services, as shown in Listing 10-23.

Listing 10-23. Listing the Kubernetes Services

```
(base) binildass-MacBook-Pro:~ binil$ kubectl get svc
NAME                TYPE          CLUSTER-IP     PORT(S)
kubernetes          ClusterIP     10.96.0.1      443/TCP
mongo               ClusterIP     10.98.30.13    27017/TCP
mongo-nodeport      NodePort      10.110.211.153 27017:30001/TCP
product-server      ClusterIP     10.102.46.205  8081/TCP
product-server-np   NodePort      10.109.197.184 8081:30002/TCP
product-web         LoadBalancer  10.98.43.63    8080:30503/TCP
(base) binildass-MacBook-Pro:~ binil$
```

Note   I have abbreviated product-server-nodeport to product-server-np in Listing 10-23 for formatting convenience.

Listing 10-24 examines one of the services from Listing 10-23 in more detail.

Listing 10-24. Describing the Kubernetes Service

```
(base) binildass-MacBook-Pro:~ binil$ kubectl describe svc
product-web
Name:                product-web
Namespace:           default
Labels:              <none>
Annotations:         <none>
Selector:            app=product-web
Type:                LoadBalancer
IP Family Policy:    SingleStack
IP Families:         IPv4
```

```
IP:                        10.98.43.63
IPs:                       10.98.43.63
Port:                      <unset>  8080/TCP
TargetPort:                8080/TCP
NodePort:                  <unset>  30503/TCP
Endpoints:                 10.244.1.104:8080
Session Affinity:          None
External Traffic Policy:   Cluster
Events:                    <none>
(base) binildass-MacBook-Pro:~ binil$
```

As you can see, services use an Endpoints resource to link to a pod. An Endpoints is a comma-separated list of IP addresses and ports exposing a service. The Endpoints resource is like any other Kubernetes resource, so you can display its basic info with the kubectl command, as shown in Listing 10-25.

Listing 10-25. Describing the Kubernetes Service Endpoint

```
(base) binildass-MacBook-Pro:~ binil$ kubectl get endpoints
product-web
NAME          ENDPOINTS            AGE
product-web   10.244.1.104:8080    13m
(base) binildass-MacBook-Pro:~ binil$
```

Before you attempt to test these services, it will help you to keep watching the terminal logs for the Product Server and Product Web microservices. You can view the logs with the help of the pod name from Listing 10-21, as shown in Listings 10-26 and 10-27.

Listing 10-26. Viewing the Product Server Microservice
Terminal Logs

```
(base) binildass-MacBook-Pro:~ binil$ kubectl --tail 15 logs -f
product-server-6fb88b6849-q2pfx
  /\\ / __'_ _ _ _(_)_ _ _ _ \ \ \ \
 ( ( )\__ | '_ | '_| | '_ \/ _` | \ \ \ \
  \\/ __)| |_)| | | | | | || (_| | ) ) ) )
   '  |___| ._|_| |_|_| |_\_, | / / / /
  =========|_|==============|___/=/_/_/_/
  :: Spring Boot ::                (v3.2.0)

...
2023-05-25 13:48:21 INFO  InitializationComponent.init:47 -
Start...
2023-05-25 13:48:21 DEBUG InitializationComponent.init:51 -
Deleting all existing data...
2023-05-25 13:48:22 DEBUG InitializationComponent.init:56 -
Creating initial data...
2023-05-25 13:48:22 INFO  InitializationComponent.
init:105 - End
2023-05-25 13:48:23 INFO  StartupInfoLogger.logStarted:57 -
Started EcomProductMicroservice...

...
```

Listing 10-27. Viewing the Product Web Microservice
Terminal Logs

```
(base) binildass-MacBook-Pro:~ binil$ kubectl --tail 15 logs -f
product-web-5dfc886d6d-8cl7t

  .   ____          _            __ _ _
 /\\ / ___'_ __ _ _(_)_ __  __ _ \ \ \ \
( ( )\___ | '_ | '_| | '_ \/ _` | \ \ \ \
 \\/  ___)| |_)| | | | | || (_| |  ) ) ) )
  '  |____| .__|_| |_|_| |_\__, | / / / /
 =========|_|==============|___/=/_/_/_/
 :: Spring Boot ::                (v3.2.0)

...
2023-05-25 13:48:20 INFO  InitializationComponent.
init:37 - Start
2023-05-25 13:48:20 DEBUG InitializationComponent.init:39 -
Doing Nothing...
2023-05-25 13:48:20 INFO  InitializationComponent.init:41 - End
2023-05-25 13:48:21 INFO  StartupInfoLogger.logStarted:57 -
Started EcomProductMicroservice...
...
```

You are now ready to test the microservices.

Testing the Microservice Pods

Once all the three pods are up and running, you can access the Product
Web microservice. For that, as mentioned in Appendix E, you must get the
Minikube IP first. See Listing 10-28.

Listing 10-28. Finding Minikube IP

```
(base) binildass-MacBook-Pro:ch07-02 binil$ minikube ip
192.168.64.5
(base) binildass-MacBook-Pro:ch07-02 binil$
```

You can now access the Product Web microservice using a browser with the URL formed with the Minikube IP.

```
http://192.168.64.5:8080/product.html
```

Refer to the section titled "Test the Microservice Using UI" in Chapter 1 to test the Product Web microservice container.

While you test the microservices, keep watching the log windows in Listings 10-26 and 10-27.

Accessing Kubernetes Deployments

Let's continue the testing, with respect to the information related to the Kubernetes services in Listing 10-23. You will first cURL from a terminal in the host machine to the URL that you tested in the previous section. See Listing 10-29.

Listing 10-29. cURL with Minikube IP Based Address

```
(base) binildass-MacBook-Pro:~ binil$ curl
http://192.168.64.6:30503/productsweb
[{"productId":"646ef0a55a32df351bf88d09","name":"Kamsung ...
(base) binildass-MacBook-Pro:~ binil$
```

You will be able to access the Product Web microservice and retrieve information.

Now try with the URL formed out of the Cluster IP, as shown in Listing 10-30.

Listing 10-30. Accessing Product Web Using cURL with Cluster IP Based URL from Host

```
(base) binildass-MacBook-Pro:~ binil$ curl
http://10.98.43.63:30503/productsweb
curl: (7) Failed to connect to 10.109.140.135 port 30012:
Connection refused
(base) binildass-MacBook-Pro:~ binil$ curl
http://10.98.43.63:8080/productsweb
curl: (7) Failed to connect to 10.109.140.135 port 30012:
Connection refused
(base) binildass-MacBook-Pro:~ binil$
```

Cluster IP provides access only inside the Kubernetes Cluster. Other apps inside your cluster can access, but there is no external access to the service, so the cURL command failed.

Now try to access the service from within the Minikube host, as shown in Listing 10-31.

Listing 10-31. Accessing Product Web Using cURL with Cluster IP Based URL from Inside Minikube

```
(base) binildass-MacBook-Pro:~ binil$ minikube ssh
```

```
$ curl http:// 10.98.43.63:30503/productsweb
curl: (7) Failed to connect to 10.109.140.135 port 30012 after
10 ms: Connection refused
$ curl http:// 10.98.43.63:8080/productsweb
[{"productId":"646ef0a55a32df351bf88d09","name":"Kamsung ...
```

501

From within the Minikube host, the command succeeded because Cluster IP provides access to other apps from inside the Kubernetes Cluster.

Now try to access the Product Server microservice. You already provided a NodePort type for the service. You should therefore be able to access it from outside the Kubernetes cluster—that is, from the host machine. See Listing 10-32.

Listing 10-32. Accessing Product Server Using cURL with Node Port IP Based URL from Host

```
(base) binildass-MacBook-Pro:~ binil$ curl
http://192.168.64.6:30002/products
[{"productId":"646ef0a55a32df351bf88d09","name":"Kamsung ...
binildass-MacBook-Pro:~ binil$
```

You can access the service since the cluster node opens a port on the node itself (hence the name NodePort) and redirects traffic received on that port to the respective service.

You may delete a pod if you want. By deleting a pod, you're instructing Kubernetes to terminate all the containers that are part of that pod. Listing 10-33 shows how to delete the Product Web pod.

Listing 10-33. Deleting a Kubernetes Pod

```
(base) binildass-MacBook-Pro:~ binil$ kubectl delete po
product-web-5dfc886d6d-8cl7t
pod "product-web-5dfc886d6d-8cl7t" deleted
(base) binildass-MacBook-Pro:~ binil$
```

Once the Product Web pod has been deleted, you can again list pods to see their statuses, as shown in Listing 10-34.

Listing 10-34. Listing the Kubernetes Pods Again

```
(base) binildass-MacBook-Pro:~ binil$ kubectl get pods
NAME                            READY STATUS    RESTARTS AGE
mongo-cluster-0                 1/1   Running   0        28m
product-server-6fb88b6849-q2pfx 1/1   Running   0        28m
product-web-5dfc886d6d-c2cps    1/1   Running   0        42s
(base) binildass-MacBook-Pro:~ binil$
```

Interestingly, you can see that the Product Web pod is not deleted. Truly speaking, it has been deleted, but then was re-created, since that is what you requested to Kubernetes when you mentioned the `replicas: 1` in `product-web-deployment.yml` in Listing 10-6. Note that pod has a new name, since it's not a stateful set.

Let's now delete a stateful set and see what happens. See Listing 10-35.

Listing 10-35. Deleting a Kubernetes Stateful Set

```
(base) binildass-MacBook-Pro:~ binil$ kubectl delete po mongo-
cluster-0
pod "mongo-cluster-0" deleted
(base) binildass-MacBook-Pro:~ binil$
```

Once the Stateful set has been deleted, you can list the pods again to see their statuses (see Listing 10-36).

Listing 10-36. Listing the Kubernetes Pods One More Time

```
(base) binildass-MacBook-Pro:~ binil$ kubectl get pods
NAME                            READY STATUS    RESTARTS AGE
mongo-cluster-0                 1/1   Running   0        3s
product-server-6fb88b6849-q2pfx 1/1   Running   0        29m
product-web-5dfc886d6d-c2cps    1/1   Running   0        116s
(base) binildass-MacBook-Pro:~ binil$
```

When you delete the stateful set, it will be re-created, since that is what you requested to Kubernetes when you mentioned `replicas: 1` in mongo-deployment.yml in Listing 10-10. The pod has been given the same name as before, since it's a stateful set.

From an ordinary command window in your host machine, you can experiment with running commands in your Product Web container. See Listing 10-37.

Listing 10-37. Running Commands from within the Kubernetes Container

```
(base) binildass-MacBook-Pro:ch10-01 binil$ kubectl exec -it
product-web-5dfc886d6d-c2cps -- ps
PID   USER      TIME  COMMAND
    1 root      0:17 java -jar /ecom.jar
  125 root      0:00 ps
(base) binildass-MacBook-Pro:ch10-01 binil$ kubectl exec -it
product-web-5dfc886d6d-c2cps -- ls
bin        etc        media      proc       sbin       tmp
dev        home       mnt        root       srv        usr
ecom.jar   lib        opt        run        sys        var
(base) binildass-MacBook-Pro:ch10-01 binil$
```

You can even use the Bourne Shell (or sh) to attach your shell console (in your host machine) to the shell in the running container, whereby you can interact with it, such as listing the processes, and so on. See Listing 10-38.

Listing 10-38. Attaching the Shell Console to a Container

```
(base) binildass-MacBook-Pro:ch10-01 binil$ kubectl exec -it
product-web-5dfc886d6d-c2cps -- sh
/ # ps -e
```

```
PID    USER      TIME  COMMAND
  1 root       0:17 java -jar /ecom.jar
144 root       0:00 sh
151 root       0:00 ps -e
/ # exit
(base) binildass-MacBook-Pro:ch10-01 binil$
```

Once you complete the tests, you can stop and remove the microservice containers and clean the environment using the clean.sh script in Listing 10-39.

Listing 10-39. The Script to Bring Down Microservices Kubernetes Pods (ch10\ch10-01\clean.sh)

```
mvn -Dmaven.test.skip=true clean
kubectl delete -f product-web-service.yml
kubectl delete -f product-web-deployment.yml
kubectl delete -f product-server-service.yml
kubectl delete -f product-server-deployment.yml
kubectl delete -f mongo-service.yml
kubectl delete -f mongo-deployment.yml
kubectl delete -f mongo-volume-claim.yml
kubectl delete -f mongo-volume.yml
docker rmi -f ecom/product-web
docker rmi -f ecom/product-server
```

Like the kubectl create command you saw in Listing 10-18, kubectl delete can be used to delete resources by filename, stdin, resources, and names, or by resources and label selector, which is done in Listing 10-39. JSON and YAML formats are accepted.

You can execute this script to stop and remove the microservice pods and clean the environment, as shown in Listing 10-40.

Listing 10-40. Stopping Microservice Pods and Cleaning the Environment

```
(base) binildass-MacBook-Pro:ch10-01 binil$ pwd
/Users/binil/binil/code/mac/mybooks/docker-04/Code/ch10/ch10-01
(base) binildass-MacBook-Pro:ch10-01 binil$ eval $(minikube
docker-env)
(base) binildass-MacBook-Pro:ch10-01 binil$ sh clean.sh
[INFO] Scanning for projects...
[INFO] ------------------------------------------------------
[INFO] Reactor Build Order:
[INFO]
[INFO] Ecom-Product-Server-Microservice      [jar]
[INFO] Ecom-Product-Web-Microservice         [jar]
[INFO] Ecom                                  [pom]
[INFO]
...
[INFO]
[INFO] Ecom-Product-Server-Microservice . SUCCESS [  0.108 s]
[INFO] Ecom-Product-Web-Microservice .... SUCCESS [  0.008 s]
[INFO] Ecom ............................. SUCCESS [  0.037 s]
[INFO] ------------------------------------------------------
[INFO] BUILD SUCCESS
[INFO] ------------------------------------------------------
[INFO] Total time:  0.366 s
[INFO] Finished at: 2023-05-19T16:40:53+05:30
[INFO] ------------------------------------------------------
 "product-web" deleted
deployment.apps "product-web" deleted
service "product-server" deleted
service "product-server-nodeport" deleted
```

```
deployment.apps "product-server" deleted
service "mongo" deleted
service "mongo-nodeport" deleted
statefulset.apps "mongo-cluster" deleted
persistentvolumeclaim "mongo-data-db" deleted
persistentvolume "mongo-data-db" deleted
Untagged: ecom/product-web:latest
Untagged: ecom/product-server:latest
(base) binildass-MacBook-Pro:ch10-01 binil$
```

This completes your first microservices example in Kubernetes.

Microservices and PostgreSQL in Kubernetes

Chapter 8 showed a full-fledged microservice example interaction with a PostgreSQL database, all in Docker containers. In Chapter 9, you modified that example to be fully deployed within a container infrastructure using Docker Compose. This section now deploys the same example in Kubernetes.

Design Microservices Deployment Topology

The Product Web and Product Server microservices are containerized, and the Product Server microservice will connect to a PostgreSQL database, again deployed within a container. All these containers will now run in Kubernetes. See Figure 10-12.

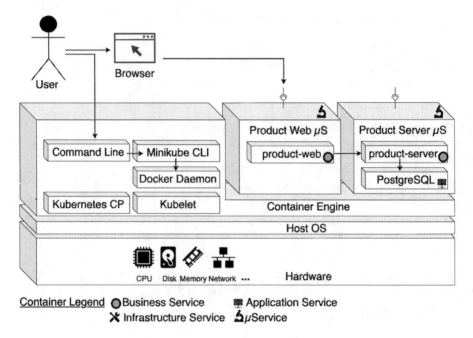

Figure 10-12. *Kubernetes based deployment topology for microservices*

Here, the Product Web and Product Server containers provide business services, whereas the PostgreSQL container provides application services for persisting state.

Understanding the Source Code

The source code for this book is available on GitHub via the book's product page, located at www.apress.com/9798868805547. The source code for the example is organized inside the ch10\ch10-02 folder. Much of the source code in this example is similar to ch03\ch03-01, which was explained in detail in Chapter 3, in the section titled "Microservices Using PostgreSQL and RestTemplate." You also saw Docker-based deployment of the topology in Figure 8-7, in the section titled "Microservice and PostgreSQL in Container" in Chapter 8 and subsequently in the Docker Compose-based deployment of the topology in Figure 9-1, in the section titled "Composing Microservice with PostgreSQL Containers" in Chapter 9. That means you can straight away get into the Kubernetes-specific aspects.

A summarized representation of the source code organization for the example inside the ch10-02 folder is shown in Listing 10-41.

Listing 10-41. Example 10-02 Source Code Organization

```
./ch10-02/
├── 01-ProductServer
│   ├── pom.xml
│   └── src
│       └── ...
├── 02-ProductWeb
│   ├── pom.xml
│   └── src
│       └── ...
├── Dockerfile
├── README.txt
├── clean.sh
├── makeandrun.sh
├── pom.xml
├── postgres-config.yml
├── postgres-deployment.yml
├── postgres-pvc.yml
├── postgres-svc.yml
├── product-server-deployment.yml
├── product-server-service.yml
├── product-web-deployment.yml
└── product-web-service.yml

32 directories, 43 files
(base) binildass-MacBook-Pro:ch10 binil$
```

The Dockerfile is similar to the one in Listing 7-35 of Chapter 7, so I do not repeat the explanation here. There are a set of .yml files, many of them you have already seen in the previous example in this chapter. There are two new descriptors required for the PostgreSQL database, which you will learn about now.

The change from MongoDB in the previous example to the PostgreSQL DB in this example starts from the Product Server microservice deployment descriptor. See Listing 10-42.

Listing 10-42. The Pod Definition YAML File for Product Server (ch10\ch10-02\product-server-deployment.yml)

```
apiVersion: apps/v1
kind: Deployment
metadata:
  name: product-server
  ...
spec:
  ...
  template:
    ...
    spec:
      containers:
      - name: product-server
        ...
        envFrom:
          - configMapRef:
              name: postgres-config
        env:
          - name: DB_SERVER
            value: postgres
```

As mentioned earlier, much of the configurations in Listing 10-42 we have already seen in the just previous example in this chapter, so it's not reproduced here or explained again.

When you have more than just a few entries as environment variables, instead of creating each environment variable from each entry individually, Kubernetes provides a way to expose all entries of a ConfigMap as environment variables, as shown in Listing 10-43. You can expose them as environment variables by using the envFrom attribute, instead of env. You still also use env the way you did in previous examples—to refer to the PostgreSQL DB address. Listing 10-43 shows the entries of this ConfigMap.

Listing 10-43. The ConfigMap YAML Referenced by the Product Server (ch10\ch10-02\postgres-config.yml)

```
apiVersion: v1
kind: ConfigMap
metadata:
  name: postgres-config
  labels:
    group: db
data:
  POSTGRES_DB: productdb
  POSTGRES_USER: postgres
  POSTGRES_PASSWORD: postgre
```

These entries are for the PostgreSQL server configuration. They are self-explanatory.

The PostgreSQL database referred to in Listing 10-42 is also new, and Listing 10-44 shows its descriptors.

Listing 10-44. Pod Description for the PostgreSQL Database
(ch10\ch10-02\postgres-deployment.yml)

```
apiVersion: apps/v1
kind: Deployment
metadata:
  name: postgres
  labels:
    app: postgres
    group: db
spec:
  replicas: 1
  selector:
    matchLabels:
      app: postgres
  template:
    metadata:
      labels:
        app: postgres
        type: db
    spec:
      volumes:
        - name: postgres-storage
          persistentVolumeClaim:
            claimName: postgres-persistent-volume-claim
      containers:
        - name: postgres
          image: postgres:15.3-alpine3.18
          ports:
            - containerPort: 5432
          envFrom:
            - configMapRef:
```

```
    name: postgres-config
volumeMounts:
  - name: postgres-storage
    mountPath: /var/lib/postgresql/data
```

Note that the PostgreSQL pod is referring to the same ConfigMap the Product Server microservice referred to. In this manner, using the same credentials the PostgreSQL DB container has been instantiated with, the Product Server Microservice can connect to that database.

Next, inspect the persistentVolumeClaim, as shown in Listing 10-45.

Listing 10-45. Description for the persistentVolumeClaim for the PostgreSQL Database (ch10\ch10-02\postgres-pvc.yml)

```
apiVersion: v1
kind: PersistentVolumeClaim
metadata:
  name: postgres-persistent-volume-claim
spec:
  accessModes:
    - ReadWriteOnce
  resources:
    requests:
      storage: 4Gi
```

The last file you will inspect is the service definition for the PostgreSQL database, as shown in Listing 10-46.

Listing 10-46. Description for the PostgreSQL Database Service (ch10\ch10-02\postgres-svc.yml)

```
apiVersion: v1
kind: Service
metadata:
  name: postgres
```

```
labels:
    group: db
spec:
  type: ClusterIP
  selector:
    app: postgres
  ports:
    - port: 5432
      targetPort: 5432
```

Only the Product Server microservice will access the PostgreSQL database from within the Kubernetes VM, so you only need a `ClusterIP`.

Run Microservices in Kubernetes

The `ch10\ch10-02` folder contains the scripts required to build and run these examples. The first step is to start a Minikube single-node Kubernetes cluster. Refer to Appendix E for a quick reference to the Kubernetes setup and commands. Subsequently, you also need to set the Minikube environment variables in your work terminal.

Assuming that your single-node Kubernetes cluster Minikube is up and running, the simple script called `makeandrun.sh` contains all the commands needed to build and run the complete application with all the deployment descriptors, as shown in Listing 10-47.

Listing 10-47. The Script to Build and Run Microservices in Kubernetes (ch10\ch10-02\makeandrun.sh)

```
mvn -Dmaven.test.skip=true clean package
docker build  --build-arg JAR_FILE=02-ProductWeb/target/
*.jar -t ecom/product-web .
docker build  --build-arg JAR_FILE=01-ProductServer/target/*.
jar -t ecom/product-server .
```

```
kubectl create -f postgres-config.yml
kubectl create -f postgres-pvc.yml
kubectl create -f postgres-deployment.yml
kubectl create -f postgres-svc.yml
kubectl create -f product-server-deployment.yml
kubectl create -f product-server-service.yml
kubectl create -f product-web-deployment.yml
kubectl create -f product-web-service.yml
minikube service product-web --url
sleep 3
kubectl get pods
kubectl get services
```

You can now execute this script, as shown in Listing 10-48.

Listing 10-48. Executing the Script to Build and Run Microservices Pods in Kubernetes

```
(base) binildass-MacBook-Pro:ch10-02 binil$ pwd
/Users/binil/binil/code/mac/mybooks/docker-04/Code/ch10/ch10-02
(base) binildass-MacBook-Pro:ch10-01 binil$ eval $(minikube
docker-env)
(base) binildass-MacBook-Pro:ch10-02 binil$ sh makeandrun.sh
[INFO] Scanning for projects...
[INFO] ------------------------------------------------------------
[INFO] Reactor Build Order:
[INFO]
[INFO] Ecom-Product-Server-Microservice                    [jar]
[INFO] Ecom-Product-Web-Microservice                       [jar]
[INFO] Ecom                                                [pom]
[INFO]
...
```

```
[INFO]
[INFO] Ecom-Product-Server-Microservice . SUCCESS [  3.001 s]
[INFO] Ecom-Product-Web-Microservice .... SUCCESS [  0.572 s]
[INFO] Ecom .......................... SUCCESS [  0.029 s]
[INFO] ------------------------------------------------------------
[INFO] BUILD SUCCESS
[INFO] ------------------------------------------------------------
[INFO] Total time:  3.762 s
[INFO] Finished at: 2023-05-25T22:47:54+05:30
[INFO] ------------------------------------------------------------
...
configmap/postgres-config created
persistentvolumeclaim/postgres-persistent-volume-claim created
deployment.apps/postgres created
service/postgres created
deployment.apps/product-server created
service/product-server created
service/product-server-nodeport created
deployment.apps/product-web created
service/product-web created
http://192.168.64.6:30263
...
(base) binildass-MacBook-Pro:ch10-02 binil$
```

You are now ready to test the microservices.

Testing the Microservice Pods

Once the pods are up and running, you can access the Product Web microservice. However, as mentioned in Appendix E, you must get the Minikube IP first. See Listing 10-49.

Listing 10-49. Finding Minikube IP

```
(base) binildass-MacBook-Pro:ch07-02 binil$ minikube ip
192.168.64.6
(base) binildass-MacBook-Pro:ch07-02 binil$
```

You can now access the Product Web microservice using a browser with the URL formed with the Minikube IP.

```
http://192.168.64.5:8080/product.html
```

Refer to the section titled "Test the Microservice Using UI" in Chapter 1 to test the Product Web microservice container.

While you test the microservices, keep watching the log windows, as was described in the previous example in this chapter, in Listings 10-26 and 10-27.

Now you'll look a little more into the PostgreSQL database. Listing 10-50 declares a persistent volume claim.

Listing 10-50. Describing the PVC

```
(base) binildass-MacBook-Pro:~ binil$ kubectl get persistent-
volumeclaims
NAME                              STATUS
VOLUME                                         CAPACITY
ACCESS MODES   STORAGECLASS   AGE
postgres-persistent-volume-claim    Bound
pvc-2c90c05e-c233-44d4-8adb-5595da8edc3e    4Gi
RWO            standard       71s
(base) binildass-MacBook-Pro:~ binil$
```

Notice that the PVC has a status of Bound and it tells you which VOLUME they are bound to. They have a set capacity of 4Gi (this was requested in the yaml file in Listing 10-45) and they have a specified access mode of RWO (read-write once), meaning one pod can use this volume at a time.

517

Even though you didn't set a storage class, it was set by default. This is done by an `AdmissionController` that's running in the Kubernetes cluster, intercepting your requests to the Kubernetes API server and modifying the incoming objects. If you had specified a storage class, the admission controller would not have injected this class.

But then, who created this storage class? You can inspect the storage class in Listing 10-51.

Listing 10-51. Describing the Storage Class

```
(base) binildass-MacBook-Pro:~ binil$ kubectl describe
storageclass standard
Name:           standard
IsDefaultClass: Yes
...
Provisioner:            k8s.io/minikube-hostpath
Parameters:             <none>
AllowVolumeExpansion:   <unset>
MountOptions:           <none>
ReclaimPolicy:          Delete
VolumeBindingMode:      Immediate
Events:                 <none>
(base) binildass-MacBook-Pro:~ binil$
```

When you started Minikube, the `StorageClass` is created for you. It's bootstrapped for you in your Minikube installation. You can read its contents. You can modify it inside of Kubernetes, by using `kubectl edit sc standard`.

Because you have a default storage class with a provisioner, you don't have to worry about creating a persistent volume explicitly. Instead, the provisioner takes care of creating those volumes based on the persistent volume claims. That is why a PV isn't provisioned explicitly, unlike the last example. Listing 10-52 shows the PV.

Listing 10-52. Listing the Persistent Volumes

```
(base) binildass-MacBook-Pro:~ binil$ kubectl get persistentvolumes
NAME                                      CAPACITY    ACCESS MODES
RECLAIM POLICY    STATUS    CLAIM
STORAGECLASS    REASON    AGE
pvc-2c90c05e-c233-44d4-8adb-5595da8edc3e    4Gi          RWO
Delete            Bound     default/postgres-persistent-volume-claim
standard                    2m33s
(base) binildass-MacBook-Pro:~ binil$
```

Note that the Capacity and Access Mode match the
PersistentVolumeClaim. Also note that PersistentVolumes point to the
PVC that has claimed it, just like PVCs point to the PersistentVolumes
that they have claimed.

Before you stop the pods and services, read the next section.

Resiliency of Kubernetes Pods

In the first example in this chapter, you saw that when a pod is killed, a new
pod is resurrected by default. You also saw that for a stateful set, when the
pod is re-created, the name of the pod is retained.

This demonstrates the resiliency of different kinds of pods and
deployments.

In the following sections, you'll perform a few more experiments with
the PostgreSQL pod.

State Retention

First list the existing pods, as shown in Listing 10-53.

519

Listing 10-53. Listing the Kubernetes Pods

```
(base) binildass-MacBook-Pro:~ binil$ kubectl get pods
NAME                                READY STATUS  RESTARTS AGE
postgres-89dbf9fd9-f5bmc            1/1   Running 0        37m
product-server-85d84cf89-kxvfw      1/1   Running 0        37m
product-web-69b5948fb9-brdnf        1/1   Running 0        37m
(base) binildass-MacBook-Pro:~ binil$
```

In Listing 10-54, you can see that the PostgreSQL pod is not defined as a stateful set, but as a deployment. Keeping that in mind, you can delete the pod.

Listing 10-54. Deleting the PostgreSQL Pod

```
(base) binildass-MacBook-Pro:~ binil$ kubectl delete po
postgres-89dbf9fd9-f5bmc
pod "postgres-89dbf9fd9-f5bmc" deleted
(base) binildass-MacBook-Pro:~ binil$
```

Now list the remaining pods again, as shown in Listing 10-55.

Listing 10-55. Listing the Kubernetes Pods Again

```
(base) binildass-MacBook-Pro:~ binil$ kubectl get pods
NAME                                READY STATUS  RESTARTS AGE
postgres-89dbf9fd9-4r5wk            1/1   Running 0        9s
product-server-85d84cf89-kxvfw      1/1   Running 0        38m
product-web-69b5948fb9-brdnf        1/1   Running 0        38m
(base) binildass-MacBook-Pro:~ binil$
```

Note that the PostgreSQL database pod has been re-created, but with a different name. What will happen to the state of the deleted pod?

To answer this question, test the Product Web microservice using the same URL so that the request will hit through the earlier existing Product Server and Product Web microservice pods.

http://192.168.64.6:30263/product.html

To your surprise, you may see that the previous state is maintained. By state, I mean, when you initialized the Product Server microservice, you inserted a few database rows, and those are retained!

You need to explore further. To do that, check out Listing 10-56, which inspects the association between pods, PVCs, and PVs.

Listing 10-56. Association Between Pods and PVCs

```
(base) binildass-MacBook-Pro:~ binil$ kubectl get pods --all-
namespaces -o=json | jq -c '.items[] | {name: .metadata.name,
namespace: .metadata.namespace, claimName: .spec |  select( has
("volumes") ).volumes[] | select( has ("persistentVolumeClaim")
).persistentVolumeClaim.claimName }'
{"name":"postgres-89dbf9fd9-4r5wk","namespace":"default","claim
Name":"postgres-persistent-volume-claim"}
(base) binildass-MacBook-Pro:~ binil$
```

This listing shows the association between the PostgreSQL pod and its PVC. You can also see the association between the PVC and PV, shown in Listing 10-57.

Listing 10-57. Association Between PV and PVC

```
(base) binildass-MacBook-Pro:~ binil$ kubectl get pvc --all-
namespaces -o json | jq -j '.items[] | "\(.metadata.namespace),
\(.metadata.name), \(.spec.volumeName)\n"'
default, postgres-persistent-volume-claim, pvc-2c90c05e-
c233-44d4-8adb-5595da8edc3e
(base) binildass-MacBook-Pro:~ binil$
```

To understand this, note what the Kubernetes documentation says:

A user creates, or in the case of dynamic provisioning, has already created, a PersistentVolumeClaim with a specific amount of storage requested and with certain access modes. A control loop in the master watches for new PVCs, finds a matching PV (if possible), and binds them together. If a PV was dynamically provisioned for a new PVC, the loop will always bind that PV to the PVC. Otherwise, the user will always get at least what they asked for, but the volume may be in excess of what was requested. Once bound, PersistentVolumeClaim binds are exclusive, regardless of how they were bound. A PVC to PV binding is a one-to-one mapping, using a ClaimRef which is a bidirectional binding between the PersistentVolume and the PersistentVolumeClaim.

—Kubernetes

This explains the behavior you saw earlier to some extent. Further details are beyond the scope of this discussion and you are advised to refer to the Kubernetes documentation.

Once you are done testing, you can stop and remove the microservice containers and clean the environment by using the clean.sh script shown in Listing 10-58.

Listing 10-58. The Script to Bring Down Microservices Kubernetes Pods (ch10\ch10-02\clean.sh)

```
mvn -Dmaven.test.skip=true clean
kubectl delete -f product-web-service.yml
kubectl delete -f product-web-deployment.yml
kubectl delete -f product-server-service.yml
kubectl delete -f product-server-deployment.yml
kubectl delete -f postgres-svc.yml
kubectl delete -f postgres-deployment.yml
```

```
kubectl delete -f postgres-pvc.yml
kubectl delete -f postgres-config.yml
docker rmi -f ecom/product-web
docker rmi -f ecom/product-server
```

You can execute this script to stop and remove the microservice pods and clean the environment, as shown in Listing 10-59, just like the way you cleaned up your environment in Listing 10-40.

Listing 10-59. Stopping Microservice Pods and Cleaning the Environment

```
((base) binildass-MacBook-Pro:ch10-02 binil$ pwd
/Users/binil/binil/code/mac/mybooks/docker-04/Code/ch10/ch10-02
(base) binildass-MacBook-Pro:ch10-02 binil$ eval $(minikube
docker-env)
(base) binildass-MacBook-Pro:ch10-02 binil$ sh clean.sh
...
```

Summary

You started your journey into containers in Chapters 7 and 8, and in Chapter 9, you extended that learning to use Docker Compose to compose multiple microservice and database containers. During the start of this chapter, you learned that when you move from monolithic to microservices, you increase the number of moving parts, and so the overall complexity also increases. This is where better container management tools like Kubernetes pay off. This chapter included a quick introduction to Kubernetes and introduced the familiar microservices example interacting with both an SQL and a NoSQL database within the Kubernetes toolset. You are not finished yet, since you have yet to investigate integrating message brokers into your Kubernetes ecosystem. This is covered in Chapter 11.

CHAPTER 11

Message Oriented Microservices in Kubernetes

In Chapter 10, you learned how Kubernetes does container orchestration, which greatly improves the manageability of operating microservices. This is even more important as the number of microservices goes up. You also saw some resiliency aspects of Kubernetes and through the examples you saw how a pod is re-created when you delete an existing pod. You also saw how a state is restored after re-creating a pod.

Scalability and resiliency are two desirable qualities for every production-grade application. When you attempt to improve these two qualities, you make the operating environment more chaotic. This is true for a microservices architecture, since you need to manage more types of services and a greater number of each type of service.

In Chapter 6, you learned about a consumer and provider microservice communicating with each other using Kafka as the messaging channel. The provider microservice stores the entity in a database. In Chapter 9, you modified those same examples, leveraging containerization as a runtime option. In this chapter, you will revisit them and use Kubernetes for deployment.

© Binildas A. Christudas 2024
B. A. Christudas, *Java Microservices and Containers in the Cloud,*
https://doi.org/10.1007/979-8-8688-0555-4_11

This chapter is a continuation of Chapter 10, so it's fully hands on and covers the following three scenarios:

- Microservices communicating over Kafka and interacting with PostgreSQL

- Microservices communicating over Kafka and interacting with MongoDB

- Using Ingress to access coordinating microservices

The following section gets straight into those examples.

Microservices Over Kafka with PostgreSQL in k8s

This example tweaks the same set of microservices from Chapter 6 in the section titled "CRUD Microservices over Kafka on PostgreSQL" and from Chapter 9 in the section titled "Composing Microservice with PostgreSQL Containers." A consumer and provider microservice communicate with each other using Kafka as the messaging channel. The provider microservice stores the entity in a PostgreSQL database. When the browser sends a request to the first (consumer) microservice, it uses async HTTP. Even though it uses async HTTP, the example emulates a sync-style user experience at the client device level, a browser in this case.

The example also contains multiple instances of the consumer and provider microservices and uses multiple clients while testing the service.

Design the Microservices Orchestration Topology

This example uses a modified version of the hexagonal microservice view shown in Figure 9-3 in Chapter 9. Both microservices communicate through an async channel. Apache Kafka is the messaging channel, which is inherently asynchronous. This modified design is shown in Figure 11-1.

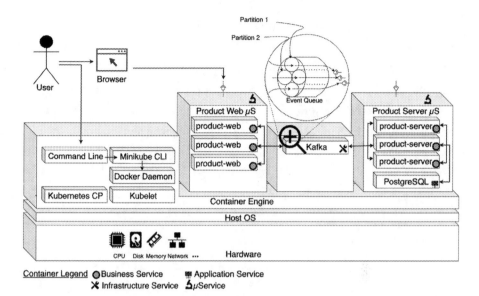

Figure 11-1. *Kubernetes orchestration topology for microservices*

Here, the Product Web and Product Server containers provide business services, whereas the Mongo container provides application services to persist the state. The Kafka container provides infrastructure services, so it's not shown as a part of any specific (business) microservice.

Another aspect you need to note in Figure 11-1 is that you have multiple instances of the Product Web and Product Server microservices. This will help you experiment with sticky and load-balanced scenarios, like you did in Chapter 6.

Understanding the Source Code

The source code for this book is available on GitHub via the book's product page, located at www.apress.com/9798868805547. The source code for this example is organized inside the ch11\ch11-01 folder. Much of the source code in this example is like ch09\ch09-03, which I explained in detail in Chapter 9. In the example in Chapter 9, the deployment architecture is similar, but it used Docker Compose instead of Kubernetes. In the second example—ch10\ch10-02—in Chapter 10, you also looked at the Kubernetes-based deployment of the two microservices and PostgreSQL. What's left is the Kubernetes deployment of Kafka alone.

A summarized representation of the source code organization for the example inside the ch11-01 folder is shown in Listing 11-1.

Listing 11-1. Example 11-01 Source Code Organization

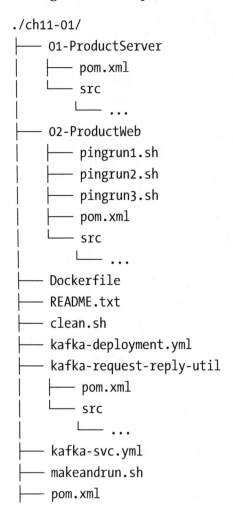

```
./ch11-01/
├── 01-ProductServer
│   ├── pom.xml
│   └── src
│       └── ...
├── 02-ProductWeb
│   ├── pingrun1.sh
│   ├── pingrun2.sh
│   ├── pingrun3.sh
│   ├── pom.xml
│   └── src
│       └── ...
├── Dockerfile
├── README.txt
├── clean.sh
├── kafka-deployment.yml
├── kafka-request-reply-util
│   ├── pom.xml
│   └── src
│       └── ...
├── kafka-svc.yml
├── makeandrun.sh
├── pom.xml
```

```
├── postgres-config.yml
├── postgres-deployment.yml
├── postgres-pvc.yml
├── postgres-svc.yml
├── product-server-deployment.yml
├── product-server-service.yml
├── product-web-deployment.yml
└── product-web-service.yml

42 directories, 53 files
(base) binildass-MacBook-Pro:ch11 binil$
```

As you can verify from Listing 11-1, all the descriptors are familiar except for kafka*.yml. Listing 11-2 shows these new descriptors.

Listing 11-2. The Zookeeper Deployment YAML File (ch11\ ch11-01\kafka-deployment.yml)

```
---
apiVersion: apps/v1
kind: Deployment
metadata:
  name: zookeeper-deployment
spec:
  replicas: 1
  selector:
    matchLabels:
      component: zookeeper
  template:
    metadata:
      labels:
        component: zookeeper
    spec:
```

```
containers:
- name: zookeeper
  image: digitalwonderland/zookeeper
  ports:
    - containerPort: 2181
```

Listing 11-2 uses digitalwonderland/zookeeper as the zookeeper image. The rest of the lines are self-explanatory. Listing 11-3 investigates the Kafka descriptors.

Listing 11-3. The Kafka Deployment YAML File (ch11\ch11-01\ kafka-deployment.yml)

```
---
apiVersion: apps/v1
kind: Deployment
metadata:
  name: kafka-1-deployment
spec:
  replicas: 1
  selector:
    matchLabels:
      component: kafka-1
  template:
    metadata:
      labels:
        component: kafka-1
    spec:
      containers:
      - name: kafka-1
        image: pharosproduction/kafka_k8s:v1
        resources:
          requests:
```

```
        memory: "256Mi"
        cpu: "250m"
      limits:
        memory: "512Mi"
        cpu: "500m"
    ports:
    - containerPort: 9092
    env:
    - name: MY_POD_IP
      valueFrom:
        fieldRef:
          fieldPath: status.podIP
    - name: KAFKA_ADVERTISED_PORT
      value: "9092"
    - name: KAFKA_ZOOKEEPER_CONNECT
      value: zookeeper-ip-service:2181
    - name: KAFKA_ADVERTISED_HOST_NAME
      value: $(MY_POD_IP)
    - name: KAFKA_BROKER_ID
      value: "1"
```

The pharosproduction/kafka_k8s:v1 image is used for the Kafka server. You can see that the kafka deployment refers to the zookeeper-ip-service, the service name for the zookeeper service that's configured in Listing 11-4.

Listing 11-4. The Zookeeper Service YAML File (ch11\ch11-01\ kafka-svct.yml)

```
---
apiVersion: v1
kind: Service
metadata:
  name: zookeeper-ip-service
```

```
spec:
  type: ClusterIP
  selector:
    component: zookeeper
  ports:
  - name: zookeeper
    port: 2181
    targetPort: 2181
  type: NodePort
```

The zookeeper-ip-service is also configured to have a NodePort.
This will help you to interact with the message broker from outside the
Kubernetes cluster to do some kind of basic queue management, which is
demonstrated later, in Listings 11-17 and 11-18.

Last but not the least, Listing 11-5 looks at the definition for the Kafka
service.

Listing 11-5. The Kafka Service YAML File (ch11\ch11-01\kafka-svct.yml)

```
---
apiVersion: v1
kind: Service
metadata:
  name: kafka-1-ip-service
spec:
  type: ClusterIP
  selector:
    component: kafka-1
  ports:
  - name: kafka
    port: 9092
    targetPort: 9092
```

The Product Server microservice pod refers to the kafka service as the message broker to receive messages from the Product Web microservice. See Listing 11-6.

Listing 11-6. The Product Server Pod YAML File (ch11\ch11-01\ product-server-deployment.yml)

```
apiVersion: apps/v1
kind: Deployment
metadata:
  name: product-server
  ...
spec:
  replicas: 3
  ...
  template:
    ...
    spec:
      containers:
      - name: product-server
        ...
        env:
          - name: DB_SERVER
            value: postgres
          - name: spring.kafka.bootstrap-servers
            value: kafka-1-ip-service:9092
```

The Product Web microservice pod also refers to the same kafka service as the message broker to send messages to the Product Server microservice. See Listing 11-7.

Listing 11-7. The Product Web Pod YAML File (ch11\ch11-01\ product-web-deployment.yml)

```
apiVersion: apps/v1
kind: Deployment
metadata:
  name: product-web
  ...
spec:
  replicas: 3
  ...
  template:
    ...
    spec:
      containers:
      ...
        env:
          - name: spring.kafka.bootstrap-servers
            value: kafka-1-ip-service:9092
```

Note that three replicas have been configured for the Product Web microservice and three for the Product Server microservice.

Run Microservices in Kubernetes

The ch11\ch11-01 folder contains the scripts required to build and run the examples. The first step is to start a Minikube single-node Kubernetes cluster (see Listing 11-8). Refer to Appendix E for a quick reference to Kubernetes setup and commands.

Listing 11-8. Starting Minikube

```
(base) binildass-MacBook-Pro:~ binil$ minikube start
  minikube v1.25.2 on Darwin 12.4
...
  Done! kubectl is now configured to use "minikube" cluster and
  "default" namespace by default
(base) binildass-MacBook-Pro:~ binil$
```

Set the Minikube environment variables in your work terminal.

Note   The examples in this chapter assume that the previous two steps connected to the Docker daemon have been executed if you are using the Minikube single-node Kubernetes cluster.

Assuming that your single-node Kubernetes cluster, Minikube is up and running, a simple script, containing a single command, can build and run the complete application with all the deployment descriptors (it's called makeandrun.sh). Listing 11-9 executes that script.

Listing 11-9. Executing the Script to Build and Run Microservices in Kubernetes (ch11\ch11-01\makeandrun.sh)

```
(base) binildass-MacBook-Pro:ch11-01 binil$ pwd
/Users/binil/binil/code/mac/mybooks/docker-04/Code/ch11/ch11-01
(base) binildass-MacBook-Pro:ch11-01 binil$ eval $(minikube
docker-env)
(base) binildass-MacBook-Pro:ch11-01 binil$ sh makeandrun.sh
[INFO] Scanning for projects...
[INFO]
[INFO] -< se.callista.blog.synch_kafka:kafka-request-
reply-util >-
```

```
[INFO] Building Kafka Request Reply utility 0.0.1-SNAPSHOT
[INFO] -------------------------------[ jar ]--------------
[INFO]
...
[INFO]
[INFO] Kafka Request Reply utility ...... SUCCESS [  1.119 s]
[INFO] Ecom-Product-Server-Microservice . SUCCESS [  2.534 s]
[INFO] Ecom-Product-Web-Microservice .... SUCCESS [  0.499 s]
[INFO] Ecom .......................... SUCCESS [  0.002 s]
[INFO] ------------------------------------------------------------
[INFO] BUILD SUCCESS
[INFO] ------------------------------------------------------------
...
http://192.168.64.6:32535
```

NAME	READY	STATUS	RESTART	AGE
kafka-1-deployment-7bcc6dd87f-rxhkd	1/1	Running	0	8s
postgres-89dbf9fd9-g9jx8	1/1	Running	0	7s
product-server-5bb6569674-9dflb	1/1	Running	0	5s
product-server-5bb6569674-g2488	1/1	Running	0	5s
product-server-5bb6569674-nzlv2	1/1	Running	0	5s
product-web-787d9ddf75-9m5c6	1/1	Running	0	4s
product-web-787d9ddf75-g82vm	1/1	Running	0	4s
product-web-787d9ddf75-tn8lk	1/1	Running	0	4s
zookeeper-deployment-886ff5f87-qmnl6	1/1	Running	0	8s

NAME	TYPE	CLUSTER-IP	PORT(S)
kafka-1-ip-service	ClusterIP	10.98.44.163	9092/TCP
kubernetes	ClusterIP	10.96.0.1	443/TCP
postgres	ClusterIP	10.97.76.252	5432/TCP
product-server	ClusterIP	10.106.100.232	8081/TCP
product-web	LoadBalan	10.110.112.90	8080:32535/TCP
zookeeper-ip-service	NodePort	10.111.204.18	2181:30059/TCP

```
(base) binildass-MacBook-Pro:ch11-01 binil$
```

Make sure all the pods are in "Running" STATUS. You are now ready to test the microservices.

Testing the Microservice Pods

Open the terminal windows of all instances of the Product Server microservice and the Product Web microservice. Remember, you configured three replicas for each microservice, as is evident in Listing 11-10.

Link your console to the Product Server microservice pod 1 terminal.

Listing 11-10. Product Server Pod 1 Terminal

```
(base) binildass-MacBook-Pro:~ binil$ kubectl --tail 30 logs -f
product-server-5bb6569674-9dflb
...
```

Next, link your console to the Product Server microservice pod 2 terminal. See Listing 11-11.

Listing 11-11. Product Server Pod 2 Terminal

```
(base) binildass-MacBook-Pro:~ binil$ kubectl --tail 30 logs -f
product-server-5bb6569674-g2488
...
```

As the last step, link your console to the Product Server microservice pod 3 terminal. See Listing 11-12.

Listing 11-12. Product Server Pod 3 Terminal

```
(base) binildass-MacBook-Pro:~ binil$ kubectl --tail 30 logs -f
product-server-5bb6569674-nzlv2


  .   ___          _            __ _ _
 /\\ / ___'_ __ _ _(_)_ __  __ _ \ \ \ \
( ( )\___ | '_ | '_| | '_ \/ _` | \ \ \ \
 \\/  ___)| |_)| | | | | || (_| |  ) ) ) )
  '  |____| .__|_| |_|_| |_\__, | / / / /
 =========|_|==============|___/=/_/_/_/
 :: Spring Boot ::                (v3.2.0)

2023-05-19 13:49:12 INFO  StartupInfoLogger.logStarting:51 -
Starting EcomProductServerMicroservice...
...
Running Changeset: db/changelog/initial-schema_inventory.
xml::product::Binildas
Running Changeset: db/changelog/initial-schema_inventory.
xml::addAutoIncrement-product::Binildas
Running Changeset: db/changelog/initial-schema_inventory.
xml::insert-product-01::Binildas
Running Changeset: db/changelog/initial-schema_inventory.
xml::insert-product-02::Binildas
...
Liquibase: Update has been successful.
2023-05-19 13:49:53 INFO  InitializationComponent.
init:42 - Start
2023-05-19 13:49:53 INFO  InitializationComponent.init:67 - End
2023-05-19 13:50:04 INFO  StartupInfoLogger.logStarted:57 -
Started EcomProductServerMicroserviceApplication in 57.979
seconds (process running for 69.734)
...
```

Next, you will get the Product Web Microservice consoles. First link your host console to the Product Web microservice pod 1 terminal. See Listing 11-13.

Listing 11-13. Product Web pod 1 Terminal

```
(base) binildass-MacBook-Pro:~ binil$ kubectl --tail 30 logs -f
product-web-787d9ddf75-9m5c6
...
```

Link your console to the Product Web microservice pod 2 terminal. See Listing 11-14.

Listing 11-14. Product Web Pod 2 Terminal

```
(base) binildass-MacBook-Pro:~ binil$ kubectl --tail 30 logs -f
product-web-787d9ddf75-g82vm
...
```

As the final step, link your console to the Product Web microservice pod 3 terminal. See Listing 11-15.

Listing 11-15. Product Web Pod 3 Terminal

```
(base) binildass-MacBook-Pro:~ binil$ kubectl --tail 30 logs -f
product-web-787d9ddf75-tn8lk
```

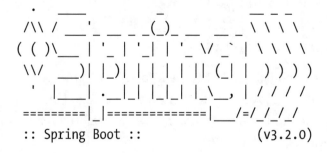

```
  .   ___          _            __ _ _
 /\\ / ___'_ __ _ _(_)_ __  __ _ \ \ \ \
( ( )\___ | '_ | '_| | '_ \/ _` | \ \ \ \
 \\/  ___)| |_)| | | | | || (_| |  ) ) ) )
  '  |____| .__|_| |_|_| |_\__, | / / / /
 =========|_|==============|___/=/_/_/_/
 :: Spring Boot ::                (v3.2.0)
```

```
2023-05-19 13:49:11 INFO  StartupInfoLogger.logStarting:51 -
Starting EcomProductWebMicroservice...
2023-05-19 13:49:43 INFO  StartupInfoLogger.logStarted:57 -
Started EcomProductWebMicroservice...
...
```

You can now access some statistics from Kafka. Remember that you defined a NodePort for the zookeeper pod. You will now connect to the zookeeper from the host machine.

To access the Kafka container, as mentioned in Appendix E, you must get the Minikube IP first. See Listing 11-16.

Listing 11-16. Finding Minikube IP

```
(base) binildass-MacBook-Pro:ch07-02 binil$ minikube ip
192.168.64.6
(base) binildass-MacBook-Pro:ch07-02 binil$
```

Now to connect to Kafka. One way to do so is to use the kafka-topics. sh script in any standard Apache Kafka extracted folder. See Listing 11-17.

Listing 11-17. Listing the Kafka Topics

```
(base) binildass-MacBook-Pro:bin binil$ pwd
/Users/binil/Applns/apache/kafka/kafka_2.13-2.5.0/bin
(base) binildass-MacBook-Pro:bin binil$ sh
./kafka-topics.sh --zookeeper 192.168.64.6:30059 --list
(base) binildass-MacBook-Pro:bin binil$
```

Note that the IP address in Listing 11-17 is the Minikube IP address and the port is the NodePort of zookeeper-ip-service in Listing 11-9.

You may now access the Product Web microservice using a browser with the URL formed with the Minikube IP:

```
http://192.168.64.5:8080/product.html
```

Refer to the section titled "Test the Microservice Using UI" in Chapter 1 to test the Product Web microservice container.

While you test the microservices, you can keep watching the log windows in Listings 11-10 through 11-15.

Let's now revisit the Kafka topics, as shown in Listing 11-18.

Listing 11-18. Listing the Kafka Topics

```
(base) binildass-MacBook-Pro:bin binil$ sh
./kafka-topics.sh --zookeeper 192.168.64.6:30059 --list
__consumer_offsets
product-req-reply-topic
product-req-topic
(base) binildass-MacBook-Pro:bin binil$
```

You can see the different topics created on the fly when you test the microservices. This is in line with the description provided in Listing 4-9 in Chapter 4.

Load Testing the Microservice Pods

I have provided a few scripts to help you load test the microservices and see how the load is evenly distributed from the Product Web to the Product Server through the Kafka messaging channel. See Listing 11-19.

Listing 11-19. Load Testing Scripts

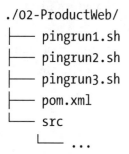

```
./02-ProductWeb/
├── pingrun1.sh
├── pingrun2.sh
├── pingrun3.sh
├── pom.xml
└── src
    └── ...
```

To load test, first open each of these scripts and tweak the URL to point to the Product Web microservice. Subsequently, you can open three different terminals and execute these scripts concurrently to fire cURL requests. See Listings 11-20 through 11-22.

Listing 11-20. Firing Requests to Product Web Microservice from Terminal 1

```
(base) binildass-MacBook-Pro:02-ProductWeb binil$ pwd
/Users/binil/binil/code/mac/mybooks/docker-04/ch11/ch11-01/02-
ProductWeb
(base) binildass-MacBook-Pro:02-ProductWeb binil$ sh pingrun1.sh
...
```

Listing 11-21. Firing Requests to Product Web Microservice from Terminal 2

```
(base) binildass-MacBook-Pro:02-ProductWeb binil$ sh
pingrun2.sh
...
```

Listing 11-22. Firing Requests to Product Web Microservice from Terminal 3

```
(base) binildass-MacBook-Pro:02-ProductWeb binil$ sh pingrun3.sh
...
```

The contents of all three scripts are the same, so you can alternatively execute the same script in three different terminals!

Once you complete testing the microservices in this example, you can stop and remove the microservice containers and clean the environment. See Listing 11-23.

Listing 11-23. Cleaning the Project and the Environment

```
(base) binildass-MacBook-Pro:ch10-03 binil$ pwd
/Users/binil/binil/code/mac/mybooks/docker-04/Code/ch11/ch11-01
(base) binildass-MacBook-Pro:ch10-03 binil$ eval $(minikube
docker-env)
(base) binildass-MacBook-Pro:ch10-03 binil$ sh clean.sh
[INFO] Scanning for projects...
[INFO] --------------------------------------
[INFO] Reactor Build Order:
[INFO]
[INFO] Kafka Request Reply utility        [jar]
[INFO] Ecom-Product-Server-Microservice   [jar]
[INFO] Ecom-Product-Web-Microservice      [jar]
[INFO] Ecom                               [pom]
[INFO]
...
service "product-web" deleted
deployment.apps "product-web" deleted
service "product-server" deleted
service "product-server-nodeport" deleted
deployment.apps "product-server" deleted
service "postgres" deleted
deployment.apps "postgres" deleted
persistentvolumeclaim "postgres-persistent-volume-
claim" deleted
configmap "postgres-config" deleted
service "zookeeper-ip-service" deleted
service "kafka-1-ip-service" deleted
deployment.apps "zookeeper-deployment" deleted
```

```
deployment.apps "kafka-1-deployment" deleted
Untagged: ecom/product-web:latest
Untagged: ecom/product-server:latest
(base) binildass-MacBook-Pro:ch11-01 binil$
```

This completes the first example.

Microservices Over Kafka with MongoDB in k8s

In this example, you will tweak the same set of microservices from Chapter 6 in the section titled "CRUD Microservices over Kafka on MongoDB" and in Chapter 9 in the section titled "Composing Microservice with MongoDB Containers." A consumer and a provider microservice communicate with each other using Kafka as the messaging channel. The provider microservice stores the entity in a MongoDB database. When the browser sends a request to the first (consumer) microservice, it uses async HTTP. Even though it uses async HTTP, the example emulates a sync-style user experience at the browser level.

This section demonstrates this example with multiple instances of the consumer and provider microservices, and you will also use multiple clients while testing the service.

Design the Microservices Orchestration Topology

This example uses a modified version of the hexagonal microservice view shown in Figure 9-4 in Chapter 9. The microservices communicate through an async channel. Apache Kafka, which is inherently asynchronous, is used as the messaging channel. See Figure 11-2.

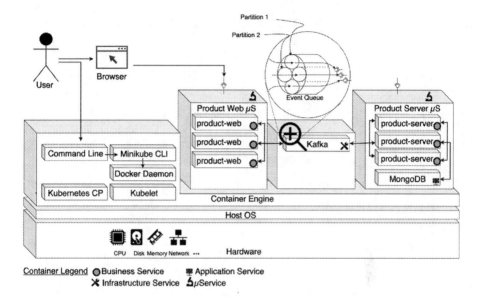

Figure 11-2. *Kubernetes orchestration topology for microservice*

The deployment architecture is very similar to the previous example in this chapter. The only difference is that this example deploys a MongoDB container in Kubernetes.

Understanding the Source Code

The source code for this book is available on GitHub via the book's product page, located at www.apress.com/9798868805547. The source code for this example is organized inside the ch11\ch11-02 folder.

A summarized representation of the source code organization for the example inside the ch11-02 folder is shown in Listing 11-24.

Listing 11-24. Example 11-02 Source Code Organization

```
ch11-02/
├── 01-ProductServer
│   ├── pom.xml
│   └── src
│       └── ...
├── 02-ProductWeb
│   ├── pingrun1.sh
│   ├── pingrun2.sh
│   ├── pingrun3.sh
│   ├── pom.xml
│   └── src
│       └── ...
├── Dockerfile
├── README.txt
├── clean.sh
├── kafka-deployment.yml
├── kafka-request-reply-util
│   ├── pom.xml
│   └── src
│       └── ...
├── kafka-svc.yml
├── makeandrun.sh
├── mongo-deployment.yml
├── mongo-service.yml
├── mongo-volume-claim.yml
├── mongo-volume.yml
├── pom.xml
├── product-server-deployment.yml
├── product-server-service.yml
├── product-web-deployment.yml
└── product-web-service.yml
```

The source code in this example is similar to ch09\ch09-04, which I explained in detail in Chapter 9. In this example from Chapter 9, the deployment architecture is similar, but it used Docker Compose instead of Kubernetes. In the first example in Chapter 10 (ch10\ch10-01), you also looked at the Kubernetes-based deployment of the two microservices and PostgreSQL, and in the previous example in this chapter, you also saw the Kubernetes deployment of Kafka. You should therefore be familiar with all the deployment descriptors in Listing 11-24, so I move to the next steps in executing the example.

Run Microservices in Kubernetes

The ch11\ch11-02 folder contains the scripts required to build and run the examples. The first step is to start a Minikube, single-node Kubernetes cluster. Refer to Appendix E for a quick reference to the Kubernetes setup and commands. As a next step, you need to create a new folder for Mongo data inside the Minikube VM, which you have configured in mongo-volume.yml.

Finally, a simple script, containing all the commands to build and run the complete application with all the defined deployments, is executed in Listing 11-25.

Listing 11-25. Executing the Script to Build and Run Microservices in Kubernetes (ch11\ch11-02\makeandrun.sh)

```
(base) binildass-MacBook-Pro:ch11-02 binil$ pwd
/Users/binil/binil/code/mac/mybooks/docker-04/Code/ch11/ch11-02
(base) binildass-MacBook-Pro:ch11-02 binil$ eval $(minikube
docker-env)
(base) binildass-MacBook-Pro:ch11-02 binil$ sh makeandrun.sh
[INFO] Scanning for projects...
[INFO]
...
[INFO]
```

```
[INFO] Kafka Request Reply utility ...... SUCCESS [  1.129 s]
[INFO] Ecom-Product-Server-Microservice . SUCCESS [  1.242 s]
[INFO] Ecom-Product-Web-Microservice .... SUCCESS [  0.481 s]
[INFO] Ecom .......................... SUCCESS [  0.002 s]
[INFO] ------------------------------------------------------
[INFO] BUILD SUCCESS
[INFO] ------------------------------------------------------
[INFO] Total time:  3.023 s
[INFO] Finished at: 2023-05-19T20:17:30+05:30
[INFO] ------------------------------------------------------
...
http://192.168.64.6:32627
NAME                                READY STATUS   RESTART AGE
kafka-1-deployment-7bcc6dd87f-jrdjx 1/1   Running 0         9s
mongo-cluster-0                     1/1   Running 0         8s
product-server-5cc8967574-6p249     1/1   Running 0         6s
product-server-5cc8967574-7gnz9     1/1   Running 0         6s
product-server-5cc8967574-jr2lv     1/1   Running 0         6s
product-web-ff4f65986-9plf7         1/1   Running 0         5s
product-web-ff4f65986-qd9bs         1/1   Running 0         5s
product-web-ff4f65986-s8hm4         1/1   Running 0         5s
zookeeper-deployment-886ff5f87-nv5xn 1/1  Running 0         9s
NAME                  TYPE        CLUSTER-IP      PORT(S)
kafka-1-ip-service    ClusterIP 10.108.5.80      9092/TCP
kubernetes            ClusterIP 10.96.0.1        443/TCP
mongo                 ClusterIP 10.103.88.174 27017/TCP
mongo-nodeport        NodePort  10.108.6.234   27017:30001/TCP
product-server        ClusterIP 10.103.49.104 8081/TCP
product-server-np     NodePort  10.109.23.86   8081:30002/TCP
product-web           LoadBalan 10.99.185.187 8080:32627/TCP
zookeeper-ip-service  ClusterIP 10.107.235.56 2181/TCP
(base) binildass-MacBook-Pro:ch11-02 binil$
```

Note   I abbreviated `product-server-nodeport` to `product-server-np` in Listing 11-25 for formatting convenience.

You are now ready to test the microservices.

Testing the Microservice Pods

You can now access the Product Web microservice using a browser with this URL formed with the Minikube IP:

`http://192.168.64.6:32627/product.html`

Refer to the section titled "Test the Microservice using UI" in Chapter 1 to test the Product Web microservice container.

You can inspect the data folder, as explained in the first example in Chapter 10. You can also repeat the related tests, as explained in the first example in Chapter 10.

Load Testing the Microservice Pods

This example provides a few scripts to help you load test the microservices and see how the load is evenly distributed from the Product Web to the Product Server through the Kafka messaging channel. See Listing 11-26.

Listing 11-26. Load Testing Scripts

```
./02-ProductWeb/
├── pingrun1.sh
├── pingrun2.sh
├── pingrun3.sh
├── pom.xml
└── src
    └── ...
```

Refer to the previous example for step-by-step instructions to load test the example.

Connect to the MongoDB Pod Using kubectl

This section investigates how to interact with MongoDB using the kubectl command. As you saw earlier, the kubectl exec command allows you to remotely run arbitrary commands inside an existing container of a pod. Based on that, you connect to the MongoDB pod. See Listing 11-27.

Listing 11-27. Connecting to MongoDB Pod Using kubectl

```
(base) binildass-MacBook-Pro:bin binil$ kubectl exec -it mongo-
cluster-0 -- sh
#
```

Next, load the Mongo shell, as shown in Listing 11-28.

Listing 11-28. Connecting to MongoDB Shell Using kubectl

```
(base) binildass-MacBook-Pro:bin binil$ kubectl exec -it mongo-
cluster-0 -- sh
# mongo
MongoDB shell version v4.2.24
connecting to: mongodb://127.0.0.1:27017/?compressors=disabled&
gssapiServiceName=mongodb
...
---

>
```

Refer to Appendix B and execute any MongoDB commands. See Listing 11-29.

Listing 11-29. Executing MongoDB Shell Commands

```
(base) binildass-MacBook-Pro:bin binil$ kubectl exec -it mongo-
cluster-0 -- sh
# mongo
...
---

> show dbs
admin    0.000GB
config   0.000GB
local    0.000GB
test     0.000GB
> db.getName()
test
> show collections
product
> db.product.find()
{ "_id" : ObjectId("64733f182a010c0eaeda6e30"), ...
{ "_id" : ObjectId("64733f182a010c0eaeda6e31"), ...
...
```

Once you test the microservices in this example, you can stop and remove the microservice containers and clean the environment, as shown in Listing 11-30.

Listing 11-30. Cleaning the Project and the Environment

```
(base) binildass-MacBook-Pro:ch11-02 binil$ pwd
/Users/binil/binil/code/mac/mybooks/docker-04/Code/ch11/ch11-02
(base) binildass-MacBook-Pro:ch11-02 binil$ eval $(minikube
docker-env)
(base) binildass-MacBook-Pro:ch11-02 binil$ sh clean.sh
```

```
[INFO] Scanning for projects...
[INFO] ------------------------------------------------------
[INFO] Reactor Build Order:
[INFO]
[INFO] Kafka Request Reply utility                     [jar]
[INFO] Ecom-Product-Server-Microservice                [jar]
[INFO] Ecom-Product-Web-Microservice                   [jar]
[INFO] Ecom                                            [pom]
[INFO]
...
[INFO]
[INFO] Kafka Request Reply utility ...... SUCCESS [  0.087 s]
[INFO] Ecom-Product-Server-Microservice . SUCCESS [  0.075 s]
[INFO] Ecom-Product-Web-Microservice .... SUCCESS [  0.013 s]
[INFO] Ecom ............................. SUCCESS [  0.003 s]
[INFO] ------------------------------------------------------
[INFO] BUILD SUCCESS
[INFO] ------------------------------------------------------
[INFO] Total time:  0.415 s
[INFO] Finished at: 2023-05-19T20:41:43+05:30
[INFO] ------------------------------------------------------
service "product-web" deleted
deployment.apps "product-web" deleted
service "product-server" deleted
service "product-server-nodeport" deleted
deployment.apps "product-server" deleted
service "mongo" deleted
service "mongo-nodeport" deleted
statefulset.apps "mongo-cluster" deleted
persistentvolumeclaim "mongo-data-db" deleted
persistentvolume "mongo-data-db" deleted
```

```
service "zookeeper-ip-service" deleted
service "kafka-1-ip-service" deleted
deployment.apps "zookeeper-deployment" deleted
deployment.apps "kafka-1-deployment" deleted
Untagged: ecom/product-web:latest
Untagged: ecom/product-server:latest
(base) binildass-MacBook-Pro:ch11-02 binil$
```

This completes the second example.

Ingress Routing of Microservices

Through the previous chapters and the previous examples in this chapter, you have seen how a typical deployment can be done in Kubernetes with multiple business, application, and infrastructure services. This section shows you how to tweak the same set of microservices in the second example in Chapter 10 to plug in an Ingress in the front to route external requests. A consumer and provider microservice communicate with each other. The provider microservice stores the entity in a PostgreSQL database. The request from the browser is intercepted by the Ingress. As seen in Chapter 10, an Ingress can expose multiple services through a single IP address.

Even though this example is included in this chapter and is titled Message Oriented Microservices as a final example, I have purposefully eliminated the messaging bridge between the microservices. This is to make the example lighter so that I can introduce a few other new components and keep the overall complexity of the example well within limits.

Design Ingress Routing Topology

The Product Web and Product Server microservices are both
containerized, and the Product Server microservice will connect to a
PostgreSQL database deployed within a container. All these containers
will reside in Kubernetes. Ingress becomes an additional component
for routing and the Adminer UI component manages the PostgreSQL
database. See Figure 11-3.

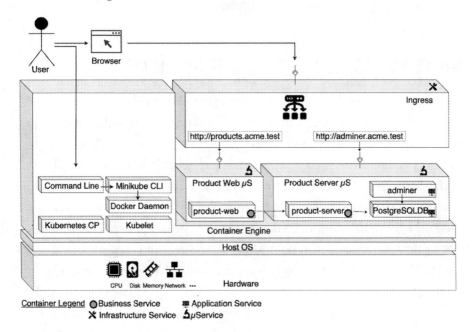

Figure 11-3. *Ingress routing topology for microservices*

Environment Configurations

To make the URLs (`http://products.acme.test` and `http://adminer.`
`acme.test`) work, you need to edit the host files in your host machine.

Every website connected to the Internet has a unique numeric address
that tells all the other devices where it is—its TCP/IP address. The Domain
Name System (DNS) translates those numeric addresses into something

more recognizable and memorable to humans, such as www.acme.com. The first time you type a web address like www.acme.com, your machine pings a DNS server—typically one automatically configured for you by your ISP (Internet Service Provider). This will resolve the TCP/IP address of the server you're trying to connect to. Your browser builds up a hidden cache file to remember those details when you visit the site again.

As specified, this example adds the names to the host files, as shown in Listing 11-31.

Listing 11-31. Adding Hostnames to the etc Hosts File

```
(base) binildass-MacBook-Pro:ch11-03 binil$ minikube ip
192.168.64.5
(base) binildass-MacBook-Pro:~ binil$ sudo nano /etc/hosts

192.168.64.5  adminer.acme.com
192.168.64.5  products.acme.com

(base) binildass-MacBook-Pro:~ binil$ ^O (To Save)
(base) binildass-MacBook-Pro:~ binil$ ^X (To Exit)
(base) binildass-MacBook-Pro:~ sudo killall -HUP mDNSResponder
```

Listing 11-31 shows how I add the two new lines to add two new hostnames to my machine. This will map your localhost (Minikube) IP address to both hostnames and make them accessible.

Figure 11-4 shows how I edited this file.

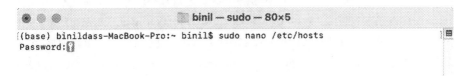

Figure 11-4. *Editing the host files*

Figure 11-5 shows how I added the two hostnames in my machine.

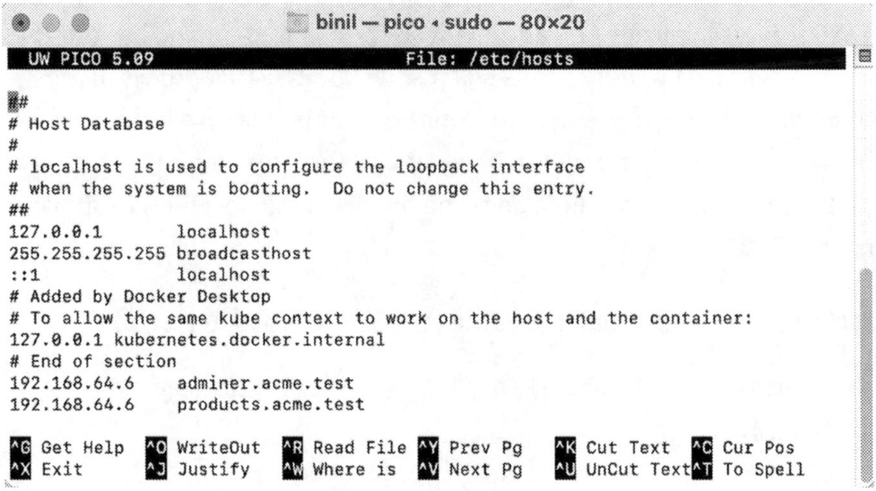

Figure 11-5. *Adding hostnames*

Once you're done, hold down the Control and O keys to save the file, and then Control and X to exit. Subsequently in a command line, type sudo killall -HUP mDNSResponder and then press Return. That will flush your DNS cache, so it isn't confused by any changes you made to the Hosts file.

Understanding the Source Code

The source code for this book is available on GitHub via the book's product page, located at www.apress.com/9798868805547. The source code for this example is organized inside the ch11\ch11-03 folder. The source code in this example is similar to ch10\ch10-01, which I explained in detail in Chapter 10. However, two new components were introduced—the Ingress and the Adminer.

A summarized representation of the source code organization for the example inside the ch11-03 folder is shown in Listing 11-32.

Listing 11-32. Example 11-03 Source Code Organization

```
./ch11-03/
├── 01-ProductServer
│   ├── make.sh
│   ├── pom.xml
│   └── src
│       └── main
├── 02-ProductWeb
│   ├── make.sh
│   ├── pom.xml
│   └── src
│       └── main
├── Dockerfile
├── README.txt
├── adminer-deployment.yaml
├── adminer-svc.yaml
├── clean.sh
├── ingress-controller.yaml
├── makeandrun.sh
├── pom.xml
├── postgres-config.yml
├── postgres-deployment.yml
├── postgres-pvc.yml
├── postgres-svc.yml
├── product-server-deployment.yml
├── product-server-service.yml
├── product-web-deployment.yml
└── product-web-service.yml
```

There are two presentation services or UI services in this project:

- `http://products.acme.test`: The user can interact with the Product Web microservice

- `http://adminer.acme.test`: The user can interact with the PostgreSQL database

Ingress and the Adminer are the two new deployments in Listing 11-32, compared to those in Listing 10-41 in Chapter 10. Let's investigate these new deployments one by one. See Listing 11-33.

Listing 11-33. The Pod Definition YAML File for Ingress (ch11\ch11-03\ingress-controller.yml)

```
apiVersion: networking.k8s.io/v1
kind: Ingress
metadata:
  name: ingress-service
  annotations:
    kubernetes.io/ingress.class: nginx
spec:
  rules:
    - host: "adminer.acme.test"
      http:
        paths:
          - path: /
            pathType: Prefix
            backend:
              service:
                name: adminer
                port:
                  number: 8080
    - host: "products.acme.test"
```

```
http:
  paths:
    - path: /
      pathType: Prefix
      backend:
        service:
          name: product-web
          port:
            number: 8080
```

First, you specify the kind of the Kubernetes object you want to create, which is Ingress. It's followed by metadata with the name of the object as usual and a new section, called annotations. You can configure the behavior of the Ingress. This example uses the simplest one, but there are many more possibilities. The spec section includes the first rule—that all requests from the adminer.acme.test host be routed to the ClusterIP with a name (adminer) and the requests from the products.acme.test host be routed to the ClusterIP with a name (product-web).

The next component is the Adminer UI, which is a UI to the PostgreSQL database. See Listing 11-34.

Listing 11-34. The Pod Definition YAML File for Adminer (ch11\ ch11-03\adminer-deployment.yml)

```
apiVersion: apps/v1
kind: Deployment
metadata:
  name: adminer
  labels:
    app: adminer
    group: db
spec:
  replicas: 1
```

```
selector:
  matchLabels:
    app: adminer
template:
  metadata:
    labels:
      app: adminer
      group: db
  spec:
    containers:
      - name: adminer
        image: adminer:4.8.1-standalone
        ports:
        - containerPort: 8080
        imagePullPolicy: IfNotPresent
        env:
          - name: ADMINER_DESIGN
            value: pepa-linha
          - name: ADMINER_DEFAULT_SERVER
            value: postgres
```

The initial section is responsible for defining what kind of object you're creating (apiVersion, kind) followed by some metadata, including name, labels, and app group (metadata). It then mentions the image to use for the container and a few other environment variables. It also defines an Adminer service. See Listing 11-35.

Listing 11-35. The Service Definition YAML File for Adminer (ch11\ ch11-03\adminer-svc.yml)

```
apiVersion: v1
kind: Service
metadata:
```

```
  name: adminer
  labels:
    group: db
spec:
  type: ClusterIP
  selector:
    app: adminer
  ports:
    - port: 8080
      targetPort: 8080
```

Run Ingress and Microservices in Kubernetes

This example assumes that your single-node Kubernetes cluster, Minikube, is up and running, and that you have already enabled the Ingress add-on in Minikube, as specified in Appendix E. You now have a simple script, containing a single command, to build and run the complete application with all the deployment descriptors, as shown in Listing 11-36.

Listing 11-36. Executing the Script to Build and Run Microservices in Kubernetes (ch11\ch11-03\makeandrun.sh)

```
(base) binildass-MacBook-Pro:ch11-03 binil$ eval $(minikube
docker-env)
(base) binildass-MacBook-Pro:ch11-03 binil$ pwd
/Users/binil/binil/code/mac/mybooks/docker-04/Code/ch11/ch11-03
(base) binildass-MacBook-Pro:ch11-03 binil$ eval $(minikube
docker-env)
(base) binildass-MacBook-Pro:ch11-03 binil$ sh makeandrun.sh
[INFO] Scanning for projects...
[INFO] ------------------------------------------------------------
[INFO] Reactor Build Order:
```

```
[INFO]
[INFO] Ecom-Product-Server-Microservice                    [jar]
[INFO] Ecom-Product-Web-Microservice                       [jar]
[INFO] Ecom                                                 [pom]
[INFO]
[INFO] -<com...product:Ecom-Product-Server-Microservice>-
[INFO] Building Ecom-Product-Server-Microservice 0.0.1-SNAPSHOT
[INFO] -------------------------------[ jar ]--------------
[INFO]
...
[INFO]
[INFO] Ecom-Product-Server-Microservice . SUCCESS [  2.975 s]
[INFO] Ecom-Product-Web-Microservice .... SUCCESS [  0.660 s]
[INFO] Ecom ........................... SUCCESS [  0.020 s]
[INFO] ----------------------------------------------------------
[INFO] BUILD SUCCESS
[INFO] ----------------------------------------------------------
[INFO] Total time:  3.850 s
[INFO] Finished at: 2023-05-28T22:17:15+05:30
[INFO] ----------------------------------------------------------
...
Successfully tagged ecom/product-web:latest
Successfully tagged ecom/product-server:latest
configmap/postgres-config created
persistentvolumeclaim/postgres-persistent-volume-claim created
deployment.apps/postgres created
service/postgres created
deployment.apps/adminer created
service/adminer created
deployment.apps/product-server created
service/product-server created
```

```
deployment.apps/product-web created
service/product-web created
ingress.networking.k8s.io/ingress-service created
http://192.168.64.6:31858
NAME                               READY   STATUS    RESTART
adminer-847f44cbd4-hg4gf           1/1     Running   0
postgres-89dbf9fd9-vr8k2           0/1     Pending   0
product-server-5bf9db77dc-v9jl7    1/1     Running   0
product-web-7496dc46f9-fqfkq       1/1     Running   0
NAME            TYPE       CLUSTER-IP      PORT(S)          AGE
adminer         ClusterIP  10.104.83.51    8080/TCP         4s
kubernetes      ClusterIP  10.96.0.1       443/TCP          11d
postgres        ClusterIP  10.104.112.235  5432/TCP         5s
product-server  ClusterIP  10.104.42.20    8081/TCP         4s
product-web     NodePort   10.106.179.41   8080:31858/TCP   4s
(base) binildass-MacBook-Pro:ch11-03 binil$
```

Describing Ingress

Once the pods are up and running, you can describe the Ingress object you
have created. See Listing 11-37.

Listing 11-37. Describing the Ingress Kubernetes Object

```
(base) binildass-MacBook-Pro:~ binil$ kubectl describe ingress
Name:             ingress-service
Labels:           <none>
Namespace:        default
Address:          192.168.64.6
Ingress Class:    <none>
Default backend:  <default>
```

```
Rules:
  Host                  Path  Backends
  ----                  ----  --------
  adminer.acme.test
                        /    adminer:8080 (10.244.1.234:8080)
  products.acme.test
                        /    product-web:8080 (10.244.1.233:8080)
Annotations:            kubernetes.io/ingress.class: nginx
Events:
  Type    Reason  Age                    From                     Message
  ----    ------  --------------------   -----------------------  --------
  Normal  Sync    7m15s (x2 over 7m44s)  nginx-ingress-controller Scheduled
                                                                  for sync
(base) binildass-MacBook-Pro:~ binil$
```

As you can see, the routes you specified while creating the Ingress Kubernetes objects are configured successfully. Let's now attempt to access those routes.

You are now ready to test the microservices.

Testing the Microservice Pods

You can access the Product Web microservice using the hostname you configured (see Figure 11-6).

```
http://products.acme.test/product.html
```

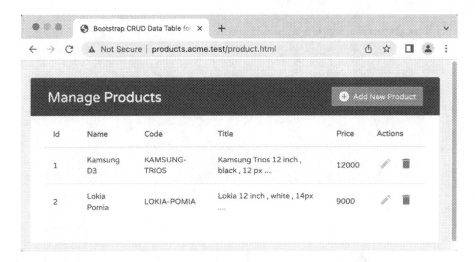

Figure 11-6. *Accessing the Product Web microservice using the hostname*

Note the URL address in Figure 11-6. Refer to the section titled "Test the Microservice Using UI" in Chapter 1 to test the Product Web microservice container. While you test the microservices, you can keep watching the log windows of the Product Web and Product Server microservices.

Recall that you also configured the Adminer UI. You can now attempt to access the PostgreSQL database through the Adminer UI. Use the second URL for that: `http://adminer.acme.test`.

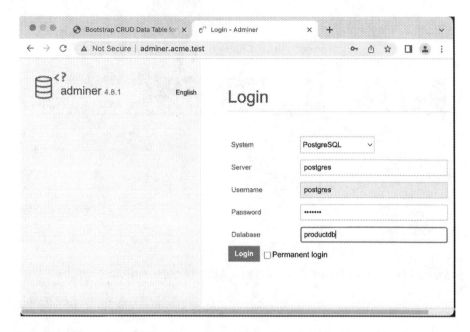

Figure 11-7. *Accessing the PostgreSQL database using the*
Adminer UI

Note the URL address in Figure 11-7. It provides the credentials
configured in `postgres-config.yml`. If you can successfully log in, you
can view the tables that the Product Server microservice initialized. See
Figure 11-8.

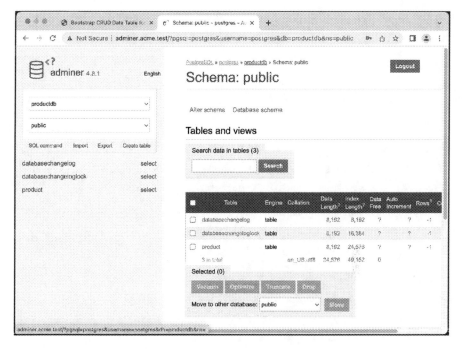

Figure 11-8. *Adminer UI displaying the new tables*

Once you test all the microservices from this example, you can stop
and remove the microservice containers and clean the environment, as
shown in Listing 11-38.

Listing 11-38. Cleaning the Project and the Environment

```
(base) binildass-MacBook-Pro:ch11-03 binil$ pwd
/Users/binil/binil/code/mac/mybooks/docker-04/Code/ch11/ch11-03
(base) binildass-MacBook-Pro:ch11-03 binil$ eval $(minikube
docker-env)
(base) binildass-MacBook-Pro:ch11-03 binil$ sh clean.sh
[INFO] Scanning for projects...
[INFO] ------------------------------------------------------
[INFO] Reactor Build Order:
[INFO]
```

```
[INFO] Ecom-Product-Server-Microservice                    [jar]
[INFO] Ecom-Product-Web-Microservice                       [jar]
[INFO] Ecom                                                [pom]
[INFO]
...
[INFO]
[INFO] Ecom-Product-Server-Microservice . SUCCESS [  0.114 s]
[INFO] Ecom-Product-Web-Microservice .... SUCCESS [  0.009 s]
[INFO] Ecom ........................... SUCCESS [  0.036 s]
[INFO] ------------------------------------------------------------
[INFO] BUILD SUCCESS
[INFO] ------------------------------------------------------------
[INFO] Total time:  0.384 s
[INFO] Finished at: 2023-05-28T22:46:54+05:30
[INFO] ------------------------------------------------------------
service "product-web" deleted
deployment.apps "product-web" deleted
service "product-server" deleted
deployment.apps "product-server" deleted
service "adminer" deleted
deployment.apps "adminer" deleted
service "postgres" deleted
deployment.apps "postgres" deleted
persistentvolumeclaim "postgres-persistent-volume-
claim" deleted
configmap "postgres-config" deleted
ingress.networking.k8s.io "ingress-service" deleted
Untagged: ecom/product-web:latest
Untagged: ecom/product-server:latest
(base) binildass-MacBook-Pro:ch11-03 binil$
```

This completes the last example in this chapter.

Summary

The last chapter introduced Kubernetes and the familiar microservices example interacting with an SQL and a NoSQL database. The current chapter is an extension of that, where you looked at Kafka in Kubernetes. You also learned that all the design primitives—including the correlation between multiple instances of the consumer and provider microservices— all work in the Kubernetes toolset as expected. Finally, you learned about Ingress, which can expose multiple services through a single IP address, giving you a practical and economic means of exposing multiple services to the external world. The next step is to look at a few more tools that can help you further reduce and manage complexity in a production scenario of microservices, where you have more than a dozen of them. This is the topic of the next chapter.

CHAPTER 12

Automating Kubernetes Deployment and Helm

The journey from monoliths to microservices includes objectives like selective scalability, parallel release, and so on. However, as you create more microservices and your application grows, it becomes increasingly difficult to manage. Kubernetes simplifies the process by grouping multiple microservices into a single deployment. Managing Kubernetes applications across the development lifecycle brings its own set of challenges, including version management, configuring environment variables, resource allocation, updating, and rollbacks. Helm provides one of the most appropriate solutions to this problem, making deployments more consistent, repeatable, and reliable. This chapter looks again at the need for automation and as a part of that it introduces Helm with the help of the multi-microservices example.

The objective here is to understand the automation steps and then introduce Helm. To start, I strip down the example application to a bare minimum so that you can concentrate just on the application automation aspects. Once I introduce Helm, I bring back the same multi-microservices example and show you how Helm makes sense when the microservices complexity increases.

© Binildas A. Christudas 2024
B. A. Christudas, *Java Microservices and Containers in the Cloud*,
https://doi.org/10.1007/979-8-8688-0555-4_12

The following concepts are covered in this chapter:

- Reintroducing the Hello World Spring Boot microservices

- Automating Docker interactions

- Automating Kubernetes interactions

- Introducing Helm

- Using Helm to deploy a multi-microservice

- Using Helmfile to deploy a multi-microservice

Let's start by reintroducing the "Hello World" microservice example.

Introducing a Simple Java Microservice

You saw one simple microservice example in Chapter 1. This section uses a similar, but even simpler, microservice to start with.

Designing Your Simple Microservices

This simple microservice has a single component or Java class, which is a REST controller (see Figure 12-1).

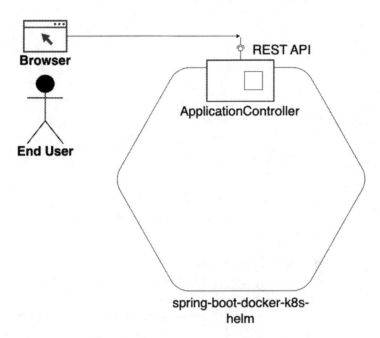

Figure 12-1. *A simple microservice*

Let's investigate the project structure as well.

Code Organization

The source code for this book is available on GitHub via the book's product page, located at www.apress.com/9798868805547. The source code for this example is organized as shown in Listing 12-1, inside the ch12\ ch12-01 folder.

Listing 12-1. Spring Boot Microservices Source Code Organization

```
./ch12-01/
├── README.txt
├── clean.sh
├── make.sh
```

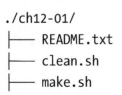

```
├── pom.xml
├── run.sh
└── src
    └── main
        ├── java
        │   └── com
        │       └── acme
        │           └── ecom
        │               └── product
        │                   └── Application.java
        └── resources
            ├── application.yml
            └── log4j2-spring.xml
```

This code follows the standard Maven structure so that the pom.xml file is in the root directory.

Understanding the Source Code

The single application component is the Application.java class, which is a REST controller (see Listing 12-2).

Listing 12-2. Application REST Controller (ch12/ch12-01/src/main/java/com/acme/ecom/product\Application.java)

```
@SpringBootApplication
@RestController
public class Application {

    private static final Logger LOGGER =
        LoggerFactory.getLogger(Application.class);

    private static volatile long times = 0L;
```

```
@RequestMapping("/")
public String home() {

    LOGGER.info("Start");
    ++times;
    LOGGER.debug("Inside hello.Application.home() : {}",
        times);
    LOGGER.info("Returning...");
    return "Hello Docker World : " + times;
}

public static void main(String[] args) {

    SpringApplication.run(Application.class, args);
    LOGGER.info("Started...");
}
}
```

This is a Spring REST annotated class, so you should be able to access it using a browser.

Build and Run the Microservice

The ch12\ch12-01 folder contains the Maven scripts required to build and run these examples. See Listing 12-3.

Listing 12-3. Building the Microservice Using Scripts

```
(base) binildass-MacBook-Pro:ch12-01 binil$ pwd
/Users/binil/binil/code/mac/mybooks/docker-04/Code/ch12/ch12-01
(base) binildass-MacBook-Pro:ch12-01 binil$ sh make.sh
[INFO] Scanning for projects...
[INFO]
...
```

```
[INFO] ------------------------------------------------------
[INFO] BUILD SUCCESS
[INFO] ------------------------------------------------------
[INFO] Total time:  1.569 s
[INFO] Finished at: 2023-05-20T11:17:49+05:30
[INFO] ------------------------------------------------------
(base) binildass-MacBook-Pro:ch12-01 binil$
```

Run the microservice as the next step, as shown in Listing 12-4.

Listing 12-4. Running the Microservice Using Scripts

```
(base) binildass-MacBook-Pro:ch12-01 binil$ pwd
/Users/binil/binil/code/mac/mybooks/docker-04/Code/ch12/ch12-01
(base) binildass-MacBook-Pro:ch12-01 binil$ sh run.sh

  .   ____          _            __ _ _
 /\\ / ___'_ __ _ _(_)_ __  __ _ \ \ \ \
( ( )\___ | '_ | '_| | '_ \/ _` | \ \ \ \
 \\/  ___)| |_)| | | | | || (_| |  ) ) ) )
  '  |____| .__|_| |_|_| |_\__, | / / / /
 =========|_|==============|___/=/_/_/_/
 :: Spring Boot ::                (v3.2.0)

2023-05-20 11:19:04 INFO  StartupInfoLogger.logStarting:51 -
Starting Application v0.0.1-SNAPSHOT ...
2023-05-20 11:19:04 DEBUG StartupInfoLogger.logStarting:52 -
Running with Spring Boot v3.0.6...
2023-05-20 11:19:04 INFO  SpringApplication.
logStartupProfileInfo:632 - No active profile set...
2023-05-20 11:19:05 INFO  StartupInfoLogger.logStarted:57 -
Started Application ...
2023-05-20 11:19:05 INFO  Application.main:50 - Started...
2023-05-20 11:19:10 INFO  Application.home:40 - Start
```

```
2023-05-20 11:19:10 DEBUG Application.home:42 - Inside hello.
Application.home() : 1
2023-05-20 11:19:10 INFO  Application.home:43 - Returning...
```

Testing the Microservice

Once the microservice is up, you can access the web application by using your browser and pointing to this URL:

```
http://127.0.0.1:8080/
```

You can alternatively use cURL to access the microservice, as shown in Listing 12-5.

Listing 12-5. Testing the Microservice Using cURL

```
(base) binildass-MacBook-Pro:~ binil$ curl
http://127.0.0.1:8080/
Hello Docker World : 1
(base) binildass-MacBook-Pro:~ binil$
```

In the next three examples, you will increase the automation level of build and packaging for container-based deployment for this microservice. After that, I introduce Helm.

Automating the Docker Build

In this section, you containerize the example and deploy it in Docker. This section uses dockerfile-maven-plugin to integrate Maven with Docker.

Understanding the Source Code

The source code for this book is available on GitHub via the book's product page, located at www.apress.com/9798868805547. The source code for this example is organized inside the ch12\ch12-02 folder.

You have the single application component, the `Application.java` class, which is a REST controller. The additional code tells the Maven script to use the `dockerfile-maven-plugin`. See Listing 12-6.

Listing 12-6. Spotify Maven Plugin (ch12/ch12-02/pom.xml)

```
</project>
    ...
    <build>
        <plugins>
            ...
            <plugin>
                <groupId>com.spotify</groupId>
                <artifactId>
                    dockerfile-maven-plugin
                </artifactId>
                <version>1.4.13</version>
                <configuration>
                    <repository>
                        ${docker.image.prefix}/
                            ${project.artifactId}
                    </repository>
                </configuration>
            </plugin>
        </plugins>
    </build>
</project>
```

The Spotify Maven plugin runs the Docker command for you using your Dockerfile, as if you were doing it on the command terminal. You can use it to automate the Docker build. There are a few configuration options for the Docker image tag, and so on, but it keeps the Docker knowledge in your application concentrated in a Dockerfile, which many people prefer.

Build and Run the Microservice

The ch12\ch12-02 folder contains the Maven scripts required to build and run the examples.

Since you need a Docker runtime, first bring Minikube up. Refer to Appendix E for a quick reference to the Minikube-based Kubernetes setup and commands. See Listing 12-7.

Listing 12-7. Starting Minikube

```
(base) binildass-MacBook-Pro:~ binil$ minikube start
😊  minikube v1.30.1 on Darwin 13.3
✦  Using the hyperkit driver based on existing profile
🔥  Starting control plane node minikube in cluster minikube
🔄  Restarting existing hyperkit VM for "minikube" ...
🐳  Preparing Kubernetes v1.26.3 on Docker 20.10.23 ...
...
🔎  Verifying ingress addon...
🌟  Enabled addons: ingress-dns, storage-provisioner,
    default-storageclass, ingress
🏃  Done! kubectl is now configured to use "minikube" cluster
    and "default" namespace by default
(base) binildass-MacBook-Pro:~ binil$
```

Also, set the minikube environment variables in your work terminal.

You have to use the mvn dockerfile:build command, which will create the Docker image, so do that now. See Listing 12-8.

Listing 12-8. Building the Microservice and the Docker Image

```
(base) binildass-MacBook-Pro:ch12-02 binil$ pwd
/Users/binil/binil/code/mac/mybooks/docker-04/Code/ch12/ch12-02
(base) binildass-MacBook-Pro:ch12-04 binil$ eval $(minikube
docker-env)
```

579

```
(base) binildass-MacBook-Pro:ch12-02 binil$ sh make.sh
[INFO] Scanning for projects...
...
[INFO]
[INFO] -< com.acme.ecom.product:spring-boot-docker-k8s-helm >-
[INFO] Building Spring Boot µS 0.0.1-SNAPSHOT
[INFO] -------------------- [ jar ]--------------------
[INFO]
...
[INFO] Successfully built 0c23b3413de1
[INFO] Successfully tagged binildas/spring-boot-docker-k8s-
helm:latest
[INFO]
...
[INFO] Successfully built binildas/spring-boot-docker-k8s-
helm:latest
[INFO] ------------------------------------------------------
[INFO] BUILD SUCCESS
[INFO] ------------------------------------------------------
[INFO] Total time:  13.935 s
[INFO] Finished at: 2023-05-20T11:54:39+05:30
[INFO] ------------------------------------------------------
(base) binildass-MacBook-Pro:ch12-02 binil$
```

This log states that `binildas/spring-boot-docker-k8s-helm:latest` has been built. You can inspect the local Docker registry to view the newly created image, as shown in Listing 12-9.

Listing 12-9. Inspecting the Docker Images

```
(base) binildass-MacBook-Pro:~ binil$ eval $(minikube
docker-env)
(base) binildass-MacBook-Pro:~ binil$ docker images
```

```
REPOSITORY                            TAG    IMAGE ID
binildas/spring-boot-docker-k8s-helm latest 0c23b3413de1
...
(base) binildass-MacBook-Pro:~ binil$
```

In this example, whatever automation you intended (image creation alone) has already been completed, so you can do the rest of the stages manually.

Now push the image to the Docker public registry. Since my Docker registry already has that image, I first delete it from the terminal. For that, I will get a token. See Listing 12-10.

Listing 12-10. Retrieving a Docker Hub Token

```
(base) binildass-MacBook-Pro:~ binil$ HUB_TOKEN=$(curl -s -H
"Content-Type: application/json" -X POST -d '{"username":
"binildas" , "password": "********" }' https://hub.docker.com/
v2/users/login/ | jq -r .token)
(base) binildass-MacBook-Pro:~ binil$ echo $HUB_TOKEN
eyJ4NWMiOlsiTUlJQytUQONBc...
(base) binildass-MacBook-Pro:~ binil$
```

Using that token, you can delete the binildas/spring-boot-docker-k8s-helm image from the public Docker registry, as shown in Listing 12-11.

Listing 12-11. Deleting Images from Public Docker Hub

```
(base) binildass-MacBook-Pro:~ binil$ curl -i -X DELETE -H
"Accept: application/json" -H "Authorization: JWT $HUB_TOKEN"
https://hub.docker.com/v2/repositories/binildas/spring-boot-
docker-k8s-helm/tags/latest/
HTTP/1.1 204 No Content
date: Sat, 20 May 2023 06:08:59 GMT
```

```
x-ratelimit-limit: 600
x-ratelimit-reset: 1684562998
x-ratelimit-remaining: 600
x-trace-id: f6de7fa45a63c1eb6b076df17971cc37
server: nginx
x-frame-options: deny
x-content-type-options: nosniff
x-xss-protection: 1; mode=block
strict-transport-security: max-age=31536000

(base) binildass-MacBook-Pro:~ binil$
```

Now, to manually push the image to the public Docker Hub, you must log in to Docker from the terminal, as shown in Listing 12-12.

Listing 12-12. Logging In to the Docker Hub from Terminal

```
(base) binildass-MacBook-Pro:~ binil$ eval $(minikube
docker-env)
(base) binildass-MacBook-Pro:~ binil$ docker login
Authenticating with existing credentials...
WARNING! Your password will be stored unencrypted in /Users/
binil/.docker/config.json.
Configure a credential helper to remove this warning. See
https://docs.docker.com/engine/reference/commandline/
login/#credentials-store

Login Succeeded
(base) binildass-MacBook-Pro:~ binil$
```

You can manually push the image to the Docker Hub (from this terminal), as shown in Listing 12-13.

Listing 12-13. Manually Pushing an Image to Docker Hub

```
(base) binildass-MacBook-Pro:~ binil$ docker push
binildas/spring-boot-docker-k8s-helm:latest
The push refers to repository [docker.io/binildas/spring-boot-
docker-k8s-helm]
250c3b6ce2b0: Pushed
1bc0685fedc8: Pushed
cc66d1dae976: Pushed
ceaf9e1ebef5: Pushed
9b9b7f3d56a0: Pushed
f1b5933fe4b5: Pushed
latest: digest: sha256:083ad89fa86e9852ba783eadb5f9c174e746ba1e
0cc8404f24cc6d76fdcd9345 size: 1575
(base) binildass-MacBook-Pro:~ binil$
```

To demonstrate the Docker pull to happen from the public Docker Hub, delete the image from the local Docker registry, as shown in Listing 12-14.

Listing 12-14. Deleting an Image from the Local Docker Registry

```
(base) binildass-MacBook-Pro:~ binil$ eval $(minikube
docker-env)
(base) binildass-MacBook-Pro:~ binil$ docker rmi binildas/
spring-boot-docker-k8s-helm
Untagged: binildas/spring-boot-docker-k8s-helm:latest
Untagged: binildas/spring-boot-docker-k8s-helm@sha256:083ad...
...
Deleted: sha256:9889cb2fe045eb9f5b7b3811796377440f5f6890fda...
(base) binildass-MacBook-Pro:~ binil$
```

You can now attempt to bring up the application. Use this command:

```
docker run -it -p 8080:8080 binildas/spring-boot-docker-k8s-
helm:latest
```

In that process, you must first pull the image from the public Docker Hub and instantiate the container. See Listing 12-15.

Listing 12-15. Pull Image and Start Container

```
(base) binildass-MacBook-Pro:ch12-02 binil$ pwd
/Users/binil/binil/code/mac/mybooks/docker-04/Code/ch12/ch12-02
(base) binildass-MacBook-Pro:ch12-02 binil$ eval $(minikube
docker-env)
(base) binildass-MacBook-Pro:ch12-02 binil$ sh run.sh
Unable to find image 'binildas/spring-boot-docker-k8s-
helm:latest' locally
latest: Pulling from binildas/spring-boot-docker-k8s-helm
5843afab3874: Already exists
53c9466125e4: Already exists
d8d715783b80: Already exists
af78a462dd1f: Pull complete
71d05ae2a767: Pull complete
04170f3d7f6b: Pull complete
Digest: sha256:275170154dd952be90cffdff0b585d28975a47070d75f59e
5f782862bb36a864
Status: Downloaded newer image for binildas/spring-boot-docker-
k8s-helm:latest
```

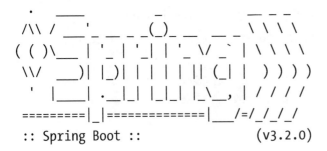

```
  .   ____          _            __ _ _
 /\\ / ___'_ __ _ _(_)_ __  __ _ \ \ \ \
( ( )\___ | '_ | '_| | '_ \/ _` | \ \ \ \
 \\/  ___)| |_)| | | | | || (_| |  ) ) ) )
  '  |____| .__|_| |_|_| |_\__, | / / / /
 =========|_|==============|___/=/_/_/_/
 :: Spring Boot ::                (v3.2.0)
```

```
2023-05-20 07:07:33 INFO  StartupInfoLogger.logStarting:51 -
Starting Application using Java...
2023-05-20 07:07:33 DEBUG StartupInfoLogger.logStarting:52 -
Running with Spring Boot v3.0.6...
2023-05-20 07:07:33 INFO  SpringApplication.
logStartupProfileInfo:632 - No active ...
2023-05-20 07:07:35 INFO  StartupInfoLogger.logStarted:57 -
Started Application ...
2023-05-20 07:07:35 INFO  Application.main:50 - Started...
...
```

Once the application is running, you are ready to test the application.

Testing the Microservice

You need to find the Minikube IP first, as shown in Listing 12-16.

Listing 12-16. Finding the Minikube IP

```
(base) binildass-MacBook-Pro:~ binil$ eval $(minikube
docker-env)
(base) binildass-MacBook-Pro:~ binil$ minikube ip
192.168.64.6
(base) binildass-MacBook-Pro:~ binil$
```

Once the microservice is up, you can access the web application using your browser and pointing to this URL:

```
http://192.168.64.6:8080/
```

You can alternatively use cURL to access the microservice, as shown in Listing 12-5.

Listing 12-17. Listing the Running Containers

```
(base) binildass-MacBook-Pro:~ binil$ eval $(minikube docker-env)
(base) binildass-MacBook-Pro:~ binil$ docker ps -a
CONTAINER ID    IMAGE
COMMAND                      CREATED              STATUS
PORTS                    NAMES
f39c79e72b6f    binildas/spring-boot-docker-k8s-helm:latest
"java -cp app:app/li..."    18 minutes ago       Up 18 minutes
0.0.0.0:8080->8080/tcp    sad_chandrasekhar
...
(base) binildass-MacBook-Pro:~ binil$ eval $
```

The next three examples increase the automation level of build and packaging.

Automating Docker Push

This example shows how to automate the Docker push of images too, which is one step more than the previous example.

The example uses Google's `jib-maven-plugin` to integrate Maven with Docker.

Understanding the Source Code

The source code for this book is available on GitHub via the book's product page, located at www.apress.com/9798868805547. The source code for this example is organized inside the ch12\ch12-03 folder.

The single application component is the Application.java class, which is a REST controller. You have already seen this level of automation in the second example in Chapter 7, but you will do this in the current example too for the sake of completeness. Also, you are doing more configurations to the jib plugin, so the Maven configurations are shown in Listing 12-18.

Listing 12-18. Maven pom xml (ch12/ch12-03/pom.xml)

```
<project>
    ...
    <build>
        <plugins>

            <plugin>
                <groupId>org.springframework.boot</groupId>
                <artifactId>
                    spring-boot-maven-plugin
                </artifactId>
            </plugin>

            <plugin>
                <groupId>com.google.cloud.tools</groupId>
                <artifactId>
                    jib-maven-plugin
                </artifactId>
                <version>3.3.2</version>
                <configuration>
                    <to>
                        <image>
                            binildas/${project.artifactId}
                        </image>
                    </to>
                    <container>
                        <creationTime>
                            USE_CURRENT_TIMESTAMP
```

```
                    </creationTime>
                    <ports>
                        <port>8080</port>
                    </ports>
                </container>
            </configuration>
        </plugin>

        </plugins>
    </build>
</project>
```

Refer to the second example in Chapter 7, where it explains how to configure the Maven settings configuration file, and so on, for the Docker Hub credential setting in Listing 7-22. This chapter goes straight to building and pushing the image.

Build and Run the Microservice

The ch12\ch12-03 folder contains the Maven scripts required to build and run the examples. The mvn clean compile jib:build command is used to build the example, as shown in Listing 12-19.

Listing 12-19. Building the Microservice and Pushing the Docker Image

```
(base) binildass-MacBook-Pro:ch12-03 binil$ pwd
/Users/binil/binil/code/mac/mybooks/docker-04/Code/ch12/ch12-03
(base) binildass-MacBook-Pro:ch12-03 binil$ eval $(minikube
docker-env)
(base) binildass-MacBook-Pro:ch12-03 binil$ sh make.sh
[INFO] Scanning for projects...
[WARNING]
```

```
...
[INFO]
[INFO] -< com.acme.ecom.product:spring-boot-docker-k8s-helm >-
[INFO] Building Spring Boot µS 0.0.1-SNAPSHOT
[INFO] --------------------------------[ jar ]----------------
[INFO]
...
[INFO] Using credentials from Docker config (/Users/binil/.
docker/config.json) for ...
[INFO] The base image requires auth. Trying again for eclipse-
temurin:17-jre...
[INFO] Using credentials from Docker config (/Users/binil/.
docker/config.json) for ...
[INFO] Using base image with digest: sha256:620beab172aa...
[INFO]
[INFO] Container entrypoint set to [java, -cp, @/app/jib-
classpath-file, com.acme.ecom.product.Application]
[INFO]
[INFO] Built and pushed image as binildas/spring-boot-
docker-k8s-helm
[INFO] Executing tasks:
[INFO] [=============================] 100.0% complete
[INFO]
[INFO] ------------------------------------------------------
[INFO] BUILD SUCCESS
[INFO] ------------------------------------------------------
[INFO] Total time:  27.088 s
[INFO] Finished at: 2023-05-20T13:09:48+05:30
[INFO] ------------------------------------------------------
(base) binildass-MacBook-Pro:ch12-03 binil$
```

You can run the microservice as the next step. Use the `docker run -it -p 8080:8080 binildas/spring-boot-docker-k8s-helm:latest` command to run this example, as shown in Listing 12-20.

Listing 12-20. Running the Microservice Using Scripts

```
(base) binildass-MacBook-Pro:ch12-03 binil$ pwd
/Users/binil/binil/code/mac/mybooks/docker-04/Code/ch12/ch12-03
(base) binildass-MacBook-Pro:ch12-03 binil$ eval $(minikube
docker-env)
(base) binildass-MacBook-Pro:ch12-03 binil$ sh run.sh

  .   ____          _            __ _ _
 /\\ / ___'_ __ _ _(_)_ __  __ _ \ \ \ \
( ( )\___ | '_ | '_| | '_ \/ _` | \ \ \ \
 \\/  ___)| |_)| | | | | || (_| |  ) ) ) )
  '  |____| .__|_| |_|_| |_\__, | / / / /
 =========|_|==============|___/=/_/_/_/
 :: Spring Boot ::                (v3.2.0)

2023-05-20 07:45:25 INFO  StartupInfoLogger.logStarting:51 -
Starting Application using Java 17-ea ...
2023-05-20 07:45:25 DEBUG StartupInfoLogger.logStarting:52 -
Running with Spring Boot v3.0.6...
2023-05-20 07:45:25 INFO  SpringApplication.
logStartupProfileInfo:632 - No active profile set...
2023-05-20 07:45:27 INFO  StartupInfoLogger.logStarted:57 -
Started Application in 2.809 seconds ...
2023-05-20 07:45:27 INFO  Application.main:50 - Started...
2023-05-20 07:46:08 INFO  Application.home:40 - Start
2023-05-20 07:46:08 DEBUG Application.home:42 - Inside hello.
Application.home() : 1
2023-05-20 07:46:08 INFO  Application.home:43 - Returning...
...
```

Once the application is running, you are ready to test the application.

Testing the Microservice

You need to find the Minikube IP first, as shown in Listing 12-6. Once the microservice is up, you can access the web application using your browser and pointing to this URL:

```
http://192.168.64.6:8080/
```

You can alternatively use cURL to access the microservice, as shown in Listing 12-5.

Automating Kubernetes Deployment

Having seen the different build automations for Docker, you automate the Kubernetes deployment in this example. In fact, you have been using automation for Kubernetes deployment in many of the examples in the previous chapters, especially in Chapters 10 and 11. Therefore, I do not explain every detail again; instead just explaining how to build and run the code. The Spotify Maven plugin is used for the automation, the details of which you learned in the second example in this chapter.

Code Organization

The source code for this book is available on GitHub via the book's product page, located at www.apress.com/9798868805547. The source code for this example is organized as shown in Listing 12-21, inside the ch12\ ch12-04 folder.

Listing 12-21. Spring Boot Microservices Source Code Organization

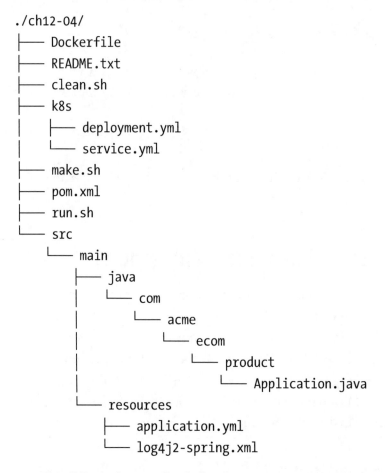

```
./ch12-04/
├── Dockerfile
├── README.txt
├── clean.sh
├── k8s
│   ├── deployment.yml
│   └── service.yml
├── make.sh
├── pom.xml
├── run.sh
└── src
    └── main
        ├── java
        │   └── com
        │       └── acme
        │           └── ecom
        │               └── product
        │                   └── Application.java
        └── resources
            ├── application.yml
            └── log4j2-spring.xml
```

This follows the standard Maven structure so that the `pom.xml` file is in the root directory.

In Chapters 10 and 11, you learned about the Kubernetes deployment descriptors, so I do not explain them here. Instead, you'll build and run the example.

Build and Run the Microservice

The ch12\ch12-04 folder contains the Maven scripts required to build
and run these examples. The mvn clean package dockerfile:build
command is used to build the example, as shown in Listing 12-22.

Listing 12-22. Building the Microservice Using Scripts

```
(base) binildass-MacBook-Pro:ch12-04 binil$ pwd
/Users/binil/binil/code/mac/mybooks/docker-04/Code/ch12/ch12-04
(base) binildass-MacBook-Pro:ch12-04 binil$ eval $(minikube
docker-env)clear
(base) binildass-MacBook-Pro:ch12-04 binil$ sh make.sh
[INFO] Scanning for projects...
[INFO]
...
```

You can run the microservice as the next step. The single script called
run.sh consolidates all the commands, as shown in Listing 12-23.

Listing 12-23. Script for Running the Microservice Containers
(ch12/ch12-04/run.sh)

```
eval $(minikube docker-env)
kubectl create -f ./k8s/deployment.yml
kubectl create -f ./k8s/service.yml
minikube service springboothelm --url
sleep 3
kubectl get pods
kubectl get services
```

You can now execute this script, as shown in Listing 12-24.

Listing 12-24. Running the Microservice Containers Using Scripts

```
(base) binildass-MacBook-Pro:ch12-04 binil$ pwd
/Users/binil/binil/code/mac/mybooks/docker-04/Code/ch12/ch12-04
(base) binildass-MacBook-Pro:ch12-04 binil$ eval $(minikube
docker-env)clear
(base) binildass-MacBook-Pro:ch12-04 binil$ sh run.sh
deployment.apps/springboothelm created
service/springboothelm created
http://192.168.64.6:30048
...
```

Once the services are up and running, you can test the example.

Testing the Microservice

You need to find the Minikube IP first, as shown in Listing 12-16. You can then access the web application by using your browser and pointing to this URL:

```
http://192.168.64.6:8080/
```

You can alternatively use cURL to access the microservice, as shown in Listing 12-5.

Helm

In the previous example and in many other examples in the previous two chapters, you saw YAML files used for Kubernetes deployments. When the number of microservices increases and when the number of deployment environments increases, you have to deal with many YAML files. For example, my current organization sells SaaS services for airline passenger reservation services and airline cargo reservation services, along with other services. We need to have a core product that can operate at Level

4 SaaS maturity, which means the same instance should functionally adapt to the requirements of multiple airlines (called tenants). At the same time, these products need to be deployed in multiple environments, like Development, Testing, Staging, and so on. Helm is a handy tool that maintains a single deployment YAML file with version information. This file lets you set up and manage a very large Kubernetes cluster with a few commands.

What Is Helm?

Helm is a package manager for Kubernetes. It helps in installing, upgrading, uninstalling, and rolling back workloads in a Kubernetes cluster. Like yum and apt, which are popular package managers for Linux distributions, Helm treats the deployments as applications being installed on a Kubernetes platform.

Helm needs you to store your Kubernetes manifest files in a specific folder structure. This folder structure is treated as one package. Helm packages are called *charts*. Helm charts can be nested to help install multiple applications using a single hierarchical folder structure. For convenience in managing the chart as well as several versions of the same Helm chart, these folders can also be archived and stored in a repository.

Helm Nomenclature

Helm uses three main concepts that you need to be familiar with:

- Chart: As explained, a chart contains all that is required for a Kubernetes deployment along with a few Helm-specific files in a certain folder structure. This includes all the YAML configuration files for deployments, services, secrets, and config maps that define the deployed state of your application.

- Config: This includes one or more YAML files that have the required configuration information for deploying a Kubernetes application. Resources in the Kubernetes cluster are deployed based on these values.

- Release: A running instance of a chart is called a release. When you run the `helm install` command, it pulls the config, merges with the chart files, and deploys all the Kubernetes resources. One chart can have multiple releases.

With these basic constructs under your belt, the next section looks at the Helm architecture.

Client-Server Helm Architecture

Helm Kubernetes has two main components—the client (CLI) and the server (Tiller). Helm works on a client-server model, as shown in Figure 12-2.

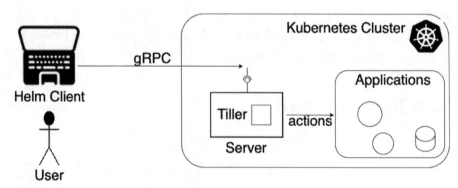

Figure 12-2. *Helm architecture*

This section investigates the two main components of the Helm architecture:

- Tiller: Tiller is a server installed in the Kubernetes cluster and Helm manages Kubernetes applications through this component. Tiller interacts with the Kubernetes API server for application release operations—install, upgrade, query, and remove Kubernetes resources. For quick development purposes, it can also be run locally and configured to talk to a remote Kubernetes cluster.

- Client (CLI): Similar to any client-server model, the Helm client lives on the local workstation of the user and the Tiller server on the Kubernetes cluster to execute what is needed. You can think of CLI as used to push the resources you need. Tiller runs inside the Kubernetes cluster and manages (creating/updating/deleting) the resources of the Helm charts.

Note   Subsequent to Helm 2 (Helm v2.16.7), the Tiller server is deprecated. However, that does not affect the examples in this book.

With this background, the next section explains how Helm works.

How Helm Works

To understand this concept, recall the first example in Chapter 11. In the Product Server microservice, you defined three replicas for the server instance, as shown in Listing 12-25.

Listing 12-25. The Product Server Pod YAML File (ch11\ch11-01\ product-server-deployment.yml)

```
apiVersion: apps/v1
kind: Deployment
metadata:
  name: product-server
  ...
spec:
  replicas: 3
  ...
  template:
    ...
    spec:
      containers:
      - name: product-server
        ...
        env:
          - name: DB_SERVER
            value: postgres
          - name: spring.kafka.bootstrap-servers
            value: kafka-1-ip-service:9092
```

Suppose that you need only one instance in staging. To do this, you need to update the `replica` value in the descriptor and deploy it in Kubernetes. A better approach is to use Helm so you can parameterize the fields depending on the environment. In this example, instead of using a static value for replicas, you can use the value for these fields from another file. This file is called `values.yaml`. In this manner, Helm helps you separate the configurable field value from the actual YAML descriptors.

In the next section, you'll learn more by doing.

Helm Package Microservice

This section shows you how to Helm-enable the previous example in this chapter. As mentioned in Appendix E, I assume that you have installed Helm on your machine.

Code Organization

The source code for this book is available on GitHub via the book's product page, located at www.apress.com/9798868805547. The source code for the example is organized as shown in Listing 12-25, inside the ch12\ ch12-05 folder. This follows the standard Maven structure so that the pom.xml file is in the root directory. This also contains a new folder called springboothelm, with many files inside it, as shown in Listing 12-26.

Listing 12-26. Spring Boot Microservices Source Code Organization

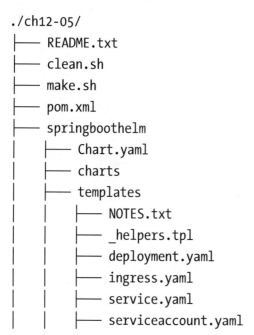

```
./ch12-05/
├── README.txt
├── clean.sh
├── make.sh
├── pom.xml
├── springboothelm
│   ├── Chart.yaml
│   ├── charts
│   ├── templates
│   │   ├── NOTES.txt
│   │   ├── _helpers.tpl
│   │   ├── deployment.yaml
│   │   ├── ingress.yaml
│   │   ├── service.yaml
│   │   ├── serviceaccount.yaml
```

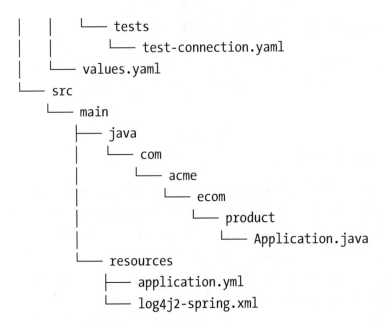

```
|   |     └── tests
|   |           └── test-connection.yaml
|   └── values.yaml
└── src
    └── main
        ├── java
        |   └── com
        |       └── acme
        |           └── ecom
        |               └── product
        |                   └── Application.java
        └── resources
            ├── application.yml
            └── log4j2-spring.xml
```

Don't panic; you don't need to hand-create all these files. Instead, you can auto-generate many of them.

Creating Your First Helm Chart

Before you start creating your first Helm chart, make sure Minikube is running as mentioned in Listing 12-7, since you need to have a Kubernetes cluster.

Next, from the source code downloaded for this example (ch12\ ch12-05), delete the springboothelm folder. Then, from the root of the project folder, create your first Helm chart. See Listing 12-27.

Listing 12-27. Creating Your First Helm Chart

```
(base) binildass-MacBook-Pro:ch12-05 binil$ pwd
/Users/binil/binil/code/mac/mybooks/docker-04/Code/ch12/ch12-05
(base) binildass-MacBook-Pro:ch12-05 binil$ helm create
springboothelm
```

```
Creating springboothelm
(base) binildass-MacBook-Pro:ch12-05 binil$ tree
./springboothelm/
./springboothelm/
├── Chart.yaml
├── charts
├── templates
│   ├── NOTES.txt
│   ├── _helpers.tpl
│   ├── deployment.yaml
│   ├── hpa.yaml
│   ├── ingress.yaml
│   ├── service.yaml
│   ├── serviceaccount.yaml
│   └── tests
│       └── test-connection.yaml
└── values.yaml

3 directories, 10 files
(base) binildass-MacBook-Pro:ch12-05 binil$
```

Let's look at Chart.yaml first. This file contains all the metadata about the Helm chart example. See Listing 12-28.

Listing 12-28. The Chart YAML File (ch12/ch12-05/ springboothelm\Chart.yaml)

```
apiVersion: v2
name: springboothelm
description: A Helm chart for Kubernetes
type: application
version: 0.1.0
appVersion: "1.16.0"
```

The apiVersion, name, and version fields are mandatory. There are no strict rules for the apiVersion. Each chart should have its own version number and it should follow the Semantic Versioning 2.0.

Listing 12-29 shows the values.yaml file.

Listing 12-29. The Values YAML File (ch12/ch12-05/ springboothelm/values.yaml)

```
# Default values for springboothelm.
# This is a YAML-formatted file.
# Declare variables to be passed into your templates.

replicaCount: 1

image:
  repository: binildas/spring-boot-docker-k8s-helm
  pullPolicy: IfNotPresent

imagePullSecrets: []
nameOverride: ""
fullnameOverride: ""
...
```

This file is quite verbose, but luckily you don't need to manage all its contents. For the purposes here, you just need to update two lines:

```
repository: binildas/spring-boot-docker-k8s-helm
port: 8080
```

The next configuration you need to update is deployment.yaml. As the name suggests, it is used for deployment purposes. Listing 12-30 shows the deployment.yaml file.

Listing 12-30. The Deployment YAML File (ch12/ch12-05/
springboothelm/templates/deployment.yaml)

```
apiVersion: apps/v1
kind: Deployment
metadata:
  name: {{ include "springboothelm.fullname" . }}
  labels:
    {{- include "springboothelm.labels" . | nindent 4 }}
spec:
  replicas: {{ .Values.replicaCount }}
  selector:
    matchLabels:
      {{- include "springboothelm.selectorLabels" . |
nindent 6 }}
...
```

This file is also quite verbose, but luckily you don't need to manage all its contents either. For the purposes here, you just need to update one line:

```
containerPort: 8080
```

You need to do this because you need to deploy the Spring Boot application on port 8080.

The `service.yaml` file is used to expose the Kubernetes springboothelm deployment as service. You don't need to make any changes to the `service.yaml` file.

Confirming Helm Chart Accuracy

You are almost ready with your first Helm chart for your Spring Boot application. It's smart to check the `service.yaml` and `deployment.yaml` files to confirm everything looks fine. For that, you should get out from the `springboothelm` directory (on the project root folder), and then execute the command in Listing 12-31.

Listing 12-31. Template Helm Chart

```
(base) binildass-MacBook-Pro:ch12-05 binil$ pwd
/Users/binil/binil/code/mac/mybooks/docker-04/Code/ch12/ch12-05
(base) binildass-MacBook-Pro:ch12-05 binil$ helm template
springboothelm
```

Running this command will return the service.yaml, deployment.
yaml, and test-connection.yaml files with actual values so that you can
verify whether all is right.

As an optional step, there is one more sanitary command provided
by Helm, called lint, which you can use to identify possible issues in
advance. See Listing 12-32.

Listing 12-32. Use lint on the Helm Chart

```
(base) binildass-MacBook-Pro:ch12-05 binil$ pwd
/Users/binil/binil/code/mac/mybooks/docker-04/Code/ch12/ch12-05

(base) binildass-MacBook-Pro:ch12-05 binil$ helm lint
springboothelm
==> Linting springboothelm
[INFO] Chart.yaml: icon is recommended

1 chart(s) linted, 0 chart(s) failed
```

You can also use the following -dry-run command to verify your
Spring Boot Helm chart. See Listing 12-33.

Listing 12-33. Dry Run of the Helm Chart

```
(base) binildass-MacBook-Pro:ch12-05 binil$ pwd
/Users/binil/binil/code/mac/mybooks/docker-04/Code/ch12/ch12-05
(base) binildass-MacBook-Pro:ch12-05 binil$ helm install
springboothelm --debug --dry-run springboothelm
...
```

If there is something wrong with your Helm chart configuration, this check will prompt you about it immediately.

Build and Run the Microservice

The ch12\ch12-05 folder contains the Maven scripts required to build and run the examples. First, you need to build the microservices and push the image to the public Docker Hub. You do this using the mvn clean compile jib:build command, as shown in Listing 12-34.

Listing 12-34. Building the Microservice and Pushing the Docker Image

```
(base) binildass-MacBook-Pro:ch12-05 binil$ pwd
/Users/binil/binil/code/mac/mybooks/docker-04/Code/ch12/ch12-05
(base) binildass-MacBook-Pro:ch12-05 binil$ sh make.sh
[INFO] Scanning for projects...
[INFO]
...
[INFO]
[INFO] Built and pushed image as binildas/spring-boot-
docker-k8s-helm
[INFO] Executing tasks:
[INFO] [===========================   ] 91.7% complete
[INFO] > launching layer pushers
[INFO]
[INFO] ------------------------------------------------
[INFO] BUILD SUCCESS
[INFO] ------------------------------------------------
[INFO] Total time:  13.205 s
[INFO] Finished at: 2023-05-20T16:06:58+05:30
[INFO] ------------------------------------------------
(base) binildass-MacBook-Pro:ch12-05 binil$
```

Once the image is pushed, you can install the application, as shown in Listing 12-35.

Listing 12-35. Helm Install the Microservice

```
(base) binildass-MacBook-Pro:ch12-05 binil$ pwd
/Users/binil/binil/code/mac/mybooks/docker-04/Code/ch12/ch12-05
(base) binildass-MacBook-Pro:ch12-05 binil$ helm install
myfirstspringboot springboothelm
NAME: myfirstspringboot
LAST DEPLOYED: Mon May 29 23:32:19 2023
NAMESPACE: default
STATUS: deployed
REVISION: 1
NOTES:
1. Get the application URL by running these commands:
     NOTE: It may take a few minutes for the LoadBalancer IP to
     be available.
            You can watch the status of by running 'kubectl
            get --namespace default svc -w myfirstspringboot-
            springboothelm'
  export SERVICE_IP=$(kubectl get svc --namespace default
  myfirstspringboot-springboothelm --template "{{ range (index
  .status.loadBalancer.ingress 0) }}{{.}}{{ end }}")
  echo http://$SERVICE_IP:8080
(base) binildass-MacBook-Pro:ch12-05 binil$
```

The installation command includes two names:

- myfirstspringboot: It's a release name for your Helm chart. If you don't provide one, Helm will generate its own release name.

- springboothelm: This is your actual chart name, which you created earlier.

You can now verify the installation, as shown in Listing 12-36.

Listing 12-36. Verify the Helm Installation

```
(base) binildass-MacBook-Pro:ch12-05 binil$ helm list -a
NAME                    NAMESPACE       REVISION
UPDATED                                 STATUS
CHART                   APP VERSION
myfirstspringboot       default         1
2023-05-29 23:32:19.571111 +0530 IST      deployed
springboothelm-0.1.0       latest
(base) binildass-MacBook-Pro:ch12-05 binil$
```

You can also verify this installation in the Kubernetes cluster, as shown in Listing 12-37.

Listing 12-37. Verify the Helm-Based Deployment in Kubernetes

```
(base) binildass-MacBook-Pro:~ binil$ kubectl get all
NAME                                                        READY
STATUS    RESTARTS    AGE
pod/myfirstspringboot-springboothelm-5575ff4d84-pvgzv       1/1
Running    0          88s

NAME                                             TYPE
CLUSTER-IP       EXTERNAL-IP      PORT(S)         AGE
service/kubernetes                               ClusterIP
10.96.0.1        <none>           443/TCP         12d
service/myfirstspringboot-springboothelm    LoadBalancer
10.103.65.93     <pending>        8080:31530/TCP  88s
```

```
NAME                                                    READY
UP-TO-DATE    AVAILABLE    AGE
deployment.apps/myfirstspringboot-springboothelm    1/1
1             1            88s

NAME
DESIRED    CURRENT    READY    AGE
replicaset.apps/myfirstspringboot-springboothelm-5575ff4d84
1          1          1        88s
(base) binildass-MacBook-Pro:~ binil$
```

Once it's all set, you are ready to test the example.

Testing the Microservice

To test the application, first find the URL for the deployed application, as shown in Listing 12-38.

Listing 12-38. Finding the URL for the Deployed Application

```
(base) binildass-MacBook-Pro:~ binil$ minikube service
myfirstspringboot-springboothelm
|-----------|---------------------------------|-------------|
---------------------------|
| NAMESPACE |               NAME              | TARGET PORT |
 URL                       |
|-----------|---------------------------------|-------------|
---------------------------|
| default   | myfirstspringboot-springboothelm | http/8080  |
 http://192.168.64.6:31530 |
|-----------|---------------------------------|-------------|
---------------------------|
🔾 Opening service default/myfirstspringboot-springboothelm in
default browser...
```

```
(base) binildass-MacBook-Pro:~ binil$ minikube service
myfirstspringboot-springboothelm --url
http://192.168.64.6:31530
(base) binildass-MacBook-Pro:~ binil$
```

You can now access the application, as shown in Listing 12-5.

Helm Release Upgrades

Helm upgrades help you create new releases of the application. To test that, you will make little changes to the application.

First, you need to update the version in Chart.yaml from 0.1.0 to 0.1.1

Next, update the replicaCount in values.yaml from 1 to 2.

You are now ready to upgrade the release, as shown in Listing 12-39.

Listing 12-39. Upgrading the Helm Release

```
(base) binildass-MacBook-Pro:ch12-05 binil$ pwd
/Users/binil/binil/code/mac/mybooks/docker-04/Code/ch12/ch12-05
(base) binildass-MacBook-Pro:ch12-05 binil$ helm upgrade
myfirstspringboot .
Error: Chart.yaml file is missing
(base) binildass-MacBook-Pro:ch12-05 binil$ pwd
/Users/binil/binil/code/mac/mybooks/docker-04/Code/ch12/ch12-05
(base) binildass-MacBook-Pro:ch12-05 binil$ helm upgrade
myfirstspringboot .
Error: Chart.yaml file is missing
(base) binildass-MacBook-Pro:ch12-05 binil$ helm upgrade
myfirstspringboot springboothelm
Release "myfirstspringboot" has been upgraded. Happy Helming!
NAME: myfirstspringboot
LAST DEPLOYED: Mon May 29 23:39:52 2023
```

```
NAMESPACE: default
STATUS: deployed
REVISION: 2
NOTES:
1. Get the application URL by running these commands:
     NOTE: It may take a few minutes for the LoadBalancer IP to
     be available.
           You can watch the status of by running 'kubectl
           get --namespace default svc -w myfirstspringboot-
           springboothelm'
     export SERVICE_IP=$(kubectl get svc --namespace default
     myfirstspringboot-springboothelm --template "{{ range (index
     .status.loadBalancer.ingress 0) }}{{.}}{{ end }}")
     echo http://$SERVICE_IP:8080
(base) binildass-MacBook-Pro:ch12-05 binil$
```

You can verify your installation again, as shown in Listing 12-40.

Listing 12-40. Verify the Helm Installation

```
(base) binildass-MacBook-Pro:ch12-05 binil$ helm list -a
NAME                    NAMESPACE      REVISION
UPDATED                                STATUS
CHART                   APP VERSION
myfirstspringboot       default        2
2023-05-29 23:39:52.906387 +0530 IST        deployed
springboothelm-0.1.1     latest
(base) binildass-MacBook-Pro:ch12-05 binil$
```

You can see that the REVISION count is now 2.

You can also verify the installation in the Kubernetes cluster, as shown in Listing 12-41.

Listing 12-41. Verify the Helm-Based Deployment in Kubernetes

```
(base) binildass-MacBook-Pro:~ binil$ kubectl get all
NAME                                                      READY
STATUS    RESTARTS    AGE
pod/myfirstspringboot-springboothelm-5575ff4d84-pvgzv    1/1
Running   0           8m2s
pod/myfirstspringboot-springboothelm-5575ff4d84-zqhq4    1/1
Running   0           29s

NAME                                    TYPE
CLUSTER-IP      EXTERNAL-IP    PORT(S)          AGE
service/kubernetes                      ClusterIP
10.96.0.1       <none>         443/TCP          12d
service/myfirstspringboot-springboothelm    LoadBalancer
10.103.65.93    <pending>      8080:31530/TCP   8m2s

NAME                                                     READY
UP-TO-DATE    AVAILABLE    AGE
deployment.apps/myfirstspringboot-springboothelm    2/2
2             2            8m2s

NAME
DESIRED    CURRENT    READY    AGE
replicaset.apps/myfirstspringboot-springboothelm-5575ff4d84
2          2          2        8m2s
(base) binildass-MacBook-Pro:~ binil$
```

You can see you have successfully upgraded the replica count from 1 to 2 for the myfirstspringboot-springboothelm service.

Helm Release Rollback

You might wonder if you can roll back the changes you made from upgrading from Release 1 to 2? See Listing 12-42 to do just that.

Listing 12-42. Roll Back the Helm Upgrade

```
(base) binildass-MacBook-Pro:ch12-05 binil$ helm rollback
myfirstspringboot 1
Rollback was a success! Happy Helming!
(base) binildass-MacBook-Pro:ch12-05 binil$
```

You can then verify that the rollback was successful by using the code in Listing 12-43.

Listing 12-43. Verify the Helm Installation

```
(base) binildass-MacBook-Pro:ch12-05 binil$ helm list -a
NAME                    NAMESPACE       REVISION
UPDATED                                 STATUS
CHART                   APP VERSION
myfirstspringboot       default         3
2023-05-29 23:42:25.252089 +0530 IST        deployed
springboothelm-0.1.0        latest
(base) binildass-MacBook-Pro:ch12-05 binil$
```

As you can see, you have successfully rolled back the release to the previous version. One interesting thing about Helm is that it still updates the REVISION to the next sequence, 3. See Listing 12-44.

Listing 12-44. Verify the Helm-Based Deployment in Kubernetes

```
(base) binildass-MacBook-Pro:~ binil$ kubectl get all
NAME                                                      READY
STATUS    RESTARTS    AGE
pod/myfirstspringboot-springboothelm-5575ff4d84-pvgzv    1/1
Running    0          10m

NAME                                        TYPE
CLUSTER-IP     EXTERNAL-IP    PORT(S)        AGE
service/kubernetes                          ClusterIP
10.96.0.1      <none>         443/TCP        12d
service/myfirstspringboot-springboothelm    LoadBalancer
10.103.65.93   <pending>      8080:31530/TCP  10m

NAME                                                    READY
UP-TO-DATE    AVAILABLE    AGE
deployment.apps/myfirstspringboot-springboothelm       1/1
1             1            10m

NAME
DESIRED    CURRENT    READY    AGE
replicaset.apps/myfirstspringboot-springboothelm-5575ff4d84
1          1          1        10m
(base) binildass-MacBook-Pro:~ binil$
```

As a last step, you can also delete the release, as shown in Listing 12-45.

Listing 12-45. Deleting a Helm Release

```
(base) binildass-MacBook-Pro:ch12-05 binil$ helm delete
myfirstspringboot
release "myfirstspringboot" uninstalled
(base) binildass-MacBook-Pro:ch12-05 binil$
```

You can then verify that it was deleted, as shown in Listings 12-46 and 12-47.

Listing 12-46. Verify the Helm Installation

```
(base) binildass-MacBook-Pro:ch12-05 binil$ helm list -a
NAME       NAMESPACE       REVISION       UPDATED       STATUS
CHART       APP VERSION
(base) binildass-MacBook-Pro:ch12-05 binil$
```

Listing 12-47. Verify the Helm-Based Deployment in Kubernetes

```
(base) binildass-MacBook-Pro:~ binil$ kubectl get all
NAME                 TYPE        CLUSTER-IP     EXTERNAL-IP   PORT(S)   AGE
service/kubernetes   ClusterIP   10.96.0.1      <none>        443/TCP   12d
(base) binildass-MacBook-Pro:~ binil$
```

I hope you enjoyed your first Helming exercise. In the next section, you will Helm-release the multi-microservice example.

Helm-Packaging Multi-Microservices

You learned how Helm can enable the packaging and deployment of microservices in Kubernetes in the previous sections. However, that example is not complex enough to enable you to appreciate the true benefits of Helm. This section shows you how to use Helm to package and deploy your multi-microservices projects.

Designing Helm-Based Deployment Topology

This example follows the deployment topology from Figure 11-3 in Chapter 11. The Product Web and Product Server microservices are containerized, and the Product Server microservice will connect to a PostgreSQL database, again deployed within a container. All these containers will now be inside Kubernetes. Ingress is an additional component for routing and an Adminer UI component manages the PostgreSQL DB. See Figure 12-3.

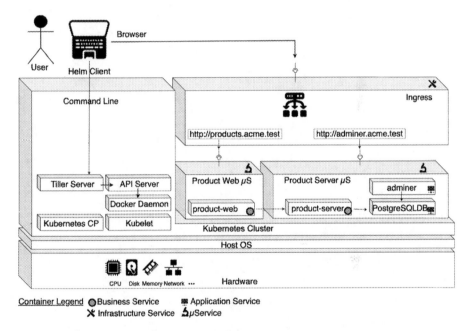

Figure 12-3. *Deployment topology for microservices*

The next sections look at the code for this deployment.

Code Organization

The source code for this book is available on GitHub via the book's product page, located at www.apress.com/9798868805547. The source code for this example is organized inside the ch12\ch12-06 folder.

615

Before you get into the source code for this example, take another look at the source code organization of the similar example (ch11\ch11-03) from Listing 11-32 in Chapter 11. It's shown again in Listing 12-48.

Listing 12-48. Example 11-03 Source Code Organization

```
./ch11-03/
├── 01-ProductServer
│   ├── make.sh
│   ├── pom.xml
│   └── src
│       └── main
├── 02-ProductWeb
│   ├── make.sh
│   ├── pom.xml
│   └── src
│       └── main
├── Dockerfile
├── README.txt
├── adminer-deployment.yaml
├── adminer-svc.yaml
├── clean.sh
├── ingress-controller.yaml
├── makeandrun.sh
├── pom.xml
├── postgres-config.yml
├── postgres-deployment.yml
├── postgres-pvc.yml
├── postgres-svc.yml
├── product-server-deployment.yml
├── product-server-service.yml
├── product-web-deployment.yml
└── product-web-service.yml
```

For two business services, you can see how many YAML files are required. A little consolidation can be done, say by merging the deployment and service definitions of Product Server microservice into a single YAML file, and so on. But it still doesn't fix another problem, the problem of duplication. How do you avoid copy-pasting major file content just to replace a couple of values? It would be nice if there was a way to define a template for both business objects (the Product Server and Product Web microservices) and then inject values into specific fields. Helm can help you in this regard.

The source code for this example is organized as shown in Listing 12-49, inside the ch12\ch12-06 folder. This is the same example you saw in Chapter 11. You will now use Helm for deployment.

Listing 12-49. Example 12-06 Source Code Organization

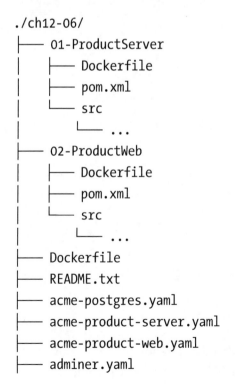

```
./ch12-06/
├── 01-ProductServer
│   ├── Dockerfile
│   ├── pom.xml
│   └── src
│       └── ...
├── 02-ProductWeb
│   ├── Dockerfile
│   ├── pom.xml
│   └── src
│       └── ...
├── Dockerfile
├── README.txt
├── acme-postgres.yaml
├── acme-product-server.yaml
├── acme-product-web.yaml
├── adminer.yaml
```

```
├── app
│   ├── Chart.yaml
│   ├── charts
│   ├── templates
│   │   ├── deployment.yaml
│   │   └── service.yaml
│   └── values.yaml
├── clean.sh
├── ingress
│   ├── Chart.lock
│   ├── Chart.yaml
│   ├── charts
│   │   └── nginx-ingress-1.36.0.tgz
│   ├── templates
│   │   └── ingress.yaml
│   └── values.yaml
├── ingress.yaml
├── make.sh
├── pom.xml
├── postgres
│   ├── Chart.yaml
│   ├── charts
│   ├── templates
│   │   ├── config.yaml
│   │   ├── deployment.yaml
│   │   ├── pcv.yaml
│   │   └── service.yaml
│   └── values.yaml
└── run.sh
```

You can see that the number of YAML configuration files at the top level of the project root folder has been reduced. There are more subfolders and many new files inside them, but I promise, it's not going to be too bad.

Understanding the Source Code

This section assumes that you have enabled Ingress in Minikube and added the required hostnames to your host files, as mentioned in the third example in Chapter 11.

This example starts by creating the Helm charts one by one. In the process, you also see how charts common for more than one component can be useful. I assume that you have a project root folder called ch12/ch12-06, which currently has only the README.txt file in it. Rather, copy the chapter code from the book's source code download and delete any files and folders not mentioned explicitly right now. Of course, after creating the charts, copy any other files required from the book's code to your project root.

Helm Chart for PostgreSQL

You'll start by creating the first chart, the chart for PostgreSQL database. See Listing 12-50.

Listing 12-50. Creating a PostgreSQL Helm Chart

```
(base) binildass-MacBook-Pro:ch12-06 binil$ pwd
/Users/binil/binil/code/mac/mybooks/docker-04/ch12/ch12-06
(base) binildass-MacBook-Pro:ch12-06 binil$ ls
README.txt
(base) binildass-MacBook-Pro:ch12-06 binil$ helm create postgres
Creating postgres
(base) binildass-MacBook-Pro:ch12-06 binil$ ls
README.txt      postgres
(base) binildass-MacBook-Pro:ch12-06 binil$ rm -r ./postgres/
templates/*
(base) binildass-MacBook-Pro:ch12-06 binil$ touch ./postgres/
templates/deployment.yaml
```

```
(base) binildass-MacBook-Pro:ch12-06 binil$ touch ./postgres/
templates/pcv.yaml
(base) binildass-MacBook-Pro:ch12-06 binil$ touch ./postgres/
templates/service.yaml
(base) binildass-MacBook-Pro:ch12-06 binil$ touch ./postgres/
templates/config.yaml
(base) binildass-MacBook-Pro:ch12-06 binil$
```

You delete all of those files generated in the ./postgres/template folder. Then you create four new files inside the ./postgres/template folder—deployment.yaml, pcv.yaml, service.yaml, and config.yaml. You will fill these new files with the files from the book's code.

Copy the contents from the respective files in BookCode/ch12/ch12-06/postgres/templates/* to the four files.

Listing 12-51 investigates selected portions of these files.

Listing 12-51. The Postgres Deployment YAML File (ch12/ch12-06/postgres/templates/deployment.yaml)

```yaml
apiVersion: apps/v1
kind: Deployment
metadata:
  name: {{ .Values.postgres.name }}
  labels:
    app: {{ .Values.postgres.name }}
    group: {{ .Values.postgres.group }}
spec:
  replicas: {{ .Values.replicaCount }}
  selector:
    matchLabels:
      app: {{ .Values.postgres.name }}
...
```

The Go template-based placeholders are referring to values located in the values.yaml file. The values.yaml files should be in the root folder of the chart. To make it clear with an example, the placeholder {{ .Values. postgres.name }} in deployment.yaml will be filled with the value in Listing 12-52.

Listing 12-52. The Postgres Values YAML File (ch12/ch12-06/ postgre/values.yaml)

```
postgres:
  name: postgres
```

Now Copy contents from BookCode/ch12/ch12-06/postgres/values. yaml to the file in your project folder ./postgres/values.yaml Listing 12-51. The postgres values YAML file (ch12/ch12-06/ postgres/values.yaml)

```
replicaCount: 1

postgres:
  name: postgres
  group: db
  container:
    image: postgres:9.6-alpine
    port: 5432
  service:
    type: ClusterIP
    port: 5432
  volume:
    name: postgres-storage
    kind: PersistentVolumeClaim
    mountPath: /var/lib/postgresql/data
    pvc:
      name: postgres-persistent-volume-claim
```

```
      accessMode: ReadWriteOnce
      storage: 4Gi
  config:
    name: postgres-config
    data:
      - key: key
        value: value
```

Let's now investigate one more file in detail, and the rest of the files will follow the same pattern. The next file to investigate is the template that you need to create for `ClusterIP`, which is required to allow other pods inside the cluster to access the pod with `postgres`. This is the `./postgres/template/service.yaml` file, as shown in Listing 12-53.

Listing 12-53. The Postgres Service YAML File (ch12/ch12-06/postgres/service.yaml)

```
apiVersion: v1
kind: Service
metadata:
  name: {{ .Values.postgres.name }}
  labels:
    group: {{ .Values.postgres.group }}
spec:
  type: {{ .Values.postgres.service.type }}
  selector:
    app: {{ .Values.postgres.name }}
  ports:
    - port: {{ .Values.postgres.service.port }}
      targetPort: {{ .Values.postgres.container.port }}
```

Here again, if you take `{{ .Values.postgres.service.port }}` for example, its value will come from the leaf of the `./postgres/values.yaml` file:

```
postgres:
  service:
    port: 5432
```

The same explanation applies to the `./postgres/pvc.yaml` and `./postgres/config.yaml` files.

You can update the metadata in the `./Chart.yaml` file, which was described in the previous example in this chapter. If you are in doubt, just copy the contents from `BookCode/ch12/ch12-06/Chart.yaml` to the file in your project folder: `./Chart.yaml`

As a final step for the `postgres` chart, you need to create another file that will hold some Postgres-specific values. Add the file outside the `postgres` chart folder.

```
(base) binildass-MacBook-Pro:ch12-06 binil$ touch ./acme-
postgres.yaml
```

Update this file with the `acme  postgres` specific values.

Then copy the contents from `BookCode/ch12/ch12-06/acme-postgres.yaml` to `./acme-postgres.yaml`

To make sure you have done everything right, you may want to execute the sanity-check commands shown in Listing 12-54.

Listing 12-54. Sanity Checking the Helmfiles

```
/Users/binil/binil/code/mac/mybooks/docker-04/ch12/ch12-06
(base) binildass-MacBook-Pro:ch12-06 binil$ helm template
postgres
(base) binildass-MacBook-Pro:ch12-06 binil$ helm lint postgres
(base) binildass-MacBook-Pro:ch12-06 binil$ helm install
postgres --debug --dry-run postgres
```

Common Chart for Microservices and Adminer

This section demonstrates another advantage of Helm—using common charts, called template charts—which can be used for more than one release. In this case, you will use it as a common template for the Product Web and Product Server microservices and the Adminer app. You need to create a new Helm chart called app and repeat the steps for creating the postgres Helm chart, as shown in Listing 12-55.

Listing 12-55. Creating the Chart for the App

```
(base) binildass-MBP:ch12-06 binil$ pwd
/Users/binil/binil/code/mac/mybooks/docker-04/ch12/ch12-06
(base) binildass-MBP:ch12-06 binil$ ls
01-ProductServer README.txt          make.sh
02-ProductWeb          acme-postgres.yaml      postgres
(base) binildass-MBP:ch12-06 binil$ eval $(minikube docker-env)
(base) binildass-MBP:ch12-06 binil$ helm create app
Creating app
(base) binildass-MBP:ch12-06 binil$ rm -r ./app/templates/*
(base) binildass-MBP:ch12-06 binil$ touch ./app/templates/
deployment.yaml
(base) binildass-MBP:ch12-06 binil$ touch ./app/templates/
service.yaml
```

To create templates for the Postgre Kubernetes objects:

Copy the contents from BookCode/ch12/ch12-06/app/templates/* to the applicable files.

Create dummy values for the Postgre Kubernetes objects:

Copy the contents from BookCode/ch12/ch12-06/app/values.yaml to ./app/values.yaml.

Update the metadata in ./app/Charts.yaml.

```
(base) binildass-MBP:ch12-06 binil$ touch ./adminer.yaml
(base) binildass-MBP:ch12-06 binil$ touch ./acme-product-
server.yaml
(base) binildass-MBP:ch12-06 binil$ touch ./acme-
product-web.yaml
```

Update these files with acme-specific values.

Copy the contents from the corresponding files BookCode/ch12/ch12-06/acme-*.yaml to ./acme-*.yaml.

Copy the contents from the corresponding files BookCode/ch12/ch12-06/adminer.yaml to ./adminer.yaml.

Helm Chart for Ingress

The last chart you create is for the Ingress controller. For this, you will create a new Helm chart called ingress and repeat the steps for creating the postgres Helm chart, as shown in Listing 12-56.

Listing 12-56. Creating a Chart for Ingress

```
(base) binildass-MBP:ch12-06 binil$ helm create ingress
Creating ingress
(base) binildass-MBP:ch12-06 binil$ rm -r ./ingress/templates/*
(base) binildass-MBP:ch12-06 binil$
```

Create Chart.yaml for Ingress Kubernetes objects:

Copy the contents from BookCode/ch12/ch12-06/ingress/Chart.yaml to ./ingress/Chart.yaml.

```
(base) binildass-MBP:ch12-06 binil$ helm dependency update
./ingress/
Saving 1 charts
Downloading nginx-ingress from repo https://charts.helm.sh/
stable
```

Deleting outdated charts
(base) binildass-MBP:ch12-06 binil$

(base) binildass-MBP:ch12-06 binil$ touch ./ingress/templates/
ingress.yaml

Copy the contents from BookCode/ch12/ch12-06/ingress/templates/
ingress.yaml to ./ingress/templates/ingress.yaml.

Copy the contents from BookCode/ch12/ch12-06/ingress/values.
yaml to ./ingress/values.yaml.

(base) binildass-MBP:ch12-06 binil$ touch ./ingress.yaml

Copy the contents from BookCode/ch12/ch12-06/ingress.yaml to ./
ingress.yaml.

Little mention needs to be done to the ./ingress/Chart.yaml file. See
Listing 12-57.

Listing 12-57.   Chart YAML for Ingress (ch12/ch12-06/ingress/
Chart.yaml)

```
apiVersion: v2
name: ingress
description: A Helm chart for Kubernetes
type: application
version: 1.1.0
appVersion: 1.17.0
keywords:
  - ingress
  - nginx
  - api-gateway
home: https://github.com/no-account/k8s-helm-helmfile/tree/
master/helm
maintainers:
```

```
  - name: Binildas
    url: https://github.com/no-account
dependencies:
  - name: nginx-ingress
    version: 1.36.0
    repository: https://charts.helm.sh/stable
```

The - dependencies: section is newly added compared to other charts. It creates a default backend service that enables the Ingress controller's features.

This declaration only defines what this chart depends on; it won't download it automatically during the installation. That is why you have you to install this dependency explicitly, by running the helm dependency update ./ingress/ command. When you run this command, a new file called nginx-ingress-1.36.0.tgz will appear inside the ./ingress/ charts folder.

Build and Run the Microservice

The ch12\ch12-06 folder contains the Maven scripts required to build and run these examples. First, you will build the microservices and release the application to Kubernetes. A single script called run.sh declares all the commands, as shown in Listing 12-58.

Listing 12-58. Script for Helm Release (ch12/ch12-06/run.sh)

```
mvn -Dmaven.test.skip=true clean package
eval $(minikube docker-env)
docker build  --build-arg JAR_FILE=02-ProductWeb/target/
*.jar -t ecom/product-web .
docker build  --build-arg JAR_FILE=01-ProductServer/target/
*.jar -t ecom/product-server .
helm install -f acme-postgres.yaml postgres ./postgres
```

```
helm install -f adminer.yaml adminer ./app
helm install -f acme-product-server.yaml product-server ./app
helm install -f acme-product-web.yaml product-web ./app
helm install -f ingress.yaml ingress ./ingress
minikube service product-web --url
sleep 3
helm list
kubectl get deployments
```

You can now execute this script, as shown in Listing 12-59.

Listing 12-59. Building and Running the Microservice

```
(base) binildass-MacBook-Pro:ch12-06 binil$ pwd
/Users/binil/binil/code/mac/mybooks/docker-04/Code/ch12/ch12-06
(base) binildass-MacBook-Pro:ch12-06 binil$ eval $(minikube
docker-env)
(base) binildass-MacBook-Pro:ch12-06 binil$ sh run.sh
[INFO] Scanning for projects...
[INFO]
...
Successfully tagged ecom/product-web:latest
Successfully tagged ecom/product-server:latest
NAME: postgres
LAST DEPLOYED: Mon May 22 23:32:05 2023
NAMESPACE: default
STATUS: deployed
REVISION: 1
TEST SUITE: None
NAME: adminer
LAST DEPLOYED: Mon May 22 23:32:06 2023
NAMESPACE: default
STATUS: deployed
```

```
REVISION: 1
TEST SUITE: None
NAME: product-server
LAST DEPLOYED: Mon May 22 23:32:06 2023
NAMESPACE: default
STATUS: deployed
REVISION: 1
TEST SUITE: None
NAME: product-web
LAST DEPLOYED: Mon May 22 23:32:06 2023
NAMESPACE: default
STATUS: deployed
REVISION: 1
TEST SUITE: None
NAME: ingress
LAST DEPLOYED: Mon May 22 23:32:06 2023
NAMESPACE: default
STATUS: deployed
REVISION: 1
TEST SUITE: None
http://192.168.64.6:32216
...
(base) binildass-MacBook-Pro:ch12-06 binil$
```

That's all; you are ready to test.

Testing the Microservice

You can access the Product Web microservice using the hostname you configured.

```
http://products.acme.test/product.html
```

Note the URL address in Figure 12-3. Refer to the section titled "Test the Microservice Using UI" in Chapter 1 to test the Product Web microservice container.

While you test the microservices, keep watching the log windows of the pods, as mentioned in Listings 11-10 through 11-15 in Chapter 11.

If you recollect, you also configured the Adminer UI. You will now attempt to access the PostgreSQL database through the Adminer UI. Use the second URL for that:

```
http://adminer.acme.test
```

Refer to the third example in Chapter 11 to get more details about testing.

Once you complete the testing process, you can stop and remove the microservice containers and clean the environment. For that, you have a single script, as shown in Listing 12-60.

Listing 12-60. Script for Cleaning the Project and the Environment (ch12/ch12-06/clean.sh)

```
eval $(minikube docker-env)
helm delete adminer
helm delete product-web
helm delete product-server
helm delete postgres
helm delete ingress-backend
helm delete ingress-controller
mvn -Dmaven.test.skip=true clean
docker rmi -f ecom/product-web
docker rmi -f ecom/product-server
```

You can now execute this script to clean the environment, as shown in Listing 12-61.

Listing 12-61. Cleaning the Project and the Environment

```
(base) binildass-MacBook-Pro:ch12-06 binil$ pwd
/Users/binil/binil/code/mac/mybooks/docker-04/Code/ch12/ch12-06
(base) binildass-MacBook-Pro:ch12-06 binil$ sh clean.sh
...
```

This completes the multi-microservices packaging example with Helm.

Helmfile Packaging Multi-Microservices

In the last example, you used Helm to package and deploy the multi-microservices project. There you defined a generic Helm chart (template) and reused it across multiple microservices only by injecting specific values into the template. In that example, even though you used a single script called run.sh, to install or update a chart in a cluster, you need to run a specific imperative command. In other words, to change the state of a cluster, you need to run a command that is specific for a given deployment. Helm doesn't have the feature to install, update, or roll back all applications from an entire cluster with a single command.

Helmfile will help you here, because it allows you to declare a definition of an entire Kubernetes cluster in a single YAML file and bundle multiple Helm releases (installation of Helm charts). It releases them depending on the type of environment (develop, test, production) on which you want to deploy your applications.

Let's deploy the example you released using Helm in the previous section, but this time using Helmfile.

Code Organization

The source code for this book is available on GitHub via the book's product page, located at www.apress.com/9798868805547. The source code for this example is organized as shown in Listing 12-62, inside the ch12\ ch12-07 folder.

Listing 12-62. Source Code Organization for Multi-Microservice Helmfile Deployment

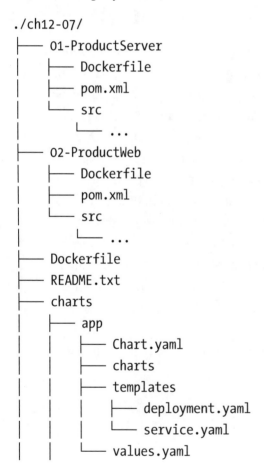

```
./ch12-07/
├── 01-ProductServer
│   ├── Dockerfile
│   ├── pom.xml
│   └── src
│       └── ...
├── 02-ProductWeb
│   ├── Dockerfile
│   ├── pom.xml
│   └── src
│       └── ...
├── Dockerfile
├── README.txt
├── charts
│   ├── app
│   │   ├── Chart.yaml
│   │   ├── charts
│   │   ├── templates
│   │   │   ├── deployment.yaml
│   │   │   └── service.yaml
│   │   └── values.yaml
```

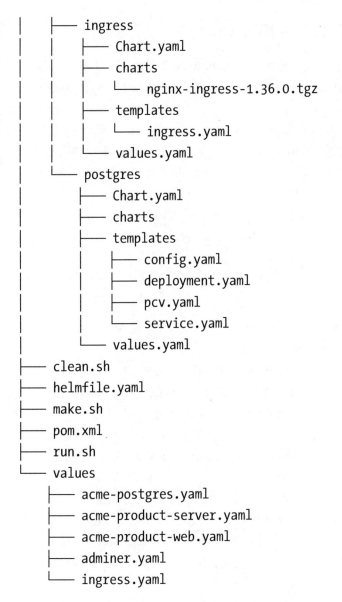

```
|       ├── ingress
|       |   ├── Chart.yaml
|       |   ├── charts
|       |   |   └── nginx-ingress-1.36.0.tgz
|       |   ├── templates
|       |   |   └── ingress.yaml
|       |   └── values.yaml
|       └── postgres
|           ├── Chart.yaml
|           ├── charts
|           ├── templates
|           |   ├── config.yaml
|           |   ├── deployment.yaml
|           |   ├── pcv.yaml
|           |   └── service.yaml
|           └── values.yaml
├── clean.sh
├── helmfile.yaml
├── make.sh
├── pom.xml
├── run.sh
└── values
    ├── acme-postgres.yaml
    ├── acme-product-server.yaml
    ├── acme-product-web.yaml
    ├── adminer.yaml
    └── ingress.yaml
```

The next section looks at the main aspects of the source code.

Understanding the Source Code

As a prerequisite, I assume that you have enabled Ingress in Minikube and added the required hostnames to your host files, as mentioned in the third example in Chapter 11.

This example assumes that you have a project root folder called ch12/ch12-07 which is empty. First, bring all the files from ch12/ch12-06 to ch12/ch12-07. Then, create two new folders called charts and values in the project root folder: ch12/ch12-07. Move ./app, ./ingress, and ./postgres to ./charts and move ./*.yaml to ./values. Then add a new helmfile.yaml file to the root directory. See Listing 12-63.

Listing 12-63. Reorganizing the Multi-Microservice Project for Helmfile

```
(base) binildass-MacBook-Pro:.Trash binil$ cd /Users/binil/
binil/code/mac/mybooks/docker-04/ch12/
(base) binildass-MacBook-Pro:ch12 binil$ pwd
/Users/binil/binil/code/mac/mybooks/docker-04/ch12
(base) binildass-MacBook-Pro:ch12 binil$ mkdir ch12-07
(base) binildass-MacBook-Pro:ch12 binil$ cp -r BookCode/ch12/
ch12-06/* /Users/binil/binil/code/mac/mybooks/docker-04/ch12/
ch12-07/
(base) binildass-MacBook-Pro:ch12-07 binil$ mkdir charts
(base) binildass-MacBook-Pro:ch12-07 binil$ mv ./charts/ ./app
(base) binildass-MacBook-Pro:ch12-07 binil$ mv ./app ./charts/
(base) binildass-MacBook-Pro:ch12-07 binil$ mv ./ingress
./charts/
(base) binildass-MacBook-Pro:ch12-07 binil$ mv ./postgres
./charts/
(base) binildass-MacBook-Pro:ch12-07 binil$ mkdir values
(base) binildass-MacBook-Pro:ch12-07 binil$ mv ./acme*.yaml
./values/
```

```
(base) binildass-MacBook-Pro:ch12-07 binil$ mv ./adminer.yaml
./values/
(base) binildass-MacBook-Pro:ch12-07 binil$ mv ./ingress.yaml
./values/
(base) binildass-MacBook-Pro:ch12-07 binil$ touch helmfile.yaml
```

I explain the major components in Listing 12-63 here.

- `helmfile.yaml`: This is a configuration for a Helmfile, currently blank.

- `./charts`: Three Helms charts that are templates for each release—app (for `adminer`, `product-web` and `product-server`), `postgres` and `ingress`.

- `./values`: The folder containing values that are specific for each application that will be released.

In the last example, in `ch12/ch12-06/ingress/Chart.yaml`, nginx-ingress version `1.36.0` is fetched from the repository. Further, you explicitly run the installation command. In this current example, you will remove this part from `ch12/ch12-07/charts/ingress/Chart.yaml` and instead mention in `./helmfile.yaml` to treat the `nginx-ingress` chart as a separate Helm release, apart from the Ingress controller configuration for routing.

You can delete the `./charts/ingress/Chart.lock` file.

Listing 12-64 shows the `./helmfile.yaml` file.

Listing 12-64. Helmfile (ch12/ch12-07/helmfile.yaml)

```
repositories:
  - name: stable
    url: https://charts.helm.sh/stable

releases:
  - name: postgres
```

```
    chart: ./charts/postgres
    values:
      - ./values/acme-postgres.yaml

  - name: adminer
    chart: ./charts/app
    values:
      - ./values/adminer.yaml

  - name: product-server
    chart: ./charts/app
    values:
      - ./values/acme-product-server.yaml

  - name: product-web
    chart: ./charts/app
    values:
      - ./values/acme-product-web.yaml

  - name: ingress-backend
    chart: stable/nginx-ingress
    version: 1.36.0

  - name: ingress-controller
    chart: ./charts/ingress
    values:
      - ./values/ingress.yaml
```

What you have done here is split the Ingress controller from the Ingress backend. The ./charts/ingress/Chart.yaml Helm chart defines only the Ingress controller; the Ingress backend has been moved to ./helmfile. yaml. In ./helmfile.yaml, you determine from which Helm repositories you would like to download charts and then mention all the releases.

Build and Run the Microservice

The ch12\ch12-07 folder contains the Maven scripts required to build and run these examples.

As a first step, you need to add the repository to your instance of Helm, which you do only once (you don't need to do this, since this is included in the single script).

```
helmfile repos
```

Next, you can install all the charts with a single command:

```
helmfile sync
```

Now perform the build and release. A single script called run.sh declares all the commands, as shown in Listing 12-65.

Listing 12-65. Script for Helm Release (ch12/ch12-07/run.sh)

```
mvn -Dmaven.test.skip=true clean package
eval $(minikube docker-env)
docker build  --build-arg JAR_FILE=02-ProductWeb/target/
*.jar -t ecom/product-web .
docker build  --build-arg JAR_FILE=01-ProductServer/target/
*.jar -t ecom/product-server .
helmfile repos
helmfile sync
minikube service product-web --url
sleep 3
helm list
kubectl get deployments
```

You can now execute this script, as shown in Listing 12-66.

Listing 12-66. Releasing the Microservice Containers

```
(base) binildass-MacBook-Pro:ch12-07 binil$ pwd
/Users/binil/binil/code/mac/mybooks/docker-04/Code/ch12/ch12-07
(base) binildass-MacBook-Pro:ch12-07 binil$ eval $(minikube
docker-env)
(base) binildass-MacBook-Pro:ch12-07 binil$ sh run.sh
[INFO] Scanning for projects...
...
[INFO]
[INFO] Ecom-Product-Server-Microservice  SUCCESS [  3.604 s]
[INFO] Ecom-Product-Web-Microservice ... SUCCESS [  0.655 s]
[INFO] Ecom .......................... SUCCESS [  0.037 s]
[INFO] ------------------------------------------------------------
[INFO] BUILD SUCCESS
[INFO] ------------------------------------------------------------
[INFO] Total time:  4.502 s
[INFO] Finished at: 2023-05-23T11:35:18+05:30
[INFO] ------------------------------------------------------------
...
Successfully tagged ecom/product-web:latest
Successfully tagged ecom/product-server:latest
Adding repo stable https://charts.helm.sh/stable
"stable" has been added to your repositories

Adding repo stable https://charts.helm.sh/stable
"stable" has been added to your repositories

Building dependency release=postgres, chart=charts/postgres
Building dependency release=adminer, chart=charts/app
Building dependency release=product-web, chart=charts/app
```

```
Building dependency release=ingress-controller,
chart=charts/ingress
Building dependency release=product-server, chart=charts/app
Upgrading release=product-server, chart=charts/app
Upgrading release=product-web, chart=charts/app
Upgrading release=ingress-controller, chart=charts/ingress
Upgrading release=adminer, chart=charts/app
Upgrading release=ingress-backend, chart=stable/nginx-ingress
Upgrading release=postgres, chart=charts/postgres
Release "product-web" does not exist. Installing it now.
NAME: product-web
LAST DEPLOYED: Tue May 23 11:35:27 2023
NAMESPACE: default
STATUS: deployed
REVISION: 1
TEST SUITE: None

...

(base) binildass-MacBook-Pro:ch12-07 binil$
```

You can also view the newly released services, as shown in
Listing 12-67.

Listing 12-67. Viewing the Releases of the Microservices

```
(base) binildass-MacBook-Pro:ch12-07 binil$ pwd
/Users/binil/binil/code/mac/mybooks/docker-04/Code/ch12/ch12-07
(base) binildass-MacBook-Pro:ch12-07 binil$ eval $(minikube
docker-env)
(base) binildass-MacBook-Pro:ch12-07 binil$ helm list
```

```
UPDATED RELEASES:
NAME                    CHART                  VERSION    DURATION
product-web             ./charts/app           0.1.0            1s
adminer                 ./charts/app           0.1.0            1s
product-server          ./charts/app           0.1.0            1s
postgres                ./charts/postgres      0.1.0            1s
ingress-controller      ./charts/ingress       1.1.0            1s
ingress-backend         stable/nginx-ingress   1.36.0           2s
(base) binildass-MacBook-Pro:ch12-07 binil$ pwd
```

Once the application is running, you can test it.

Testing the Microservice

Next you can access the Product Web microservice using the hostname you configured.

```
http://products.acme.test/product.html
```

Note the URL address in Figure 12-3. Refer to the section titled "Test the Microservice Using UI" in Chapter 1 to test the Product Web microservice container.

While you test the microservices, keep watching the log windows of the pods, as mentioned in Listings 11-10 through 11-15 in Chapter 11.

If you recollect, you also configured the Adminer UI. You will now attempt to access the PostgreSQL database through the Adminer UI. Use the second URL for that:

```
http://adminer.acme.test
```

Refer to the third example in Chapter 11 to get more details about testing.

Once you complete the testing process, you can stop and remove the microservice containers and clean the environment, using the clean.sh script provided, which is like the script in Listing 12-60. See Listing 12-68.

Listing 12-68. Cleaning the Project and the Environment

```
(base) binildass-MacBook-Pro:ch12-02 binil$ pwd
/Users/binil/binil/code/mac/mybooks/docker-04/Code/ch12/ch12-07
(base) binildass-MacBook-Pro:ch12-07 binil$ sh clean.sh
...
```

This completes the multi-microservice example with Helmfile.

Summary

Helm simplifies the process of application development in Kubernetes by automating the distribution of your applications using a packaging format called a *Helm chart*. Helmfile allows you to declare a definition of an entire Kubernetes cluster in a single YAML file and bundles multiple Helm releases. These are handy tools to use while installing, managing, and updating hundreds of configurations, which is a normal process in a microservices environment. You saw examples with just enough complexity that you can appreciate their benefits. So far so good. Now isn't it time to also investigate CI (Continuous Integration) and CD (Continuous Deployment) in the context of containers and microservices? That's what you'll do in the next chapter.

CHAPTER 13

CI/CD for Microservice Containers

When the number of microservices and the number of deployment environments increase, you have to deal with many YAML files. In the last chapter, you learned that Helm is a handy tool that maintains a single deployment YAML file with version information. This file lets you set up and manage very large Kubernetes clusters with a few commands.

Another problem with a large number of microservices is that you can have as many teams building code as you have microservices, if you need true parallelism to improve release speed. An app is an aggregate of many microservices, and code changes must be regularly built, tested, and merged to a shared repository. You may have a single repository or multiple repositories for an app, such as a separate repository for each microservice. When there are many branches in a single repository, this can lead to merge conflicts in the build cycles. If there are multiple repositories, there could be conflicts during the integration process. Regardless of the repository strategy, there must be a process to minimize such conflicts and enable a continuous, frictionless release. CI (Continuous Integration) and CD (Continuous Deployment) are intended to minimize these issues.

© Binildas A. Christudas 2024
B. A. Christudas, *Java Microservices and Containers in the Cloud,*
https://doi.org/10.1007/979-8-8688-0555-4_13

This chapter covers the following concepts:

- Introduction to CI and CD

- Example demonstrating a simple CI/CD pipeline

CI and CD

The motivations for modern day software release automation and several standard DevOps practices—such as automated build and test, Continuous Integration (CI), and Continuous Delivery (CD)—originated in the Agile world of software engineering.

DevOps

DevOps is a methodology from the software development industry. Used as a set of practices and tools, DevOps is intended to integrate and automate the work of software development (Dev) and IT operations (Ops) as a means for improving and shortening the software development lifecycle. Microservices-based architecture is intended to increase delivery speed, and to enable releases of parts of an app independent of other parts. Microservices are smaller in size, which allows the architecture of an individual service to emerge through continuous refactoring. Shared repositories and artefacts, which are version controlled, are the essence of DevOps practices, and the roles of Dev and Ops personnel are converging into a single pipeline of stages. Each stage identifies the discrete steps of the Dev and Ops processes with a blurred boundary between the Dev and Ops. If you look at the typical stages in a release process, these concepts will become clearer. See Figure 13-1.

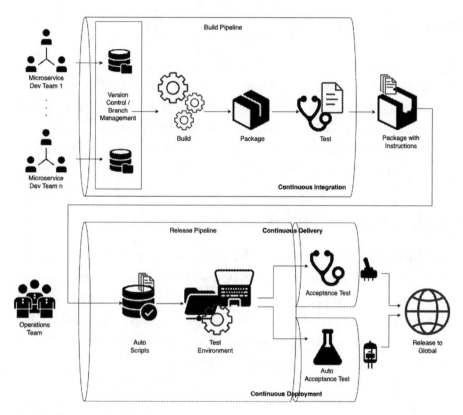

Figure 13-1. *CI and CD*

CI/CD stands for Continuous Integration and Continuous Delivery (or Continuous Deployment). This chapter investigates each component.

Continuous Integration (CI)

Continuous Integration defines how developers integrate code using a shared repository, multiple times a day with the help of automation. New code changes are regularly built, tested, and merged to a shared repository.

Continuous Delivery (CD)

Continuous Delivery is about automatically releasing software to the test or production environment. Continuous Delivery usually means a developer's changes to an app are automatically bug tested and uploaded to a repository (like GitHub or a container registry like Docker Hub), where they can then be deployed to a live production environment by the operations team.

Continuous Deployment (CD)

Continuous Deployment is about releasing software to production automatically, without human intervention. It addresses the problem of overloading operations teams with manual processes of testing and pushing buttons, which slow down app delivery. Continuous Deployment builds over the benefits of Continuous Delivery by automating the next stage in the pipeline, as shown in Figure 13-1.

The following section investigates these aspects in the context of a tool, Skaffold.

Google Skaffold

Skaffold is an open-source command-line tool that facilitates developer productivity by orchestrating Continuous Development, Continuous Integration (CI), and Continuous Delivery (CD). It handles the workflow for building, pushing, and deploying your application and you can use it to easily configure a local development workspace. Due to how easy it is to set up, this chapter uses Skaffold to show a few of the aspects of CI/CD in the microservice example.

Skaffold Workflow

Skaffold provides a single, simple command that will simplify your development workflow by organizing common development stages. Here's a typical workflow when you execute the Skaffold dev command:

- Collects and watches your source code for changes.

- Syncs files directly to pods if the user marks them as able to be synced.

- Builds artifacts from the source.

- Tests the built artifacts using container-structure-tests or custom scripts.

- Tags the artifacts.

- Pushes the artifacts.

- Deploys the artifacts.

- Monitors the deployed artifacts.

- Cleans up the deployed artifacts on exit (Ctrl+C).

Skaffold is flexible so that if you are coding on a local machine, you can configure it to build artifacts with your local Docker daemon and deploy them to Minikube using kubectl, which is what you will do next in the example. In production, you can switch to your production profile and start building with different profiles and then deploy with Helm.

CI and CD Example for Microservices

You will use Skaffold to enable CI/CD to the example in the previous chapter. This example assumes that Skaffold is already installed in your machine. On the Mac, you can install it using brew:

```
brew skaffold
```

This section starts by investigating the project structure.

Code Organization

The source code for this book is available on GitHub via the book's product page, located at www.apress.com/9798868805547. The source code for this example is organized as shown in Listing 13-1, inside the ch13\ ch13-01 folder.

Listing 13-1. Spring Boot Microservices Source Code Organization

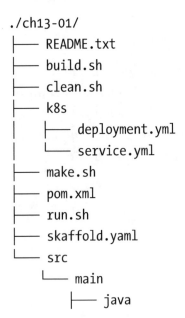

```
./ch13-01/
├── README.txt
├── build.sh
├── clean.sh
├── k8s
│   ├── deployment.yml
│   └── service.yml
├── make.sh
├── pom.xml
├── run.sh
├── skaffold.yaml
└── src
    └── main
        ├── java
```

```
|        └── com
|             └── acme
|                  └── ecom
|                       └── product
|                            └── Application.java
└── resources
     ├── application.yml
     └── log4j2-spring.xml
```

```
9 directories, 12 files
binildass-MacBook-Pro:ch13 binil$
```

Since you are using Google jib-maven-plugin to automate the Docker image creation, Docker daemon does not have to be running on your local machine, nor do you need a Docker file for your Spring Boot application.

Understanding the Source Code

The single application component is the Application.java class, which is a REST controller. You saw this code in the third example in Chapter 12, and there are more configurations to the jib plugin, so the Maven configurations are shown in Listing 13-2.

Listing 13-2. Maven pom.xml (ch13/ch13-01/pom.xml)

```
<project>
    ...
    <build>
        <plugins>

            <plugin>
                <groupId>com.google.cloud.tools</groupId>
                <artifactId>jib-maven-plugin</artifactId>
                <version>3.3.2</version>
```

```
            <configuration>
                <to>
                    <image>
                        binildas/${project.artifactId}
                    </image>
                </to>
                <container>
                    <creationTime>
                        USE_CURRENT_TIMESTAMP
                    </creationTime>
                    <ports>
                        <port>8080</port>
                    </ports>
                </container>
            </configuration>
        </plugin>

    </plugins>
  </build>
</project>
```

You are mainly configuring the container port in Listing 13-2.

This example also looks at the application source code. The single application component is the `Application.java` class, which is a REST controller (see Listing 13-3).

Listing 13-3. Application REST Controller (ch13/ch13-01/src/main/java/com/acme/ecom/product\Application.java)

```
@SpringBootApplication
@RestController
public class Application {
```

```java
private static final Logger LOGGER =
    LoggerFactory.getLogger(Application.class);

private static volatile long times = 0L;
private static String appVersion = "1";

@RequestMapping("/")
public String home() {

    LOGGER.info("Start");
    ++times;
    LOGGER.debug("Inside hello.Application.home() :
        Counted {} times by App Version: {}", times,
            appVersion);
    LOGGER.info("Returning...");
    return "Hello Docker World : Counted " + times +
        " times by App Version: " + appVersion;
}

public static void main(String[] args) {

    SpringApplication.run(Application.class, args);
    LOGGER.info("Started...");
}
}
```

An `appVersion` field is introduced in the Java class file in Listing 13-3. You will make changes to this field to understand the Skaffold CI/CD feature.

Next, take a look at the Skaffold descriptor, as shown in Listing 13-4.

Listing 13-4. Skaffold Descriptor (ch13/ch13-01/skaffold.yaml)

```
apiVersion: skaffold/v1beta4
kind: Config
build:
  local:
    push: false
  artifacts:
    - image: binildas/spring-boot-docker-k8s-helm
      # jibGradle: {}
      jibMaven: {}
deploy:
  kubectl:
    manifests:
      - k8s/*.yml
```

A few of the descriptor fields are explained here:

- `build.local.push`: False enforces Skaffold to use `jibDockerBuild`.

- `build.artifacts` is a list of images you're going to build.

- `build.artifacts.jibMaven` configures Skaffold to use jib during the image-building phase, with type maven, since you are using Maven as a build tool.

- `deploy.kubectl.manifests` sets the folder name where you have the Kubernetes manifest files. If you skip this attribute, the default directory name would be k8s.

You are almost done setting up a CI/CD pipeline in this Dev environment.

Build and Run the Microservice

The ch13\ch13-01 folder contains the Maven scripts required to build and run the examples. You will build using the mvn clean compile jib:build command, as shown in Listing 13-5.

Listing 13-5. Building the Microservice Using Scripts

```
(base) binildass-MacBook-Pro:ch13-01 binil$ pwd
/Users/binil/binil/code/mac/mybooks/docker-04/Code/ch13/ch13-01
(base) binildass-MacBook-Pro:ch13-01 binil$ sh build.sh
[INFO] Scanning for projects...
[INFO]
[INFO] -< com.acme.ecom.product:spring-boot-docker-k8s-helm >-
[INFO] Building Spring Boot µS 0.0.1-SNAPSHOT
[INFO] --------------------[ jar ]--------------------
[INFO]
...
[INFO]
[INFO] Built and pushed image as binildas/spring-boot-
docker-k8s-helm
[INFO] Executing tasks:
[INFO] [============================  ] 91.7% complete
[INFO] > launching layer pushers
[INFO]
[INFO] ------------------------------------------------------
[INFO] BUILD SUCCESS
[INFO] ------------------------------------------------------
[INFO] Total time:  33.855 s
[INFO] Finished at: 2023-05-23T15:43:14+05:30
[INFO] ------------------------------------------------------
(base) binildass-MacBook-Pro:ch13-01 binil$
```

This build will push the image to Docker Hub. When you execute the dev mode of the Skaffold, it will build the application, create the image, deploy in your local cluster, and keep watching your sources to see if there is a change. When there is a change, it will repeat the same flow upon code change so that you have a fresh deployment for testing and debugging.

Before you trigger any changes to the code, first run the microservice as the next step. Note that you are going to use the skaffold command to run the microservices. See Listing 13-6.

Listing 13-6. Running the Microservice Using Skaffold

```
(base) binildass-MacBook-Pro:ch13-01 binil$ pwd
/Users/binil/binil/code/mac/mybooks/docker-04/Code/ch13/ch13-01
(base) binildass-MacBook-Pro:ch13-01 binil$ eval $(minikube
docker-env)
(base) binildass-MacBook-Pro:ch13-01 binil$ skaffold
dev --trigger notify -v debug
DEBU[0000] skaffold API not starting as it's not
requested   subtask=-1 task=DevLoop
...
[INFO]
[INFO] Built image to Docker daemon as binildas/spring-boot-
docker-k8s-helm
[INFO]
[INFO] ------------------------------------------------------------
[INFO] BUILD SUCCESS
[INFO] ------------------------------------------------------------
...
Press Ctrl+C to exit
DEBU[0017] Change detected<nil>        subtask=-1 task=DevLoop
Watching for changes...
...
```

```
[springboothelm]
[springboothelm]   .   ___                        _ _ _
[springboothelm]  /\\ / ___'_ __ _ _(_)_ __  __ _ \ \ \ \
[springboothelm] ( ( )\___ | '_ | '_| | '_ \/ _` | \ \ \ \
[springboothelm]  \\/  ___)| |_)| | | | | || (_| |  ) ) ) )
[springboothelm]   '  |____| .__|_| |_|_| |_\__, | / / / /
[springboothelm]  =========|_|==============|___/=/_/_/_/
[springboothelm]  :: Spring Boot ::                (v3.2.0)
[springboothelm]
...
[springboothelm] 2023-06-01 12:55:42 INFO  StartupInfoLogger.
logStarted:57 - Started Application ...
[springboothelm] 2023-06-01 12:55:42 INFO  Application.
main:51 - Started...
...
```

This will build your image and deploy it to Minikube for every change you make in your project.

Testing the Microservices

Once the microservice is up, you can access the web application using your browser and pointing to the URL, which you will discover in Listing 13-7.

Listing 13-7. Finding the Service URL

```
(base) binildass-MacBook-Pro:~ binil$ minikube service
springboothelm --url
http://192.168.64.6:31831
(base) binildass-MacBook-Pro:~ binil$
```

You can test using this URL in a browser or by using cURL, as shown in Listing 13-8.

Listing 13-8. Testing the Microservice Using cURL

```
(base) binildass-MacBook-Pro:~ binil$ curl
http://192.168.64.6:31831
Hello Docker World : Counted 1 times by App Version: 1
(base) binildass-MacBook-Pro:~ binil$
```

The corresponding logs will also be visible in the microservice terminal window, as shown in Listing 13-9.

Listing 13-9. Microservice Terminal Window Logs

```
[springboothelm]
[springboothelm]   .   ___          _            __ _ _
[springboothelm]  /\\ / ___'_ __ _ _(_)_ __  __ _ \ \ \ \
[springboothelm] ( ( )\___ | '_ | '_| | '_ \/ _` | \ \ \ \
[springboothelm]  \\/  ___)| |_)| | | | | || (_| |  ) ) ) )
[springboothelm]   '  |____| .__|_| |_|_| |_\__, | / / / /
[springboothelm]  =========|_|==============|___/=/_/_/_/
[springboothelm]  :: Spring Boot ::                (v3.2.0)
[springboothelm]
...
[springboothelm] 2023-06-01 12:55:42 INFO  StartupInfoLogger.
logStarted:57 - Started Application ...
[springboothelm] 2023-06-01 12:55:42 INFO  Application.
main:51 - Started...
...
[springboothelm] 2023-06-01 12:59:50 INFO  Application.
home:41 - Start
[springboothelm] 2023-06-01 12:59:50 DEBUG Application.
home:43 - Inside hello.Application.home() : Counted 1 times by
App Version: 1
```

```
[springboothelm] 2023-06-01 12:59:50 INFO  Application.
home:44 - Returning...
...
```

You will now make some changes to the source code of the project. While making the change, keep watching the terminal window. Make this change (see Listing 13-10):

```
private static String appVersion = "2";
```

Listing 13-10. Microservice Terminal Window Logs on Redeployment

```
[springboothelm]
[springboothelm]   .    ___               _          _ _ _
[springboothelm]  /\\ / ___'_ _ _ _(_)_ _   _ _ _ \ \ \ \
[springboothelm] ( ( )\__ | '_ | '_| | '_ \/ _` | \ \ \ \
[springboothelm]  \\/  ___)| |_)| | | | | | || (_| |  ) ) ) )
[springboothelm]   '  |___| ._|_| |_|_| |_\__, | / / / /
[springboothelm]  ========|_|==============|___/=/_/_/_/
[springboothelm]  :: Spring Boot ::             (v3.0.6)
[springboothelm]
...
[springboothelm] 2023-06-01 13:01:23 INFO  Application.
main:51 - Started...
```

Any small change will be picked up and Skaffold and will automatically trigger a new build of the Docker image, create a new pod, and redeploy the application.

You can test the application again using cURL, as in Listing 13-11.

Listing 13-11. Testing the Microservice Using cURL

```
(base) binildass-MacBook-Pro:~ binil$ curl
http://192.168.64.6:31831
Hello Docker World : Counted 1 times by App Version: 2
(base) binildass-MacBook-Pro:~ binil$
```

The corresponding logs are also visible in the terminal window, as shown in Listing 13-12.

Listing 13-12. Microservice Terminal Window Logs After Redeployment

```
[springboothelm]
[springboothelm]   .   ____          _            __ _ _
[springboothelm]  /\\ / ___'_ __ _ _(_)_ __  __ _ \ \ \ \
[springboothelm] ( ( )\___ | '_ | '_| | '_ \/ _` | \ \ \ \
[springboothelm]  \\/  ___)| |_)| | | | | || (_| |  ) ) ) )
[springboothelm]   '  |____| .__|_| |_|_| |_\__, | / / / /
[springboothelm]  =========|_|==============|___/=/_/_/_/
[springboothelm]  :: Spring Boot ::                (v3.0.6)
[springboothelm]
...
[springboothelm] 2023-06-01 13:01:23 INFO  Application.
main:51 - Started...
[springboothelm] 2023-06-01 13:04:58 INFO  Application.
home:41 - Start
[springboothelm] 2023-06-01 13:04:58 DEBUG Application.
home:43 - Inside hello.Application.home() : Counted 1 times by
App Version: 2
[springboothelm] 2023-06-01 13:04:58 INFO  Application.
home:44 - Returning...
```

You can clearly view the change you have made in the source code (appVersion = "2"). Even the private static volatile long times = 0L counter has been reset since the class binaries have been reloaded by the new container. See Listing 13-13.

You can stop the application by typing Ctrl+C in the terminal window.

Listing 13-13. Terminating the Microservice Application

```
^CCleaning up...
...
DEBU[0972] Running command: [kubectl --context minikube
delete --ignore-not-found=true -f -]
 - deployment.apps "springboothelm" deleted
 - service "springboothelm" deleted
INFO[0972] Cleanup complete in 273.772602ms
(base) binildass-MacBook-Pro:ch13-01 binil$
```

This completes the simple CI/CD pipeline example for microservices.

Summary

Faster release cycles are one of the major promises of microservices architectures. However, without a good CI/CD process, you won't achieve the agility that microservices promise.

> *"We try to create teams that are no larger than can be fed by two pizzas. We call that the two-pizza team rule."*
>
> —Bezos

When this becomes the norm, it is more important to have a strong CI/CD process, since you will have multiple teams working in their own separate repositories of microservices. You have seen an example demonstrating these concepts. Although the example and pipeline are simple, they served the purpose of introducing the concepts. Having looked at different aspects of microservices and containers, you are now ready to get into the public cloud, which you will do in the next chapter.

CHAPTER 14

Microservices in AWS Elastic Compute Cloud

In a manufacturing enterprise, dead stock refers to products that are not selling and are no longer in production, but remain on the shelf. Similarly, obsolete stock refers to products that are no longer being sold and are discontinued, and often cannot be used or sold anymore. The IT industry is also not shielded from similar obsoleteness. Compute, network, and storage devices may become obsolete or useless, and the investment done on this in the past may become unprotected. Cloud computing attempts to address this obsoleteness to some extent as one of its objectives.

This chapter introduces the notion of a public cloud and explains how to deploy microservices in the public cloud.

The following concepts are covered in this chapter:

- Introduction to cloud computing

- Introduction to Amazon Web Services (AWS)

- Introduction to Terraform

- Provisioning an EC2 in AWS Cloud

- Deploying a microservice example in AWS Cloud

© Binildas A. Christudas 2024
B. A. Christudas, *Java Microservices and Containers in the Cloud,*
https://doi.org/10.1007/979-8-8688-0555-4_14

Cloud Computing

Cloud computing is the on-demand availability of computer system resources as network accessible services—especially computing power, storage, and networking resources—without direct, active management by the user enterprise. Clouds often have such functions distributed over multiple locations of geography, each of which is a *data center*. Cloud computing relies on sharing these resources to achieve coherence and typically uses a pay-per-usage model, which can help in reducing capital expenses of the user enterprise.

Public Clouds

Around the year 2000, Amazon created the subsidiary called Amazon Web Services (AWS) and before too long they introduced Simple Storage Service (S3) and Elastic Compute Cloud (EC2). With this, instead of buying, owning, and maintaining physical data centers and servers, enterprises could access technology services, such as computing power, storage, and databases, on an as-needed basis from AWS.

Before too long, many other players also offered similar cloud computing services. See Figure 14-1.

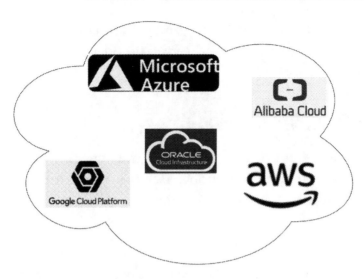

Figure 14-1. *Major cloud service providers*

A few of the advantages of cloud computing are worth mentioning:

- Agility: The long cycles of hardware and software purchasing followed by further delays of provisioning and testing are cut short by cloud computing, since an enterprise or even an individual developer can spin up resources the instance they need them.

- Elasticity: Over-provisioning or extra provisioning for just a few hours or days of seasonal peak in a year is not required since cloud computing allows you to add or reduce resources as and when your scalability needs change. This is like having zero "dead inventory" on the shelf.

- Cost savings: There is less upfront investment in IT infrastructure and middleware, so your Capex is greatly reduced. Since cloud providers operate at huge volumes, they achieve economies of scale, a part of which could also be extended to cloud users.

Cloud is fast becoming the de facto mode of IT infrastructure services. Figure 14-1 shows a few of the cloud service providers; there are many more in the industry.

Cloud Deployment Models

There are differences in who owns the cloud computing service and how the service is offered to its customers. Based on that, the Cloud Deployment models are classified into three or more.

Public Cloud

A *public cloud* is a subscription service that is offered to all customers who want similar services from their cloud provider. See Figure 14-2.

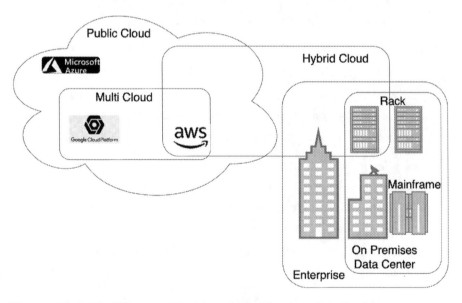

Figure 14-2. *Public vs. private vs. hybrid vs. multi-cloud*

Public cloud services are offered over the Internet so that any consumer can subscribe to the service.

Private Cloud

A *private cloud* is infrastructure operated solely for a single organization. It can be managed internally by the organization's own IT or by a third party and hosted internally or externally.

Hybrid Cloud

A *hybrid cloud* service is composed of some combination of private, public, and community cloud services, from different service providers. Some organizations use public cloud computing resources to meet temporary high-capacity needs that cannot be met by the private cloud. This capability enables hybrid clouds to employ cloud bursting for scaling across clouds.

Multi-Cloud

A *multi-cloud* leverages computing services from multiple providers in a single but heterogeneous architecture to reduce reliance on single vendors. The reason might be to increase flexibility through choice so that you are not dependent on a single provider, to mitigate against disasters, and so on.

While data consistency and synchronization are aspects to be taken care of, managing hybrid and multi-cloud modes involves more complexities compared to pure private or public modes. Even with single providers, taking care of those aspects in an errorless manner is a non-trivial task. That is a bigger topic with many technical complexities involved, and could be the subject matter for another book in the future.

Distributed Computing

The cloud service model is based on the kind of control users have over how the resources are utilized. Figure 14-3 shows the different models.

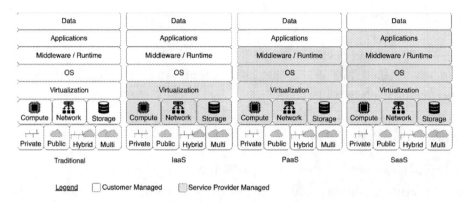

Figure 14-3. *Cloud service models (adapted from "Practical Microservices Architectural Patterns," ISBN-13: 978-1484245002)*

Typically, the cloud architecture can be mapped to the cloud service model. In the traditional service model, the user, or the enterprise itself, is responsible for managing the whole stack (e.g., the hardware, data center facilities, software, and data), whereas in the cloud service model it varies as follows:

- Infrastructure as a Service (IaaS): In the IaaS service model, the users request compute power, storage, network, and their associated resources alone and pay for what they use.

- Platform as a Service (PaaS): In the PaaS model, the users have no control over the underlying infrastructure, such as CPU, network, and storage, as they are abstracted away, below the platform. Instead, it allows application development platforms the creation of applications with supported programming languages and related tools hosted in the cloud and accessed through an interface, mainly a browser. Many times, the application runtime and middleware are also provided by the CSP, and the user develops, installs, manages, and operates the software application alone and its data.

- Software as a Service (SaaS): This is the "forget everything" model, where the user doesn't even own, manage, or operate the application. Applications are run on the cloud infrastructure and are accessible from various client devices. Limited user-configurations are available. Sometimes the same application instance serves the end users of more than one enterprise (tenant); such applications are called multi-tenant.[1]

IaaS and PaaS are both covered in the examples in this book.

Amazon Web Services (AWS)

Amazon Web Services (AWS) offers public cloud services over different levels of abstractions of compute, storage, and networking. AWS infrastructure is distributed globally, and the AWS website provides a glimpse of the global distribution of its data centers. See Figure 14-4.

---

[1] The author's company IBS Software provides SaaS services to the airline passenger, cargo, and hospitality industries and the author has patented in-house multi-tenant frameworks from the USPTO on behalf of his company.

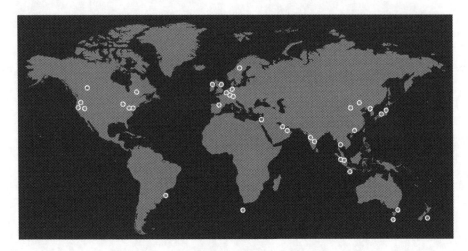

Figure 14-4. *AWS data center locations (Source:* https://aws. amazon.com/about-aws/global-infrastructure/*)*

These services can be accessed by machines using HTTP protocols. Users can also access AWS services through the AWS command terminal or through the web UI.

The next section looks at a few of the AWS services used in the example in the next section.

VPC

A Virtual Private Cloud (VPC) is a virtual network dedicated to your AWS account. It is logically isolated from other virtual networks in AWS Cloud. You can specify an IP address range for the VPC, add subnets, add gateways, and associate security groups.

Subnet

A *subnet* is a range of IP addresses in your VPC. You can create AWS resources, such as EC2 instances, in specific subnets. When you create a subnet, you specify its IP addresses, depending on the configuration of the

VPC. The IPv4 subnet has an IPv4 CIDR block, but does not have an IPv6 CIDR block. Similarly, an IPv6 subnet has an IPv6 CIDR block, but does not have an IPv4 CIDR block. Dual stack subnets have both blocks.

There are two subnet types:

- Public subnets: Have a direct route to an Internet gateway. Resources in a public subnet can access the public Internet.

- Private subnets: Do not have a direct route to an Internet gateway. Resources in a private subnet require a NAT device to access the public Internet.

Public Proxy Subnet

If the EC2 instance running in a subnet needs to be reachable via the Internet, you can create a proxy subnet. Use these steps to do so:

1. Create a subnet spanning a subsection of the IP address range assigned to the VPC.

2. Create a route table and attach it to the subnet.

3. Add the `0.0.0.0/0` route pointing the Internet gateway to the route table.

NAT Gateway

A NAT gateway is a Network Address Translation (NAT) service. You can use a NAT gateway so that instances in a private subnet can connect to services outside your VPC, but external services cannot initiate a connection with those instances.

EC2

Amazon EC2 is a web service that provides secure, resizable compute capacity in the cloud. You will use the T2 instance in a later example. T2 instances are a low-cost, general-purpose instance types that provide a baseline level of CPU performance with the ability to burst above the baseline when needed. T2 instances are one of the lowest-cost Amazon EC2 instance options and are ideal for a variety of general-purpose applications like microservices.

Route Tables

A route table contains a set of rules, called *routes*, that determine where network traffic from your subnet or gateway is directed.

The *Main* route table automatically comes with your VPC, and it is an implicit route table. It controls the routing for all subnets that are not explicitly associated with any other route table.

Each subnet in your VPC must be associated with a route table, which controls the routing for the subnet (the subnet route table).

Internet Gateway

An Internet Gateway (IGW) enables your instances to connect to the Internet through the Amazon EC2 network edge. The IGW will translate the public IP addresses of your virtual machines to their private IP addresses using network address translation (NAT). All public IP addresses used in the VPC are controlled by this IGW.

These AWS services are just representative, not exhaustive. Detailed discussions on these or discussions on more services are beyond the scope of this book.

Infrastructure as Code (IaC)

Infrastructure as Code (IaC) is where you write and execute code to define, deploy, update, and destroy your infrastructure. Typically, you have been automating infrastructure management using ad hoc scripts, such as .sh bash scripts. Such ad hoc scripts provide a general-purpose tool-based approach, so you need to write complete custom code for every task. But specific and purpose-built tools for IaC provide concise APIs for accomplishing complicated tasks, thus enforcing a particular structure for your code. Ad hoc scripts are great for small, one-off tasks but when it comes to infrastructures involving multiple moving parts, especially when you want to take care of a number of microservices, bash scripts become a mess of unmaintainable spaghetti. This is where the IaC tools come to your help.

Let's look at a few benefits of IaC:

- Self-service: Since you are reading this book, most probably your role in your daily job is that of an application developer, not a system administrator. However, there could be times when you need to have an infrastructure to deploy and test your application components. In my years of experience, I have seen a few system administrators serving the entire big team or the entire organization. Then how do you, as a developer, get an infrastructure in time? If your infrastructure is defined in code, the infrastructure deployment process can be automated, and you can kick off your own deployments to provision the infrastructure whenever necessary.

- Version control: When you have your infrastructure provisioning as code, you can store the IaC in version control so that the entire history of your infrastructure is captured in the commit log. This means, when problems occur and you suspect this is due to changes in your infrastructure, you can simply revert to your previous, known-good version of your provisioning code.

The next section looks at one of the tools in the IaC space—Terraform.

Terraform

Terraform is an open source IaC tool created by HashiCorp. Terraform is written in the Go language. Terraform can use the authentication mechanism you're already using with cloud service providers like AWS, Azure, Google Cloud, and so on, and then make API calls. You need to create Terraform configurations, which are text files that specify the infrastructure you want to create.

You can define your entire infrastructure, starting with Internet gateways, load balancers, VPCs, subnets, servers, and so on. You do this in Terraform configurations and commit those files to a version control system. You can then run `terraform apply` to create your infrastructure on the target cloud. When you need to make some changes to your infrastructure, you make those changes in the Terraform configuration files, validate those changes through code reviews and tests, commit the updated code to version control, and then run the `terraform apply` command again. One aspect to note is that there is no straight way to deploy the same infrastructure in a different cloud provider using the same Terraform configuration, because the cloud providers don't offer the same types of infrastructure.

That's a quick introduction to public cloud and IaC. The next section puts these learnings into some code.

Setting Up AWS EC2 Using Terraform

In this section, you use Terraform to create an EC2 compute infrastructure in AWS. I assume that you already have the following prerequisites in your development machine:

- An AWS account that you know how to manage using the AWS web console

- An AWS CLI (Command Line Interface) and terminal with secret keys to access the AWS account (optional)

- A key pair to access your EC2 instances

- Terraform

I don't intend to cover those aspects in this book. If you aren't familiar with these steps, refer to an appropriate book.[2] Appendix F also provides some guidance in using a few of these tools.

The next sections use a few of the AWS infrastructure components already discussed for this demonstration.

Design a Mini Data Center in the Cloud

You will have a very minimal Compute module in AWS Cloud. Even though the intention is to set up a minimal Compute infrastructure, note that you need a full set of Compute and Network infrastructures for this, which is not trivial. Thanks to Terraform, it will make even such non-trivial tasks accessible to developers like you and me. Figure 14-5 shows the targeted Compute module in AWS Cloud.

---

[2] *Programming Amazon EC2,* O'Reilly Media; ISBN-13: 978-1449393687

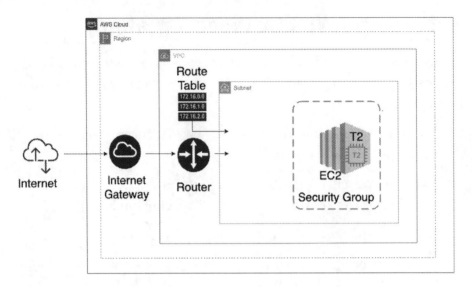

Figure 14-5. *A mini data center in AWS Cloud*

The next section gets into the code. It starts by investigating the project structure.

Code Organization

The source code for this book is available on GitHub via the book's product page, located at www.apress.com/9798868805547. The source code for this example is organized as shown in Listing 14-1, inside the ch14\ ch14-01 folder.

Listing 14-1. Terraform EC2 Project Source Code Organization

```
./ch14-01/
├── README.txt
├── connections.tf
├── gateways.tf
├── network.tf
├── security.tf
```

```
├── servers.tf
├── subnets.tf
└── variables.tf
```

You can guess what many of these Terraform files are intended to do from the name of the files, but the next section also covers them.

Understanding the Source Code

This section starts from the first step of selecting which cloud provider to use and in which geography. See Listing 14-2.

Listing 14-2. AWS Region Configuration (ch14/ch14-01/ connections.tf)

```
provider "aws" {
  region = "ap-southeast-1"
}
```

As mentioned, Terraform helps you manage IT infrastructure across a variety of public cloud providers (e.g., Amazon Web Services, Microsoft Azure, DigitalOcean) and private cloud and virtualization platforms (e.g., OpenStack, VMware). In this example, it intends to use aws as the cloud provider. I am using ap-southeast-1, which is the Singapore region. You can use whichever region you prefer.

The next step is to define the VPC, as shown in Listing 14-3.

Listing 14-3. AWS VPC Configuration (ch14/ch14-01/network.tf) .

```
resource "aws_vpc" "test-env" {
  cidr_block = "10.0.0.0/16"
  enable_dns_hostnames = true
  enable_dns_support = true
  tags = {
```

```
    Name = "bdca-Instance-03"
  }
}
resource "aws_eip" "ip-test-env" {
  instance = "${aws_instance.test-ec2-instance.id}"
  domain   = "vpc"
}
```

Amazon Virtual Private Cloud (Amazon VPC) allows you to launch AWS resources in a logically isolated virtual network. Your AWS account includes a default VPC in each AWS region. Your default VPCs are configured so that you can immediately start launching and connecting to EC2 instances; however, in the example you will be creating your own VPC called test-env.

While creating a VPC in AWS, the CIDR block is used to configure the expanse of your network. The IP CIDR block gives the range of IP addresses to be allocated to this VPC. It has the format 10.0.0.0/16. The number after the slash /, 16denotes that any IP address in the range of this CIDR block must consist of the first 16 bits exactly.

- Since the first 16 bits must remain unchanged, it still has remained with 16 bits to take any value.

- To understand this further, you can calculate the range of IP addresses in the provided CIDR block 10.0.0.0/16.

Remaining bits = 32 - the number after the / in the cidr prefix

```
= 32 - 16
= 16
```

The total number of IP addresses in the cidr block:

```
= 2 ^ remaining bits
= 2 ^ 16
= 65536
```

This calculation is just for your information; a detailed discussion is beyond the scope of this book.

The tag called `Name = "bdca-Instance-03"` is added so you can identify the VPC.

Elastic IP is a static public IPv4 address, which is not free. You can attach an Elastic IP to the `aws_instance.test-ec2-instance.id` instance, which you will see subsequently.

Next, you create a subnet. See Listing 14-4.

Listing 14-4. AWS Subnet Configuration (ch14/ch14-01/subnets.tf)

```
resource "aws_subnet" "subnet-uno" {
  cidr_block = "${cidrsubnet(aws_vpc.test-env.cidr_
  block, 3, 1)}"
  vpc_id = "${aws_vpc.test-env.id}"
  availability_zone = "ap-southeast-1a"
}
resource "aws_route_table" "route-table-test-env" {
  vpc_id = "${aws_vpc.test-env.id}"
route {
    cidr_block = "0.0.0.0/0"
    gateway_id = "${aws_internet_gateway.test-env-gw.id}"
  }
tags = {
    Name = "test-env-route-table"
  }
}
```

```
resource "aws_route_table_association" "subnet-association" {
  subnet_id       = "${aws_subnet.subnet-uno.id}"
  route_table_id = "${aws_route_table.route-table-test-env.id}"
}
```

This subnet part also introduces an important feature in Terraform, showing how it references other existing resources by name. Note how the vpc_id is defined. It refers to an existing resources attribute (the id), referencing its full terraform name aws_vpc.test-env.id, which was defined in the previous step.

To calculate the subnet address in a given IP network address prefix, you must use the cidrsubnet function provided by Terraform, which requires three arguments:

- CIDR prefix: This should be in a CIDR notation, as defined in RFC 4632 Section 3.1, and here you refer to the CIDR of the VPC of which the subnet should be part

- newbits: The CIDR prefix will get extended by this many bits. If the CIDR prefix ends with /16 and the newbits provided is 4, the CIDR prefix is extended to /20. (Adding four bits to the 16 bits provided in the CIDR prefix.)

- netnum: Used to populate the additional bits in the prefix. This whole number value cannot contain bits greater than the newbits provided.

To know what value it will finally have, you can use the Terraform console utility. From your development machine terminal, first connect to the Terraform console, and then execute the function, as shown in Listing 14-5.

Listing 14-5. Terraform cidrsubnet Function

```
(base) binildass-MacBook-Pro:~ binil$ terraform console
> cidrsubnet("10.0.0.0/16", 3, 1)
"10.0.32.0/19"
>
```

Let's investigate the routing next.

Terraform currently provides both a standalone route resource and a route table resource with routes defined inline. You cannot use both methods for the same table. In other words, if you create routes in the aws_ route_table, you cannot associate routes created with aws_route.

aws_route_table_association ties the routing table to your subnet.

The resource aws_route_table route-table-test-env block creates a new route table in the VPC specified by the vpc_id attribute aws_vpc.test-env.id. It also defines a route that sends all traffic with destination CIDR 0.0.0.0/0 to the Internet gateway specified by the gateway_id = "${aws_ internet_gateway.test-env-gw.id} attribute. The tags attribute sets a test-env-route-table name for the route table for easy identification.

The aws_route_table_association block associates the newly created route table with a subnet_id = "${aws_subnet.subnet-uno.id}" subnet. The route_table_id attribute refers to the ID of the route table created in the previous block.

Listing 14-6 looks at the test-env-gw referred to in the previous route.

Listing 14-6. AWS Internet Gateway Configuration (ch14/ch14-01/ gateways.tf)

```
resource "aws_internet_gateway" "test-env-gw" {
  vpc_id = "${aws_vpc.test-env.id}"
tags = {
    Name = "test-env-gw"
  }
}
```

Attaching this Internet gateway will allow public traffic to come through to the subnet.

AWS by default will allow all traffic outside, but when you use Terraform, this is disabled and therefore has to be explicitly stated to allow traffic. To do that, you need to first create a security group to suit your needs. See Listing 14-7.

Listing 14-7. AWS Security Group Configuration (ch14/ch14-01/ security.tf)

```
resource "aws_security_group" "ingress-all-test" {
name = "allow-all-sg"
vpc_id = "${aws_vpc.test-env.id}"
ingress {
    cidr_blocks = [
      "0.0.0.0/0"
    ]
    from_port = 22
    to_port = 22
    protocol = "tcp"
  }
ingress {
    cidr_blocks = [
      "0.0.0.0/0"
    ]
    from_port = 8080
    to_port = 8080
    protocol = "tcp"
  }
  egress {
   from_port = 0
   to_port = 0
```

```
  protocol = "-1"
  cidr_blocks = ["0.0.0.0/0"]
 }
}
```

When you create VPC, it automatically comes with a default security group. Each EC2 instance that you launch in your VPC is automatically associated with the default security group if you don't specify a different security group when you launch the instance.

A security group acts as a virtual firewall for your instance to control inbound and outbound traffic. Security groups act at the instance level, not at the subnet level. Therefore, each instance in a subnet in your VPC can be assigned to a different set of security groups. If you don't specify a particular group at launch time, the instance is automatically assigned to the default security group for the VPC.

For each security group, you add rules that control the inbound traffic to instances, and a separate set of rules that control the outbound traffic. The default route in Internet Protocol Version 4 (IPv4) is designated as the zero-address 0.0.0.0/0 in CIDR notation, often called the *quad-zero route.* The subnet mask is given as /0, which effectively specifies all networks. 0.0.0.0/0, ::/0. This means the source can be any IP address, from any system request. 0.0.0.0/0 represents IPv4 and ::/0 represents IPv6.

The ingress-all-test you defined allows anyone to connect through port 22. It will also forward all traffic without restriction. Using vpc_id = "${aws_vpc.test-env.id}" you can attach it to the VPC you created. The ingress block describes how incoming traffic will be treated. This example defined a rule to accept connections from all IPs on port 22. The egress block defines the rule for outgoing traffic and this example defined it to allow all.

As a final step, you need to define EC2 instances, which are the actual compute module where you want the AWS Cloud to expend computing to crunch the workload. See Listing 14-8.

681

Listing 14-8. AWS EC2 Configuration (ch14/ch14-01/servers.tf)

```
resource "aws_instance" "test-ec2-instance" {
  ami = "${var.ami_id}"
  instance_type = "t2.micro"
  key_name = "${var.ami_key_pair_name}"
  security_groups = ["${aws_security_group.ingress-all-
  test.id}"]
tags = {
    Name = "${var.ami_name}"
  }
subnet_id = "${aws_subnet.subnet-uno.id}"
}
```

This code requests an AWS instance of `t2.micro`. You then do the security group and subnet associations. One thing you want to note is that we are using variables in three places—for `ami_id`, `ami_key_pair_name`, and `ami_name`. The values come from a few variables defined in another file. See Listing 14-9.

Listing 14-9. Terraform Variables Configuration (ch14/ch14-01/variables.tf)

```
variable "ami_name" {}
variable "ami_id" {}
variable "ami_key_pair_name" {}
```

These variables are defined for convenience so that the entire Terraform plan can be used as a template to launch multiple instances if required, providing the option for those variables to take different values. Since you keep the variables empty as shown, Terraform will prompt for them to be given in the terminal as input during Terraform plan execution. The `ami_name` variable will be used as a tag and the `ami_id` variable is used to find the instance to be launched.

You now have almost everything completed, so it's time to spin up the servers in the cloud.

Build and Spin EC2 Server in the Cloud

Go to the ch14\ch14-01 root folder and run the terraform init command, as shown in Listing 14-10.

Listing 14-10. Terraform init

```
(base) binildass-MacBook-Pro:ch14-01 binil$ pwd
/Users/binil/binil/code/mac/mybooks/docker-04/Code/ch14/ch14-01
(base) binildass-MacBook-Pro:ch14-01-temp binil$ terraform init

Initializing the backend...

Initializing provider plugins...
- Finding latest version of hashicorp/aws...
- Installing hashicorp/aws v5.1.0...
- Installed hashicorp/aws v5.1.0 (signed by HashiCorp)

Terraform has created a lock file .terraform.lock.hcl to record
the provider
selections it made above. Include this file in your version
control repository
so that Terraform can guarantee to make the same selections by
default when
you run "terraform init" in the future.

Terraform has been successfully initialized!

You may now begin working with Terraform. Try running
"terraform plan" to see
any changes that are required for your infrastructure. All
Terraform commands
should now work.
```

If you ever set or change modules or backend configuration for
Terraform,
rerun this command to reinitialize your working directory. If
you forget, other
commands will detect it and remind you to do so if necessary.
(base) binildass-MacBook-Pro:ch14-01-temp binil$

The Terraform binary installed in your machine only contains the
basic functionality for Terraform; it does not come with the code for any of
the providers (e.g., the AWS Provider, Azure provider, GCP provider, etc.).
When you use Terraform the first time, you need to run terraform init to
tell Terraform to inspect the code, determine which providers you're using,
and download the code for them—in this case, it is AWS. This provider
code is downloaded into a terraform folder, which is Terraform's scratch
directory. Terraform will also record information about the provider code
it downloaded into a .terraform.lock.hcl file.

You can now sanity check your code, as shown in Listing 14-11.

Listing 14-11. Validate Terraform Scripts

```
(base) binildass-MacBook-Pro:ch14-01 binil$ pwd
/Users/binil/binil/code/mac/mybooks/docker-04/Code/ch14/ch14-01
(base) binildass-MacBook-Pro:ch14-01-temp binil$ terraform
validate
Success! The configuration is valid.
```

```
(base) binildass-MacBook-Pro:ch14-01-temp binil$
```

The plan command lets you see what Terraform will do before making
any changes. Next, you can validate the Terraform plan, as shown in
Listing 14-12.

Listing 14-12. Terraform Plan

```
(base) binildass-MacBook-Pro:ch14-01-temp binil$ terraform plan
var.ami_id
  Enter a value: ami-061058b2c8f7fb264

var.ami_key_pair_name
  Enter a value: bdca-key-01

var.ami_name
  Enter a value: bdca-Instance-03
...
```

This is a nice way to sanity-check your code before attempting to create the actual infrastructure. Next you can go about applying the scripts. The apply command shows you the same plan output and asks you to confirm whether you want to proceed with this plan. See Listing 14-13.

Listing 14-13. Terraform Apply

```
(base) binildass-MacBook-Pro:005-aws-ec2-ssh binil$
terraform apply
var.ami_id
  Enter a value: ami-061058b2c8f7fb264

var.ami_key_pair_name
  Enter a value: bdca-key-01

var.ami_name
  Enter a value: bdca-Instance-03
...
Apply complete! Resources: 8 added, 0 changed, 0 destroyed.
(base) binildass-MacBook-Pro:005-aws-ec2-ssh binil$
```

Accessing Your EC2 in AWS Cloud Using SSH

Once your Compute infrastructure is created in AWS, you can access it using SSH. You can log in to the AWS console and inspect the newly created EC2 instance and get the public IP of it. Further, this example assumes that you have created a key pair in the Amazon EC2 console for the region where you plan to receive data.

If you plan to use an SSH client on a macOS or Linux computer to connect to your cloud instance, use the commands in Listing 14-14 to set the permissions of your private key file and then ssh to the instance.

Listing 14-14. Accessing AWS Cloud EC2 Using SSH

```
(base) binildass-MacBook-Pro:AWS binil$ ls
BDCA-01.pem    bdca-key-01.pem
(base) binildass-MacBook-Pro:AWS binil$ chmod 600 ./bdca-
key-01.pem
(base) binildass-MacBook-Pro:001-aws-ec2-ssh-http binil$ ssh -i
"/Users/binil/AWS/bdca-key-01.pem" ubuntu@ec2-13-228-93-93.ap-
southeast-1.compute.amazonaws.com
The authenticity of host 'ec2-13-228-93-93.ap-southeast-1.
compute.amazonaws.com (13.228.93.93)' can't be established.
ECDSA key fingerprint is SHA256:TK4sg3Pw8w1crRgI/KebZJ///
AavY8uSnKwZmFzqTJw.
Are you sure you want to continue connecting (yes/no)? yes
Warning: Permanently added 'ec2-13-228-93-93.ap-southeast-1.
compute.amazonaws.com,13.228.93.93' (ECDSA) to the list of
known hosts.
Welcome to Ubuntu 16.04.4 LTS (GNU/Linux 4.4.0-1114-aws x86_64)
...
ubuntu@ip-10-0-53-123:~$
```

You can next inspect if you have Java runtime in your EC2 instance, as shown in Listing 14-15.

Listing 14-15. Verifying Java Runtime in Your AWS Cloud EC2

```
ubuntu@ip-10-0-53-123:~$ java -version
java version "1.8.0_161"
Java(TM) SE Runtime Environment (build 1.8.0_161-b12)
Java HotSpot(TM) 64-Bit Server VM (build 25.161-b12,
mixed mode)
ubuntu@ip-10-0-53-123:~$ pwd
/home/ubuntu
ubuntu@ip-10-0-53-123:~$ ls
Nessus-7.0.2-ubuntu1110_amd64.deb
ubuntu@ip-10-0-53-123:~$
...
```

Installing JRE in AWS EC2

If you don't have Java by default, you can install it. Before that, update the software. Use the `sudo apt update` command, which is a Linux/ Debian system administration command that updates the list of available packages and their versions stored in the system's package index. See Listing 14-16.

Listing 14-16. Updating AWS Cloud EC2 packages

```
ubuntu@ip-10-0-53-123:~$ sudo apt update
...
```

Then install Java, as shown in Listing 14-17.

Listing 14-17. Installing JRE in AWS Cloud EC2

```
ubuntu@ip-10-0-53-123:~$ java -version
Command 'Java' not found, but can be installed with:
sudo apt install openjdk-11-jre-headless
sudo apt install default-jre
sudo apt install openjdk-17-jre-headless
sudo apt install openjdk-18-jre-headless
sudo apt install openjdk-19-jre-headless
sudo apt install openjdk-8-jre-headless
ubuntu@ip-10-0-53-123:~$ sudo apt install openjdk-17-
jre-headless
...
```

Now that you have successfully accessed the new server that you provisioned and set up with JRE in AWS Cloud, you can deploy your microservice in the cloud.

Deploying Microservice in AWS EC2

This example uses the simplest microservice in this book, found in ch01/ ch01-01/. Assuming that you built the microservice as shown in Listing 14-18 and the .jar file Ecom-Product-Web-Microservice-0.0.1-SNAPSHOT.jar is available in the ch01/ch01-01/target folder, you need to first upload this .jar file to the EC2 in AWS Cloud using the secure copy command.

Listing 14-18. Commands to Build the Microservice (from Listing 1-5)

```
mvn -Dmaven.test.skip=true clean package
java -jar -Dserver.port=8080 ./02-ProductWeb/target/Ecom-
Product-Web-Microservice-0.0.1-SNAPSHOT.jar
```

The next step is to copy the .jar file to the cloud.

Copy the Microservice Executable to the Cloud

You will now copy the microservice .jar file from your localhost to the
AWS EC2 instance, as shown in Listing 14-19.

Listing 14-19. Upload Microservice Jar File to the Cloud EC2
Using scp

```
(base) binildass-MacBook-Pro:target binil$ pwd
/Users/binil/binil/code/mac/mybooks/docker-03/ch01/
ch01-01/target
(base) binildass-MacBook-Pro:target binil$ scp -i "/Users/
binil/AWS/bdca-key-01.pem" /Users/binil/binil/code/mac/mybooks/
docker-03/ch01/ch01-01/02-ProductWeb/target/Ecom-Product-Web-
Microservice-0.0.1-SNAPSHOT.jar ubuntu@ec2-13-228-93-93.ap-
southeast-1.compute.amazonaws.com:/home/ubuntu/
Ecom-Product-Web-Microservice-0.0.1-SNAPSHOT.jar
    100%   20MB   1.6MB/s   00:12
(base) binildass-MacBook-Pro:target binil$
```

Once the microservice .jar file is copied to the cloud, you can run the
Microservice.

Run the Microservice

Since you have the microservice .jar file, you can use Java to run the
application. See Listing 14-20.

Listing 14-20. Run the Microservice in EC2 in AWS

```
ubuntu@ip-10-0-53-123:~$ pwd
/home/ubuntu
ubuntu@ip-10-0-53-123:~$ ls
```

Ecom-Product-Web-Microservice-0.0.1-SNAPSHOT.jar Nessus-7.0.2-
ubuntu1110_amd64.deb
ubuntu@ip-10-0-53-123:~$ java -jar -Dserver.port=8080 ./Ecom-
Product-Web-Microservice-0.0.1-SNAPSHOT.jar

```
  .   ____          _            __ _ _
 /\\ / ___'_ __ _ _(_)_ __  __ _ \ \ \ \
( ( )\___ | '_ | '_| | '_ \/ _` | \ \ \ \
 \\/  ___)| |_)| | | | | || (_| |  ) ) ) )
  '  |____| ._|_| |_|_| |_\__, | / / / /
 =========|_|==============|___/=/_/_/_/
 :: Spring Boot ::                (v3.2.0)
```

2021-07-03 00:38:41 INFO StartupInfoLogger.logStarting:55 -
Starting EcomProductMicroserviceApplication v0.0.1-SNAPSHOT
using Java 1.8.0_161 on ip-10-0-53-123 with PID 4892 (/home/
ubuntu/Ecom-Product-Web-Microservice-0.0.1-SNAPSHOT.jar started
by ubuntu in /home/ubuntu)
2021-07-03 00:38:41 DEBUG StartupInfoLogger.logStarting:56 -
Running with Spring Boot v2.4.4, Spring v5.3.5
2021-07-03 00:38:41 INFO SpringApplication.
logStartupProfileInfo:662 - No active profile set, falling back
to default profiles: default
2021-07-03 00:38:46 INFO InitializationComponent.
init:58 - Start
2021-07-03 00:38:46 DEBUG InitializationComponent.init:60 -
Doing Nothing...
2021-07-03 00:38:46 INFO InitializationComponent.init:62 - End
2021-07-03 00:38:49 INFO StartupInfoLogger.logStarted:61 -
Started EcomProductMicroserviceApplication in 9.914 seconds
(JVM running for 12.273)

```
2021-07-03 00:41:09 INFO  ProductRestController.
getAllProducts:84 - Start
2021-07-03 00:41:09 DEBUG ProductRestController.
lambda$getAllProducts$0:94 - Product [productId=1, name=Kamsung
D3, code=KAMSUNG-TRIOS, title=Kamsung Trios 12 inch ,
black , 12 px ...., description=, imgUrl=, price=12000.0,
productCategoryName=]
2021-07-03 00:41:09 DEBUG ProductRestController.
lambda$getAllProducts$0:94 - Product [productId=2,
name=Lokia Pomia, code=LOKIA-POMIA, title=Lokia 12 inch ,
white , 14px ...., description=, imgUrl=, price=9000.0,
productCategoryName=]
2021-07-03 00:41:09 INFO  ProductRestController.
getAllProducts:95 - Ending
...
```

You can see from the log that the application is built and deployed and is in the running state. You can now test the application.

Test the Microservice Using UI

Once the microservice is up, you can access the web application using your browser and pointing to the public URL of your EC2:

```
http://ec2-13-228-93-93.ap-southeast-1.compute.amazonaws.
com:8080/product.html
```

Refer to the section titled "Test the Microservice Using UI" in Chapter 1 to test the Product Web microservice.

Once the testing is complete, you can destroy the cloud infrastructure using the terraform destroy command, as shown in Listing 14-21.

Listing 14-21. Releasing AWS Resources

```
(base) binildass-MacBook-Pro:ch14-01 binil$ pwd
/Users/binil/binil/code/mac/mybooks/docker-04/Code/ch14/ch14-01
(base) binildass-MacBook-Pro:ch14-01-temp binil$
terraform destroy
...
```

Summary

From the starting chapter of this book up to the previous chapter, you
have traveled from the simplest of microservices to Docker containers and
Kubernetes. You have seen multiple, non-trivial design patterns, including
NoSQL and messaging brokers. In this chapter, you used IaC to provision
an EC2 in AWS Cloud. You also deployed the microservice example
from the first chapter in the EC2 and accessed it from your host machine
through the Internet. This is a good start, and you can now try to deploy
many of these examples from other chapters in the cloud. What is left is
Containers and Orchestration in the cloud, which is covered in the next
chapter.

## CHAPTER 15

Microservices in AWS Elastic Kubernetes Service

You learned in the previous chapter how to create a minimal compute infrastructure in AWS using the IaC tool Terraform. In this chapter, you extend that knowledge by setting up a Kubernetes-based infrastructure using the same toolset. You have already seen how a single-node Kubernetes based on Minikube enables you to run all the examples in this book up to the previous chapter. Now you will attempt to deploy those microservices in a multi-node Kubernetes-based infrastructure on the AWS cloud.

This chapter covers the following concepts:

- Elastic Kubernetes Service (EKS)

- Setting up an AWS EKS using Terraform

- Running microservice containers in AWS EKS

© Binildas A. Christudas 2024
B. A. Christudas, *Java Microservices and Containers in the Cloud,*
https://doi.org/10.1007/979-8-8688-0555-4_15

The Amazon Elastic Kubernetes Service

Amazon Elastic Kubernetes Service (Amazon EKS) runs the Kubernetes management infrastructure across Availability Zones. Applications running on any standard Kubernetes environment are fully compatible and can be migrated to Amazon EKS, so this chapter demonstrates how the microservices you deployed in Minikube can be deployed in EKS in AWS.

Amazon EKS cluster consists of two primary components—the EKS control plane and the EKS worker nodes.

EKS Control Plane

The EKS control plane consists of nodes that run the Kubernetes software, such as etcd and the Kubernetes API server. (Refer to Chapter 10 for an overview of these components.) The control plane runs in an account managed by AWS, and the Kubernetes API is exposed via the Amazon EKS endpoint associated with your cluster. Each Amazon EKS cluster control plane runs on its own set of Amazon EC2 instances. These control plane nodes are also provisioned across multiple Availability Zones and fronted by an Elastic Load Balancing Network Load Balancer. Amazon EKS also provisions elastic network interfaces in your VPC subnets to provide connectivity from the control plane instances to the nodes.

EKS Worker Nodes

EKS worker nodes are part of the Kubernetes cluster, where the user's workload is processed. Amazon EKS worker nodes are created in your AWS account, and they establish a connection to your cluster's control plane instance running in an AWS managed account. Amazon EKS worker nodes are registered with the control plane.

As of this writing, a related solution called Amazon EKS Blueprints was introduced. However, Amazon EKS still works.

Setting Up AWS EKS Using Terraform

This section illustrates a working demonstration of an AWS EKS based microservices deployment. This chapter is built over the fundamentals of AWS Cloud, which you learned about in Chapter 14, so you are advised to refer to Chapter 14 prior to reading this chapter. This chapter will also leverage Terraform, so that it is relatively easy for you to set up the infrastructure and run the examples. If you are already familiar with AWS Cloud and Terraform, you can read this chapter without referring back to Chapter 14.

Since this example uses Terraform to create an EKS compute infrastructure in AWS, I assume that you have the following prerequisites on your development machine:

- An AWS account that you know how to manage using the AWS web console

- AWS CLI (Command Line Interface) installed and the terminal configured with secret keys to access the AWS account

- A key pair to access your EC2 instances

- Terraform installed

I don't cover those aspects in this book. If you aren't familiar with these steps, you are advised to refer to an appropriate book.[1] Appendix F also provides some guidance for using a few of these tools.

Designing an EKS Topology in an AWS Cloud

You will have a very minimal EKS cluster in an AWS cloud (see Figure 15-1). Even though the intention is to set up a minimal EKS infrastructure, note that you also need a full set of compute and network

---

[1] *Programming Amazon EC2,* O'Reilly Media; ISBN-13: 978-1449393687.

infrastructures for this, which is nontrivial. Thanks to Terraform, which makes even such nontrivial tasks accessible to developers like you and me, as you learned in the previous chapter.

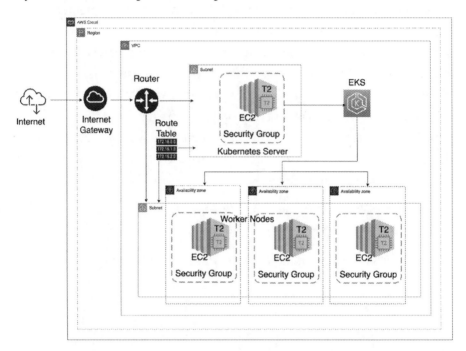

Figure 15-1. *EKS cluster in an AWS cloud*

A typical EKS cluster is shown in Figure 15-1. However, note that, for the Kubernetes server you could have redundancy by having multiple nodes. Even though the diagram depicts three nodes for the worker cluster, this example will be a customized one to keep the infrastructure simple.

Let's get into the code now. Let's start by investigating the project structure.

Code Organization

The source code for this book is available on GitHub via the book's product page, located at www.apress.com/9798868805547. The source code for this example is organized as shown in Listing 15-1, inside the ch15\ ch15-01 folder.

Listing 15-1. Terraform EKS Project Source Code Organization

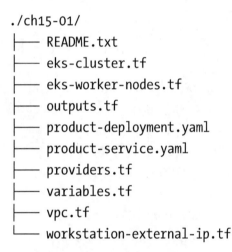

```
./ch15-01/
├── README.txt
├── eks-cluster.tf
├── eks-worker-nodes.tf
├── outputs.tf
├── product-deployment.yaml
├── product-service.yaml
├── providers.tf
├── variables.tf
├── vpc.tf
└── workstation-external-ip.tf
```

Chapter 14 showed the contents of a few of these files. In addition, you adapted a few new files from the EKS example provided on the Terraform website to create this demonstration. Let's investigate the new aspects in this example.

Understanding the Source Code

Start with the first step of selecting which cloud provider you want to use. See Listing 15-2.

Listing 15-2. AWS Region Configuration (ch15/ch15-01/ providers.tf)

```
terraform {
  required_version = ">= 0.12"
}
provider "aws" {
  region = var.aws_region
}
data "aws_availability_zones" "available" {}
provider "http" {}
```

After specifying the Terraform version, you have to mention that you intend to use aws as the cloud provider. I am using ap-southeast-1, which is the Singapore region, but you may use whichever region you prefer.

The Availability Zones data source allows access to the list of AWS Availability Zones that can be accessed by an AWS account in the region configured in the provider.

The HTTP provider is used to interact with generic HTTP servers. It provides a data source that issues an HTTP request exposing the response headers and a body for use within a Terraform deployment. You use this HTTP provider to determine your own external IP gateway address (see Listing 15-3). If you have that, you can configure inbound EC2 Security Group access to the Kubernetes cluster. You'll do that in the next descriptor.

Listing 15-3. Discover External IP Gateway Address (ch15/ch15-01/ workstation-external-ip.tf)

```
data "http" "workstation-external-ip" {
  url = "http://ipv4.icanhazip.com"
}
```

```
locals {
  workstation-external-cidr = "${chomp(data.http.workstation-
  external-ip.body)}/32"
}
```

As you can guess, this example overrides in the runtime the value of
workstation-external-cidr with the value of the external IP gateway
address. Assuming you want the external IP gateway address, you'll need
to either determine it from the gateway device manually or ask an external
service. icanhazip.com is one such service that can show your Internet-
facing IPv4 and IPv6 addresses, among other things.

There are a couple of ways to use this service:

- In a configuration file, point to (http://)ipv4.
  icanhazip.com (or ipv6 if you need that).

- In a script, get the address using curl like this: echo
  This external IP address is $(curl -s http://ipv4.
  icanhazip.com).

Before you proceed, you need to configure the region = var.aws_
region in the variables configuration. See Listing 15-4.

Listing 15-4. Terraform Variables Configuration (ch15/ch15-01/
variables.tf)

```
variable "aws_region" {
  default = "ap-southeast-1"
}
variable "cluster-name" {
  default = "bdca-tf-eks-01"
  type    = string
}
```

That is self-explanatory.

You started with the provider as AWS, now you'll investigate the network infrastructure definitions. See Listing 15-5.

Listing 15-5. Terraform EKS Network Infrastructure Configuration (ch15/ch15-01/vpc.tf)

```
resource "aws_vpc" "demo" {
  cidr_block = "10.0.0.0/16"

  tags = tomap(
    {"Name" = "terraform-eks-demo-node",
    "kubernetes.io/cluster/${var.cluster-name}" = "shared"}
  )
}

resource "aws_subnet" "demo" {
  count = 2

  availability_zone        = data.aws_availability_zones.
                             available.names[count.index]
  cidr_block               = "10.0.${count.index}.0/24"
  map_public_ip_on_launch  = true
  vpc_id                   = aws_vpc.demo.id

  tags = tomap(
    {"Name" = "terraform-eks-demo-node",
    "kubernetes.io/cluster/${var.cluster-name}" = "shared"}
  )
}

resource "aws_internet_gateway" "demo" {
  vpc_id = aws_vpc.demo.id
```

```
  tags = {
    Name = "terraform-eks-demo"
  }
}

resource "aws_route_table" "demo" {
  vpc_id = aws_vpc.demo.id

  route {
    cidr_block = "0.0.0.0/0"
    gateway_id = aws_internet_gateway.demo.id
  }
}

resource "aws_route_table_association" "demo" {
  count = 2

  subnet_id      = aws_subnet.demo.*.id[count.index]
  route_table_id = aws_route_table.demo.id
}
```

Refer to Chapter 14 for a detailed explanation of many of these configurations.

There are a few new aspects, which I explain here.

This specification will create a 10.0.0.0/16 VPC, two 10.0.X.0/24 subnets, and an Internet gateway, and it will set up the subnet routing to route external traffic through the Internet gateway.

The count = 2 is a meta-argument in Terraform. It can be used with modules and with every resource type. The count meta-argument accepts a whole number and creates that many instances of the resource or module. Each instance has a distinct infrastructure object associated with it, and each is separately created, updated, or destroyed when the configuration is applied. The intention is to create two subnets.

In blocks where count is set, an additional count object is available in expressions, so you can modify the configuration of each instance. This object has one attribute:

- count.index: The distinct index number (starting with 0) corresponding to this instance.

You are using the count = 2 as a meta-argument in the aws_subnet demo resource and in the aws_route_table_association demo resource. In the first case, you are using count.index to specify the cidr_block and in the second case, you are using count.index to specify the subnet_id for the route table association.

Now comes the cluster and worker specifications. First the cluster description. The cluster in Amazon EKS can be configured in Terraform with the resource name aws_eks_cluster. See Listing 15-6.

Listing 15-6. Terraform EKS Cluster Configuration (ch15/ch15-01/eks-cluster.tf)

```
resource "aws_iam_role" "demo-cluster" {
  name = "terraform-eks-demo-cluster"

  assume_role_policy = <<POLICY
{
  "Version": "2012-10-17",
  "Statement": [
    {
      "Effect": "Allow",
      "Principal": {
        "Service": "eks.amazonaws.com"
      },
      "Action": "sts:AssumeRole"
    }
  ]
```

```
}
POLICY
}

resource "aws_iam_role_policy_attachment" "demo-cluster-
AmazonEKSClusterPolicy" {
  policy_arn = "arn:aws:iam::aws:policy/AmazonEKSClusterPolicy"
  role       = aws_iam_role.demo-cluster.name
}

resource "aws_iam_role_policy_attachment" "demo-cluster-
AmazonEKSVPCResourceController" {
  policy_arn = "arn:aws:iam::aws:policy/
  AmazonEKSVPCResourceController"
  role       = aws_iam_role.demo-cluster.name
}

resource "aws_security_group" "demo-cluster" {
  name        = "terraform-eks-demo-cluster"
  description = "Cluster communication with worker nodes"
  vpc_id      = aws_vpc.demo.id

  egress {
    from_port   = 0
    to_port     = 0
    protocol    = "-1"
    cidr_blocks = ["0.0.0.0/0"]
  }

  tags = {
    Name = "terraform-eks-demo"
  }
}
```

```
resource "aws_security_group_rule" "demo-cluster-ingress-
workstation-https" {
  cidr_blocks       = [local.workstation-external-cidr]
  description       = "Allow workstation to communicate with
                      cluster API Server"
  from_port         = 443
  protocol          = "tcp"
  security_group_id = aws_security_group.demo-cluster.id
  to_port           = 443
  type              = "ingress"
}

resource "aws_eks_cluster" "demo" {
  name     = var.cluster-name
  role_arn = aws_iam_role.demo-cluster.arn

  vpc_config {
    security_group_ids = [aws_security_group.demo-cluster.id]
    subnet_ids         = aws_subnet.demo[*].id
  }

  depends_on = [
    aws_iam_role_policy_attachment.demo-cluster-
    AmazonEKSClusterPolicy,
    aws_iam_role_policy_attachment.demo-cluster-AmazonEKSVPC
    ResourceController,
  ]
}
```

The security group of worker nodes and the security group that handles the communication of the worker nodes with the control plane have been constructed in a way to avoid communication via the privileged ports in the worker nodes.

You need a few operator-managed resources beforehand so that Kubernetes can properly manage other AWS services and allow inbound networking communication from your local workstation (if desired) and worker nodes.

`aws_iam_role` and `aws_iam_role_policy_attachment` are required to allow the EKS service to manage or retrieve data from other AWS services.

`aws_security_group` controls networking access to the Kubernetes masters. You then configure this with an `ingress` rule to allow traffic from the worker nodes. In both `egress` and `ingress`, you specify the protocol. Here, the IP protocol name (`tcp`, `udp`, `icmp`) or number for the protocol can be used. When you specify -1 in the `egress`, or when you specify a protocol number other than `tcp`, `udp`, `icmp`, or 58 (ICMPv6), traffic on all ports is allowed, regardless of any ports you specify. For `tcp`, `udp`, and `icmp`, you must specify a port range. For protocol 58 (ICMPv6), you can optionally specify a port range. If you don't specify anything, traffic of all types and codes is allowed.

`aws_security_group_rule` allows the worker nodes networking access to the EKS master cluster.

Next is the worker nodes configuration. AWS EKS does not currently provide managed resources for running worker nodes. Hence, you need to create a few operator-managed resources so that Kubernetes can properly manage other AWS services, networking access, and so on.

Listing 15-7. Terraform EKS Worker Configuration (ch15/ch15-01/ eks-worker-nodes.tf)

```
resource "aws_iam_role" "demo-node" {
  name = "terraform-eks-demo-node"

  assume_role_policy = <<POLICY
{
  "Version": "2012-10-17",
  "Statement": [
```

```
    {
      "Effect": "Allow",
      "Principal": {
        "Service": "ec2.amazonaws.com"
      },
      "Action": "sts:AssumeRole"
    }
  ]
}
POLICY
}

resource "aws_iam_role_policy_attachment" "demo-node-
AmazonEKSWorkerNodePolicy" {
  policy_arn = "arn:aws:iam::aws:policy/
               AmazonEKSWorkerNodePolicy"
  role       = aws_iam_role.demo-node.name
}

resource "aws_iam_role_policy_attachment" "demo-node-AmazonEKS_
CNI_Policy" {
  policy_arn = "arn:aws:iam::aws:policy/AmazonEKS_CNI_Policy"
  role       = aws_iam_role.demo-node.name
}

resource "aws_iam_role_policy_attachment" "demo-node-AmazonEC2C
ontainerRegistryReadOnly" {
  policy_arn = "arn:aws:iam::aws:policy/
               AmazonEC2ContainerRegistryReadOnly"
  role       = aws_iam_role.demo-node.name
}
```

```
resource "aws_eks_node_group" "demo" {
  cluster_name    = aws_eks_cluster.demo.name
  node_group_name = "demo"
  node_role_arn   = aws_iam_role.demo-node.arn
  subnet_ids      = aws_subnet.demo[*].id

  scaling_config {
    desired_size = 1
    max_size     = 1
    min_size     = 1
  }

  depends_on = [
    aws_iam_role_policy_attachment.demo-node-
    AmazonEKSWorkerNodePolicy,
    aws_iam_role_policy_attachment.demo-node-AmazonEKS_
    CNI_Policy,
    aws_iam_role_policy_attachment.demo-node-AmazonEC2Container
    RegistryReadOnly,
  ]
}
```

As stated earlier, you are running with a minimal number in the scaling configuration even though in production deployments you may want to have three or more nodes for high availability. The aws_eks_node_group resource will manages an EKS node group, which can provision and optionally update an auto-scaling group of Kubernetes worker nodes compatible with EKS.

The aws_iam_role and policy will allow the worker nodes to manage or retrieve data from other AWS services. It is used by Kubernetes to allow worker nodes to join the cluster.

Setups Required to Operate an EKS Cluster

There are a few setups that come in handy when managing and operating an EKS. I list them here. You may also refer to Appendix F to see a few of these setups in detail.

You are advised to do the following:

1. Install AWS CLI.

2. Install AWS IAM Authenticator.

3. Configure kunectl for EKS.

4. Join the worker nodes to the Kubernetes cluster.

Start by completing the first two steps. Subsequently you may complete the next subsection titled "Build and Spin Your EKS Cluster in AWS," and once the EKS cluster is formed, you can execute the last two steps.

Build and Spin Your EKS Cluster in AWS

To form an EKS cluster in AWS, you need to go to the root folder ch15\ ch15-01 and run the terraform init command first. See Listing 15-8.

Listing 15-8. Terraform init

```
(base) binildass-MacBook-Pro:ch15-01 binil$ pwd
/Users/binil/binil/code/mac/mybooks/docker-04/Code/ch15/ch15-01
(base) binildass-MacBook-Pro:ch15-01 binil$ terraform init

Initializing the backend...
...
(base) binildass-MacBook-Pro:ch15-01 binil$
```

You then sanity check your code. See Listing 15-9.

Listing 15-9. Terraform validate

```
(base) binildass-MacBook-Pro:ch15-01 binil$ pwd
/Users/binil/binil/code/mac/mybooks/docker-04/Code/ch15/ch15-01
(base) binildass-MacBook-Pro:ch15-01 binil$ terraform validate
Success! The configuration is valid.

(base) binildass-MacBook-Pro:ch15-01 binil$
```

The plan command lets you see what Terraform will do before making any changes, as shown in Listing 15-10.

Listing 15-10. Terraform plan

```
(base) binildass-MacBook-Pro:ch15-01 binil$ terraform plan
```

The apply command shows you the same plan output and asks you to confirm whether you want to proceed with this plan, as shown in Listing 15-11.

Listing 15-11. Terraform apply

```
(base) binildass-MacBook-Pro:001-aws-eks-tf binil$
terraform apply
aws_eks_node_group.demo: Creation complete after 2m12s
[id=bdca-tf-eks-01:demo]

Apply complete! Resources: 18 added, 0 changed, 0 destroyed.

Outputs:

config_map_aws_auth = <<EOT
apiVersion: v1
kind: ConfigMap
...
EOT
(base) binildass-MacBook-Pro:001-aws-eks-tf binil$
```

You can now apply the commands mentioned previously in Steps 3 and 4 (configure kunectl for EKS and Join the worker nodes to Kubernetes cluster). Then watch the status of your nodes and wait for them to reach the Ready status. Refer to Appendix F for more information.

Deploying Containers in AWS EKS

This example uses a relatively simple microservice you have seen in this book, from ch01/ch01-01/. I assume that you have executed the required commands, in Listings 7-41 through 7-43 in Chapter 7, and that you already have the binildas/product-web image in the public Docker Hub.

You will use this image in Docker Hub and deploy it to the AWS EKS.

Note   This example assumes that kubectl is configured for the EKS cluster.

You might have noticed that product-deployment.yaml and product-service.yaml are already in the EKS terraform project root folder ch15/ch15-01/. They are shown in Listings 15-12 and 15-13.

Listing 15-12. Product Web Microservice Deployment Description (ch15/ch15-01/product-deployment.yaml)

```
apiVersion: apps/v1
kind: Deployment
metadata:
  name: product-deployment
  labels:
    app: product
spec:
  replicas: 1
```

```
selector:
  matchLabels:
    app: product
template:
  metadata:
    labels:
      app: product
  spec:
    containers:
    - name: product
      image: binildas/product-web
      ports:
      - containerPort: 8080
```

Listing 15-13. Product Web Microservice Service Description
(ch15/ch15-01/product-service.yaml)

```
apiVersion: v1
kind: Service
metadata:
  name: product-service-loadbalancer
spec:
  type: LoadBalancer
  selector:
    app: product
  ports:
    - protocol: TCP
      port: 8080
      targetPort: 8080
```

You can now deploy the specified microservice, as shown in
Listing 15-14.

Listing 15-14. Deploying a Product Web Microservice Image into EKS (ch15/ch15-01/product-deployment.yaml)

```
(base) binildass-MBP:ch15-01 binil$ kubectl get pods -l
'app=nginx' -o wide | awk {'print $1" " $3 " " $6'} | column -t
No resources found in default namespace.
(base) binildass-MBP:ch15-01 binil$ kubectl get pods -l
'app=product' -o wide | awk {'print $1" " $3 " " $6'} |
column -t
No resources found in default namespace.
(base) binildass-MBP:ch15-01 binil$ kubectl apply -f product-
deployment.yaml
deployment.apps/product-deployment created
(base) binildass-MBP:ch15-01 binil$ kubectl get pods -l
'app=product' -o wide | awk {'print $1" " $3 " " $6'} |
column -t
NAME                                  STATUS              IP
product-deployment-84b9777c5-9kpz8  ContainerCreating  <none>
(base) binildass-MBP:ch15-01 binil$ kubectl get pods -l
'app=product' -o wide | awk {'print $1" " $3 " " $6'} |
column -t
NAME                                  STATUS    IP
product-deployment-84b9777c5-9kpz8  Running   10.0.0.180
(base) binildass-MBP:ch15-01 binil$
```

As shown in Listing 15-14, you first assert that you don't have any valid deployments in your newly formed EKS and subsequently deploy the new container. Once the deployment is ready, you can then deploy the service definition. See Listing 15-15.

Listing 15-15. Exposing Product Web Microservice Service in EKS (ch15/ch15-01/product-service.yaml)

```
(base) binildass-MBP:ch15-01 binil$ kubectl get svc
NAME         TYPE         CLUSTER-IP    EXTERNAL-IP   PORT(S)    AGE
kubernetes   ClusterIP    172.20.0.1    <none>        443/TCP    11m
(base) binildass-MBP:ch15-01 binil$ kubectl create -f product-
service.yaml
service/product-service-loadbalancer created
(base) binildass-MBP:ch15-01 binil$ kubectl get svc
NAME                            TYPE            CLUSTER-IP
EXTERNAL-IP            PORT(S)            AGE
kubernetes                      ClusterIP       172.20.0.1
<none>                443/TCP            12m
product-service-loadbalancer    LoadBalancer    172.20.15.199
a2473f05176a6444bb676cf3927fd363-1434093128.ap-southeast-1.elb.
amazonaws.com           8080:32087/TCP     49s
(base) binildass-MBP:ch15-01 binil$
```

Once all is set, you are ready to test the example. You can also view the EKS console using the appropriate URL formation, which in my case is as follows:

```
https://ap-southeast-1.console.aws.amazon.com/eks/
home?region=ap-southeast-1#/clusters
```

Testing the Microservice in EKS

Once the microservice is up in the EKS cluster in the AWS Cloud, you can access the web application by using your browser. Point to the application URL, which you can determine from the AWS UI console.

You can test the microservice using the URL in Listing 15-16 in a browser.

Listing 15-16. Testing the Service in EKS Using a Browser

```
http://a2473f05176a6444bb676cf3927fd363-1434093128.ap-
southeast-1.elb.amazonaws.com:8080/product.html
```

You can also test the service using cURL, as shown in Listing 15-17.

Listing 15-17. Testing the Service in EKS Using cURL

```
(base) binildass-MBP:ch15-01 binil$ curl -silent http://
a2473f05176a6444bb676cf3927fd363-1434093128.ap-southeast-1.elb.
amazonaws.com:8080/product.html | grep title
<title>Bootstrap CRUD Data Table for Database with Modal
Form</title>
    .table-title {
    .table-title h2 {
    .table-title .btn-group {
    .table-title .btn {
    .table-title .btn i {
    .table-title .btn span {
    .modal .modal-title {
            <div class="table-title">
                        <td><span ng-bind="p.title">
                        </span></td>
                            data-toggle="tooltip"
                            title="Edit">&#xE254;
                            </i></a> <a
                            class="material-icons"
                            data-toggle="tooltip"
                            title="Delete" ng-click=
                            "openDeleteForm(p)">
                            &#xE872;</i></a>
                    <h4 class="modal-title">Product
                    Details</h4>
```

```
                <textarea class="form-control" ng-
                model="product.title" required>
                </textarea>
                <h4 class="modal-title">Delete
                Product</h4>
(base) binildass-MBP:ch15-01 binil$
```

Note   Do not forget to release the AWS resources once your testing is finished, because unreleased resources might drain your credit card!

Once the testing is complete, you can destroy the cloud infrastructure using the terraform destroy command, as in Listing 15-18.

Listing 15-18. Releasing AWS Resources

```
(base) binildass-MacBook-Pro:ch15-01 binil$ pwd
/Users/binil/binil/code/mac/mybooks/docker-04/Code/ch15/ch15-01
(base) binildass-MacBook-Pro:ch15-01 binil$ terraform destroy
...
```

Summary

Every end is a new beginning. You have reached the end of this book; however, you have just started your microservices and cloud journey. I demystified a few dilemmas around architecture choices and investigated many details. You started with the simplest microservice example in Chapter 1, and as you pause your journey in Chapter 15, you have even deployed this microservice container to EKS in the cloud.

I hope you have enjoyed many parts of this book in the same way I have enjoyed getting into the intricacies of the code to explain them. I have tried to balance theory with code to give you a hands-on feel of almost all the concepts explained. Frameworks will come and go, and specifications will keep evolving, since "change is the only constant thing." However, the architectural foundations discussed throughout the book will still be relevant and valid—at least that is what I have experienced in my 25-plus years in IT. Keep moving and keep a fast pace.

APPENDIX A

Using cURL and Postman

cURL is a command-line tool for getting or sending files using the URL syntax. cURL supports a range of common Internet protocols, including HTTP, HTTPS, FTP, FTPS, SCP, SFTP, TFTP, and LDAP, out of which HTTP is of interest for the discussions in different chapters in this book.

Postman is an API platform for building and using APIs. Postman simplifies each step of the API lifecycle.

The "Build Your First Java Microservice" section in Chapter 1 introduced an example Spring Boot application. You used Spring Data REST to create implementations of a simple in-memory database repository. Then Spring Boot directed Spring MVC to create RESTful endpoints at /productsweb. For this appendix, you need to build that example and have it up and running. That way, you can perform the basic operations of cURL and Postman.

The following concepts are covered in this appendix:

- How to use cURL for HTTP operations

- How to use Postman for HTTP operations

© Binildas A. Christudas 2024
B. A. Christudas, *Java Microservices and Containers in the Cloud*,
https://doi.org/10.1007/979-8-8688-0555-4

cURL Operations for HTTP

Basic cURL operations involve typing `curl` at the command line, followed by the URL pointing to the output to retrieve it. For example, to retrieve the apple.com home page, you type:

```
curl https://www.apple.com/
```

cURL defaults to displaying the output it retrieves from the URL to the standard output specified on the system, normally the terminal window (on the Mac). So running this command will, on most systems, display www.apple.com's source code of the web page in the terminal window.

The next section looks at executing the main HTTP actions using cURL.

Using HTTP GET to Retrieve an Entity

HTTP GET can be used to retrieve contents from an URL, as shown in Listing A-1.

Listing A-1. cURL HTTP GET

```
binildass-MacBook-Pro:~ binil$ curl http://localhost:8080/
productsweb
[{"productId":"1","name":"Kamsung D3","code":"KAMSUNG-TRIOS",
"title":"Kamsung Trios 12 inch , black , 12 px ....",
"price":12000.0},{"productId":"2","name":"Lokia Pomia",
"code":"LOKIA-POMIA","title":"Lokia 12 inch , white ,
14px ....","price":9000.0}]
binildass-MacBook-Pro:~ binil$
```

Assuming the Spring Boot example titled "Build Your First Java Microservice" from Chapter 1 is up and running, you will see the terminal output representing the entities retrieved, as shown in Listing A-1.

Using HTTP POST to Create an Entity

You can now create a new product entity using HTTP POST, as shown in Listing A-2.

Listing A-2. cURL HTTP POST

```
binildass-MacBook-Pro:~ binil$ curl -i -X POST -H "Content-
Type:application/json" -d '{"productId":"3","name":"Mapple
J-Phone","code":"MAPPLE-J-PHONE","title":"Mapple Smart Phone,
black , 20 px ....","price":30000.0}' http://localhost:8080/
productsweb
HTTP/1.1 200
Vary: Origin
Vary: Access-Control-Request-Method
Vary: Access-Control-Request-Headers
Content-Type: application/json
Transfer-Encoding: chunked
Date: Wed, 13 Dec 2023 09:02:34 GMT

{"productId":"3","name":"Mapple J-Phone","code":"MAPPLE-
J-PHONE","title":"Mapple Smart Phone, black , 20 px
....","price":30000.0}
binildass-MacBook-Pro:~ binil$
```

Here are the meanings of the options provided in HTTP POST:

- -i indicates that you need to see the response message including the headers. The URI of the newly created person is also shown.

- -X POST signals that this is a POST used to create a new entry.

- `-H "Content-Type:application/json"` hints at the content type, so the application expects the payload to contain a JSON object.

- `-d '{"productId":"3","name":"Mapple J-Phone","code":"MAPPLE-J-PHONE","title": "Mapple Smart Phone, black , 20 px ....", "price":30000.0}'` is the data being sent, in JSON format in this case.

If you run into trouble when you copy these commands across platforms (from Windows to Linux or Mac, etc.), you may want to type them into the terminal window directly using the keyboard.

Using HTTP PUT to Replace an Entity

If you want to replace an entire group, use HTTP PUT. The server may opt to create a new group and throw the old one out, so the IDs may stay the same. But the client should assume that they will get an entirely new item, based on the server's response.

In the case of a PUT request, the client should always send the entire resource, therefore having all the data needed to create a new item, as shown in Listing A-3.

Listing A-3. cURL HTTP PUT

```
binildass-MacBook-Pro:~ binil$ curl -i -X PUT -H "Content-
Type:application/json" -d '{"productId":"3", "name":"Giomi-
New", "code":"GIOME-KL-NEW", "title":"Giome New 10 inch gold",
"price":33000.0}' http://localhost:8080/productsweb/3
HTTP/1.1 200
Vary: Origin
Vary: Access-Control-Request-Method
```

```
Vary: Access-Control-Request-Headers
Content-Type: application/json
Transfer-Encoding: chunked
Date: Wed, 13 Dec 2023 09:07:14 GMT
```

```
{"productId":"3","name":"Giomi-New","code":"GIOME-KL-
NEW","title":"Giome New 10 inch gold","price":33000.0}
binildass-MacBook-Pro:~
```

You can query and see the changes you made via the code in Listing A-4 using the HTTP GET method you saw earlier.

Listing A-4. cURL HTTP GET

```
binildass-MacBook-Pro:~ binil$ curl http://localhost:8080/
productsweb
[{"productId":"1","name":"Kamsung D3","code":"KAMSUNG-
TRIOS","title":"Kamsung Trios 12 inch , black , 12 px
....","price":12000.0},{"productId":"2","name":"Lokia
Pomia","code":"LOKIA-POMIA","title":"Lokia 12 inch , white
, 14px ....","price":9000.0},{"productId":"3","name":"Gio
mi-New","code":"GIOME-KL-NEW","title":"Giome New 10 inch
gold","price":33000.0}]
binildass-MacBook-Pro:~ binil$
```

Using HTTP PATCH to Modify an Entity

If you want to update an attribute, such as price, that is an attribute of a group that can be set, use PATCH. An attribute such as status is often a good candidate to limit to a whitelist of values, but in Listing A-5 you use PATCH on the price attribute.

Listing A-5. cURL HTTP PATCH

```
binildass-MacBook-Pro:~ binil$ curl -i -X PATCH -H "Content-
Type:application/json" -d '{"productId":"3", "price":33300.0}'
http://localhost:8080/productsweb/3
HTTP/1.1 200
Vary: Origin
Vary: Access-Control-Request-Method
Vary: Access-Control-Request-Headers
Content-Type: application/json
Transfer-Encoding: chunked
Date: Wed, 13 Dec 2023 10:32:06 GMT

{"productId":"3","name":"Giomi-New","code":"GIOME-KL-
NEW","title":"Giome New 10 inch gold","price":33300.0}
binildass-MacBook-Pro:~ binil$
```

You can again query and see the changes you made via the code in Listing A-6.

Listing A-6. cURL HTTP GET

```
binildass-MacBook-Pro:~ binil$ curl http://localhost:8080/
productsweb/3
{"productId":"3","name":"Giomi-New","code":"GIOME-KL-
NEW","title":"Giome New 10 inch gold","price":33300.0}
binildass-MacBook-Pro:~ binil$
```

As you can verify, the ID of the entity remains the same, with changes in the values of some of the other attributes, which is what I mean by modifying an entity.

Using HTTP DELETE to Delete an Entity

HTTP DELETE can be used to delete the entity, as shown in Listing A-7.

Listing A-7. cURL HTTP DELETE

```
binildass-MacBook-Pro:~ binil$ curl -i -X DELETE http://
localhost:8080/productsweb/3
HTTP/1.1 204
Vary: Origin
Vary: Access-Control-Request-Method
Vary: Access-Control-Request-Headers
Date: Wed, 13 Dec 2023 10:36:07 GMT
binildass-MacBook-Pro:~ binil$
```

Postman for HTTP Operations

Postman is a Google Chrome app for interacting with HTTP APIs. It presents you with a friendly GUI for constructing requests and reading responses. The app is available from www.getpostman.com/. As of this writing, the Postman app is available for the Mac, Windows, and Linux platforms.

Using HTTP GET to Retrieve an Entity with Postman

Figure A-1 shows the execution of the GET action on the http://localhost:8080/productsweb link using Postman.

Figure A-1. *HTTP GET using Postman*

Note how the example provides the URL where the entity resource is available, and the method selected is GET.

Using HTTP POST to Create an Entity with Postman

Figure A-2 shows the execution of the POST action on the http://localhost:8080/productsweb link using Postman, to create a new entity.

Figure A-2. *HTTP POST using Postman*

Note that raw and JSON are the options stipulated for the payload body.

The rest of the HTTP operations demonstrated using cURL in the previous section can be executed in a similar manner using Postman, so they are not included here.

Summary

cURL and Postman are both great and handy utilities for quickly interacting with REST endpoints and performing basic HTTP operations. You will use them extensively when executing the examples in this book.

Using MongoDB

The Community version of MongoDB database offers a flexible document data model along with support for ad hoc queries. It provides powerful ways to access and analyze your data. This appendix covers installing and running MongoDB. The following concepts are covered:

- Installing MongoDB on macOS

- Installing MongoDB in Windows OS

- Running commands against a MongoDB server

Install MongoDB on the macOS

This section explains how to install and create a MongoDB on the macOS.

Downloading and Extracting the MongoDB Tarball

The tarball (.tgz) for the Community version of the MongoDB distributed database could be downloaded from this link:

https://www.mongodb.com/try/download/community?tck=docs_server

In the Version drop-down, select the version of MongoDB to download.

In the Platform drop-down, select macOS.

© Binildas A. Christudas 2024
B. A. Christudas, *Java Microservices and Containers in the Cloud*,
https://doi.org/10.1007/979-8-8688-0555-4

In the Package drop-down, select tgz.

Click Download (see Figure B-1).

Figure B-1. *Downloading the MongoDB tarball*

Extract the files from the downloaded archive to an appropriate folder location, as shown in Listing B-1.

Listing B-1. Extracting the MongoDB Tarball

```
binildass-MacBook-Pro:~ binil$ tar -xzf ~/Downloads/mongodb-
macos-x86_64-4.2.8.tar -C ~/Applns/mongodb/
binildass-MacBook-Pro:~ binil$ cd ~/Applns/mongodb/
binildass-MacBook-Pro:mongodb binil$ ls
mongodb-macos-x86_64-4.2.8
binildass-MacBook-Pro:mongodb binil$ cd mongodb-
macos-x86_64-4.2.8/
binildass-MacBook-Pro:mongodb-macos-x86_64-4.2.8 binil$ ls
LICENSE-Community.txt        THIRD-PARTY-NOTICES
MPL-2                   THIRD-PARTY-NOTICES.gotools
README                  bin
binildass-MacBook-Pro:mongodb-macos-x86_64-4.2.8 binil$ cd bin/
binildass-MacBook-Pro:bin binil$ ls
```

```
bsondump     mongod      mongofiles    mongorestore    mongotop
install_compass   mongodump    mongoimport    mongos
mongo        mongoexport    mongoreplay    mongostat
```

Note that, if your web browser automatically unzips the file as part of the download, the file will end in .tar instead.

Installing the Tarball

Create symbolic links to the binaries from a directory listed in your PATH variable, such as /usr/local/bin. (Update /Users/binil/Applns/ mongodb/mongodb-macos-x86_64-4.2.8/bin/* /usr/local/ with your installation directory, based on the location in your machine.) See Listing B-2.

Listing B-2. Creating Links to MongoDB

```
binildass-MacBook-Pro:bin binil$ sudo ln -s /Users/binil/
Applns/mongodb/mongodb-macos-x86_64-4.2.8/bin/* /usr/local/bin/
Password:
binildass-MacBook-Pro:bin binil$
```

Create the folders for MongoDB to create the database and log files, as shown in Listing B-3.

Listing B-3. Creating Folders for MongoDB

```
binildass-MacBook-Pro:bin binil$ mkdir -p /usr/local/
var/mongodb
binildass-MacBook-Pro:bin binil$ mkdir -p /usr/local/var/
log/mongodb
```

Next ensure that the user account running mongod has read and write permissions for these two directories. If you are running mongod as your own user account, and you just created the two directories, they should already be accessible to your user. Otherwise, you need to change the file and folder ownerships. The chown command is used to change the file owner or group. Whenever you want to change ownership, you can use chown command.

First, find the current user, as shown in Listing B-4.

Listing B-4. Finding the Current User

```
binildass-MacBook-Pro:var binil$ whoami
binil
binildass-MacBook-Pro:var binil$
```

Next, grant the required permissions for the user, as shown in Listing B-5.

Listing B-5. Granting Permissions for the MongoDB Folder

```
binildass-MacBook-Pro:bin binil$ sudo chown binil /usr/local/
var/mongodb
Password:
binildass-MacBook-Pro:bin binil$ sudo chown binil /usr/local/
var/log/mongodb
binildass-MacBook-Pro:bin binil$
```

Running the MongoDB Server

You can now run the mongod process at the system prompt by providing the two necessary parameters directly on the command-line, as shown in Listing B-6.

Listing B-6. Starting the MongoDB Server

```
binildass-MacBook-Pro:bin binil$ pwd
/Users/binil/Applns/mongodb/mongodb-macos-x86_64-4.2.8/bin
binildass-MacBook-Pro:bin binil$ mongod --dbpath /usr/local/
var/mongodb --logpath /usr/local/var/log/mongodb/mongo.log
```

Alternatively, you can create a script and reuse it, as shown in Listing B-7.

Listing B-7. Creating a Shell Script

```
binildass-MacBook-Pro:mongodb-macos-x86_64-4.2.8 binil$ touch
startmongodb.sh
binildass-MacBook-Pro:mongodb-macos-x86_64-4.2.8 binil$ ls
LICENSE-Community.txt        THIRD-PARTY-NOTICES
startmongodb.sh
MPL-2                        THIRD-PARTY-NOTICES.gotools
README                       bin
binildass-MacBook-Pro:mongodb-macos-x86_64-4.2.8 binil$
```

Open startmongodb.sh and update it with the content in Listing B-8.

Listing B-8. Editing the Shell Script

```
mongod --dbpath /usr/local/var/mongodb --logpath /usr/local/
var/log/mongodb/mongo.log
```

Now you can start mongodb using the script, as shown in Listing B-9.

Listing B-9. Starting MongoDB Server Using the Script

```
binildass-MacBook-Pro:mongodb-macos-x86_64-4.2.8 binil$ sh
startmongodb.sh
binildass-MacBook-Pro:var binil$
```

Verify that MongoDB has started successfully, as shown in Listing B-10.

Listing B-10. Verifying the MongoDB Server Running

```
binildass-MacBook-Pro:var binil$ ps aux | grep -v grep |
grep mongod
binil      1091   0.0  0.3  5563288   42432 s001  S+   11:45AM
0:00.75 mongod --dbpath /usr/local/var/mongodb --logpath /usr/
local/var/log/mongodb/mongo.log
binil      1090   0.0  0.0  4268636    1124 s001  S+   11:45AM
0:00.01 sh startmongodb.sh
binildass-MacBook-Pro:var binil$
```

If you do not see a mongod process running, check the logfile for any error messages.

Opening the MongoDB Terminal

The Mongo terminal can be brought up by executing the command in Listing B-11 in the terminal.

Listing B-11. Bringing Up the MongoDB Terminal

```
binildass-MacBook-Pro:bin binil$ pwd
/Users/binil/Applns/mongodb/mongodb-macos-x86_64-4.2.8/bin
binildass-MacBook-Pro:~ binil$ mongo
MongoDB shell version v4.2.8
connecting to: mongodb://127.0.0.1:27017/?compressors=disabled&
gssapiServiceName=mongodb
Implicit session: session { "id" : UUID("08f3204a-
ac4e-4cec-8f51-bc0ebc767704") }
MongoDB server version: 4.2.8
...
>
```

You can now interact with the MongoDB Server from this terminal.

Install MongoDB on Windows

MongoDB 5.0 Community Edition supports 64-bit versions of Windows on the x86_64 architecture. This section explains how to install and create a MongoDB database on Windows OS.

Downloading and Extracting the MongoDB Archive

The ZIP file (.zip) for the Community version of the MongoDB distributed database can be downloaded from this link:

```
https://www.mongodb.com/try/download/community?tck=docs_server
```

In the Version drop-down, select the version of MongoDB to download.

In the Platform drop-down, select Windows.

In the Package drop-down, select ZIP.

Click Download (see Figure B-2).

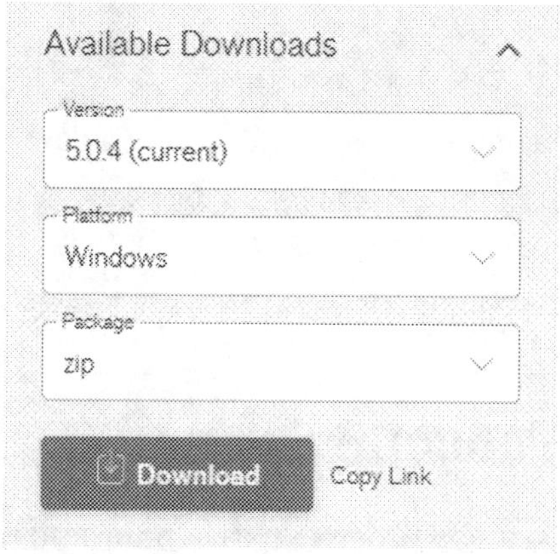

Figure B-2. *Downloading the MongoDB ZIP archive*

Installing the ZIP Archive

Extract the files from the downloaded archive to an appropriate folder location. I explicitly avoid a location with a space in the file path, such as the space in the Program Files folder. Hence, on my Windows machine, I use the following location:

D:\Applns\mongodb\mongodb-win32-x86_64-windows-5.0.4

The MongoDB server requires a data directory to store all the data. You can run MongoDB from any folder you choose. MongoDB's default data directory path is the absolute path \data\db on the drive where you start MongoDB. You can create this folder by running the command in Listing B-12 from a Windows command prompt.

Listing B-12. Creating Folders for MongoDB

```
Microsoft Windows [Version 10.0.19041.1348]
(c) Microsoft Corporation. All rights reserved.

C:\Users\A-####.TRV_IBS_INDIA>cd D:\Applns\mongodb\mongodb-
win32-x86_64-windows-5.0.4
C:\Users\A-####.TRV_IBS_INDIA>d:
D:\Applns\mongodb\mongodb-win32-x86_64-windows-5.0.4>md data\db
D:\Applns\mongodb\mongodb-win32-x86_64-windows-5.0.4>md
data\log
D:\Applns\mongodb\mongodb-win32-x86_64-windows-5.0.4>
```

Running the MongoDB Server

You can now run the mongod process at the command prompt by providing the two necessary parameters directly on the command-line, as shown in Listing B-13.

Listing B-13. Starting the MongoDB Server

```
C:\Users\A-####.TRV_IBS_INDIA>D:\Applns\mongodb\mongodb-win32-
x86_64-windows-5.0.4\bin\mongod --dbpath D:\Applns\mongodb\
mongodb-win32-x86_64-windows-5.0.4\data\db --logpath
D:\Applns\mongodb\mongodb-win32-x86_64-windows-5.0.4\data\
log\mongo.log
```

```
{"t":{"$date":"2021-11-24T07:13:08.532Z"},"s":"I",
"c":"CONTROL",  "id":20697,   "ctx":"-","msg":"Renamed existing
log file","attr":{"oldLogPath":"D:\\Applns\\mongodb\\mongodb-
win32-x86_64-windows-5.0.4\\data\\log\\mongo.log","newLogPath":
"D:\\Applns\\mongodb\\mongodb-win32-x86_64-windows-5.0.4\\data
\\log\\mongo.log.2021-11-24T07-13-08"}}
```

You may want to create a .bat script with this code in it to start the server easily next time.

Opening the MongoDB Terminal

The Mongo terminal can be brought up by executing the command in Listing B-14 in the terminal.

Listing B-14. Bringing Up the MongoDB Terminal

```
C:\Users\A-####.TRV_IBS_INDIA>D:\Applns\mongodb\mongodb-win32-
x86_64-windows-5.0.4\bin\mongo
MongoDB shell version v5.0.4
connecting to: mongodb://127.0.0.1:27017/?compressors=disabled&
gssapiServiceName=mongodb
Implicit session: session { "id" : UUID("c8f686ba-f644-4a47-
a043-ec2489081f79") }
MongoDB server version: 5.0.4
...
>
```

You can now interact with the MongoDB server from this terminal.

Run Commands Against the MongoDB Server

This section looks at how to interact with the MongoDB server using the Mongo terminal.

From the Mongo terminal, you can list the existing databases, the current database names, and the collections in the current database, as shown in Listing B-15.

Listing B-15. Listing Database Names and Collections

```
> show dbs
admin    0.000GB
config   0.000GB
local    0.000GBsee
> db.getName()
test
> show collections
>
```

Creating a New Document

The following example inserts a new document into the students collection. If the document does not specify an _id field, MongoDB adds the _id field with an ObjectId value to the new document. See Listing B-16.

Listing B-16. Creating a New Document in Existing Collection

```
> db.students.insert({name: "bob", class: 2})
WriteResult({ "nInserted" : 1 })
>
```

Reading a Document

The newly created document can be queried using the `find` command, as shown in Listing B-17.

Listing B-17. Querying Documents from an Existing Collection

```
> db.students.find()
{ "_id" : ObjectId("5efedd82e5c023296c347cd0"), "name" : "bob",
"class" : 2 }
>
```

This operation corresponds to the following SQL statement:

```
SELECT * FROM students
```

Updating a Document

Sometimes you might need to update an inventory collection. To update the first document where the name equals bob, for example, use the code in Listing B-18.

Listing B-18. Updating an Existing Document

```
> db.students.update({"name":"bob"}, {$set:{"class":3}})
WriteResult({ "nMatched" : 1, "nUpserted" : 0,
"nModified" : 1 })
> db.students.find()
{ "_id" : ObjectId("5efedd82e5c023296c347cd0"), "name" : "bob",
"class" : 3 }
>
```

737

Deleting a Document

You can delete the document you created, as shown in Listing B-19.

Listing B-19. Deleting an Existing Document

```
> db.students.remove({"name":"bob"})
WriteResult({ "nRemoved" : 1 })
> db.students.find()
>
```

You can also delete all documents from a collection, as shown in Listing B-20.

Listing B-20. Deleting All Documents from an Existing Collection

```
> db.students.remove( { } )
WriteResult({ "nRemoved" : 1 })
> db.students.find()
>
```

Dropping a Collection

The collection that was auto-created earlier can also be deleted, as shown in Listing B-21.

Listing B-21. Dropping a Collection

```
> show collections
students
> db.students.drop()
true
> show collections
>
```

Exiting the Mongo Terminal

You can exit the Mongo terminal by executing the command shown in Listing B-22 in the terminal.

Listing B-22. Exiting the Mongo Terminal

```
> exit
bye
binildass-MacBook-Pro:~ binil$
```

Summary

MongoDB is a production-grade, NoSQL database and in this appendix you learned how to install, run, and interact with MongoDB. You use MongoDB extensively when executing many of the examples in this book.

Using PostgreSQL

PostgreSQL is a free and open-source relational database management system (RDBMS). PostgreSQL runs on all major operating systems and has been ACID-compliant since 2001. This appendix covers installing and running PostgreSQL.

Install PostgreSQL on macOS

This section explains how to install and create a PostgreSQL database on macOS.

Downloading and Extracting the Image

The mountable disk image (.dmg) for the Community version of the PostgreSQL database can be downloaded from this link:

`https://www.enterprisedb.com/downloads/postgres-postgresql-downloads`

Click the button shown in Figure C-1.

© Binildas A. Christudas 2024
B. A. Christudas, *Java Microservices and Containers in the Cloud*,
https://doi.org/10.1007/979-8-8688-0555-4

741

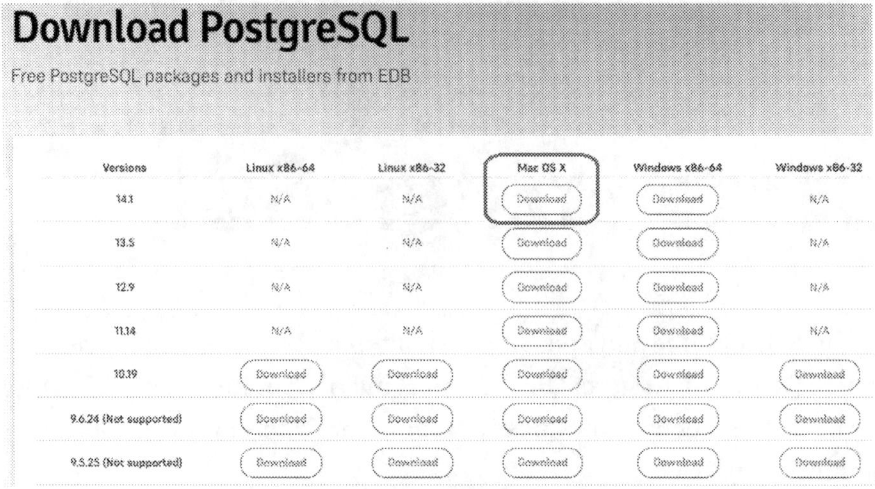

Figure C-1. *Downloading the PostgreSQL image for the Mac*

As a next step, navigate to the location where the .dmg installer was downloaded.

Double-click the installer file. You will be provided with another folder containing two files.

Double-click the file inside the folder.

You will be asked to choose Cancel or Open. To continue the installation, click Open.

You will then be prompted to enter your password for your macOS X.

After entering your password, click OK. You will then see the installation wizard.

Installing the Image

You can now follow the instructions shown by the wizard (see Figure C-2).

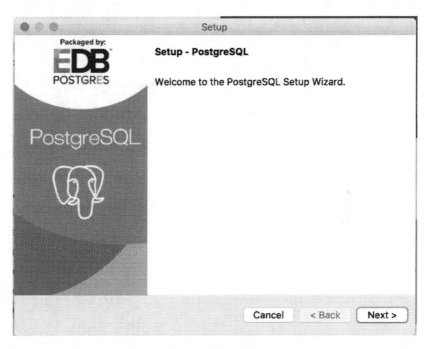

Figure C-2. *Install Wizard for PostgreSQL on a Mac*

Click Next. You will be prompted to specify the path of the destination folder in which you want to install PostgreSQL (see Figure C-3).

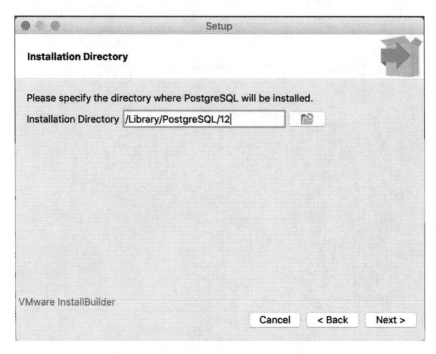

Figure C-3. *Providing an installation path for PostgreSQL on a Mac*

Specify the path and click Next. On the next screen, you can select the components you want to install (see Figure C-4).

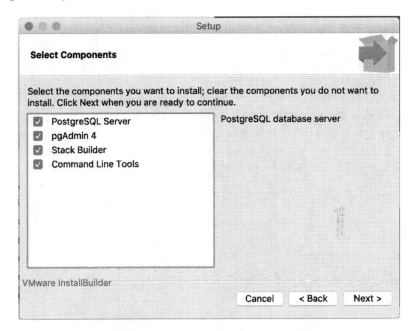

Figure C-4. *Selecting PostgreSQL components to be installed on a Mac*

Next, you'll see a dialog box asking you to specify the data directory of the PostgreSQL database (see Figure C-5). It is best to leave it as it appears.

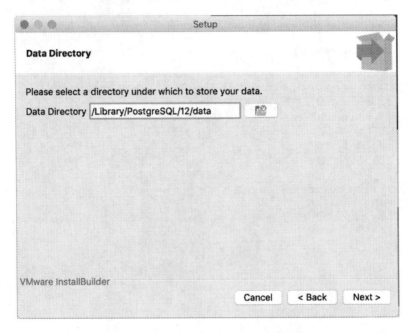

Figure C-5. *Providing a path to the data folder for PostgreSQL*

You will now be asked to enter a password to protect your PostgreSQL database system. It is highly advised that you provide a password. I have provided postgre as the default password (see Figure C-6).

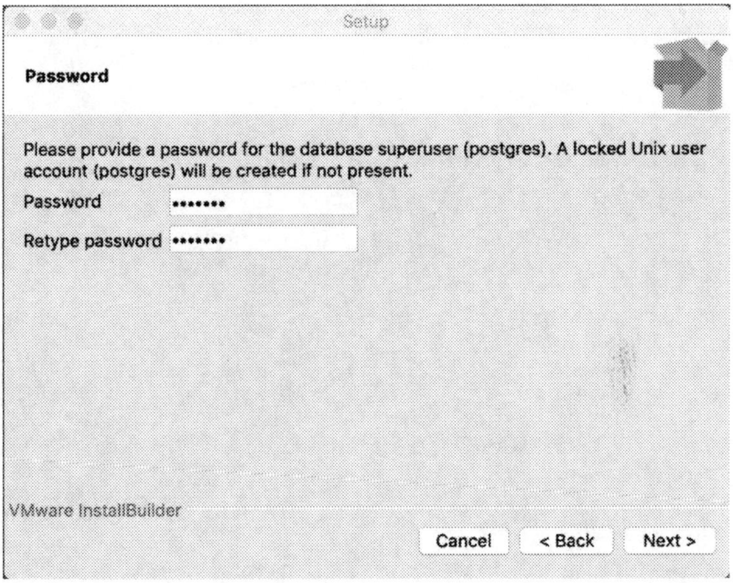

Figure C-6. *Providing a database admin password for PostgreSQL*

By default, PostgreSQL's services run on port number 5432. But PostgreSQL also lets you specify that after you enter and confirm your password. It's best to leave the port unchanged. See Figure C-7.

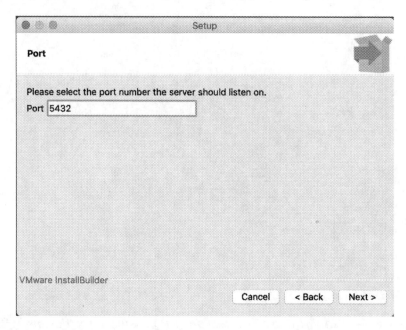

Figure C-7. *Configuring the listen port for PostgreSQL*

You will then be asked to provide the locale of the database. It is better to leave it to the default one, as shown the Figure C-8. Click Next.

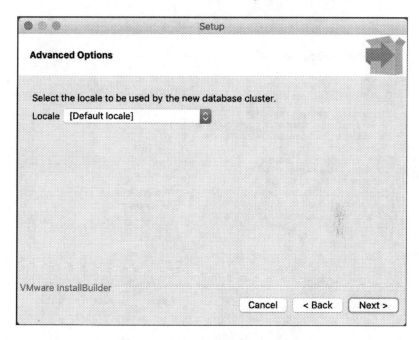

Figure C-8. *Configuring the locale for PostgreSQL*

The next screen shows a summary of the installation decisions you've made, as shown in Figure C-9.

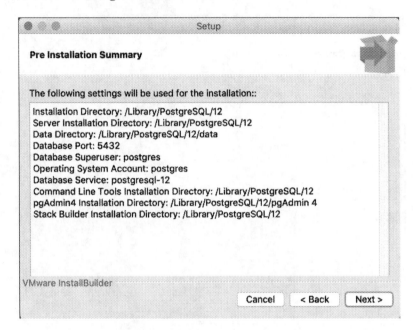

Figure C-9. *Installation summary for PostgreSQL*

Click Next. PostgreSQL is now ready to be installed on your Mac. You are left with just one more click (Next). See Figure C-10.

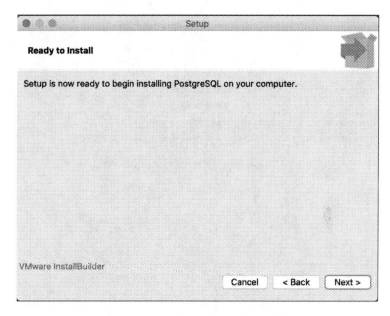

Figure C-10. *PostgreSQL installation final go ahead*

Your PostgreSQL installation should now start. It won't take much time to complete. See Figure C-11.

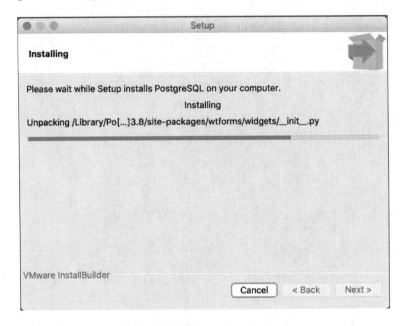

Figure C-11. *PostgreSQL installation in progress*

Toward the end of the installation process, you will be prompted to check/uncheck to launch Stack Builder. You can uncheck that and click Finish. See Figure C-12.

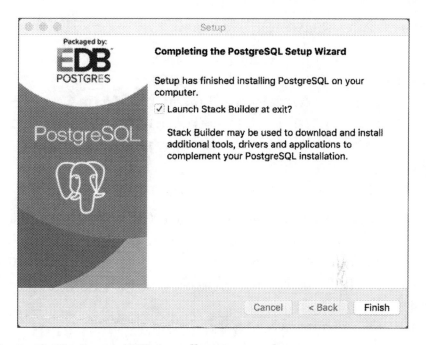

Figure C-12. *PostgreSQL installation complete*

Finally, it's best to enter the PostgreSQL `bin` folder to your path. Edit the files, as shown in Listing C-1.

Listing C-1. Editing the Path Variables

```
binildass-MacBook-Pro:nginx binil$ sudo nano /etc/paths
```

Go to the bottom of the file and enter this path: `/Library/PostgreSQL/12/bin`

Press Control+X to quit. Then enter Y to save the modified buffer.

To test this, type the code in Listing C-2 in a new terminal window.

Listing C-2. Viewing the Path Variables

```
Last login: Fri Aug  7 13:19:35 on ttys003
binildass-MacBook-Pro:~ binil$ echo $PATH
/Users/binil/Library/Python/2.7/bin:/usr/local/bin:/usr/
bin:/bin:/usr/sbin:/sbin:/Users/mike/Applns/apache/maven/
apache-maven-3.6.2/bin:/usr/local/nginx/sbin:/Library/
PostgreSQL/12/bin
binildass-MacBook-Pro:~ binil$
```

Next, ensure that the user account running PostgreSQL has read and write permissions for the required directories. You need to change the file and folder ownerships. The chown command is used to change the file owner or group. Whenever you want to change ownership, you can use chown command.

First, find the current user, as shown in Listing C-3.

Listing C-3. Finding the Current User

```
binildass-MacBook-Pro:var binil$ whoami
binil
binildass-MacBook-Pro:var binil$
```

Next, grant the required permissions to the user, as shown in Listing C-4.

Listing C-4. Granting Permissions for the PostgreSQL Folder

```
binildass-MacBook-Pro:local binil$ sudo chown -R binil
/Library/PostgreSQL/12/data
Password:
binildass-MacBook-Pro:~ binil$
```

Your PostgreSQL installation is now complete.

Starting and Stopping PostgreSQL Server

To start the server, execute the command in Listing C-5.

Listing C-5. Starting the PostgreSQL Server

```
binildass-MacBook-Pro:~ binil$ pg_ctl -D /Library/
PostgreSQL/12/data start
waiting for server to start....2020-08-07 16:41:53.401 IST
[1220] LOG:  starting PostgreSQL 12.3 on x86_64-apple-darwin,
compiled by Apple LLVM version 6.0 (clang-600.0.54) (based on
LLVM 3.5svn), 64-bit
2020-08-07 16:41:53.401 IST [1220] LOG:  listening on IPv6
address "::", port 5432
2020-08-07 16:41:53.401 IST [1220] LOG:  listening on IPv4
address "0.0.0.0", port 5432
2020-08-07 16:41:53.401 IST [1220] LOG:  listening on Unix
socket "/tmp/.s.PGSQL.5432"
2020-08-07 16:41:53.408 IST [1220] LOG:  redirecting log output
to logging collector process
2020-08-07 16:41:53.408 IST [1220] HINT:  Future log output
will appear in directory "log".
 done
server started
binildass-MacBook-Pro:~ binil$
```

You can stop the server by running the code in Listing C-6.

Listing C-6. Stopping the PostgreSQL Server

```
binildass-MacBook-Pro:~ binil$ pg_ctl -D /Library/
PostgreSQL/12/data stop
waiting for server to shut down.... done
server stopped
binildass-MacBook-Pro:~ binil$
```

Interacting Using psql Terminal

Once the PostgreSQL server has started, you can connect to the server using the psql client and perform database operations. Click the Mac Launchpad and type psql, then click the application. See Listing C-7.

Listing C-7. Connecting to the PostgreSQL Server Using psql

```
Last login: Tue Aug  4 20:28:16 on ttys000
binildass-MBP:~ binil$ /Library/PostgreSQL/12/scripts/
runpsql.sh
Server [localhost]:
Database [postgres]:
Port [5432]:
Username [postgres]:
Password for user postgres:
psql (12.3)
Type "help" for help.

postgres=#

You can now execute commands against your PostgreSQL Server.

Type "exit" to exit.
```

Opening the PostgreSQL Server for Remote Clients

To allow PostgreSQL server to accept connections from remote hosts, you need to do two things:

First, in the postgresql.conf file, change the line shown in Listing C-8.

Listing C-8. Opening the PostgreSQL Server

```
listen_addresses = 'localhost'
```

to

```
listen_addresses = '*'
```

Next, to the pg_hba.conf file, add the line shown in Listing C-9.

Listing C-9. More Config for Opening the PostgreSQL Server

```
host    all    all    192.168.0.0/16    md5
```

Both of these files are located on my Mac in the following location:

```
/Library/PostgreSQL/12/data/
```

Also, in my case, my client machine as well as my PostgreSQL server machine have the IP in the pattern 192.168.x.y and they are both in the same network.

To find the IP address of your Mac, type the code in Listing C-10.

Listing C-10. Finding an IP Address on a Mac

```
(base) binildass-MacBook-Pro:~ binil$ ipconfig getifaddr en0
192.168.8.104
(base) binildass-MacBook-Pro:~ binil$
```

Opening PostgreSQL on the Host Machine for Docker Clients

To allow the PostgreSQL server in the (local) host machine to accept connections from the Docker container in the same host, you need to add the line shown in Listing C-11 to the pg_hba.conf file.

Listing C-11. Config for Opening the PostgreSQL Server for Docker Clients

```
host   all    all    172.17.0.1/16    md5
```

This will allow connections to the PostgreSQL server from the 172.17.0.1/16 range of addresses. They belong to Docker and when running a container, Docker will assign an IP to a container from this range.

Install PostgreSQL in Windows OS

This section explains how to install and create a PostgreSQL database in Windows OS.

Downloading and Extracting the ZIP Archive

You can download the files to be installed by the PostgreSQL installer. You can either download the installer or download the ZIP archive and install it manually. I show the manual installation here.

The zipfile (.zip) for the Community version of the PostgreSQL database can be downloaded from this link:

```
https://www.enterprisedb.com/download-postgresql-binaries
```

In the Version drop-down, select the version of PostgreSQL to download.

For Windows 64-bit, select Win x86-64.

Click Download (see Figure C-13).

Binaries from installer Version 14.1

Binaries from installer Version 13.5

Figure C-13. ZIP archive for PostgreSQL installation for Windows

Installing the ZIP Archive

Extract the files from the downloaded archive to an appropriate folder location. I explicitly avoid a location with a space in the path, such as the space in the Program Files folder. Hence in my Windows machine, I extracted the ZIP file to the following location:

D:\Applns\postgresql

It extracts to this folder:

D:\Applns\postgresql\pgsql

On my machine, I renamed this folder so I can easily track the version info with the name of the ZIP file to:

D:\Applns\postgresql\postgresql-14.1-1-windows-x64-binaries

Next, you need to create a folder where your server's configurations (such as data, user, and so on) will be stored. I created a pgsql_data folder in my PostgreSQL installation. So the folder in my case is as follows:

D:\Applns\postgresql\postgresql-14.1-1-windows-x64-binaries\
pgsql_data

You have now set up the user, the password with encryption type, and the encoding for the database, using only a few commands along with `initdb.exe`. The `initdb.exe` file on my machine is found in this folder:

```
D:\Applns\postgresql\postgresql-14.1-1-windows-x64-
binaries\bin.
```

The main parameters are as follows:

-U: Postgres creates the superuser as `postgres`

-W: Prompts for the password of the superuser

-E: Creates the database with UTF-8 encoding

-A: Enables password authentication.

I entered `postgre` as the password. See Listing C-12.

Listing C-12.   Configuring PostgreSQL in Windows

```
D:\Applns\postgresql\postgresql-14.1-1-windows-x64-binaries\
bin>D:\Applns\postgresql\postgresql-14.1-1-windows-
x64-binaries\bin\initdb.exe -D D:\Applns\postgresql\
postgresql-14.1-1-windows-x64-binaries\pgsql_data -U postgres
-W -E UTF8 -A scram-sha-256
The files belonging to this database system will be owned by
user "A-4345".
This user must also own the server process.

The database cluster will be initialized with locale "English_
Indonesia.1252".
The default text search configuration will be set to "english".

Data page checksums are disabled.

Enter new superuser password:
Enter it again:
```

fixing permissions on existing directory D:/Applns/postgresql/
postgresql-14.1-1-windows-x64-binaries/pgsql_data ... ok
creating subdirectories ... ok
selecting dynamic shared memory implementation ... windows
selecting default max_connections ... 100
selecting default shared_buffers ... 128MB
selecting default time zone ... Asia/Calcutta
creating configuration files ... ok
running bootstrap script ... ok
performing post-bootstrap initialization ... ok
syncing data to disk ... ok

Success. You can now start the database server using:

"D:\Applns\postgresql\postgresql-14.1-1-windows-x64-binaries\
bin\pg_ctl" -D "D:\Applns\postgresql\postgresql-14.1-1-windows-
x64-binaries\pgsql_data" -l logfile start

Starting and Stopping PostgreSQL Server

To start the server, execute the command in Listing C-13.

Listing C-13. Starting the PostgreSQL Server

D:\Applns\postgresql\postgresql-14.1-1-windows-x64-binaries\
bin>D:\Applns\postgresql\postgresql-14.1-1-windows-
x64-binaries\bin\pg_ctl.exe -D D:\Applns\postgresql\
postgresql-14.1-1-windows-x64-binaries\pgsql-data -l D:\Applns\
postgresql\postgresql-14.1-1-windows-x64-binaries\pgsql-log\
logfile start
waiting for server to start..... done
server started

D:\Applns\postgresql\postgresql-14.1-1-windows-x64-binaries\bin>

To shut down PostgreSQL, execute the command in Listing C-14.

Listing C-14. Stopping the PostgreSQL Server

```
D:\Applns\postgresql\postgresql-14.1-1-windows-x64-binaries\
bin>D:\Applns\postgresql\postgresql-14.1-1-windows-
x64-binaries\bin\pg_ctl.exe -D D:\Applns\postgresql\
postgresql-14.1-1-windows-x64-binaries\pgsql-data stop
waiting for server to shut down.... done
server stopped

D:\Applns\postgresql\postgresql-14.1-1-windows-x64-
binaries\bin>
```

Interacting Using the psql Terminal

Once the PostgreSQL server has started, you can connect to the server using the psql client and perform database operations. See Listing C-15.

Listing C-15. Connecting to the PostgreSQL Server Using psql

```
C:\Users\USER>D:\Applns\postgresql\postgresql-14.1-1-windows-
x64-binaries\bin\psql -U postgres
Password for user postgres:
psql (14.1)
WARNING: Console code page (437) differs from Windows code
page (1252)
         8-bit characters might not work correctly. See psql
         reference
         page "Notes for Windows users" for details.
Type "help" for help.

postgres=#
```

You can now execute commands against your PostgreSQL Server.

Create a Database Using pgAdmin

pgAdmin is a web-based GUI tool used to interact with the Postgres database sessions, both locally and with remote servers. In this section, you will use pgAdmin to create a new database.

Logging In to PostgreSQL Server

On my Mac, I have an icon of pgAdmin on my desktop. Clicking that icon will open the GUI. See Figure C-14.

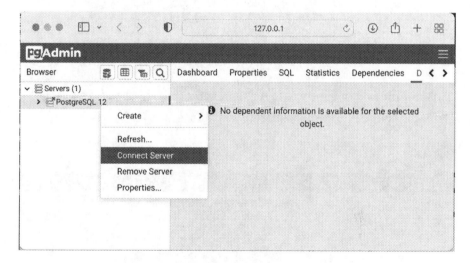

Figure C-14. *The pgAdmin screen*

Once your database is up, you need to manually connect your pgAdmin console to it. To do that, right-click and select Connect Server, as shown in Figure C-15.

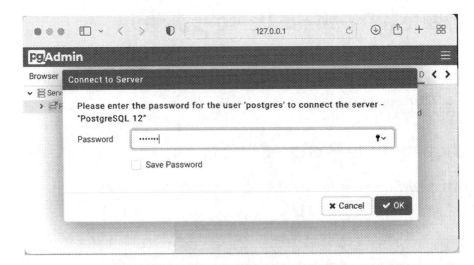

Figure C-15. *Enter login credentials into the pgAdmin screen*

As mentioned in Figure C-6, if you haven't changed postgre as the
default password, you can use that to log in (see Figure C-16).

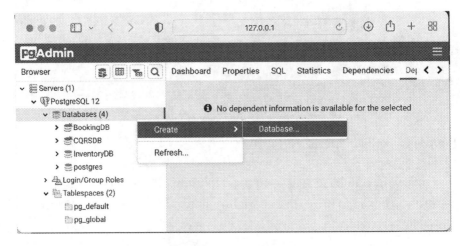

Figure C-16. *Creating a database using the pgAdmin screen*

From the Databases menu, you can right-click and select Create and then Database... to create a new database (see Figure C-17).

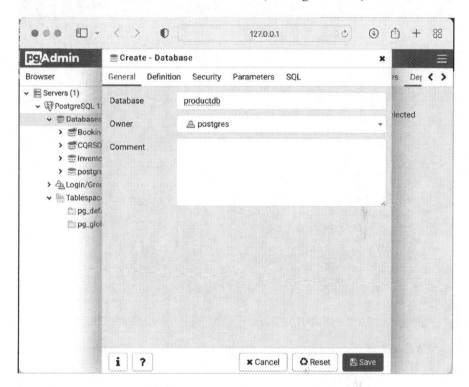

Figure C-17. *Creating a productdb database using the pgAdmin screen*

You can provide a name for the database and perhaps keep all other options to the defaults. Click Save when you're ready.

When a database is newly created, it will not contain any tables. You can right-click the Tables menu and select Create. Then select Table... to create a new table. See Figure C-18.

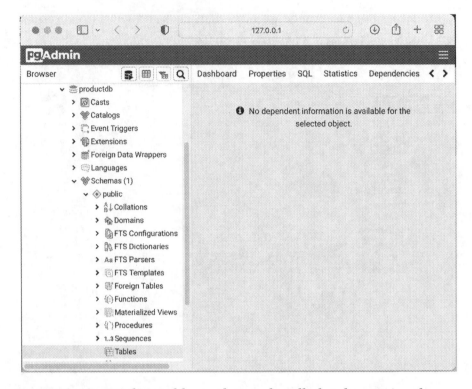

Figure C-18. *Finding tables in the productdb database using the pgAdmin screen*

Alternatively, you can use the terminal command explained in the next section to create a new table. Once you create a table, you can insert data into it.

If a table contains data, you can view the data (see Figure C-19).

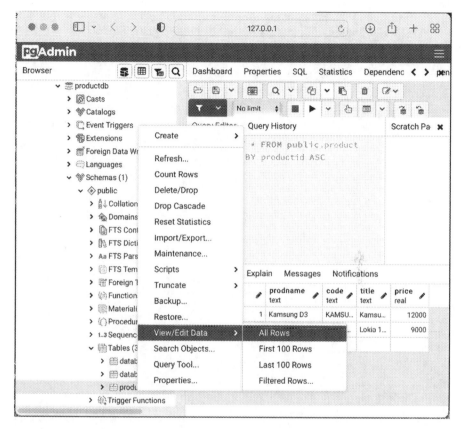

Figure C-19.   *Screen Query Table in the productdb database using the pgAdmin screen*

You can also view any inserted data. For that, select the specific table, right-click it, and then select View/Edit Data. Select the required option. See Figure C-20.

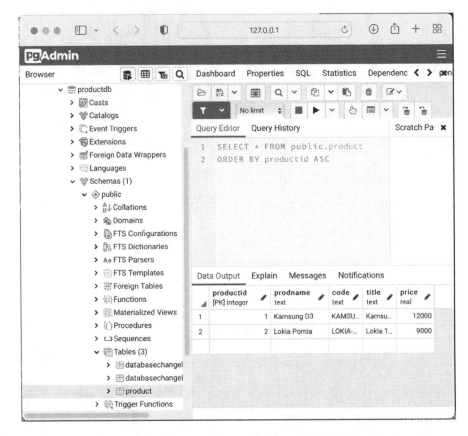

Figure C-20. *View Data in Table in the productdb database using the pgAdmin screen*

Run Command Against PostgreSQL Using psql

This section looks into how to interact with the PostgreSQL server using the psql terminal introduced earlier.

Type help and execute to see the help commands, as shown in Listing C-16.

Listing C-16. Connecting to the PostgreSQL Server Using psql

```
postgres=# help
You are using psql, the command-line interface to PostgreSQL.
Type:  \copyright for distribution terms
       \h for help with SQL commands
       \? for help with psql commands
       \g or terminate with semicolon to execute query
       \q to quit

To list all databases use command: \list or \l

postgres=# \list
                    List of databases
   Name    | Owner    |Encod |Collate |Ctype |Access privilege
-----------+----------+------+--------+------+----------------
 postgres  |postgres  |UTF8  |C       |C     |
 template0 |postgres  |UTF8  |C       |C     | =c/postgres +
 template1 |postgres  |UTF8  |C       |C     | =c/postgres +
(3 rows)

To know which database you are currently connected:

postgres=# SELECT current_database();
 current_database
------------------
 postgres
(1 row)

postgres=# \connect productdb

To connect to a different database:

postgres=# \connect productdb
You are now connected to database "productdb" as user
```

```
"postgres".
productdb=# SELECT current_database();
 current_database
------------------
 productdb
(1 row)

productdb=#
```

The next section looks at executing the basic commands that are helpful when running the examples in this book.

Creating a New Table

If a table with the same name as your new table exists, you may want to (optionally) drop it first and then create the required table, as shown in Listing C-17.

Listing C-17. Creating a Table Using psql

```
postgres=# DROP TABLE IF EXISTS links;
DROP TABLE
postgres=# CREATE TABLE links (id SERIAL PRIMARY KEY, url
VARCHAR(255) NOT NULL,            name VARCHAR(255) NOT
NULL, description VARCHAR (255),            last_update DATE);
CREATE TABLE
postgres=#
```

Listing Existing Tables

You can view any existing tables in the database, as shown in Listing C-18.

Listing C-18. List Existing Tables Using psql

```
postgres=# \dt
          List of relations
 Schema | Name  | Type  |  Owner
--------+-------+-------+----------
 public | links | table | postgres
(1 row)

postgres=#
```

Describing the Structure of an Existing Table

You can inspect the schema of the table by running the code in Listing C-19.

Listing C-19. Describing Table Schema Using psql

```
productdb-# \d product
                Table "public.product"
  Column   |        Type         |Nullable | Default
-----------+---------------------+---------+------------
 productid|bigint                |not null | nextval('pr
 prodname |character varying(30)|         |
 code     |character varying(30)|         |
 title    |character varying(60)|         |
 price    |double precision     |         |
Indexes:
    "product_pk" PRIMARY KEY, btree (productid)

productdb=#
```

Inserting a Row into a Table

Once a table is created, you can insert rows with the required values, as shown in Listing C-20.

Listing C-20. Inserting a Row into a Table Using psql

```
postgres=# INSERT INTO links (url, name)
VALUES('https://www.test.com',Test');
INSERT 0 1
postgres=# select * from links;
id |         url          |name | description |last_update
---+----------------------+-------------------+-----------
 1 | https://www.test.com |Test |             |
(1 row)

postgres=#
```

Reading Data from the Table

To view all column data from a table, use the code in Listing C-21.

Listing C-21. Reading Full Data from Tables Using psql

```
productdb=# select * from product;
 productid |  prodname    | code     |    title          | price
-----------+--------------+----------------+------------------
         1 | Kamsung D3   | KAMSUNG | Kamsung Trios 12 in..
         2 | Lokia Pomia  | LOKIA   | Lokia 12 inch..
(2 rows)
```

Use the code in Listing C-22 to select a few columns of data from the table.

Listing C-22. Reading Select Column Data from Tables Using psql

```
productdb=# select productid, prodname, code from product;
 productid |   prodname   |      code
-----------+--------------+----------------
         1 | Kamsung D3   | KAMSUNG-TRIOS
         2 | Lokia Pomia  | LOKIA-POMIA
(2 rows)

productdb=#
```

Updating a Table

You can update the rows in an existing table by selecting the row using a where clause, as shown in Listing C-23.

Listing C-23. Updating Select Column Data in Tables Using psql

```
productdb=# update product set price=9009 where productid=2;
UPDATE 1
productdb=# select * from product;
 productid |   prodname   |  code    |    title      | price
-----------+--------------+----------+---------------+-----
         1 | Kamsung D3   | KAMSUNG  | Kamsung Tr..  | 12000
         2 | Lokia Pomia  | LOKIA    | Lokia 1.      |  9009
(2 rows)

productdb=#
```

Deleting Rows from a Table

You can delete the rows in an existing table by selecting the row using a where clause, as shown in Listing C-24.

Listing C-24. Updating Select Row Data from Tables Using psql

```
productdb=# delete from product where productid=2;
DELETE 1
 productid |  prodname   |  code   |  title       | price
-----------+-------------+---------+--------------+-----
         1 | Kamsung D3  | KAMSUNG | Kamsung Tr.. | 12000
(1 row)

postgres=#
```

Dropping a Table

You can also drop an existing table, as shown in Listing C-25.

Listing C-25. Drop an Existing Table Using psql

```
postgres=# DROP TABLE IF EXISTS links;
DROP TABLE
postgres=#
```

Exiting the psql Terminal

You can close the psql session by running the code in Listing C-26.

Listing C-26. Drop an Existing Table Using psql

```
postgres=# \q
logout
Saving session...
...copying shared history...
...saving history...truncating history files...
...completed.
Deleting expired sessions...342 completed.

[Process completed]
```

Summary

PostgreSQL is a production-grade SQL database and in this appendix you learned how to install, run, and interact with a PostgreSQL database. You use PostgreSQL database extensively when executing many of the examples in this book.

Using Kafka

Apache Kafka is a distributed messaging system consisting of servers and clients that communicate via a high-performance TCP network protocol. Kafka can be deployed on bare-metal hardware, virtual machines, containers, and on on-premise as well as on cloud environments. This appendix explains how to install Kafka and operate it on your laptop. This appendix also contains examples where you operate Kafka in a container environment.

The following concepts are covered in this appendix:

- Downloading and installing Kafka

- Starting and stopping a Kafka Broker

- Creating Kafka Topics

- Doing operations on Kafka Topics

Installing Kafka

Installing Kafka is more or less similar on Mac and Windows, as this section explains.

Downloading and Extracting the Image

Download the latest Kafka archive. It's available for download from the Kafka site at `https://kafka.apache.org/downloads` (see Figure D-1).

© Binildas A. Christudas 2024
B. A. Christudas, *Java Microservices and Containers in the Cloud*,
https://doi.org/10.1007/979-8-8688-0555-4

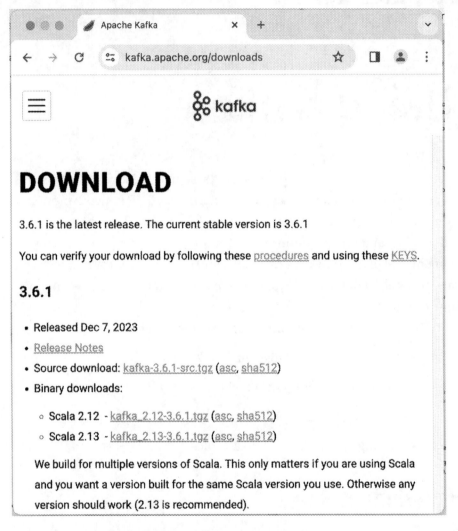

Figure D-1. *Downloading Kafka*

The current archive is available from this URL:

```
https://downloads.apache.org/kafka/3.6.1/kafka_2.12-3.6.1.tgz
```

Once the archive is downloaded, you can extract it. See Listing D-1.

Listing D-1. Extracting the Kafka Tar File

```
binildass-MacBook-Pro:~ binil$ tar -xzf kafka_2.13-3.0.0.tgz
binildass-MacBook-Pro:~ binil$ cd kafka_2.13-3.0.0
```

Starting and Stopping Kafka Broker

To start the Kafka Broker, follow these steps.

Open the command terminal and change the directory to the kafka bin folder. Start zookeeper using the command shown in Listing D-2.

Listing D-2. Starting zookeeper

```
binildass-MacBook-Pro:~ binil$ cd /Users/binil/Applns/apache/
kafka/kafka_2.13-2.5.0/bin
binildass-MacBook-Pro:bin binil$ pwd
/Users/binil/Applns/apache/kafka/kafka_2.13-2.5.0/bin
binildass-MacBook-Pro:bin binil$ sh ./zookeeper-server-start.
sh /Users/binil/Applns/apache/kafka/kafka_2.13-2.5.0/config/
zookeeper.properties
```

Next open another command prompt and change the directory to the kafka bin folder. Run kafka broker using the command shown in Listing D-3.

Listing D-3. Starting Kafka Broker

```
binildass-MacBook-Pro:bin binil$ sh ./kafka-server-start.sh
/Users/binil/Applns/apache/kafka/kafka_2.13-2.5.0/config/
server.properties
```

Kafka should be up and running now.

To stop Kafka, first terminate the Kafka server and then stop the zookeeper, as shown in Listing D-4.

Listing D-4. Stopping Kafka Broker and Zookeeper

```
binildass-MacBook-Pro:~ binil$ cd /Users/binil/Applns/apache/
kafka/kafka_2.13-2.5.0/bin
binildass-MacBook-Pro:bin binil$ pwd
/Users/binil/Applns/apache/kafka/kafka_2.13-2.5.0/bin
binildass-MacBook-Pro:bin binil$ sh ./kafka-server-stop.sh
binildass-MacBook-Pro:bin binil$ sh ./zookeeper-server-stop.sh
```

The next section looks at main operations you can do against a
Kafka Broker.

Run Commands Against Kafka Broker

This section investigates how to interact with the Kafka server using the
command terminal.

Creating a Topic

Kafka lets you read, write, store, and process events (also called records or
messages in the documentation) across many machines. Before you can
write your events, you must create a topic. Open another terminal session
and change the directory to the kafka bin folder. Then run the code in
Listing D-5.

Listing D-5. Creating a Kafka Topic

```
binildass-MacBook-Pro:bin binil$ sh ./kafka-topics.sh --create
--bootstrap-server localhost:9092 --replication-factor 1
--partitions 1 --topic test
```

You may view a topic like a folder in a filesystem, and the events as the
files in that folder.

Viewing a Topic

Once a topic is created, you can view its details.

You can list all the topics by running the code in Listing D-6.

Listing D-6. View All Kafka Topics

```
binildass-MacBook-Pro:bin binil$ sh ./kafka-topics.sh
--zookeeper localhost:2181 --list
__consumer_offsets
test
binildass-MacBook-Pro:bin binil$
```

You can also view or describe the details of a particular topic, as shown in Listing D-7.

Listing D-7. View a Particular Kafka Topic

```
binildass-MacBook-Pro:bin binil$ sh ./kafka-topics.sh
--zookeeper localhost:2181 --describe --topic test
Topic: test       PartitionCount: 1       ReplicationFactor:
1       Configs:
Topic: test       Partition: 0 Leader: 0 Replicas:
0               Isr: 0
binildass-MacBook-Pro:bin binil$
```

Reading Events from a Topic

Once a topic is created, you can listen to that topic using a consumer client. Open another terminal session and run, as shown in Listing D-8.

Listing D-8. Reading Events from a Kafka Topic

```
binildass-MacBook-Pro:bin binil$ sh ./kafka-console-consumer.sh
--bootstrap-server localhost:9092 --topic test --from-beginning

binildass-MacBook-Pro:bin binil$
```

Note the use of `--from-beginning` to consume all historical and future messages in the Kafka topic test. You may also use without that flag.

Publishing Events to a Topic

A Kafka producer can then communicate with the Kafka brokers via the network for writing events. Once the events are received, the brokers will store them in a durable and fault-tolerant manner as long as you need them, even forever.

To publish an event, open another terminal session and run the code shown in Listing D-9.

Listing D-9. Publishing Events to a Kafka Topic

```
binildass-MacBook-Pro:bin binil$ sh ./kafka-console-producer.sh
--bootstrap-server localhost:9092 --topic test

binildass-MacBook-Pro:bin binil$ Type Message Here and
hit Enter
```

Once the producer is running, you can type messages into the console and press Enter to send them to the Kafka cluster. The messages will be added to the test topic and made available for consumption by any listening Kafka consumers.

Deleting a Topic

Finally, you can also delete the previously created topic, as shown in Listing D-10.

Listing D-10. Deleting a Kafka Topic

```
binildass-MacBook-Pro:bin binil$ sh ./kafka-topics.sh
--zookeeper localhost:2181 --topic test --delete
Topic test is marked for deletion.
Note: This will have no impact if delete.topic.enable is not
set to true.
binildass-MacBook-Pro:bin binil$
```

Summary

Kafka provides publish-subscribe, event storage, and stream processing in a distributed, highly scalable, elastic, fault-tolerant, and secure manner. Kafka can be deployed on bare-metals, virtual machines, and containers, and on-premises as well as in the cloud. You can use a local Kafka Broker installation to run many of the examples in this book.

APPENDIX E

Container Tools

This appendix explains how to equip yourself with container tools. I had been using Docker Desktop, which used to provide a container environment and a UI-based container management tool. When Docker changed the licensing for Docker Desktop, I uninstalled Docker Desktop and followed a lightweight approach to have Docker running on my local machine. You learn how to will follow that procedure here.

The following concepts are covered in this appendix:

- Installing Docker in Intel based Mac

- Installing Docker in Apple Silicon based Mac

- Installing Minikube, a convenient Kubernetes environment

- Various operations using kubectl

- Installing Helm

This appendix provides instructions for on a Mac; however, similar or appropriate procedures can be followed based on which OS environment you are using as a development machine.

Docker Env for Intel based Mac

This section assumes you are using homebrew as the package manager for your Mac.

© Binildas A. Christudas 2024
B. A. Christudas, *Java Microservices and Containers in the Cloud*,
https://doi.org/10.1007/979-8-8688-0555-4

Uninstalling the Existing Docker Desktop

You need to first clean up any existing Docker (Desktop) on your machine. To do that, execute the following command:

```
brew uninstall docker
```

This is shown in Listing E-1.

Listing E-1. Uninstalling Docker

```
(base) binildass-MacBook-Pro:~ binil$ pwd
/Users/binil
(base) binildass-MacBook-Pro:~ binil$ brew uninstall docker
Warning: Treating docker as a formula. For the cask, use
homebrew/cask/docker
Uninstalling /usr/local/Cellar/docker/20.10.10...
(12 files, 56.8MB)
(base) binildass-MacBook-Pro:~ binil$
```

This command will get rid of Docker, which includes HyperKit, Docker Daemon, which allows building images, Docker CLI, which is used to interact with the Docker Daemon, and any Kubernetes clusters and kubectl binary (unless you it deployed separately).

Installing HyperKit

HyperKit is an open-source hypervisor for macOS, optimized for lightweight virtual machines and container deployment. If Docker for Desktop is installed, you already have HyperKit. If you uninstalled the existing Docker for Desktop instance in the last section, you need to run Brew Package Manager to install it. Use this command:

```
brew install hyperkit
```

This is shown in Listing E-2.

Listing E-2. Installing HyperKit

```
(base) binildass-MacBook-Pro:~ binil$ brew install hyperkit
Running 'brew update --preinstall'...
==> Auto-updated Homebrew!
Updated 4 taps (hashicorp/tap, homebrew/core, homebrew/cask and
aws/tap).
==> New Formulae
...
Warning: hyperkit 0.20200908 is already installed and
up-to-date.
To reinstall 0.20200908, run:
  brew reinstall hyperkit
(base) binildass-MacBook-Pro:~ binil$
```

You can verify if you have correctly installed HyperKit, as shown in Listing E-3.

Listing E-3. Verifying HyperKit Installation

```
(base) binildass-MacBook-Pro:~ binil$ hyperkit -v
hyperkit: 0.20200908

Homepage: https://github.com/docker/hyperkit
License: BSD

(base) binildass-MacBook-Pro:~ binil$
```

Installing Docker CLI

You have uninstalled any existing Docker to get rid of Docker Desktop but not Docker itself. You still need Docker since it is an open-source container management tool and if you have a bunch of Dockerfiles to deal with, Docker CLI will help you interact with Docker Daemon. Use this command:

```
brew install docker
```

This is shown in Listing E-4.

Listing E-4. Installing Docker CLI

```
(base) binildass-MacBook-Pro:~ binil$ brew install docker
Warning: Treating docker as a formula. For the cask, use
homebrew/cask/docker
...
==> Downloading https://storage.googleapis.com/golang/go1.16.
darwin-amd64.tar.gz
Already downloaded: /Users/binil/Library/Caches/Homebrew/
downloads/c50278859eacb3397c41a3baef31fd7b40fa2c5f08912812051
bb36f777c3b7c--go1.16.darwin-amd64.tar.gz
==> Downloading https://go.dev/dl/go1.18.2.src.tar.gz
==> Downloading from https://dl.google.com/go/
go1.18.2.src.tar.gz
...
==> Installing docker
==> go build -ldflags=-X "github.com/docker/cli/cli/version.
BuildTime=2022-05-11T16:22:17Z" -X github.com/doc
...
==> Caveats
```

Bash completion has been installed to:
  /usr/local/etc/bash_completion.d
==> Summary
  /usr/local/Cellar/docker/20.10.16: 12 files, 55.9MB, built in
35 seconds
==> 'brew cleanup' has not been run in the last 30 days,
running now...
Disable this behaviour by setting HOMEBREW_NO_INSTALL_CLEANUP.
Hide these hints with HOMEBREW_NO_ENV_HINTS (see 'man brew').
Removing: /Users/binil/Library/Caches/Homebrew/docker-compose-
-2.3.3.tar.gz... (263.8KB)
Removing: /usr/local/Cellar/go/1.17.8... (10,831 files, 566MB)
Removing: /Users/binil/Library/Caches/Homebrew/go--1.17.8.tar.
gz... (21.2MB)
Removing: /usr/local/Cellar/go-md2man/2.0.1... (6 files, 2.2MB)
Removing: /Users/binil/Library/Caches/Homebrew/go_mod_cache...
(72 files, 552.8KB)
Removing: /Users/binil/Library/Caches/Homebrew/go_cache...
(4,310 files, 510.1MB)
Removing: /Users/binil/Library/Logs/Homebrew/docker-compose...
(2 files, 7.0KB)
Error: Permission denied @ apply2files - /usr/local/lib/docker/
cli-plugins
(base) binildass-MacBook-Pro:~ binil$

Take care *not* to run the following:

brew install --cask docker

This command will install Docker Desktop and you will be back to
where you started.

The command in Listing E-4 will install the Docker CLI but not the Docker Daemon (dockerd). I explain shortly how to get the Docker Daemon. For the time being, you can verify Docker by running this command:

```
docker info
```

This is shown in Listing E-5.

Listing E-5. Verifying Docker

```
(base) binildass-MacBook-Pro:~ binil$ docker info
Client:
 Context:    default
 Debug Mode: false

Server:
ERROR: Cannot connect to the Docker daemon at unix:///var/run/
docker.sock. Is the docker daemon running?
errors pretty printing info
(base) binildass-MacBook-Pro:~ binil$
```

Container Orchestration

Container orchestration aids to provision, deploy, scale, and manage containerized applications, including those deployed into Docker Container, without worrying about the underlying infrastructure. Container orchestration can help you anywhere containers are, thus allowing you to automate the lifecycle management of containers. This section covers the minimum container orchestration toolset required to use the examples in this book.

Installing kubectl

The Kubernetes command-line tool, kubectl, allows you to run commands against Kubernetes clusters. You can use kubectl to deploy applications, inspect and manage cluster resources, and view logs. Install kubectl with this command:

```
brew install kubectl
```

This is shown in Listing E-6.

Listing E-6. Installing kubectl

```
(base) binildass-MacBook-Pro:~ binil$ brew install kubectl
kubernetes-cli 1.22.3 is already installed but outdated (so it
will be upgraded).
==> Downloading https://ftp.gnu.org/gnu/bash/bash-5.1-patches/
bash51-001
...
HEAD is now at 4ce5a895401 Release commit for
Kubernetes v1.24.0
==> Upgrading kubectl
  1.22.3 -> 1.24.0
...
  /usr/local/Cellar/coreutils/9.1: 566 files, 19.6MB, built in
1 minute 55 seconds
==> Installing kubernetes-cli
==> make WHAT=cmd/kubectl
==> hack/update-generated-docs.sh
==> Caveats
Bash completion has been installed to:
  /usr/local/etc/bash_completion.d
==> Summary
```

```
/usr/local/Cellar/kubernetes-cli/1.24.0: 228 files, 56.3MB,
built in 4 minutes 7 seconds
==> 'brew cleanup' has not been run in the last 30 days,
running now...
Disable this behaviour by setting HOMEBREW_NO_INSTALL_CLEANUP.
Hide these hints with HOMEBREW_NO_ENV_HINTS (see 'man brew').
Removing: /usr/local/Cellar/bash/5.1.8... (157 files, 9.7MB)
Removing: /usr/local/Cellar/coreutils/9.0... (480 files, 9.0MB)
Removing: /usr/local/Cellar/kubernetes-cli/1.22.3... (226
files, 57.2MB)
Error: Permission denied @ apply2files - /usr/local/lib/docker/
cli-plugins
(base) binildass-MacBook-Pro:~ binil$
```

Even though I explained the Kubernetes command-line tool here, you haven't looked at Kubernetes yet. The next section does just this.

Installing Minikube

Minikube is a tool that lets you run Kubernetes locally. Minikube runs a single-node Kubernetes cluster on your personal computer (including Windows, macOS, and Linux PCs) so that you can try out Kubernetes, or use it for your daily development work. With HyperKit deployed in the previous step, you are ready to deploy a Kubernetes cluster by deploying Minikube. In the process of setting up Minikube, you also get a Docker Daemon, and this Docker Daemon is sufficient for all local testing purposes. Run this command:

```
brew install minikube
```

This is shown in Listing E-7.

Listing E-7. Installing Minikube

```
(base) binildass-MacBook-Pro:~ binil$ brew install minikube
Running 'brew update --preinstall'...
minikube 1.24.0 is already installed but outdated (so it will
be upgraded).
...
==> Cloning https://github.com/kubernetes/minikube.git
Cloning into '/Users/binil/Library/Caches/Homebrew/
minikube--git'...
==> Checking out tag v1.25.2
HEAD is now at 362d5fdc0 Merge pull request #13668 from
sharifelgamal/v1.25.2
...
==> Installing minikube
==> make
==> Caveats
Bash completion has been installed to:
  /usr/local/etc/bash_completion.d
==> Summary
  /usr/local/Cellar/minikube/1.25.2: 9 files, 70.2MB, built in
1 minute 50 seconds
==> 'brew cleanup' has not been run in the last 30 days,
running now...
Disable this behaviour by setting HOMEBREW_NO_INSTALL_CLEANUP.
Hide these hints with HOMEBREW_NO_ENV_HINTS (see 'man brew').
Removing: /usr/local/Cellar/go-bindata/3.22.0_1... (7
files, 3.5MB)
Removing: /usr/local/Cellar/minikube/1.24.0... (9
files, 69.3MB)
Removing: /Users/binil/Library/Caches/Homebrew/go_mod_cache...
(28,632 files, 829MB)
```

```
Removing: /Users/binil/Library/Caches/Homebrew/go_cache...
(4,087 files, 423.2MB)
Error: Permission denied @ apply2files - /usr/local/lib/docker/
cli-plugins
(base) binildass-MacBook-Pro:~ binil$
```

Configuring Minikube

You can deploy Kubernetes in VMs, containers, or directly in bare-metal setups. In this case, you will use the HyperKit driver for Mac (my machine is 2.8 GHz Quad-Core Intel Core i7). If you are using the M1 version of the processor for your Mac, you may have to use the Podman driver for M1 instead. You can configure HyperKit like so:

```
--driver=hyperkit
```

Multiple options of the container technology can be used with this Kubernetes cluster, including docker, containerd, and cri-o. Since you want the Docker Daemon to be able to build Docker images, it's best to use Docker by specifying:

```
--container-runtime=docker
```

Earlier, you set the CPU and memory using Docker Desktop. Now it is advised to set the correct CPU and memory limits, especially if you intend to run many pods:

```
minikube config set cpus 6
minikube config set memory 12g
```

You can also specify the CPU and memory while starting the Minikube, like so:

```
--cpus 4
--memory 8192
```

794

Starting Minikube

Having seen the way to minimally configure Kubernetes using Minikube, we could now start Minikube like so:

```
minikube start --kubernetes-version=v1.25.2 --driver=hyperkit
--container-runtime=docker
```

You can use the --kubernetes-version flag to deploy a specific Kubernetes version. Omit this flag to simply deploy the latest version, as shown in Listing E-8.

Listing E-8. Starting Minikube

```
(base) binildass-MacBook-Pro:~ binil$ minikube start
  minikube v1.25.2 on Darwin 12.4
✦ Automatically selected the hyperkit driver. Other choices:
virtualbox, ssh
  Downloading driver docker-machine-driver-hyperkit:
    > docker-machine-driver-hyper...: 65 B / 65 B [----------]
    100.00% ? p/s 0s
    > docker-machine-driver-hyper...: 8.35 MiB / 8.35
    MiB   100.00% 2.37 MiB p/s
The 'hyperkit' driver requires elevated permissions. The
following commands will be executed:

    $ sudo chown root:wheel /Users/binil/.minikube/bin/docker-
    machine-driver-hyperkit
    $ sudo chmod u+s /Users/binil/.minikube/bin/docker-machine-
    driver-hyperkit

Downloading VM boot image ...
    > minikube-v1.25.2.iso.sha256: 65 B / 65 B [-------------]
    100.00% ? p/s 0s
```

```
> minikube-v1.25.2.iso: 237.06 MiB / 237.06 MiB  100.00%
2.14 MiB p/s 1m51s
Starting control plane node minikube in cluster minikube
Downloading Kubernetes v1.23.3 preload ...
> preloaded-images-k8s-v17-v1...: 505.68 MiB / 505.68
MiB  100.00% 2.05 MiB
Creating hyperkit VM (CPUs=2, Memory=4000MB,
Disk=20000MB) ...
Preparing Kubernetes v1.23.3 on Docker 20.10.12 ...
■ kubelet.housekeeping-interval=5m
■ Generating certificates and keys ...
■ Booting up control plane ...
■ Configuring RBAC rules ...
Verifying Kubernetes components...
■ Using image gcr.io/k8s-minikube/storage-provisioner:v5
Enabled addons: storage-provisioner, default-storageclass
Done! kubectl is now configured to use "minikube" cluster and
"default" namespace by default
(base) binildass-MacBook-Pro:~ binil$
```

If dnsmasq is running locally, DNS resolution could fail within the cluster. You can either uninstall it or add listen-address=192.168.64.1 to dnsmasq.conf. Refer to https://minikube.sigs.k8s.io/docs/drivers/hyperkit/ for more information.

Once Minikube is running, you can check the cluster with kubectl using this command:

```
kubectl get nodes
```

This is shown in Listing E-9.

Listing E-9. Verifying Minikube Kubernetes

```
(base) binildass-MacBook-Pro:~ binil$ minikube kubectl
get nodes
    > kubectl.sha256: 64 B / 64 B [--------------------------]
    100.00% ? p/s 0s
    > kubectl: 50.65 MiB / 50.65 MiB [---------------] 100.00%
    2.04 MiB p/s 25s
NAME        STATUS    ROLES                   AGE    VERSION
minikube    Ready     control-plane,master    55s    v1.23.3
(base) binildass-MacBook-Pro:~ binil$
```

Starting Docker env in the Terminal

Since Minikube is up now, you have a Kubernetes cluster, so the Docker Daemon is also running. Before you can use the daemon, you need to set the environment variables in the command terminal where you want to work. You can do so using this command:

```
eval $(minikube docker-env)
```

This is shown in Listing E-10.

Listing E-10. Setting the Terminal to Work with Kubernetes

```
(base) binildass-MacBook-Pro:~ binil$ eval $(minikube docker-env)
(base) binildass-MacBook-Pro:~ binil$
```

Accessing Docker from the Terminal

Once the Docker environment is set, from the same terminal, try accessing the Docker Daemon to make sure all is right. Use this command to do so:

```
docker info
```

This is shown in Listing E-11.

Listing E-11. Verifying Docker Access

```
(base) binildass-MacBook-Pro:~ binil$ docker info
Client:
 Context:    default
 Debug Mode: false

Server:
 Containers: 15
  Running: 14
  Paused: 0
  Stopped: 1
 Images: 10
 Server Version: 20.10.12
...
 Product License: Community Engine

WARNING: No blkio throttle.read_bps_device support
WARNING: No blkio throttle.write_bps_device support
WARNING: No blkio throttle.read_iops_device support
WARNING: No blkio throttle.write_iops_device support
(base) binildass-MacBook-Pro:~ binil$
```

Installing Docker Compose

Docker Compose defines and runs multi-container Docker applications. With Compose, you use a YAML file to configure your application's services. Then, with a single command, you create and start all the services from your configuration. You can install Docker Compose using this command:

```
brew install docker-compose
```

This is shown in Listing E-12.

Listing E-12. Installing Docker Compose

```
(base) binildass-MacBook-Pro:~ binil$ brew install
docker-compose
docker-compose 2.3.3 is already installed but outdated (so it
will be upgraded).
...
==> Downloading https://github.com/docker/compose/archive/
v2.5.1.tar.gz
==> Downloading from https://codeload.github.com/docker/
compose/tar.gz/refs/tags/v2.5.1
######################################################## 100.0%
==> Upgrading docker-compose
  2.3.3 -> 2.5.1
...
/usr/local/Cellar/docker-compose/2.5.1: 6 files, 27.7MB, built
in 1 minute 4 seconds
==> 'brew cleanup' has not been run in the last 30 days,
running now...
Disable this behaviour by setting HOMEBREW_NO_INSTALL_CLEANUP.
Hide these hints with HOMEBREW_NO_ENV_HINTS (see 'man brew').
Removing: /usr/local/Cellar/docker-compose/2.3.3... (6
files, 27.7MB)
Removing: /Users/binil/Library/Caches/Homebrew/go_mod_cache...
(19,324 files, 343.3MB)
Removing: /Users/binil/Library/Caches/Homebrew/go_cache...
(3,405 files, 289.7MB)
Error: Permission denied @ apply2files - /usr/local/lib/docker/
cli-plugins
(base) binildass-MacBook-Pro:~ binil$
```

In my Minikube-based Docker environment, I received the following error when I tried to build using Docker Compose the first time:

```
"exec: "docker-credential-desktop.exe": executable file not
found in $PATH, out:"
```

I changed credsStore to credStore in ~/.docker/config.json, as shown in Listing E-13.

Listing E-13. Correcting the Docker Compose Error

```
(base) binildass-MacBook-Pro:~ binil$ sudo nano ~/.docker/
config.json
```

Make the change, then press Control+X to quit. Enter Y to save the modified buffer. You need to open a new terminal after making these changes.

Stopping Minikube

To stop Minikube, you can execute the command shown in Listing E-14.

Listing E-14. Stopping Minikube

```
(base) binildass-MacBook-Pro:~ binil$ minikube stop
🖐  Stopping node "minikube"  ...
1 node stopped.
(base) binildass-MacBook-Pro:~ binil$
```

Deleting Minikube

If for any reason you want to delete Minikube, you can do so by executing the command in Listing E-15.

Listing E-15. Deleting Minikube

```
(base) binildass-MacBook-Pro:~ binil$ minikube delete
Deleting "minikube" in hyperkit ...
Removed all traces of the "minikube" cluster.
(base) binildass-MacBook-Pro:~ binil$ rm -rf ~/.kube
(base) binildass-MacBook-Pro:~ binil$ rm -rf ~/.minikube
(base) binildass-MacBook-Pro:~ binil$ sudo rm -rf /var/lib/
minikube
Password:
(base) binildass-MacBook-Pro:~ binil$ sudo rm /var/lib/
kubeadm.yaml
rm: /var/lib/kubeadm.yaml: No such file or directory
(base) binildass-MacBook-Pro:~ binil$ sudo rm -rf /etc/
kubernetes
(base) binildass-MacBook-Pro:~ binil$
```

Troubleshooting Minikube

There can be scenarios in which your Minikube cluster does not start, perhaps as shown in Listing E-16.

Listing E-16. Troubleshooting Minikube

```
(base) binildass-MacBook-Pro:~ binil$ minikube start
--kubernetes-version=v1.26.3 --driver=hyperkit --container-
runtime=docker
  minikube v1.30.1 on Darwin 13.3
✦ Using the hyperkit driver based on existing profile
  Starting control plane node minikube in cluster minikube
  Restarting existing hyperkit VM for "minikube" ...
```

✗ Exiting due to RUNTIME_ENABLE: Failed to enable container runtime: sudo systemctl restart docker: Process exited with status 1
stdout:

stderr:
Job for docker.service failed because the control process exited with error code.
See "systemctl status docker.service" and "journalctl -xe" for details.

   If the above advice does not help, please let us know:
   https://github.com/kubernetes/minikube/issues/new/choose
Please run 'minikube logs --file=logs.txt' and attach logs.txt to the GitHub |

(base) binildass-MacBook-Pro:~ binil$

In such scenarios, it is advised that you delete your existing Minikube by following the procedure mentioned in previous section, and then attempt to start it over, as shown in Listing E-17.

Listing E-17. Troubleshooting and Restarting Minikube

(base) binildass-MacBook-Pro:~ binil$ minikube start --kubernetes-version=v1.26.3 --driver=hyperkit --container-runtime=docker
   minikube v1.30.1 on Darwin 13.3
✦ Using the hyperkit driver based on user configuration
   Starting control plane node minikube in cluster minikube
   Creating hyperkit VM (CPUs=2, Memory=4000MB, Disk=20000MB) ...

```
Preparing Kubernetes v1.26.3 on Docker 20.10.23 ...
    ■ Generating certificates and keys ...
    ■ Booting up control plane ...
    ■ Configuring RBAC rules ...
Configuring bridge CNI (Container Networking Interface) ...
    ■ Using image gcr.io/k8s-minikube/storage-provisioner:v5
Verifying Kubernetes components...
Enabled addons: storage-provisioner, default-storageclass
Done! kubectl is now configured to use "minikube" cluster and
"default" namespace by default
(base) binildass-MacBook-Pro:~ binil$
```

Expose Minikube Services

For local development and testing, it is easy to access the services from the laptop or desktop via a browser or CLI. This section investigates some handy utility methods.

Enabling the Ingress Addon

To access the Kubernetes services, port forwarding is always an option. However, you can also enable an ingress using this command:

```
minikube addons enable ingress
```

This is shown in Listing E-18.

Listing E-18. Enabling the Ingress Addon

```
(base) binildass-MacBook-Pro:~ binil$ minikube addons
enable ingress
    ■ Using image k8s.gcr.io/ingress-nginx/controller:v1.1.1
```

- Using image k8s.gcr.io/ingress-nginx/kube-webhook-certgen:v1.1.1
- Using image k8s.gcr.io/ingress-nginx/kube-webhook-certgen:v1.1.1

```
Verifying ingress addon...
The 'ingress' addon is enabled
(base) binildass-MacBook-Pro:~ binil$
```

This code will deploy the Nginx Ingress Controller. While doing so, the Nginx service is deployed as NodePort and the MINIKUBE IP is pointed to the ingress directly. You can now find the minikube IP, as shown in Listing E-19.

Listing E-19. Showing the Minikube IP

```
(base) binildass-MacBook-Pro:~ binil$ minikube ip
192.168.64.5
(base) binildass-MacBook-Pro:~ binil$
```

You can now access the Nginx using the IP, as shown in Listing E-20.

Listing E-20. Accessing nginx in Minikube

```
(base) binildass-MacBook-Pro:~ binil$ curl http://192.168.64.5
<html>
<head><title>404 Not Found</title></head>
<body>
<center><h1>404 Not Found</h1></center>
<hr><center>nginx</center>
</body>
</html>
(base) binildass-MacBook-Pro:~ binil$
```

Note that the 404 Not Found message is normal and expected.

Enabling the Ingress DNS Addon

Once you have enabled the Ingress addon, it works on DNS and it should resolve to the Minikube IP. However, if one of the backend services calls that DNS, it will fail unless explicitly configured. To enable this, you need to enable the Ingress DNS addon, as shown in Listing E-21.

Listing E-21. Enabling the Ingress DNS Addon

```
(base) binildass-MacBook-Pro:~ binil$ minikube addons enable
ingress-dns
    ■ Using image gcr.io/k8s-minikube/minikube-ingress-
      dns:0.0.2
The 'ingress-dns' addon is enabled
(base) binildass-MacBook-Pro:~ binil$
```

There is a known issue that prevents the ingress from being exposed on macOS (Issue #7332). The Ingress addon is currently not supported on the Docker Driver on macOS. This is due to a limitation of the Docker Bridge on the Mac.

Manage Kubernetes Applications

In the previous sections, you set up a running, single-node Kubernetes cluster. In this section, you learn how to deploy an application and access the service.

Deploying Kubernetes Applications

One easy way to deploy a service to the Kubernetes cluster is to deploy the deployment manifest using its direct URL, as shown in Listing E-22.

Listing E-22. Deploying a Kubernetes Application

```
(base)binildass-MacBook-Pro:~binil$kubectl apply -f https://
raw.githubusercontent.com/scriptcamp/minikube/main/nginx.yaml
configmap/index-html-configmap created
deployment.apps/nginx-deployment created
service/nginx-service created
(base) binildass-MacBook-Pro:~ binil$
```

Inspecting the Kubernetes Deployment

The status of the deployment can be accessed as shown in Listing E-23.

Listing E-23. Listing Kubernetes Deployment

```
(base) binildass-MacBook-Pro:~ binil$ kubectl get deployments
NAME                READY   UP-TO-DATE   AVAILABLE   AGE
nginx-deployment    0/2     2            0           40s
(base) binildass-MacBook-Pro:~ binil$
```

The status of the service can be accessed as shown in Listing E-24.

Listing E-24. Inspecting Kubernetes Service

```
(base) binildass-MacBook-Pro:~ binil$ kubectl get service
NAME            TYPE        CLUSTER-IP      EXTERNAL-IP
PORT(S)         AGE
kubernetes      ClusterIP   10.96.0.1       <none>
443/TCP         22m
nginx-service   NodePort    10.111.23.105   <none>
80:32000/TCP    49s
(base) binildass-MacBook-Pro:~ binil$
```

The status of the services can be accessed using the Minikube command shown in Listing E-25.

Listing E-25. Listing Minikube Services

```
(base) binildass-MacBook-Pro:~ binil$ minikube service list
|---------------|----------------------|--------------|
|NAMESPACE      | NAME                 | TARGET PORT  |
|---------------|----------------------|--------------|
|default        |kubernetes            |No node port  |
|default        |nginx-service.        |80            |
|ingress-nginx  |ingress-nginx-contr...|http/80       |
|...                                                   |
|---------------|----------------------|--------------|
(base) binildass-MacBook-Pro:~ binil$
```

Accessing the Kubernetes Application

You can get the URL for a specific service by using the command shown in Listing E-26.

Listing E-26. Getting Minikube Service URL

```
(base) binildass-MacBook-Pro:~ binil$ minikube service --url
nginx-service
http://192.168.64.5:32000
(base) binildass-MacBook-Pro:~ binil$
```

Now use the URL in a browser:

```
http://192.168.64.5:32000
```

Docker Env for Apple Silicon-Based Mac

The latest Macs use Apple M1 processors based on ARM64. HyperKit does not work on M1, so you need to use Podman to create your virtual machines.

Installing Podman

Podman is a daemon-less container engine for developing, managing, and running OCI containers on your Linux system. The initial versions of Podman only supported Intel-based Apple machines. From Podman 3.4 onward, it has supported Apple silicon hardware. You can install Podman using this command.

```
brew install podman
```

Creating and Starting a VM

The next step is to initialize Podman. To do so, you need to create a virtual machine with the desired specs, as shown in Listing E-27.

Listing E-27. Initializing Podman

```
(base) binildass-MacBook-Pro:~ binil$ podman machine init
--cpus 6 --memory 12288 --disk-size 50 --image-path next
Downloading VM image: fedora-coreos-35.20220131.1.0-qemu.
aarch64.qcow2.xz: done
Extracting compressed file
...
(base) binildass-MacBook-Pro:~ binil$
```

To list the VMs and their status, the `list` command helps. The example in Listing E-28 shows the names of all my VMs, the date they were created, and the last time they were up.

Listing E-28. Listing Podman VMs

```
(base) binildass-MacBook-Pro:~ binil$ podman machine list
NAME                     VM TYPE  CREATED        LAST UP
podman-machine-default*  qemu     6 days ago     Currently running
vm2                      qemu     11 minutes ago 11 minutes ago
(base) binildass-MacBook-Pro:~ binil$
```

To start the VM, use the command in Listing E-29.

Listing E-29. Starting Podman VM

```
(base) binildass-MacBook-Pro:~ binil$ podman machine start
INFO[0000] waiting for clients...
INFO[0000] listening tcp://127.0.0.1:7777
INFO[0000] new connection from  to /var/folders/2x/wz0vrff9o3q
0p3lpn959b8zw0000gn/T/podman/qemu_podman-machine-default.sock
Waiting for VM ...
Machine "podman-machine-default" started successfully
(base) binildass-MacBook-Pro:~ binil$
```

Next, you need to use the root destination of the Podman service to make it work with Minikube, as shown in Listing E-30.

Listing E-30. Configuring Podman for Minikube

```
(base) binildass-MacBook-Pro:~ binil$ podman system connection
default podman-machine-default-root
(base) binildass-MacBook-Pro:~ binil$
```

```
(base) binildass-MacBook-Pro:~ binil$ podman system
connection list
Name                     Identity                          URI
podman-machine-default    /Users/x/.ssh/podman-machine-default
ssh://core@localhost:57623/run/user/1000/podman/podman.sock
podman-machine-default-root*  /Users/x/.ssh/podman-machine-
default  ssh://root@localhost:57623/run/podman/podman.sock
(base) binildass-MacBook-Pro:~ binil$
```

Starting Minikube

To start the Minikube cluster using a Podman driver, you need to make a small change and compile Minikube locally to make it work with Podman (see Listing E-31). This is due to an unexposed listener endpoint. The details are provided here:

https://github.com/kubernetes/minikube/issues/12658#issuecomment-999840079

Listing E-31. Building Minikube

```
(base) binildass-MacBook-Pro:~ binil$ git clone https://github.
com/kubernetes/minikube.git
(base) binildass-MacBook-Pro:~ binil$ cd minikube
(base) binildass-MacBook-Pro:~ binil$ sed -i.bak
's/fmt.Sprintf("--publish=%s::%d", pm.ListenAddress,
pm.ContainerPort)/fmt.Sprintf("--publish=%d",
pm.ContainerPort)/g' pkg/drivers/kic/oci/oci.go && rm
pkg/drivers/kic/oci/oci.go.bak
(base) binildass-MacBook-Pro:~ binil$ make minikube-
darwin-arm64
```

As a next step, you can start the cluster with a Podman driver and a cri-o container runtime. Make sure to use the compiled binary in the previous step, and then start Minikube as shown in Listing E-32.

Listing E-32. Starting Minikube

```
(base) binildass-MacBook-Pro:~ binil$ ./out/minikube-darwin-
arm64 start --kubernetes-version=v1.22.5 --driver=podman
--container-runtime=cri-o -p minipod
[minipod] minikube v1.25.1 on Darwin 12.2 (arm64)
✦ Using the podman (experimental) driver based on user
configuration
Starting control plane node minipod in cluster minipod
Pulling base image ...
E0205 23:11:56.616067   71622 cache.go:203] Error downloading
kic artifacts:  not yet implemented, see issue #8426
Creating podman container (CPUs=6, Memory=11264MB) ...
Preparing Kubernetes v1.22.5 on CRI-O 1.22.1 ...
E0205 23:13:05.499833   71622 start.go:126] Unable to get host
IP: RoutableHostIPFromInside is currently only implemented
for linux
    ▪ kubelet.housekeeping-interval=5m
    ▪ Generating certificates and keys ...
    ▪ Booting up control plane ...
    ▪ Configuring RBAC rules ...
Configuring CNI (Container Networking Interface) ...
Verifying Kubernetes components...
    ▪ Using image gcr.io/k8s-minikube/storage-provisioner:v5
Enabled addons: storage-provisioner, default-storageclass
Done! kubectl is now configured to use "minipod" cluster and
"default" namespace by default
(base) binildass-MacBook-Pro:~ binil$
```

Installing Helm on the Mac

Helm is a package manager for Kubernetes. You can install Helm using brew and this command:

```
brew install helm
```

This is shown in Listing E-33.

Listing E-33. Installing Helm

```
To verify the installation use the following command
(base) binildass-MacBook-Pro:~ binil$ which helm
/usr/local/bin/helm
(base) binildass-MacBook-Pro:~ binil$
```

Summary

Minikube is a quick and easy way to create a Kubernetes environment that you can use to develop and test your container applications. You can use Minikube, which provides both a container runtime and a container orchestration service. You use them in many of the examples in this book.

Cloud Tools

This appendix covers how to equip yourself with some essential cloud tools. Amazon Web Services (AWS) is used as the cloud provider for the examples in this book, so the tools listed in this appendix are targeted toward AWS.

The following concepts are covered in this appendix:

- Installing and configuring AWS CLI

- Downloading and configuring AWS IAM

- Configuring kubectl for AWS EKS

- Setting up Terraform

The following sections investigate these tools one by one.

AWS CLI

You can install the AWS Command Line Interface (AWS CLI), and its dependencies on macOS, by following the steps mentioned in this section.

You can also refer to the AWS website for the latest information:

```
https://docs.aws.amazon.com/cli/latest/userguide/getting-
started-install.html
```

© Binildas A. Christudas 2024
B. A. Christudas, *Java Microservices and Containers in the Cloud*,
https://doi.org/10.1007/979-8-8688-0555-4

Downloading AWS CLI

One quick way to download the .pkg version is using a direct URL, as shown in Listing F-1.

Listing F-1. Downloading the AWS CLI .pkg

```
binildass-MacBook-Pro:biniltemp binil$ curl "https://awscli.
amazonaws.com/AWSCLIV2.pkg" -o "AWSCLIV2.pkg"
  % Total    % Received % Xferd  Average Speed   Time
Time     Time     Current
                                 Dload   Upload  Total
Spent    Left     Speed
100 37.5M  100 37.5M    0       0   4460k        0  0:00:08
0:00:08  --:--:-- 6240k
binildass-MacBook-Pro:biniltemp binil$
```

Installing AWS CLI

Double-click the downloaded file called AWSCLIV2.pkg to launch the installer. Follow the onscreen instructions to install it.

Then verify your AWS CLI installation, as shown in Listing F-2.

Listing F-2. Verifying AWS CLI Installation

```
(base) binildass-MacBook-Pro:001-Init-EC2 binil$ which aws
/usr/local/bin/aws
(base) binildass-MacBook-Pro:001-Init-EC2 binil$ aws --version
aws-cli/2.2.3 Python/3.8.8 Darwin/18.7.0 exe/x86_64 prompt/off
Last login: Wed May 12 22:25:12 on ttys001
(base) binildass-MBP:001-Init-EC2 binil$
```

Configuring AWS CLI

You can also configure your AWS CLI with your access credentials, as shown in Listing F-3.

Listing F-3. Configuring AWS CLI Installation

```
(base) binildass-MBP:001-Init-EC2 binil$ aws configure
AWS Access Key ID [None]: XYZ
AWS Secret Access Key [None]: xyzzy
Default region name [None]: ap-southeast-1
Default output format [None]:
(base) binildass-MBP:001-Init-EC2 binil$
```

AWS IAM

The AWS Identity and Access Management (IAM) principal (role or user) is a type of identity that can access your Amazon EKS cluster. When users use this identity, IAM can:

- Assign users Kubernetes permissions so that they can work with Kubernetes objects on your cluster.

- Assign users IAM permissions so that they can work with your Amazon EKS cluster and its resources using Amazon EKS API, AWS CLI, AWS CloudFormation, AWS Management Console, or eksctl.

Downloading AWS IAM

One quick way to download the IAM Authenticator binary is using a direct URL, as shown in Listing F-4.

Listing F-4. Downloading AWS IAM

```
(base) binildass-MacBook-Pro:001-Init-EC2 binil$ curl -o aws-
iam-authenticator https://amazon-eks.s3-us-west-2.amazonaws.
com/1.13.7/2019-06-11/bin/linux/amd64/aws-iam-authenticator
```

Configuring AWS IAM

You must first provide execute permissions to the AWS IAM, as shown in Listing F-5.

Listing F-5. Providing Permissions to AWS IAM

```
(base) binildass-MacBook-Pro:001-Init-EC2 binil$ chmod +x
./aws-iam-authenticator
```

Next, copy the binary to a folder and include it in your path. See Listing F-6.

Listing F-6. Configuring the Path

```
binildass-MacBook-Pro:nginx binil$ sudo nano /etc/paths
```

Go to the bottom of the file and enter this path: `:/Users/binil/Applns/AWS/IAM/aws-iam-authenticator`

Pres Control+X to quit. Then enter Y to save the modified buffer. This process is shown in Figure F-1.

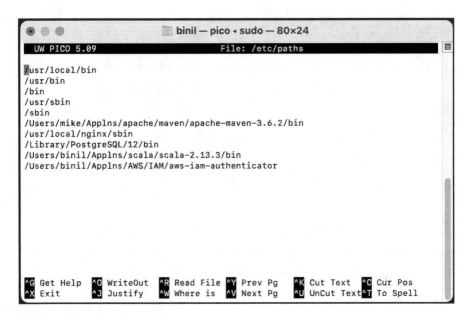

Figure F-1. *Configuring the path*

To test your configuration, open a new terminal and check the path, as shown in Listing F-7.

Listing F-7. Verifying the Path

```
Last login: Fri Jul 17 12:07:55 on ttys002
binildass-MacBook-Pro:~ binil$ echo $PATH
/Users/binil/Library/Python/2.7/bin:/usr/local/bin:/usr/bin:/
bin:/usr/sbin:/sbin:/Users/mike/Applns/apache/maven/apache-
maven-3.6.2/bin:/usr/local/nginx/sbin:/Users/binil/Applns/AWS/
IAM/aws-iam-authenticator
binildass-MacBook-Pro:~ binil$
```

kubectl for EKS

You can configure the local kubectl to target EKS in AWS. To do that, you first have to complete the two prerequisites in the previous two subsections:

- Installed and configured AWS CLI: Get the access key and the secret access key for the Production EKS Cluster user and configure AWS CLI by running aws configure.

- Downloaded and configured AWS IAM: Amazon EKS uses IAM to provide authentication to your Kubernetes cluster through the AWS IAM Authenticator for Kubernetes.

Note   This section can be applied after you create the EKS infrastructure in AWS.

Next, create the required kubeconfig file using this format:

```
aws eks --region region update-kubeconfig --name cluster_name
```

This is shown in Listing F-8.

Listing F-8. Configuring kubectl for EKS

```
Last login: Sat Jul  3 10:01:11 on ttys000
(base) binildass-MBP:ch15-01 binil$ pwd
/Users/binil/binil/code/mac/mybooks/docker-04/ch15/ch15-01
(base) binildass-MBP:ch15-01 binil$ aws eks --region
ap-southeast-1 update-kubeconfig --name bdca-tf-eks-01
Updated context arn:aws:eks:ap-southeast-1:023577096755:
cluster/bdca-tf-eks-01 in /Users/binil/.kube/config
```

Joining Worker Nodes to EKS

This is required for the AWS EKS Cluster, but you should not execute this section until you apply the AWS EKS Terraform scripts to create the EKS infrastructure, or until you create the EKS clusters through any other means.

Note   This section can be applied after you create the EKS infrastructure in AWS.

First, download the AWS IAM Authenticator configuration map, as shown in Listing F-9.

Listing F-9. Downloading the AWS IAM Authenticator Configuration Map

```
(base) binildass-MacBook-Pro:001-Init-EC2 binil$ curl -o
aws-auth-cm.yaml https://amazon-eks.s3-us-west-2.amazonaws.com/
cloudformation/2019-02-11/aws-auth-cm.yaml
```

Open the `aws-auth-cm.yaml` file with any editor and replace the ARN (Amazon Resource Names) of the instance role (not instance profile), taking care not to make any other changes. ARNs uniquely identify AWS resources. You need an ARN when you have to specify a resource unambiguously across all of AWS, such as in IAM policies, Amazon Relational Database Service (Amazon RDS) tags, and API calls. See Listing F-10.

Listing F-10. Configuration for EKS Cluster vs Worker Sync

```
apiVersion: v1
kind: ConfigMap
metadata:
```

```
name: aws-auth
  namespace: kube-system
data:
  mapRoles: |
    - rolearn: <ARN of instance role (not instance profile)>
      username: system:node:{{EC2PrivateDNSName}}
      groups:
        - system:bootstrappers
        - system:nodes
```

You can apply this configuration using `kubectl`, for the AWS Region configured. See Listing F-11.

Listing F-11. Applying Configuration for EKS Cluster vs Worker Sync

```
kubectl apply -f aws-auth-cm.yaml
```

This command may take a few minutes to finish. You can watch the status of your nodes and wait for them to reach the **Ready** status.

```
kubectl get nodes — watch
```

Terraform

Terraform is an infrastructure as code (IaS) tool that helps you build, change, and version infrastructure.

You can install Terraform and its dependencies on macOS by following the steps in this section.

You can also refer to the Terraform website for the latest information:

```
https://developer.hashicorp.com/terraform/tutorials/aws-get-
started/install-cli
```

Installing Terraform

I assume you have homebrew, which is a free and open-source package management system for macOS X.

As a first step, install the HashiCorp tap, a repository of all Terraform homebrew packages. See Listing F-12.

Listing F-12. Installing Hashicorp Tap

```
(base) binildass-MacBook-Pro:~ binil$ brew tap hashicorp/tap
...
```

Next, Install Terraform, as shown in Listing F-13.

Listing F-13. Installing Hashicorp Terraform

```
(base) binildass-MacBook-Pro:~ binil$ brew install hashicorp/
tap/terraform
...
```

Upgrading Terraform

If you want to update to the latest version of Terraform, first update homebrew, as shown in Listing F-14.

Listing F-14. Updating Homebrew

```
(base) binildass-MacBook-Pro:~ binil$ brew upgrade hashicorp/
tap/terraform
...
```

Now you can run the upgrade command to download and use the latest Terraform version. See Listing F-15.

Listing F-15. Upgrading Terraform

```
(base) binildass-MacBook-Pro:~ binil$ brew upgrade hashicorp/
tap/terraform
...
```

Verifying Terraform

One easy way to verify the Terraform installation is to list Terraform's available subcommands, as shown in Listing F-16.

Listing F-16. Verifying Terraform

```
binildass-MacBook-Pro:biniltemp binil$ terraform -help
Usage: terraform [global options] <subcommand> [args]

The available commands for execution are listed below.
The primary workflow commands are given first, followed by
less common or more advanced commands.

Main commands:
  init      Prepare your working directory for other commands
  validate  Check whether the configuration is valid
...
binildass-MacBook-Pro:biniltemp binil$
```

Summary

Cloud computing is a de facto means of infrastructure provisioning, and this appendix has taken you through a few tools that will help you interact with AWS Cloud. You use these tools in the last two chapters of this book.

Index

A

© Binildas A. Christudas 2024
B. A. Christudas, *Java Microservices and Containers in the Cloud*,
https://doi.org/10.1007/979-8-8688-0555-4

Q

R

Y

Z

Printed in the United States
by Baker & Taylor Publisher Services